THE Great Migration Directory

Immigrants to New England, 1620–1640

A Concise Compendium

Robert Charles Anderson, FASG

NEW ENGLAND HISTORIC GENEALOGICAL SOCIETY
AmericanAncestors.org
2015

Copyright © 2015 by the New England Historic Genealogical Society.

All rights reserved. No part of this publication may be reproduced or transmitted in any form or by any means, electronic or mechanical, including photocopying, recording, or any information storage or retrieval system, without permission in writing from the copyright holder, except for the inclusion of brief quotations in a review.

ISBN: 978-0-88082-327-2
Library of Congress Control Number: 2015942387

Cover design by Carolyn Sheppard Oakley
Printed by King Printing Company, Lowell, Massachusetts

NEW ENGLAND HISTORIC
GENEALOGICAL SOCIETY
Boston, Massachusetts
www.AmericanAncestors.org

TABLE OF CONTENTS

ACKNOWLEDGMENTS vii
INTRODUCTION ix
    Source List xix
    Maps xxii
KEY TO TITLES xxv
CHAPTERS BY SURNAME
    A. 1
    B. 13
    C. 55
    D. 87
    E. 101
    F. 111
    G. 125
    H. 145
    I 179
    J 181
    K. 191
    L. 201
    M 217
    N. 237
    O. 245
    P. 245
    Q. 275
    R. 277
    S. 293
    T. 329
    U. 347
    V. 349
    W 353

Y 389
   Africans 391
INDEX SECTION
   Index of Supplemental Names 395
   Index of European Places 399
   Index of American Places 409
   Index of Ship Names 421

ACKNOWLEDGMENTS

On a rainy day in September 2010, I had lunch at Clapham, Yorkshire, with Sharon Atkinson-Mallory, Kate Van Demark, and Peter Van Demark and presented to them my earliest concepts for the present volume. Their comments in response were constructive and helpful in encouraging me to proceed.

About two years later I presented the idea for the book to the NEHGS management team of D. Brenton Simons, Tom Wilcox, and Ryan Woods. They responded positively to my presentation, and we soon reached an agreement to proceed with the project.

Henry B. Hoff, FASG; Roger D. Joslyn, FASG; and Patricia Law Hatcher, FASG, viewed early samples of some entries for the book and provided constructive criticism which further advanced the work. At a later stage, each of them also provided comments on specific entries within their personal areas of expertise.

Others who also commented on specific entries within their own expertise were Gale Ion Harris, FASG; Sandra M. Hewlett, CG; David Curtis Dearborn, FASG; Gordon L. Remington, FASG; and William B. Saxbe Jr., FASG.

Leslie Mahler, FASG, kindly read the entire manuscript and provided many valuable comments deriving from his deep knowledge of the English origins of Great Migration immigrants.

Melinde Lutz Byrne, FASG, drew on her unparalleled knowledge of Africans in early New England to assist me in that section of this book, although the conclusions stated here are mine.

In the NEHGS Publications Department, Penelope L. Stratton and Leslie A. Weston expertly guided the preparation and production of this volume at every stage of work; Lynn Betlock and Scott C. Steward read the entire manuscript and pointed out many omissions and infelicities; and Carolyn Oakley Sheppard designed the dust jacket and text for the case.

Every member of the NEHGS library staff watched me over the six months of this book's preparation as I worked through the alphabet and created mountainous stacks of books on the library's research tables. They responded cheerfully and promptly to my endless barrage of requests for items from the vault or rare books, and they worked with me to track down volumes that had gone astray in the Society's collections.

Thanks also to Linda Skinner Austin for her work on the text layout, and to Steve Csipke for his keen eye while compiling the indexes. Jeff King at Mapping Specialists created the custom maps.

To all of these colleagues my sincere appreciation for their efforts. Any remaining errors and omissions are mine alone.

Robert Charles Anderson
Jaffrey, New Hampshire
24 May 2015

INTRODUCTION

The Great Migration is the term used for the movement of Europeans, mostly English men, women and children, to New England between the sailing of the *Mayflower* in 1620 and the outbreak of the English Civil War in 1640. During that period, about 20,000 immigrants crossed the Atlantic, most of them between 1634 and 1640. In twelve volumes published over the last two decades, the Great Migration Study Project has presented detailed genealogical and biographical sketches for nearly half of these immigrants, covering the years from 1620 to 1635. These books are:

- *The Great Migration Begins: Immigrants to New England, 1620–1633*, three-volume set
- *The Great Migration: Immigrants to New England, 1634–1635*, seven volumes
- *The Pilgrim Migration: Immigrants to Plymouth Colony, 1620–1633*
- *The Winthrop Fleet: Massachusetts Bay Company Immigrants to New England, 1629–1630*

The present volume takes a different approach, providing concise entries for all immigrant families for the entirety of the Great Migration, from 1620 to 1640. Each entry contains at a minimum the English origin (if known), the year of arrival, and the best treatment of that immigrant in the secondary literature. Where appropriate, the information in these entries has been extracted from the sketches already published in the various volumes published by the Great Migration Study Project (see above). For the remaining entries, this data has been gathered and compiled through an abbreviated version of the procedure established over the last two decades in creating the published Great Migration sketches.

I used a three-step process to generate the entries for *The Great Migration Directory*. The first step was to compile a list of all available records generated in New England between 1636 and 1640.[1] The result was a five-page list of town, church, court, colony, and other miscellaneous records. I read each of these sources systematically and extracted all names appearing by May of 1641 (other than those of persons known to have arrived by 1635, for whom this step had been completed earlier) into a simple database, which listed first name, last name, residence, date of record, and volume and page citation of the record. (See the end of this introduction for a list of the sources consulted.)

In some cases this database might include only one record for a given immigrant, but in others it might include two or more records. Then I created a new database, by merging entries that pertained to the same individual. The result was a list with about 3,200 entries. This first step is identical with the procedure I have used in the past in generating the lists of immigrants who were covered in the Great Migration volumes for the years 1620 to 1635.

In the second step, I merged this checklist with the list of sketches already created for the three volumes of *Great Migration Begins* and the seven volumes of the *The Great Migration*, as well as *The Pilgrim Migration* and *The Winthrop Fleet*.[2] Since the published volumes, covering the years from 1620 to 1635, contained about 2,400 sketches, this means that the current best estimate of the total number of families and unattached individuals in the Great Migration is about 5,600. This merged list consisted of limited information on each immigrant.

Finally, as a third step, from this merged list of all Great Migration immigrants, I created concise entries for each head of family or isolated individual, each entry to include a limited amount of information about the immigrant. For those persons in the checklist who arrived between 1620 and 1635, the entries comprise information extracted from the published sketches (and, when relevant, taking note of more recent research). For those who arrived between 1636 and 1640, I composed entries by adding to the checklist whatever additional data points were required to generate a useful entry, especially English origins, and then searching out the best treatment of the immigrant in the secondary literature. The result is a reference work that presents enough information about every Great Migration immigrant to provide the researcher with an easy path to the best treatments of an immigrant of interest (or to indicate that no useful treatment yet exists).

Preparing the entries for *The Great Migration Directory* had some similarities to the writing of full sketches in the previous Great Migration volumes. In both instances I made every effort to distinguish carefully between two or more persons of the same name. Work on the *Directory* required treating thousands of immigrants within a fixed period of time, so some cases warrant further investigation. As always, much work remains to be done.

SOME SAMPLE ENTRIES

Each entry in *The Great Migration Directory* has a limited number of standard fields:

> **Last name, First name:** English origin (if known); year of arrival in New England; New England residence(s); departure from New England (if applicable) [citations (keyed to a master list of titles)]. (Occasional comments.)

The reader will notice, for the most part, that the data included in an entry corresponds to the first section of a full Great Migration sketch, and incorporates the information specifically pertaining to the migration process for that immigrant. In the Great Migration Study Project, "English origin" always means the last known English residence before migration, not place of birth or any other known residence. This emphasizes the interest in the migration process itself, as the last known residence is likely to be the context within which the decision to migrate was made.

The entries deriving from the previously published volumes, representing families or individuals who arrived between 1620 and 1635, are in general shorter and simpler than those for later arrivals. In our first example the sole citation is to one of the Great Migration sketches, examination of which will provide the evidence for all the statements made in the entry.

> **Dady, William:** Unknown; 1631; Charlestown [GMB 505-8].

Given the fact that many of the Great Migration sketches are now twenty years old, there has been ample opportunity for new research, and the next entry reflects this situation, as the new research provides the English origin for the immigrant.

> **Thomson, James:** Fishtoft, Lincolnshire; 1633; Charlestown, Woburn [GMB 1809-11; TAG 74:101-4].

The passage of twenty years has also revealed that a few immigrants were missed in the process of research on the published volumes. In most cases, these were relatively minor immigrants, represented by only one or two records. But a few significant immigrants were omitted, as in the next example.

> **Blake, William:** Pitminster, Somerset; 1635 on *Hopewell*; Springfield, Dorchester [NGSQ 71:173; DChR 3; MBCR 1:375;

SpTR 159; TAG 74:15-28; NEHGR 163:85-97, 199-211, 278-88, 164:73-74, 175-83].

In general, *Directory* entries for immigrants from 1620 to 1635 who were missed in earlier publications may be identified as those which have a year of arrival in that range but do not have a citation to a published Great Migration volume.

This William Blake entry also demonstrates how the entries for those who arrived between 1636 and 1640 were created. While the entries for the 1620–1635 immigrants refer to earlier published Great Migration sketches and perhaps one or two other more recent sources, the entries for 1636–1640 immigrants usually contain a longer string of citations within the square brackets. The listing will almost always begin with a contemporaneous source that documents the year of arrival in New England, in this case a ship's passenger list published in the *National Genealogical Society Quarterly*. This item is here followed by three more citations to seventeenth-century sources, providing evidence for the two New England residences of William Blake. Finally, there are citations to the best treatments by modern genealogists.

No attempt is made in any of the entries to include references to all reliable secondary sources. In the case of the William Blake example, the multipart article in the *Register* provides ample references to earlier important research. In some cases more than one secondary source may be cited. Sometimes this indicates that two earlier researchers provide slightly different information on the immigrant; sometimes more than one secondary source is cited just because each is interesting.

In instances where no secondary source is cited, the immigrant and his or her family may not yet have been treated properly in print. Alternatively, any existing secondary treatments may be lacking in proper documentation, or may have serious and misleading defects. Whatever the explanation, when no secondary source is cited, I have not found any treatment that represents a significant advance on what James Savage composed a century and a half ago in his *Genealogical Dictionary of New England* (1860). Hundreds of the Great Migration immigrants have as yet not been the subjects of modern genealogical research and writing.

Many Great Migration immigrants returned permanently to England, and this may be noted at the end of the data string of the appropriate entries. In many of the entries of this type, the last citation will be to Susan Hardman Moore's *Abandoning America: Life-Stories from Early New England* (2013).

Introduction

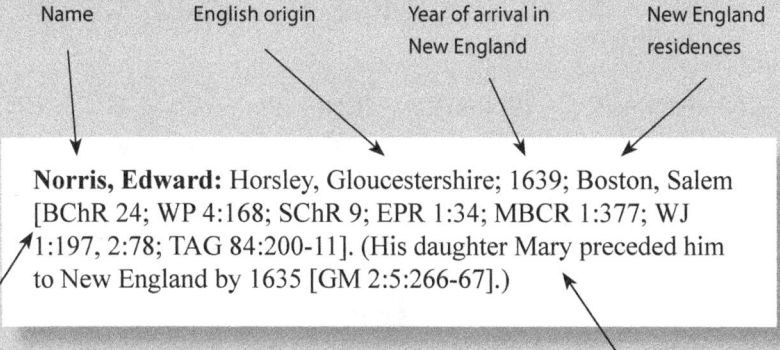

An entry from *The Great Migration Directory*

Name | English origin | Year of arrival in New England | New England residences

Norris, Edward: Horsley, Gloucestershire; 1639; Boston, Salem [BChR 24; WP 4:168; SChR 9; EPR 1:34; MBCR 1:377; WJ 1:197, 2:78; TAG 84:200-11]. (His daughter Mary preceded him to New England by 1635 [GM 2:5:266-67].)

Citations: *The Records of the First Church in Boston, 1630–1868*; *Winthrop Papers, 1498–1654*; *The Records of the First Church in Salem, Massachusetts, 1629–1736*; *The Probate Records of Essex County, Massachusetts, 1635–1681*; *Records of the Governor and Company of the Massachusetts Bay in New England, 1628–1686*; John Winthrop, *The History of New England from 1630 to 1649*, James Savage, ed.; and *The American Genealogist*

Additional comment with a citation to *The Great Migration: Immigrants to New England, 1634–1635*.

Hall, Samuel: Unknown; 1633; Ipswich, Salisbury; returned permanently to England after 1662 [GMB 844-48; Abandoning 362-63].

Sometimes immigrants, after some documented period of residence in New England, will simply disappear from the records. They may have returned to England, or removed to a colony outside New England, or died without leaving a death record or a probate file or any descendants. The standard annotation for such immigrants is "not seen after" the year of the last discovered record.

Martin, Ambrose: Unknown; 1637; Dorchester, Concord; not seen after 1642 [DTR 24, 28, 30; DChR 4; CoVR 2; MBCR 1:252].

Hundreds of immigrants in the *Directory* are represented by only one or two records. Such entries include a parenthetic note indicating that the record or records cited are all that have been found for this particular person. Such parenthetic notes will always include the word "only."

Hadson, John: Unknown; 1639; Newport (court appearance only) [RICR 1:94].

As these last few examples indicate, many of the Great Migration immigrants have left behind unresolved puzzles. The annotations to these entries are intended as a challenge to future researchers.

SCOPE

The Great Migration Directory attempts to include all those who immigrated to New England during the Great Migration, and only those immigrants. After much examination of the historical record, and particularly of the activities of the passenger vessels each spring, I determined that the Great Migration ended during 1640,[3] and so this volume is designed to include every head of household or unattached individual who arrived between 1620 and 1640.

This basic conclusion must be tempered by two other considerations, which have always guided the Great Migration Study Project. First, because published errors are immortal, an error of omission is always preferable to an error of commission. If someone who was not a Great Migration immigrant is included in this volume, that mistaken conclusion will live forever on library shelves. If, on the other hand, a demonstrable Great Migration immigrant is omitted from this volume, he or she can always be added to the list. Thus, when deciding whether or not to include a given immigrant in this volume, I have always taken a conservative approach.

Second, because very few passenger vessels sailed from England to New England during the winter months, the Great Migration Study Project has always assumed that anyone who appears in New England records by May of a given year must have arrived no later than the previous calendar year. This explains the decision noted above, in discussing the creation of the checklist, to survey all contemporaneous sources through May of 1641.

With this background in mind, let's review some examples of who has been included and who has been excluded. The largest source of false claims of participation in the Great Migration is the corpus of published genealogies of the last century and a half, which includes many undocumented and unsupported statements that this or that immigrant arrived in

1630 or at some other date between 1620 and 1640. One of the most egregious of such sources is the *History of Lynn* by Newhall, which includes a long list of immigrants said to have come in 1630, but with no justification or evidence. Unfortunately, James Savage, in compiling his *Genealogical Dictionary of New England* (1860), picked up many of these claims without expressing any doubts, and, more recently, Meredith Colket included many of these same statements in his *Founders of Early American Families* (1985). None of these immigrants, nor any of the hundreds more similarly claimed in other genealogies and journal articles, has been included in this volume, unless there exists independent evidence in contemporaneous sources for their arrival by 1640.

Conversely, however, I did not include in the *Directory* all those who appear in contemporaneous sources. For example, on a number of occasions crew members of the many vessels that came to New England, and especially those who came to Boston, ran afoul of the law during their brief time ashore, and thus made an appearance in the colony court records. When those who made a single appearance in the records may be identified as transient crew members or merchants, I have not listed them here.

Other men and women appear in the surviving records who never came to New England. Andrew Coleman, for example, appeared twice in New England sources in 1640, once in a Quarter Court session record in Boston and once in the notarial records maintained by Thomas Lechford.[4] These were in fact two versions of the same document, created by Lechford and then entered in the court records. Careful reading of the item shows that all the actions attributed to Coleman took place in England, and that he had authorized John Haynes of Hartford to act for him in New England. Andrew Coleman does not get an entry in the *Directory*.

A similar situation may be found with the ships' passenger lists. Many names appear on the lists of ships bound for New England with no evidence that the passenger ever arrived in New England. On such occasions, the *Directory* entry for that passenger will have the annotation "passenger list only" in the space where New England residences are usually given. When this notation is applied to a servant or a young single person, the passenger may simply have died during the passage or soon after arrival in New England. When such a person is a woman, she may possibly have married soon after arrival in New England, at a time when few marriage records were maintained. She may, therefore, have had a long life in New England, but we usually have no way of knowing this. However, when a passenger list records an entire family, comprising a husband, wife, and several children, and there is no New England record, the more likely explanation is that the family, having signed up for passage on the ship, changed their minds at the last moment and remained in England. An interesting research project would be to collect a number of instances of such families and attempt to find them in English records after the date of the ship's sailing.

On some occasions when the annotation "passenger list only" is employed, there is added the additional statement "(with caveat)." This indicates that some researchers have attempted to connect this passenger with a man or woman of the same name found at a later date in New England records. In these cases, my conclusion has been that there is not sufficient evidence to make the connection, but I do take note of these suggestions by earlier researchers.

A different but not very common problem arises when there is a defect in the contemporary sources. Such inconsistencies usually became apparent during the secondary source phase of the survey process. Savage has an entry for a Robert Pond who was supposed to have died at Dorchester in 1637. Indeed, there is a probate record for Robert Pond, consisting of one document, an inventory which was said to have been taken on 27 December 1637.[5] Closer examination of this record raises some questions, however. On 10 May 1648, the widow and one of the sons petitioned the court for an order to administer the estate, and the court ordered them to bring in an inventory.[6] And the widow remarried in 1649 or 1650.[7] Another look at the inventory reveals a description of land held by the decedent as "4 acres of meadow . . . he bought of Mrs. Burre." The only available "Mrs. Burre" in Dorchester was Frances Burr, the widow of Rev. Jonathan Burr, who had not arrived in New England until 1639 and who died in 1641. Robert Pond, therefore, must have been alive after 1641 to purchase land from Jonathan Burr's widow. The most parsimonious explanation is that the date on the inventory is simply wrong, and should be 27 December 1647 (on the assumption that the inventory had already been prepared prior to the court order of 10 May 1648). Robert Pond does not get an entry in the *Directory*.

Occasionally we are able to determine that an immigrant arrived in New England by 1640 without the existence of a contemporaneous record created during the years from 1620 to 1640.

One way to arrive at this conclusion is by implication. William B. Saxbe Jr. demonstrated that, although there is no record of Richard Bowen in New England by 1640, the first grandchild of Richard Bowen was born in 1641, and that the marriage that produced this grandchild must have taken place in New England. Richard Bowen's eldest child, his daughter Alice Bowen, married Robert Wheaton and their eldest known child was born in 1641. Robert Wheaton had arrived in Salem by 1636. One could construct a complicated scenario in which Robert Wheaton returned to England in the late 1630s, that the marriage of Robert Wheaton and Alice Bowen took place there, and that the Bowen and Wheaton families had then sailed for New England in 1641 or soon after. But the more likely solution is that Richard Bowen, although he did not immediately appear in New England records, must have arrived in New England by 1640 in order for his daughter Alice to marry Robert Wheaton and produce a child by early 1641. The result is a *Directory* entry such as the following:

> **Bowen, Richard:** Unknown; 1640; Salem, Weymouth, Rehoboth [William B. Saxbe Jr., *Richard Bowen (1594?-1675), of Rehoboth, Massachusetts, and His Descendants* (Williamstown, Massachusetts, 2011)].

Another way in which we may learn of the arrival of an immigrant during the Great Migration without there being a contemporaneous record is through a late deposition. Scott Andrew Bartley recently demonstrated, through a deposition made in 1681, that John Cooper, who first appeared in New England records at Scituate in late 1634 or early 1635,[8] had actually migrated to New England about four years earlier.[9] Immigrants whose year of arrival may be dated by such depositions are frequently servants who had arrived in the 1630s, but did not appear in New England records until the 1640s or even later. No way exists to search systematically for these depositions, so future research will undoubtedly reveal many more Great Migration immigrants in this way.

Should an ancestor of interest to you not appear in the *Directory*, please consider all these possible scenarios described above as the possible reason. If, however, you believe you have reliable documentation for a Great Migration immigrant not included in this volume, please let us know by emailing GreatMigration@nehgs.org, as we will be collecting additions and corrections for future publication.

RCA

Notes

1. This process is described in Robert Charles Anderson, "Editor's Effusions," *The Great Migration Newsletter* 22 (2013):2, 10.
2. Some of the most recently updated versions of Great Migration sketches came from the *The Pilgrim Migration: Immigrants to Plymouth Colony, 1620–1633*

(2004) and *The Winthrop Fleet: Massachusetts Bay Company Immigrants to New England, 1629–1630* (2012). Both of these Great Migration Study Project volumes by Robert Charles Anderson cover subsets of Great Migration immigrants.

3. Robert Charles Anderson, "When Did the Great Migration End?" *The Great Migration Newsletter* 22 (2013):3, 6.
4. Nathaniel B. Shurtleff, ed., *Records of the Governor and Company of the Massachusetts Bay in New England, 1628–1686*, 5 vols. in 6 (Boston: W. White, 1853–54) 1:298; Edward Everett Hale, ed., *Note-book Kept by Thomas Lechford, Esq., Lawyer, in Boston, Massachusetts Bay, from June 27, 138, to July 29, 1641* (Cambridge, 1885; rpt. Camden, Maine: Picton Press, 1988), 308.
5. Suffolk County Probate Records, Case #6.
6. Shurtleff, ed., *Records of the Governor and Company of the Massachusetts Bay in New England, 1628–1686* [note 4], 2:247.
7. Charles Henry Pope, *The Pioneers of Massachusetts . . .* (Boston 1900; rpt. Boston: NEHGS 2013), 366.
8. Robert Charles Anderson, *The Great Migration: Immigrants to New England, 1634–1635* (Boston: NEHGS, 2001), vol. 2, C–F, 200–2.
9. Scott Andrew Bartley, "John Cooper of Barnstable, Nephew of Sabin Staresmore," *Mayflower Descendant* 63 (Autumn 2014):152–74.

An earlier version of this introduction appeared in American Ancestors *magazine, Spring 2015 (vol. 16, no. 2, pp. 25-30).*

GREAT MIGRATION SOURCES

An essential step in creating *The Great Migration Directory* was the compilation of the checklist of those immigrants who arrived from 1636 to 1640. The following list comprises all those contemporary sources consulted for this group—as well as for the immigrants who arrived earlier—using the abbreviated titles as entered in the *Key to Titles*. For each of the items listed below, all pages were read, and names extracted, covering June 1636 through May 1641. For several of the New England towns settled in 1640 or earlier, no records created in 1640 or earlier survive. (New England towns are listed roughly north to south.)

Colony Court Records
Maine Provincial Court Records: MPCR
New Hampshire Provincial Papers: NHPP volume 40
Massachusetts Bay Court Records: MBCR
Records of the Court of Assistants (Massachusetts Bay): RCA
Plymouth Colony Records: PCR
Rhode Island Colony Records: RICR
Connecticut Colony Court Records: CCCR
New Haven Colony Court Records: NHCR

County Court Records
Essex Quarter Courts: EQC
Hampshire County Courts: Pynchon Court
Connecticut Particular Court Records: RPCC

Probate Records
Province of Maine: Maine Wills
New Hampshire: NHPP volume 31
Essex County: EPR
Suffolk County: SPR
Plymouth Colony: PCPR
Connecticut Colony: CCCR; Manwaring

Maine Towns
Richmond Island: Trelawny

New Hampshire Towns
Dover: NHPP volume 1
Strawbery Bank (Portsmouth): NHPP volume 1
Hampton: HmTR; HampVR; NHPP volume 1
Exeter: NHPP volume 1; Exeter Hist 435-43

Massachusetts Towns

Salisbury: SyTR
Haverhill: Births, Marriages and Deaths [FHL film #893120]
Newbury: NeTR; NewBOP
Ipswich: ITR
Gloucester: GlTR
Wenham: Fiske Notebook
Salem: STR; SChR; Perley 1:268-72
Lynn: EQC 2:270-71
Boston: BTR; BVR; BBOP; BChR
Dorchester: DTR; DChR; DVR
Roxbury: RBOP ; RChR; NEHGR 5:334, 6:183-84, 377-78
Charlestown: ChTR 1:36-120; ChBOP; ChVR; ChChR
Cambridge: CaTR; CaBOP; CaVR; Shepard
Watertown: WaTR; WaVR; WaBOP
Woburn: WoTR; WoVR
Dedham: DeTR; DeVR; DeChR
Concord: CoVR
Sudbury: SuTR; SuBOP
Hingham: HiBOP; HiTR; NEHGR 15:25-27 (Cushing record), 121:10-17 (Hobart record)
Weymouth: Weymouth Hist 1:183-99
Braintree: BrTR 1-2; BrVR; NEHGR 3:126-27, 247-48
Springfield: Springfield Hist 1:156-68; SpVR

Plymouth Towns

Plymouth: PTR
Scituate: ScitTR; NEHGR 9:280-87, 10:37-43
Duxbury: DuTR
Marshfield: MaTR; MaVR
Barnstable: Barnstable VR in MD volume 2
Sandwich: Sandwich TR in CCL #104:1-5
Rehoboth: ReTR

Rhode Island Towns

Providence: RICR; PrTR
Portsmouth: RICR; PoTR
Newport: RICR; RICR (MS); NHM 2:1-4, 65-69, 172-75, 220-22, 236-40 {22}
Warwick: RICR

Connecticut Towns
    Hartford: HaBOP; HaTR
    Wethersfield: WetLR
    Windsor: WiLR; Grant; CTVR
    Southampton: SoTR

New Haven Towns
    New Haven: NHChR
    Guilford: Guilford Hist 25
    Milford: MiTR; MiChR
    Stamford: SmTR

Correspondence
    Winthrop Family: WP
    John Cotton: Cotton Corr
    Roger Williams: RWCorr
    Thomas Gorges: Gorges
    Miscellaneous: Letters from NE

Passenger Lists
    Outports: Hotten; Drake's Founders; NGSQ 71:175-77; NEHGR 75:221-23

Miscellaneous
    Winthrop Journal: WJ
    Notarial Records: Lechford
    Harvard Graduates: Sibley
    Pequot War Narratives:
        Lyon Gardiner MHSC 3:3:131-60
        John Underhill MHSC 3:6:1-28
        John Mason MHSC 2:8:126-53
        Philip Vincent MHSC 3:6:29-43

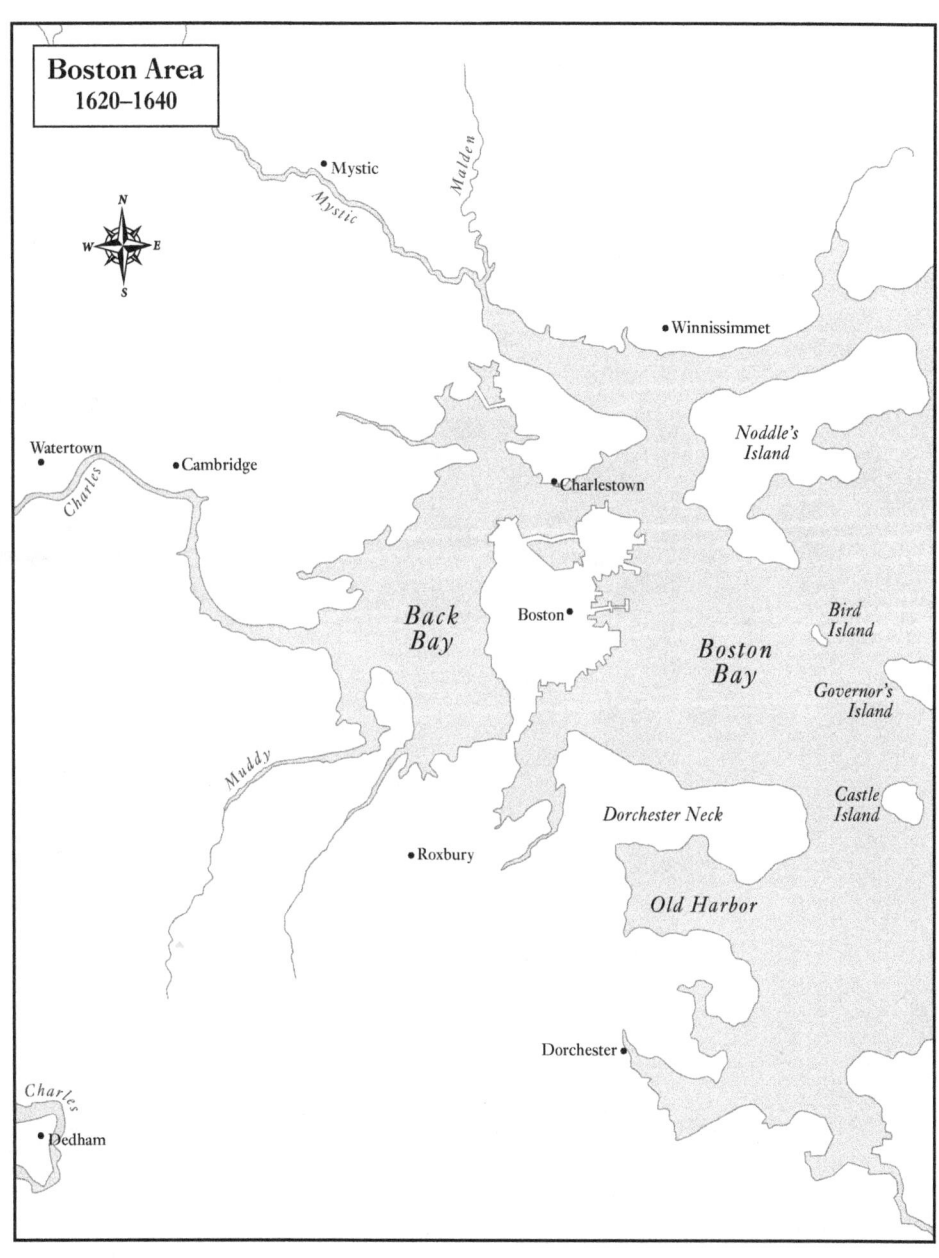

KEY TO TITLES

Abandoning	Susan Hardman Moore, *Abandoning America: Life-stories from Early New England* (Woodbridge, Suffolk, 2013)
Abel Lunt Anc	Walter Goodwin Davis, *The Ancestry of Abel Lunt, 1769-1806, of Newbury, Massachusetts* (Portland, Maine, 1963)
Ackley-Bosworth	Nathan Grier Parke II, *The Ancestry of Lorenzo Ackley & His Wife, Emma Arabella Bosworth*, Donald Lines Jacobus, ed. (Woodstock, Vermont, 1960)
Angell Anc	Dean Crawford Smith, *The Ancestry of Emily Jane Angell, 1844-1910* (Boston 1992)
Annis Spear Anc	Walter Goodwin Davis, *The Ancestry of Annis Spear, 1775-1858, of Litchfield, Maine* (Portland, Maine, 1945)
Aspinwall	"A Volume Relating to the Early History of Boston Containing the Aspinwall Notarial Records from 1644 to 1651," in *Reports of the Record Commissioners of the City of Boston*, Volume 32 (Boston 1903)
Austin	John Osborne Austin, *The Genealogical Dictionary of Rhode Island . . .* (Albany 1887; rpt. Baltimore 1969 [with *addenda et corrigenda* as published in TAG])
Backus Anc	Mary E.N. Backus, comp. and ed., *The New England Ancestry of Dana Converse Backus* (Salem 1949)
BarnPR	Barnstable County, Massachusetts, Probate Records

Bartlett-Jenkins	Edith Bartlett Sumner, *Ancestry and Descendants of Samuel Bartlett and Lucy Jenkins* (Los Angeles 1951)
Bassett-Preston	Belle Preston, *Bassett-Preston Ancestors* (New Haven 1930)
BBOP	"The Book of Possessions" for Boston, in *Second Report of the Record Commissioners of the City of Boston; containing the Boston Records, 1634-1660, and the Book of Possessions*, 2nd ed. (Boston 1881)
BChR	*The Records of the First Church in Boston, 1630-1868*, Publications of the Colonial Society of Massachusetts, Volumes 39, 40 and 41, Richard D. Pierce, ed. (Boston 1961)
Bethia Harris Anc	Walter Goodwin Davis, *The Ancestry of Bethia Harris, 1748-1833, Wife of Dudley Wildes of Topsfield, Massachusetts* (Portland, Maine 1934)
Blake-Glidden	Edith Bartlett Sumner, *Ancestry of Edward Wales Blake and Clarissa Matilda Glidden with Ninety Allied Families* (Los Angeles 1948)
Blakeney-Sabin	Josephine C. Frost, *Ancestors of Benjamin Ferris Blakeney and His Wife Stella Peronne Sabin* (Brooklyn 1926)
Blake-Torrey	Almira Torrey Blake Fenno-Gendrot, *The Ancestry and Allied Families of Nathan Blake 3rd and Susan (Torrey) Blake, Early Residents of East Corinth, Vermont* (Boston 1916)
Boardman Anc	William F. J. Boardman, *The Ancestry of William Francis Joseph Boardman* (Hartford 1906)
Bodge	George Madison Bodge, *Soldiers in King Philip's War being A Critical Account of That War with A Concise History of the Indian Wars of New England From*

	1620-1677 (Leominster, Massachusetts, 1896; rpt. Baltimore 1967)
Bond	Henry Bond, *Genealogies of the Families and Descendants of the Early Settlers of Watertown, Massachusetts* . . . , two volumes in one, second edition (Boston 1860)
Botsford-Marble	Donald Lines Jacobus, *An American Family: Botsford-Marble Ancestral Lines* (New Haven 1933)
Bradford	William Bradford, *Of Plymouth Plantation, 1620-1647*, Samuel Eliot Morison, ed. (New York 1952)
Bradford LB	*Governor William Bradford's Letter Book* (Boston, 1906; rpt. from *Mayflower Descendant*, 1904-6)
Brady Anc	L. Effingham deForest and Anne Lawrence deForest, *James Cox Brady and His Ancestry* (New York 1933)
Brainerd Anc	Thomas Chalmers Brainerd, *Ancestry of Thomas Chalmers Brainerd*, Donald Lines Jacobus, ed. (Montreal 1948)
Bridgewater Hist	Nahum Mitchell, *History of the Early Settlement of Bridgewater in Plymouth County, Massachusetts, Including an Extensive Family Register* (Boston 1840)
BrLR	Bristol County, Massachusetts, Land Records
BrPR	Bristol County, Massachusetts, Probate Records
BrTR	*Records of the Town of Braintree, 1640 to 1793*, Samuel A. Bates, ed. (Randolph 1886), pp. 1-625
BrVR	*Records of the Town of Braintree, 1640 to 1793*, Samuel A. Bates, ed. (Randolph 1886), pp. 627-940
BTR	"Boston Town Records," in *Second Report of the Record Commissioners of the City of Boston; containing the Boston Records,*

	1634-1660, and the Book of Possessions, 2nd ed. (Boston 1881)
BTR2	*A Report of the Record Commissioners of the City of Boston Containing the Boston Records from 1660 to 1701* (Boston 1881)
Builders of the Bay	Samuel Eliot Morison, *Builders of the Bay Colony* (Boston 1930)
Bulkeley Gen	Donald Lines Jacobus, *The Bulkeley Genealogy, Rev. Peter Bulkeley* (New Haven 1933)
Bushnell Anc	J. Gardner Bartlett, *The Ancestry of Daniel Bushnell* . . . (Boston 1918)
BVR	*Boston Births, Baptisms, Marriages, and Deaths, 1630-1699*, Ninth Report of the Boston Record Commissioners (Boston 1883; rpt. Baltimore 1978)
CA	*Connecticut Ancestry*, Volume 1 through present (1958+) [early volumes titled *Bulletin of the Stamford Genealogical Society*]
CaBOP	*The Register Book of the Lands and Houses in the "New Towne" and the Town of Cambridge* . . . (Cambridge 1896)
CaChR	Stephen Paschall Sharples, ed., *Records of The Church of Christ at Cambridge in New England, 1632-1830* (Boston 1906)
Calamy	Edmund Calamy, *The Nonconformist's Memorial* . . . , 3 volumes (London 1802)
Cambridge Hist	Lucius R. Paige, *History of Cambridge, Massachusetts. 1630-1877. With a Genealogical Register* (Boston 1877)
Cameos	Roger Thompson, *Camridge Cameos: Stories of Life in Seventeenth-Century New England* (Boston 2005)
CaTR	*The Records of the Town of Cambridge (Formerly Newtowne) Massachusetts, 1630-1703* . . . (Cambridge 1901)

CCCR	*The Public Records of the Colony of Connecticut, 1636-1776*, 15 volumes (Hartford 1850-1890)
CCL	Leonard H. Smith Jr., comp., *Cape Cod Library of Local History and Genealogy*, 2 vols. (Baltimore 1992)
Chapin	Howard M. Chapin, *Documentary History of Rhode Island*, 2 vols. (Providence 1916, 1919)
Chase-Wigglesworth	Alicia Crane Williams, *Chase-Wigglesworth Genealogy: The Ancestors and Descendants of Philip Putnam Chase and His Wife Anna Cornelia Wigglesworth* (Baltimore 1990)
ChBOP	*Charlestown Land Records, 1638-1802*, Third Report of the Boston Record Commissioners, 2nd ed. (Boston 1883)
ChChR	*Records of the First Church in Charlestown, Massachusetts, 1632-1789*, James Frothingham Hunnewell, ed. (Boston 1880)
Chelsea Hist	Mellen Chamberlain, *A Documentary History of Chelsea, Including the Boston Precincts of Winnisimmet, Rumney Marsh, and Pullen Point, 1624-1824*, 2 volumes (Boston 1908)
ChTR	Charlestown Town Records (from microfilm of original)
ChVR	*Vital Records of Charlestown, Massachusetts, to the Year 1850*, Volume I, Roger D. Joslyn, ed. (Boston 1984)
CN	*Connecticut Nutmegger*, Volume One through present (1968+)
Coldham	Peter Wilson Coldham, *The Complete Book of Emigrants, 1607-1660* (Baltimore 1987)
Coltman Anc	Edith Bartlett Sumner, *Ancestry and Descendants of James Hensman Coltman and Betsey Tobey* (Los Angeles 1957)

Comstock-Thomas	H. Minot Pitman, *Comstock-Thomas Ancestry of Richard Wilmot Comstock* (Bronxville, New York, 1964)
Conant Gen	Frederick Odell Conant, *A History . . . of the Conant Family* (Portland, Maine, 1887)
Cotton Corr	*The Correspondence of John Cotton*, ed. Sargent Bush Jr. (Chapel Hill 2001)
Council NE	"Records of the Council for New England," *Proceedings of the American Antiquarian Society*, Meeting of April 24, 1867, pp. 53-131
CoVR	*Concord, Massachusetts[:] Births, Marriages, and Deaths[:] 1635-1850* (Concord, n.d.)
CP	*The Complete Peerage of England, Scotland, Ireland, Great Britain and the United Kingdom*, The Hon. Vicary Gibbs, ed., 13 volumes in 14 (London 1910-1940)
Crucial Decade	Robert Emmet Wall Jr., *Massachusetts Bay: The Crucial Decade, 1640-1650* (New Haven 1972)
CSM	*Publications of the Colonial Society of Massachusetts*, Volume 1 to present (1895+)
CSPD	Calendar of State Papers, Domestic
CTLR	Connecticut Colony Land Records, Connecticut State Archives, Hartford, Connecticut
CTVR	*Births Marriages and Deaths Returned from Hartford, Windsor and Fairfield and Entered in the Early Land Records of the Colony of Connecticut . . .* , Edwin Stanley Welles, ed. (Hartford 1898)
DAB	*Dictionary of American Biography*
Davenport	Isabel MacBeath Calder, *Letters of John Davenport, Puritan Divine* (New Haven 1937)

Davis Fam	Samuel Forbes Rockwell, *Davis Families of Early Roxbury and Boston* (North Andover 1932)
Dawes-Gates	Mary Walton Ferris, *Dawes-Gates Ancestral Lines*, 2 vols. (n.p., 1943, 1931)
DChR	*Records of the First Church at Dorchester in New England, 1636-1734* (Boston 1891)
DeChR	*The Record of Baptisms, Marriages and Deaths . . . from the Church Records in the Town of Dedham, Massachusetts, 1638-1845 . . .* , Don Gleason Hill, ed. (Dedham 1888)
Deerfield Hist	George Sheldon, *A History of Deerfield, Massachusetts . . .* , 2 volumes (Deerfield 1895-1896)
DeHR	*The Dedham Historical Register*, 14 volumes (Dedham 1890-1903)
DeTR	*The Early Records of the Town of Dedham, Massachusetts. 1636-1659 . . . being Volume Three of the Printed Records of the Town*, Don Gleason Hill, ed. (Dedham 1892)
DeVR	*The Record of Births, Marriages and Deaths . . . in the Town of Dedham*, Volumes 1 & 2 . . . , Don Gleason Hill, ed. (Dedham 1886)
Doc Hist ME	*Documentary History of the State of Maine*, 24 vols. in *Collections of the Maine Historical Society, Second Series* (Portland, 1869-1916)
Doc Hist NY	*The Documentary History of the State of New York*, 4 vols., E.B. O'Callaghan, ed. (Albany 1849)
Doc Rel NY Hist	*Documents Relative to the Colonial History of the State of New York*, 15 vols., E.B. O'Callaghan, ed. (Albany 1853-1887)
Dover Hist	John Scales, *History of Dover, New Hampshire* (Dover 1923; rpt. Bowie, Maryland, 1977)

DoVR	*Vital Records of Dover, New Hampshire, 1686-1850* (Bowie, Maryland, 1977) (reprint of *Collections of the Dover, N.H., Historical Society*, Volume 1 [Dover 1894])
Drake's Boston	Samuel G. Drake, *The History and Antiquities of Boston, the Capital of Massachusetts and Metropolis of New England From its Settlement in 1630 to the Year 1770* (Boston 1856)
Drake's Founders	Samuel G. Drake, *Result of Some Researches Among the British Archives for Information Relative to the Founders of New England: Made in the Years 1858, 1859 and 1860* (Boston 1860)
Driver Gen	Harriet Ruth (Waters) Cooke, *The Driver Family: A Genealogical Memoir of the Descendants of Robert and Phebe Driver, of Lynn, Mass. . . .* (New York 1889)
DSGRM	*Detroit Society for Genealogical Research Magazine*, Volume 1 to present (Detroit, Michigan, 1937+)
DTR	*Fourth Report of the Record Commissioners of the City of Boston. 1880. Dorchester Town Records* (Boston 1883)
Dudley	Thomas Dudley, Letter to Lady Bridget, Countess of Lincoln, 12 and 28 March 1630/1, in *Letters from New England: The Massachusetts Bay Colony, 1629-1638,* Everett Emerson, ed. (Amherst, Massachusetts, 1976), pp. 66-83
Dudley Wildes Anc	Walter Goodwin Davis, *The Ancestry of Dudley Wildes, 1759-1820, of Topsfield, Massachusetts* (Portland, Maine, 1959)
DukesLR	Dukes County, Massachusetts, Deeds
Dunn	*The Journal of John Winthrop, 1630-1649*, edited by Richard S. Dunn, James Savage, and Laetitia Yeandle (Cambridge, Massachusetts, 1996)

DuTR	*Copy of the Old Records of the Town of Duxbury, Mass. From 1642 to 1770* (Plymouth 1893)
DuVR	*Vital Records of Duxbury, Massachusetts, to the Year 1850* (Boston 1911)
DVR	*Dorchester Births, Marriages, and Deaths to the End of 1825, Twenty-first Report of the Boston Record Commissioners* (Boston 1890)
Early Rehoboth	Richard LeBaron Bowen, *Early Rehoboth: Documented Historical Studies of Families and Events in This Plymouth Colony Township*, 4 volumes (Rehoboth 1945-1950)
Eastchester TR	Eastchester Historical Society, *Records of the Town of Eastchester, Book One*, typescript (Eastchester 1964)
Edgartown TR	Edgartown, Massachusetts, Town Records
EIHC	*Essex Institute Historical Collections*, Volume 1 to present (1859+)
ELR	Essex County, Massachusetts, Deeds, microfilm copies
Emerson-Benson	Edmund K. Swigart, *An Emerson-Benson Saga: The Ancestry of Charles F. Emerson and Bessie Benson and the Struggle to Settle the United States* (Baltimore 1994)
English Adventurers	Peter Wilson Coldham, *English Adventurers and Emigrants, 1609-1660* (Baltimore 1984)
EPR	*The Probate Records of Essex County, Massachusetts, 1635-1681*, 3 volumes (Salem 1916-1920; rpt. Newburyport, Massachusetts, 1988). Citations to the unpublished probate records are to case numbers, or to register volumes (which begin with volume 301).

EQC	*Records and Files of the Quarterly Courts of Essex County, Massachusetts, 1636-1686*, 9 volumes (Salem 1911-1975)
Essex Ant	*The Essex Antiquarian*, Volume 1 through 13, Sidney Perley, ed. (Salem 1897-1909)
Evans Festschrift	*Studies in Genealogy and Family History in Tribute to Charles Evans On the Occasion of His Eightieth Birthday*, Lindsay L. Brook, ed. (Salt Lake City 1989)
Exeter Hist	Charles H. Bell, *History of the Town of Exeter, New Hampshire* (Exeter 1888; rpt. Bowie, Maryland, 1979)
Fairfield LR	Fairfield, Connecticut, Deeds
Fairfield PR	Fairfield County, Connecticut, Probate Records
FANH	Donald Lines Jacobus, *Families of Ancient New Haven*, 9 volumes in 3 (Baltimore 1974; originally published as *New Haven Genealogical Magazine,* Volumes 1 through 8 [New Haven 1922-1932]; these were the first 8 volumes of TAG)
Farmington LR	Farmington, Connecticut, Deeds
Farm VR Barbour	Farmington Vital Records, Barbour Collection, Connecticut State Library, Hartford, Connecticut
Farr Anc	Edith Bartlett Sumner, *Descendants of Thomas Farr of Harpswell, Maine, and Ninety Allied Families* (Los Angeles 1959)
Farwell Gen	John Dennis Farwell, Jane Harter Abbott and Lillian M. Wilson, *The Farwell Family*, 2 volumes (n.p. 1929)
Fiske Notebook	*The Notebook of the Reverend John Fiske, 1644-1675*, Publications of the Colonial Society of Massachusetts, Volume 47 (Boston 1974)
Flagg Anc	Ernest Flagg, *Genealogical Notes on the Founding of New England, My Ancestors'*

	Part in that Undertaking (n.p. 1926; rpt. Baltimore 1973)
FOOF	Donald Lines Jacobus, comp. and ed., *History and Genealogy of the Families of Old Fairfield*, 3 volumes (Fairfield, Connecticut, 1930; rpt. Baltimore 1976, 1991)
Ford	William Bradford, *History of Plymouth Plantation, 1620-1647*, Worthington Chauncey Ford, ed., 2 volumes (Boston 1912)
Foster	Joseph Foster, *Alumni Oxonienses: The Members of the University of Oxford, 1500-1714* ..., 4 volumes (Oxford 1891-1892)
Foundations	*Foundations: Journal of the Foundation for Medieval Genealogy*
Gardiner	Lyon Gardiner, "Relation of the Pequot War," in Charles Orr, *History of the Pequot War* (Cleveland 1897)
GDMNH	Sybil Noyes, Charles Thornton Libby and Walter Goodwin Davis, *Genealogical Dictionary of Maine and New Hampshire* (Portland, Maine, 1928-1939; rpt. Baltimore 1972)
Gen Adv	*The Genealogical Advertiser*, v. 1-4 (Cambridge, 1898-1901; rpt. Baltimore, GPC, 1974)
Gen Bull	*The Genealogical Bulletin*
Gen Mag	*The Genealogical Magazine* (Salem, Massachusetts 1810-1915)
Gilbert Gen	Homer Worthington Brainard, Harold Simeon Gilbert and Clarence Almon Torrey, *The Gilbert Family, Descendants of Thomas Gilbert, 1582(?)-1659* (New Haven 1953)
Gilberts of NE	George Gordon Gilbert and Geoffrey Gilbert, *Gilberts of New England. Part I:*

	Descendants of John Gilbert of Dorchester, and Homer W. Brainard and Clarence A. Torrey, *Gilberts of New England. Part II: Descendants of Mathew Gilbert of New Haven, Humphrey Gilbert of Ipswich, and William Gilbert of Boston, from the Gilbert Family Manuscript Genealogy* (Victoria, British Columbia, 1959)
Giles Memorial	John Adams Vinton, *The Giles Memorial: Genealogical Memoirs of the Families Bearing the Names of Giles, Gould, Holmes, Jennison, Leonard, Lindall, Curwen, Marshall, Robinson, Sampson, and Webb . . .* (Boston 1864)
Gillespie Anc	Paul W. Prindle, *Ancestry of Elizabeth Barrett Gillespie (Mrs. William Sperry Beinecke)* (New Orleans 1976)
Gleaner	*Gleaner Articles*, Fifth Report of the Boston Record Commissioners (Boston revised 1887)
Gloucester Hist	John J. Babson, *History of the Town of Gloucester, Cape Ann, Including the Town of Rockport* (Gloucester 1860)
Glover Gen	Anna Glover, *Glover Memorials and Genealogies. An Account of John Glover of Dorchester and His Descendants . . .* (Boston 1867)
GlTR	Gloucester, Massachusetts, Town Records
GM	Robert Charles Anderson, George F. Sanborn Jr. and Melinde Lutz Sanborn, *The Great Migration: Immigrants to New England, 1634-1635*, Volume I, A-B (Boston 1999), Volume II, C-F (Boston 2001), Volume III, G-H (Boston 2003), Volume IV, I-L (Boston 2005), Volume V, M-P (Boston 2007), Volume VI, R-S (Boston 2009), Volume VII, T-Y (Boston 2011)

GMB	Robert Charles Anderson, *The Great Migration Begins: Immigrants to New England, 1620-1633*, 3 volumes (Boston 1995)
GMC26	John Brooks Threlfall, *Twenty-Six Great Migration Colonists To New England & Their Origins* (Madison, Wisconsin, 1993)
GMC50	John Brooks Threlfall, *Fifty Great Migration Colonists To New England & Their Origins* (Madison, Wisconsin, 1990)
GMN	*Great Migration Newsletter*, Volume 1 through present (1990+)
GMNJ	*Genealogical Magazine of New Jersey*, Volume 1 through present (1925+)
Goodman	Harrison Black, *The Ancestry of Frances Maria Goodman 1829-1912, Wife of Learner Blackman Harrison* (Boston 2001)
Goodwin-Morgan Anc	Frank Farnsworth Starr, *Various ancestral lines of James Goodwin and Lucy (Morgan) Goodwin, Hartford, Connecticut*, 2 vols. (Hartford 1915)
Gorges	*The Letters of Thomas Gorges, Deputy Governor of the Province of Maine, 1640-1643*, Robert E. Moody, ed. (Portland 1978)
GQM	*The Genealogical Quarterly Magazine*, Volume 1 through 5 (1900-1905)
Granberry	Donald Lines Jacobus, *The Granberry Family and Allied Families* (Hartford 1945)
Grant	"Matthew Grant Record, 1639-1681" in *Some Early Records and Documents of and Relating to The Town of Windsor, Connecticut, 1639-1703* (Hartford 1930)
Gravesend TR	Gravesend, New York, Town Records
Greenwich Hist	Spencer P. Mead, *Ye Historie of ye Town of Greenwich, County of Fairfield and State of Connecticut* (New York 1911)
Greenwich LR	Greenwich, Connecticut, Deeds

Gregory Stone Gen	J. Gardner Bartlett, *Gregory Stone Genealogy, Ancestry and Descendants of Dea. Gregory Stone of Cambridge, Mass., 1320-1917* (Boston 1918)
Guilford Fam	Alvan Talcott, *Families of Early Guilford, Connecticut* (Baltimore 1984)
Guilford Hist	Bernard C. Steiner, *A History of the Plantation of Menunkatuck and of the Original Town of Guilford, Connecticut* (Baltimore, Maryland, 1897)
HaBOP	*Original Distribution of the Lands in Hartford Among the Settlers, 1639*, Collections of the Connecticut Historical Society, Volume 14 (Hartford 1912; rpt. Bowie, Maryland, 1989)
HaCR	Helen Schatvet Ullmann, transcriber, *Hartford County, Connecticut, County Court Minutes, Volumes 3 and 4, 1663-1687, 1697* (Boston 2005)
Hadley Hist	Sylvester Judd, *The History of Hadley, Massachusetts* (1905; rpt. Somersworth, New Hampshire, 1976)
HadVR	Hadley, Massachusetts, Vital Records
HAHAC	Oliver Ayer Roberts, *History of . . . the Ancient and Honorable Artillery Company of Massachusetts, 1637-1888*, 4 volumes (Boston 1895-1901)
Hale, House	Donald Lines Jacobus and Edgar Francis Waterman, *Hale, House and Related Families, Mainly of the Connecticut River Valley* (Hartford 1952; rpt. Baltimore 1978)
Hall-Baldwin	Edith Bartlett Sumner, *Ancestry and Descendants of Amaziah Hall and Betsey Baldwin* (Los Angeles 1954)
HamCCR	Hampshire County, Massachusetts, Court Records
HamLR	Hampshire County, Massachusetts, Deeds, Springfield, Massachusetts

Hammatt Papers	Abraham Hammatt, *The Hammatt Papers. Early Inhabitants of Ipswich, Massachusetts. 1633-1700* (Ipswich 1880-1899; rpt. Baltimore 1980)
HamPR	Hampshire County, Massachusetts, Probate Records, Northampton, Massachusetts (and on microfilm)
Hampton Hist	Joseph Dow, *History of the Town of Hampton, New Hampshire: From Its Settlement in 1638, To the Autumn of 1892* (Salem 1893)
HampVR	*Vital Records of Hampton, New Hampshire To The End of the Year 1900*, Vol. 1, George Freeman Sanborn Jr. and Melinde Lutz Sanborn, eds. (Boston 1992)
HamVR	Manuscript volume of vital records kept at Hadley Town Hall; same hand, same format and similar time span as Pynchon VR; covers Hadley, Hatfield, Deerfield and Northampton
HaPR	Hartford County, Connecticut, Probate Registers (two sets of records in some volumes, "probate" side and "court" side)
Hartford First	George Leon Walker, *History of the First Church in Hartford, 1633-1883* (Hartford 1884)
Hartford PD	Hartford Probate District, original files, Connecticut State Archives (and on microfilm)
Hartford Second	Edwin Pond Parker, *History of the Second Church of Christ in Hartford* (Hartford 1892)
HarVR	Louise H. Kelley and Dorothy Straw, *Vital Records, Town of Harwich, Massachusetts, 1694-1850* (Harwich 1982)
HaTR	"Hartford Town Votes, Volume I. 1635-1716" in *Collections of the Connecticut Historical Society*, Volume 6 (Hartford 1897)

HaVR	"Early Hartford Vital Records" in *Collections of the Connecticut Historical Society*, Volume 14, pp. 575-632 (Hartford 1912; rpt. Bowie, Maryland, 1989)
HaVR Barbour	Hartford Vital Records, Barbour Collection, Connecticut State Library, Hartford, Connecticut
Hempstead TR	*Records of the Towns of North and South Hempstead, Long Island, New York, 1654-1880*, 8 volumes, Benjamin D. Hicks, ed. (Jamaica, New York, 1896-1904)
HiBOP	Hingham, Massachusetts, Book of Possessions (original)
Higginson	Francis Higginson, *New-Englands Plantation with The Sea Journal and Other Writings* (Salem 1908)
Hingham Hist	George Lincoln, *History of the Town of Hingham, Massachusetts*, 3 volumes (Hingham 1893; rpt. Somersworth, New Hampshire, 1982)
Hinsdale Gen	Alfred L. Holman, *Hinsdale Genealogy[:] Descendants of Robert Hinsdale of Dedham, Medfield, Hadley and Deerfield* . . . (Lombard, Illinois, 1906)
HiTR	Hingham, Massachusetts, Town Records (original)
HiVR	Hingham, Massachusetts, Vital Records (original)
HmTR	Hampton, New Hampshire, Town Records (from microfilm of original)
Holden Gen	Eben Putnam, *The Holden Genealogy*, 2 volumes (Boston 1923-26)
Hotten	*The Original Lists of Persons of Quality* . . . , John Camden Hotten, ed. (London 1874; rpt. Baltimore 1974)

Hoyt	David Webster Hoyt, *The Old Families of Salisbury and Amesbury, Massachusetts*, 3 vols. (Providence, R.I., 1897-1919)
Hubbard	William Hubbard, *A General History of New England from the Discovery to MDCLXXX* (Cambridge 1815)
Hubbard Indian Wars	William Hubbard, *The History of the Indian Wars in New England . . .* , ed. Samuel G. Drake (Roxbury, Massachusetts, 1865)
Hull	"Diary of John Hull" *in Transactions and Collections of the American Antiquarian Society*, Volume 3 (Worcester 1857)
Huntington TR	Charles R. Street, *Huntington Town Records, Including Babylon, Long Island, N.Y.*, 5 vols. in 8 (n.p. 1887-1889, 1981)
Hutchinson	Thomas Hutchinson, *The History of the Colony and Province of Massachusetts Bay*, 3 volumes, ed. Lawrence Shaw Mayo (Cambridge 1936)
Hutchinson Papers	*The Hutchinson Papers*, 2 volumes (Albany 1865
HvBOP	Haverhill Book of Possessions
IHSP	*Publications of the Ipswich Historical Society*, 29 volumes (1894-1935)
ILR	Ipswich Land Records, manuscript, Essex County Courthouse, Salem, Massachusetts
Ipswich Hist	Thomas Franklin Waters, *Ipswich in the Massachusetts Bay Colony*, 2 vols. (Ipswich 1905, 1917)
ITR	Ipswich, Massachusetts, Town Records (both the originals and the limited records that have been published are muddled and unpaginated, so no volume or page citations are given with this citation)
JIC	*A Tribute to John Insley Coddington on the Occasion of the Fortieth Anniversary of The American Society of Genealogists,*

	Neil D. Thompson and Robert Charles Anderson, eds. (New York 1980)
John White	Frances Rose-Troup, *John White, The Patriarch of Dorchester [Dorset] and The Founder of Massachusetts, 1575-1648* . . . (New York 1930)
Johnson	Edward Johnson, *Johnson's Wonder-Working Providence, 1628-1651*, J. Franklin Jameson, ed. (New York 1910)
Joseph Neal Anc	Walter Goodwin Davis, *The Ancestry of Joseph Neal, 1769-c.1835* (Portland, Maine, 1945)
Kempton Anc	Dean Crawford Smith, *The Ancestry of Eva Belle Kempton, 1878-1908, Part I: The Ancestry of Warren Francis Kempton, 1817-1879* (Boston 1996), *Part II: The Ancestry of Amanda Spiller, 1823-1873* (Boston 2008), *Part III: The Ancestry of Henry Clay Bartlett, 1832-1892* (Boston 2004), and *Part IV: The Ancestry of Linda Anna Powers, 1839-1879* (Boston 2000)
Kings County Settlers	Teunis G. Bergen, *Register in Alphabetical Order of the Early Settlers of Kings County, Long Island, N.Y.* . . . (rpt. Cottonport, Louisiana, 1973)
Kittery Hist	Everett S. Stackpole, *Old Kittery and Her Families* (Lewiston, Maine, 1903; rpt. Somersworth, New Hampshire, 1981)
KitVR	Joseph Crook Anderson II and Lois Ware Thurston, *Vital Records of Kittery, Maine, To The Year 1892*, Maine Genealogical Society Special Publication No. 8 (Camden, Maine, 1991)
Lancaster Records	Henry S. Nourse, *The Early Records of Lancaster, Massachusetts. 1643-1752* (Lancaster, Massachusetts, 1884; rpt. Bowie, Maryland, 1993)
LanVR	Henry S. Nourse, ed., *The Birth, Marriage and Death Register, Church Records and*

	Epitaphs of Lancaster, Massachusetts. 1643-1850 (Lancaster 1890; rpt. Bowie, Maryland, 1993)
LCVR	James N. Arnold, *Vital Record of Rhode Island, 1636-1850*, First Series, Volume 4, Part VI, Little Compton (Providence 1893)
Lechford	*Note-book Kept by Thomas Lechford, Esq., Lawyer, in Boston, Massachusetts Bay, from June 27, 1638, to July 29, 1641*, Edward Everett Hale, Jr., ed. (Cambridge 1885; rpt. Camden, Maine, 1988). Citations herein refer to the pagination as printed (and not to the manuscript pagination) and will therefore differ from the index entries of the 1885 edition.
Legal Executions	Daniel Allen Hearn, *Legal Executions in New England, 1623-1960* (Jefferson, North Carolina, 1999)
Letters of NE	*Letters from New England. The Massachusetts Bay Colony, 1629-1638*, Everett Emerson, ed. (Amherst, Massachusetts, 1976)
Lewis	Samuel Lewis, *A Topographical Dictionary of England ...*, 4 volumes (London 1831; rpt. Baltimore 1996 as four volumes in two)
Little Compton Fam	Benjamin Franklin Wilbour, *Little Compton Families* (Little Compton, Rhode Island, 1967)
LI Wills	William Smith Pelletreau, *Early Long Island Wills of Suffolk County, 1691-1703* (New York 1897)
London Depositions	Peter Wilson Coldham, *Lord Mayor's Court of London Depositions Relating to Americans, 1641-1736* (Washington, D.C., 1980)
Lydia Harmon Anc	Walter Goodwin Davis, *The Ancestry of Lydia Harmon, 1755-1836, Wife of Joseph Waterhouse of Standish, Maine* (Boston 1924)

Lyme VR	Verne M. Hall and Elizebeth B. Plimpton, comps., *Vital Records of Lyme, Connecticut to the End of the Year 1850* (Lyme 1976)
Lynn Hist	Alonzo Lewis and James Newhall, *History of Lynn* . . . (Lynn, Massachusetts, 1890)
LynnHSR	*The Register of the Lynn Historical Society*, Numbers 1 through 23, 1897-1926
Lyon-Rice	Patty Barthell Myers, *Ancestors and Descendants of Thomas Rice and His Wife Harriet Wade Rice with Related Families* (San Antonio 2003)
M&JCH	*Search for the Passengers of the Mary & John 1630*, Volume 1 through present (Toledo, Ohio, 1985+)
MA Arch	"Massachusetts Archives," being bound volumes of loose papers at the Commonwealth Archives of Massachusetts, Boston, Massachusetts
MA Civil List	William H. Whitmore, *The Massachusetts Civil List for the Colonial and Provincial Periods, 1630-1774* (Albany 1870; rpt. Baltimore 1969)
Magnalia	Cotton Mather, *Magnalia Christi Americana* . . . , 2 volumes (Hartford 1855)
Maine PR	John Eldridge Frost, *Maine Probate Abstracts*, 2 volumes (Camden, Maine, 1991)
Maine Wills	William M. Sargent, *Maine Wills, 1640-1760* (Portland 1887; rpt. Baltimore 1972)
Malden Hist	Deloraine Pendre Corey, *The History of Malden, Massachusetts, 1633-1785* (Malden 1899)
Manwaring	*A Digest of the Early Connecticut Probate Records, Volume One, Hartford Probate District, 1635-1700*, Charles William Manwaring, comp. (Hartford 1904)
Marblehead	Thomas E. Gray, *The Founding of Marblehead* (Baltimore 1984)

MarVR	*Vital Records of Marshfield, Massachusetts, to the year 1850*, Robert M. Sherman and Ruth Wilder Sherman, eds. (n.p. 1970)
Martha's Vineyard Hist	Charles Edward Banks, *The History of Martha's Vineyard, Dukes County, Massachusetts in Three Volumes* (Edgartown 1966)
Mason	John Mason, "Brief History of the Pequot War," in Charles Orr, *History of the Pequot War* (Cleveland 1897), pp. 1-46
MBCR	*Records of the Governor and Company of the Massachusetts Bay in New England, 1628-1686*, Nathaniel B. Shurtleff, ed., 5 volumes in 6 (Boston 1853-1854)
McArthur-Barnes	Selim Walker McArthur, *McArthur-Barnes Ancestral Lines*, Donald Lines Jacobus, ed. (Portland, Maine, 1964)
McCormick-Hamilton	Elizabeth Day McCormick and Robert Hall McCormick III, patrons, *McCormick-Hamilton, Lord-Day Ancestral Lines* (privately printed, 1957)
MCF	Middlesex County Court Files, deposited at the Commonwealth Archives of Massachusetts, Boston, Massachusetts
MCR	Middlesex County, Massachusetts, Court Record Books (microfilm)
MD	*Mayflower Descendant*, Volume 1 through present (1899-1937, 1985+)
Medfield Hist	William S. Tilden, ed., *History of the Town of Medfield, Massachusetts. 1650-1886* (Boston 1887)
MeHGR	*The Maine Historical and Genealogical Recorder*
MF	*Mayflower Families* (the "silver" books)
MFIP	*Mayflower Families in Progress* (the "pink" books)
MHGR	*Maine Historical & Genealogical Recorder*

MHSC	*Collections of the Massachusetts Historical Society*, Volume 1 through present (1792+). This serial is divided into a number of series, so the citations will sometimes be in three parts, designating series, volume and page.
MHSP	*Proceedings of the Massachusetts Historical Society*, Volume 1 through present (1791+). This serial is divided into a number of series, so the citations will sometimes be in three parts, designating series, volume and page.
MidChR	Middletown, Connecticut, Church Records
Middleboro Hist	Thomas Weston, *History of the Town of Middleboro, Massachusetts* (Cambridge 1906)
MiddleVR	*Middleborough, Massachusetts Vital Records*, Barbara Lambert Merrick and Alicia Crane Williams, eds., 2 vols. (Boston 1986, 1990)
MidLR	Middletown, Connecticut, Deeds
MidVR	Middletown, Connecticut, Vital Records
MidVR Barbour	Middletown, Connecticut, Vital Records, Barbour transcript
Milford ChR	Milford, Connecticut, Church Records
Milford Fam	Susan Woodruff Abbott, *Families of Early Milford, Connecticut* (Baltimore 1979)
Milford LR	Milford, Connecticut, Land Records
Milford VR Barbour	Milford, Connecticut, Vital Records, Barbour transcript
Miner Anc	Lillian Lounsberry (Miner) Selleck (and Donald Lines Jacobus), *One Branch of the Miner Family . . . and Fifty Other Allied Families of Connecticut and Long Island* (New Haven 1928)
Minor Diary	*The Diary of Thomas Minor, Stonington, Connecticut. 1653 to 1684* (n.p. 1899; rpt. n.p. 1993 [with the diary of Manasseh Minor, 1696 to 1720])

MLR	Middlesex County, Massachusetts, Deeds
Moore Anc	L. Effingham deForest and Anne Lawrence deForest, *Moore and Allied Families: The Ancestry of William Henry Moore* (New York 1938)
Morison	Samuel Eliot Morison, *The Founding of Harvard College* (Cambridge 1935) [especially for Appendix B, "English University Men Who Emigrated to New England Before 1646," pp. 359-410]
Morton	Nathaniel Morton, *New-England's Memorial . . .* (Plymouth 1826)
Mourt	*A Journal of the Pilgrims at Plymouth. Mourt's Relation. A Relation or Journal of the English Plantations Settled at Plymouth in New England, by Certain English Adventurers Both Merchants and Others*, Dwight B. Heath, ed. (New York 1963)
Mower Anc	Lyman Mower, *The Ancestry of Calvin Robinson Mower (1840-1927)* (Durham, New Hampshire, 2004)
MPCR	*Province and Court Records of Maine*, 6 volumes (Portland 1928-1975; volumes 1-3 rpt. Newburyport, Massachusetts, 1991)
MPR	Middlesex County, Massachusetts, Probate Records
MQ	*Mayflower Quarterly*, Volume 1 to present (1935+)
Nantucket Hist	Alexander Starbuck, *The History of Nantucket: County, Island, and Town, Including Genealogies of the First Settlers* (Rutland, Vermont, 1969)
Nantucket Land	Henry Barnard Worth, *Nantucket Lands and Land Owners* (Bowie, Maryland, 1992)
NanTR	Nantucket, Massachusetts, Town Records (as with many other early New England towns, this volume contains deeds, and, since the

	town and county are co-extensive, county court records are also included)
NanVR	Nantucket, Massachusetts, Vital Records
NEA	*New England Ancestors*, Volumes 1-11 (2000-2010)
NEHGR	*New England Historical and Genealogical Register*, Volume 1 through present (1847+)
NeTR	Newbury, Massachusetts, Town Records
NewBOP	Newbury, Massachusetts, Proprietors' Records
Newbury Hist	Joshua Coffin, *A Sketch of the History of Newbury, Newburyport & West Newbury* (Hampton, New Hampshire, 1845)
Newbury Hist (Currier)	John J. Currier, *History of Newbury, Mass., 1635-1902* (Boston 1902)
Newell Anc	William M. Emery, *Newell Ancestry: The Story of the Antecedents of William Stark Newell* (n.p. 1944)
New English Canaan	Thomas Morton, *New English Canaan* (Amsterdam 1637; rpt. Boston 1883)
New London Hist	Frances Mannering Caulkins, *History of New London, Connecticut* (New London 1852)
New London PD	New London County, Connecticut, Probate District
Newport Gleanings	Jane Fletcher Fiske, *Gleanings from Newport Court Files, 1659-1783* (Boxford, Massachusetts, 1998)
Newton Gen	Ermina Elizabeth Newton Leonard, comp., *Newton Genealogy, Genealogical, Biographical, Historical: Being a Record of the Descendants of Richard Newton of Sudbury and Marlborough, Massachusetts, 1638* . . . (DePere, Wisconsin, 1915)
NewtownTR	Newtown, New York, Town Records

New York Wills	Original wills of New York (microfilm)
NGSQ	*National Genealogical Society Quarterly*, Volume 1 through present (1912+)
NHChR	New Haven, Connecticut, Church Records
NHCR	*Records of the Colony and Plantation of New Haven, 1638-1649, 1653-1664*, 2 volumes, Charles J. Hoadly, ed. (Hartford 1857-1858)
NHGR	*New Hampshire Genealogical Record*, Volume 1 through present (1903-1910; 1990+)
NHLR	New Haven, Connecticut, Land Records
NHM	"Extracts from Rhode Island Colonial Records," *The Newport Historical Magazine* 1:236-40, 2:1-4, 65-69, 172-75, 220-22
NHPCR	New Hampshire Province Court Records, manuscript records at New Hampshire Division of Records Management and Archives, Concord, New Hampshire
NHPLR	New Hampshire Provincial Deeds, New Hampshire Division of Records Management and Archives, Concord, New Hampshire
NHPP	*Provincial Papers, Documents and Records Relating to the Province of New Hampshire from 1686 to 1722*, 40 volumes, Nathaniel Boulton, ed. (Manchester, N.H., 1867-1943)
NHPPR	New Hampshire Provincial Probate Records, New Hampshire Division of Records Management and Archives, New Hampshire
NHPR	New Haven, Connecticut, Probate Records
NHTR	*New Haven Town Records*, 3 volumes, Franklin Bowditch Dexter, ed. (New Haven 1917-1962)

NHVR	*Vital Records of New Haven, 1649-1850*, 2 volumes (Hartford 1917, 1924)
NJArch	New Jersey Archives
NJHSP	*New Jersey Historical Society Proceedings*, four series, 1845 to present
NLChR	New London, Connecticut, Church Records
NLCR	New London County, Connecticut, Court Records
NLLR	New London, Connecticut, Deeds
NLPR	New London, Connecticut, Probate Records
NLR	(Old) Norfolk County, Massachusetts, Deeds
NLVR Barbour	New London Vital Records, Barbour Collection, Connecticut State Library, Hartford, Connecticut
Northampton Hist	James Russell Trumbull, *History of Northampton, Massachusetts, from Its Settlement in 1654* (Northampton 1902)
North Brookfield Hist	J.H. Temple, *History of North Brookfield, Massachusetts* (North Brookfield 1887)
NorthVR	Northampton, Massachusetts, Vital Records
Norwalk Hist	Charles M. Selleck, *Norwalk* (Norwalk 1896)
Norwalk Records	Edwin Hall, comp., *The Ancient Historical Records of Norwalk, Conn.* (Norwalk 1847)
Norwich Cem	George S. Porter, *Inscriptions from Gravestones in the Old Burying Ground, Norwich Town, Connecticut* (Norwich 1933)
NoVR	*Vital Records of Norwich, 1659-1848*, 2 volumes (Hartford 1913)
Noyes-Gilman	Charles Phelps Noyes, *Noyes-Gilman Ancestry* (St. Paul, Minnesota, 1907)
NYCalendar	E.B. O'Callaghan, ed., *Calendar of Historical Manuscripts in the Office of the Secretary of State, Albany, N.Y.* (Albany 1865)
NYChR	*Marriages from 1639 to 1801 in the Reformed Dutch Church, New York*, Collections of the New York Genealogical and

Biographical Society, Volume I (New York 1890), and *Baptisms from 1639 to 1730 in the Reformed Dutch Church, New York*, Collections of the New York Genealogical and Biographical Society, Volume II (New York 1901)

NYCM	New York Council Minutes
NYGBR	*The New York Genealogical and Biographical Record*, Volume 1 through present (1869+)
NY Lists	E.B. O'Callaghan, *Lists of Inhabitants of Colonial New York*, ed. Rosanne Conway (Baltimore 1979)
NYHM:D	New York Historical Manuscripts: Dutch
NYHM:E	New York Historical Manuscripts: English
NYMarr	*New York Marriages Previous to 1784 . . .* (Baltimore 1968, 1984)
NYWills	[William S. Pelletreau], *Abstracts of Wills on File in the Surrogate's Office, City of New York*, 17 volumes, New-York Historical Society Collections 25-41 (New York 1893-1909)
ODNB	*Oxford Dictionary of National Biography*
OED	*Oxford English Dictionary*
Old Dover	John Scales, *Historical Memoranda concerning Persons and Places in Old Dover, N.H.* (Dover 1900)
Old South Hist	[Hamilton Andrews Hill and George Frederick Bigelow], *An Historical Catalogue of the Old South Church (Third Church) Boston, 1669-1882* (Boston 1883)
ONGQ	*Old Northwest Genealogical Quarterly*, Volume 1 through 15 (1898-1912)
Ordway Anc	Dean Crawford Smith, *The Ancestry of Samuel Blanchard Ordway, 1844-1916* (Boston 1990)

Otis	Amos Otis, *Genealogical Notes of Barnstable Families* . . . , 2 volumes (Barnstable, Massachusetts, 1888, 1890; rpt. Baltimore 1979, in 1 volume)
Oyster Bay TR	*Oyster Bay Town Records, 1653-1878*, 8 vols. (New York 1916-1940)
Parke-Gildersleeve	Nathan Grier Parke II, *The Ancestry of Rev. Nathan Grier & his Wife, Ann Elizabeth Gildersleeve*, Donald Lines Jacobus, ed. (Woodstock 1959)
Parker-Ruggles	John William Linzee, Jr., *The History of Peter Parker and Sarah Ruggles of Roxbury, Mass., and Their Ancestors and Descendants* (Boston 1913)
PCC	Prerogative Court of Canterbury, England
PCCR	David Thomas Konig, ed., *Plymouth Court Records, 1686-1859*, 16 vols. (Wilmington, Delaware, 1978-1981)
PChR	*Plymouth Church Records, 1620-1859, Part 1 and Part 2* in Publications of the Colonial Society of Massachusetts, volumes 22 and 23 (Boston 1920, 1923)
PCLR	Plymouth Colony Deeds (from microfilm; Volume 1 has been published as Volume 12 of PCR)
PCR	*Records of the Colony of New Plymouth in New England*, Nathaniel B. Shurtleff and David Pulsifer, eds., 12 volumes in 10 (Boston 1855-1861)
PCPR	Plymouth Colony Probate Records (from microfilm)
PCY	Prerogative Court of York
Pemaquid Papers	"Pemaquid Papers," in *Collections of the Maine Historical Society*, vol. 5 (Portland 1857), pp. 1-138

Perley	Sidney Perley, *The History of Salem, Massachusetts*, 3 volumes (Salem 1924-1928)
PGM	*Pennsylvania Genealogical Magazine*
Phoebe Tilton Anc	Walter Goodwin Davis, *The Ancestry of Phoebe Tilton, 1775-1847, The Wife of Capt. Abel Lunt of Newburyport, Massachusetts* (Portland 1947)
Pillsbury Anc	Mary Lovering Holman, *Ancestry of Charles Stinson Pillsbury and John Sargent Pillsbury* . . . 2 vols. (Concord, N.H., 1938)
Plain Dealing	Thomas Lechford, *Plain Dealing: or, Newes From New-England* (London 1642)
Planters	Charles Edward Banks, *The Planters of the Commonwealth, 1620-1640* (Boston 1930; rpt. Baltimore 1972)
PLR	Plymouth County, Massachusetts, Deeds (from microfilm)
Plymouth Wills	C.H. Simmons, Jr., *Plymouth Colony Records, Volume 1, Wills and Inventories, 1633-1669* (Camden, Maine, 1996)
PM	Robert Charles Anderson, *The Pilgrim Migration: Immigrants to Plymouth Colony, 1620-1633* (Boston 2004)
PN&Q	*Pilgrim Notes and Queries*
PoLE	Portsmouth, Rhode Island, Land Evidences
Pope	Charles Henry Pope, *The Pioneers of Massachusetts* . . . (Boston 1900; rpt. Baltimore 1965)
Pope MNH	Charles Henry Pope, *The Pioneers of Maine and New Hampshire, 1623 to 1660* . . . (Boston 1908; rpt. Baltimore 1973)
Portland Hist	William Willis, *The History of Portland, From Its First Settlement* . . . (Portland 1833)
Portsmouth Misc	Loose papers at the Portsmouth, Rhode Island, Town Hall

Portsmouth TR	Frank W. Hackett, *1645-1656[,] Portsmouth Records[:] A Transcript of the First Thirty-Five Pages of the Earliest Town Book[,] Portsmouth[,] New Hampshire[,] With Notes* (Portsmouth 1886)
PoTR	*The Early Records of the Town of Portsmouth* (Providence 1901)
PoVR	Portsmouth, Rhode Island, Vital Records
PPR	Plymouth County, Massachusetts, Probate Records (from microfilm)
Prince	Thomas Prince, *A Chronological History of New England* . . . , Samuel G. Drake, ed., third edition (Boston 1852)
PRO	Public Record Office, London, England
Providence Home Lots	Charles Wyman Hopkins, *The Home Lots of the Early Settlers of the Providence Plantations* (Providence 1886)
PrTR	*The Early Records of the Town of Providence*, 21 volumes (Providence 1892-1915)
PTR	*Records of the Town of Plymouth*, Volume 1, 1636 to 1705 (Plymouth 1889)
Putnam's Mag	*Putnam's Monthly Historical Magazine*, Volumes 1-7 (1892-99)
PVR	*Vital Records of Plymouth, Massachusetts, to the Year 1850*, Lee D. van Antwerp, comp., and Ruth Wilder Sherman, ed. (Camden, Maine, 1993)
Pynchon Court	*Colonial Justice in Western Massachusetts (1639-1702), The Pynchon Court Record. An Original Judges' Diary of the Administration of Justice in the Springfield Courts in the Massachusetts Bay Colony*, Joseph H. Smith, ed. (Cambridge, Massachusetts, 1961)
Pynchon Papers	*The Pynchon Papers, Volume I: Letters of John Pynchon, 1654-1700* and *Volume II: Selections from the Account Books of*

	John Pynchon, 1651-1697, Publications of the Colonial Society of Massachusetts, Volumes 60 and 61, Carl Bridenbaugh, ed. (Boston 1982)
Pynchon VR	Manuscript volume of vital records kept by John Pynchon, at Connecticut Valley Historical Museum, Springfield, Massachusetts
RBOP	*Roxbury Book of Possessions* in Sixth Report of the Boston Record Commissioners (Boston 1884), pp. 11-51
RCA	*Records of the Court of Assistants*, 3 volumes (Boston 1901-1928)
RChR	*Roxbury Land and Church Records*, Sixth Report of the Boston Record Commissioners (Boston 1884), pp. 74-191
ReadingChR	James F. Cooper Jr. and Kenneth P. Minkema, eds., *The Colonial Church Records of the First Church of Reading (Wakefield) and the First Church of Rumney Marsh (Revere)* (Boston 2006)
ReVR	James N. Arnold, *Vital Record of Rehoboth, 1642-1896* . . . (Providence 1897)
RICR	*Records of the Colony of Rhode Island and Providence Plantations* . . . , 1636-1692, 10 volumes, John Russell Bartlett, ed. (Providence 1856-1865)
RICR (MS)	Rhode Island Court Records, Volume One (manuscript volume, from which court records were abstracted for the published RICR; some records, mostly deeds, were not included in the published RICR, and are available only in this manuscript volume)
RICT	*Rhode Island Court Records: Records of the Court of Trials of the Colony of Providence Plantations, 1647-1662*, Volume I (Providence 1920) [RICT 1]; *Rhode Island Court Records: Records*

	of the Court of Trials of the Colony of Providence Plantations, 1662-1670, Volume II (Providence 1922) [RICT 2]; Jane Fletcher Fiske, trans., *Rhode Island General Court of Trials, 1671-1704* (Boxford, Massachusetts, 1998) [RICT 3]
RIGR	*Rhode Island Genealogical Register*, Volume 1 through present (1978+)
RIHSC	*Rhode Island Historical Society Collections*, Volume 1 through present (1827+)
RILE	*Rhode Island Land Evidences, Volume I, 1648-1696* (Providence 1921; rpt. Baltimore 1970)
RIRoots	*Rhode Island Roots*, Volume 1 through present (1975+)
RIVR	James N. Arnold, *Vital Record of Rhode Island, 1636-1850*, Volumes 1 through 21 (Providence 1891-1912)
Rodgers	Robert H. Rodgers, *Middlesex County in the Colony of the Massachusetts Bay in New England: Records of Probate and Administration, Volume One, October 1649-December 1660* (Boston 1999), *Volume Two: March 1660/61-December 1670* (Boston 2001) and *Volume Three, February 1670/71-June 1676* (Rockport, Maine, 2005)
Rowley Fam	George Brainard Blodgette, comp., *Early Settlers of Rowley, Massachusetts* (Rowley 1933)
Rowley Records	Benjamin P. Mighill and George B. Blodgette, *The Early Records of the Town of Rowley, Massachusetts. 1639-1672. Being Volume One of the Printed Records of the Town* (Rowley 1894)
RPCC	*Records of the Particular Court of Connecticut, 1639-1663*, Collections of the Connecticut

	Historical Society, Volume 22 (Hartford 1928; rpt. Bowie, Maryland, 1987)
RTR	Robert J. Dunkle & Ann S. Lainhart, *The Town Records of Roxbury, Massachusetts, 1647 to 1730, Being Volume One of the Original* (Boston 1997)
RVR MS	Roxbury Vital Records, manuscript copy at New England Historic Genealogical Society, Boston
RWCorr	*The Correspondence of Roger Williams, Volume One 1629-1653, Volume Two 1654-1682*, Glenn W. LaFantasie, ed. (Providence 1988)
Saints	George F. Willison, *Saints and Strangers . . .* (New York 1945)
Saints and Sectaries	Emery Battis, *Saints and Sectaries: Anne Hutchinson and the Antinomian Controversy in the Massachusetts Bay Colony* (Chapel Hill 1962)
Saltonstall Papers	Robert E. Moody, *The Saltonstall Papers, 1607-1815, Volume 1: 1607-1789*, Collections of the Massachusetts Historical Society, Volume 80 (Boston 1972)
SandVR	Caroline Lewis Kardell and Russell A. Lovell, Jr., *Vital Records of Sandwich, Massachusetts, to 1885*, 3 volumes (Boston 1996)
Sarah Hildreth Anc	Walter Goodwin Davis, *The Ancestry of Sarah Hildreth, 1773-1857, Wife of Annis Spear of Litchfield, Maine* (Portland, Maine, 1958)
Sarah Johnson Anc	Walter Goodwin Davis, *The Ancestry of Sarah Johnson, 1775-1824, Wife of Joseph Neal of Litchfield, Maine* (Portland 1960)
Sarah Miller Anc	Walter Goodwin Davis, *The Ancestry of Sarah Miller, 1755-1840, Wife of Lieut. Amos Towne of Arundel (Kennebunkport), Maine* (Portland 1939)

Sarah Stone Anc	Walter Goodwin Davis, *The Ancestry of Sarah Stone, Wife of James Patten of Arundel (Kennebunkport) Maine* (Portland 1930)
Savage	James Savage, *A Genealogical Dictionary of the First Settlers of New England*, 4 volumes (Boston 1860-1862; rpt. Baltimore 1965)
SChR	*The Records of the First Church in Salem, Massachusetts, 1629-1736*, Richard D. Pierce, ed. (Salem 1974)
SCC	*Records of the Suffolk County Court, 1671-1680*, 2 vols., in *Publications of The Colonial Society of Massachusetts*, vols. 29 and 30 (Boston, 1933)
SCHSR	*Suffolk County Historical Society Register*
Scituate Hist	Samuel Deane, *History of Scituate, Massachusetts, From Its First Settlement to 1831* (Boston 1831)
ScitTR	Jeremy Dupertuis Bangs, *The Seventeenth-Century Town Records of Scituate, Massachusetts*, 2 volumes (Boston 1997, 1999)
Scott Gen	Mary Lovering Holman, *The Scott Genealogy* . . . (Boston 1919)
Scrapbook	*The Plymouth Scrap Book, The Oldest Original Documents Extant In Plymouth Archives . . .*, Charles Henry Pope, ed. (Boston 1918)
ScVR	*Vital Records of Scituate, Massachusetts, to the Year 1850*, 2 volumes (Boston 1909)
Seversmith	Herbert Furman Seversmith, *Colonial Families of Long Island, New York and Connecticut Being the Ancestry & Kindred of Herbert Furman Seversmith . . .* , typescript (Washington DC 1939-1958)
Sewall	*The Diary of Samuel Sewall,* Volume One 1674-1708, Volume Two 1709-1729, M. Halsey Thomas, ed. (New York 1973)
Sex in Middlesex	Roger Thompson, *Sex in Middlesex: Popular Mores in a Massachusetts County, 1649-1699* (Amherst, Massachusetts, 1986)

Key to Titles

Shepard	*Thomas Shepard's Confessions*, Publications of the Colonial Society of Massachusetts, Volume 58, George Selement & Bruce C. Woolley, eds. (Boston 1981)
Shepard Fam	Donald Lines Jacobus, ed., *The Shepard Families of New England*, 3 volumes, comp. Gerald Faulkner Shepard (New Haven 1971-1973)
Sibley	John Langdon Sibley, *Biographical Sketches of Graduates of Harvard University, 1642-1689*, 3 volumes (Cambridge 1873-1885)
Simon Stone Gen	J. Gardner Bartlett, *Simon Stone Genealogy . . .* (Boston 1926)
Shattuck	Lemuel Shattuck, *A History of the Town of Concord . . .* (Boston 1835)
Sir Ferdinando Gorges	James Phinney Baxter, *Sir Ferdinando Gorges and His Province of Maine . . .* , 3 volumes (Boston 1890)
SJC	Supreme Judicial Court, Massachusetts
SLR	*Suffolk Deeds*, Volumes 1 through 14 (Boston 1880-1906). Citations to later volumes are from the microfilm copies of the originals.
Small Gen	Lora Altine Woodbury Underhill, *Descendants of Edward Small of New England and the Allied Families with Tracings of English Ancestry*, revised edition, 3 volumes (Boston and New York, 1934)
Smith-Hale	Mary Audentia Smith Anderson, *Ancestry and Posterity of Joseph Smith and Emma Hale* (Independence, Missouri, 1929)
SmTR	Paul R. Finch, ed., *Stamford Town Records, Volume 1:1641-1723* (Boston 2011)
Snow-Estes	Nora E. Snow, *The Snow-Estes Ancestry*, 2 volumes (Hillburn, New York, 1939)
Southampton Hist	George Rogers Howell, *The Early History of Southampton, L.I., New York, with Genealogies* (Albany 1887)

Southampton TR	*The First Book of Records of the Town of Southampton* . . . (Sag-Harbor, New York, 1874)
Southold TR	J. Wickham Case, ed., *Southold Town Records Copied and Explanatory Notes Added*, 2 volumes (Riverhead 1882, 1884)
Spencer	Wilbur D. Spencer, *Pioneers on Maine Rivers with Lists to 1651* . . . (Portland, Maine, 1930; rpt. Bowie, Maryland, 1990)
SPR	Suffolk County, Massachusetts, Probate Records
SPR NS	Suffolk County, Massachusetts, Probate Records, New Series
Springfield Fam	Thomas B. Warren, *Springfield Families*, 3 vols. (Springfield 1934-1935)
Springfield Hist	Henry M. Burt, *The First Century of the History of Springfield. The Official Records from 1636 to 1736*, 2 volumes (Springfield 1898 & 1899)
SpTR	Springfield, Massachusetts, Town Records
SpVR	Clifford L. Stott, comp., *Vital Records of Springfield, Massachusetts to 1850*, 6 vols. (Boston 2003)
Stevens-Miller Anc	Mary Lovering Holman (and Winifred Lovering Holman), *Ancestry of Colonel John Harrington Stevens and his wife Frances Helen Miller*, 2 volumes (n.p. 1948, 1951)
Stillwell	John E. Stillwell, *Historical and Genealogical Miscellany: Data Relating to the Settlement and Settlers of New York and New Jersey*, 5 vols. (n.p. 1903-32; rpt. Baltimore 1970)
Stone-Gregg	Alicia Crane Williams, *Stone-Gregg Genealogy: The Ancestors and Descendants of Galen Luther Stone and His Wife Carrie Morton Gregg* (Baltimore 1987)

Stonington Hist	Richard Anson Wheeler, *History of the Town of Stonington, County of New London, Connecticut, From Its First Settlement in 1649 to 1900, With a Genealogical Register of Stonington Families* (1900; rpt. Mystic 1966)
StonVR Barbour	Stonington Vital Records, Barbour Collection, Connecticut State Library, Hartford, Connecticut
STR	*Town Records of Salem, Massachusetts*, 1634-1691, 3 volumes (Salem 1868, 1913, 1934)
Stratton	Eugene Aubrey Stratton, *Plymouth Colony: Its History & People, 1620-1691* (Salt Lake City 1986)
SuBOP	Sudbury, Massachusetts, Book of Possesions
Suffolk Sessions	Thomas W. Cooper, comp., *The Records of the Court of Sessions of Suffolk County in the Province of New York, 1670-1688* (Bowie, Maryland, 1993)
SuTR	Sudbury, Massachusetts, Town Records
SVR	*Vital Records of Salem, Massachusetts, to the End of the Year 1849*, 6 volumes (Salem 1916-1925; rpt. Newburyport, Massachusetts, 1988)
SwVR	*Vital Records of Swansea, Massachusetts to 1850*, transcribed by H.L. Peter Rounds (Boston 1992)
SyTR	Salisbury, Massachusetts, Town Records
TAG	*The American Genealogist*, Volume 9 to present (1932+)
Taunton Hist	Samuel Hopkins Emery, *History of Taunton, Massachusetts, from Its Settlement to the Present Time* (Syracuse 1893)
TEG	*The Essex Genealogist*, Volume 1 to present (1981+)
TG	*The Genealogist*, Volume 1 to present (1980+)

Three Episodes	Charles Francis Adams, *Three Episodes of Massachusetts History*, 2 volumes (Boston and New York, 1903)
Three Visitors	Sydney V. James, Jr., *Three Visitors to Early Plymouth* (Plymouth 1963)
TMG	*The Maine Genealogist*, Volume 1 through present (1977+) [early issues titled *Maine Seine*]
TNA	The National Archives, London, England (formerly PRO)
Topo Dict	Charles Edward Banks, *Topographical Dictionary of 2885 English Emigrants to New England, 1620-1650*, Elijah Ellsworth Brownell, ed. (Philadelphia 1937; rpt. Baltimore 1957)
TopsHC	*The Historical Collections of the Topsfield Historical Society*, Volume 1 to present (1895+)
TopsTR	*Town Records of Topsfield, Massachusetts*, 2 vols. (Topsfield 1917-1920)
Torrey	Clarence Almon Torrey, *New England Marriages Prior to 1700*, 12 volumes, original manuscript, New England Historic Genealogical Society
Trelawny	*The Trelawny Papers*, James Phinney Baxter, ed., in *Collections of the Maine Historical Society, 2nd Series*, Volume 3 (Portland, Maine, 1884)
Two Voyages	John Josselyn, *Colonial Traveler. A Critical Edition of Two Voyages to New England*, Paul J. Lindholdt, ed. (Hanover, N.H., and London, 1988)
Venn	John Venn and J.A. Venn, *Alumni Cantabrigienses, Part I (From the Earliest Times to 1751)*, 4 volumes (Cambridge 1922-1927)

Vinton Memorial	John Adams Vinton, *The Vinton Memorial, Comprising a Genealogy of the Descendants of John Vinton of Lynn, 1648 . . .* (Boston 1858)
WaBOP	"Lands, Grants, Divisions, Allotments, Possessions and Proprietors' Book," Section Two in *Watertown Records Comprising the First and Second Books of Town Proceedings . . .* (Watertown 1894)
WaChR	Watertown Church Records, Watertown Town Records, volume 4
WarLE	Warwick, Rhode Island, Land Evidences
WarTR	*The Early Records of the Town of Warwick* (Providence 1926)
Warner-Harrington	Frederick Chester Warner, *The Ancestry of Samuel, Freda and John Warner*, typescript (Boston 1949-55)
Waterhouse Anc	Walter Goodwin Davis, *The Ancestry of Joseph Waterhouse, 1754-1837, of Standish, Maine* (Portland 1949)
Waterman Gen	E.F. Waterman, *The Waterman Family*, Donald Lines Jacobus, ed., 3 volumes (New Haven 1939-1954)
Waters	Henry FitzGilbert Waters, *Genealogical Gleanings In England*, 2 volumes (Boston 1901)
WaTR	"Records of Town Proceedings—First and Second Books," Section One in *Watertown Records Comprising the First and Second Books of Town Proceedings . . .* (Watertown 1894)
WaVR	"Records of Births, Deaths and Marriages - First Book and Supplement," Section Three in *Watertown Records Comprising the First and Second Books of Town Proceedings . . .* (Watertown 1894)

Webster	Tom Webster, *Godly Clergy in Early Stuart England: The Caroline Puritan Movement, c.1620-1643* (Cambridge, England, 1997)
Wentworth Gen	John Wentworth, *The Wentworth Genealogy: English and American*, 3 volumes (Boston 1878)
Westchester Court	Dixon Ryan Fox, ed., *The Minutes of the Court of Sessions (1657-1696), Westchester County, New York*, Publications of the Westchester County Historical Society, Volume II, Source Series, Volume I (White Plains, New York, 1924)
WetLR	Wethersfield, Connecticut, Land Records
Wethersfield Hist	Henry Reed Stiles, *The History of Ancient Wethersfield*, 2 vols. (New York 1904; rpt. Somersworth, New Hampshire, 1987)
WetVR Barbour	Wethersfield Vital Records, Barbour Collection, Connecticut State Library, Hartford, Connecticut
WeVR	*Vital Records of Weymouth, Massachusetts, to the Year 1850*, 2 volumes (Boston 1910)
Weymouth Hist	George Walter Chamberlain, *History of Weymouth, Massachusetts, Volumes Three and Four, Genealogy of Weymouth Families* (Weymouth 1923; rpt. Baltimore 1984, 2 volumes in 1)
WeyTR	Weymouth, Massachusetts, Town Records, original manuscript at town hall, Weymouth, Massachusetts
WF	Robert Charles Anderson, *The Winthrop Fleet: Massachusetts Bay Company Immigrants to New England, 1629-1630* (Boston 2012)
WiLR	Windsor, Connecticut, Deeds (microfilm of original at Connecticut State Library, Hartford, Connecticut)

Windsor Hist	Henry Reed Stiles, *The History and Genealogies of Ancient Windsor, Connecticut* . . . , 2 vols. (Hartford, 1891-92)
Witchhunting	David D. Hall, *Witchhunting in Seventeenth-Century New England: A Documentary History, 1638-1693* (Boston 1991)
WiVR	Windsor Vital Records, typescript, Connecticut State Library (1918-29)
WiVR Barbour	Windsor Vital Records, Barbour Collection, Connecticut State Library, Hartford, Connecticut
WJ	John Winthrop, *The History of New England from 1630 to 1649*, James Savage, ed., 2 volumes (Boston 1853). Citations herein refer to the pagination of the 1853 and not the 1826 edition, even though the index to the 1853 edition continues to use the 1826 pagination.
WMJ	Medical Journals of John Winthrop Jr., 1657-1669, manuscript, Massachusetts Historical Society, Boston, Massachusetts
WMQ	*William and Mary Quarterly*
Wood	William Wood, *New England's Prospect*, Alden T. Vaughan, ed. (Amherst 1977)
Woolson-Fenno	Lula May Fenno Woolson, *The Woolson-Fenno Ancestry and Allied Lines with Biographical Sketches* (n.p. 1907)
Worthley	Harold Field Worthley, *An Inventory of the Records of the Particular (Congregational) Churches of Massachusetts Gathered 1620-1805*, in *Harvard Theological Studies*, volume 25 (Cambridge 1970)
WoVR	Edward F. Johnson, *Woburn Records of Births, Deaths, and Marriages, from 1640 to 1873*, 4 parts (Woburn 1890-1894)
WP	*Winthrop Papers, 1498-1654*, 6 volumes, various editors (Boston 1925-1992)

WWP	Johnson's *Wonder-Working Providence, 1628-1651*, J. Franklin Jameson, ed. (New York 1910; rpt. 1952)
Wyllys Papers	"The Wyllys Papers. Correspondence and Documents Chiefly of Descendants of Gov. George Wyllys of Connecticut. 1590-1796" in *Collections of the Connecticut Historical Society*, Volume 21 (Hartford 1924)
Wyman	Thomas Bellows Wyman, *The Genealogies and Estates of Charlestown, Massachusetts: 1629-1818*, 2 volumes (Boston 1879; rpt. in 1 volume Somersworth, New Hampshire, 1982)
YarVR	Robert M. Sherman and Ruth Wilder Sherman, *Vital Records of Yarmouth, Massachusetts To The Year 1850*, 2 vols. (Warwick, Rhode Island, 1975)
YLR	*York Deeds*, 18 volumes (Portland, Maine, 1887-1910)
York Hist	Charles Edward Banks, *History of York, Maine*, 2 volumes (Boston 1931, 1935)
Young's First Planters	*Chronicles of the First Planters of the Colony of Massachusetts Bay* . . . , Alexander Young, ed. (Boston 1846; rpt. Baltimore 1975)
Young's Pilgrim Fathers	*Chronicles of the Pilgrim Fathers of the Colony of Plymouth* . . . , Alexander Young, ed. (Boston 1844; rpt. Baltimore 1974)

Abbey, John: Unknown; 1636; Salem, Wenham [STR 1:22, 28, 79; EQC 1:12, 22; Granberry 139-42; Cleveland Abbe and Josephine Genung Nichols, *Abbe-Abbey Genealogy* (New Haven 1916)].

Abbott, Daniel: Unknown; 1630; Watertown, Cambridge, Providence [GMB 1-3; WF 61-64].

Abbott, George: Unknown; 1639; Windsor, Norwalk [CCCR 1:49; FOOF 1:5; Lemuel Abijah Abbott, *Descendants of George Abbott of Rowley, Mass.*, 2 volumes (n.p. 1906), 2:975-78].

Abbott, John: Unknown; 1635 on *Hopewell*; possibly killed at Cambridge in 1637, otherwise no New England record [GM 2:1:1].

Abbott, Mary: Unknown; 1635 on *Hopewell*; passenger list only [GM 2:1:1].

Abbott, Robert: Unknown; 1634; Watertown, Wethersfield, New Haven, Branford [GM 2:1:1-6].

Abdy, Matthew: London; 1635 on *Abigail*; Boston [GM 2:1: 6-8].

Abell, Robert: London; 1630; Weymouth, Rehoboth [GMB 3-6; WF 64-68; TG 9:89].

Ackerly, Henry: Unknown; 1639; New Haven, Stamford [NHCR 1:32; SmTR 6, 25, 63-64, 72-73].

Adams, Dorothy: Unknown; 1635 on *Defence*; passenger list only [GM 2:1:8].

Adams, Edward: Unknown; 1640; Massachusetts Bay (court appearance only) [MBCR 1:316].

Adams, Edward: Unknown; 1640; New Haven, Milford, Fairfield [NHCR 1:46; FOOF 1:7-11].

Adams, Ferdinando: Ipswich, Suffolk; 1637; Dedham; returned permanently to England in 1641 [WP 3:439-40; DeTR 1:32; DeChR 22, 36-37; MBCR 1:377; Abandoning 31-32].

Adams, Henry: Kingweston, Somerset; 1639; Braintree [BTR 1:49; BrVR 629; SPR 1:27; TAG 53:18-20, 79:217, 85:382-85; NEHGR 153:213-14; J. Gardner Bartlett, *Henry Adams of Somersetshire, England, and Braintree, Mass.* (New York 1927)].

Adams, Jeremy: Unknown; 1633; Cambridge, Hartford [GMB 6-11].

Adams, John: Unknown; 1621 on *Fortune*; Plymouth [GMB 11-12; PM 1-2].

Adams, John: Unknown; 1636; Salem (servant; court appearance only) [EQC 1:3].

Adams, Nathaniel: Unknown; 1640; Newport, Weymouth, Boston [RICR 1:92; TAG 30:65-73].

Adams, Richard: Batcombe, Somerset; 1635 on *Marygould*; Weymouth, Malden [GM 2:1:8-11].

Adams, Richard: Unknown; 1635 on *Abigail*; Salem [GM 2:1:11-12].

Adams, Robert: Unknown; 1638; Salem, Newbury [STR 1:74; EQC 1:21; NEHGR 9:126, 59:322, 151:308-12; Andrew N. Adams, *A Genealogical History of Robert Adams of Newbury, Mass., and His Descendants, 1635-1900* (Rutland, Vermont, 1900)].

Adams, William: Unknown; 1635; Cambridge, Ipswich [GM 2:1:13-14; MBCR 1:375; NEQ 82:136-69; Essex Ant 2:87]. (His son William came to New England in 1635 on the *Elizabeth & Ann* [GM 2:1:13]. The *New England Quarterly* article cited here connects, corrects and amplifies these two Great Migration sketches.)

Addington, Isaac: Unknown; 1639; Boston [BChR 30; NEHGR 4:116-20].

Addis, Henry: Unknown; 1639; Salem (court appearance only) [EQC 1:17, 20].

Adey, Webb: Unknown; 1632; Plymouth [GMB 12-14; PM 2-4].

Ager, William: Unknown; 1630; Salem [GMB 14-15].

Aires (or Arres), Samuel: Norwich, Norfolk; 1637 on *John & Dorothy* or *Rose* or *Mary Anne*; passenger list only (servant) [Hotten 289, 294].

Albee, Benjamin: Unknown; 1639; Braintree, Medfield, Mendon, Swansea [BTR 1:49; NEHGR 3:126, 163:212, 164:295; SPR 2:17; Medfield Hist 293-94; TAG 40:213].

Albee, John: Unknown; 1640; Braintree [NEHGR 3:126; BrTR 2; MBCR 2:293].

Albon, Alice: Unknown; 1635 on *Hopewell*; passenger list only [GM 2:1:14].

Albro, John: Unknown; 1634 on *Francis*; Boston, Portsmouth [GM 2:1:15-20].

Alcock, Agnes: Unknown; 1635 on *Abigail*; passenger list only [GM 2:1:20].

Alcock, Francis: Unknown; 1638 on *Bevis*; passenger list only [Drake's Founders 61].

Alcock, George: Leicester, Leicestershire; 1630; Roxbury [GMB 15-18; WF 68-71].

Alcock, John: Mancetter, Warwickshire; 1639; York [YLR 2:176-77, 4:20; Gorges 4; GDMNH 59-60; York Hist 1:114-15; NEHGR 36:400-1; NHGR 26:49-56].

Alcock, Thomas: Unknown; 1630; Boston, Dedham [GMB 18-20; WF 71-74].

Alden, John: Southampton; 1620 on *Mayflower*; Plymouth, Duxbury [GMB 21-26; PM 4-10].

Alderedg, Widow: Unknown; 1638; Plymouth (court appearance only) [PCR 1:100].

Alderman, John: Unknown; 1634 on *Recovery*; Dorchester, Salem [GM 2:1:20-23].

Aldis, Nathan: Fressingfield, Suffolk; 1639; Dedham [DeChR 22; DeTR 1:67; DeHR 14:18-23; NEHGR 150:473-94].

Aldrich, George: Unknown; 1636; Dorchester, Braintree, Mendon [DChR 4; MBCR 1:372; DTR 28; Alvin James Aldrich, *The George Aldrich Genealogy, 1605-1971* (n.p. 1971)].

Aleworth, Francis: Unknown; 1630; Massachusetts Bay; returned permanently to England in 1632 [GMB 26].

Alexander, John: Unknown; 1637; Plymouth Colony; banished in 1637 [PCR 1:64].

Alford, William: London; 1634; Salem, Boston [GM 2:1:23-26].

Alger, Andrew: Yealmpton, Devon; 1632; Richmond Island, Scarborough [GMB 27-29].

Alger, Thomas: Unknown; 1630; Casco, Richmond Island [GMB 29-30].

Alger, Tristram: Unknown; 1637; Richmond Island [Trelawny 112, 184, 194, 290; GDMNH 61].

Allen, Arnold: London; 1640; Casco [MPCR 1:61, 64, 65, 70, 78, 100; Trelawny 234; SLR 1:75; Aspinwall 272-73; WP 5:66-67, 77, 151-52; Spencer 212-13, 236-37].

Allen, Bozoun: King's Lynn, Norfolk; 1638 on *Diligent*; Hingham, Boston [NEHGR 5:299-300, 8:60-61, 15:26; HiTR 3; HiBOP 87; Lechford 304-5; MBCR 1:378; Waters 601-2, 1447; WJ 2:271-88; Hingham Hist 2:8; Robert Emmet Wall Jr., *Massachusetts Bay: The Crucial Decade, 1640-1650* (New Haven 1972), 93-120].

Allen, Elizabeth: Unknown; 1638; Boston [BChR 24, 34]. (She married Samuel Stone.)

Allen, George: Unknown; 1635; Weymouth, Sandwich [GM 2:1:27-35; TAG 80:27-37; NEHGR 155:212-14].

Allen, Henry: Unknown; 1639; Massachusetts Bay (court appearance only) [MBCR 1:297].

Allen, Joan: Unknown; 1630; Weymouth [GMB 30]. (She married Clement Briggs.)

Allen, John: Unknown; 1634; Dorchester, Springfield [GM 2:1:35; WP 4:296, 330].

Allen, John: Hernehill, Kent; 1635 on *Abigail*; Plymouth, Scituate [GM 2:1:36-39].

Allen, John: Unknown; 1639; Charlestown [ChTR 46; ChBOP 10, 50; MBCR 1:378; NEHGR 4:183; SPR 2:8; Wyman 17-18; Flagg Anc 263-64; HAHAC 1:85].

Allen, Robert: Unknown; 1633; Marblehead [GMB 31].

Allen, Robert: Unknown; 1636; Salem, Manchester, New London [STR 1:22; Perley 2:13; Granberry 152-53; Waterman Gen 1:603-6].

Allen, Samuel: Unknown; 1634; Massachusetts Bay [GM 2:1:39-40]. (Possibly one of the following.)

Allen, Samuel: Unknown; 1638; Windsor [NEHGR 30:444-46; Hale, House 447-52].

Allen, Samuel: Unknown; 1639; Braintree [BTR 1:49; Martha's Vineyard Hist 3:3; NEHGR 83:507-11].

Allen, Samuel: Unknown; 1639; Newport (admission as inhabitant only; possibly the Braintree man) [RICR 1:92].

Allen, Thomas: Braunton, Devon; 1636; Dorchester, Barnstable [CCCR 1:4, 33, 43, 45; Lechford 328, 352, 378, 418; MD 2:213; PCPR 4:1:49; Hale, House 447-48; TAG 57:115-19; Otis 5-12; Bond 668].

Allen, Thomas: Norwich, Norfolk; 1638; Boston, Charlestown; returned permanently to England in 1651 [BChR 22; ChChR 10, 48; MBCR 1:284; ChTR 51; NEHGR 4:183; Wyman 16-17; ODNB; Abandoning 32-35].

Allen, Walter: Bury St. Edmunds, Suffolk; 1638; Newbury, Charlestown, Watertown [WP 4:97; Wyman 18; Bond 3-4; DeHR 11:41-44; TAG 83:13-18; TG 28:137-54; Allen H. Bent, *Walter Allen of Newbury, Mass., 1640, and Some of His Descendants* (Boston 1896)].

Allen, William: Unknown; 1624; Cape Ann, Salem, Manchester [GMB 31-35].

Allen, William: Unknown; 1637; Newbury, Salisbury [NeTR 21; SyTR 4; EIHC 68:190; Moore Anc 10-15; Abel Lunt Anc 91-94].

Allen, William: Milbrook, Cornwall; 1638; Richmond Island; left New England permanently in 1638 [Trelawny 136, 146, 181, 190, 194].

Allerton, Isaac: Leiden, Holland; 1620 on *Mayflower*; Plymouth, Marblehead, New Amsterdam, New Haven [GMB 35-39; PM 10-15; MQ 75:46-48, 54-56].

Allerton, John: Leiden, Holland; 1620 on *Mayflower*; Plymouth [GMB 39; PM 16].

Alley, Hugh: Stepney, Middlesex; 1635 on *Abigail*; Lynn [GM 2:1:40-42].

Alleyne, Edward: Unknown; 1636; Dedham [DeTR 1:20; DeChR 6-9, 13, 39; DeVR 127; MBCR 1:231, 261, 374, 2:22, 162, 164; SPR 1:10, 2:4; SLR 1:34, 232-33; RCA 2:127-28; WP 4:508-9].

Allin, James: Unknown; 1637; Dedham [DeTR 1:42; DeVR 1:126; Medfield Hist 294-95; Frank Allen Hutchinson, *Genealogical and*

Historical Sketches of the Allen Family of Dedham and Medfield, Mass., 1837-1890 (Lowell, Massachusetts, 1896)].

Allin, John: Saxlingham-juxta-Mare, Norfolk; 1637; Dedham [DeTR 1:32; DeChR 5; MBCR 1:374; NEHGR 41:68-69; ODNB; TAG 67:29]. (This John Allin was not son of Reginald Allin of Colby, Norfolk, and was not minister at St. Mary Quay, Ipswich, Suffolk.)

Alling, Roger: Kempston, Bedford; 1639; New Haven [NHCR 1:33; NEHGR 46:330-31, 81:121; FANH 15-17; TAG 27:7-9; George P. Allen, *A History and Genealogical Record of the Alling-Allens of New Haven, Conn.* (New Haven 1899)].

Allis, Richard: Unknown; 1632 on *Lyon*; passenger list only [GMB 40].

Allis, William: Unknown; 1639; Braintree, Hadley, Hatfield [BTR 1:49; MBCR 1:377; NEHGR 3:127; TAG 38:203; Horatio D. Allis, *Genealogy of William Allis of Hatfield, Mass., and Descendants, 1630-1919* (Hartford 1919)].

Allyn, Matthew: Braunton, Devon; 1633; Cambridge, Hartford, Windsor [GMB 40-44; Legal Executions 26-28].

Almy, William: Unknown; 1631; Charlestown [GMB 44-45].

Almy, William: South Kilworth, Leicestershire; 1635 on *Abigail*; Lynn, Sandwich, Portsmouth [GM 2:1:42-47].

Alsop, Joseph: London; 1635 on *Elizabeth & Ann*; New Haven [GM 2:1:47-51].

Alsop, Thomas: Unknown; 1635 on *Elizabeth & Ann*; Stratford [GM 2:1:51-52].

Alvord, Benedict: Broadway, Somerset; 1637; Windsor [CCCR 2:150; PCR 1:160; Grant 22; Manwaring 1:268; TAG 65:13-16; M&JCH 19:108-10].

Alwood, Richard: Unknown; 1637 on *Prosperous*; passenger list only [NGSQ 71:177].

Alxarson, Anne: Unknown; 1637 on *Rose* or *John & Dorothy*; passenger list only [Hotten 289].

Alxarson, Mary: Unknown; 1637 on *Rose* or *John & Dorothy*; passenger list only [Hotten 289].

Ambler, Richard: Unknown; 1639; Watertown, Stamford [NEHGR 7:160; WaBOP 63; NYGBR 64:15-19; FOOF 1:16-17].

Ambrose, Henry: Kersey, Suffolk; 1640; Hampton, Salisbury, Boston, Charlestown [HmTR 48; HampVR 1:4; GDMNH 55; NHGR 9:49-56].

Ames, Joan: Great Yarmouth, Norfolk; 1637 on *Mary Anne*; Salem, Cambridge [Hotten 294; WP 4:109; STR 1:98; MBCR 1:208; SChR 7; Sibley 1:107-10; Shepard 209-12; NEHGR 33:196]. (She was widow of Reverend William Ames, 1576-1633 [ODNB].)

Ames, William: Unknown; 1640; Braintree [NEHGR 3:126; Kempton Anc 3:41-45; Ann Theopold Chaplin, *Descendants of William Ames of Braintree, Massachusetts* (Boston 2004)].

Ammidowne, Roger: Unknown; 1637; Salem, Weymouth, Boston, Rehoboth [STR 1:102; Lechford 282; BChR 293; MD 19:70, 25:122; Christopher D. Amaden and Nancy K. Ameden Mullen, *Descendants of Jacob Amidown (1720-1790)* (Westminster, Maryland, 2007)].

Amory, John: Chudleigh, Devon; 1637; Richmond Island; left New England in 1638 [Trelawny 129-30, 136, 146, 172, 181, 185, 194].

Anderson, David: Unknown; 1639; New Haven [NHCR 1:28, 59; Lechford 342; SPR 1:22].

Anderson, Gowen: Unknown; 1639; Roxbury, Boston [RChR 84; MBCR 1:377; BTR 1:60].

Anderson, Robert: Unknown; 1636; Massachusetts Bay (court appearance only) [MBCR 1:198, 199, 245].

Andrews, Edward: Unknown; 1637; Massachusetts Bay (court appearance only) [WJ 2:426].

Andrews, Francis: Unknown; 1639; Hartford, Fairfield [HaTR 23; HaBOP 235; FOOF 1:18].

Andrews, Henry: Unknown; 1638; Taunton [PCR 1:53, 105, 7:36; Lechford 318; MD 11:152-56, 12:246-47; NEHGR 52:16-23].

Andrews, John: Unknown; 1636; Ipswich [EPR 1:5-8; ITR 43; NEHGR 70:102-4].

Andrews, John: Unknown; 1639; Kittery [MPCR 1:42; GDMNH 65; NEA 8:3:55-57].

Andrews, Mabel: Unknown; 1636; Boston (church admission only) [BChR 21].

Andrews, Robert: Unknown; 1634; Ipswich [GM 2:1:52-56].

Andrews, Samuel: London; 1635 on *Increase*; Saco [GM 2:1:56-59].

Andrews, Thomas: Unknown; 1631; Massachusetts Bay [GMB 45].

Andrews, Thomas: Unknown; 1634; Dorchester [GM 2:1:59-60].

Andrews, Thomas: Unknown; 1635; Hingham [GM 2:1:61-62; TAG 87:1-10].

Andrews, William: Unknown; 1633; Lynn [GMB 45-46].

Andrews, William: Unknown; 1634; Cambridge, Hartford [GM 2:1:63-67].

Andrews, William: Landford, Wiltshire; 1635 on *James*; passenger list only [GM 2:1:62].

Andrews, William: Ipswich, Suffolk; 1636; Charlestown, Cambridge [ChTR 27, 49; NEHGR 3:248; Shepard 111-13; WaBOP 50; TAG 71:26-27, 82:142-52; Craig Partridge, *The Descendants of William Andrews of Cambridge, Massachusetts* (Camden, Maine, 1995)].

Andrews, William: Unknown; 1638; Dorchester, Salem (servant; two court appearances only) [MBCR 1:246, 269].

Andrews, William: Unknown; 1639; New Haven [NHCR 1:20; NhCHR 1; FANH 40-41].

Angell, Thomas: Unknown; 1637; Providence [PrTR 1:1, 15:5; Angell Anc 1-177].

Angells (or Anglesey), Margaret: Eastwell, Kent; 1637; Dorchester (servant) [NEHGR 75:221; DChR 5].

Anger, Sampson: Lezant, Cornwall; 1640; York [Lechford 265-66; GDMNH 66; York Hist 1:117].

Angier, Edmond: Dedham, Essex; 1636; Cambridge [CaBOP 40, 50; CaTR 43; Lechford 232; MBCR 1:377; Abel Lunt Anc 163-72].

Annable, Anthony: Cambridge, Cambridgeshire; 1623 on *Anne*; Plymouth, Scituate, Barnstable [GMB 47-50; PM 16-20].

Anthony, John: Unknown; 1634 on *Mary & John* (but probably did not sail); passenger list only [GM 2:1:67].

Anthony, John: Unknown; 1640; Newport [RICR 1:108, 110; Charles L. Anthony, *Genealogy of the Anthony Family from 1495 to 1904* (Sterling, Illinois, 1904)].

Antrobus, Joan: St. Albans, Hertfordshire; 1635; Unknown [GM 2:1:67-69].

Antrum, Thomas: Salisbury, Wiltshire; 1635 on *James*; Salem [GM 2:1:69-71].

Applegate, Thomas: Unknown; 1635; Weymouth, Newport, Gravesend [GM 2:1:72-75].

Appleton, Samuel: Little Waldingfield, Suffolk; 1636; Ipswich, Rowley [WP 3:346, 432; EPR 1:4; MBCR 1:193, 371; Phoebe Tilton Anc 59-77; TAG 27:208-10; NEHGR 147:3-10, 160:109-11; Walter Goodwin Davis, *The Ancestry of Mary Isaac, c.1549-1613, Wife of Thomas Appleton of Little Waldingfield, Suffolk, and Mother of Samuel Appleton of Ipswich, Massachusetts* (Portland, Maine, 1955)].

Archer, Giles: Unknown; 1638; Boston (land record only) [SLR 3:170].

Archer, Henry: Epping, Essex; 1638; Roxbury, Ipswich [ITR 36; MBCR 1:378; NEHGR 158:117-23, 341-46].

Archer, Samuel: Unknown; 1630; Salem [GMB 50-53].

Armitage, Godfrey: Unknown; 1638; Lynn, Boston [MBCR 1:375; EQC 2:270; TEG: 18:233-34].

Armitage, Joseph: Unknown; 1636; Lynn [MBCR 1:373; EQC 2:270; Lechford 139, 362; NEHGR 33:60-61; TEG 18:229-33].

Armitage, Thomas: Unknown; 1635 on *James*; Plymouth, Sandwich, Stamford, Hempstead, Oyster Bay [GM 2:1:76-81].

Armstrong, Gregory: Unknown; 1638; Yarmouth [PCR 1:95, 8:11, 12:33-34, 37-38, 93-95; MF 5:34, 35, 21:1, 5, 6, 9].

Arnold, Edward: Unknown; 1640; Boston [BTR 1:58; TAG 35:204-5; Hale, House 544, 790-91].

Arnold, Jasper and Ann: London; 1635 on *Abigail*; passenger list only [GM 2:1:81].

Arnold, John: Unknown; 1634; Cambridge, Hartford [GM 2:1:81-83].

Arnold, John: Unknown; 1638; Portsmouth [RICR 1:60, 91]. (Possibly the same as the next.)

Arnold, John: Unknown; 1639; Boston [BTR 1:49, 57; BBOP 8, 91; BChR 39; MBCR 2:293; SPR 4:28-29; SLR 3:512, 10:19; TAG 35:204].

Arnold, Thomas: Unknown; 1636; Watertown, Providence [WaBOP 4, 62; WaVR 1:8; MBCR 1:377; NEHGR 69:64-69; TAG 20:120; Richard H. Benson, *The Arnold Family of Smithfield, Rhode Island* (Boston 2009)].

Arnold, William: Ilchester, Somerset; 1635; Hingham, Providence [GM 2:1:84-91; M&JCH 25:8].

Arnoll, Richard: Unknown; 1633; Winnissimmett [GMB 53-54].

Arratt, John: Unknown; 1636; Boston (grant of land only) [BTR 1:14; see also Coldham 194].

Arres *see* **Aires**

Arresby, Richard: Unknown; 1639 on *John*; Dorchester, Connecticut, Piscataqua [WP 4:294]. (Could this be Richard Ormsby?)

Arrowsmith, Thomas: Unknown; 1634; Richmond Island [GM 2:1:91].

Ashby, Alice: Unknown; 1635 on *Defence*; passenger list only [GM 2:1:92].

Ashby, Thomas: Unknown; 1639; New Haven (court appearance only) [NHCR 1:31].

Ashley, Edward: Unknown; 1628; Maine; returned permanently to England in 1631 [GMB 54; PM 20].

Ashley, Robert: Unknown; 1638; Springfield [SpTR 161; Pynchon 205, 210-11; Francis Bacon Trowbridge, *The Ashley Genealogy: A History of the Descendants of Robert Ashley of Springfield, Massachusetts* (New Haven 1896).]

Ashley, Thomas: Unknown; 1638 on *Castle*; Charlestown, Gloucester [Lechford 118, 406; EQC 1:16, 17, 28, 33, 42, 43, 48; GDMNH 67].

Askew, John: Yarmouth, Norfolk; 1640; Cambridge (servant; court appearance only) [Lechford 365].

Aspinwall, William: Manchester, Lancashire; 1630; Charlestown, Boston, Portsmouth, New Haven; returned permanently to England in 1652 [GMB 55-60; WF 74-80; Abandoning 39-40].

Astwood, James: Unknown; 1638; Roxbury, Boston; his widow and children returned permanently to England in 1653 [RChR 84; MBCR 1:376; RBOP 2; HAHAC 1:51; NEHGR 5:334, 10:71; Aspinwall 106-7, 340-41, 354-55; SPR Case #134; SLR 3:463-64; Abandoning 42].

Astwood, John: Little Hadham, Hertfordshire; 1635 on *Hopewell*; Roxbury, Milford; returned permanently to England in 1653 [GM 2:1:92-95; Abandoning 41].

Atherson, John: Unknown; 1635 on *Susan & Ellen*; passenger list only [GM 2:1:95].

Atherton, Humphrey: Unknown; 1636; Dorchester [DChR 2; DTR 30; MBCR 1:235, 295, 374; PCPR 1:31; HAHAC 1:52; SPR Case #275; Manwaring 1:174-75; NEHGR 2:382, 35:67-72; Putnams Mag 7:98-104].

Atkins, Thomas: Unknown; 1639; Plymouth [PTR 1:6; PCR 2:4, 5]. (Possibly the same as Thomas Atkinson of Plymouth. See also NEHGR 121:241-45.)

Atkinson, Theodore: Unknown; 1634; Boston [GM 2:1:95-103].

Atkinson, Thomas: Unknown; 1635; Plymouth [GM 2:1:103-4].

Atkinson, Thomas: Unknown; 1636; Concord [MBCR 1:372; CoVR 1; SPR 2:27; Rodgers 2:402-4].

Atwater, David: Lenham, Kent; 1640; New Haven [NHCR 1:41, 93; Stevens-Miller 1:467-72; Francis Atwater, *Atwater History and Genealogy*, 4 volumes (Meriden, Connecticut, 1901-1927)].

Atwater, Joshua: Ashford, Kent; 1640; New Haven, Milford, Boston [NHCR 1:41, 93; RChR 193; Stevens-Miller 1:467-70; Francis Atwater, *Atwater History and Genealogy*, 4 volumes (Meriden, Connecticut, 1901-1927)].

Atwell, Benjamin: Unknown; 1639; Richmond Island [Trelawny 299; GDMNH 68].

Atwood, Elizabeth: Unknown; 1633; Charlestown (church admission only) [GMB 60].

Atwood, John: London; 1636; Plymouth [PCR 1:12, 47, 48, 78, 7:10, 8:173, 188, 12:28; PTR 1:7; WP 4:437; MD 5:153-59, 11:200-6, 44:137].

Atwood, Philip: Unknown; 1635; Charlestown, Malden, Worcester, Bradford [GM 2:1:104-6].

Audley, Edmund: Unknown; 1637; Lynn [EQC 1:7, 11, 12, 32, 48; WP 4:95; RCA 2:82; MBCR 1:249, 266].

Ault, John: Unknown; 1640; Dover [GDMNH 68; GM 2:7:41].

Austin, _____: Unknown; 1638; New Haven [WJ 2:14; Abandoning 42].

Austin, Francis: Unknown; 1636; Dedham, Hampton [DeTR 1:20; DeChR 8; GDMNH 55, 68-69; HmTR 45; HampVR 1:4; NEHGR 63:282-83, 67:77-78; TAG 61:19-23].

Austin, Jonas: Tenterden, Kent; 1635 on *Hercules*; Cambridge, Hingham, Taunton [GM 2:1:106-9].

Austin, Richard: Bishopstoke, Hampshire; 1638 on *Bevis*; passenger list only [Drake's Founders 60]. (Claims that he settled at Charlestown lack supporting evidence [Wyman 28].)

Averill, William: Chipping Norton, Oxford; 1637; Ipswich [ITR 27; Dudley Wildes Anc 39-44; Legal Executions 80-83].

Avery, Joseph: Romsey, Hampshire; 1635 on *James* of Southampton; Newbury [GM 2:1:109-13].

Avery, Matthew: Wapping, Middlesex; 1638; Charlestown; returned permanently to England by 1641 [ChBOP 44; MLR 2:89-95; Wyman 40; NYGBR 47:252].

Avery, Thomas: Unknown; 1634 on *Mary & John*; Salem [GM 2:1:113-15].

Awards, Richard: Unknown; 1637; Boston, Portsmouth [BTR 1:31; PoTR 2; RICR 1:70, 91, 100, 111, 127].

Awkley, Miles: Unknown; 1635; Boston [GM 2:1:115]. (A forthcoming NEHGR article by Patricia Law Hatcher FASG demonstrates that this man was Miles Oakley of Saffron Walden, Essex, and that he arrived in New England after spring 1638, possibly after 1640.)

Axey, James: Unknown; 1638; Lynn [EQC 2:270; EPR 2:158-60, 209-11].

Axtell, Nathaniel: St. Albans, Hertfordshire; 1639; New Haven [NHCR 1:31, 35, 91; NEHGR 44:50-51; TAG 13:205-8; GMN 13:5, 14].

Ayer, John: Unknown; 1639; Salisbury, Haverhill [SyTR 3; HvBOP 4; EPR 1:260-63; EIHC 65:450; Moore Anc 20-22; Pillsbury Anc 2:1085-89; Granberry 158-59].

B

Baber, Francis: Unknown; 1635; Scituate [GM 2:1:117; NEHGR 10:43].

Babson, Isabel: Wookey, Somerset; 1637; Salem, Gloucester [NGSQ 71:176; STR 1:58; EQC 1:12, 29; Ann Theopold Chaplin, *The Babson Genealogy, 1606-1997: Descendants of Thomas and Isabel Babson* (Baltimore 1997)].

Bachelor, Henry: Dover, Kent; 1637; Ipswich [NEHGR 75:222, 163:12-13; EPR 3:294-97; Essex Ant 7:186-87; Scott Gen 207-9].

Bachelor, John: Unknown; 1634; Watertown, Dedham, Reading [GM 2:1:117-22].

Bachelor, John: Canterbury, Kent; 1637; Salem [NEHGR 75:222, 163:13; SChR 8; STR 1:86; MBCR 1:377; EPR 3:41-42; Essex Ant 7:186-87; Scott Gen 207-9; Dawes-Gates 2:96-102].

Bachelor, Joseph: Canterbury, Kent; 1637; Salem [NEHGR 75:222, 163:13; SChR 7; MBCR 1:374; Lechford 114; Essex Ant 7:105, 186-87; Scott Gen 207-9].

Bachelor, Stephen: South Stoneham, Hampshire; 1632 on *William & Francis*; Lynn, Ipswich, Yarmouth, Newbury, Hampton, Strawberry Bank; returned permanently to England in 1650 or 1651 [GMB 61-69; Abandoning 44-45].

Bachelor, William: Dover, Kent; 1634; Charlestown [GM 2:1:122-26; TAG 80:23-24].

Bacon, Andrew: Dedham, Essex; 1637; Hartford [CCCR 1:11, 49, 442; HaTR 23; HaBOP 237-39; Manwaring 1:270-71; TAG 47:136-37; NEHGR 168:33].

Bacon, George: Unknown; 1635 on *Increase*; Hingham [GM 2:1:127-29].

Bacon, Michael: Winston, Suffolk (by way of Ireland); 1640; Dedham [MBCR 1:316; DeChR 25; WoTR 2; WoVR; SPR Case #80; NEHGR 57:329-31; NEA 7:2:54-55; Stevens-Miller 1:192-200; Thomas W.

Baldwin, *Michael Bacon of Dedham, 1640, and His Descendants* (Cambridge, Massachusetts, 1915)].

Bacon, Nicholas: Unknown; 1640; Boston (court appearance only) [MBCR 1:315].

Bacon, Rebecca: Unknown; 1638; Cambridge (probate proceedings only) [SPR NS 1:14, 2:14].

Bacon, Thomas: Unknown; 1640; Massachusetts Bay (witness only) [SPR NS 1:19, 2:19].

Bacon, William: Coventry, Warwickshire (by way of Ireland); 1639; Dedham, Salem [DeTR 1:68; STR 1:111; SChR 10, 18; EPR 1:161-62, 227-30; Essex Ant 7:73-74; NEHGR 13:272, 39:28; Perley 2:98; TAG 73:23-32, 79:309-15].

Badcock, George: Unknown; 1640; New Haven (servant; two court appearances only) [NHCR 1:46, 80].

Baddiver, John: Unknown; 1632; Richmond Island [GMB 70; Trelawny 470].

Badger, Giles: Gloucester, Gloucestershire; 1639; Newbury [NeBOP 42v; TAG 58:1-11, 91-98, 167; Alice W. Badger, *Four Ancestral Lines of Erastus Beethoven and Fanny Babcock (Campbell) Badger* (Chestnut Hill, Massachusetts, 1982) 17-27].

Badger, Thomas: Unknown; 1639; New Haven (servant; two court appearances only) [NHCR 1:24, 61, 67].

Bagley, John: Unknown; 1636; Saybrook (mention by Lyon Gardiner only) [MHSC 3:3:159].

Bagnall, Walter: Unknown; 1631; Richmond Island [GMB 70-71].

Baguley, Thomas: Unknown; 1640; Concord [MBCR 1:299; CoVR 1; SPR 1:20, 2:16].

Bailey, Anne: Unknown; 1639; Dorchester (church admission only) [DChR 4].

Bailey, Henry: Unknown; 1638; Salem (two grants of land only) [STR 1:74, 80, 87, 89].

Bailey, Hilkiah: Unknown; 1640; Saco [MPCR 1:58; GDMNH 72; YLR 2:53].

Bailey, John: Bromham, Wiltshire; 1636; Salisbury, Newbury [MBCR 1:199, 266; SyTR 5; Phoebe Tilton Anc 179-81; TAG 29:110-13, 77:241-47].

Bailey, Jonas: Unknown; 1638; Richmond Island, Scarborough [Trelawny 169, 189; MBCR 4:1:358; Maine Wills 15-17; GDMNH 72-73, 190, 370; YLR 1:1:64, 78, 99].

Bailey, Richard: Unknown; 1638 on *Bevis*; Boston (servant) [Drake's Founders 61; Lechford 150]. (Claims that he was the Rowley settler lack evidence.)

Bailey, Robert: Upton Grey, Hampshire; 1638 on *Confidence*; passenger list only [Drake's Founders 58].

Bailey, Samuel: Unknown; 1640; New Haven (list of landholdings only) [NHCR 1:91; GMN 13:13].

Bailey, Thomas: Unknown; 1639; Weymouth [MBCR 1:377; SPR 1:29, 2:18; Louis G. Bailey and Billie Cooke Bailey, *Bailey Genealogy: Descendants of Thomas Bayley/Bailey of Weymouth, Massachusetts* (Dallas 1999)].

Baily, Christopher: Unknown; 1634; Richmond Island [GM 2:1:130].

Baker, Alexander: London; 1635 on *Elizabeth & Ann*; Boston [GM 2:1:130-32].

Baker, Ann: Unknown; 1638; Dedham [DeChR 21; DeVR 126]. (She married Thomas Bayes.)

Baker, Edmond: Unknown; 1630; Casco [GMB 72].

Baker, Edward: Unknown; 1638; Lynn, Northampton [EQC 2:270; MBCR 1:375; TAG 80:265-77; TEG 18:147-49; Dawes-Gates 1:66-68].

Baker, Francis: St. Albans, Hertfordshire; 1635 on *Planter*; passenger list only [GM 2:1:132].

Baker, Francis: Unknown; 1640; Yarmouth, Boston [PCR 2:17, 19; NEHGR 2:76, 87:50, 52; MD 31:107-8; CCL #106].

Baker, George: Unknown; 1634; Richmond Island [GM 2:1:133].

Baker, John: Unknown; 1630; Charlestown, Newbury, York, Boston [GMB 72-78; WF 81-87].

Baker, John: Norwich, Norfolk; 1637 on *John & Dorothy* or *Rose*; Ipswich [Hotten 289; Lechford 216; ITR 67; MBCR 1:379; WP 4:13; GMB 74; WF 84; Essex Ant 5:158; William S. Appleton, *Ancestry of Priscilla Baker* (Cambridge, Massachusetts, 1870)].

Baker, John: Unknown; 1639; Dover [WP 4:143; NHPP 40:11; GMB 75; WF 84].

Baker, John: Unknown; 1639; Massachusetts Bay (court appearance only) [WP 4:128]. (This record probably pertains to one of the three men above.)

Baker, John: Unknown; 1640; Charlestown [ChChR 10, 49; ChTR 51; ChBOP 119; MBCR 1:378; GMB 75; WF 84; Wyman 47].

Baker, Nathaniel: Unknown; 1635; Hingham [GM 2:1:133-39].

Baker, Nicholas: Unknown; 1634; Roxbury, Hingham, Hull, Scituate [GM 2:1:139-45; RChR 80; GMN 6:185; NEHGR 161:123].

Baker, Richard: Unknown; 1639; Dorchester [DChR 4, 153; Frame-Dana 156-57].

Baker, Robert: Unknown; 1636; Salem [STR 1:47; WJ 2:29; EQC 1:25; EPR 1:13; MBCR 1:314].

Baker, Samuel: Benenden, Kent; 1635 on *Elizabeth & Ann*; passenger list only [GM 2:1:145-46].

Baker, Thomas: Hothfield, Kent; 1639; Milford, Easthampton [MiTR 2; NEHGR 54:203; TAG 9:201-4; NYGBR 138:178-88].

Baker, Walter: Unknown; 1639; Salem (servant; mention in letter only) [WP 4:145; see also NHPP 40:11].

Baker, William: Unknown; 1632; Plymouth [GMB 78-80; PM 21-23].

Baker, William: Unknown; 1633; Charlestown, Billerica [GMB 80-83].

Baker, William: Unknown; 1636; Watertown, Plymouth [WaBOP 5; PCR 1:102, 2:13, 12:69; GMB 79].

Baker, William: Unknown; 1638; Portsmouth [RICR 1:59, 91, 92; GMB 79; Austin 10].

Balch, John: Unknown; 1624; Cape Ann, Salem, Beverly [GMB 84-86].

Baldin, George: Unknown; 1639; Boston [NEHGR 2:76; BChR 49, 310].

Baldin, John: Unknown; 1635 on *Pied Cow*; passenger list only [GM 2:1:146].

Baldin, William: Unknown; 1635 on *Pied Cow*; passenger list only [GM 2:1:146].

Baldwin, John: Unknown; 1638; passenger list only [Savage 1:105]. (Shipboard witness to the will of Sylvester Baldwin; possibly the same as John Baldwin Sr. of Milford [Moore Anc 247-50; Ackley-Bosworth 247-50; TAG 35:226-27].)

Baldwin, Joseph: Cholesbury, Buckinghamshire; 1639; Milford [MiTR 2; NEHGR 156:103-11; Charles Candee Baldwin, *The Baldwin Genealogy From 1500 to 1881* (Cleveland 1881) 23-24, 479-82].

Baldwin, Nathaniel: Cholesbury, Buckinghamshire; 1639; Milford [MiTR 2; FOOF 1:22-23; Charles Candee Baldwin, *The Baldwin Genealogy From 1500 to 1881* (Cleveland 1881) 23-24, 406-8].

Baldwin, Richard: Unknown; 1637; Braintree (court appearance only) [WJ 2:426].

Baldwin, Sarah: Cholesbury, Buckinghamshire; 1638; Springfield [SpVR 19; Pynchon 212-14; NEHGR 38:164-65]. (She married John Searles.)

Baldwin, Sylvester: Aston Clinton, Buckinghamshire; 1638 on *Martin*; died at sea (his widow and children settled at Milford) [MBCR 1:235; NHCR 1:92; MiTR 2; MiChR 2; Ackley-Bosworth 182-86; TG 11:111-15; Charles Candee Baldwin, *The Baldwin Genealogy From 1500 to 1881* (Cleveland 1881); NEHGR 26:294-303, 38:160-70, 289-99, 372-76, 110:310, 113:245-48].

Baldwin, Timothy: Cholesbury, Buckinghamshire; 1639; Milford [MiTR 2; NHCR 1:44; Pynchon 212-13; Charles Candee Baldwin, *The Baldwin Genealogy From 1500 to 1881* (Cleveland 1881) 23-24, 403-5].

Ballard, Elizabeth: Unknown; 1633; Roxbury [GMB 86]. (She married Robert Seaver.)

Ballard, William: Unknown; 1634 on *Mary & John*; passenger list only [GM 2:1:151].

Ballard, William: Unknown; 1635; Lynn [GM 2:1:146-51].

Banbridge, Guy: Newcastle-upon-Tyne; Northumberland; 1634; Cambridge [GM 2:1:151-53].

Bancraft, Widow: Unknown; 1638; Lynn [EQC 2:270; TAG 37:154-60, 42:210-16].

Bancroft, Roger: Unknown; 1639; Cambridge [CaBOP 70; MBCR 2:292; Rodgers 1:136-40].

Banes, Martha: Unknown; 1635 on *Defence*; passenger list only [GM 2:1:154].

Bangs, Edward: Unknown; 1623 on *Anne*; Plymouth, Eastham [GMB 86-91; PM 23-29].

Banks, Lydia: Maidstone, Kent; 1636; Salem; returned to England about 1642 [SChR 6, 102; EQC 1:192, 193, 2:394, 8:174-81; Waters 1294-1300, 1306].

Bannister, Edward: Unknown; 1638; New Haven [NHCR 1:13, 35, 92, 460, 479; NEHGR 81:121; FANH 1012, 1805].

Banshott, Thomas: Unknown; 1638 on *Bevis*; passenger list only [Drake's Founders 60].

Barber, George: Unknown; 1640; Dedham, Medfield [DeTR 1:74; DeChR 27; SPR 1:19; SPR Case #1404; Medfield Hist 312-15; NGSQ 74:3-6; Bassett-Preston 21].

Barber, John: Unknown; 1636; Salem; removed from Salem by 1653 [STR 1:22, 82, 103, 132, 171; SChR 11, 18; EQC 1:75, 85-86, 118; ELR 1:17v].

Barber, Richard: Unknown; 1638; Dedham [DeTR 1:50, 52, 57, 75, 95, 100, 173; DeChR 21, 39 (as "Edward Barber"); DeVR 127; MBCR 1:377; SPR Case #33; SPR Case #40].

Barber, Thomas: London; 1635 on *Christian*; Windsor [GM 2:1:154-57].

Barber, William: Unknown; 1637; Dorchester, Marblehead [DTR 1:32, 39; STR 1:95; EQC 1:29, 48, 56-58; EPR 3:143; Marblehead 43-44]. ("William Baber" of London who bought land in Watertown and resided in Boston was a different man [Pope 32; SLR 1:95, 258].)

Barcroft, John: Unknown; 1632 on *James*; (probably) Winnissimmet; removed to Virginia by 1637 [GMB 91-92].

Barden, William: Unknown; 1638; Marshfield, Concord, Barnstable, Middleborough [PCR 1:110, 8:196; MaTR 1:4; MD 3:51, 17:109, 111; PPR Case #878; Kempton Anc 4:65].

Barding, Nathaniel: Unknown; 1639; Hartford [HaBOP 38-40; HaTR 7; WMJ 69; Manwaring 1:182-83, 271; TAG 35:55-59].

Barker, Dorothy: Unknown; 1639; Dorchester [DChR 4; SPR 1:68, 2:84; Weymouth Hist 3:22, 349-50]. (She remarried to Enoch Hunt and then John King.)

Barker, James: Stradishall, Suffolk; 1640; Rowley [MBCR 1:378; RowBOP 3; Rowley Fam 14-15; Essex Ant 6:101; GMN 18:28-29; NEHGR 161:22-26; Elizabeth Frye Barker, *Barker Genealogy* (New York 1927) 389].

Barker, John: Unknown; 1638; Plymouth, Marshfield [PCR 1:101, 3:28-37; Lechford 194; MD 11:156-57, 17:109, 111; NEHGR 53:427; Elizabeth Frye Barker, *Barker Genealogy* (New York 1927) 231].

Barker, Robert: Unknown; 1632; Plymouth, Marshfield, Duxbury [GMB 92-97; PM 29-34].

Barker, Thomas: Unknown; 1639; Rowley [MBCR 1:308, 376; Lechford 208; RowBOP 6; HAHAC 1:112; EPR 1:128-30; Rowley Fam 14; GMN 18:22].

Barker, William: Unknown; 1635; Massachusetts Bay [GM 2:1:157].

Barlow, George: Unknown; 1637; Massachusetts Bay, Exeter, Saco, Scarborough [MBCR 1:203; NHPP 1:133; GDMNH 76; GMB 1950-51]. (George Barlow of Sandwich was a different man.)

Barnard, Bartholomew: Westminster, Middlesex; 1636; York, Boston [MPCR 1:54; York Hist 1:82; GDMNH 76; Goodwin-Morgan 1:47-54].

Barnard, John: Unknown; 1634 on *Francis*; Cambridge, Hartford, Hadley [GM 2:1:158-61].

Barnard, John: Unknown; 1634 on *Elizabeth*; Watertown [GM 2:1:161-66].

Barnard, Richard: Unknown; 1635; Watertown [GM 2:1:166-67].

Barnard, Thomas: Unknown; 1639; Salisbury, Amesbury [SyTR 8; EPR 3:167-70; Pillsbury Anc 537-39; Stone-Gregg 59-64; NEXUS 6:146-48; TEG 8:29-38].

Barnardiston, Katherine: Unknown; 1639; Salem (church admission only) [SChR 9].

Barnes, John: Unknown; 1632; Plymouth [GMB 97-103; PM 35-42].

Barnes, Joshua: Unknown; 1632; Massachusetts Bay (court appearance only, with caveat) [GMB 104].

Barnes, Joshua: Unknown; 1638; Yarmouth, Edgartown, Southampton [PCR 1:117, 2:17, 20, 29, 31, 36, 41; NEHGR 123:81-83; GMB 104].

Barnes, Richard: Clatford, Hampshire; 1639 on *Jonathan*; Sudbury [NEHGR 32:407-11, 49:65-67].

Barnes, Thomas: Unknown; 1637; Hingham [HiBOP 70; Angell Anc 194-201].

Barnes, Thomas: Unknown; 1637; Hartford, Farmington [CCCR 2:161; HaBOP 167; TAG 9:40-41, 35:84; Legal Executions 40; McArthur-Barnes 57-60].

Barnes, William: Unknown; 1639; Salisbury, Amesbury [SyTR 5; MBCR 1:378; Pillsbury Anc 161-62; GMC50 9-12].

Barnett, Alice: Unknown; 1640; Salem (church admission only) [SChR 9].

Barney, Jacob: Unknown; 1633; Salem [GMB 104-8; Eugene Dimon Preston, *Genealogy of the Barney Family in America* (Springfield, Virginia, 1990)].

Barrell, George: South Elmham St. Michael; 1638; Boston [Lechford 33, 159; BTR 1:36, 49; NEHGR 2:79, 61:69, 65:74-75, 165:5-10; SPR 1:27, 2:16; RCA 2:119; Farr Anc 19-22].

Barrell, William: Unknown; 1639; Boston (death record only) [NEHGR 2:76].

Barrett, John: Unknown; 1636; York, Wells [GDMNH 77; Lydia Harmon Anc 48-50; York Hist 1:113].

Barrett, Stephen: Unknown; 1639; Massachusetts Bay (servant; indenture only) [Lechford 101].

Barrett, Thomas: Unknown; 1635 on *Increase*; passenger list only (with caveat) [GM 2:1:167].

Barron, Ellis: Unknown; 1640; Watertown [WaVR 1:8; WaBOP 31; MBCR 1:378; TAG 20:135-36; Kempton Anc 118-31].

Barsham, William: Unknown; 1630; Watertown [GMB 108-11; WF 87-92].

Barstow, George: Halifax, Yorkshire; 1635; Watertown, Dedham, Scituate, Cambridge [GM 2:1:167-70].

Barstow, Michael: Halifax, Yorkshire; 1635; Charlestown, Watertown [GM 2:1:171-74].

Barstow, William: Halifax, Yorkshire; 1635 on *Truelove*; Watertown, Dedham, Hingham, Scituate [GM 2:1:174-80].

Bartholomew, Henry: Unknown; 1636; Salem, Boston [STR 1:22, 73; SChR 6; EQC 1:28; EPR 1:51-52; EIHC 2:163-65; George Wells Bartholomew Jr., *Record of the Bartholomew Family* (Austin, Texas, 1885) 43-52].

Bartholomew, Richard: Unknown; 1637; Salem [STR 1:64; SChR 10; MBCR 1:378; HAHAC 1:127; EPR 1:51-52; George Wells Bartholomew Jr., *Record of the Bartholomew Family* (Austin, Texas, 1885) 52-54].

Bartholomew, William: London; 1634 on *Griffin*; Ipswich, Boston, Charlestown [GM 2:1:180-86].

Bartlett, John: Unknown; 1639; Newport [RICR 1:92]. (Possibly John Bartlett of Newbury, son of Richard [GMN 23:3].)

Bartlett, John: Unknown; 1640; Windsor [Grant 28; WMJ 703; Windsor Hist 2:61; NEHGR 168:180].

Bartlett, Richard: Unknown; 1640; Newbury [ILR 1:3; Kempton Anc 2:38-46; Pillsbury Anc 653-57; NEHGR 40:192-204]. (His son John had preceded him to New England, arriving in 1634 [Drake's Founders 70; MBCR 1:373].)

Bartlett, Robert: Unknown; 1623 on *Anne*; Plymouth [GMB 112-17; PM 42-48].

Bartlett, Robert: Unknown; 1632 on *Lyon*; Cambridge, Hartford Northampton [GMB 117-20].

Bartlett, Thomas: Unknown; 1630; Watertown [GMB 120-22; WF 92-95].

Bartlett, William: Unknown; 1639; Medford (servant) [WP 4:217; MBCR 1:265, 310].

Bartoll, John: Crewkerne, Somerset; 1640; Marblehead [EQC 1:20; Lechford 432; EPR 1:456-57; NEHGR 61:385, 63:160-61; Marblehead 45-46; *The Westcustogo Chronicle* 1 (1885):4-11].

Barton, Edward: Unknown; 1639; Salem, Piscataqua, Cape Porpus [EQC 1:19, 21; ELR 1:81v; NEHGR 84:401-3; GDMNH 79].

Barton, Marmaduke: Unknown; 1637; Massachusetts Bay; not seen after 1642 (servant) [EQC 1:6 ("Barniston"), 8, 20, 24, 35; MBCR 2:21; RCA 2:118].

Barton, Rufus: Unknown; 1640; Portsmouth, New Amsterdam, Warwick [PoTR 16; NEHGR 12:304-5; TAG 27:136-38; NYGBR 54:284; Austin 250-51].

Bascom, Thomas: Unknown; 1634 on *Recovery*; Dorchester, Windsor, Northampton [GM 2:1:186-88; CN 28:186-88].

Bass, Samuel: Saffron Walden, Essex; 1633; Roxbury, Braintree [GMB 122-27].

Bassett, Thomas: Unknown; 1635 on *Christian*; Windsor, Stratford, Fairfield [GM 2:1:188-90].

Bassett, William: Unknown; 1621 on *Fortune*; Plymouth, Duxbury, Bridgewater [GMB 127-30; PM 48-52].

Bassett, William: Dorking, Surrey; 1635 on *Abigail*; Lynn [GM 2:1:190-95; TAG 79:181-83].

Bassingthwait, Mrs.: Unknown; 1640; Sudbury (land grant only) [SuTR 13].

Bate, Clement: Biddenden, Kent; 1635 on *Elizabeth*; Hingham [GM 2:1:195-98].

Bate, James: Lydd, Kent; 1635 on *Elizabeth*; Dorchester [GM 2:1:198-200].

Bateman, Edward: Unknown; 1639; Pemaquid [GDMNH 82 (citing YLR 35:55); Spencer 283, 325, 399].

Bateman, William: Unknown; 1630; Charlestown [GMB 130-31; WF 95-96].

Bateman, William: Unknown; 1630; Massachusetts Bay [GMB 130-31; WF 95-96].

Bateman, William: Unknown; 1638; Charlestown (land grant only) [ChTR 41].

Bateman, William: Unknown; 1640; Concord, Fairfield [MBCR 1:379; FOOF 1:38; Lyon-Rice 185-86 (clue)].

Bates, Edward: Unknown; 1633; Boston [GMB 131-32].

Bates, Edward: Aston Clinton, Buckinghamshire; 1638; Weymouth [MBCR 1:375; WP 4:310; RCA 2:116; TAG 65:33-43, 89-96].

Bates, George: Unknown; 1635; Boston [BTR 1:25; BChR 20, 23, 29, 37, 61, 62; MBCR 1:372; SPR 6:116].

Bates, Robert: Unknown; 1640; Wethersfield, Stamford [WetLR 1:71, 155; SmTR 4; FOOF 1:38-39].

Batson, Stephen: Unknown; 1636; Saco [MPCR 1:6; Lechford 81; GDMNH 82; GM 2:7:101-4].

Batt, Christoper: Salisbury, Wiltshire; 1638 on *Bevis*; Newbury, Salisbury, Boston [Drake's Founders 60; Lechford 181; SyTR 1; MBCR 1:237, 277, 375; NEHGR 51:181-88, 348-57, 52:44-51, 321-22; Abel Lunt Anc 175-255; TG 17:86-95; TAG 79:85-99].

Batt, Dorothy: Salisbury, Wiltshire; 1638 on *Bevis*; passenger list only [Drake's Founders 60; Abel Lunt Anc 183].

Batt, Nicholas: The Devizes, Wiltshire; 1635 on *James*; Newbury [GM 2:1:200-4].

Batte, Theodore: Unknown; 1637; passenger list only [NGSQ 71:177].

Batter, Edmund: Salisbury, Wiltshire; 1635 on *James*; Salem [GM 2:1:204-13].

Battey, Nicholas: Unknown; 1638; Lynn [MBCR 1:375; EQC 1:84, 131, 2:270; GM 2:1:204].

Baulston, William: Sudbury, Suffolk; 1630; Boston, Portsmouth [GMB 133-37; WF 97-102].

Baunsh, William: Unknown; 1638 on *Confidence*; passenger list only [Drake's Founders 59].

Baver *see* **Baber**

Baxter, Daniel: Unknown; 1638; Salem [STR 1:71; Perley 2:61].

Baxter, Gregory: Unknown; 1631; Roxbury, Braintree [GMB 137-39].

Baxter, Nicholas: Unknown; 1639; Boston [BTR 1:43; NEHGR 2:76; BChR 41; SPR Case #1944].

Baxter, Richard: Hingham, Norfolk; 1638 on *Diligent*; passenger list only (servant) [NEHGR 15:26].

Bayes, Thomas: Unknown; 1637; Dedham, Boston, Edgartown [DeTR 1:42; DeChR 27; DeVR 126; NEHGR 8:350, 53:130; Aspinwall 69, 165, 322-23; EQC 1:17; Martha's Vineyard Hist 2:Edgartown:38-41].

Baylie, Robert: Unknown; 1635 on *Hopewell*; passenger list only [GM 2:1:213].

Baysey, John: Dedham, Essex; 1639; Hartford [HaTR 22; HaBOP 200; TAG 82:32-38].

Bazill, Ellen: Unknown; 1640; Boston (servant; church admission only) [BChR 31].

Beacham, Edward: Unknown; 1636; Salem [STR 1:22, 32; SChR 9; EPR 1:35; Lydia Harmon Anc 47; Driver Gen 397].

Beal, Sarah: Unknown; 1635 on *James*; no certain record found in New England [GM 2:1:213].

Beal, Thomas: Unknown; 1634; Cambridge [GM 2:1:214-17].

Beale, John: Hingham, Norfolk; 1638 on *Diligent*; Hingham [NEHGR 15:26, 121:13; MBCR 1:375; HiBOP 54; PCR 1:53; TAG 13:263-65, 27:94; Stone-Gregg 65-70].

Beale, William: Unknown; 1621 on *Fortune*; Plymouth [GMB 139; PM 52].

Beamon, Gamaliel: Unknown; 1635 on *Elizabeth & Ann*; Dorchester, Lancaster [GM 2:1:217-19].

Beamon, John: Bridgenorth, Shropshire; 1635 on *Elizabeth*; Salem [GM 2:1:219-20].

Beamon, William: Bridgenorth, Shropshire; 1635 on *Elizabeth*; Salem, Saybrook [GM 2:1:220-22].

Beamsley, William: Unknown; 1632; Boston [GMB 139-42].

Bear, Philip: Unknown; 1637; Marblehead [STR 1:59, 63, 74; EQC 1:17, 3:102, 286, 287, 300; MBCR 1:220, 233 (as "Philip Deare")].

Bearce, Augustine: Unknown; 1638 on *Confidence*; Barnstable [Drake's Founders 59; MD 2:213; NEHGR 9:280; Otis 52-59; TAG 15:111-18, 83:122-30; Brainerd Anc 32].

Beard, Martha: Epping, Essex; 1640; Milford [MiChR 2; NGSQ 64:219-20; Ruth Beard, *A Genealogy of the Descendants of Widow Martha Beard of Milford, Conn.* (Ansonia, Connecticut, 1915)].

Beard, Richard: Unknown; 1640; Massachusetts Bay (servant; court appearance only) [MBCR 1:331].

Beard, Thomas: London; 1629; hired but probably never came to New England [WF 102].

Beard, William: Unknown; 1640; Dover [Lechford 282; NHPP 40:6; GDMNH 85].

Beards, Elizabeth: Unknown; 1635 on *Increase*; passenger list only [GM 2:1:222].

Beardsley, William: Ilkeston, Derby; 1635 on *Planter*; Concord, Stratford [GM 2:1:222-27].

Beats, Richard: Unknown; 1635; Cambridge (land grant only, with caveat) [GM 2:1:227]. (Possibly error for John Betts [GM 2:1:275].)

Beaven, John: Unknown; 1633; Plymouth [GMB 142; PM 52].

Beck, Alexander: Unknown; 1632; Boston [GMB 143-45].

Beck, Henry: (possibly) Warwickshire; 1635 on *Blessing*; Dover, Portsmouth [NH] [GM 2:1:228-30; NHPP 10:701].

Becket, Stephen: Unknown; 1634 on *Francis*; passenger list only [GM 2:1:231].

Beckley, Richard: Unknown; 1637; Salem (court appearance only) [EQC 1:7]. (See Alice Beggarly [WF 105-7].)

Beckley, Richard: Unknown; 1637; Sandwich (mention in will only) [PCPR 1:32; MD 3:74].

Beckley, Richard: Unknown; 1639; New Haven, Wethersfield [NHCR 1:28; Manwaring 1:404; Goodwin-Morgan 2:222-28].

Beckwith, Matthew: Unknown; 1639; Connecticut [CCCR 1:29; WMJ 379; TAG 18:15-16, 21:259-65, 22:49-52; Moore Anc 73-112; Angell Anc 222-30].

Becon, Richard: Unknown; 1635 on *James* of Bristol; passenger list only [Young's First Planters 475].

Beech, Richard: Unknown; 1638; New Haven [NHCR 1:13, 32; FANH 147-48].

Beech, Richard: Unknown; 1639; Watertown [WaVR 1:7; WaBOP 39; Bond 19].

Beecher, Ann: Lewes, Sussex; 1639; New Haven [NHCR 1:92; TAG 34:218-20, 79:28-33, 81:133-40].

Beecher, Thomas: Unknown; 1630; Charlestown [GMB 145-46; WF 103-5].

Beeder, Thomas: Unknown; 1638; Portsmouth, Newport [RICR 1:66, 70, 91; PoTR 1; GMN 22:27].

Beefer, Richard: Unknown; 1636; Lynn [EQC 1:5]. (Possibly Richard Beefer or Beeford of Gloucester more than a decade later [EQC 1:240; Essex Ant 8:95, 140].)

Beers, Richard: Unknown; 1636; Duxbury, Marshfield [PCR 1:44, 45, 78, 8:182, 196; PCPR 3:1:100; MD 25:90; PCPR 1:30].

Beers, Richard: Unknown; 1636; Watertown [WaBOP 3, 54; WaVR 1:6; MBCR 1:316, 372; Mary Louise Regan, *The Beers Genealogy, Volume One, The Beers Families of Massachusetts and Rhode Island* (Palatine, Illinois, 1972) 56-65].

Beggarly, Alice: Unknown; 1630; Salem, Providence [GMB 147-48; WF 105-7].

Belcher, Andrew: Unknown; 1639; Cambridge, Sudbury [SuTR 1; CaChR 9; HAHAC 1:120; NEHGR 27:239-40 (clue)].

Belcher, Edward: Guilsborough, Northamptonshire; 1630; Boston [GMB 149-51; WF 107-10].

Belcher, Gregory: Mancetter, Warwickshire; 1639; Braintree [MBCR 1:377; EQC 3:256; NHGR 26:52; NEHGR 60:128-29].

Belcher, Jeremy: Unknown; 1635 on *Susan & Ellen*; Ipswich [GM 2:1:231-37].

Belden, Richard: Heptonstall, Yorkshire; 1640; Wethersfield [WetLR 1:80, 138; TAG 45:135-38, 76:20-28, 122-28].

Belknap, Abraham: North Weald, Essex; 1638; Lynn [EQC 2:270; EPR 1:26-27; NEHGR 68:83-92, 190-97, 85:265-88, 104:316-17].

Bell, Abraham: Unknown; 1639; New Haven, Charlestown [NHCR 1:35; Wyman 75; Rodgers 2:138-41].

Bell, Francis: Unknown; 1640; Stamford [SmTR 4; NYGBR 28:153-54; FOOF 1:59-61].

Bell, Thomas: Bury St. Edmunds, Suffolk; 1634; Roxbury; returned permanently to England by 1648 [GM 2:1:237-43; NEHGR 157:31-33; Abandoning 47-48].

Bell, Thomas: Unknown; 1637; Boston [BTR 1:31; NEHGR 2:77; BChR 290; TAG 74:281-91; PM 340].

Bell, William: Unknown; 1640; Massachusetts Bay (court appearance only) [MBCR 1:314; WP 4:324].

Bellingham, Richard: Boston, Lincolnshire; 1634; Boston, Rowley [GM 2:1:243-50; Abandoning 49].

Bellingham, William: Unknown; 1638; Rowley [Lechford 3; WP 4:151; MBCR 1:378; RowBOP 5; EPR 1:120-21; EQC 2:360-62, 367, 395-401; Pillsbury Anc 411-13].

Bellows, John: Unknown; 1635 on *Hopewell*; Concord, Marlborough [GM 2:1:250-53; NEHGR 164:153-60].

Bemis, Joseph: Unknown; 1640; Watertown [Lechford 330; WaBOP 58; Stevens-Miller 1:162-64].

Bemont, ____: Hadleigh, Suffolk; 1637; passenger list only [WP 3:395].

Bendall, Edward: Kersey, Suffolk; 1630; Boston; returned permanently to England by 1653 [GMB 151-56; WF 110-16; Abandoning 50-51].

Benfield, John: Unknown; 1636; Medford, Watertown [WJ 2:424; MBCR 1:198; WaVR 1:16; GM 2:3:20].

Benham, John: Unknown; 1630; Dorchester, New Haven [GMB 156-60].

Benjamin, John: Unknown; 1632 on *Lyon*; Cambridge, Watertown [GMB 160-64].

Benjamin, Richard: Unknown; 1632 on *Lyon*; Cambridge, Watertown, Southold [GMB 164-66].

Bennett, Edward: Unknown; 1635; Weymouth, Rehoboth [GM 2:1:253-54].

Bennett, Elizabeth: Unknown; 1640; Massachusetts Bay (court appearance only) [MBCR 1:297].

Bennett, James: Tenterden, Kent; 1635 on *Hercules*; Cambridge, Concord, Fairfield [NEHGR 75:218; CaTR 23; CoVR 1; MBCR 1:375; FOOF 1:65-66; Ackley-Bosworth 47-51].

Bennett, John: Unknown; 1630; Marblehead [GMB 167-68].

Bennett, John: Unknown; 1639; Connecticut (court appearance only) [CCCR 1:29]. (Compare similar behavior by a John Bennett in 1648 and 1649 [CCCR 1:164, 167, 171, 190, 191, 201; Windsor Hist 2:71].)

Bennett, Richard: Unknown; 1635; Salem (land grant only) [GM 2:1:254].

Bennett, Richard: Unknown; 1640; Boston [BTR 1:58, 104, 105; BBOP 46; NEHGR 11:200; Waters 72-73, 294-95; SPR Case #908].

Bennett, Samuel: Unknown; 1635 on *James*; Lynn, Boston [GM 2:1:255-60; Gorges 52; TEG 17:87-91].

Bennett, William: Unknown; 1632; Plymouth, Salem, Manchester [GMB 168-71; PM 52-56].

Benson, John: Caversham, Oxfordshire; 1638 on *Confidence*; Hingham [Drake's Founder 59; HiBOP 85; Scott Gen 290-91; Richard H. Benson, *The Benson Family of Colonial Massachusetts* (Boston 2003)].

Bent, John: Weyhill, Hampshire; 1638 on *Confidence*; Sudbury [Drake's Founders 58; SuTR 3; Lechford 293; MBCR 1:377; NEHGR 48:288-89, 49:65-67, 153:219-20; Allen H. Bent, *The Bent Family in America* (Boston 1900)].

Bentley, Mary: Unknown; 1635 on *Defence*; passenger list only [GM 2:1:260-61].

Bentley, William: Unknown; 1635 on *Truelove*; passenger list only [GM 2:1:261].

Bernard, Musachiell: Batcombe, Somerset; 1635; Weymouth; probably returned to England soon after 1643 [GM 2:1:261-63; M&JCH 25:10-12; Abandoning 52].

Bernard, William: Unknown; 1639; Charlestown [Lechford 226, 313; ChTR 63; Wyman 59].

Berry, Ambrose: Unknown; 1636; Saco [MPCR 1:lxii, 46; Lechford 278; NEHGR 71:126, 127; GDMNH 89].

Berry, Christopher: Unknown; 1639; Salem; returned permanently to England in 1640 [EQC 1:19, 22, 2:136].

Berry, William: Unknown; 1639; Newbury [NeTR 36; MBCR 2:292].

Berry, William: Unknown; 1639; Piscataqua [NHPP 1:113; GDMNH 90].

Besbeech, Thomas: Ashford, Kent; 1635 on *Hercules*; Cambridge, Scituate, Duxbury, Sudbury, Marshfield [GM 2:1:263-66].

Bessey, Anthony: London; 1635 on *James*; Lynn, Sandwich [GM 2:1:266-70].

Best, Edward: Milbrook, Cornwall; 1638 on *Fortune*; Richmond Island; soon ran away [Trelawny 136, 181, 190].

Best, John: Canterbury, Kent; 1635 on *Hercules*; Salem [GM 2:1:270].

Best, Robert: Unknown; 1639; Sudbury [SuTR 3; Rodgers 1:174-77].

Beton, Thomasine: Unknown; 1639; Dorchester (church admission only) [DChR 4].

Betscombe, Richard: Bridport, Dorset; 1635; Hingham; returned permanently to England in 1647 [GM 2:1:271-72; Abandoning 52].

Betts, John: Unknown; 1634 on *Francis*; Cambridge [GM 2:1:273-77].

Betts, Mary: Claydon, Oxfordshire; 1639; Hartford [HaBOP 116; Hale, House 458-59; TAG 80:177-87].

Betts, Robert: Unknown; 1636; Watertown; not seen after 1637 [WaBOP 3, 6, 10].

Betts, William: Unknown; 1635; Scituate, Barnstable, Dorchester, Westchester [GM 2:1:278-81; TAG 78:38].

Bewett, Hugh: Unknown; 1640; Massachusetts Bay, Providence [MBCR 1:312; WJ 2:22; PrTR 15:5; RICR 1:252-53; RWCorr 384; MHSC 3:1:2-4].

Bibble, John: Stepney, Middlesex; 1637; Boston, Malden, Hull [BTR 1:21; EQC 1:16; Lechford 325-26; Aspinwall 322; NEHGR 9:306-7; TAG 31:90-101; M&JCH 26:10-12].

Bickerstaff, John: Unknown; 1638; Watertown (court appearance only) [MBCR 1:246].

Bickett, John: Unknown; 1639; Massachusetts Bay (court appearance only) [EQC 1:16].

Bickford, Old: Unknown; 1636; Richmond Island [Trelawny 108; GDMNH 90].

Bickford, Priscilla: Unknown; 1636; Richmond Island [Trelawny 166-68, 189, 291, 300; GDMNH 90].

Bicknell, Zachary: Unknown; 1635; Weymouth [GM 2:1:282-83; M&JCH 27:1-10].

Biddle, Joseph: Unknown; 1635; Plymouth, Duxbury, Marshfield [GM 2:1:283-84].

Biddlecombe, Richard: Sutton Mandeville, Wiltshire; 1638 on *Confidence*; passenger list only [Drake's Founders 57].

Bidgood, Richard: Romsey, Hampshire; 1638 on *Confidence*; Boston, Ipswich; returned permanently to England by 1650 [Drake's Founders 59; BTR 1:41; EQC 1:87, 94, 128, 143, 199, 266; Ipswich Hist 1:361; Abandoning 52-53].

Bidwell, John: Unknown; 1639; Hartford [HaBOP 116; HaTR 24; Manwaring 1:274-75; Hale, House 459-65; Bidwell Family Association, *The Bidwell Family*, 2 volumes (Baltimore 2011)].

Bigg, Rachel: Cranbrook, Kent; 1635 on *Elizabeth*; Dorchester [GM 2:1:284-89; TAG 56:219-20].

Biggs, John: Unknown; 1630; Boston, Ipswich [GMB 171-73; WF 116-18].

Biggs, Thomas: Unknown; 1635 on *Blessing*; passenger list only [GM 2:1:289; see GDMNH 92].

Bigsby, Mary: Unknown; 1640; Boston (church admission only) [BChR 30].

Bill, James: Ringstead, Northamptonshire; 1638; Boston [NEHGR 2:77; BTR 1:37; TAG 60:193-201].

Bill, John: Unknown; 1635 on *Hopewell*; passenger list only [GM 2:1:289].

Bill, Mary: Unknown; 1635 on *Planter*; passenger list only [GM 2:1:289].

Billing, Nathaniel: Unknown; 1640; Concord [MBCR 1:379; Rodgers 3:220-21].

Billing, Richard: Unknown; 1640; Hartford, Hadley [HaTR 32; Hadley Hist 12].

Billings, John: Unknown; 1635 on *Speedwell*; Richmond Island, Piscataqua [GM 2:1:290-92].

Billings, Roger: Unknown; 1639; Dorchester [DChR 5; NEHGR 5:97, 9:152, 92:261-64; TAG 74:28-30; M&JCH 25:12].

Billington, John: Spalding, Lincolnshire; 1620 on *Mayflower*; Plymouth [GMB 173-74; PM 56-58; TG 3:228-48].

Bills, Robert: Unknown; 1635 on *Pied Cow*; Charlestown [GM 2:1:292-93].

Binks, Bryan: Unknown; 1632; Massachusetts Bay; removed to Virginia in 1632 [GMB 175].

Birchard, Thomas: Terling, Essex; 1635 on *Truelove*; Roxbury, Hartford, Saybrook, Edgartown, Norwich [GM 2:1:293-98].

Bircher, Nathan: Unknown; 1636; Massachusetts Bay (court appearance only) [WJ 2:425].

Bird, Jathnell: Unknown; 1638; Ipswich [ITR 42; GM 2:2:563].

Bird, Simon: Unknown; 1635 on *Susan & Ellen*; Boston, Billerica [GM 2:1:298-301].

Bird, Thomas: Unknown; 1636; Scituate [NEHGR 10:43; PCR 6:66, 7:29; MD 16:123-24].

Bird, Thomas: Unknown; 1638; Ipswich (land grant only) [ITR 47]. (Some authorities claim that this was the Thomas Bird who appeared at Hartford in 1644 [Goodwin-Morgan 2:11-14].)

Bird, Thomas: Unknown; 1639; Braintree (land grant only) [BTR 1:50].

Bird, Thomas: Unknown; 1639; Dorchester [NEHGR 5:97, 25:21-22; DChR 5; SPR Case #454; Blake-Glidden 45-46].

Birdsall, Henry: Norwich, Norfolk; 1635; Boston, Salem [GM 2:1:301-2].

Birdsey, John: Unknown; 1639; Milford, Stratford [MiTR 2; MiChR 1; FOOF 1:76; TAG 10:12; Hale, House 732-33; Bassett-Preston 35].

Birge, Richard: Unknown; 1640; Windsor [WiLR 1:76; Grant 26; CTVR 32-33, 42; Manwaring 1:98; Windsor Hist 2:74; Blackman Anc 48-49].

Births, Christian: Unknown; 1640; Woburn [WoVR]. (She married George Farley.)

Biscoe *see also* **Briscoe**

Biscoe, Nathaniel: Unknown; 1639; Watertown; returned permanently to England by 1652 [Lechford 356; WaBOP 46; WJ 1:373, 2:110; Morison 234-35; Bond 42-43, 683-84; Ackley-Bosworth 274; Abandoning 53-54].

Bishop, Anne: Unknown; 1639; Dorchester [DChR 4]. (She possibly married John Holman as his second wife [NEHGR 72:189].)

Bishop, Henry: Unknown; 1640; Newport [RICR 1:92, 108, 111, 112; GMN 23:4].

Bishop, James: Unknown; 1638; Taunton (servant; court appearance only) [PCR 1:128].

Bishop, John: Unknown; 1637; Newbury, Nantucket, Woodbridge [NJ] [NeTR 8; EPR 1:23; NEHGR 20:144; TAG 75:184-85; NYGBR 47:112; *The Genealogical Register* 1 (1913):107-17; Nantucket Land 62-63].

Bishop, John: Unknown; 1639; Guilford [Guilford Hist 25; TAG 29:127-28; Goodman 71-74].

Bishop, John: Unknown; 1640; Taunton, Stamford [PCR 2:17; Plain Dealing 96; TAG 16:196; Gillespie 33-40].

Bishop, Nathaniel: Unknown; 1634; Ipswich, Boston [GM 2:1:302-6; WP 3:433].

Bishop, Richard: Unknown; 1635; Salem [GM 2:1:307-10].

Bishop, Richard: Unknown; 1638; Plymouth [PCR 1:103, 2:6, 79, 132-33, 134, 137, 138, 4:18, 136, 5:30].

Bishop, Thomas: Unknown; 1637; Ipswich [ITR 26, 62; Putnam's Mag 4:239-45; Essex Ant 8:124].

Bishop, Thomas: Unknown; 1637 on *Prosperous*; passenger list only [NGSQ 71:177].

Bishop, Townsend: Unknown; 1634; Salem; left New England permanently, perhaps to return to England, in 1645 [GM 2:1:310-12; Abandoning 54-55].

Bissell, John: Unknown; 1639; Windsor [Grant 10, 23; CCCR 1:55; WiLR 1:53; TAG 26:84-94, 185-86, 27:100-1, 232-33; Windsor Hist 2:76-77].

Bitfield, Samuel: Wrington, Somerset; 1639; Braintree, Boston [BTR 1:50; MBCR 1:378; TAG 67:236-42].

Bittlestone, Thomas: Newcastle-upon-Tyne, Northumberland; 1640; Cambridge [NEHGR 2:263, 3:248; 61:69; SPR 1:25, 2:17; Ackley-Bosworth 274].

Bittlestone, William: Newcastle-upon-Tyne, Northumberland; 1639; Cambridge [NEHGR 3:248; CaBOP 63; CaTR 40; NEHGR 61:69].

Bitton, James: Unknown; 1635 on *Increase*; passenger list only [GM 2:1:312].

Black, John: Unknown; 1629 on *Talbot*; Salem, Beverly [GMB 175-77].

Blackborne, Walter: London; 1638; Roxbury, Boston; returned permanently to England in 1640 [RChR 83; MBCR 1:376; Lechford 60, 203-8, 250, 255, 393-95, 429; HAHAC 1:54; NEHGR 151:408-16; Abandoning 55].

Blackett, Martha: Unknown; 1634; Boston [GM 2:1:313].

Blackleach, John: London; 1634; Winnissimmett, Salem, Boston, New Haven, Hartford, Wethersfield [GM 2:1:313-18].

Blackley, Edward: Unknown; 1637; Roxbury [RVR MS 96; SPR NS 1:7, 2:7].

Blackley, Thomas: London; 1635 on *Hopewell*; passenger list only [GM 2:1:318-19].

Blackstone, Elizabeth: Salisbury, Wiltshire; 1638 on *Bevis*; passenger list only (servant) [Drake's Founders 60].

Blackstone, William: Cambridge, Cambridgeshire; 1623; Wessagusset; Boston, Study Hill [GMB 177-81].

Blackwell, Jeremy: Unknown; 1635 on *Truelove*; Exeter [GM 2:1:319; Exeter Hist 436; GDMNH 94].

Blackwood, Christopher: Rye, Sussex; 1640; Scituate; returned permanently to England in 1642 [PCR 12:67, 81; ScitTR 3:360; Plain Dealing 96; Morison 366; Abandoning 55-56; ODNB].

Blaisdell, Ralph: Unknown; 1635; York, Salisbury [GM 2:1:319-23; SyTR 10; TAG 66:74].

Blage, Henry: Unknown; 1638; Duxbury, Braintree, Boston [PCR 1:102, 12:32; Lechford 166; NEHGR 3:126, 30:103; SPR Case #310].

Blake, Richard: Unknown; 1638 in *Confidence*; passenger list only [Drake's Founders 58].

Blake, Thomas: Unknown; 1633; Piscataqua [GMB 181-82].

Blake, William: Pitminster, Somerset; 1635 on *Hopewell*; Springfield, Dorchester [NGSQ 71:173; DChR 3; MBCR 1:375; SpTR 159; TAG 74:15-28; NEHGR 163:85-97, 199-211, 278-88, 164:73-74, 175-83].

Blakeman, Adam: Duffield, Derbyshire; 1639; Stratford [CCCR 1:53; FOOF 1:81-82; Sibley 2:140-44; Goodwin Anc 2:75-83; TAG 74:128-30, 78:185, 81:104].

Blakemore, John: Unknown; 1639; Sandwich [PCR 1:130, 150, 8:184, 193].

Blanchard, Joseph: Unknown; 1637; Boston (death record only) [NEHGR 2:77]. (The claim that widow Anne Blanchard of Salem had been his wife lacks evidence.)

Blanchard, Anne: Unknown; 1638; Marblehead [STR 1:74; EQC 1:79; NEHGR 93:162-67]. (The claim that she was widow of Joseph Blanchard of Boston lacks evidence.)

Blanchard, Thomas: Clatford, Hampshire; 1639; Braintree, Charlestown [EQC 1:268; EPR 1:23, 137; Rodgers 1:45-47, 156-66; NEHGR 32:407-10, 68:107, 140:312-16; Wyman 88; Weymouth Hist 3:97-98; Essex Ant 9:26].

Blandfield, Elizabeth: Unknown; 1640; Roxbury (mention in will only) [SPR 1:7].

Blanford, John: Sutton Mandeville, Wiltshire; 1638 on *Confidence*; Sudbury [Drake's Founders 57; SuTR 4; NEHGR 39:163; Dawes-Gates 1:678-86].

Blanton, William: Unknown; 1638; Boston [MBCR 1:246, 249; BTR 1:44, 48; BChR 290; SPR Case #306 (clue); NEHGR 72:194].

Blason, Anne: Unknown; 1635 on *Susan & Ellen*; passenger list only [GM 2:1:323].

Blatchford, Peter: Unknown; 1637; Hartford [CCCR 1:33, 2:161; Manwaring 1:185; TAG 27:170; GM 2:6:424].

Blatchley, Thomas: Unknown; 1640; Hartford, New Haven, Branford, Boston [HaTR 32; TAG 12:102; NEHGR 58:357, 59:105; Seversmith 1:326-32; Shirley Hathaway Stebbings, *Blatchley Physicians and Pioneers: A Family History of the Descendants of Thomas Blatchley, 1635-1929* (Baltimore 1983)].

Blinman, Richard: Holt, Denbighshire; 1640; Marshfield, Gloucester, New London, New Haven; returned permanently to England in 1659 [WP 4:292; PCR 2:8; WJ 2:77; GlTR 1:4; NEHGR 53:234-41, 54:39-44; TG 4:173-86; Abandoning 56-58].

Bliss, George: Unknown; 1639; Sandwich, Newport [PCR 1:149; Austin 22; Aaron Tyler Bliss, *Genealogy of the Bliss Family in America*, 3 volumes (Midland, Michigan, 1982) {but see TAG 59:25-27}]. (The proposed English origin for this immigrant should be revisited.)

Bliss, Thomas: Unknown; 1639; Braintree, Rehoboth [BTR 1:50; ReTR 1:2; NEHGR 151:31-37; Aaron Tyler Bliss, *Genealogy of the Bliss Family in America*, 3 volumes (Midland, Michigan, 1982) {but see TAG 59:25-27}; Hale, House 476-77]. (The proposed English origin for this immigrant should be revisited.)

Bliss, Thomas: Rodborough, Gloucestershire; 1639; Hartford [HaBOP 256; TAG 52:193-97, 60-202; Aaron Tyler Bliss, *Genealogy of the Bliss Family in America*, 3 volumes (Midland, Michigan, 1982) {but see TAG 59:25-27}].

Blodgett, Thomas: Stowmarket, Suffolk; 1635 on *Increase*; Cambridge [GM 2:1:324-26].

Blois, Edmund: Unknown; 1634; Watertown [GM 2:1:326-29].

Bloise, Francis: Unknown; 1640; Cambridge [MBCR 1:379; SPR NS 1:34].

Blood, James: Unknown; 1640; Concord [CoVR 1; MBCR 1:379; Farr Anc 30-31; NEHGR 161:217-18].

Bloomfield, Henry: Unknown; 1638; Salem (mention in will only; possibly not in New England) [EPR 1:37].

Bloomfield, John: Unknown; 1637; Newbury [NeTR 2; EPR 1:12; MBCR 1:286; NYGBR 68:58; Freeman 529 (incorrectly gives immigrant's name as Thomas)].

Bloomfield, William: Unknown; 1634 on *Elizabeth*; Cambridge, Hartford, New London, Newtown [NY] [GM 2:1:329-33].

Blossom, Thomas: Leiden, Holland; 1629; Plymouth [GMB 182-84; PM 58-60; MQ 59:10-15].

Blott, Robert: Puddington, Bedfordshire; 1634; Charlestown, Concord, Boston [GM 2:1:334-38]. (His daughter Mary preceded him to New England, settling in Roxbury in 1632; she married Thomas Woodford [GMB 184].)

Blower, Thomas: Sudbury, Suffolk; 1635 on *Truelove*; Boston [GM 2:1:338-40; TAG 61:161-66, 63:134, 65:241-47].

Blumfield, Thomas: Unknown; 1640; Massachusetts Bay (probate inventory only) [SPR 2:6]. (This is probably the inventory for John Bloomfield of Newbury.)

Blush, Abraham: Unknown; 1637; Duxbury, Barnstable [PCR 2:17, 8:182, 193, 12:23, 39; PCPR 1:30; MD 17:111; James Knox Blish, *Genealogy of the Blish Family in America, 1637-1905* (Kewanee, Illinois, 1905)].

Boade, Henry: Unknown; 1636; Saco, Wells [MPCR 1:lxii, 57; Trelawny 238; GDMNH 96-97].

Boaden, John: Unknown; 1639; Black Point [Trelawny 299; GDMNH 97].

Boaden, William: Unknown; 1640; Dover [NHPP 10:701; GDMNH 98].

Boaneo, Elizabeth: Unknown; 1635; Boston (church admission only) [GM 2:1:340].

Boardman, William: Cambridge, Cambridgeshire; 1638 on *John*; Cambridge [Waters 1076-77; NEHGR 77:305-12].

Boggust, John: Unknown; 1630; Massachusetts Bay [GMB 184].

Bolden, Henry: Unknown; 1640; Woburn (signed founding covenant of Woburn only) [WoTR 2].

Bolles, Joseph: Worksop, Nottinghamshire; 1639; Saco [MPCR 1:49, 51; Trelawny 210; GDMNH 101; TAG 37:114-16, 38:180; Small Gen 3:1186].

Bolt, Francis: Unknown; 1638 on *Martin*; Milford [Savage 1:105; MiTR 2; MiChR 1; GMN 20:21].

Bone, Thomas: Saltash, Cornwall; 1638; Richmond Island [Trelawny 136, 181].

Bonham, George: Unknown; 1640; Plymouth [PCR 2:6, 7:27, 12:61; TAG 35:145-47; Scott Gen 279-81].

Bonner, Mary: Unknown; 1634; Boston [GM 2:1:340]. (She married Daniel Maude.)

Bonney, Thomas: Sandwich, Kent; 1635 on *Hercules*; Charlestown, Duxbury [GM 2:1:340-43].

Bonython, Richard: St. Breage, Cornwall; 1635; Saco [GM 2:1:343-47].

Boosey, James: Colchester, Essex (or vicinity); 1635; Wethersfield [GM 2:1:347-50].

Borden, John: Lenham, Kent; 1635 on *Elizabeth & Ann*; Watertown [GM 2:1:350-51; NEHGR 164:114-20].

Borden, Richard: Unknown; 1638; Portsmouth [PoTR 14; RICR 1:55, 91, 111; NEHGR 75:226-35, 84:70-84, 225-29].

Boreman, Samuel: Claydon, Oxfordshire; 1639; Ipswich, Wethersfield [ITR 55; WetLR 1:10; Charlotte Goldthwaite, *Boardman Genealogy, 1525-1895: The English Home and Ancestry of Samuel Boreman, Wethersfield, Conn. [and] Thomas Boreman, Ipswich, Mass., with Some Account of Their Descendants (Now Called Boardman) in America* (Hartford 1895)].

Boreman, Thomas: Unknown; 1632; Plymouth [GMB 185-86; PM 60-61].

Boreman, Thomas: London; 1634; Ipswich [GM 2:1:352-55].

Boreman, Thomas: London; 1638; Sandwich, Yarmouth [PCR 1:93, 150; GMB 185-86; PM 60-61].

Boreman, William: Unknown; 1639; Concord, Boston (servant) [Lechford 162, 210, 235].

Bosworth, Edward: Unknown; 1634 on *Elizabeth Dorcas*; Boston [GM 2:1:356-57]. (His son Jonathan had arrived in New England by 1633 [GMB 187-91].)

Bosworth, Haniel: Lincolnshire; 1638; Ipswich [EQC 1:381; ITR 58; Essex Ant 11:38; Dawes-Gates 1:105-6; GM 2:6:212].

Bosworth, John: Unknown; 1630; Boston [GMB 186-87; WF 118-20].

Bosworth, Zaccheus: Unknown; 1630; Boston [GMB 191-93; WF 120-23].

Botfish, Robert: Unknown; 1634; Lynn, Sandwich [GM 2:1:357-58].

Botsford, Henry: Unknown; 1639; Milford [MiTR 2; MiChR 1; TAG 14:58-76; NEHGR 141:358; Botsford-Marble].

Boule, Bridget: Norwich, Norfolk; 1637 on *Rose* or *John & Dorothy*; passenger list only (servant) [Hotten 289].

Bourne, Henry: Unknown; 1634; Scituate, Barnstable [GM 2:1:358-60].

Bourne, Jared: Unknown; 1634; Boston, Portsmouth, Swansea [GM 2:1:360-63].

Bourne, John: Unknown; 1636; Salem, Gloucester [STR 1:21, 81; EPR 1:34-36; Perley 3:30].

Bourne, John: Unknown; 1639; Boston (servant) [Lechford 203].

Bourne, Nehemiah: Wapping, Middlesex; 1638; Charlestown; returned permanently to England in 1648 [ChTR 39; DChR 4; NEHGR 2:77, 8:139, 27:26-36, 159:235-36; MBCR 1:378; WP 4:153; Lechford 195 BChR 288; HAHAC 1:54; ODNB; Abandoning 58-62].

Bourne, Richard: Unknown; 1636; Plymouth, Sandwich [PCR 1:47, 150, 7:5; NEHGR 118:83-89].

Bourne, Thomas: Unknown; 1636; Plymouth, Marshfield [PCR 1:49, 74, 138, 12:28; PCPR 1:28; MD 16:24-25; Moore Anc 118-24].

Boutwell, James: Unknown; 1638; Lynn [EQC 2:270; MBCR 1:375; EPR 1:143].

Boutwell, Mary: Unknown; 1640; Lynn (court appearance only) [EQC 1:20]. (Probably sister of James Boutwell.)

Bowditch, William: Unknown; 1639; Salem [SChR 9; EQC 1:21; NEHGR 72:223-24; TAG 30:122-24].

Bowen, Goodman: Unknown; 1640; Dover (mention in letter only) [Gorges 29].

Bowen, Griffin: Unknown; 1638; Boston, Roxbury; returned permanently to England by about 1650 [BChR 23; BTR 1:38; MBCR 1:376; Lechford 258; NEHGR 47:453-59; Parker-Ruggles 511-20; NGSQ 67:163-66, 69:124; TAG 76 266-67; CN 19:335-41, 558-96].

Bowen, Richard: Unknown; 1640; Salem, Weymouth, Rehoboth [William B. Saxbe Jr., *Richard Bowen (1594?-1675), of Rehoboth, Massachusetts, and His Descendants* (Williamstown, Massachusetts, 2011); TAG 76:263-78].

Bowen, Robert: Unknown; 1639; Boston [Lechford 240].

Bowers, George: Unknown; 1636; Scituate, Cambridge [PCR 1:53, 75, 116, 129, 7:7, 12:21, 52; NEHGR 10:42, 79:288; Makepeace Anc 96-101 (clue)].

Bowis, Elizabeth: Unknown; 1635; Roxbury (church admission only) [GM 2:1:363].

Bowler, Mary: Unknown; 1636; Massachusetts Bay (court appearance only) [MBCR 1:194].

Bowles, John: Unknown; 1639; Roxbury [RChR 84; MBCR 1:377; TAG 23:151; Annis Spear Anc 31].

Bowman, John: Unknown; 1632; Plymouth (two tax lists only) [GMB 193; PM 62].

Bowman, Nathaniel: Unknown; 1630; Watertown, Cambridge [GMB 193-96; WF 123-27].

Bowne, William: Unknown; 1635 on *Recovery*; Salem, Gravesend, Middletown [NJ] [GM 2:1:363-66].

Bowstreet, William: Unknown; 1638; Concord [MBCR 1:375; CoVR 1; SPR 1:30, 2:18].

Boyden, Thomas: Unknown; 1634 on *Francis*; Scituate, Watertown, Boston, Medfield [GM 2:1:366-68].

Boykin, Jarvis: Thanington, Kent; 1637; Charlestown, New Haven [NEHGR 75:222, 81:122; ChTR 31; NHCR 1:50, 93; FANH 237; Boardman Anc 239-40].

Boylston, Thomas: London; 1635 on *Defence*; Watertown [GM 2:1:368-72; Goodman 87-93].

Boynton, William: Unknown; 1639; Rowley [MBCR 1:376; RowBOP 2; Rowley Fam 24-26].

Boyse, Joseph: Burford, Oxfordshire; 1640; Salem [STR 1:105; SChR 10; WP 4:285; Essex Ant 6:98-100, 10:58; TAG 73:23-32; Chase-Wigglesworth 107].

Boyse, Matthew: Leeds, Yorkshire; 1637; Roxbury, Rowley; returned permanently to England in 1656 [RChR 83; MBCR 1:318, 376; RowBOP 3; NEHGR 12:65-67, 61:385; Rowley Fam 23; Abandoning 62-63; ODNB (son Joseph)].

Boyse, Thomas: Unknown; 1638; Massachusetts Bay (court appearance only) [MBCR 1:249].

Brabrook, John: Unknown; 1639; Hampton, Watertown [HmTR 45; WaVR 1:8; WaBOP 33; SLR 1:85; Rodgers 2:194-98; EPR 1:391-92; GDMNH 102; Bond 92, 705].

Brackenbury, Richard: Unknown; 1628 in *Abigail*; Salem, Beverly [GMB 196-99].

Brackenbury, William: Unknown; 1630; Charlestown, Malden [GMB 199-202; WF 127-31].

Brackett, Anthony: Unknown; 1639; Piscataqua [NHPP 1:113; GDMNH 102; Herbert I. Brackett, *Brackett Genealogy* (Washington DC 1907)].

Brackett, Peter: Sudbury, Suffolk; 1639; Braintree, Boston [BTR 1:49; NEHGR 3:126, 155:279-94; TAG 28:215-20, 52:65-75, 92, 55:215-17, 56:94-96].

Brackett, Richard: Sudbury, Suffolk; 1632; Boston, Braintree [GMB 203-6; NEHGR 157:199-208].

Bracy, Thomas: London; 1634; Ipswich, Newport, New Haven [GM 2:1:372-75; NEHGR 118:251-62, 119:71, 314; TG 7-8:132-36; TAG 81:224-37].

Bradbury, Thomas: London; 1635; York, Salisbury [GM 2:1:375-81; NEHGR 153:259-77, 161:27-36].

Bradfield, Leslie: Unknown; 1640; Wethersfield, Branford [CCCR 1:445; TAG 12:100, 103, 37:255-56].

Bradford, Robert: Unknown; 1639; Boston [BTR 1:46; BChR 29; MBCR 2:291; SLR 9:105; Bethia Harris Anc 121; TAG 30:67; MD 53:1-4].

Bradford, William: Leiden, Holland; 1620 on *Mayflower*; Plymouth [GMB 207-9; PM 62-66; MQ 61:110-18; NEQ 65:389-421].

Bradish, Robert: Bury St. Edmunds, Suffolk; 1635; Cambridge, Boston [GM 2:1:381-84; TAG 75:47-50, 78:96-102; Juanita Bradish Curley,

A Genealogy & History of Robert Bradish in America (Northville, Michigan, 2000)].

Bradley, John: Unknown; 1636; Salem [STR 1:22, 65; EQC 1:17; EPR 1:18; SPR 1:21; GMB 35].

Bradshaw, John: Unknown; 1640; Lynn (court appearance only) [EQC 1:21; Lechford 329].

Bradshaw, Richard: Unknown; 1628; Pejepscot, Richmond Island, Spurwink [Council NE 98-99; Trelawny 207; MPCR 1:59; WP 3:70; GDMNH 105; Spencer 245-46; English Adventurers 36, 88; NYGBR 47:76].

Bradstreet, Humphrey: Unknown; 1634 on *Elizabeth*; Ipswich [GM 2:1:384-88].

Bradstreet, Simon: Horbling, Lincolnshire; 1630; Boston, Cambridge, Ipswich, Salem, Andover [GMB 209-15; WF 131-39; NEQ 71:517-42].

Bradwick, Joyce: Unknown; 1632; Boston (court appearance only) [GMB 215].

Brady, Elizabeth: Unknown; 1640; Saco (court appearance only) [MPCR 1:lxi, 58, 70-71].

Bragdon, Arthur: Unknown; 1636; York [YLR 1:119, 8:210; Gorges 42; York Hist 1:106-7; GDMNH 105-6].

Branch, Arthur: Unknown; 1636; Saybrook (single mention in narrative of Lyon Gardiner) [MHSC 3:3:143].

Branch, Peter: High Halden, Kent; 1638 on *Castle*; died aboard ship bound for New England [SPR 1:16, 2:2; NEHGR 65:286; Scott Gen 270-72; William Farrand Branch and Roger Eddy Branch, *The Branch Family of New England: The Line of William Farrand Branch* (Champlain, New York, 1935)].

Brand, Benjamin: Edwardstone, Suffolk; 1630; Massachusetts Bay; returned permanently to England by 1631 [GMB 215; WF 139-40].

Brand, Thomas: Unknown; 1629; hired by Massachusetts Bay Company but not seen in New England [WF 140].

Brane, Thomas: Unknown; 1635 on *Abigail*; Lynn [GM 2:1:388-89].

Branker, John: Dorchester, Dorset; 1632; Dorchester, Windsor [GMB 215-17; M&JCH 26:13-15].

Brasier, Henry: Unknown; 1639; New Haven (court appearance only) [NHCR 1:29].

Bratcher, Austin: Unknown; 1630; Mystic [GMB 217-18; WF 141].

Braybrooke, William: Unknown; 1639; Sandwich (land grant only) [PCR 1:149].

Brayne, Agnes: Unknown; 1636; Salem (church admission only) [SChR 6].

Breck, Edward: Prescot, Lancashire; 1638; Dorchester, Lancaster [DTR 1:34; DChR 4, 5; MBCR 1:313, 376; NEHGR 164:175-83; Samuel Breck, *Genealogy of the Breck Family Descended from Edward of Dorchester and His Brothers in America* (Omaha, Nebraska, 1889)].

Breed, Allen: Pulloxhill, Bedfordshire; 1638; Lynn [EQC 2:270; Lechford 153; SoTR 1:2; TAG 14:2; EIHC 40:147-53; TEG 11:196-201].

Brenton, William: Unknown; 1633; Boston, Portsmouth, Newport, Boston, Taunton [GMB 218-24].

Brett, Isabel: Unknown; 1630; Boston, Salem (church admission only) [GMB 225]. (Possibly married William Robinson.)

Brett, William: Unknown; 1639; Duxbury, Bridgewater [PCR 1:144, 6:81; PCPR 1:40, 4:1:105-6; TAG 61:129-32; L. B. Goodenow, *The Brett Genealogy* (n.p. 1915)].

Brewer, Daniel: Unknown; 1632 on *Lyon*; Roxbury [GMB 225-27].

Brewer, Thomas: Unknown; 1638; Ipswich (land grant only) [ITR 46, 47]. (Claims that he was later of Roxbury and Hampton lack sufficient evidence [NEHGR 9:159-60, 30:424-26].)

Brewster, Francis: Bristol; 1640; New Haven, died at sea 1646 while returning to England [NHCR 1:50, 93; NEHGR 81:122; TAG 12:199-210, 13:8-21, 113-16, 154-63, 221-33, 14:105-9; FOOF 1:101-2; Seversmith 1:389-401; Abandoning 65-67].

Brewster, William: Leiden, Holland; 1620 on *Mayflower*; Plymouth, Duxbury [GMB 227-30; PM 66-70; MQ 72:239-41].

Brian, Thomas: Unknown; 1632; Plymouth (servant; court appearance only) [GMB 230; PM 70].

Bridge, Edward: Unknown; 1637; Roxbury [RChR 82; MBCR 1:376; Dawes-Gates 1:112-18].

Bridge, John: Unknown; 1634; Cambridge [GM 2:1:393-97].

Bridges, Edmund: Unknown; 1635 on *James*; Lynn, Rowley, Ipswich, Salem [GM 2:1:389-92].

Bridges, Elisha: Unknown; 1639; Massachusetts Bay (appearance in legal transaction only) [Lechford 180; GM 2:2:531-32].

Bridges, Robert: Unknown; 1640; Lynn [MBCR 1:378; HAHAC 1:112; EQC 1:383-86; EIHC 17:13-16; Waters 508-9; TAG 43:100-2; NEQ 71:290-97].

Bridges, William: Unknown; 1623 on *Anne*; Plymouth, Watertown, Charlestown [GMB 231-34; PM 70-75].

Bridgham, Henry: Thelnetham, Suffolk; 1640; Dorchester, Boston [DChR 5; TAG 33:113-21, 34:210-11, 58:129-30].

Brigden, Thomas: Faversham, Kent; 1635 on *Hercules*; Charlestown [GM 2:1:397-400].

Briggs, Clement: Southwark, Surrey; 1621 on *Fortune*; Plymouth, Weymouth [GMB 234-37; PM 76-80].

Briggs, John: Unknown; 1635 on *Blessing*; passenger list only (with caveat) [GM 2:1:400-1].

Briggs, John: Unknown; 1638; Portsmouth [PoTR 2, 16; RICR 1:67, 91, 111; NEHGR 125:77; Austin 25-26].

Briggs, John: Unknown; 1639; Sandwich [PCR 1:149, 2:18, 8:184; PCPR 1:39; NEHGR 125:77; MD 3:224-25; GM 2:1:400-1; Edna Anne Hannibal, *John Briggs of Sandwich, Massachusetts, and His Descendants* (n.p. 1962)].

Brigham, Sebastian: Holme-upon-Spalding-Moor, Yorkshire; 1638; Cambridge, Rowley; returned permanently to England by 1652 [CaBOP 59, 65; RowBOP 6; Rowley Fam 42-43; GMN 1:13, 18:27; Abandoning 67].

Brigham, Thomas: Holme-upon-Spalding-Moor, Yorkshire; 1635 on *Susan & Ellen*; Cambridge [GM 2:1:401-6; Rhonda R. McClure, *The History of the Brigham Family: Descendants of Thomas Brigham* (Boston 2010)].

Bright, Francis: Rayleigh, Essex; 1629 on *Lyon's Whelp*; Salem, Charlestown; returned permanently to England in 1630 [GMB 238; WF 142-44].

Bright, Henry: Bury St. Edmunds, Suffolk; 1630; Boston, Watertown [GMB 239-43; WF 144-49; HmTR 45; GDMNH 110].

Bright, Margaret: Unknown; 1636; Salem [SChR 6; STR 1:60]. (Sister of John Holgrave.)

Bright, Thomas: Unknown; 1640; Watertown (two land records only) [Lechford 286; WaBOP 19].

Brighton, Thomas: Unknown; 1635 on *Truelove*; passenger list only [GM 2:1:404].

Brinsmead, John: Unknown; 1636; Charlestown, Stratford [ChTR 22; ChChR 9, 10; ChBOP 34; NEHGR 4:183; MBCR 1:374; Wyman 130; FOOF 1:102-3; M&JCH 25:13-21 (clue)].

Briscoe *see also* **Biscoe**

Briscoe, Nathaniel: Unknown; 1639; Milford [MiTR 2; Ackley-Bosworth 173-74, 274; Bond 684-85].

Briscoe, William: Unknown; 1639; Boston, Milford [BTR 1:48; BChR 32, 33, 36, 49; MBCR 1:378; WJ 2:80; SPR Case #449].

Bristow, Goodman: Unknown; 1639; Hampton [HmTR 43; GDMNH 111].

Bristow/Briskow, Widow: Unknown; 1635; Ten Hills [WP 3:211, 275].

Brittell, John: Unknown; 1637; Salem (land grant only) [STR 1:102].

Britteridge, Richard: Unknown; 1620 on *Mayflower*; Plymouth [GMB 243-44; PM 80].

Britton, James: Unknown; 1638; Weymouth [MBCR 1:254, 296; WJ 1:347, 2:190; WP 4:445-46; Weymouth Hist 3:130].

Britton, James: Unknown; 1640; Woburn [WoTR 2; Dawes-Gates 1:285-86; GM 2:2:155-56].

Brock, Henry: Stradbroke, Suffolk; 1638; Dedham [DeTR 1:48; DeVR 126; DeChR 23; SPR 1:19, 67, 2:60; NEHGR 144:124-37; DeHR 3:158-59, 161-62; Sibley 1:127-31; GDMNH 111].

Brock, Richard: Westminster, Middlesex; 1635 on *Elizabeth & Ann*; passenger list only [GM 2:1:404].

Brockett, John: Unknown; 1638; New Haven, Wallingford [NHCR 1:13, 26; Babcock Anc 32-35; Gen Journal 12:129-35 (clue); Edward J. Brockett, *The Descendants of John Brockett* (East Orange, New Jersey, 1905)].

Brodley, Daniel: London; 1635 on *Elizabeth*; passenger list only (with caveat) [GM 2:1:405].

Bromfield, William: Unknown; 1637; Massachusetts Bay, New Haven (servant; three court appearances only; see George Spencer) [MBCR 1:203; NHCR 1:28, 29].

Broock, William: Unknown; 1639; Salem (admitted town inhabitant only) [STR 1:93].

Brook, Henry: Unknown; 1638; Concord, Woburn [MBCR 1:375; CoVR 1; TAG 53:94, 54:234-35; Snow-Estes 2:282-85].

Brook, Thomas: Unknown; 1636; Watertown, Concord [WaBOP 4; WP 4:124; SPR 2:12; MBCR 1:295, 372; TAG 53:94-100, 54:234-35].

Brooke, Thomas: Unknown; 1639; died at sea during passage to New England [Lechford 176].

Brooke, Richard: Unknown; 1635 on *Susan & Ellen*; passenger list only (but possibly Richard Brooks of Lynn) [GM 2:1:405-6].

Brooke, Robert: Maidstone, Kent; 1635 on *Hercules*; passenger list only [GM 2:1:406; NEHGR 79:108].

Brooke, Thomas: Unknown; 1635 on *Susan & Ellen*; Lynn [GM 2:1:406-7].

Brooks, Gilbert: Unknown; 1635 on *Blessing*; Scituate, Marshfield, Rehoboth [GM 2:1:407-11].

Brooks, Richard: Unknown; 1638; Lynn [EQC 2:270; Lechford 153; GM 2:1:405-6].

Brooks, Thomas: Unknown; 1639; Piscataqua [MPCR 1:xiii-xiv, 42; GDMNH 112]. (This man also used the name Basil Parker.)

Brooks, William: Unknown; 1635 on *Blessing*; Scituate, Marshfield [GM 2:1:412-15].

Broome, Roger: Unknown; 1635 on *Truelove*; passenger list only [GM 2:1:415].

Broomell, John: Unknown; 1638; Duxbury (business transaction only) [Lechford 167].

Broomer, Joan: Unknown; 1635 on *Susan & Ellen*; passenger list only [GM 2:1:415].

Broomer, Mary: Unknown; 1635 on *Elizabeth & Ann*; passenger list only [GM 2:1:415].

Brough, Edmond: Unknown; 1640; Plymouth, Marshfield, Boston [PCR 1:164; TAG 27:1-6, 37:212-17; MF 15:9].

Browce, Edward: Unknown; 1639; Newport (admission as town inhabitant only; surname possibly corrupted) [RICR 1:92; GMN 23:4].

Brown, Abraham: Childerditch, Essex; 1631; Watertown [GMB 244-46; TAG 56:24; Kempton Anc 1:168-86].

Brown, Arthur: Unknown; 1633; Casco; not seen after 1642 [Trelawny 106, 232, 269-72, 326, 328; MPCR 1:6, 56-57, 67, 72, 75, 79-81; Lechford 224, 402; TAG 40:29; GDMNH 114].

Brown, Chad: High Wycombe, Buckinghamshire; 1638 on *Martin*; Providence [PrTR 1:1, 15:2; NEHGR 65:84; TAG 62:193-201; A Descendant, *The Chad Browne Memorial* (Brooklyn 1888)].

Brown, Christian: Salisbury, Wiltshire; 1639; Salisbury [SyTR 1, 13, 14; HvBOP 7]. (She was the widowed mother of George, Henry and William Brown of Salisbury.)

Brown, Edmund: Sawbridgeworth, Hertfordshire; 1634; Boston; removed to the Caribbean by the early 1660s [GM 2:1:416-18].

Brown, Edmund: Unknown; 1638; Watertown, Sudbury [Letters from NE 224; MBCR 1:377; SuTR 2; WaTR 1:9; Lechford 130-33; MPR Case #2984; NEHGR 7:344; Stevens-Miller 1:175-77; Morison 368-69; GM 2:4:354-57].

Brown, Edward: Unknown; 1637; Ipswich [ITR 25, 43, 63; MBCR 1:379; EPR 1:306-8; TAG 41:8-12; Parker-Ruggles 434-38; Granberry 178-79].

Brown, Francis: Unknown; 1640; Braintree (servant; death record only) [NEHGR 3:126].

Brown, Francis: Unknown; 1640; New Haven [NHCR 1:42, 50; NEHGR 81:122-23; FANH 346-47 (clue)].

Brown, George: Unknown; 1634 on *Mary & John*; Newbury [GM 2:1:418-20].

Brown, Hugh: Unknown; 1629; Salem; returned permanently to England in 1641 [GMB 246-47; Abandoning 67-68].

Brown, James: Unknown; 1630; Boston [GMB 248-49; WF 150-52].

Brown, James: Unknown; 1633; Charlestown, Newbury, Salem [GMB 249-54].

Brown, James: Hampshire; 1635 on *James*; passenger list only [GM 2:1:420].

Brown, James: Unknown; 1636; Newbury [MBCR 1:373; NeTR 4; EQC 1:40; GMB 253]. (See Savage 1:268 and GDMNH 115.)

Brown, John: Roxwell, Essex; 1629; Salem; returned permanently to England in 1629 [GMB 255; WF 152-54].

Brown, John: Unknown; 1632 on *Lyon*; Watertown [GMB 255-57].

Brown, John: Dorking, Surrey; 1632; Duxbury [GMB 257-59; PM 80-82].

Brown, John: [Great?] Baddow, Essex; 1635 on *Defence*; passenger list only [GM 2:1:420].

Brown, John: London; 1635 on *Elizabeth*; Plymouth, Taunton, Rehoboth [GM 2:1:420-29; MQ 57:318-22, 58:16-20, 126-30].

Brown, John: Unknown; 1637; Salem [STR 1:51, 93; SChR 7; MBCR 1:374; Essex Ant 13:147; Perley 1:430-32; TG 2:132-33; EIHC 4:171, 8:33-35].

Brown, John: Unknown; 1639; Hampton [HmTR 45; GDMNH 44, 115; Sarah Stone Anc 143].

Brown, John: Unknown; 1639; Ipswich [ITR 68; Phoebe Tilton Anc 81-83; Essex Ant 12:156].

Brown, John: Bristol; 1639; Pemaquid [GDMNH 115 (citing YLR 35:55); NYGBR 51:29-30].

Brown, Lydia: London; 1635 on *Abigail*; passenger list only (with caveat) [GM 2:1:429].

Brown, Nathaniel: Unknown; 1635; Cambridge, Hartford, Springfield, Middletown [GM 2:1:429-31].

Brown, Nicholas: Unknown; 1638; Portsmouth [PoTR 2; RICR 1:91; Austin 28].

Brown, Nicholas: Inkberrow, Worcestershire; 1638; Lynn, Reading [EQC 1:14, 18, 2:270; MBCR 1:295, 374; SPR 1:15; NEHGR 103:182; TEG 8:178-81; Aspinwall 266].

Brown, Peter: Dorking, Surrey; 1620 on *Mayflower*; Plymouth [GMB 259-61; PM 82-85].

Brown, Peter: Unknown; 1639; New Haven, Stamford [NHCR 1:29; FOOF 1:104-5].

Brown, Richard: London; 1630; Watertown, Charlestown [GMB 262-66; WF 154-59; TAG 56:24].

Brown, Richard: Unknown; 1634 on *Mary & John*; Ipswich, Newbury [GM 2:1:432-35].

Brown, Robert: Unknown; 1635 on *Truelove*; passenger list only [GM 2:1:435].

Brown, Samuel: Roxwell, Essex; 1629; Salem; returned permanently to England in 1629 [GMB 255; WF 159-60].

Brown, Susan: Unknown; 1635 on *Elizabeth & Ann*; passenger list only (servant) [GM 2:1:435].

Brown, Thomas: Christian Malford, Wiltshire; 1635 on *James*; Newbury [GM 2:1:435-38].

Brown, Thomas: Unknown; 1635 on *James*; passenger list only [GM 2:1:438-39].

Brown, Thomas: Unknown; 1638; Sudbury, Concord, Cambridge [SuTR 3; MBCR 1:307, 374; CoVR 1; NEHGR 140:317-20; MPR Case #3212].

Brown, William: Unknown; 1633; Boston [GMB 266-67].

Brown, William: Brundish, Suffolk; 1635 on *Love*; Salem [GM 2:1:439-45; NEHGR 25:352-55].

Brown, William: Unknown; 1639; Boston (servant; apprenticeship record only) [Lechford 188].

Brown, William: Unknown; 1639; Sudbury [SuTR 3; MBCR 1:378; NEHGR 52:336-37; MPR Case #3233].

Brown, William: Unknown; 1640; Salem, Gloucester [Lechford 406; WP 4:165-66; SChR 11; EPR 1:102, 386-88; Farr Anc 43-44 (some items included from the William Brown of Salem above)].

Brownell, Thomas: London; 1639; Braintree, Portsmouth [Lechford 252; Waters 646-47; TAG 36:126-27; RIR 21:99-114; Austin 29].

Browning, Henry: Unknown; 1639; New Haven; not seen after 1647 [CCCR 1:43; Lechford 342; WP 4:222; NHChR 1; NHCR 1:32, 50, 93; FANH 357; GMN 13:19].

Browning, Mr.: Unknown; 1639; Massachusetts Bay (court appearance only) [MBCR 1:296].

Browning, Thomas: Unknown; 1636; Salem, Topsfield [STR 1:21; SChR 6; MBCR 1:373; Amos Towne Anc 19-22].

Bruen, Obadiah: Shrewsbury, Shropshire; 1640; Marshfield, Gloucester, New London, Newark [MA Arch 3:440; PCR 2:8; GITR 1:1; TAG 26:12-25].

Brundish, John: Unknown; 1634; Watertown, Wethersfield [GM 2:1:445-48].

Brunson, John: Earls Colne, Essex; 1635; Hartford, Farmington [HaTR 7; HaBOP 182; TAG 38:193-211, 39:113-22, 71:206-14].

Brunson, Mary: Earls Colne, Essex; 1635; Hartford [CCCR 1:45, 50; TAG 38:193-211]. (She married Nicholas Desborough.)

Brunson, Richard: Earls Colne, Essex; 1635; Hartford, Farmington [TAG 38:193-211].

Bryan, Alexander: Aylesbury, Buckinghamshire; 1639; Milford [MiTR 2; MiChR 1; TAG 9:89-90, 10:90-100; Miner Anc 81-83; Goodwin-

Morgan 2:285-95; Charles Candee Baldwin, *The Baldwin Genealogy From 1500 to 1881* (Cleveland 1881) 46-47].

Bryan, John: Unknown; 1638; Scituate [PCR 1:118, 132, 2:12; NEHGR 48:46-47].

Bryan, Widow: Unknown; 1639; Salem (land grant only) [STR 1:97].

Bryant, John: Unknown; 1637; Taunton [PCPR 1:31; MD 2:210-11].

Buck, Christian: Unknown; 1635 on *Blessing*; passenger list only [GM 2:1:448].

Buck, James: Hingham, Norfolk; 1638 on *Diligent*; Hingham [NEHGR 15:26, 121:11; HiBOP 80; MBCR 1:376; Hingham Hist 2:96].

Buck, John: Unknown; 1637; passenger list only (servant) [NEHGR 75:222].

Buck, Susan: Unknown; 1637; Ipswich [NEHGR 75:222; EQC 1:87, 109].

Buck, William: Unknown; 1635 on *Increase*; Cambridge [GM 2:1:448-50].

Buckett, Mary: Unknown; 1623 on *Anne*; Plymouth [GMB 267; PM 85]. (She married George Soule.)

Buckingham, Thomas: Minsden, Hertfordshire; 1639; Milford [MiChR 1; MiTR 2; NHCR 1:28; TAG 13:205-8].

Buckland, Thomas: Unknown; 1634; Dorchester, Windsor [GM 2:1:450-53; M&JCH 19:19-21 (clue)].

Buckland, William: Unknown; 1631; Massachusetts Bay [GMB 267-68].

Buckland, William: Unknown; 1634; Hingham, Rehoboth [GM 2:1:454-56].

Buckmaster/Buckminster, Thomas: Unknown; 1639; Sudbury, Boston [SuTR 4; MBCR 1:287; SPR 1:283, 3:57; Frame-Dana 142-43].

Bucknall, Roger: Unknown; 1638; Richmond Island [Trelawny 188, 194].

Bucknam, William: Unknown; 1638; Charlestown [ChBOP 66; Lechford 411; Ann Theopold Chaplin, *A Bucknam-Buckman Genealogy* (Baltimore 1988)].

Budd, John: Unknown; 1640; New Haven, Southold [Lechford 314; NHCR 1:91; NYGBR 52:75; 57:243].

Buell, William: Unknown; 1639; Windsor [Grant 27, 78; WiLR 1:19; Manwaring 1:280-81; TAG 54:65-71; Goodwin-Morgan 1:123-31].

Buffam, Robert: Great Yarmouth, Norfolk; 1638; Salem [STR 1:73; EPR 2:174-77; EIHC 50:245-52; Dudley Wildes Anc 119-20; Sarah Johnson Anc 37-39; NEQ 74:355-84; Owen A. Perkins, *Buffum Family, Volume II* (n.p. 1983)].

Bugby, Edward: Unknown; 1634 on *Francis*; Roxbury [GM 2:1:456-59; TAG 67:8-10].

Bugby, Richard: Unknown; 1630; Roxbury [GMB 268-69; WF 161-62].

Buitt, George: Unknown; 1639; Sandwich [PCR 1:149, 2:83, 115, 155, 162, 163, 3:188, 8:180, 193; PCPR 3:1:153; MD 34:114].

Bulfinch, John: Unknown; 1639; Salem [EQC 1:19, 28, 44, 55, 86; SChR 10; STR 1:110, 121; MBCR 2:291; ELR 1:19v; Perley 1:133].

Bulgar, Richard: Unknown; 1630; Boston, Roxbury, Exeter, Dover, Portsmouth [GMB 269-71; WF 162-64].

Bulkeley, Peter: Odell, Bedfordshire; 1635 on *Susan & Ellen*; Cambridge, Concord [GM 2:1:459-65; TAG 42:129-35, 46:256, 65:24-32].

Bull, Dixey: London; 1631; York [GMB 272].

Bull, Henry: Unknown; 1635 on *James*; Roxbury, Boston, Portsmouth, Newport [GM 2:1:465-69; TG 28:26-57, 155-79].

Bull, Henry: Southwark, Surrey; 1635 on *Elizabeth*; passenger list only (with caveat) [GM 2:1:469].

Bull, Thomas: Unknown; 1635 on *Hopewell*; Cambridge, Hartford [GM 2:1:469-76].

Bull, William: Unknown; 1638; Cambridge [Pope 77 (citing MCF); Wyman 149; SPR Case #1602½].

Bullard, George: Barnham, Suffolk; 1639; Watertown [WaVR 1:7; MBCR 1:379; NEHGR 154:172-88; Kempton Anc 1:198-206].

Bullard, John: Barnham, Suffolk; 1638; Dedham; Medfield [DeTR 1:45; DeChR 21; NEHGR 146:279-80, 154:172-88; Kempton Anc 1:198-214].

Bullard, Robert: Barnham, Suffolk; 1639; Watertown [WaVR 1:7; NEHGR 146:279-80, 154:172-88; Kempton Anc 1:198-206].

Bullard, William: Bradwell, Suffolk; 1638; Dedham [DeTR 1:45; DeChR 22; MBCR 1:377; SPR 1:11; TAG 72:135-36; NEHGR 154:172-88; Kempton Anc 1:198-206].

Bullen, Samuel: Unknown; 1639; Dedham, Medfield [DeTR 1:68; DeChR 26; MBCR 1:379; Medfield Hist 334; SPR Case #2259].

Bullock, Edward: Barkham, Berkshire; 1635 on *Elizabeth*; Dorchester [GM 2:1:476-77].

Bullock, Erasmus: Unknown; 1633; Boston [GMB 273].

Bullock, Henry: St. Lawrence, Essex; 1635 on *Abigail*; Charlestown, Salem [GM 2:1:477-80].

Bumpas, Edward: Unknown; 1621 on *Fortune*; Plymouth, Duxbury, Marshfield [GMB 273-76; PM 85-88].

Bumstead, Thomas: Unknown; 1639; Roxbury [RChR 84; NEHGR 5:334, 15:193-94, 140:312-16; MBCR 1:377; TAG 85:92-104, 86:53; Dawes-Gates 1:123-27; GMN 7:3-6, 21:9-10].

Bunce, Thomas: Unknown; 1637; Hartford [CCCR 2:154; HaBOP 205; Manwaring 1:283-84, 416; Wethersfield Hist 2:164].

Bundy, John: Unknown; 1635; Plymouth, Boston, Taunton [GM 2:1:480-83].

Bunell, William: Unknown; 1630; Massachusetts Bay [GMB 276-77; WF 165-66].

Bunnell, William: Unknown; 1640; Watertown [MBCR 1:307; ChTR 54; WF 165].

Bunker, George: Odell, Bedfordshire; 1634; Charlestown [GM 2:1:483-87].

Bunt, George: Unknown; 1638; Richmond Island [Trelawny 187, 194, 280, 282, 300].

Burbank, John: Unknown; 1639; Rowley [MBCR 1:376; RowBOP 2; Rowley Fam 54; George Burbank Sedgley, *Genealogy of the Burbank Family* (Farmington, Maine, 1928)].

Burbank, Joseph: Unknown; 1635 on *Abigail*; passenger list only [GM 2:1:487; see also NEHGR 94:393-94].

Burcham, Edward: Unknown; 1638; Lynn [EQC 1:1, 410, 2:270, 8:254-56, 399; MBCR 1:375; NEHGR 19:31; TAG 27:21-22].

Burcher, Edward: Unknown; 1623 on *Anne*; Plymouth [GMB 277-78; PM 88-89].

Burden, George: Newcastle-upon-Tyne, Northumberland; 1635 on *Abigail*; Boston [GM 2:1:487-91; NEHGR 155:91-104].

Burdett, George: Great Yarmouth, Norfolk; 1635; Salem, Dover, York, Pemaquid; returned permanently to England in 1641 [GM 2:1:491-97].

Burgess, James: Unknown; 1635 on *Hopewell*; Boston [GM 2:1:497-98].

Burgess, John: Unknown; 1638; Sandwich (court appearance only) [PCR 1:107].

Burgess, Thomas: Unknown; 1637; Duxbury, Sandwich [PCR 1:63, 100, 149, 155, 12:38; TAG 61:69, 80:304-7, 81:152].

Burgess, _____: Unknown; 1637; passenger list only (servant) [Hotten 294].

Burkbee, Thomas: Unknown; 1639; Massachusetts Bay (court appearance only) [MBCR 1:270]. (Almost certainly not the same as Thomas Burpee of Rowley.)

Burles, John: Unknown; 1635 on *Blessing* or *Defence*; passenger list only [GM 2:1:498].

Burley, Phebe: Unknown; 1638; Boston (servant; church admission only) [BChR 24].

Burne, William: Unknown; 1638; Duxbury (court appearance only) [PCR 1:101].

Burnell, _____: Unknown; 1638; Sandwich (court appearance only) [PCR 1:109].

Burnham, John: Unknown; 1637; Ipswich [ITR 43; GM 2:1:54; Elizabeth Puckett Martin, *Deacon John Burnham of Ipswich and Ebenezer Martin of Rehoboth, Massachusetts, with Some of their Descendants* (Baltimore 1987)].

Burns, Margaret: Unknown; 1634; Boston (church admission only) [GM 2:1:498].

Burr, Benjamin: Unknown; 1636; Cambridge, Hartford [CaTR 23; HaBOP 165; HaTR 24; Manwaring 1:284-85; WMJ 726, 761, 787; Charles Burr Todd, *A General History of the Burr Family* (New York 1902) 278-81].

Burr, Jehu: Unknown; 1630; Roxbury, Springfield, Fairfield [GMB 278-80; WF 166-69].

Burr, Jonathan: Rickinghall Superior, Suffolk; 1639; Dorchester [DChR 5, 16, 23, 151, 250; WJ 2:26-27; WoTR 4; Magnalia 1:368-75; Morison 370; Sibley 1:309-10].

Burr, Rebecca: Unknown; 1639; Dorchester (church admission only) [DChR 5].

Burrage, John: Unknown; 1637; Charlestown [ChTR 31; ChBOP 13; ChChR 10; NEHGR 4:183; EIHC 50:151; Wyman 157-58].

Burrage, John: Unknown; 1638; Richmond Island, Scarborough [Trelawny 164, 182; GDMNH 121].

Burrell, George: Boston, Lincolnshire; 1636; Lynn [EQC 1:5, 8, 2:270; EPR 1:177-81; EIHC 51:271-72; NEHGR 83:117-21; Ruth Burell-Brown, *The Burell/Burrill Genealogy* (Baltimore 1990); Chase-Wigglesworth 125-33].

Burrill, John: Unknown; 1634; Roxbury, Boston [GM 2:1:499-500].

Burrow, William: Unknown; 1635 on *Susan & Ellen*; passenger list only (with caveat) [GM 2:1:500].

Burrowes, William: Unknown; 1640; Providence [PrTR 15:5; Macdonough-Hackstaff 436-43].

Burrows, John: Great Yarmouth, Norfolk; 1637 on *Mary Anne*; Salem; not seen after 1644 [Hotten 294; STR 1:54, 60, 102, 128].

Burrows, John: Unknown; 1638; Salisbury (servant; three court appearances only) [MBCR 1:241, 271, 300].

Bursley, John: Unknown; 1623; Weymouth, Barnstable [GMB 280-83; PM 89-92].

Burt, Henry: Harberton, Devonshire; 1639; Roxbury, Springfield [MBCR 1:278; Pynchon 209, 211; NEHGR 86:77-84, 216-20, 247-52; Hale, House 486-91; Stevens-Miller 1:359-66; Henry M. Burt and Silas W. Burt, *Life and Times of Henry Burt of Springfield and Some of His Descendants* (Springfield, Massachusetts, 1893)].

Burt, Hugh: Dorking, Surrey; 1635 on *Abigail*; Lynn [GM 2:1:501-4; TAG 79:181-83].

Burt, James: Unknown; 1639; Newport, Taunton [RICR 1:92; WP 4:245; TAG 75:109-16, 206, 319; GMN 23:3].

Burt, John: Unknown; 1638; Springfield (land grant only) [SpTR 161].

Burton, Boniface: Unknown; 1635; Lynn, Reading [GM 2:1:504-6].

Burton, Edward: Unknown; 1632; Charlestown, Hingham [GMB 283-85].

Burton, John: Unknown; 1636; Salem [STR 1:22; Putnam's Mag 7:302-6; EPR Case #4289].

Burton, Thomas: London; 1639; Boston, Newport, Portsmouth [Lechford 231, 235; RICR 1:92; TAG 59:84-89; NEHGR 161:101-12, 301; Robert Emmet Wall Jr., *Massachusetts Bay: The Crucial Decade, 1640-1650* (New Haven 1972) 237].

Burwell, John: Hitchin, Hertfordshire; 1639; Milford [MiTR 2; MiChR 1; Parke-Gildersleeve 64-68].

Burwood, Alice: Unknown; 1638; Watertown (court appearance only) [MBCR 1:246, 270].

Burwood, Thomas: Unknown; 1639; Salem; returned permanently to England in 1640 [EQC 1;19, 22, 2:136; NEHGR 154:159-71].

Busby, Nicholas: Norwich, Norfolk; 1637 on *John & Dorothy* or *Rose*; Newbury, Watertown, Boston [Hotten 289; NeTR 4; MBCR 1:374; WaBOP 11, 50; Anna C. Kingsbury, *A Historical Sketch of Nicholas Busby the Emigrant* (n.p. 1924); TAG 85:242-53].

Busby, William: Unknown; 1637; Massachusetts Bay (court appearance only) [MBCR 1:233].

Bushell, Ruth: Buttercrambe, Yorkshire; 1635 on *Abigail*; Cambridge [GM 2:1:507; God's Plot 52-53]. (She married Edward Mitchelson.)

Bushnell, Edmond: Horsham, Sussex; 1635; Boston [GM 2:1:507-9].

Bushnell, Francis: Horsham, Sussex; 1635 on *Planter*; Boston, Salem, Guilford, Saybrook [GM 2:1:510-12; Guilford Hist 25].

Bushnell, John: Horsham, Sussex; 1635 on *Hopewell*; Salem, Boston [GM 2:1:512-14].

Bushrod, Thomas: Dorchester, Dorset; 1635 on *Hopewell*; Massachusetts Bay; removed to Virginia by 1643 [NGSQ 71:174; EQC 1:4; MBCR 1:262, 265, 269; NEHGR 167:183-84].

Busicot, Peter: Hartland, Devonshire; 1636; Salem, Hartford, Warwick [MBCR 1:177, 244, 248; EQC 1:7-9, 54; HaBOP 310; CCCR 1:102, 111, 114, 115, 123, 157, 160, 168, 169, 177, 181; PrTR 15:25-26; Austin 33-34; TAG 58:230].

Busket, James: Unknown; 1635 on *Christian*; passenger list only [GM 2:1:515].

Buss, William: Unknown; 1638; Concord [MBCR 1:375; CoVR 1; NHGR 26:57-64].

Buswell, Isaac: Husbands Bosworth, Leicestershire; 1639; Salisbury [SyTR 5; MBCR 1:378; NEHGR 158:33-39; Pillsbury Anc 317-19].

Butler, Giles: Marlborough, Wiltshire; 1635 on *James*; passenger list only [GM 2:1:515].

Butler, Nicholas: Eastwell, Kent; 1637; Dorchester, Edgartown [NEHGR 58:404, 75:221; Lechford 243; DChR 4; DTR 25, 28, 40; MBCR 1:375; Martha's Vineyard Hist 2:Edgartown:54-58, 3:47-66; Henry Langdon Butler, *Tales of Our Kinsfolk Past and Present: The Story of Our Butler Ancestors for Ten Generations from 1602 to 1919* (New York 1919)].

Butler, Richard: Unknown; 1633; Cambridge, Hartford [GMB 285-88].

Butler, Thomas: Unknown; 1637; Duxbury, Sandwich [PCR 1:63, 150; PCPR 1:45; NEHGR 127:18-22].

Butler, William: Unknown; 1634; Cambridge, Hartford [GM 2:1:515-17; WetLR 1:71].

Butterfield, Benjamin: Unknown; 1638; Charlestown, Woburn; Chelmsford [ChTR 41; WoTR 2; WoVR; Fiske Notebook 105; NEHGR 44:33-34].

Butterfield, Samuel: Halifax, Yorkshire; 1635; Charlestown, Concord, Springfield, Saybrook [SpTR 1:159; WJ 1:236; MHSC 3:3:143; NYGBR 120:98-99; GM 2:5:128-30].

Butterworth, Henry: Halifax, Yorkshire; 1635; Weymouth [MBCR 1:313; NEHGR 168:58-61].

Butterworth, Samuel: Halifax, Yorkshire; 1635; Charlestown, Weymouth, Rehoboth [MBCR 1:377; ReTR 1:2; NEHGR 168:58-61].

Buttles, Leonard: Unknown; 1639; Boston [Lechford 174-75, 215-16, 384; Aspinwall 189; BTR 1:44, 48, 56, 59, 66; BChR 34; MBCR 1:296; SLR 1:42, 111, 126, 142, 2:258, 3:301; MD 14:155].

Buttolph, Thomas: Little Baddow, Essex; 1635 on *Abigail*; Boston [GM 2:1:517-22; Boreham, Essex, parish register].

Button, John: Unknown; 1633; Boston [GMB 288-92].

Button, Matthias: Unknown; 1633; Boston, Ipswich, Haverhill [GMB 292-98].

Button, William: Unknown; 1620 on *Mayflower*; died at sea [GMB 298; PM 92].

Buttrick, William: Unknown; 1635; Concord [GM 2:1:522-26].

Buttry, Nicholas: Unknown; 1635 on *James*; Cambridge [GM 2:1:526].

Buxton, Anthony: Wookey, Somerset; 1637; Salem [NGSQ 71:176; EQC 1:8; STR 1:59; EPR Case #4387; Sarah Johnson Anc 81-83; NEHGR 12:138; M&JCH 26:15-21; Perley 1:450-53].

Buxton, Thomas: Wookey, Somerset; 1639; Salem [STR 1:93, 110; EPR 1:182-83; Sarah Johnson Anc 81].

Byam, George: Unknown; 1640; Salem, Wenham, Chelmsford [SChR 10; Fiske Notebook 105, 215; MPR Case #3833; Edwin Colby Byam, *Descendants of George Byam (?-1680) (Suffield, Connecticut, 1975)*].

Byam, Nathaniel: Unknown; 1635 on *Blessing*; Scituate [GM 2:1:526-27].

Byley, Henry: Salisbury, Wiltshire; 1638 on *Bevis*; Newbury, Salisbury [Drake's Founders 60; SyTR 2; MBCR 1:237; Essex Ant 1:20; Noyes-Gilman 271-74; NEHGR 42:308-9. 51:181-88, 348-57, 52:44-51, 321-22].

Byley, John: Salisbury, Wiltshire; 1638 on *Bevis*; died soon after arrival in New England [Drake's Founders 60; NEHGR 52:50; Noyes-Gilman 271-74].

Byley, Mary: Salisbury, Wiltshire; 1638 on *Bevis*; passenger list only [Drake's Founders 60; NEHGR 52:50]. (She married Samuel Dudley, son of Thomas Dudley.)

Byram, Nicholas: Unknown; 1637; Weymouth, Bridgewater [MBCR 1:309, 374; SPR 1:10; Lechford 329; PPR Case #3508; Weymouth Hist 3:149-50].

C

Cable, John: Unknown; 1630; Roxbury, Springfield, Fairfield [GMB 299-301; WF 171-74].

Cabot, Mr.: Unknown; 1636; Cambridge (land record only) [CaTR 26].

Cade, James: Unknown; 1635; Hingham (land grant only) [GM 2:2:1-2].

Cade, James: Northam, Devon; 1638; Boston [Lechford 42; NEHGR 2:191; BChR 138; Waters 1213-14; M&JCH 18:27-29].

Cade, James: Unknown; 1639; Yarmouth (freemanship records only) [PCR 2:3, 8:185].

Caffinch, John: Tenterden, Kent; 1639; Guilford, New Haven; returned permanently to England by 1658 [Guilford Hist 29; NHCR 1:93; FANH 375; TAG 9:101; Abandoning 74].

Cakebread, Thomas: Unknown; 1633; Watertown, Sudbury [GMB 301-3].

Call, Thomas: Faversham, Kent; 1637; Charlestown [NEHGR 4:183, 75:222, 225, 85:280-83; ChChR 10 (as "John Caule"); MBCR 1:376; ChTR 29; ChBOP 65; Wyman 166; Dawes-Gates 1:132-40; TAG 85:280-83].

Callow, Oliver: Unknown; 1630; Penobscot, Watertown, Scituate, Boston [GMB 304-5].

Cammock, Thomas: London (probably); 1630; Piscataqua, Black Point; died in the West Indies [GMB 305-7; Gen Mag NS 4:7-13].

Cammond, Abel: Unknown; 1640; Dover [NHPP 10:701; GDMNH 126].

Camp, Nicholas: Nazeing, Essex; 1639; Milford [MiTR 2; Parke-Gildersleeve 51-57; TAG 15:125-26].

Campion, Clement: Unknown; 1640; Dover [NHPP 40:3; WP 4:322; GDMNH 126].

Campion, Robert: Unknown; 1639; New Haven [NHCR 1:28, 42, 88, 138].

Cane, Christopher: Unknown; 1634; Cambridge [GM 2:2:2-6; NEA 10:4:54-55].

Cannage, Matthew: Unknown; 1633; Richmond Island, Monhegan [GMB 307-8].

Canney, Thomas: Unknown; 1640; Dover [NHPP 10:701; NHGR 19:1-7].

Cannon, John: Unknown; 1623 on *Fortune*; Plymouth [GMB 308; PM 93].

Cantlebury, William: Unknown; 1638; Salem [STR 1:85; EIHC 4:63; EPR 1:420-22; EQC 9:300-1; Perley 2:62, 3:117].

Capen, Bernard: Dorchester, Dorset; 1633; Dorchester [GMB 309-11; NEHGR 158:110-11].

Card, Mr.: Unknown; 1633; Piscataqua [NHPP 1:78; GDMNH 127].

Carder, Richard: Unknown; 1635; Roxbury, Boston, Portsmouth, Warwick [GM 2:2:6-10].

Carew *see also* **Cary**

Carew, John: Unknown; 1637; Duxbury, Braintree, Bridgewater [PCR 1:67, 109, 135; 2:79, 8:182, 202; MD 2:90-91, 17:155-56; TAG 78:187-95; Seth C. Cary, *John Cary the Plymouth Pilgrim* (Boston 1911)].

Carleton, Edward: York, Yorkshire; 1639; Rowley; returned permanently to England in 1650 [WP 4:201, 279; RowBOP 2; Pillsbury 361-72; TAG 17:105-9; NEHGR 93:3-46, 94:3-18, 111:195-200, 260-65; Abandoning 74-75].

Carman, John: Unknown; 1631; Roxbury, Hempstead [GMB 311-13].

Carpenter, Priscilla: Leiden, Holland; 1633; Plymouth [GMB 313-14; PM 93-95; M&JCH 27:10-12]. (She married William Wright and John Cooper.)

Carpenter, Thomas: Amesbury, Wiltshire; 1635 on *James*; passenger list only [GM 2:2:10]. (This passenger list entry is almost certainly an error for William Carpenter.)

Carpenter, Thomasine: Unknown; 1635 on *Susan & Ellen*; passenger list only [GM 2:2:10].

Carpenter, William: Amesbury, Wiltshire; 1635 on *James*; Salem, Providence [Drake's Founders 56 (as "Thomas Carpenter"); NEHGR 159:54-68, 164:36-40, 296-97].

Carpenter, William: Wherwell, Hampshire; 1638 on *Bevis*; Weymouth [Drake's Founders 60; WP 4:232; MBCR 1:313, 377; ReTR 1:2; TAG 70:193-204; NEHGR 159:54-68]. (Some of these records are probably for William Carpenter, son of the immigrant, who soon moved to Rehoboth.)

Carr, Caleb: Unknown; 1635 on *Elizabeth & Ann*; Newport [GM 2:2:11-16].

Carr, George: Unknown; 1634; Ipswich, Salisbury [GM 2:2:17-22].

Carr, Richard: Unknown; 1635 on *Abigail*; Ipswich, Salisbury [GM 2:2:23-24].

Carr, Robert: Unknown; 1635 on *Elizabeth & Ann*; Portsmouth, Newport [GM 2:2:24-27].

Carrington, Edward: Unknown; 1633; Charlestown, Malden [GMB 315-18].

Carrington, Thomas: Unknown; 1632 on *Lyon*; passenger list only [GMB 318].

Carsley, William: Unknown; 1637; Hingham, Barnstable [HiBOP 97v; MBCR 1:206, 373; PCR 1:125, 137, 141, 8:176, 193, 200; NEHGR 9:285, 286, 10:41; Otis 147].

Carter, Joseph: London; 1639; Newbury; returned permanently to England soon after 1640 [WP 4:114; ITR 73; EQC 1:386; NEHGR 35:373-74; Abandoning 75-76].

Carter, Joshua: Unknown; 1633; Dorchester, Windsor [GMB 318-20].

Carter, Martha: Unknown; 1635 on *Hopewell*; passenger list only (with caveat) [GM 2:2:27].

Carter, Richard: Unknown; 1639; Boston [BTR 1:41, 49, 53; Lechford 228; MBCR 1:317; NEHGR 18:156; SPR 3:201; TAG 40:82-84].

Carter, Robert: Unknown; 1620 on *Mayflower*; Plymouth [GMB 320; PM 95].

Carter, Thomas: Unknown; 1635 on *Planter*; Ipswich, Salisbury [GM 2:2:27-30].

Carter, Thomas: Unknown; 1636; Charlestown [ChChR 9, 49; MBCR 1:315, 373; Lechford 183; NEHGR 4:184; ChBOP 69; Wyman 186-87; Dawes-Gates 1:141-53; Stevens-Miller 1:112-15].

Carter, Thomas: Cambridge, Cambridgeshire; 1636; Watertown, Dedham, Woburn [WJ 1:209; WaBOP 11, 18; WaVR 1:7; DeTR 1:29, 42; DeChR 5, 16, 25; NEHGR 27:364-65, 68:373; NEA 8:2:48-49; Venn 1:301; Sibley 2:65-67; Howard Williston Carter, *Carter: A Genealogy of the Descendants of Thomas Carter* (Norfolk, Connecticut, 1909); Stevens-Miller 1:112].

Carthrick, Michael: Unknown; 1635; Ipswich [GM 2:2:31-32].

Cartwright, Bethia: Unknown; 1639; Salem [EPR 1:12; EQC 1:18; NEA 7:3:26-29 (clue)].

Carver, John: Leiden, Holland; 1620 on *Mayflower*; Plymouth [GMB 320-22; PM 95-97].

Carver, Richard: Scratby, Norfolk; 1637 on *John & Dorothy* or *Rose*; Watertown [Hotten 291; SPR 1:24; NEHGR 146:230-34; GDMNH 131].

Carver, Robert: Unknown; 1638; Duxbury, Marshfield [PCR 1:94, 158; NEHGR 88:215-17, 119:92-94; Clifford N. Carver, *The Carver Family of New England: Robert Carver of Marshfield and His Descendants* (n.p. 1935)].

Carwithy, David: Unknown; 1639; Taunton, Salem, Boston, Southold [PCR 1:132; SChR 12, 13, 106; NYWills 25:3; Perley 2:157; NEHGR 48:466; NYGBR 14:68].

Carwithy, ____: Unknown; 1640; Roxbury (mention in will of George Alcock only) [SPR 1:8].

Cary *see also* **Carew**

Cary, Nicholas: Unknown; 1636; Salem; not seen after 1637 [STR 1:22, 53, 102; EQC 1:6, 7].

Case, Edward: Unknown; 1638; Taunton; not seen after 1658 [PCR 1:53, 105, 155, 2:41, 53, 56, 85, 117, 123, 144, 155, 175, 176, 7:32, 41, 8:176, 195, 199].

Castell, Robert: Unknown; 1637; Ipswich, Hampton [ITR 43; GDMNH 55].

Castle, Mary: Unknown; 1640; Watertown [WP 4:286]. (She married Richard Gale.)

Cattell, Robert: Unknown; 1635 on *Unity*; passenger list only [GM 2:2:32].

Caulkin, Hugh: Waverton, Cheshire; 1640; Plymouth, Gloucester, New London, Norwich [PCR 2:8; GlTR 1:1; Granberry 191-92; Kenneth W. Calkins, *Calkins Family in America* (n.p. 2000)].

Chadbourne, William: Tamworth, Staffordshire; 1634 on *Pied Cow*; Kittery [GM 2:2:33-36].

Chadwell, Richard: Unknown; 1636; Lynn, Sandwich [MBCR 1:199; EQC 1:6; PCR 1:57, 107, 8:9; Lechford 371, 403; Gen Adv 4:10; PCPR 4:1:102b].

Chadwell, Thomas: Unknown; 1636; Salem, Lynn, Sandwich, Boston, Charlestown [STR 1:40, 53; EQC 2:270; SPR Case #374; GDMNH 134; Parker-Ruggles 283-86; GM 2:7:553-54; Backus Anc 67-68].

Chadwick, Charles: Unknown; 1630; Watertown [GMB 322-24; WF 174-77].

Chaffee, Matthew: Unknown; 1636; Boston, Newbury; returned permanently to England soon after 1655 [BChR 21, 56; MBCR 1:373; BTR 1:32; EQC 1:27; NEHGR 70:184; William H. Chaffee, *The Chaffee Genealogy* (New York 1909) 573-75].

Chaffee, Thomas: Unknown; 1637; Hingham, Rehoboth, Swansea [HiBOP 68; NEHGR 142:350-51; William H. Chaffee, *The Chaffee Genealogy* (New York 1909)].

Chairye, John: Unknown; 1638; Massachusetts Bay (court appearance only) [MBCR 1:268]. (This may be a corruption of some more common surname.)

Challis *see* **Watson Challis**

Chamberlin, Henry, blacksmith: Unknown; 1638; Hingham; returned permanently to England by 1649 [HiBOP 71; NEHGR 121:109, 139:126-38].

Chamberlin, Henry, shoemaker: Hingham, Norfolk; 1638 on *Diligent*; Hingham [HiBOP 75; NEHGR 15:26, 121:11, 139:126-38, 142:351-52; MBCR 1:375].

Chambers, Amy: Assington, Suffolk; 1632; Boston [GMB 324-26].

Chambers, Elizabeth: Unknown; 1634; Boston (church admission only) [GM 2:2:36].

Chambers, Robert: Unknown; 1635 on *Hopewell*; Marshfield; "departed the government" by 1655 [GM 2:2:36-37].

Chambers, Thomas: Ash-juxta-Sandwich, Kent; 1638; Scituate [PCR 1:106, 5:132; PCPR 1:34; GDMNH 135; MD 24:136-37; Harold Dunham Curtis, *A Genealogy of the Curtiss-Curtis Family of Stratford, Connecticut* (Stratford, Connecticut, 1953)]. (Thomas Chambers was accompanied to New England by his Curtis stepchildren [Scott Gen 267-69].)

Chambers, Thomas: Unknown; 1640; New Haven (court appearance only) [NHCR 1:39].

Champernown, Francis: Dartington, Devonshire; 1637; York, Kittery [WP 3:492; NHPP 10:701, 40:8; Gorges 2, 42; MPCR 1:31, 42, 254; GDMNH 135-37; NEHGR 5:246, 27:146-48].

Champion, Thomas: Ashford, Kent; 1635 on *Hercules*; passenger list only (with caveat) [GM 2:2:37].

Champlin, Jeffrey: Unknown; 1638; Portsmouth, Westerly [RICR 1:91; TAG 20:106-9 (clue), 32:8-9; NEHGR 82:69-70; Austin 274-77].

Champney, John: Unknown; 1635; Cambridge [GM 2:2:37-39].

Champney, Richard: Stisted, Essex; 1635 on *Defence*; Cambridge [GM 2:2:39-46].

Champnois, Henry: Unknown; 1639; Pemaquid, Winnegance [GDMNH 137 (witnessed a deed in 1639)].

Chandler, Edmund: Leiden, Holland; 1632; Plymouth, Duxbury [GMB 326-30; PM 97-101].

Chandler, John: Unknown; 1639; Concord [MBCR 1:377; CoVR 1].

Chandler, John: Unknown; 1640; Boston (apprenticeship record only) [Lechford 362].

Chandler, John: Unknown; 1640; Plymouth (two court appearances only) [PCR 1:162, 7:22, 26].

Chandler, Roger: Leiden, Holland; 1632; Plymouth, Duxbury [GMB 330-32; PM 101-3].

Chandler, William: Bishop's Stortford, Hertfordshire; 1637; Roxbury [RChR 83; MBCR 1:377; Cotton 340; TAG 73:50-57, 80:27-37; NEHGR 85:133-45; George Chandler, *The Chandler Family: Descendants of William and Annis Chandler* (Worcester, Massachusetts, 1883)].

Chapin, Samuel: Berry Pomeroy, Devonshire; 1638; Roxbury, Springfield [RChR 83; RBOP 1; MBCR 1:378; Pynchon 214; NEHGR 83:351-56; Goodwin-Morgan 2:123-43; Gilbert Warren Chapin, *The Chapin Book,* two volumes (Hartford, Connecticut, 1924)].

Chaplin, Clement: Rushbrooke, Suffolk; 1635 on *Elizabeth & Ann*; Cambridge, Hartford, Wethersfield; returned permanently to England after 1646 [GM 2:2:46-51; TAG 82:250-60; Abandoning 76].

Chapman, Henry: Unknown; 1639; Boston [MBCR 1:296; EQC 1:27; NHPP 40:11].

Chapman, Jacob: Unknown; 1637; Boston [EQC 1:7; RCA 2:119; BTR 1:68].

Chapman, John: Unknown; 1633; Watertown, Wethersfield, New Haven, Fairfield, Stamford [GMB 332-35].

Chapman, Ralph: Southwark, Surrey; 1635 on *Elizabeth*; Duxbury, Marshfield [GM 2:2:51-55].

Chapman, Robert: Unknown; 1635; Saybrook [MHSC 3:3:143; TAG 66:30-32; NEHGR 159:316; Dawes-Gates 2:185-98].

Chapman, William: Unknown; 1639; Hingham [NEHGR 121:12; SPR 7:120].

Chappell, Anthony: Unknown; 1636; Richmond Island; returned permanently to England in 1638 (servant) [Trelawny 124, 193].

Chappell, George: Unknown; 1635 on *Christian*; Wethersfield, New London [GM 2:2:55-59; NEHGR 157:394].

Chappell, Mary: Unknown; 1638; Boston (church admission only) [BChR 24; see GM 2:2:59-60].

Chappell, Nathaniel: Unknown; 1634; Boston [GM 2:2:59-60].

Chappell, William: Unknown; 1636 on *Hercules*; Richmond Island; returned permanently to England in 1637 [Trelawny 106, 113, 114, 123, 160, 194; GDMNH 4, 138].

Charles, John: Unknown; 1636; Charlestown, New Haven, Branford [ChTR 23, 28, 31; WP 3:320; NHCR 1:29; FANH 391; Granberry 192-94].

Charles, William: Unknown; 1637; Salem [STR 1:59; EPR 2:372-74, 3:143-44; Marblehead 52-53].

Chase, Aquila: Unknown; 1639; Hampton, Newbury [HmTR 44; Annis Spear Anc 129-30; Pillsbury Anc 1099-1103; John Carroll Chase and George Walter Chamberlain, *Seven Generations of the Descendants of Aquila and Thomas Chase* (Derry, New Hampshire, 1928)].

Chase, Thomas: Unknown; 1639; Hampton [HmTR 45; GDMNH 55; John Carroll Chase and George Walter Chamberlain, *Seven Generations of the Descendants of Aquila and Thomas Chase* (Derry, New Hampshire, 1928)].

Chase, William: Unknown; 1630; Roxbury, Yarmouth [GMB 336-39; WF 177-81].

Chatfield, Francis: North Mundham, Sussex; 1639; Guilford [Guilford Hist 25; NEHGR 70:55-65, 125-36, 150:260-79; TG 22:212-20].

Chatterton, Michael: Unknown; 1639; Strawberry Bank [NHPP 1:113, 40:13; GDMNH 139].

Chaulkley, Robert: Unknown; 1638; Charlestown, Woburn [MBCR 1:249; Rodgers 3:175-77; Wyman 197].

Chauncy, Charles: Marston St. Lawrence, Northamptonshire; 1638; Plymouth, Scituate, Cambridge [Lechford 45; WJ 1:397, 2:86; WP 4:129, 291; Davenport 78; Cotton 299; Waters 107-9; NEHGR 10:106-20, 251-62, 323-36, 11:148-53, 148:161-66; TG 16:183-88; William Chauncy Fowler, *Chauncy Memorials* (Boston 1858); MHSC 1:10:171; Morison 371].

Chauner, Margery: Unknown; 1631; Boston (church admission only) [GMB 339].

Checkett, Josias: Unknown; 1638; Scituate; not seen after 1643 [PCR 1:110, 2:34, 40, 66, 7:36, 8:183, 12:66-68, 82].

Checkley, John: Unknown; 1640; Boston [Lechford 313-14; EQC 1:21] (Probably a transient merchant. No obvious connection with the John Checkley who appeared at Boston a decade later.)

Cheeseborough, William: Boston, Lincolnshire; 1630; Boston, Braintree, Rehoboth, New London, Stonington [GMB 339-45; WF 181-88].

Cheever, Ezekiel: London; 1637; Boston, New Haven, Ipswich, Charlestown [NHCR 1:20; NHChR 1; Venn 1:328; NEHGR 33:164-202, 38:170-93, 45:61-68, 57:40-50, 115:254-55; TAG 11:118-20, 81:54-65; EIHC 54:123].

Chenery, Lambert: Unknown; 1636; Dedham [DeTR 1:20; DeChR 24; RBOP 2; HmTR 44; SPR Case #721; Bond 157-58, 740-41; Medfield Hist 338-39; Scott Gen 192].

Cheney, John: Lawford, Essex; 1635; Roxbury, Newbury [GM 2:2:60-63; TAG 76:245-47; NEHGR 162-115-16].

Cheney, William: Unknown; 1639; Roxbury [Lechford 116, 203; NEHGR 5:334; RChR 84; GMN 21:12; TAG 76:246; Kempton Anc 1:224-39; Charles Henry Pope, *The Cheney Genealogy* (Boston 1897)].

Cherral, William: Unknown; 1635 on *Love*; passenger list only [GM 2:2:63].

Chesholm, Thomas: Newcastle-upon-Tyne, Northumberland; 1635; Cambridge [GM 2:2:63-66].

Chesson, Roger: Unknown; 1640; Ipswich (land grant only) [ITR 84].

Chester, Dorothy: Leicester, Leicestershire; 1634; Cambridge, Hartford [GM 2:2:67-68].

Chester, Leonard: Blaby, Leicestershire; 1633; Watertown, Wethersfield [GMB 345-49].

Chickering, Francis: Ringsfield, Suffolk; 1637; Dedham [DeTR 1:42; DeVR 1; DeChR 22; MBCR 1:295, 377; SPR Case #197; HAHAC 1:128; NEHGR 4:180, 63:282-83, 64:136-37, 68:105, 88:273; TAG 17:70-71; Ackley-Bosworth 113-14].

Chickering, Henry: Wrentham, Suffolk; 1639; Salem, Dedham [STR 1:96, 98; DeChR 24; DeTR 1:78; MBCR 1:328, 379; NEHGR 61:189, 63:282-83, 64:136-37, 68:105, 69:226-29].

Chickin, Joseph: Unknown; 1635; passenger list only [GM 2:2:68].

Child, Ephraim: Nayland, Suffolk; 1630; Watertown [GMB 349-53; WF 188-93].

Child, Robert: London; 1639; Massachusetts Bay; returned permanently to England in 1647 [WJ 2:320; WP 4:333; HAHAC 1:86; Morison 371-72; Samuel Eliot Morison, *Builders of the Bay Colony* (Boston 1930) Chapter VIII; CSMP 21:1-146; Abandoning 79-80].

Chillingworth, Thomas: Unknown; 1637; Sandwich, Marshfield [PCPR 1:32; PCR 1:107, 133, 150, 3:21-22, 45; MaTR 1:8; MD 11:157; TAG 56:209, 61:234-37; GMN 14:13; Frank Mortimer Hawes, *Foster Record:*

An Account of Thomas Foster of Billerica, Massachusetts (Somerville, Massachusetts, 1889) 49].

Chilton, James: Leiden, Holland; 1620 on *Mayflower*; Plymouth [GMB 353-55; PM 103-5; MQ 75:137-40; NEA 8:2:39-40].

Chinn, George: Unknown; 1638; Marblehead [STR 1:74; EQC 1:10; EPR 1:162; Marblehead 55-56].

Chipman, John: Affpuddle, Dorset; 1637; Plymouth [NEHGR 4:23-24, 35:127; TAG 61:2-6; Elizabeth Pearson White, *John Howland of the Mayflower*, volume three (Camden, Maine, 2008); Makepeace Anc 112-27]. (John Chipman's letter describing his arrival in New England is properly dated 8 February 1657/8 [NEHGR 79:248].)

Chipperfield, Edward: Unknown; 1635 on *Hopewell*; New Haven [GM 2:2:68-70].

Chittenden, Thomas: Wapping, Middlesex; 1635 on *Increase*; Scituate [GM 2:2:70-72].

Chittenden, William: Hawkhurst, Kent; 1639; Guilford [Guilford Hist 25; NEHGR 160:199-214, 312].

Chittwood, Mary: St. Albans, Hertfordshire; 1635 on *Planter*; passenger list only [GM 2:2:73].

Choppin, Philip: Unknown; 1639; Marblehead (court appearance only) [EQC 1:16].

Chubb, Thomas: Crewkerne, Somerset; 1630; Noddle's Island, Dorchester, Salem, Manchester, Beverly [GMB 355-58].

Chubbock, Thomas: Hingham, Norfolk; 1634; Charlestown, Hingham [GM 2:2:73-75].

Church, Garrett: Unknown; 1633; Watertown [GMB 358-60].

Church, George: Salisbury, Wiltshire; 1638 on *Confidence*; Newbury (servant) [Drake's Founders 58; MBCR 2:46].

Church, Richard: Unknown; 1630; Weymouth, Plymouth, Eastham, Charlestown, Hingham [GMB 360-64; PM 105-9; WF 193-97].

Church, Richard: Unknown; 1639; Hartford, Hadley [HaBOP 326; CCCR 1:56; Hale, House 491-92; Brainerd Anc 85-86; Gen Mag NS 3:192-94].

Churchill, Josias: Unknown; 1639; Wethersfield [WetLR 1:15, 132; Manwaring 1:287-88; NEHGR 61:311; Brainerd Anc 88; Gardner Asaph

Churchill and Nathaniel Wiley Churchill, *The Churchill Family in America* (Boston 1904) 323-25].

Churchman, Ann: Unknown; 1638; Duxbury [PCR 1:120]. (She married John Rogers [MF 19:7-10; Brainerd Anc 89].)

Churchman, Hugh: Unknown; 1640; Lynn [EPR 1:32-34; EQC 1:56].

Churchman, John: Unknown; 1632 on *Lyon*; passenger list only [GMB 364].

Chusmore, Richard: Unknown; 1637; Salem (land grant only) [STR 1:60].

Chute, Lionel: Dedham, Essex; 1639; Ipswich [ITR 57; Waters 1201, 1203; EPR 1:46-48; NEHGR 163:137-38; Wm. E. Chute, *A Genealogy and History of the Chute Family in America* (Salem, Massachusetts, 1894)].

Clap, Edward: Salcombe Regis, Devon; 1635 on *Hopewell*; Dorchester [GM 2:2:76-81].

Clap, Nicholas: Sidbury, Devon; 1636; Dorchester [DChR 3; NEHGR 5:97; DTR 28; Scott Gen 224-30; Joseph Neal Anc 87-89; Kempton Anc 4:114-30; M&JCH 27:12].

Clap, Roger: Exeter, Devon; 1630 on *Mary & John*; Dorchester, Boston [GMB 364-70].

Clap, Thomas: Sidbury, Devon; 1637; Hingham, Weymouth, Scituate [NGSQ 71:176 (as "Claff"); HiBOP 76; Lechford 80; MBCR 1:375; Joseph Neal Anc 87-93; Kempton Anc 4:114-39].

Clark, Anthony: Unknown; 1638; Richmond Island; not seen after 1640 [Trelawny 187, 194, 282, 295, 301].

Clark, Arthur: Unknown; 1639; Hampton, Boston [HmTR 44; GDMNH 55, 143; MBCR 1:377; BChR 40, 42, 45, 57, 295, 305; SPR Case #388].

Clark, Bray: Unknown; 1634; Dorchester (land grant only) [GM 2:2:81].

Clark, Cicely: Unknown; 1635 on *Planter*; passenger list only (with caveat) [GM 2:2:81-82].

Clark, Daniel: Unknown; 1634; Ipswich [GM 2:2:82; Lechford 181].

Clark, Edmond: Unknown; 1639; Sandwich [PCR 1:150, 8:192].

Clark, Edward: Unknown; 1639; Marblehead, Cape Porpus [EQC 1:15, 31; GDMNH 143; Lydia Harmon Anc 6-8].

Clark, Frances: Unknown; 1639; Boston [BChR 28, 37]. (She married John Reyner.)

Clark, George: Unknown; 1636; Plymouth [PCR 1:75, 108, 2:29, 33, 79, 132-34, 138, 7:5, 12:26, 55; Moore Anc 179-80].

Clark, George Sr.: Unknown; 1639; Milford [MiTR 2; MiChR 2; Ackley-Bosworth 189-93; George Clarke Bryant, *Deacon George Clark(e) of Milford, Connecticut, and Some of His Descendants* (Ansonia, Connecticut, 1949)].

Clark, George Jr.: Great Munden, Hertfordshire; 1639; Milford [MiTR 2; TAG 74:72-73; George Clarke Bryant, *Deacon George Clark(e) of Milford, Connecticut, and Some of His Descendants* (Ansonia, Connecticut, 1949) 3-16].

Clark, Henry: Unknown; 1639; Windsor, Hadley [CCCR 1:46; Windsor Hist 2:155].

Clark, James: Unknown; 1635; Massachusetts Bay (mention in probate inventory only) [SPR NS 1:17].

Clark, James: Unknown; 1636; Massachusetts Bay (court appearance only) [MBCR 1:177].

Clark, James: Unknown; 1639; Braintree, Rehoboth, Roxbury [BTR 1:50; ReTR 1:2; Waters 1256-57 (clue); Early Rehoboth 3:129; Joseph Neal Anc 100; TAG 67:38].

Clark, James: Unknown; 1640; New Haven [NHCR 1:92; Ackley-Bosworth 164-65; Gillespie Anc 65-70; Waters 1256-57 (clue)].

Clark, Jeremy: London; 1638; Portsmouth [RICR 1:87, 91; NHM 238; TG 10:167-94; George Austin Morrison Jr., *"Clarke Genealogies" The "Clarke" Families of Rhode Island* (New York 1902); Alfred Rudulph Justice, *Ancestry of Jeremy Clarke of Rhode Island and Dungan Genealogy* (Philadelphia 1922)]. (Jeremy Clark was accompanied to New England by his Dungan stepchildren.)

Clark, John: Unknown; 1632; Boston [GMB 370-71].

Clark, John: Unknown; 1633; Cambridge, Hartford [GMB 371-72].

Clark, John: Unknown; 1637; Boston, Portsmouth, Newport [BTR 1:31; MBCR 1:212; WP 3:514; RICR 1:52, 87; WJ 1:326; NEHGR

75:273-301; Austin 45-46; Sydney V. James, *John Clarke and His Legacies* (University Park, Pennsylvania, 1999)].

Clark, John: London; 1638; Newbury, Boston [NeTR 31; MBCR 1:261, 376; Lechford 311; SPR Case #371½; NEHGR 33:19-20, 33:226-29, 95:389-91; Scott C. Steward, *The Descendants of Dr. Nathaniel Saltonstall of Haverhill, Massachusetts* (Boston 2013) 19-20].

Clark, John: Unknown; 1638; New Haven [NHCR 1:12, 20, 92; NEHGR 81:123; FANH 403-4].

Clark, John: Unknown; 1640; Wethersfield [WetLR 1:122; Wethersfield Hist 1:260]. (This may be the same as the New Haven John Clark.)

Clark, Joseph: Unknown; 1634; Dorchester, Windsor [GM 2:2:82-85].

Clark, Joseph: Westhorpe, Suffolk; 1638; Portsmouth, Newport [RICR 1:67, 91; Austin 47; NEHGR 75:273-301; George Austin Morrison Jr., *"Clarke Genealogies" The "Clarke" Families of Rhode Island* (New York 1902)].

Clark, Joseph: Banham, Norfolk; 1640; Dedham [DeTR 1:71; SPR 1:19; NEHGR 152:3-23, 153:180-82].

Clark, Mary: Unknown; 1635 on *Hopewell*; passenger list only [GM 2:2:85].

Clark, Mr.: Unknown; 1636; Massachusetts Bay (minister; mention in letter only) [WP 3:385].

Clark, Nicholas: Unknown; 1632 on *Lyon*; Cambridge, Hartford [GMB 373-75; TAG 83:68-73].

Clark, Oliver: Unknown; 1635; Richmond Island [GM 2:2:85].

Clark, Priscilla: Unknown; 1639; Dedham [DeVR 126]. (She married Nathaniel Colburne [NEHGR 152:3-23, 153:180-82].)

Clark, Richard: Unknown; 1620 on *Mayflower*; Plymouth [GMB 375; PM 109].

Clark, Richard: Unknown; 1638; Plymouth (servant; apprenticeship record only) [PCR 1:100].

Clark, Rowland: Barnham, Suffolk; 1637; Dedham [DeTR 1:34; DeVR 127; NGSQ 74:5; NEHGR 152:3-23].

Clark, Samuel: Unknown; 1640; Wethersfield, Stamford, Hempstead, Southampton [Wethersfield Hist 1:260; SmTR 4; Suffolk Sessions 84-87; TAG 34:225-30, 35:112-13, 36:92-94; TG 5:41, 50].

Clark, Thomas: Unknown; 1623 on *Anne*; Plymouth, Boston, Barnstable [GMB 375-80; PM 109-15].

Clark, Thomas: Unknown; 1634; Ipswich [GM 2:2:86-98].

Clark, Thomas: Unknown; 1638; Dorchester, Boston [DTR 1:37; NEHGR 5:98; Lechford 243; DChR 4; MBCR 1:375; BChR 49; SPR Case #1274; GDMNH 148-49; TW 222-24].

Clark, Thomas: Unknown; 1639; Boston [BTR 1:44; BChR 30, 38; NEHGR 2:78; MBCR 1:379; SPR Case #966; TW 221-22].

Clark, Thomas: Westhorpe, Suffolk; 1639; Newport [RICR 1:91; NEHGR 75:273-301; Austin 47-48].

Clark, Thurston: Ipswich, Suffolk; 1634 on *Francis*; Plymouth, Duxbury [GM 2:2:99-101].

Clark, William: Unknown; 1630; Watertown, Ipswich; returned permanently to England by 1639 [GMB 380-83; WF 197-200].

Clark, William: Unknown; 1634 on *Mary & John*; passenger list only [GM 2:2:101].

Clark, William: Unknown; 1636; Massachusetts Bay (court appearance only) [MBCR 1:184].

Clark, William: Unknown; 1636; Dorchester, Northampton [DChR 3; NEHGR 5:98; DTR 1:37; TAG 12:255; Waterman 1:637-40]. (The William Clark admitted to freemanship on 22 May 1639 was probably this man or the second Watertown William Clark [MBCR 1:376].)

Clark, William: Unknown; 1637; Salem [STR 1:49, 103; EQC 1:10; MBCR 1:332; TAG 14:83-86, 39:100-12, 55:120, 72:183-86].

Clark, William: Unknown; 1639; Hartford, Haddam [CCCR 1:41; Manwaring 1:290-91; Dawes-Gates 2:206-9; TAG 17:19; CN 30:190].

Clark, William: Unknown; 1640; Watertown, Woburn [WaVR 1:8; WaBOP 53; MPR Case #4585; GMB 382; WF 199; Farr Anc 67-68].

Clary, John: Unknown; 1639; Watertown, Hadley [MBCR 1:287 (as "John Clare"); WaVR 1:10, 13, 15, 30, 50; Bond 162, 742].

Clay, Thomas: Unknown; 1640; Massachusetts Bay, Scituate [MBCR 1:309; PCR 8:191].

Clayton, Richard: Sutton, Bedfordshire; 1629; died before taking passage [WF 200-1]. (This sketch replaces an earlier one for Barnabas and Richard Claydon [GMB 383].)

Clear, George: Unknown; 1636; Plymouth, Portsmouth; not seen after 1642 [PCR 1:57, 98, 12:36; PCPR 1:48; PoTR 2; RICR 1:70, 91; RICR (MS) 11; GMN 22:27]. (For later scattered occurrences of this name, see NYHM:D, Register of the Provincial Secretary, 1642-1647, Volume II, 326-27, 351-52; WMJ 883; DeVR 126.)

Clear, Mary: Unknown; 1638; Boston (servant; mention in two letters only) [WP 4:63, 68].

Cleemond, John: Unknown; 1640; Boston (servant; church admission only) [BChR 30].

Cleeve, George: Shrewsbury, Shropshire; 1630; Spurwink, Falmouth [GMB 383-89; NEQ 82:490-513].

Clement, Augustine: Reading, Berkshire; 1635 on *James*; Dorchester, Boston [GM 2:2:101-6].

Clements, William: Unknown; 1636; Cambridge [MBCR 1:179; Cameos 75-80; Rodgers 2:609-14].

Cleven, Joan: Unknown; 1635 on *Hopewell*; passenger list only [GM 2:2:106-7].

Clifford, John: Unknown; 1639; Salisbury, Hampton [SyTR 6; Nicholas Davis Anc 75-83].

Clifford, Mary: Unknown; 1635 on *Susan & Ellen*; passenger list only (with caveat) [GM 2:2:107].

Clifton, Thomas: Unknown; 1640; Weymouth, Rehoboth, Newport [MBCR 1:313, 379 (as "Clipton"); ReTR 1:2; RIVR 7:51, 95; NEHGR 168:60; Weymouth Hist 3:165; Austin 48; Stevens-Miller 259].

Clough, John: Unknown; 1635 on *Elizabeth*; Ipswich, Salisbury [GM 2:2:107-14].

Clough, Richard: Manchester, Lancashire; 1630; Massachusetts Bay, Plymouth, New Amsterdam, Gravesend [GMB 389-92; PM 115-18; WF 201-4].

Cloyse, John: Unknown; 1638; Watertown, Charlestown, Falmouth [WaVR 1:6; MBCR 1:282; WaBOP 51; Stevens-Miller 1:165-67; GDMNH 152; Stone-Gregg 71-74].

Coake, John: Unknown; 1638; Plymouth (mention in letter only) [ScitTR 3:348].

Cobb, Henry: Unknown; 1632; Plymouth, Scituate, Barnstable [GMB 392-95; PM 118-22; Susan E. Roser, *Early Descendants of Henry Cobb of Barnstable, Massachusetts* (Milton, Ontario, 2008)].

Cobb, Peter: Unknown; 1638; Richmond Island [Trelawny 170, 193].

Cobbett, _____: Unknown; 1630; Massachusetts Bay; returned permanently to England in 1631 [GMB 2076; WF 204].

Cobbett, James: Unknown; 1635 on *Elizabeth & Ann*; passenger list only [GM 2:2:114].

Cobbett/Cobham, Josiah: Unknown; 1635 on *Elizabeth & Ann*; Cambridge, Hingham, Salisbury, Boston [GM 2:2:114-21].

Cobbett, Thomas: Newbury, Berkshire; 1637; Lynn, Ipswich [MBCR 1:374; EQC 2:270, 9:546-56; Sibley 2:135-38; NEHGR 7:209-19, 60:250; GM 2:3:326-27; Waters 5, 97-98 (clue); Morison 372; Hammatt 54-59; Magnalia 1:518-21].

Coccrey, Thomas: Unknown; 1640; Salisbury (apprenticeship record only) [Lechford 393].

Cockerill, John: Unknown; 1639; New Haven; not seen after 1640 [NHCR 1:26, 31, 32, 39, 41, 436, 444; CCCR 1:55].

Cockerill, William: Unknown; 1635; Hingham, Salem [GM 2:2:121-22].

Cockerum, William: Southwold, Suffolk; 1635; Hingham; returned permanently to England in 1642 [GM 2:2:122-25; Abandoning 80-81].

Codd, Ellen: Unknown; 1640; Boston (court appearance and church admission only) [EQC 1:22; BChR 34].

Coddington, William: Boston, Lincolnshire; 1630; Boston, Portsmouth, Newport [GMB 395-401; WF 205-11].

Codman, John: Unknown; 1637; Massachusetts Bay (court appearance only) [EQC 1:7].

Codman, Robert: Unknown; 1637; Salem, Salisbury, Hartford, Saybrook, Edgartown [STR 1:51; EQC 1:7, 9; SyTR 5; WP 4:288 (as "Goodman Codmore"); Martha's Vineyard Hist 2:Edgartown:59-61, 3:95].

Coe, Jane: Unknown; 1635 on *Susan & Ellen*; passenger list only [GM 2:2:125].

Coe, Matthew: Unknown; 1639; Piscataqua, Gloucester, Falmouth [NHPP 1:113; GDMNH 153; J. Gardner Bartlett, *Robert Coe, Puritan, His Ancestors and Descendants, 1340-1910, with Notices of Other Coe Families* (Boston 1911) 531-32].

Coe, Robert: Boxford, Suffolk; 1634 on *Francis*; Watertown, Wethersfield, Stamford, Hempstead, Newtown [NY], Jamaica [NY] [GM 2:2:125-32; TAG 78:37-41].

Coggan, Henry: Taunton, Somerset; 1634; Dorchester, Scituate, Barnstable; returned permanently to England in 1649 [GM 2:2:132-36; NGSQ 71:176; M&JCH 27:12-15; Abandoning 81-82].

Coggan, John: Exeter, Devon; 1633; Dorchester, Boston [GMB 401-5].

Coggan, William: Unknown; 1637 in *Prosperous*; passenger list only [NGSQ 71:177].

Coggeshall, John: Castle Hedingham, Essex; 1632 on *Lyon*; Roxbury, Boston, Portsmouth, Newport [GMB 405-9].

Cogswell, John: Westbury Leigh, Wiltshire; 1635 on *Angel Gabriel*; Ipswich [GM 2:2:137-40; NEHGR 162:5-7].

Cogswell, Robert: Unknown; 1640; New Haven [NHCR 1:41, 47, 92; GMN 13:15].

Coit, John: Unknown; 1637; Marblehead, Gloucester, New London [STR 1:63, 74; EQC 1:12; PCR 1:108; Manwaring 1:118; EPR 1:358-59; Dawes-Gates 1:190-96; Goodwin-Morgan 2:433-36; Marblehead 59-60].

Coitmore, Thomas: Unknown; 1636; Charlestown [ChTR 22; MBCR 1:376; ChChR 9; ChBOP 20; TAG 32:9-23, 82:172-77; NEHGR 32:253-59, 138:39-41].

Coke, John: Unknown; 1635 on *Abigail*; passenger list only [GM 2:2:141].

Coke, Mary: Unknown; 1635 on *Hopewell*; passenger list only [GM 2:2:141].

Coker, Richard: Unknown; 1634; Massachusetts Bay [GM 2:2:141]. (Possibly the same as the next.)

Coker, Richard: Unknown; 1640; Connecticut [CCCR 1:54, 172].

Coker, Robert: Unknown; 1634 on *Mary & John*; Newbury [GM 2:2:142-44].

Colbron, William: Brentwood, South Weald, Essex; 1630; Boston [GMB 409-13; WF 212-16].

Colburn, Edward: Unknown; 1635 on *Defence*; Ipswich, Dracut [GM 2:2:144-49].

Colburn, Robert: Unknown; 1635 on *Defence*; Ipswich [GM 2:2:149-52].

Colburne, Nathaniel: Woolverstone, Suffolk; 1637; Dedham [DeTR 1:34; DeVR 1:136; DeChR 24; MBCR 1:379; NEHGR 153:180-82; Lyon-Rice 277-80].

Colburne, Samuel: Unknown; 1637; Salem; not seen after 1641 [STR 1:102; EQC 1:28, 29].

Colby, Anthony: Horbling, Lincolnshire; 1630; Boston, Cambridge, Ipswich, Salisbury [GMB 413-16; WF 216-20].

Colcord, Edward: Unknown; 1637; Salem, Dover, Hampton [STR 1:67; NHPP 1:128, 135, 10:701, 40:3; WP 4:179; TAG 16:65-81, 17:216; NEHGR 66:183, 141:114-21; GDMNH 154].

Coldham, Thomas: Unknown; 1633; Lynn [GMB 417-20].

Cole, Clement: Unknown; 1635 on *Susan & Ellen*; Boston, Braintree [GM 2:2:152-53].

Cole, Daniel: Unknown; 1639; Plymouth, Duxbury, Eastham [PCR 1:144; WP 4:295, 297, 414; MD 5:23, 6:204, 23:67-68; TAG 75:124-29; MF 6:24, 31, 44, 66; Susan E. Roser, *Early Descendants of Daniel Cole of Eastham, Massachusetts* (Milton, Ontario, 2010).]

Cole, Elizabeth: Unknown; 1635 on *Bachelor*; passenger list only [GM 2:2:153].

Cole, George: Unknown; 1637; Lynn [PCPR 1:32; PCR 1:150; EPR 1:154-55]. (Probably never removed to Sandwich.)

Cole, Isaac: Sandwich, Kent; 1635 on *Hercules*; Charlestown, Woburn [GM 2:2:153-56].

Cole, James: Barnstaple, Devon; 1633; Plymouth [GMB 420-24; PM 122-26; WP 4:295-97; NEHGR 115:255-56; TAG 81:122-32, 238-45, 83:258].

Cole, James: Unknown; 1636; Saco, Casco; not seen after 1640 [MPCR 1:1, 5, 51, 53, 79-80, 98; GDMNH 155 (see also Gorges 87)].

Cole, James: London; 1639; Hartford [HaBOP 195; Manwaring 1:49, 108-9, 3:vii; NYGBR 62:116-20, 70:104-10; Hale, House 524-35].

Cole, Job: Unknown; 1633; Plymouth, Duxbury, Yarmouth, Eastham [GMB 424-26; PM 126-28].

Cole, John: Unknown; 1635; Massachusetts Bay (court appearance only) [GM 2:2:157].

Cole, John: Unknown; 1637; Plymouth [PCR 1:75; PCPR 1:30; GMB 425; PM 127-28].

Cole, John: Unknown; 1638 on *Confidence*; Salisbury [Drake's Founders 58; SyTR 7; EQC 8:443; Hoyt 111].

Cole, Margaret: Unknown; 1638; Dedham [DeChR 21, 37]. (She married Henry Dow.)

Cole, Rice: Great Bowden, Leicestershire; 1630; Charlestown [GMB 426-29; WF 221-25].

Cole, Samuel: Unknown; 1630; Boston [GMB 430-35; WF 225-32].

Cole, Thomas: Unknown; 1634 on *Mary & John*; passenger list only (with caveat) [GM 2:2:157].

Cole, Thomas: Navestock, Essex; 1639; New England [NEHGR 31:324]. (The New England resident who produced this record may not have been Thomas Cole of Navestock.)

Cole, Thomas: Unknown; 1638; Saco [MPCR 1:51; YLR 1:1:34, 79-80; GDMNH 157 (see also Gorges 87)].

Cole, William: Unknown; 1636; Boston, Exeter, Hampton [BTR 1:15; GDMNH 55, 157; NHPP 1:133, 135; HmTR 44].

Cole, William: Unknown; 1638; Massachusetts Bay (business transaction only) [WP 4:134].

Cole, William: Chew Magna, Somerset; 1639; Boston, Saco, Wells [Lechford 133-37; WP 4:128, 281; MPCR 1:43; GDMNH 157-58; TAG 77:16-17].

Cole, William: Unknown; 1640; Weymouth (business transaction only) [Lechford 268].

Coleman, Anne: Colchester, Essex; 1639; Watertown (letter of attorney only) [Lechford 151].

Coleman, Joseph: Sandwich, Kent; 1637; Charlestown, Hingham, Scituate [NEHGR 75:222; ChTR 29; PCR 1:110, 8:182; PCPR 3:1:140-42; MD 34:73-75].

Coleman, Thomas: Marlborough, Wiltshire; 1635 on *James*; Newbury, Hampton, Nantucket [GM 2:2:157-62].

Coleman, Thomas: Unknown; 1639; Wethersfield, Hadley [CCCR 1:41; TAG 28:227-35; NEHGR 146:28-34, 298].

Coles, Robert: Unknown; 1630; Roxbury, Ipswich, Salem, Providence, Warwick [GMB 435-39; WF 232-37].

Coley, Samuel: Unknown; 1639; Milford [MiTR 2; MiChR 1; FOOF 1:153-54; Ackley-Bosworth 201; TAG 16:28, 50:93-95 (clue); Goodwin-Morgan 2:163-70].

Colfax, William: Unknown; 1640; Saco (court appearance only) [MPCR 1:79].

Collamore *see also* **Cullimore**

Collamore, Peter: Northam, Devon; 1639; Scituate [PCR 1:164, 12:47; PCPR 4:2142; TAG 32:38; Scott Gen 265-66; Davis Fam 150-51; Charles Hatch, *Genealogy of the Descendants of Anthony Collamer of Scituate, Massachusetts* (Salem, Massachusetts, 1915) 9-20; *Pilgrim Notes and Queries* 2:97-100].

Collen, Sarah: Unknown; 1640; Dorchester (church admission only) [DChR 5].

Collicott, Richard: Barnstaple, Devon; 1632 on *Charles*; Dorchester, Boston, Casco, Falmouth [GMB 439-46].

Collier, Thomas: Unknown; 1635; Hingham, Hull [GM 2:2:162-64].

Collier, William: Southwark, Surrey; 1633; Plymouth, Duxbury [GMB 446-30; PM 128-33].

Collins, Christopher: Unknown; 1639; Braintree, Lynn, Scarborough [BTR 1:50; Aspinwall 14; EQC 1:274, 276; MPCR 1:316; GDMNH 159].

Collins, Edward: Framlingham, Suffolk; 1639; Cambridge [NEHGR 4:55, 61:281-83, 89:72-79, 148-51; Shepard 81; HAHAC 1:114; MBCR 1:377; CaTR 43; TAG 23:149-53; Jack L. White and D. Jolene White, *The Bramford-Earls Colne Connection* (Baltimore 2012)].

Collins, Henry: Stepney, Middlesex; 1635 on *Abigail*; Lynn [GM 2:2:164-69; TEG 10:145-52].

Collins, John: Unknown; 1639; Braintree (land grant only) [BTR 1:50].

Collins, Mary: New Windsor, Berkshire; 1640; Windsor [WiLR 1:24; Windsor Hist 1:153, 545; NEHGR 149:401-32].

Collins, William: Unknown; 1640; New Haven, Hartford, Portsmouth, New Netherland [PoTR 16; WJ 2:10-11, 46-48, 163-64; GM 2:3:481].

Collishawe, William: Unknown; 1633; Boston [GMB 450].

Colt, Richard: Unknown; 1640; Saco (court appearance only) [MPCR 1:80].

Coltman, John: Wistow, Leicestershire; 1640; Wethersfield [Lechford 280-81; TAG 77:248-57].

Comberbach, Thomas: Unknown; 1637; passenger list only [Hotten 290].

Comins, William: Unknown; 1636; Salem [EQC 1:5, 32; STR 1:21, 22, 102, 105, 176; NEHGR 153:53-54; NEA 7:3:28-29].

Compton, John: Unknown; 1634; Roxbury, Boston, Exeter [GM 2:2:170-71; Cotton Corr 309; NHPP 1:134].

Comstock, John: Unknown; 1639; Weymouth (servant; mentioned in will only) [SPR 1:25]. (He was not likely the John Comstock who appeared at Saybrook in the early 1660s.)

Comstock, William: Unknown; 1640; Wethersfield, New London [WetLR 1:84, 128; Miner Anc 91-92; Comstock-Thomas 1-2].

Conant, Christopher: London; 1623; Plymouth, Massachusetts Bay [GMB 450-51; PM 133-34].

Conant, Roger: London; 1624; Plymouth, Nantasket, Cape Ann, Salem, Beverly [GMB 451-59; PM 134-43; M&JCH 26:21-22].

Conklin, Ananias: Nottingham, Nottinghamshire; 1638; Salem, Southold, Easthampton [STR 1:70; SChR 9, 10; NEHGR 61:386; TAG 11:139-43, 21:48-58, 133-47, 71:195; EIHC 31:43-53].

Conklin, John: Nottingham, Nottinghamshire; 1640; Salem, Southold, Huntington [STR 1:107; NEHGR 61:386; EIHC 31:43-53; TAG 21:48-51, 210-15, 246-53, 22:111-21, 226-36; Miner Anc 93-95; CA 50:80-82].

Conley, Abraham: Wittersham, Kent; 1638; Kittery [MPCR 1:42; YLR 5:1:30, 102, 5:2:33; TAG 84:89-94].

Conner, William: Unknown; 1621 on *Fortune*; Plymouth [GMB 459; PM 143-44].

Constable, Katherine: Everingham, Yorkshire; 1640; New Haven [NHCR 1:50, 93; GMN 18:27; TAG 31:24-29].

Converse, Allen: South Weald, Essex; 1638; Salem, Woburn [STR 1:96; WoVR; NEHGR 50:346-52, 153:95-96; TAG 75:329-30; Stevens Miller 1:233-36].

Converse, Edward: South Weald, Essex; 1630; Charlestown, Woburn [GMB 459-63; WF 237-43; NEHGR 146:130-32, 153:81-96].

Cook, Henry: Unknown; 1638; Salem [STR 1:73; EQC 1:383-84; FANH 435-36].

Cook, John: Unknown; 1636; Salem; not seen after 1644 [STR 1:22, 53, 61, 75, 102, 117; EQC 1:14-16, 19, 20, 23, 27, 66; SChR 10 (annotated "removed"), 18, 19; MBCR 2:291].

Cook, Mary: Unknown; 1639; Dorchester (church admission only) [DChR 5].

Cook, Richard: Unknown; 1640; Marblehead [EQC 1:19, 62; Marblehead 60].

Cook, Robert: Unknown; 1638; Charlestown [WP 4:55, 244, 268; ChChR 10 (as "Richard Cook"); ChTR 53; Lechford 413; Aspinwall 41-42; MBCR 1:307, 338, 378; Wyman 235].

Cook, Samuel: Dublin, Ireland; 1639; Dedham [Aspinwall 39; DeTR 1:68, 68, 77, 175; WP 4:414; MBCR 2:162, 164, 3:290, 4:1:117].

Cook, Thomas: Netherbury, Dorset; 1637 on *Speedwell*; Taunton, Portsmouth [NGSQ 71:176; PCR 8:195; TAG 56:93-94; NEHGR 128:152-53, 306-8; Jane Fletcher Fiske, *Thomas Cook of Rhode Island*, two volumes (Boxford, Massachusetts, 1987).]

Cooke, Aaron: Dorchester, Dorset; 1630 on *Mary & John*; Dorchester, Windsor, Northampton, Westfield [GMB 464-67].

Cooke, Francis: Leiden, Holland; 1620 on *Mayflower*; Plymouth [GMB 467-471; PM 144-48; MD 56:150-62].

Cooke, George: Earls Colne, Essex; 1635 on *Defence*; Cambridge; returned permanently to England in 1645 [GM 2:2:171-77; Abandoning 84-85].

Cooke, John: Unknown; 1633; Plymouth [GMB 471-72; PM 148-49].

Cooke, John: Unknown; 1635 on *Abigail*; passenger list only [GM 2:2:177].

Cooke, Joseph: Earls Colne, Essex; 1635 on *Defence*; Cambridge; returned permanently to England in or soon after 1659 [GM 2:2:178-83; Abandoning 85].

Cooke, Josias: Unknown; 1633; Plymouth, Eastham [GMB 472-75; PM 149-53].

Cooke, Margaret: Unknown; 1630; Boston [GMB 475; WF 244].

Cooke, Payton: Unknown; 1634; Saco [GM 2:2:183-84].

Cooke, Richard: Unknown; 1634; Boston [GM 2:2:185-91].

Cooke, Thomas: Unknown; 1639; Guilford [Guilford Hist 25; NEHGR 62:218-20; Goodwin-Morgan 2:437-51].

Cooley, John: Unknown; 1638; Ipswich [ITR 40, 45; EPR 1:173-74; Pillsbury Anc 70-71; GM 2:2:197].

Cooley, William: Unknown; 1633; Massachusetts Bay [GMB 476].

Coolidge, John: Cottenham, Cambridgeshire; 1635; Watertown [GM 2:2:191-98; DeTR 1:20, 33, 48; Kempton Anc 3:82-111].

Coombs, John: Unknown; 1633; Plymouth [GMB 476-79; PM 153-56].

Cooper, Anthony: Hingham, Norfolk; 1635; Hingham [GM 2:2:198-99; NEHGR 156:6].

Cooper, Benjamin: Brampton, Suffolk; 1637 on *Mary Anne*; passenger list only [Hotten 293; SPR NS 1:6-7].

Cooper, Elizabeth: Sudbury, Suffolk; 1635 on *Defence*; passenger list only [GM 2:2:199].

Cooper, Humility: Leiden, Holland; 1620 on *Mayflower*; Plymouth; returned permanently to England by 1638 [GMB 479; PM 156-57; MQ 76:125-31].

Cooper, Jane: Unknown; 1638; Scituate [PCR 1:97; NEHGR 10:40, 42]. (She married Christopher Winter.)

Cooper, John: London; 1630; Scituate, Barnstable [GM 2:2:200-2; MD 63:152-74].

Cooper, John: Olney, Buckinghamshire; 1635 on *Hopewell*; Lynn, Southampton [GM 2:2:202-4; EQC 2:270; TAG 64:193-202; NYGBR 121:72-73; Seversmith 2:757-66].

Cooper, John: Unknown; 1640; New Haven [NHCR 1:93; Gillespie Anc 80-91].

Cooper, Lydia: Unknown; 1635; Plymouth [GM 2:2:205]. (She married Nathaniel Morton.)

Cooper, Mrs.: Unknown; 1639; Dorchester (church admission only) [DChR 5].

Cooper, Peter: Unknown; 1635 on *Susan & Ellen*; passenger list only (with caveat) [GM 2:2:205].

Cooper, Tace: Unknown; 1634; Dorchester, Windsor [*New England Magazine of History* 1:172-75]. (She married Samuel Hubbard.)

Cooper, Thomas: Unknown; 1635 on *Christian*; Windsor, Springfield [GM 2:2:205-12].

Cooper, Thomas: Unknown; 1636; Watertown (death record only) [WaVR 1:5].

Cooper, Thomas: Hingham, Norfolk; 1638 on *Diligent*; Hingham, Rehoboth [NEHGR 15:26; HiBOP 74; MBCR 1:258, 375; ReTR 1:2; Waters 1120-22; TAG 13:151-54].

Cooper, Thomas: Little Bowden, Northamptonshire; 1639; Boston (apprenticeship record only) [Lechford 174-75].

Cooper, Timothy: Unknown; 1638; Lynn [EQC 2:270; EPR 1:276-77; TEG 11:212-14; TAG 25:32-33; Waters 142-43 (clue)].

Cooper, William: Unknown; 1633; Piscataqua [GMB 479-80].

Cope, Edward: Unknown; 1637; Providence [PrTR 1:1, 15:5; RICR 1:14, 15, 31; WP 4:59; RWCorr 186].

Cope, Richard: Unknown; 1635 on *Blessing*; passenger list only [GM 2:2:212].

Cope, William: Unknown; 1635 on *Blessing*; passenger list only [GM 2:2:212; NYGBR 64:152].

Copeland, Lawrence: Unknown; 1637; Exeter [NHPP 1:135; NEHGR 9:154, 37:286; Warner Turner Copeland, *The Copeland Family* (Rutland, Vermont, 1937)].

Copp, William: Hatton, Warwickshire; 1640; Boston [BChR 29; NEHGR 2:78; MBCR 1:379; NYGBR 62:338-70, 64:150-52, 79:1-16; Pillsbury Anc 681-83].

Coppyn, Thomas: Unknown; 1631; York [GMB 480].

Corber, Richard: Unknown; 1634; Richmond Island [GM 2:2:212-13].

Corbin, Hugh: Unknown; 1635 on *Unity*; passenger list only [GM 2:2:213].

Corby, William: Unknown; 1640; Hartford (servant; mention in will only) [CCCR 1:446]. (Possibly the same as the William Corby who appeared in the same area in the 1650s [RPCC 103, 104; Manwaring 1:189].)

Cornall, James: Unknown; 1637; Exeter (witnessed deed only) [NHPP 1:135].

Cornelius, Daniel: Unknown; 1639; Massachusetts Bay (business transaction only) [Lechford 224].

Cornell, Thomas: Saffron Walden, Essex; 1638; Boston, Portsmouth [BTR 1:35; MBCR 1:238; Lechford 85, 235; RICR 1:104; PoTR 19; TAG 19:132, 35:107, 36:16-18, 39:2, 58:77-83; John Cornell, *Genealogy of the Cornell Family, Being an Account of the Descendants of Thomas Cornell of Portsmouth, R.I.* (New York 1902); Elaine Forman Crane, *Killed Strangely: The Death of Rebecca Cornell* (Ithaca, New York, 2002)].

Corning, Samuel: Unknown; 1637; Salem, Beverly [STR 1:69; SChR 9; MBCR 1:378; EPR 1:34-35; EPR Case #6381; EQC 7:11; NEHGR 100:261-62; Perley 2:11; Stone Anc 5].

Cornish, John: Unknown; 1637; passenger list only [NGSQ 71:176].

Cornish, Richard: Unknown; 1634; Weymouth, York [GM 2:2:213-14; Legal Executions 11-12].

Cornwall, William: Fairstead, Essex; 1633; Roxbury, Hartford, Middletown [GMB 481-84].

Cornwell, Thomas: Unknown; 1639; Connecticut (court appearance only) [CCCR 1:29].

Corrington, John: Unknown; 1635 on *Susan & Ellen*; passenger list only [GM 2:2:214-15].

Corvanell, William: Unknown; 1637; Duxbury; not seen after 1638 [PCR 1:68, 75, 85; PCPR 1:29].

Cotta, Robert: Unknown; 1634; Lynn; Salem [GM 2:2:215-17].

Cotterell, Nicholas: Unknown; 1639; Newport, Westerly [RICR 1:92; Austin 57-58; Thomas H. Bierce and Lisle Cottrell, *Ancestors in the*

United States of Byron H. Bierce and His Wife Mary Ida Cottrell (n.p. 1902) 94-95].

Cottle, William: Landford, Wiltshire; 1638 on *Confidence*; Newbury [Drake's Founders 58; EQC 1:336, EPR 1:438-39, 2:129-30; Hoyt 115-16].

Cotton, John: Boston, Lincolnshire; 1633; Boston [GMB 484-87; TG 21:108-28, 191-217; NHGR 16:145-70; NEQ 56:78-102, 76:73-107; NEA 11:2:38-42].

Cotton, William: Unknown; 1640; Strawberry Bank [NHPP 40:4; EQC 1:28; Coltman Anc 43-45; GDMNH 164; NEHGR 58:294-95].

Couchman, Sarah: Tenterden, Kent; 1635 on *Hercules*; possibly married William Hoskins, otherwise no further record [GM 2:2:217-18].

Courser, William: Unknown; 1635 on *Elizabeth & Ann*; Boston [GM 2:2:218-21].

Cousins, John: Unknown; 1626; Casco [Trelawny 194, 239; MPCR 1:65; GDMNH 165].

Coussens, George: Marlborough, Wiltshire; 1635 on *James*; passenger list only [GM 2:2:221].

Covell, Ezra: Unknown; 1635 on *Abigail*; Plymouth [GM 2:2:222]. (See Martha's Vineyard Hist 2:Edgartown:61-62.)

Covey, James: Unknown; 1639; Braintree; not seen after 1651 [BTR 1:50 (as "James Covey"); MBCR 1:377 (as "James Copie"); NEHGR 3:126-27 (as "James Coney"); BrVR 628 (as "James Couve"); BrTR 3, 4, 7 (as "James Couvey")]. (Banks thought this man might be the same as James Covell of Edgartown, but none of the children's names match [Martha's Vineyard Hist 3:115-16].)

Covington, John: Unknown; 1635; Ipswich [GM 2:2:222; WP 3:433].

Cowdrey, William: Unknown; 1638; Lynn [EQC 2:270; SPR 1:25; Bailey 3:79; TAG 10:14 (clue), 41:206-8; Mary Bryant Alverson Mehling, *Cowdrey-Cowdery-Cowdray Genealogy: William Cowdery of Lynn, Massachusetts, 1630, and His Descendants* (New York 1911)].

Cowland, Ralph: Unknown; 1639; Portsmouth [PoTR 5; RICR 1:104; RIVR 7:12, 97; TAG 20:112; Austin 58].

Cowley, William: Unknown; 1638; Portsmouth, Newport, New London [RICR 1:49, 69, 91, 95; WP 5:95, 339; GMN 22:27].

Cox, Moses: Unknown; 1639; Hampton [GDMNH 55, 167; HmTR 41; Lechford 318; NHPP 31:261-62; Pillsbury Anc 1:347-48; Sarah Stone Anc 132].

Coy, Matthew: Boston, Lincolnshire; 1638; Boston [EQC 1:381-82; NEHGR 11:199, 113:236 (clue)].

Coy, Richard: Boston, Lincolnshire; 1638; Salisbury, Boston, Ipswich, Wenham, Brookfield [EQC 1:381-82; Hoyt 118, 699, 897; NEHGR 113:236 (clue)].

Crabb, John: Unknown; 1630; Dorchester [GMB 488].

Crabb, Richard: Unknown; 1638; Wethersfield, Stamford, Greenwich, Oyster Bay [CCCR 1:27; WetLR 1:85, 167; SmTR 4; NYGBR 3:36-37, 6:109, 7:39, 65:115; TAG 12:125-26].

Crackbone, Gilbert: Great Coggeshall, Essex; 1635; Cambridge [GM 2:2:223-26].

Crackstone, John: Leiden, Holland; 1620 on *Mayflower*; Plymouth [GMB 488-89; PM 157-58; TAG 80:100-1].

Craddock, Isabel: Unknown; 1635 on *Rebecca*; passenger list only [GM 2:2:226-27].

Crafts, Griffin: Unknown; 1630; Roxbury [GMB 489-91; WF 244-47].

Craine, Elizabeth: Unknown; 1640; Dorchester (church admission only) [DChR 5].

Cram, John: Farlsthorpe, Lincolnshire; 1635; Boston, Exeter, Hampton [GM 2:2:227-80].

Crampton, Henry: Unknown; 1640; Plymouth (servant; court appearance only) [PCR 2:14].

Crane, Jasper: Unknown; 1640; New Haven, Branford, Newark [NHCR 1:39; Lechford 286; Ellery Bicknell Crane, *Genealogy of the Crane Family*, Volume Two (Worcester, Massachusetts, 1900) 295-406].

Crane, Richard: Unknown; 1638; Newbury; apparently returned permanently to England in 1640 [WP 4:106, 238].

Crane, Robert: Unknown; 1638; Ipswich; returned permanently to England by about 1639 [ITR 33; EQC 1:176; Ipswich Hist 1:341, 501; Hammatt 290-91; Abandoning 335-36].

Cranwell, John: Unknown; 1630; Boston [GMB 492-93; WF 247-48].

Crase, Joseph: Unknown; 1634; Richmond Island [GM 2:2:230].

Craver, Morgan: Unknown; 1640; Weymouth (servant; mention in deposition only) [Lechford 373].

Crawford, ____: Unknown; 1634; Watertown [GM 2:2:230-31; Manwaring 1:119].

Crawford, Stephen: Unknown; 1639; Kittery, Isles of Shoals [MPCR 1:42, 52, 120-23; GDMNH 170; York Hist 1:115].

Crawley, Thomas: Unknown; 1638; Exeter [NHPP 1:133]. (The reading of this name in the surviving copy of the Exeter Combination is doubtful, and so may not pertain to the Thomas Crawley who later appeared in New Hampshire [GDMNH 53, 170].)

Cribb, Benjamin: Unknown; 1630; Massachusetts Bay [GMB 493]. (See Benjamin Crisp.)

Cribb, John: Unknown; 1635 on *Christian*; passenger list only [GM 2:2:231].

Crisp, Benjamin: Unknown; 1630; Charlestown, Watertown, Groton [GMB 493-95; WF 248-51].

Crisp, George: Unknown; 1640; Plymouth, Eastham [Lechford 376; PCR 8:184, 187; Aspinwall 87 (clue), 132 (clue); PCPR 4:2:14-15; CCL 32:17-18].

Crispe, Mr.: London; 1631; Massachusetts Bay [GMB 2077].

Critchley, Richard: Unknown; 1639; Boston [SLR 2:105; Lechford 240; BTR 1:46; NEHGR 2:79, 91:91].

Crocker, John: Unknown; 1637 on *Speedwell*; Scituate, Barnstable [NGSQ 71:176; PCR 1:110, 141; MD 17:116-17].

Crocker, William: Unknown; 1636; Scituate, Barnstable [NEHGR 9:280, 112:194-95; PCR 1:110, 141; PCPR 1:34; MD 3:150-52, 18:58-59, 24:73; TAG 16:207-20; Makepeace Anc 128-47].

Crockett, Thomas: Unknown; 1633; Piscataqua, Kittery, York [GMB 495-98; M&JCH 25:31].

Croft, William: Unknown; 1638; Lynn [EQC 2:270, 8:290; EPR 302:180, 181; EIHC 4:234, 235; GMB 711; WF 322].

Cromwell, Thomas: Unknown; 1637; Newbury, Hampton [NeTR 11; MBCR 1:236; EPR 1:53; EIHC 53:235-37; GDMNH 173].

Crosby, Dorothy: Unknown; 1640; Massachusetts Bay [MBCR 1:318, 334]. (She married William Pillsbury.)

Crosby, Thomas: Holme-upon-Spalding-Moor, Yorkshire; 1639; Cambridge, Rowley [SLR 1:38; RowBOP 26; Rowley Fams 89-92; Paul W. Prindle, *Ancestors and Descendants of Timothy Crosby Jr.* (Orleans, Massachusetts, 1981)]. (His son Simon Crosby preceded him to New England in 1635 [GM 2:2:232-36].)

Cross, Daniel: Unknown; 1638; Plymouth (court appearance only) [PCR 1:96, 97].

Cross, Henry: Unknown; 1635 on *Increase*; passenger list only [GM 2:2:236].

Cross, John: Unknown; 1634 on *Elizabeth*; Ipswich, Newbury, Hampton [GM 2:2:237-40].

Cross, John: Unknown; 1640; Dover, Wells [NHPP 10:701; GDMNH 174].

Cross, John: Unknown; 1640; Watertown [WaVR 1:8, 9; MLR 8:147; GDMNH 607].

Cross, Margaret: Ripplingham, Yorkshire; 1638; Boston, Rowley [BChR 23; EPR 1:120; Pillsbury Anc 847; Rowley Fam 93; GMN 18:21].

Cross, Robert: Unknown; 1635; Ipswich [GM 2:2:240-45; M&JCH 27:15-19].

Cross, William: Unknown; 1637; Windsor, Wethersfield, Fairfield [Manwaring 1:111; FOOF 1:167; Miner Anc 96-98; TAG 20:Supp:9 (clue)].

Crow, John: Unknown; 1634; Charlestown, Yarmouth [GM 2:2:245-48; NEHGR 167:180].

Crow, John: Unknown; 1639; Hartford, Hadley [CCCR 1:41; HaTR 22; HaBOP 45; Manwaring 1:297; FOOF 1:169].

Crowther, John: Unknown; 1639; Strawberry Bank [NHPP 1:113, 40:12; GDMNH 174].

Crugott, James: Unknown; 1630; Mystic [GMB 498; WF 252].

Crumwell, Samuel: Unknown; 1634; Massachusetts Bay (admission to freemanship only) [GM 2:2:249].

Cruse, Richard: Unknown; 1639; Boston (probate inventory only) [SPR NS 1:425].

Cruttenden, Abraham: Hawkhurst, Kent; 1639; Guilford [Guilford Hist 25; NEHGR 52:466-69, 160:199-214, 165:15-26].

Cudworth, James: Aller, Somerset; 1634; Scituate, Barnstable [GM 2:2:249-58].

Cullick, John: Unknown; 1639; Charlestown, Hartford, Boston [ChBOP 93; HaTR 33; HaBOP 358-61; HaVR 580, 582, 608; BChR 58; BVR 76, 86; SLR 4:325-28 (clue), 7:285-86; SPR Case #325; Sibley 2:249-50; Glover Gen 460-62].

Cullimore *see also* **Collamore**

Cullimore, Isaac: Unknown; 1634; Charlestown, Boston [GM 2:2:258-61].

Culver, Edward: Unknown; 1637; Dedham, Roxbury, New London [DeTR 1:37; DeVR 1, 126; DeChR 25; TAG 22:107-10, 31:129-54, 64:56-57].

Cummings, Richard: Sheviock, Cornwall; 1638; Richmond Island [Trelawny 187; GDMNH 175-76; NEHGR 153:53].

Cummins, Isaac: Mistley, Essex; 1636; Watertown, Ipswich, Topsfield [WaBOP 5, 91; ITR 55; NEHGR 145:239-40, 165:35-41; TEG 20:174-75; Parker-Ruggles 279-86].

Cunliffe, Henry: Unknown; 1638; Dorchester, Northampton [DChR 3; Warner-Harrington 158-59].

Curkeitt, Ellis: Unknown; 1638; Richmond Island (business transaction only) [Trelawny 182].

Currier, Richard: Salisbury, Wiltshire; 1639; Salisbury [SyTR 9; EQC 3:253; Pillsbury Anc 149-50; Philip Joseph Currier, *Currier Family Records of U.S.A. and Canada*, Volume I (Henniker, New Hampshire, 1984); Philip Joseph Currier, *Ancestry of Philip Joseph Currier* (Henniker, New Hampshire, 2000)].

Curtis, Deodatus: Unknown; 1639; Braintree [Lechford 252; BrVR 628; Laura Guthrie (Curtis) Preston, *The Curtis Family: A Record of Some of the Descendants of Deodatus Curtis of Braintree, Massachusetts* (Marietta, Ohio, 1945)].

Curtis, George: Unknown; 1639; Boston; not seen after 1645 [BChR 24; BTR 1:44, 83; MBCR 1:377].

Curtis, Henry: Unknown; 1635 on *Elizabeth & Ann*; Watertown, Sudbury [Hotten 76; WaBOP 4, 57; MBCR 1:310; SuTR 4; TAG 65:17-23; NEHGR 61:258-65, 393 (clue)].

Curtis, Thomas: Unknown; 1639; Wethersfield [WetLR 1:12; Manwaring 1:297-98; Wethersfield Hist 2:262; TAG 71:235-41; CN 25:192-98].

Curtis, William: Nazeing, Essex; 1632; Roxbury [GMB 499-501; NEHGR 160:181-84, 161:85-91, 186-98, 250-59, 162:65-72, 128-39, 300-1].

Curtis, Zaccheus: Downton, Wiltshire; 1635 on *James*; Salem, Reading, Gloucester, Rowley [GM 2:2:261-64; Kempton Anc 2:111-26].

Curwen, George: Northampton, Northamptonshire; 1638; Salem [STR 1:72; SChR 9; EIHC 17:331-47; NEHGR 150:180-85, 190-97, 163:192-93].

Curwen, Matthias: Sibbertoft, Northamptonshire; 1634; Ipswich, Southold [GM 2:2:264-67].

Cushing, Matthew: Hingham, Norfolk; 1638 in *Diligent*; Hingham [NEHGR 15:26; HiBOP 73; Chase-Wigglesworth 155-60; James S. Cushing, *The Genealogy of the Cushing Family* (Montreal 1905)].

Cushing, Theophilus: Hingham, Norfolk; 1633; Charlestown, Hingham [GMB 501-2].

Cushman, James: Unknown; 1638; Scituate [PCR 1:106, 8:191; ScitTR 1:506-512; MD 9:81-82].

Cushman, Robert: Leiden, Holland; 1621 on *Fortune*; Plymouth; returned permanently to England in 1621 [GMB 502-4; PM 158-60; Robert E. Cushman and Franklin P. Cole, *Robert Cushman of Kent* (n. p. 2005)].

Cuthbertson *see* **Godbertson**

Cutler, James: Unknown; 1635; Watertown, Cambridge [GM 2:2:267-72].

Cutler, John: Unknown; 1637; Hingham [NEHGR 15:27, 86:257 (clue), 121:10; HiBOP 52; Brainerd Anc 98-99; Snow-Estes 2:182-84; Nahum S. Cutler, *A Cutler Memorial and Genealogical History* (Greenfield, Massachusetts, 1889) 315-507].

Cutler, Robert: Unknown; 1636; Charlestown [MBCR 1:183, 374; ChChR 9, 49; ChTR 26; ChBOP 13; Nahum S. Cutler, *A Cutler*

Memorial and Genealogical History (Greenfield, Massachusetts, 1889) 508-16].

Cutter, Elizabeth: Newcastle-upon-Tyne, Northumberland; 1636; Cambridge [MBCR 1:373; CaBOP 53; NEHGR 61:69; Shepard 89, 144, 179; Abandoning 86-87; TAG 74:292-98; Benjamin Cutter and William Richard Cutter, *A History of the Cutter Family in New England* (Boston 1871)].

Cutting, John: Ipswich, Suffolk; 1636; Watertown [WaBOP 3, 109; Lechford 384; WP 4:89; Abel Lunt Anc 81-87; TAG 83:13-18].

Cutting, Richard: Great Bromley, Essex; 1634 on *Elizabeth*; Watertown [GM 2:2:272-75].

Cutting, William: Unknown; 1634 on *Elizabeth*; passenger list only [GM 2:2:275].

Cutts, William: Unknown; 1639; Saco (servant) [MPCR 1:49-50; Trelawny 210-11; Gorges 100].

D

Dabyn, Robert: Unknown; 1635 on *Marygould*; passenger list only [Hotten 283].

Dady, William: Unknown; 1631; Charlestown [GMB 505-8].

Dalton, Philemon: Dennington, Suffolk; 1635 on *Increase*; Watertown, Dedham, Hampton [GM 2:2:277-80].

Dalton, Timothy: Woolverstone, Suffolk; 1637; Dedham, Hampton [DeChR 8; DeTR 1:32; WP 3:387; MBCR 1:202, 373; HmTR 40; NEHGR 154:259-89].

Dam, John: Unknown; 1640; Dover [NHPP 1:128, 10:701, 31:13, 40:10; NEHGR 65:212-19, 310-14, 89:192-95, 92:101-16, 220-31, 359-65, 111:45-55]. (Evidence for claimed arrival in 1633 not seen.)

Damon, Jane: Dover, Kent; 1635 on *Elizabeth & Ann*; Dedham [GM 2:2:280; Richard A. Damon Jr., *The Damon Family of Reading, Massachusetts* (Rockport, Maine, 1999)]. (She married John Plimpton.)

Dane, James: Unknown; 1640; Massachusetts Bay (court appearance only) [MBCR 1:316].

Dane, John: Hatfield Broadoak, Essex; 1638; Ipswich [ITR 35; EPR 1:30; MBCR 1:379; NEHGR 8:148-56, 132:18-19; Tom Webster and Kenneth Shipps, ed., *The Diary of Samuel Rogers, 1634-1638* (Woodbridge, Suffolk, 2004) 29, 102-4; Dawes-Gates 1:238-48].

Dane, Thomas: Unknown; 1635 on *Elizabeth & Ann*; passenger list only (with caveat) [GM 2:2:281].

Danford, John: Unknown; 1638; Weymouth (two court appearances only) [PCR 7:12, MBCR 1:287].

Danforth, Nicholas: Framlingham, Suffolk; 1635; Cambridge [GM 2:2:281-85].

Daniel, Robert: Unknown; 1636; Watertown, Cambridge [WaBOP 4, 49; CaTR 43; CaBOP 61; Shepard 60; MBCR 1:375; NEHGR 49:341-42,

55:226, 88:383-86, 89:154]. (His daughter Elizabeth Daniel preceded him to New England in 1635 [GM 2:2:285].)

Darby, Thomas: Unknown; 1637 on *Elizabeth*; passenger list only [NGSQ 71:177].

Darloe, Penelope: Unknown; 1635 on *Pied Cow*; Boston [GM 2:2:285-86]. (She married Robert Turner.)

Darrell, John: Unknown; 1637 on *Mary Anne*; passenger list only [Hotten 294].

Darvell, Robert: Unknown; 1639; Sudbury [SuTR 1; Aspinwall 329 (clue); NEHGR 55:226; Rodgers 2:70-73].

Dassett (or Dorset), John: Unknown; 1639; Braintree [MBCR 1:377; BTR 1:50; NEHGR 3:127; SLR 10:125; SPR 6:186, 12:140].

Dastin (or Dustin), Josiah: Unknown; 1639; Charlestown, Medford, Reading [Lechford 177; SLR 1:11; Reading ChR 69, 75-76; Savage 2:25, 83].

Daukings, William: Unknown; 1635; Scituate (not seen after 1636) [ScitTR 1:241, 245; NEHGR 10:43].

Dause/Dawse, Priscilla: Unknown; 1638; Boston [BChR 24, 33]. (She married John Rogers of Watertown.)

Davenish, Thomas: Unknown; 1639; Salem [STR 1:89, 113; SChR 11, 18, 19; MBCR 1:378; EQC 2:148].

Davenport, John: London; 1637 on *Hector*; New Haven [WJ 1:272; WP 4:4; NHCR 1:20; Lechford 2; Francis J. Bremer, *Building a New Jerusalem: John Davenport, a Puritan in Three Worlds* (New Haven 2012); NEQ 70:265-84; TAG 52:216-17].

Davenport, Richard: Unknown; 1628 on *Abigail*; Salem, Boston [GMB 509-14; Waters 43-44, 1032].

Davenport, Thomas: Unknown; 1639; Dorchester [MBCR 1:286; DChR 5; Dawes-Gates 1:270-78; Mower Anc 106-17].

Davis, Barnabas: Tetbury, Gloucestershire; 1635 on *Blessing*; Connecticut, Charlestown [GM 2:2:286-92].

Davis, Christopher: Unknown; 1636; Massachusetts Bay (court appearance only) [MBCR 1:187, 245].

Davis, Dolor: East Farleigh, Kent; 1634; Cambridge, Duxbury, Scituate, Barnstable, Concord [GM 2:2:292-97; Hotten 68].

Davis, Elizabeth: Unknown; 1635; Charlestown (church admission only) [GM 2:2:297].

Davis, Isaac: Unknown; 1636; Salem; returned permanently to England in 1638 [STR 1:22, 58, 65, 77; MBCR 1:198].

Davis, James: Boston, Lincolnshire; 1634; Boston [GM 2:2:298-300; Davis Fam 241-47].

Davis, James: Unknown; 1636; Plymouth [PCR 1:50, 70, 71, 12:24].

Davis, James: Unknown; 1638; Portsmouth, Boston [PoTR 2; RICR 1:91; MBCR 1:296; WP 4:259].

Davis, James: Gloucester, Gloucestershire; 1639; Hampton, Haverhill [MBCR 1:377; HmTR 40; GDMNH 55, 184; HvBOP 17; TAG 73:81-90, 209-19; Pillsbury 153-57]. (This James Davis did not reside at Newbury; the freeman of 4 March 1634/5 was not of Newbury but was the first James Davis of Boston.)

Davis, Jenkin: Unknown; 1636; Lynn [MBCR 1:372; EPR 1:11; EQC 1:7, 2:270, 8:290; WJ 2:54; EPR 1:357-58; EIHC 3:188-89].

Davis, John: Unknown; 1635 on *Increase*; Boston; may have returned to England after 1646 [GM 2:2:301-3].

Davis, John: Unknown; 1637; Massachusetts Bay [PCR 7:7; MBCR 1:187, 245]. (These three records do not necessarily pertain to the same man, and cannot be connected to any of the other men named John Davis.)

Davis, John: Unknown; 1638; Ipswich, Gloucester [MBCR 1:248, 269; Dawes-Gates 1:280-83].

Davis, John: Unknown; 1640; New Haven (servant; two court appearances only) [NHCR 1:46-47, 58].

Davis, Margaret: Unknown; 1635 on *Elizabeth*; Boston [GM 2:2:303-4]. (The Great Migration sketch should not have been created. The passenger on the *Elizabeth* in 1635 was the wife of Dolor Davis, accompanied by their three children. The remainder of the material in the sketch belonged to another woman who did not appear in New England until the mid-1640s.)

Davis, Margaret: Weyhill, Hampshire; 1638 on *Confidence*; Sudbury [Drake's Founders 58]. (She married (1) _____ Gurgefield and (2) Richard Bennett [Stevens-Miller 1:143; NEHGR 11:200]).

Davis, Nathaniel: Unknown; 1634 on *Mary & John* or *Hercules*; probably never left England [GM 2:2:304].

Davis, Nicholas: St. Dunstan, Stepney, Middlesex; 1635 on *Planter*; Charlestown, Woburn, York [GM 2:2:304-9].

Davis, Nicholas: Unknown; 1638; Portsmouth (admission as inhabitant of Portsmouth only) [RICR 1:91; GMN 22:22].

Davis, Philip: Unknown; 1638 on *Confidence*; passenger list only (servant) [Drake's Founders 59].

Davis, Philip: Unknown; 1638; Plymouth (servant, court appearance only) [PCR 2:6]. (Possibly the same as the man immediately above.)

Davis, Richard: Unknown; 1635 on *Unity*; passenger list only [GM 2:2:309].

Davis, Robert: Weyhill, Hampshire; 1638 on *Confidence*; Sudbury [Drake's Founders 58; SuTR 11; Stevens-Miller 1:82, 143; NEHGR 55:226].

Davis, Sergeant: Unknown; 1637; Connecticut [MHSC 2:8:140, 3:6:27, 170]. (These records for service in the Pequot War probably pertain to one of the other early Davis immigrants.)

Davis, Susan: Unknown; 1635 on *Blessing*; passenger list only [GM 2:2:309].

Davis, Theophilus: Unknown; 1636; Saco (court appearances in 1636 and 1637 only) [MPCR 1:lxii, 1, 5, 7, 8].

Davis, Thomas: Marlborough, Wiltshire; 1635 on *James* of Southampton; Newbury, Haverhill [GM 2:2:310-16].

Davis, William: Unknown; 1635; Boston [GM 2:2:316-20].

Davis, William: Unknown; 1638; Salem (land grant only) [STR 1:84].

Davis, William: Gloucester, Gloucestershire; 1640; New Haven [NHCR 1:50; TAG 48:208-14; NEHGR 81:123; FANH 524; Brainerd Anc 290-92].

Davis, William: Unknown; 1640; York [Gorges 23; GDMNH 188].

Davison, Nicholas: Unknown; 1639; Charlestown, Pemaquid [WP 4:128; Rodgers 2:229-36; GDMNH 189; NYGBR 47:86; Essex Ant 5:179; Wyman 283-84; H. R. Remsen Coles, *Genealogical Record of the Davison, Davidson, Davisson Family of New England* (New York 1899)].

Davol, William: Unknown; 1640; Duxbury, Braintree, Rehoboth, Newport [PCR 1:159; NEHGR 3:127; Austin 284-87; Josephine C. Frost, *Ancestors of Frank Herbert Davol and His Wife Phebe Downing Willits* (New York 1925)].

Dawe, John: Unknown; 1631; Massachusetts Bay (court appearance only) [GMB 514].

Dawes, William: Unknown; 1635 on *Planter*; Boston, Braintree [GM 2:2:320-25].

Dawse *see* **Dause**

Dawson, Henry: Unknown; 1640; Boston [BTR 1:58; BChR 34, 44-46; MBCR 1:378; WJ 2:305-6].

Day, Hannah: Unknown; 1635 on *Elizabeth & Ann*; passenger list only [GM 2:2:325].

Day, Robert: Unknown; 1634 on *Elizabeth*; Cambridge, Hartford [GM 2:2:325-29].

Day, Robert: Stanstead Abbots, Hertfordshire; 1635 on *Hopewell*; Ipswich [GM 2:2:329-33].

Day, Steven: Cambridge, Cambridgeshire; 1638 on *John*; Cambridge [NEHGR 4:55, 77:305-12; Rodgers 2:534-39; Waters 1076-77; George Parker Winship, *The Cambridge Press, 1638-1692* (Philadelphia 1945)]. (Steven Day was accompanied to New England by his stepson William Boardman.)

Day, Wentworth: Unknown; 1640; Boston; returned permanently to England by about 1650 [BChR 31, 287, 293; BTR 1:57; HAHAC 1:100; Abandoning 88-89].

Dayton, Ralph: Ashford, Kent; 1640; New Haven [NHCR 1:50; Donald Lines Jacobus and Arthur Bliss Dayton, *The Early Daytons and Descendants of Henry, Jr.* (New Haven, Connecticut, 1959); NEHGR 128:147-48; NYGBR 138:178-88].

Deacon, John: Unknown; 1631; Penobscot [GMB 514-15; PM 161-62].

Deacon, John: Unknown; 1635 on *Abigail*; Lynn, Salem, Boston [GM 2:2:333-35].

Deacon, Mr.: Unknown; 1638; Massachusetts Bay (mention in letter only) [WP 4:232].

Deane, John: South Chard, Somerset; 1637; Taunton [PCR 1:53, 105; PCPR 2:2:61; NEHGR 51:432-34, 139:324-25; TAG 59:224-27; McArthur-Barnes 87-89; M&JCH 26:22-25, 27:19, 87-99].

Deane, Rachel: Unknown; 1635; Marshfield [GM 2:2:335-36].

Deane, Stephen: Unknown; 1621 on *Fortune*; Plymouth [GMB 515-17; PM 162-62].

Deane, Walter: South Chard, Somerset; 1637; Taunton [NGSQ 71:176; PCR 1:53, 105, 7:12; NEHGR 51:432-34, 80:336, 139:324-25, 147:240-54; TAG 23:174-77, 59:224-30; M&JCH 26:22-25, 27:19, 87-99; James

Eldon Dean and H. Clark Dean, *The Ancestry and Descendants of Walter Deane, 1612-1697*, two volumes (Rockport, Maine, 2013)].

Dearborn, Godfrey: Hannah, Lincolnshire; 1638; Exeter [NHPP 1:133; NEHGR 68:68-72; Hampton Hist 659-72; GDMNH 189-90].

Dearing, George: Unknown; 1634; Richmond Island, Black Point [GM 2:2:336-38].

Deengaine, Henry: Unknown; 1636; Watertown, Dedham, Roxbury [WaBOP 3, 7, 9; DeTR 1:48; SLR 1:240; MLR 10:52; DeHR 6:11-15; Bond 198, 752].

Delano, Philip: Leiden, Holland; 1621 on *Fortune*; Plymouth, Duxbury [GMB 517-21; PM 164-68; MD 56:70-90, 150-84].

Deming, John: Unknown; 1640; Wethersfield [WetLR 1:147; Goodwin-Morgan 2:229-45; TAG 55:28-32, 62:140-42].

Denison, William: Bishop's Stortford, Hertfordshire; 1631; Roxbury [GMB 521-24; TAG 73:50-57; NEHGR 158:361-62].

Denning, William: Unknown; 1633; Boston [GMB 525-26].

Dennis, Edward: Unknown; 1635; Boston [BChR 21, 26; MBCR 1:373 (as "Edward Dinny"); Ordway Anc 67].

Dennis, Robert: Unknown; 1640; Yarmouth [PCR 2:9, 128, 129, 154, 4:116, 7:30, 118, 8:9, 10, 185, 194; MD 10:142-43].

Dennis, William: Unknown; 1638; Scituate [PCR 12:42; TAG 33:153-56].

Denny, Mary: Baddow, Essex; 1635 on *Defence*; passenger list only [GM 2:2:338].

Denslow, Nicholas: Unknown; 1632; Dorchester, Windsor [GMB 526-29; M&JCH 27:19-22].

Dent, Francis: Unknown; 1633; Lynn, Salem [GMB 529-30].

Denton, Richard: Halifax, Yorkshire; 1639; Wethersfield, Stamford, Hempstead; returned permanently to England in 1658 [CCCR 1:63; WetLR 1:139; SmTR 4; NYGBR 117:163-66, 211-12, 120:10-17; CA 47:107-18; Abandoning 89-90].

Derby, John: Burton Bradstock, Dorset; 1637; Plymouth, Yarmouth [NGSQ 71:176; PCR 1:64, 69, 79, 3:96, 4:98, 8:194; MD 14:112; PCPR 2:1:29, 4:2:32; NEHGR 35:127-28, 79:410-49].

Derby, Richard: Burton Bradstock, Dorset; 1637; Plymouth; returned permanently to England in 1640 [NGSQ 71:176; PCR 1:94, 95, 96, 97,

99, 100, 120-21, 128, 2:50, 4:98, 7:10, 12, 18, 12:20, 38-39, 46, 47; NEHGR 35:127-18, 79:410-49].

Desborough, Isaac: Eltisley, Cambridgeshire; 1635 on *Hopewell*; Lynn; returned permanently to England late 1639 or soon after [GM 2:2:338-42; Abandoning 337].

Desborough, Nicholas: Saffron Walden, Essex; 1637; Hartford [HaBOP 138; CCCR 1:45; TAG 38:208-11; GM 2:2:341, 343-44; Goodwin-Morgan 2:203-10].

Desborough, Samuel: Eltisley, Cambridgeshire; 1639; Guilford; returned permanently to England in 1650 [Guilford Hist 25; GM 2:2:339-41; Abandoning 90-91; ODNB].

Desborough, Walter: Bishops Stortford, Hertfordshire; 1634; Roxbury [GM 2:2:342-44; TAG 80:261-63, 82:81-90, 187-95, 273-89].

Desbre, Thomas: Unknown; 1633; Massachusetts Bay (probate record only) [GMB 530].

Devell, Walter: Unknown; 1637; Yarmouth; not seen after 1642 [PCR 1:68, 109, 2:20, 35, 43, 52, 7:19, 20, 24, 29, 30].

Devereux, John: Unknown; 1630; Salem, Marblehead [GMB 530-37].

Devotion, Margaret: Unknown; 1635 on *Abigail*; passenger list only [GM 2:2:344].

Dewey, Thomas: Unknown; 1633; Dorchester, Windsor [GMB 537-39].

Dewhurst, Henry: Unknown; 1635 on *Defence*; passenger list only [GM 2:2:344-45].

Dewhurst, Roger: Unknown; 1639; New Haven, Salem [NHCR 1:26; EQC 1:75, 81-83, 114, 178, 182].

Dewsbury, Hester: Unknown; 1634; Plymouth [GM 2:2:345]. (She married Philip Delano.)

Dexter, Francis: Unknown; 1635 on *Planter*; passenger list only [GM 2:2:345].

Dexter, Thomas: Great Bowden, Leicestershire; 1630; Lynn, Sandwich, Barnstable, Boston [GMB 540-45; WF 253-58].

Diamonts, John: Unknown; 1640; Windsor (land grant only) [WiLR 1:40; Windsor Hist 1:548].

Dibble, John: Unknown; 1640; Springfield [SpTR 167; Pynchon Court 206, 209, 212, 214, 215; SpVR 10, 11, 20].

Dibble, Robert: Unknown; 1634 on *Recovery*; Dorchester [GM 2:2:345-47].

Dickerman, Thomas: Little Missenden, Buckinghamshire; 1637; Dorchester [DChR 3; DTR 1:30; MBCR 1:375; SPR Case #175; NEHGR 5:98; TAG 26:165-67; Gillespie Anc 108-10; Edward Dwight Dickerman and George Sherwood Dickerman, *Dickerman Genealogy: Descendants of Thomas Dickerman* (New Haven 1922)].

Dickerson, Philemon: Brampton, Suffolk; 1637 on *Mary Anne*; Salem, Southold [Hotten 293; SChR 10; STR 1:83; SPR 1:3; MBCR 1:378; Suffolk Sessions 35-36; TAG 84:213-20; Wesley L. Baker, *Dickerson & Dickinson Descendants of Philemon Dickerson of Southold, Long Island, N. Y.* (Chicago 1978)].

Dickinson, Nathaniel: Billingborough, Lincolnshire; 1638; Wethersfield, Hadley [WetLR 1:10; CCCR 1:452; NEHGR 152:159-78]. (Nathaniel Dickinson was accompanied to New England by his stepson William Gull.)

Dickinson, Thomas: Unknown; 1639; Lynn, Rowley [MBCR 1:284, 300; WJ 1:387; RowBOP 2; EPR 1:372-73; Rowley Fams 94-100].

Dickison, John: Unknown; 1639; Salisbury [SyTR 7; EPR Case #7661; Hoyt 132].

Didcutt, John: Unknown; 1638; Sandwich [PCR 1:113, 2:31, 8:184].

Diffy, Richard: Unknown; 1630; Watertown [GMB 545; WF 259].

Dike, Anthony: Unknown; 1623 on *Anne*; Plymouth, Cape Ann, Salem [GMB 545-47; PM 169-71].

Dill, George: Unknown; 1638; Salem, Boston [WP 4:119; STR 1:89; EQC 1:14; BChR 322; WJ 2:381-82; SPR Case #286; Parker-Ruggles 420-21; NEHGR 8:77, 13:149].

Dillingham, Edward: Cottesbach, Leicestershire; 1636; Sandwich [PCR 1:57, 4:155; Lechford 51; MD 14:173; PCPR 2:2:36; Gen Adv 4:12; Winthrop Alexander, *A Genealogy of the Dillingham Family of New England* (typescript, n.p., n.d.) 18a-21].

Dillingham, John: Cottesbach, Leicestershire; 1630; Boston, Lynn, Ipswich [GMB 547-50; WF 259-63].

Dimmock, Thomas: Unknown; 1635 on *Hopewell* of Weymouth; Dorchester, Barnstable [GM 2:2:347-51; MJCH 27:22-23].

Dinely, William: Boston, Lincoln; 1635; Boston [GM 2:2:351-55].

Dingley, John: Unknown; 1638; Sandwich, Marshfield [PCR 1:107; MaTR 1:8; PPR Case #6500; TAG 56:207-10, 61:234-40; Moore Anc 227-32].

Dix, Edward: Unknown; 1639; Boston, Watertown [GMB 551-53; WF 263-67].

Dix, Margaret: Unknown; 1635 on *Susan & Ellen*; passenger list only (servant) [GM 2:2:355].

Dix, Samuel: Norwich, Norfolk; 1637 on *John & Dorothy* or *Rose*; passenger list only [Hotten 290].

Dix, Widow: Unknown; 1637; Ipswich (land grant only) [ITR 25].

Dixey, Katherine: Unknown; 1639; Salem (church admission only) [SChR 8].

Dixey, Thomas: Unknown; 1637; Salem, Marblehead [STR 1:55; EQC 1:28; Sarah Stone Anc 28; Marblehead 64-65].

Dixey, William: Unknown; 1629; Lynn, Salem, Beverly [GMB 553-57; WF 267-73].

Dixon, Jeremy: Unknown; 1638; New Haven (not seen after 1641) [NHCR 1:16, 20, 43, 44, 50, 93, 444; GMN 13:20].

Dixon, Rebecca: Unknown; 1634; Boston; church admission only (servant) [GM 2:2:355].

Dixon, William: Unknown; 1633; Massachusetts Bay [GMB 557-58].

Dixon, William: Unknown; 1636; York [WP 4:322; YLR 8:210; York Hist 1:108; GDMNH 197; Kempton 2:217-21]. (May be the same man as the William Dixon above.)

Dixson, Rachel: Great Yarmouth, Norfolk; 1637 on *Mary Ann*; passenger list only [Hotten 293; NEHGR 154:216-17].

Doane, John: Unknown; 1630; Plymouth, Eastham [GMB 558-63; PM 171-77].

Dodd, James: Unknown; 1635 on *Abigail*; passenger list only [GM 2:2:355-56].

Dodge, Richard: East Coker, Somerset; 1638; Salem, Beverly [STR 1:73; NEHGR 44:297-98; Dawes-Gates 2:315-17; Joseph Thompson Dodge, *Genealogy of the Dodge Family of Essex County, Mass., 1629-1894* (Madison, Wisconsin, 1894); M&JCH 26:25-29].

Dodge, William: Middle Chinnock, Somerset; 1629 on *Lyon's Whelp*; Salem, Beverly [GMB 563-68; TAG 79:278-82].

Doggett, John: Woburn, Bedfordshire; 1630; Watertown, Rehoboth, Martha's Vineyard [GMB 568-70; WF 273-76; TAG 72:89-100; NEHGR 161:5-21].

Doggett, Thomas: Norwich, Norfolk; 1637 on *Mary Anne*; Concord, Weymouth, Marshfield [Hotten 295; CoVR 2; PPR Case #6540; Weymouth Hist 3:194-95; Samuel Bradlee Doggett, *A History of the Doggett-Daggett Family* (Boston 1894) 325-41)].

Dole, Richard: Thornbury, Gloucestershire; 1639; Newbury [Phoebe Tilton Anc 216, 221; TAG 74:53-57].

Doliber, Joseph: Stoke Abbot, Dorset; 1639; Salem [STR 1:98; NEHGR 31:312-13, 32:94-95; Waters 828; Marblehead 65-66].

Done, John: Unknown; 1635 on *Truelove*; passenger list only [GM 2:2:356].

Donley, Jude: Unknown; 1638 on *Confidence*; passenger list only (servant) [Drake's Founders 59].

Donn, Thomas: Unknown; 1635 on *Defence*; passenger list only [GM 2:2:356].

Donnard, Mary: Unknown; 1635 on *Abigail*; passenger list only [GM 2:2:360].

Donnell, Henry: Unknown; 1636; York, Casco [GDMNH 199; York Hist 1:142-44].

Donnil, William: Unknown; 1633; Piscataqua [GMB 571].

Dorety, ____: Unknown; 1634; Massachusetts Bay [GM 2:2:356-57].

Dorman, Thomas: Unknown; 1634; Ipswich, Topsfield [GM 2:2:357-60].

Dorryfall, Anne: Unknown; 1634 on *Elizabeth*; Boston [GM 2:2:360]. (She married Thomas Spencer.)

Dorryfall, Barnaby: Unknown; 1633; Boston, Braintree [GMB 571-73].

Dorset *see* Dassett

Dotteris, John: Unknown; 1637; Massachusetts Bay (court appearance only) [WJ 2:426].

Doty, Edward: Unknown; 1620 on *Mayflower*; Plymouth [GMB 573-77; PM 177-82; NEHGR 166:85-97].

Doud, Henry: Unknown; 1639; Guilford [Guilford Hist 25; TAG 13:93, 76:296-99; W. W. Doud, *The Descendants of Henry Doude* (Hartford 1885)].

Doughty, Francis: Rangeworthy, Gloucestershire; 1639; Dorchester, Taunton, Newtown [NY], New Amsterdam, Virginia, Maryland [Lechford 137; WP 4:128, 281; PCR 2:8, 7:35; NYGBR 43:273-78; TG 2:141; TAG 74:57, 77:1-17, 127-36, 289; M&JCH 26:29-32; SCHSR 4:24-25; John Frederick Dorman, *Adventurers of Purse & Person: Virginia, 1607-1624/5*, three volumes (Baltimore 2004-7) 1:133-35].

Douglas, William: Unknown; 1640; Boston [BTR 1:55]. (This man may be the same as the William Douglas who appeared at Ipswich in 1641, but almost certainly not the William Douglas who appeared at Boston in 1646 and then moved on to New London [TAG 74:275-80].)

Dove, Francis: Unknown; 1637 on *Elizabeth*; Salisbury; returned permanently to England by 1664 [NGSQ 71:177; SyTR 2; Hoyt 132-33, 742, 949; Waters 676-80; NEHGR 51:185, 52:48; Abel Lunt Anc 182].

Dove, Matthew: Unknown; 1640; Salem [Lechford 254; Driver Gen 218; Perley 2:213].

Dow, Henry: Ormesby St. Michael, Norfolk; 1637 on *John & Dorothy* or *Rose*; Watertown, Hampton [Hotten 292; WaBOP 11, 30; WaVR 1:5; MBCR 1:374; HmTR 45; NEHGR 142:255-58; TAG 60:75-76].

Dowell, Elizabeth: Ware, Hertfordshire; 1636; Roxbury [RChR 82; NEHGR 148:57]. (She married Giles Payson.)

Downe, James: Unknown; 1631; Piscataqua (witness only) [GMB 578].

Downes, William: Unknown; 1635; Massachusetts Bay [GM 2:2:360-61].

Downes, William: Unknown; 1640; Dover; about to sail for the West Indies (business transaction only) [Lechford 282-83].

Downes, William: Unknown; 1640; Taunton (business transaction only) [Lechford 319].

Downham, John: Unknown; 1639; Braintree [MBCR 1:297; BrVR 632, 637, 638, 642; BChR 310].

Downing, Emanuel: London; 1638; Salem; returned permanently to England in 1654 [SChR 7; MBCR 1:375; Hale, House 514-21; NEHGR 115:151; TAG 36:68-73, 74:161-74, 299-308, 76:137; TEG 30:90-93, 125-32, 171-76; Abandoning 91-94]. (His son James Downing came to New England in 1630 [GMB 578-79; WF 276-78]. His daughters Mary and Susan Downing came to New England in 1633 [GMB 579-81].)

Dowse, Francis: Unknown; 1639; Boston [BTR 1:45; BChR 30; MBCR 1:379; SPR 6:336, 9:19; Azro Milton Dows, *The Dows or Dowse Family in America* (Lowell, Massachusetts, 1890) 296].

Drake, Abraham: Colchester, Essex; 1640; Hampton [HmTR 51; Alice Smith Thompson and Sir Anthony Richard Wagner, *The Drake Family of New Hampshire* (Concord, New Hampshire, 1962); TAG 61:19-23].

Drake, Elizabeth: Unknown; 1639; Dorchester (church admission only) [DChR 5].

Drake, Joan: Unknown; 1634; Boston [GM 2:2:361-62].

Drake, John: Unknown; 1630; Massachusetts Bay [GMB 581].

Drake, John: Hampton in Arden, Warwickshire; 1640; Windsor [WiLR 1:45; Manwaring 1:111-12; TAG 63:193-206, 65:87-88; Frank B. Gay, *The Descendants of John Drake of Windsor, Connecticut* (Rutland, Vermont, 1933); Frederick Lewis Weis, *Ancestral Roots of Certain American Colonists*, seventh edition (Baltimore 1992) 197].

Drake, Widow: Unknown; 1639; Windsor (death record only) [Grant 10].

Draper, Clear: Unknown; 1634 on *Francis*; passenger list only [GM 2:2:362].

Draper, Nicholas: Unknown; 1636; Salem; removed from Salem by 1642 (two land transactions only) [STR 1:22, 102, 114].

Draper, Roger: Unknown; 1638; Concord [MBCR 1:375; CoVR 2; Wyman 308-9; Granberry 235].

Drinker, Philip: Hernehill, Kent; 1635 on *Abigail*; Charlestown [GM 2:2:362-65].

Driver, Robert: Unknown; 1634; Lynn [GM 2:2:365-68].

Driver, Robert: Unknown; 1635 on *Abigail*; passenger list only [GM 2:2:368].

Druce, Vincent: Unknown; 1637; Hingham [HiBOP 86; NEHGR 121:13; SPR 6:107, 214; Hingham Hist 2:195; GM 2:7:465-69; Francis Jackson, *A History of the Early Settlement of Newton, County of Middlesex, Massachusetts* (Boston 1854) 271-73].

Drury, George: Unknown; 1635 on *Abigail*; passenger list only [GM 2:2:368].

Drury, Hugh: Unknown; 1640; Sudbury, Boston [SuTR 16; Stevens-Miller 2:53-71].

Duabant, John: Unknown; 1635 on *Hopewell* of Weymouth; passenger list only [GM 2:2:369; NEHGR 167-82].

Dudley, Thomas: Sempringham, Lincolnshire; 1630; Charlestown, Cambridge, Ipswich, Roxbury [GMB 581-88; WF 279-87; TAG 44:129-37; TG 22:29-31].

Dudley, William: Ockley, Surrey; 1639; Guilford [Guilford Hist 25; TAG 10:73-78, 82:63-75, 83:232-33].

Duke, John: Unknown; 1635 on *Elizabeth*; passenger list only [GM 2:2:369].

Dumbleton, John: Unknown; 1639; Windsor, Springfield [Hale, House 521-24; Windsor Hist 1:155; TAG 67:11-14].

Dummer, Joan: Bishopstoke, Hampshire; 1638 on *Bevis*; Newbury [Drake's Founders 61; NEHGR 35:269-71]. (She married Thomas Nelson.)

Dummer, Richard: Bishopstoke, Hampshire; 1632 on *Whale*; Roxbury, Newbury [GMB 588-95].

Dummer, Stephen: Bishopstoke, Hampshire; 1638 on *Bevis*; Newbury; returned permanently to England in 1647 [Drake's Founders 61; MBCR 1:375; RICR 1:59; NEHGR 35:254-71, 321-31, 160:273-79; Abandoning 94-95].

Dummer, Thomas: Bishopstoke, Hampshire; 1638 on *Bevis*; Salisbury; returned permanently to England by 1650 [MBCR 1:376; RICR 1:59; NEHGR 35:254-71, 321-31; Waters 200; Hoyt 141].

Duncan, Nathaniel: Exeter, Devonshire; 1633; Dorchester, Boston [GMB 595-99].

Dunford, John: Unknown; 1638; Plymouth Colony; not seen after 1639 [PCR 1:126, 128, 7:12 (as "John Danford")].

Dunham, John: Leiden, Holland; 1632; Plymouth [GMB 599-603; PM 182-86; MQ 54:201-3].

Dunkin, Samuel: Unknown; 1635 on *Hercules*; Newbury, Boston, Roxbury [NeTR 24; GM 2:2:369-71].

Dunster, Henry: Bury, Lancashire; 1640; Cambridge, Scituate [MBCR 1:378; Shepard 156; SuTR 7; HAHAC 1:100; Rodgers 1:393-401; Morison 376-77; Stevens-Miller 1:36-42; NEHGR 80:86-95; Samuel Dunster, *Henry Dunster and His Descendants* (Central Falls, Rhode Island, 1876)].

Dunton, Elizabeth: Unknown; 1638; Salem (church admission only) [SChR 8].

Durdall, Hugh: Unknown; 1638 on *Bevis*; Newport, Hingham [Drake's Founders 60; RICR 1:48, 92; RICR (MS) 32; WP 4:248; Lechford 390; GMN 22:30].

Dustin *see* also Dastin

Dustin, Thomas: Unknown; 1640; Richmond Island, Dover, Kittery [Trelawny 40; NHPP 1:128, 10:701, 40:8; GDMNH 212; EIHC 46:350-53; Duston-Dustin Family Association Genealogists, *The Duston-Dustin Family: Thomas and Elizabeth Wheeler Duston and Their Descendants* (Decorah, Iowa, 1990)].

Dutch, Osmund: Bridport, Dorset; 1638; Portsmouth, Gloucester [RICR 1:59, 66, 91; EQC 1:28; Lechford 109; Phoebe Tilton Anc 87-96; Nicholas Davis Anc 207-14; David Earle Dutch, *The Dutch Family: Pioneers of New England, Descendants of Osmund Dutch of Gloucester, Massachusetts* (Portsmouth, New Hampshire, 2004)].

Dutchfield, Thomas: London; 1640; Boston [WP 4:249, 251; MBCR 1:335; NEHGR 2:79].

Dutton, John: Unknown; 1640; Massachusetts Bay (court appearance only) [MBCR 1:309].

Dwight, John: Woolverstone, Suffolk; 1635; Watertown, Dedham [GM 2:2:371-78; NEHGR 164:135-38].

Dwight, Timothy: Burstall, Suffolk; 1638; Dedham, Medfield [DeTR 1:47; DeChR 24; MBCR 1:379; HmTR 45; NEHGR 164:135-38; GDMNH 212-13; Medfield Hist; 372-74; Parker-Ruggles 265].

Dyer, George: Unknown; 1630; Dorchester [GMB 603-6].

Dyer, John: Unknown; 1635 on *Christian*; Windsor [GM 2:2:378-79; MHSC 2:8:152, 3:6:174 (Pequot War service)]. (The connection of this passenger with the records for Pequot War service derives from the association in both cases with Thomas Stiles. For possible later records for this man see NHCR 1:32; CCCR 1:218, 341.)

Dyer, William: London; 1635; Boston, Portsmouth, Newport [GM 2:2:379-85; NEHGR 158:27-28; Legal Executions 29-32].

E

Eaborne, Samuel: Unknown; 1636; Salem [STR 1:22; GM 2:6:366; NEHGR 55:324; TEG 16:30-32].

Eaborne, Thomas: Unknown; 1633; Salem [GMB 607-8].

Eaglesfield, Mary: Unknown; 1638; Charlestown [Lechford 25-32; ChChR 9; Aspinwall 34, 103, 145; Henry Adams Gen 77]. (She married Samuel Adams, son of Henry Adams.)

Eale, Samuel: Unknown; 1639; Ipswich (servant) [WP 4:142].

Eames, Anthony: Fordington, Dorset; 1634 on *Recovery*; Charlestown, Hingham, Marshfield [GM 2:2:387-92; M&JCH 27:23].

Eames, Thomas: Unknown; 1637; Dedham, Medford, Cambridge, Sudbury [MA Arch 67:128; DeTR 1:71; DeChR 26; DeVR 1; NEHGR 32:408; Goodman 181-83].

Earl, Ralph: Bishops Stortford, Hertfordshire; 1638; Portsmouth, Newport [PoTR 2; RICR 1:91; TAG 19:135; NYGBR 67:390-93; Scott Gen 238; Pliny Earle, *Ralph Earle and His Descendants* (Worcester, Massachusetts, 1888)].

Early, Robert: Unknown; 1634 on *Hercules* (but probably did not sail); passenger list only [GM 2:2:392].

Earning, Katherine: London; 1639; Dorchester, Boston; returned permanently to England by 1648 [Lechford 195; DChR 5; BChR 37; WP 5:244; Abandoning 96].

East, Francis: Unknown; 1636; Boston [BChR 21; BTR 1:30; MBCR 1:373; NEHGR 2:79, 31:332; SPR Case #1402 (son David); MG 20:165-66].

East, William: Unknown; 1639; Milford [MiTR 2; MiChR 1; TAG 12:112, 16:29; Milford Fam 243].

Eastman, Roger: Unknown; 1638 on *Confidence*; Salisbury [Drake's Founders 58; SyTR 7; NYGBR 46:58-62; Pillsbury Anc 111-15; Guy S.

Rix, *History and Genealogy of the Eastman Family of America*, 2 volumes (Concord, New Hampshire, 1901)].

Easton, Joseph: Unknown; 1634; Cambridge, Hartford [GM 2:2:392-96].

Easton, Nicholas: Romsey, Hampshire; 1634 on *Mary & John*; Ipswich, Newbury, Portsmouth, Newport [GM 2:2:396-403; NEHGR 162:245-54, 163:51-65].

Eastwick, Widow: Unknown; 1640; Salem [SChR 9 (with later annotation "removed")]. (She was possibly mother of Edward Eastwick of Salem [Sarah Johnson Anc 43; Dudley Wildes Anc 125]. Isolated records of 1643 and 1646 for "Elizabeth Estick" may pertain to her or to "Goodwife Estrick" [EQC 1:53, 101].)

Eaton, Francis: Bristol; 1620 on *Mayflower*; Plymouth [GMB 608-10; PM 187-89].

Eaton, John: Dover, Kent; 1635 on *Elizabeth & Ann*; Watertown, Dedham [GM 2:2:403-7].

Eaton, John: Hatton, Warwickshire; 1639; Salisbury, Haverhill [SyTR 7; HvBOP 6; TAG 68:48-54; Pillsbury Anc 1119-21; GMC 26 63-67].

Eaton, Jonas: Staple, Kent; 1637; Watertown, Reading [NEHGR 75:222, 76:73; Granberry 212-13].

Eaton, Nathaniel: London; 1637 on *Hector*; Cambridge; removed to Virginia in 1639 [CaTR 33; CaBOP 54; ChTR 36; MBCR 1:374; WP 4:142; NEHGR 2:79; Shepard 53; WJ 1:371; Sibley 1:1-6; Morison 228-40, 377; ODNB; John Frederick Dorman, *Adventurers of Purse and Person, Virginia 1607-1624/5*, fourth edition, three volumes (Baltimore 2004-2007) 2:133-35].

Eaton, Samuel: London; 1637; Boston, New Haven; returned permanently to England in 1640 [NHCR 1:20, 24, 40; Abandoning 97-101; ODNB].

Eaton, Theophilus: London; 1637 on *Hector*; Boston, New Haven [WJ 1:272; WP 4:4; NHCR 1:20; NEHGR 38:29-31, 81:123-24; FANH 591; TAG 52:142-44; ODNB]. (His widow and their children returned to England in 1658 [Abandoning 96-97].)

Eaton, William: Staple, Kent; 1637; Watertown, Reading [NEHGR 37:378, 75:222, 76:73-74; WaBOP 134; WaVR 1:6; Granberry 213].

Eccles, Richard: Unknown; 1638; Cambridge [CaTR 36; Shepard 114-16; NEHGR 8:345; CaChR 15-16; EQC 1:335; MLR 4:448, 452; Cameos 183-88, 307].

Eddenden, Edmond: Tenterden, Kent; 1637; Scituate, Boston [NEHGR 10:43, 67:37-44; PCR 1:110, 2:3, 7:20, 12:67; GM26 83-88].

Eddy, John: Boxted, Essex; 1630 on *Handmaid*; Plymouth, Watertown [GMB 610-14; PM 189-94; WF 289-94].

Eddy, Samuel: Cranbrook, Kent; 1630; Plymouth, Swansea [GMB 614-18; PM 194-98].

Eden, Alice: Ormesby, Norfolk; 1637 on *John & Dorothy* or *Rose*; passenger list only [Hotten 291]. (She may have married John Marston, who was also from Ormesby and was on the same passenger list.)

Edge, Robert: Unknown; 1635 on *Hopewell*; passenger list only [GM 2:2:407].

Edgecomb, Nicholas: Unknown; 1637; Richmond Island, Scarborough [Trelawny 190; Charity Haley Anc 29-49; Nicholas Davis Anc 87-94].

Edmonds, Henry: Milbrook, Cornwall; 1638; Richmond Island; left New England permanently in 1638 [Trelawny 136, 181, 190, 194].

Edmonds, John: Unknown; 1638; Connecticut (court appearance only) [CCCR 1:28]. (Another isolated record for this name appears in Connecticut in 1648 [CCCR 1:171].)

Edmonds, Walter: Nottingham, Nottinghamshire; 1638; Concord, Charlestown [MBCR 1:314, 375; CoVR 2; GMC26 89-106; Rodgers 2:400-3].

Edmonds, William: Unknown; 1633; Lynn [ELR 4:203; GM 2:2:407-11; TEG 16:202-4].

Edmunds, John: Unknown; 1630; Boston [GMB 620; WF 295].

Edson, Samuel: Fillongley, Warwickshire; 1639; Salem, Bridgewater [STR 1:89; MD 34:181; GMC26 107-22; Jarvis Bonesteel Edson, *Edsons in England and America and Genealogy of the Edsons* (New York 1903)].

Edwards, Edward: Unknown; 1639; Sandwich, Plymouth [PCR 1:132 (as "Edmond Edwards"), 8:188, 12:87-88].

Edwards, Henry: Unknown; 1640; Massachusetts Bay (court appearance only) [MBCR 1:309].

Edwards, John: Unknown; 1638; Watertown, Wethersfield [SChR 16; MLR 2:356; CCCR 1:55; WetLR 1:148; NEHGR 145:317-41, 149:41-45, 150:215-16; TAG 71:235-41; Bond 204, 756].

Edwards, John: Unknown; 1638; Plymouth (servant; apprenticeship record only) [PCR 1:110].

Edwards, John: Unknown; 1640; Charlestown (servant) [Lechford 316, 411, 414-16].

Edwards, Mathew: Unknown; 1639; Massachusetts Bay (court appearance only) [MBCR 1:269].

Edwards, Robert: Unknown; 1635 on *Hopewell*; Concord [GM 2:2:411-12].

Edwards, Thomas: Unknown; 1637; Salem, Marblehead; returned permanently to England by 1649 [STR 1:51, 71; SChR 8, 17; EQC 1:233; EPR 1:133-36; Abandoning 101].

Edwards, William: Unknown; 1638; Richmond Island (witness only) [Trelawny 181].

Edwards, William: London; 1639; Hartford [Lechford 184; Hale, House 524-35; TAG 10:83-84, 42:65-76, 63:33-45; NYGBR 62:116-20, 71:217-21].

Eedes, William: Dorset or Somerset; 1629 on *Lyon's Whelp*; unknown [GMB 618; WF 295].

Eeles, John: Unknown; 1633; Dorchester, Windsor; returned to England permanently in 1641 [GMB 618-20; Abandoning 102].

Egelden, Elizabeth: Unknown; 1634 on *Hercules*; passenger list only [GM 2:2:413-15]. (In 2009 Nancy L. Dodge published tantalizing but inconclusive evidence and discussion regarding this passenger and the next three [CN 42:172, 282-83].)

Egelden, Jane: Unknown; 1634 on *Hercules*; passenger list only [GM 2:2:413-15].

Egelden, John: Unknown; 1634 on *Hercules*; passenger list only [GM 2:2:413-15].

Egelden, Sarah: Unknown; 1634 on *Hercules*; passenger list only [GM 2:2:413-15].

Eggleston, Bigod: Norwich, Norfolk; 1630; Dorchester, Windsor [GMB 620-24].

Elderkin, John: Unknown; 1638; Lynn, Dedham, Reading, Providence, New London, Norwich [EQC 2:270; DeChR 25; Wethersfield 2:98; Snow-Estes 1:447-50; New London Hist 158-59].

Eldon, Edward: Unknown; 1639; Massachusetts Bay (court appearance only) [WP 4:128].

Eldred, John: Unknown; 1640; Hampton (land grant only) [HmTR 45].

Eldred, Mrs.: London; 1640; New Haven [NHCR 1:50, 93, 94, 95, 298-99, 427, 502]. (Probably never came to New England.)

Eldred, Robert: Unknown; 1638; Plymouth, Yarmouth [PCR 1:122, 6:104-5; PCPR 4:2:25-26; Nelson B. Eldred III, *Robert Eldred (Eldredge) of Yarmouth and Chatham, Cape Cod, Massachusetts, and Some of His Descendants* (Marietta, Georgia, 1996) 73-76].

Elford, John: Unknown; 1630; Massachusetts Bay [GMB 625-26].

Eliot, Francis: Nazeing, Essex; 1637; Boston [BTR 1:19, 31; NEHGR 3:127, 160:181-84, 161:85-91, 186-98, 250-59, 162:65-72, 128-39, 300-1; MBCR 1:378; BrVR 633].

Eliot, Jacob: Nazeing, Essex; 1631; Boston [GMB 626-30; NEHGR 146:377-82, 154:3-16, 160:181-84, 161:85-91, 186-98, 250-59, 162:65-72, 128-39, 300-1].

Eliot, John: Nazeing, Essex; 1631 on *Lyon*; Boston, Roxbury [GMB 630-32; NEHGR 160:181-84, 161:85-91, 186-98, 250-59, 162:65-72, 128-39, 300-1; NEQ 62:346-68, 66:416-33, 69:3-32].

Eliot, Philip: Nazeing, Essex; 1635 on *Hopewell*; Roxbury [GM 2:2:413-16; TAG 80:208-16; NEHGR 160:181-84, 161:85-91, 186-98, 250-59, 162:65-72, 128-39, 300-1].

Elkins, Henry: Unknown; 1634; Boston, Exeter, Hampton [GM 2:2:417-19].

Elkins, Thomas: Unknown; 1634; Massachusetts Bay (court appearance only, with caveat) [GM 2:2:420].

Elkins, Thomas: Unknown; 1639; Saco [MPCR 1:42, 75; GDMNH 218].

Ellen, Nicholas: Unknown; 1638; Dorchester [MBCR 1:267; DChR 162, 169; SPR 5:98, 6:20; Fulton Anc 382].

Ellenwood (or Elwood), Ralph: Unknown; 1635 on *Truelove*; Salem, Beverly [GM 2:2:420-24; MG 17:59-68].

Ellerd, Gertrude: Unknown; 1636; Salem (church admission only) [SChR 6].

Ellery, Henry: Unknown; 1639; Massachusetts Bay (court appearance only) [MBCR 1:298].

Ellet, John: Unknown; 1633; Watertown, Stamford [GMB 632-34].

Elliott, Richard: Unknown; 1637; Massachusetts Bay (court appearance only) [WP 3:333].

Elliott, William: Unknown; 1634 on *Hercules*; Ipswich (possibly) [GM 2:2:417].

Ellis, Ann: Unknown; 1638; Dedham [DeVR 126]. (She married Edward Culver.)

Ellis, Arthur: Unknown; 1630; Mystic (court appearance only) [GMB 634; WF 295-96].

Ellis, Elizabeth: Unknown; 1635 on *Abigail*; passenger list only [GM 2:2:420].

Ellis, John: Unknown; 1636; Dedham, Medfield [DeTR 1:20; DeChR 23; DeVR 126; MBCR 1:379; Medfield Hist 374; SPR Case #2376].

Elmer, Edward: Unknown; 1632 on *Lyon*; Cambridge, Hartford, Northampton [GMB 634-38].

Elmes, Rhodolphus: Unknown; 1635 on *Planter*; Scituate [GM 2:2:424-26].

Else, Roger: Unknown; 1640; Yarmouth, Boston, Weymouth, Charlestown [PCR 7:21, 50, 8:7, 194; NEHGR 9:284; BTR 1:116; ChChR 12; ChVR 1:58, 82; Weymouth Hist 3:221-22; Wyman 333; Rodgers 2:541-42].

Elsey, Nicholas: Merstham, Surrey; 1640; New Haven [NHCR 1:91; FANH 594; NEHGR 64:347; GM 2:5:128].

Elston, John: Unknown; 1631; Massachusetts Bay [GMB 638].

Elwell, Robert: Unknown; 1634 on *Recovery*; Dorchester, Marblehead, Gloucester [GM 2:2:426-31; NGSQ 71:171].

Elwood *see also* **Ellenwood**

Elwood, William: Unknown; 1635 on *Unity*; passenger list only [GM 2:2:432].

Ely, Nathaniel: Unknown; 1634; Cambridge, Hartford, Norwalk, Springfield [GM 2:2:432-39].

Ely, ____: Unknown; 1620 on *Mayflower*; Plymouth [GMB 638; PM 198].

Emans, Edward: Unknown; 1639; Massachusetts Bay (servant; court appearance only) [Lechford 343].

Emerson, John: Unknown; 1635 on *Abigail*; Scituate; possibly returned permanently to England in 1640 [GM 2:2:439-41].

Emerson, Thomas: Bishops Stortford, Hertfordshire; 1638; Ipswich [ITR 32; EPR 1:11; Stone-Gregg 105-11].

Emery, Anthony: Romsey, Hampshire; 1635 on *James*; Newbury, Dover, Kittery, Portsmouth [GM 2:2:441-46; NHPP 10:701; EIHC 121:210-20].

Emery, George: Unknown; 1636; Salem [STR 1:22, 65, 2:444; SChR 13; Essex Ant 3:65; Perley 1:390].

Emery, John: Romsey, Hampshire; 1635 on *James*; Newbury [GM 2:2:446-52; EIHC 121:210-20].

Emmons, Thomas: Unknown; 1639; Portsmouth, Boston [RICR 1:91, 100, 111; PoTR 17, 28; GDMNH 222 (son Joseph); SPR 1:425, 4:183].

Endicott, John: Unknown; 1628 on *Abigail*; Salem, Boston [GMB 639-46; TEG 27:79-84].

Enfling, Nathaniel: Unknown; 1638; Boston (servant; deposition only) [Lechford 147].

England, John: Unknown; 1637; passenger list only (servant) [NEHGR 75:221]. (This entry and the next two could all pertain to the same man.)

England, John: Unknown; 1637; Lynn (servant) [EQC 1:7; Lechford 41; MBCR 1:247].

England, John: Unknown; 1637; Plymouth (coroner's inquest only) [PCR 1:88].

English, Thomas: Unknown; 1620 on *Mayflower*; Plymouth [GMB 646; PM 199].

English, William: Unknown; 1637; Ipswich, Hampton, Boston [ITR 23; HmTR 45; GDMNH 55, 223].

Ensign, James: Rye, Sussex; 1634; Cambridge, Hartford [GM 2:2:452-58].

Ensign, Thomas: Cranbrook, Kent; 1638; Scituate [PCR 1:108; NEHGR 121:13; MD 16:22-24; TAG 56:219-20, 60:97-100, 61:46-49, 73:241-55, 75:1-15, 130-44, 229-40; NYGBR 42:97-98].

Epes, Daniel: Unknown; 1637; Ipswich [WP 3:518; NEHGR 71:91-92; Bethia Harris Anc 74].

Epes, Elizabeth: Unknown; 1635 on *Abigail*; Ipswich [GM 2:2:458]. (She married James Chute, son of Lionel Chute.)

Errington, Ann: Newcastle-upon-Tyne, Northumberland; 1638; Cambridge [MLR 1:87; NEHGR 132:44-50].

Errington, Thomas: Unknown; 1639; Charlestown, Lynn, Warwick [Lechford 110; SLR 1:42, 89, 110, 129, 131; ELR 1:8, 10; EQC 2:211, 3:292; WarTR 39, 73, 208-9; RICR 1:302 (as "Thomas Evington")].

Essex, Anne: Unknown; 1633; Boston (church admission only) [GMB 646]. (She may have married Thomas Bell [TAG 74:281-91].)

Estow, William: Ormesby St. Margaret, Norfolk; 1637; Newbury, Hampton [NeTR 4; GDMNH 55; MBCR 1:126, 375; HmTR 39; Sarah Stone Anc 137-39; NEHGR 142:258-60].

Estrick, Goodwife: Unknown; 1640; Salem (church admission only) [SChR 10]. (Isolated records of 1643 and 1646 for "Elizabeth Estick" may pertain to "Goodwife Estrick" or to "Widow Eastwick" [EQC 1:53, 101].)

Esty, Jeffrey: Freston, Suffolk; 1636; Salem, Southold, Huntington [STR 1:22; EQC 1:12; EIHC 36:129-34, 47:259-52; TopsHC 5:105-10].

Evance, John: London; 1639; New Haven; returned permanently to England by 1655 [NHCR 1:25; PCR 12:120-25; FANH 596; WetLR 1:153; Wethersfield Hist 2:320; NEHGR 165:273-79; EIHC 17:27-33, 89-98, 28:144; Abandoning 102].

Evans, Elizabeth: Bridgend, Glamorganshire; 1639; Massachusetts Bay (servant; indenture only) [Lechford 107].

Evans, Richard: Unknown; 1639; Dorchester [Lechford 344; DChR 6; MBCR 2:293; NEHGR 5:98, 398-99; SPR Case #294].

Evans, Thomas: Unknown; 1634; Plymouth [GM 2:2:458-59].

Evans, Thomas: Unknown; 1640; Boston (court appearance only) [MBCR 1:312].

Evans, William: Unknown; 1639; Dorchester (court appearance only) [Lechford 343].

Evarts, John: Unknown; 1637; Concord, Guilford [MBCR 1:374; CoVR 2; NEHGR 61:25; FOOF 1:193-94; Hall-Baldwin 65-68].

Eve, Henry: Unknown; 1638; Sandwich [PCR 1:106, 150].

Evens, John: Unknown; 1640; Connecticut (court appearance only) [CCCR 1:55].

Evered *alias* Webb, John: Marlborough, Wiltshire; 1635 on *James*; Boston, Chelmsford [GM 2:2:459-68].

Evered *alias* Webb, Stephen: Marlborough, Wiltshire; 1635 on *James*; passenger list only [GM 2:2:469].

Everett, Richard: Woolverstone, Suffolk; 1636; Dedham [DeTR 1:20; DeChR 29; DeVR 1; Lechford 57; NEHGR 154:259-89; Kempton Anc 4:197-216].

Everett, Richard: Unknown; 1637; Springfield, Jamaica [NY] (possibly) [SpTR 161, 162; Pynchon 206; GM 2:7:453-54; PGM 28:141-42, 154-55; Kempton Anc 4:197, 207].

Everett, William: Unknown; 1639; Dover [MPCR 1:42; NHPP 40:3; GDMNH 226; Coltman Anc 71; TAG 84:88-89, 92; MG 33:3-6].

Everill, James: Unknown; 1634; Boston [GM 2:2:469-76].

Ewell, Henry: Sandwich, Kent; 1634 on *Hercules*; Scituate, Barnstable [GM 2:2:476-79].

Ewer, Thomas: Strood, Kent; 1635 on *James*; Charlestown [GM 2:2:479-83].

Ewstead, Richard: Unknown; 1629; unknown [GMB 646; WF 296].

Eyre, Simon: Bury St. Edmunds, Suffolk; 1635 on *Increase*; Watertown, Boston [GM 2:2:483-89].

F

Faber, Joseph: Unknown; 1635 on *Elizabeth & Anne*; Boston; probably returned permanently to England in 1640 or soon after [GM 2:2:491-92].

Fabin, Elizabeth: Unknown; 1635 on *Elizabeth & Anne*; passenger list only [GM 2:2:492].

Fairbanks, Jonathan: Halifax, Yorkshire; 1636; Dedham [DeTR 1:28; Lorenzo Sayles Fairbanks, *Genealogy of the Fairbanks Family in America, 1633-1897* (Boston 1897); Kempton Anc 3:130-39; TAG 37:65-72; NEHGR 166:165-87].

Fairbanks, Richard: Unknown, 1633, Boston [GMB 647-50].

Fairchild, Thomas: Unknown; 1640; Stratford [Stratford Deeds 1:44; Moore Anc 468-69; W. Bruce Fairchild, *Thomas Fairchild: Puritan Merchant & Magistrate, The Life and Times of an American Colonizer & Patriarch (c. 1610-1670)* (New York 2006)].

Fairfield, Daniel: Unknown ("half Dutchman"); 1639; Salem; returned permanently to England in 1652 [EQC 1:12, 24; NEHGR 2:79; WJ 2:54; MBCR 3:67, 161, 273-74, 421; Abandoning 104].

Fairfield, John: Unknown; 1638; Charlestown [ChTR 39; ChBOP 4, 26, 28, 30].

Fairfield, John: Unknown; 1639; Salem [SChR 8; STR 1:91; MBCR 1:377; Connie Fairfield Ganz, *The Fairfields of Wenham* (Lake Oswego, Oregon, 2013)].

Fairweather, Thomas: Unknown; 1630; Boston [GMB 650-51; WF 297-98].

Faldoe, Bartholomew: Unknown; 1635 on *Planter*; passenger list only [GM 2:2:493].

Falland, Thomas: Unknown; 1639; Yarmouth [PCR 1:140, 7:21; BarnPR 1:5; MD 3:176; TAG 31:124-25, 48:4-7].

Fallowell, Gabriel: Unknown; 1636; Boston, Plymouth [PCR 1:43, 63, 82; BTR 1:41; NEHGR 148:315-27].

Fane *see also* **Vane**

Fane (or Vane), Henry: Unknown; 1638; Boston [MBCR 1:254, 261; EQC 7:127].

Farebrother, Susan: Unknown; 1635 on *Defence*; passenger list only [GM 2:2:493].

Farle, John: Canterbury, Kent; 1637 on *Hercules*; passenger list only (servant) [NEHGR 75:221].

Farley, George: Unknown; 1640; Woburn, Billerica [NEHGR 136:43-62, 133-47].

Farnham, John: Unknown; 1638; Dorchester, Boston [NEHGR 5:243; MBCR 1:375; DChR 4]. (John Farnham was not father of Henry Farnham of Roxbury [TAG 62:33-40].)

Farnham, Ralph: Rochester, Kent; 1635 on *James*; Ipswich [GM 2:2:493-94].

Farnsworth, Joseph: Unknown; 1636; Dorchester [NEHGR 5:243; DTR 27; DChR 3; MBCR 1:375; Moses Franklin Farnsworth and R. Glen Nye, *Farnsworth Memorial II, Second Edition of the Farnsworth Memorial* (n.p. 1974) 749-58].

Farr, George: Unknown; 1630; Lynn [GMB 2077-79; WF 299-301].

Farrington, Edmund: Olney, Buckinghamshire; 1635 on *Hopewell*; Lynn [GM 2:2:494-98].

Farrow, John: Hingham, Norfolk; 1635; Hingham [GM 2:2:498-501].

Farwell, Henry: Boston, Lincolnshire; 1638; Concord, Chelmsford [MBCR 1:375; CoVR 2; John Dennis Farwell, *The Farwell Family*, Volume 1 (n.p. 1929); Bulkeley Gen 22-23].

Farwell, Thomas: Unknown; 1637; Taunton [NGSQ 71:176; PCR 1:128, 132].

Faunce, John: Unknown; 1623 on *Anne*; Plymouth [GMB 651-54; PM 201-3].

Fawer, Barnabas: Unknown; 1635 on *James* of Bristol; Dorchester, Boston [GM 2:2:501-5].

Fawne, John: St. Olave Old Jewry, London; 1634; Ipswich, Haverhill; perhaps returned to England after 1650 [GM 2:2:505-7; TAG 77:28-31].

Feake, Henry: London; 1633; Lynn, Sandwich, Newtown (Long Island) [GMB 654-56].

Feake, Robert: London; 1630; Watertown, Greenwich [GMB 656-60; WF 301-6].

Fearing, John: Cambridge, Cambridgeshire; 1638 on *Diligent*; Hingham [NEHGR 13:331-32, 15:27; HiBOP 30; Hingham Hist 2:217-18; Jeri James, *Ancestors and Descendants of John Fearing 1612/1613 – 1665 of Hingham, Massachusetts* (Riverton, Utah, 2005)].

Fellows, Samuel: Unknown; 1640; Salisbury [SyTR 18; Hoyt 156; NEHGR 138:17-23; Louis Dow Scisco, *Fellows, Fallowes, Fellow and Like Names* (New York 1926) 14-18, 22].

Fellows, William: Unknown; 1635 on *Planter*; Ipswich [GM 2:2:507-12].

Felmingham, Francis: Brampton, Suffolk; 1637; Salem [Hotten 293; STR 1:54; EQC 1:13; MBCR 1:247; Perley 1:443].

Felt, George: Unknown; 1633; Charlestown, Malden, Casco [GMB 660-64].

Felton, Benjamin: Great Yarmouth, Norfolk; 1635; Salem [GM 2:2:512-16].

Felton, Ellen: Great Yarmouth, Norfolk; 1636; Salem [SChR 6; STR 1:21; Waters 1399-1403; William Reid Felton, *A Genealogical History of the Felton Family* (Rutland, Vermont, 1935)].

Fenn, Benjamin: Buckinghamshire; 1639; Milford [MiTR 2; MiChR 1; NHCR 1:91; TAG 24:129-32; Waters 695-96; Ackley-Bosworth 182-84; Charles Candee Baldwin, *The Baldwin Genealogy From 1500 to 1881* (Cleveland 1881) 49-51].

Fenn, Richard: London; 1635 on *Planter*; passenger list only [GM 2:2:516].

Fenn, Robert: Unknown; 1640; Salem, Boston; returned to England by 1655, leaving wife in New England [MBCR 1:311; SChR 11; BChR 296, 302, 309; Waters 603-4; SLR 3:86-87; Stevens-Miller 2:53].

Fenner *see also* **Venner**

Fenner (or Venner), Rebecca: Unknown; 1635 on *Truelove*; Dorchester [GM 2:2:517].

Fennick, Elizabeth: Unknown; 1635 on *Defence*; passenger list only [GM 2:2:517].

Fenwick, George: London; 1636; Saybrook; returned to England permanently in 1645 [WP 3:261-62; Davenport 75; Abandoning 105-7; ODNB].

Fermayes *see* **Vermayes**

Fernald, Renald: Unknown; 1639; Piscataqua [Joseph Waterhouse Anc 35-43].

Ferris, Jeffrey: Unknown; 1634; Watertown, Wethersfield, Stamford, Greenwich [GM 2:2:517-21].

Fessenden, John: Unknown; 1638; Cambridge [Lechford 165; Shepard 176; MBCR 1:378; ChBOP 94; SPR 1:21; CaBOP 46; NEHGR 25:105].

Fever, William: Batcombe, Somerset; 1635 on *Marygould*; passenger list only [GM 2:2:521].

Fibbin, Robert: Unknown; 1633; Dorchester (servant) [GMB 664].

Field, Alexander: Unknown; 1640; Charlestown, Salem, (possibly) New Haven [ChTR 50, 53].

Field, Darby: Ireland; 1636; Piscataqua [NEHGR 36:41; NHPP 1:133, 134, 40:8; Gorges 115; WJ 2:80; GDMNH 232].

Field, John: Unknown; 1637; Providence [PrTR 1:1, 15:5; Austin 75-76; NEHGR 51:359 (clue); TAG 20:181 (clue)].

Field, Richard: Unknown; 1638; Richmond Island [Trelawny 189, 282].

Field, Robert: Eling, Hampshire; 1635; passenger list only [GM 2:2:522]. (Possibly the same as the next.)

Field, Robert: Unknown; 1638; Portsmouth, Newport (and possibly later of Flushing) [RICR 1:59, 92; NHM 67; NEHGR 113:197-203].

Field, William: Unknown; 1640; Providence [PrTR 15:5; Austin 77].

Field, Zachariah: Unknown; 1639; Hartford, Northampton [HaBOP 193; HaTR 23; Warner-Harrington 203-5].

Fiennes, Charles: Sempringham, Lincolnshire; 1630; Boston; returned to England permanently in late 1630 or early 1631 [WF 307].

Fifield, William: Unknown; 1634 on *Hercules*; Newbury, Hampton [GM 2:2:522-26; NHGR 20:60-63, 22:8-14].

Filer, Walter: Unknown; 1633; Dorchester, Windsor [GMB 665-67].

Filley, William: Unknown; 1640; Windsor [WiLR 1:68; Windsor Hist 2:250; Warner-Harrington 206].

Finch, Daniel: Unknown; 1630; Watertown, Wethersfield, Stamford, Fairfield [GMB 667-69; WF 307-10].

Finch, John: Unknown; 1632; Watertown, Stamford [GMB 669-71].

Finch, Samuel: Unknown; 1633; Roxbury [GMB 671-73].

Finney, Robert: Lenton, Nottinghamshire; 1638; Plymouth [NEHGR 148:315-27].

Firmin, Giles: Sudbury, Suffolk; 1633; Boston [GMB 673-75].

Firmin, John: Nayland, Suffolk; 1630; Watertown [GMB 675-78; WF 310-15].

Firmin, Josiah: Unknown; 1639; Boston [BChR 30; MBCR 1:379]. (Possibly son of John Firmin. See also NEHGR 56:182-82.)

Firmin, Thomas: Unknown; 1635; Ipswich [ITR; EPR 1:95].

Firnwell, William: Unknown; 1639; Newbury (servant; court appearance only) [WP 4:128].

Fish, Gabriel: Unknown; 1639; Exeter [Lechford 141; WJ 1:394; BChR 290; GDMNH 233].

Fish, John: Great Bowden, Leicestershire; 1639; Sandwich [PCR 1:150; Michael E. Leveridge, *A Godly Minister* (Cambridge, England, 2008) 44-48; Lester Warren Fish, *The Fish Family in England and America* (Rutland, Vermont, 1948)].

Fish, Jonathan: Great Bowden, Leicestershire; 1639; Sandwich, Newtown [NY] [PCR 1:150; Michael E. Leveridge, *A Godly Minister* (Cambridge, England, 2008) 44-48; Lester Warren Fish, *The Fish Family in England and America* (Rutland, Vermont, 1948); NEHGR 138:30-33; TAG 80:53-55].

Fish, Nathaniel: Great Bowden, Leicestershire; 1639; Sandwich [PCR 1:150; Michael E. Leveridge, *A Godly Minister* (Cambridge, England, 2008) 44-48; Lester Warren Fish, *The Fish Family in England and America* (Rutland, Vermont, 1948); NEHGR 138:30-33; TAG 80:53-55].

Fishcock, Edward: Plymouth, Devon; 1634; Richmond Island, New Amsterdam [GM 2:2:526-28].

Fisher, Anthony: Denton, Norfolk; 1637; Dedham [DeTR 1:32; DeChR 6; NEHGR 151:171-91, 291-99, 300-7, 154:495-96; Kempton Anc 4:218-44].

Fisher, Constance: Unknown; 1638; Dedham (death record only) [DeVR 127].

Fisher, Edward: Unknown; 1639; Portsmouth [PoTR 6; TAG 67:193-200; GM 2:6:394; Austin 79].

Fisher, Joshua: Syleham, Suffolk, and Redenhall, Norfolk; 1639; Dedham [DeChR 21; DeTR 1:38; MBCR 1:377; TAG 66:133-34; NEHGR 151:171-91, 291-99, 300-7, 154:495-96, 159:25-34; Kempton Anc 4:218-44].

Fisher, Robert: Unknown; 1640; Stamford [SmTR 4, 6, 10, 13].

Fisher, Thomas: Saxlingham-juxta-mare, Norfolk; 1634; Cambridge, Dedham [GM 2:2:528-32].

Fiske, David: Weeley, Essex; 1637; Watertown [MBCR 1:374; WaBOP 11, 36; WaTR 1:5; NEHGR 86:406-35, 87:40-45, 141-46, 217-24, 367-74, 88:142-46, 265-73, 92:177-83, 287-88].

Fiske, John: South Elmham, Suffolk; 1637; Salem, Wenham, Chelmsford [WP 3:394; MBCR 1:206, 235, 373; EPR 1:20; STR 1:51; WnTR 1:1; NEHGR 86:406-35, 87:40-45, 141-46, 217-24, 367-74, 88:142-46, 265-73, 92:177-83, 287-88; Robert G. Pope, ed., *The Notebook of the Reverend John Fiske, 1644-1675*, Publications of the Colonial Society of Massachusetts, Volume XLVII (Boston 1974)].

Fiske, Phineas: Wingfield, Suffolk; 1640; Salem, Wenham [SChR 10; WnTR 1:1; NEHGR 86:406-35, 87:40-45, 141-46, 217-24, 367-74, 88:142-46, 265-73, 92:177-83, 287-88].

Fiske, William: South Elmham, Suffolk; 1638; Salem, Wenham [MBCR 1:235; STR 1:72; EQC 1:14; NEHGR 86:406-35, 87:40-45, 141-46, 217-24, 367-74, 88:142-46, 265-73, 92:177-83, 287-88; 149:232-33].

Fitch, James: Unknown; 1635 on *Defence*; Boston [GM 2:2:532-33].

Fitch, John: Unknown; 1635 on *Defence*; Massachusetts Bay [GM 2:2:533]. (He may have been the John Fitch who appeared at Rehoboth in the early 1640s [ReTR 1:2; NEHGR 63:381-82].)

Fitch, Richard: Unknown; 1635; Boston [BTR 1:24; NEHGR 16:367].

Fitch, Zachary: St. Albans, Hertfordshire; 1638; Lynn, Reading [EQC 2:270; MBCR 1:374; NEHGR 55:288-89, 57:415-16, 63:162-64, 69-88-89].

Fitcher, _____: Unknown; 1624; Massachusetts Bay; soon returned to England permanently [GMB 679].

Fitchew, Peter: Unknown; 1639; Massachusetts Bay (probate only) [SPR 2:1].

Fitts, Richard: Unknown; 1637; Newbury [NeTR 11; Pillsbury Anc 731-32; Ordway Anc 73].

Fitts, Robert: Unknown; 1638, Cambridge, Salisbury [CaBOP 57; SyTR 8; EQC 3:236-37; Hoyt 156-57].

Fitzrandolph, Edward: Sutton-in-Ashfield, Nottinghamshire; 1636; Scituate, Barnstable, Piscataway [NJ] [NEHGR 9:280, 97:275-80, 295-99, 99:35-36; PCR 1:53, 87; Louise Aymar Christian and Howard Stelle

Fitz Randolph, *The Descendants of Edward Fitz Randolph and Elizabeth Blossom, 1630–1950* (n.p. 1950); TAG 83:29].

Flack, Cotton: Saffron Walden, Essex; 1633; Boston [GMB 679-80].

Flagg, Thomas: Scratby, Norfolk; 1637; Watertown [Hotten 291; WaBOP 38; WaVR 1:8; Flagg 437-40; Ackley-Bosworth 269-70; NEHGR 163:19-26, 139-46].

Flatman, Thomas: Unknown; 1637; Salem, Braintree [STR 1:104; MBCR 1:377; BrTR 2; NEHGR 3:127].

Flavell, Thomas: Unknown; 1621 on *Fortune*; Plymouth [GMB 681; PM 203-4].

Flawne, Thomas: Unknown; 1639; Yarmouth [PCR 8:185, 194].

Fleming, Abraham: Unknown; 1635 on *Increase*; passenger list only [GM 2:2:533].

Fleming, John: Unknown; 1639; Watertown [WaVR 1:7; WaBOP 43].

Fletcher, Edward: Unknown; 1639; Boston [BTR 1:48; BChR 30, 36-37; MBCR 1:378; HAHAC 1:130; SLR 3:120, 8:123, 9:262, 392, 13:64; SPR Case #427; NEHGR 15:78; Stevens-Miller 1:465; Henry Jessey, *The Lord's Loud Call to England* (London 1660) 18, 20-24; Abandoning 110-11].

Fletcher, John: Unknown; 1640; Wethersfield, Milford [CCCR 1:452; WetLR 1:159; MiTR 2; Emerson-Benson 217-18].

Fletcher, John: Unknown; 1640; Richmond Island [Trelawny 289].

Fletcher, Moses: Leiden, Holland; 1620 on *Mayflower*; Plymouth [GMB 681-82; PM 204-5].

Fletcher, Robert: Unknown; 1637; Concord [MBCR 1:206, 267; Kempton Anc 4:272-79].

Flint, Henry: Matlock, Derbyshire; 1635; Boston, Braintree [GM 2:2:534-37; Edward E. Flint Jr. and Gwendolyn S. Flint, *Flint Family History of The Adventuresome Seven*, two volumes (Baltimore 1984)].

Flint, Thomas: Matlock, Derbyshire; 1636; Boston, Concord [BTR 1:18; Lechford 70; MBCR 1:221, 264, 374; SPR 1:20, 2:12; SuTR 8; CoVR 2; NEHGR 14:58-59; Edward E. Flint Jr. and Gwendolyn S. Flint, *Flint Family History of The Adventuresome Seven*, two volumes (Baltimore 1984)].

Flood, Edmund: Unknown; 1623 on *Anne*; Plymouth [GMB 682; PM 205].

Flood, Joseph: Stepney, Middlesex; 1635 on *Abigail*; Dorchester, Lynn; left New England permanently in 1646, perhaps returning to England [GM 2:2:537-39].

Floyd, Thomas: London; 1640; Duxbury, Scituate, Boston [Lechford 297].

Flute, John: Unknown; 1635; Lynn (servant) [EQC 1:14; WP 4:236-37].

Fobes *see* **Vobes**

Fogg, Ralph: London; 1633; Plymouth, Salem; returned to England permanently after 1652 [GMB 682-86; PM 206-10; Abandoning 111-12].

Fogg, Samuel: Theydon Garnon, Essex; 1640; Hampton [Phyllis O. Whitten, *Samuel Fogg, 1628-1672: His Ancestors and Descendants* (Annandale, Virginia, 1976); GDMNH 235-36].

Fokar, John: Unknown; 1635 on *Increase*; passenger list only (with caveat) [GM 2:2:539].

Folger, John: Norfolk; 1638; Dedham, Watertown, Edgartown [DeTR 1:48; WaBOP 53; NEHGR 86:257; Martha's Vineyard Hist 2:Edgartown:66-70; Nantucket Hist 740; *Pennsylvania Magazine of History and Biography* 23:17-21].

Folland *see* **Falland**

Follett, John: Unknown; 1640; Dover [NHPP 1:128, 10:701; GDMNH 236].

Folsom, Adam: Hingham, Norfolk; 1639; Hingham (immigration record only) [NEHGR 15:27].

Folsom, John: Hingham, Norfolk; 1638; Hingham, Exeter [NEHGR 15:26; Lechford 176; HiBOP 81; Abel Lunt Anc 141-49].

Foote, Nathaniel: Shalford, Essex; 1634; Watertown, Wethersfield [GM 2:2:540-44].

Foote, Pasco: Unknown; 1636; Salem, Salisbury [STR 1:19; Pillsbury 1:141-46].

Footman, Thomas: Unknown; 1639; York, Dover [YLR 3:85; GDMNH 239].

Ford, ____: Unknown; 1621 on *Fortune*; Plymouth [GMB 686-87; PM 211-12].

Ford, Barbara: Unknown; 1635 on *Susan & Ellen*; passenger list only [GM 2:2:544].

Ford, Edward: Tenterden, Kent; 1635 on *Hercules*; passenger list only (servant) [GM 2:2:544].

Ford, John: Unknown; 1635 on *Marygould*; passenger list only (servant) [GM 2:2:545].

Ford, Thomas: Dorchester, Dorset; 1630 in *Mary & John*; Dorchester, Windsor, Northampton [GMB 688-90].

Ford, Timothy: Unknown; 1636; Charlestown, New Haven, Fairfield [ChTR 25; NHCR 1:32; FANH 611-12; FOOF 1:207; Charles R. Ford, *Timothy Ford of New Haven, Connecticut* (South Windsor, Connecticut, 2004)].

Fordham, Robert: Flamstead, Hertfordshire; 1640; Sudbury, Hempstead, Southampton [SuTR 27; SPR 1:25; SPR NS 1:19, 2:19; TAG 13:67-76; NEHGR 2:263; NYGBR 105:144; Miner Anc 212-16].

Forten, John: Unknown; 1635 on *Hopewell*; passenger list only [GM 2:2:545].

Mr. Fosbrook: Unknown; 1637; Sandwich (land grant only) [PCPR 1:32].

Fosdick, Stephen: Great Wenham, Suffolk; 1635; Charlestown [GM 2:2:545-51].

Foster, Christopher: Ewell, Surrey; 1635 on *Abigail*; Lynn, Hempstead, Southampton [GM 2:2:551-54].

Foster, Edward: Unknown; 1632; Scituate [GMB 690-92; PM 212-14].

Foster, George: Unknown; 1630; Lynn, Plymouth (mention in probate record) [GMB 692; PM 215; WF 315].

Foster, Lettis: Unknown; 1639; Plymouth (marriage record only) [PCR 1:134].

Foster, Patience: Biddenden, Kent; 1635 on *Elizabeth*; Dorchester [GM 2:2:554-55; TAG 80:26].

Foster, Renald: Theydon Garnon, Essex; 1638; Ipswich [ITR 37; NEHGR 30:83-102; Dudley Wildes Anc 177-83].

Foster, Thomas: Unknown; 1634 on *Hercules* (but probably did not sail); passenger list only [GM 2:2:555-56].

Foster, Thomas: Ipswich, Suffolk; 1639; Boston [Lechford 135, 377; BTR 1:42; BChR 35; MBCR 2:291; TAG 49:95-97 (use with caution)].

Foster, Thomas: Wendover, Buckinghamshire; 1640; Weymouth, Braintree, Billerica [TAG 68:14-22; Weymouth Hist 3:233; NEHGR 26:394-99].

Foster, William: Unknown; 1634 on *Hercules* (but probably did not sail); passenger list only [GM 2:2:556].

Foster, William: Unknown; 1634; Ipswich, Newport [GM 2:2:556-58].

Foulfoot, Thomas: Unknown; 1635 on *Christian*; passenger list only [GM 2:2:558].

Fountaine, Edward: Unknown; 1635 on *Abigail*; passenger list and one court appearance only [GM 2:2:558-59].

Fowkes, Henry: Unknown; 1634; Dorchester, Windsor [GM 2:2:559].

Fowle, Ann: Unknown; 1635 on *Susan & Ellen*; passenger list only [GM 2:2:560].

Fowle, George: Unknown; 1638; Concord, Charlestown [MBCR 1:256, 309, 375; NEHGR 2:188; CoVR 2; SPR 1:20; Eugene Chalmers Fowle, *Descendants of George Fowle (1610/11?-1682) of Charlestown, Massachusetts* (Boston 1990)].

Fowle, Thomas: Unknown; 1639; Boston; returned to England permanently in 1646 [BTR 1:42; BChR 32, 287; Lechford 261; HAHAC 1:88; WJ 2:241, 320, 347, 391, 430; Abandoning 112-14].

Fowler, Philip: Marlborough, Wiltshire; 1634 on *Mary & John*; Ipswich [GM 2:2:560-64].

Fowler, Richard: Unknown; 1640; Massachusetts Bay (court appearance only) [EQC 1:25].

Fowler, William: Ippollitts, Hertfordshire; 1639; Milford [MiChR 1; MiTR 2; NHCR 1:27; NEHGR 54:352; Daniel W. Fowler, *A Genealogical Memoir of the Descendants of Capt. William Fowler of New Haven, Connecticut* (Milwaukee 1870)].

Fownell, John: Hertford, Hertfordshire; 1638; Cambridge, Charlestown [NEHGR 4:56; Shepard 203; TAG 40:29-30].

Fox, Daniel: Unknown; 1636; Hingham [HiBOP 58; SLR 1:250].

Fox, John and Richard: Unknown; 1635 on *Abigail*; passenger list only [GM 2:2:565].

Fox, Thomas: Unknown; 1630; Mystic (servant, court appearance only) [GMB 2079-80].

Fox, Thomas: Unknown; 1637; Concord [MBCR 1:315, 374; CoVR 2; TAG 53:94, 54:234-35].

Foxwell, Richard: Unknown; 1630; Boston, Piscataqua, Scarborough [GMB 693-98].

Foxwell, Richard: Unknown; 1634; Scituate, Barnstable [GM 2:2:565-68].

Fraile, George: Unknown; 1637; Charlestown, Lynn [ChTR 31; EQC 2:270; NEHGR 7:169; Wyman 373; TEG 17:17-19].

Francis, Richard: Unknown; 1639; Cambridge [MBCR 1:377; Stevens-Miller Anc 1:237-39].

Franckland, Thomas: Unknown; 1640; New Haven (two court appearances only) [NHCR 1:42, 46].

Franklin, William: Unknown; 1634 on *Mary & John*; Ipswich, Boston; returned to England permanently by 1658 [GM 2:2:568-73; Abandoning 114].

Frary, John: Norwich, Norfolk; 1637; Dedham [DeTR 1:37; DeVR 1; DeChR 6; MBCR 1:374; Margaret Murphy Frary and Anne Frary Lepak, *The Frary Family in America, 1637-1980* (n.p. 1981)].

Free, John: Unknown; 1639; Newport [NHM 2:173; RICR (MS) 32].

Freeborn, William: Maldon, Essex; 1634 on *Francis*; Roxbury, Boston, Portsmouth [GM 2:2:573-75].

Freeman, Anthony: Unknown; 1635 on *Hopewell*; passenger list only [GM 2:2:575].

Freeman, Edmond: Billingshurst, Sussex; 1635 on *Abigail*; Lynn, Sandwich [GM 2:2:576-82; NEHGR 164:104-11].

Freeman, John: Unknown; 1635 on *Abigail*; passenger list only [Hotten 93; GM 2:2:580-81].

Freeman, John: Unknown; 1639; Sudbury [SuTR 4; Blake-Torrey 120-21; Warner-Harrington 216-17]. (Claimed as brother of Edmond Freeman of Lynn and Sandwich, but not likely [TAG 17:88-89, 94]. Also not likely the passenger of 1635.)

Freeman, Samuel: London; 1630; Watertown [GMB 698-700; WF 316-19; TAG 86:170-72].

Freestone, Anne: Horncastle, Lincolnshire; 1634; Boston (church admission record only) [GM 2:2:582-83].

Freestone, Elizabeth: Alford, Lincolnshire; 1640; Boston [Lechford 327]. (She married by 1643 Robert Turner of Boston [EIHC 48:263-75, 89:211-12; TAG 30:158-67; NEHGR 72:51-63, 74:140-45, 79:170-75].)

Freestone, Frances: Horncastle, Lincolnshire; 1634; Boston [GM 2:2:583]. (She married by 1638 Valentine Hill [GM 2:3:318-28].)

Freethy, Alexander: Unknown; 1636; Richmond Island; returned to England permanently in 1638 [Trelawny 120, 125, 137; GDMNH 245].

Freethy, William: Unknown; 1635; Richmond Island, Piscataqua, York [GM 2:2:583-87].

French, Edward: Unknown; 1637; Ipswich, Salisbury [ITR 25; SyTR 3; EPR 2:441-46; Hoyt 166-70, 750, 962; TAG 71:50-51].

French, John: Unknown; 1637; Cambridge [CaTR 28; NEHGR 4:55, 142:250; CaChR 23; Pillsbury 1:489].

French, John: Unknown; 1639; Braintree, Dorchester [BTR 1:50; NEHGR 5:243; DChR 7; Stone-Gregg 117-27].

French, Judith: Broadway, Somerset; 1635 on *Marygould*; passenger list only (servant) [Hotten 283].

French, Stephen: Unknown; 1632; Dorchester, Windsor [GMB 700-3].

French, Thomas: Assington, Suffolk; 1639; Ipswich [MBCR 1:278; Parker-Ruggles 412-20; Dudley Wildes Anc 63-64; Granberry 218-20; NEHGR 142:250-52, 393, 143:213-20, 363-64]. (Thomas French was preceded to New England by four of his children: Thomas, Alice, Dorcas and Susan [GMB 703-6, 1024-28, 1413-14].)

French, Thomas: Unknown; 1639; Charlestown, Guilford [ChTR 46; Parker-Ruggles 419-23; NEHGR 47:357-61].

French, William: Unknown; 1635 on *Defence*; Cambridge, Billerica [GM 2:2:588-93].

Friar, Thomas: Unknown; 1638; Salem, Gloucester [STR 1:80; GlTR 1:1; Gloucester Hist 94].

Friend, John: Unknown; 1635; Saybrook, Hartford, Salem [MHSC 3:3:159; WP 3:269; HaTR 15; HaBOP 10, 195, 247, 248, 306, 307, 341; STR 1:58; EQC 1:7; RPCC 99; HAHAC 1:103; TEG 16:138-40].

Friend, John: Unknown; 1639; Boston, Barnstable [Lechford 385; BTR 1:51; BChR 37; SLR 1:100; PCR 1:149; GMB 543, 1356].

Frost, Edmond: Earls Colne, Essex; 1635; Cambridge [GM 2:2:593-97].

Frost, George: Unknown; 1636; Saco [MPCR 1:lxii, 43; Trelawny 214; GDMNH 247].

Frost, Nicholas: Unknown; 1632; Damariscove, Kittery [GMB 706-8].

Frost, William: Nottingham, Nottinghamshire; 1638; Fairfield [Plain Dealing 98; Ackley-Bosworth 93-94; TAG 64:161-67, 208-13].

Frothingham, William: Unknown; 1630; Charlestown [GMB 708-11; WF 319-22].

Fry, George: Combe St. Nicholas, Somerset; 1640; Weymouth [SLR 8:392; Granberry 220].

Fry, John: Basing, Hampshire; 1638 on *Bevis*; Newbury, Salisbury, Andover [Drake's Founders 60; NEHGR 8:226-27; TAG 41:77-80; Ellen Frye Barker, *Frye Genealogy* (New York 1920)].

Fry, Richard: Unknown; 1634; Dorchester (land grant only) [GM 2:2:597-98].

Fry, William: Unknown; 1636; Weymouth [Weymouth Hist 199; SPR 1:29, 2:18; NEHGR 156:145-46].

Fryers, James: Unknown; 1640; Cambridge (death record of wife only) [NEHGR 4:56].

Fugill, Thomas: Buttercrambe, Yorkshire; 1639; New Haven; returned to England permanently by 1647 [NHCR 1:20; NHChR 1; WP 4:161; Young's First Planters 525; FANH 635; TAG 10:208-12; Abandoning 114-15].

Fuller, Daniel: Unknown; 1640; New Haven (one court appearance only) [NHCR 1:38].

Fuller, Edward: Leiden, Holland; 1620 on *Mayflower*; Plymouth [GMB 712-13; PM 215-17].

Fuller, Edward: Unknown; 1639; Charlestown (three court appearances only) [MBCR 1:270, 282; SPR 2:9].

Fuller, Giles: Topcroft, Norfolk; 1638; Dedham, Hampton [DeTR 1:50; GDMNH 249; TAG 61:197-98; NEHGR 55:193-94; EIHC 57:313-15].

Fuller, John: Chelmsford, Essex; 1635 on *Abigail*; Ipswich [GM 2:2:598-602; TAG 77:267-70].

Fuller, John: Olney, Buckinghamshire; 1639; Boston, Lynn [WP 4:239; Lechford 152; SyTR 14; TAG 65:67-68; NEHGR 50:533, 100:255; TEG 17:154-56; *Lynn Historical Society Register* 18:72-108].

Fuller, Mary: Sudbury, Suffolk; 1635 on *Planter;* passenger list only (servant) [GM 2:2:602].

Fuller, Robert: Unknown; 1639; Dorchester, Dedham [DChR 5; MBCR 1:378; TAG 24:92-95].

Fuller, Robert: Unknown; 1639; Salem, Rehoboth [STR 1:91; EQC 1:25; ReTR 1:2; TAG 76:274-77; Clarrence C. Fuller, *Records of Robert Fuller of Salem and Rehoboth and Some of His Descendants* (Norwood, Massachusetts, 1969); William B. Saxbe Jr., *Richard Bowen (1594?-1675), of Rehoboth, Massachusetts, and His Descendants* (Williamstown, Massachusetts, 2011) 20-24].

Fuller, Samuel: Leiden, Holland; 1620 on *Mayflower*; Plymouth [GMB 713-17; PM 217-21].

Fuller, Samuel: Unknown; 1640; Salem (one court appearance only) [EQC 1:25].

Fuller, Thomas: Unknown; 1640; Woburn [WoTR 2; Stevens-Miller 1:127; Bassett-Preston 116-17; Elizabeth Abercrombie, *Fuller Genealogy: A Record of Joseph Fuller, Descendant of Thomas Fuller of Woburn and Middleton, Mass.* (Boston 1897)].

Fuller, William: Chelmsford, Essex; 1635 on *Abigail*; Ipswich, Hampton [GM 2:2:602-6; TAG 77:267-70].

Fuller, William: Unknown; 1638; Concord [MBCR 1:267; CoVR 2; GM 2:2:606].

Furber, William: Unknown; 1635 on *Angel Gabriel*; Ipswich, Dover [GM 2:2:606-12; TAG 55:120; NHPP 1:128, 135].

Furnell, John: Unknown; 1636; Saco (two court appearances only, unless he is the same as **Fownell, John** of Cambridge) [MPCR 1:7, 79].

Furness, Elizabeth: Unknown; 1639; Concord (court appearance only) [WP 4:128; GM 2:4:95].

Fussell, John: Unknown; 1640; Weymouth, Medfield [SLR 1:16; Weymouth Hist 3:245; Medfield Hist 396].

G

Gabilloe, Michael: Unknown (Frenchman); 1638; Massachusetts Bay (servant; apprenticeship record only) [Lechford 76].

Gage, John: Unknown; 1630; Boston, Ipswich, Bradford [GMB 719-22; WF 323-27].

Gager, William: Little Waldingfield, Suffolk; 1630; Boston [GMB 722-24; WF 327-29; Edmund R. Gager, *The Gager Family* (Baltimore 1985)].

Gaines, Henry: Olney, Buckinghamshire; 1638; Lynn [EQC 2:28, 270; MBCR 1:375; NEHGR 85:30-56; TAG 65:68; NHGR 9:180-81].

Gaines, Thomas: Unknown; 1639; Connecticut, New Haven (two court appearances only) [CCCR 1:29; NHCR 1:39]. (Possibly the same as Thomas Gainer, a merchant from Stepney, Middlesex, active in New England in the late 1640s [MBCR 2:247-49, 274, 3:*passim*; Aspinwall *passim*].)

Gale, Richard: Unknown; 1640; Watertown [WP 4:286; WaBOP 47, 131; Edward Chenery Gale, *Richard Gale, Yeoman, of Watertown in the Massachusetts Bay Colony, 1614-1678* (Minneapolis 1932)].

Gallant, Abraham: Maidstone, Kent; 1635 on *Hercules*; passenger list only [GM 2:3:1].

Gallant, James: Maidstone, Kent; 1635 on *Hercules*; passenger list only [GM 2:3:1].

Galley, John: Unknown; 1635; Salem, Beverly [GM 2:3:1-4].

Gallop, Humphrey: Unknown; 1632; Dorchester [GMB 724-25].

Gallop, John: Bridport, Dorset; 1630; Boston [GMB 725-28].

Galloway, George: Unknown; 1637; Lynn (mention in will only) [PCPR 1:32].

Game, William: Unknown; 1640; Weymouth (servant; apprenticeship record only) [Lechford 389].

Gamlin, Robert: Unknown; 1632 on *William & Francis*; Roxbury, Concord [GMB 728-29].

Garde, Roger: Bideford, Devon; 1637; York [YLR 1:118; MPCR 1:42; Gorges 12; NEHGR 35:343-45, 82:69-70, 185; TAG 20:106-9; GDMNH 252-53; York Hist 1:104-6].

Gardiner, Christopher: Unknown; 1630; Massachusetts Bay, Pejepscot; returned permanently to England in 1632 [GMB 729-30; Abandoning 338-39].

Gardiner, George: Unknown; 1638; Portsmouth, Newport [Lechford 63; NHM 66; RICR 1:91; PoTR 5; TAG 14:243-46, 17:50-52, 19:222, 20:53-54, 21:191-200, 39:2].

Gardiner, John: Unknown; 1635; Plymouth, Scituate, Duxbury [GM 2:3:5].

Gardiner, Lyon: Rotterdam, Holland; 1635 on *Bachelor*; Boston, Saybrook [GM 2:3:6-12].

Gardiner, Richard: Unknown; 1620 on *Mayflower*; Plymouth [GMB 730-31; PM 223].

Gardner, Edward: Unknown; 1635 on *James*; passenger list only (with caveat) [GM 2:3:12].

Gardner, Samuel: Unknown; 1640; Hartford, Wethersfield, Hadley [HaTR 32; HaBOP 165, 345; Wethersfield Hist 1:271; Hadley Hist 55; Parker-Ruggles 309].

Gardner, Thomas: Unknown; 1624; Cape Ann, Salem [GMB 731-37].

Gardner, Thomas: Unknown; 1638; Roxbury [NEHGR 6:183; Dawes-Gates 1:308-9; Granberry 225-27]. (His son Peter came to New England in 1635 on the *Elizabeth* and also settled at Roxbury [GM 2:3:12-16; NEHGR 159:40-42].)

Garfield, Edward: Coventry, Warwickshire; 1634; Watertown [GM 2:3:16-23].

Garford, Jarvis: Unknown; 1634; Salem [GM 2:3:23-25].

Garland, John: Unknown; 1638; Richmond Island (servant) [Trelawny 172, 193].

Garland, Peter: Unknown; 1626; Casco, Charlestown, Dover, Saco [Trelawny 239; ChTR 27, 29, 33, 36, 38, 42; ChBOP 46; Lechford 60-61; NHPP 10:701, 40:17; GDMNH 254].

Garlick, Joseph: Unknown; 1639; Lynn, Marblehead, Easthampton [EQC 1:13, 16, 19, 21, 23; NEHGR 93:163-64; CCCR 1:573; MHSC 3:10:183; Easthampton TR 1:128-36, 139-40, 152-55, 487-91; Entertaining Satan 213-41, 281; Marblehead 70-71; TAG 21:118-20].

Garner, Edmund: Unknown; 1634; Cambridge, Ipswich [GM 2:3:25-26].

Garnett, Judith: Unknown; 1634 on *Francis*; Boston [GM 2:3:26-27]. (She married Robert Shelley.)

Garrett, Daniel: Unknown (but possibly from Bocking, Essex); 1639; Hartford [HaBOP 163; HaTR 24; CCCR 1:46; TAG 71:93-104].

Garrett, Herman: Unknown; 1637; Charlestown, Concord, Lancaster, Boston [ChTR 38; Lechford 316, 411; SLR 3:388; Wyman 403; Pope 182].

Garrett, Hugh: Unknown; 1630; Charlestown [GMB 737; WF 329]. (Possible clerical error for Richard Garrett.)

Garrett, James: Unknown; 1637; Charlestown [ChTR 31; MBCR 1:376; ChChR 9, 49; ChBOP 43; NEHGR 4:184; MLR 2:53, 158; GDMNH 254; Wyman 403].

Garrett, Richard: Unknown; 1630; Charlestown [GMB 737-39; WF 330-32].

Garrett, Richard: Unknown; 1638; Scituate, Boston [PCR 1:119; TAG 38:74-81].

Garrold, Henry: Unknown; 1638; Boston [BTR 1:37; Lechford 159; SPR 1:27].

Gary, Arthur: Little Hadham, Hertfordshire; 1637; Roxbury [RChR 82; RBOP 1; MBCR 1:375; TG 20:191-210, 22:78-79].

Gaskell, Edward: Unknown; 1636; Salem [STR 1:23, 102; SChR 8, 17; Snow-Estes 2:67-71; Gussie Esther Gaskill, *The Gaskill Family: One Line of Descendants of Edward Gaskill of Salem, Massachusetts, Since 1636* (n.p. 1986)].

Gatchell, John: Unknown; 1635 on *Hopewell*; Marblehead [GM 2:3:27-33; TG 21:3-41; M&JCH 27:25-29].

Gatchell, Samuel: Unknown; 1635 on *Hopewell*; Marblehead, Hampton, Salisbury [GM 2:3:33-35; M&JCH 27:25-29; Sylvia Fitts Getchell, *Getchell/Gatchell: A Family Genealogy of Maine Pioneers* (Newmarket, New Hampshire, 2005)].

Gates, Stephen: Hingham, Norfolk; 1638 on *Diligent*; Hingham, Cambridge, Lancaster [NEHGR 15:26, 120:161-63, 137:146, 160:7-14, 163:134-36; HiBOP 49; TAG 10:19-200; Sarah Miller Anc 41-46].

Gaud, Mark: St. John, Cornwall; 1638 on *Fortune*; Richmond Island; soon ran away [Trelawny 136, 172, 181, 190, 194].

Gault, William: Great Yarmouth, Norfolk; 1637 on *Mary Ann*; Salem [Hotten 294; SChR 8; STR 1:71, 72; EPR 1:316-17; Essex Ant 10:139; Perley 2:30-31].

Gaunt, Peter: Unknown; 1637; Sandwich [PCPR 1:32; MD 3:74-75; PCR 1:107, 149; NGSQ 62:247-54].

Gay, John: Unknown; 1634; Watertown, Dedham [GM 2:3:36-42; NEHGR 164:114-20].

Gayle, John: Unknown; 1634; Boston (church admission only) [GM 2:3:42-43].

Gaylord, William: Crewkerne, Somerset; 1630 on *Mary & John*; Dorchester, Windsor [GMB 739-43; M&JCH 26:35-39, 27:29-31].

Gedney, John: Norwich, Norfolk; 1637 on *Mary Anne*; Salem [Hotten 294; Fiske 243; MBCR 1:374; SChR 7; STR 1:53; TAG 14:83-86, 21:205-6, 39:108-12; EIHC 16:241-70].

Gedney, John: Norwich, Norfolk; 1637 on *John & Dorothy* or *Rose*; passenger list only (servant) [Hotten 290].

Gee, Ralph: Unknown; 1633; Piscataqua [GMB 744-45].

Geere, Dennis: Ovingdean, Sussex; 1635 on *Abigail*; Lynn [GM 2:3:43-45; NYGBR 119:81-82].

Geere, William: Unknown; 1639; Salem, Wenham [STR 1:93; MBCR 1:378; SChR 10; Fiske Notebook 9-10, 13, 45-47; EPR 3:144; TEG 5:27-28].

Gell, Richard: Unknown; 1639; Salem (servant; two court appearances only) [EQC 1:18, 60].

Genere *see* **Chenery**

George, John: Unknown; 1640; Massachusetts Bay (apprenticeship record only) [MBCR 1:314].

Gibbins, William: Unknown; 1623; Casco, Richmond Island [GMB 2080].

Gibbons, Ambrose: Unknown; 1630; Piscataqua, Dover [GMB 745-49].

Gibbons, Edward: Unknown; 1623; Wessagusset, Charlestown, Boston [GMB 749-55].

Gibbons, James: London; 1635 on *Increase*; Saco, Kittery [GM 2:3:45-48].

Gibbons, John: Unknown; 1639; Massachusetts Bay (court appearance only) [MBCR 1:265].

Gibbons, William: Unknown; 1636; Saco [MPCR 1:2, 43, 80; Trelawny 191, 231, 353; GDMNH 259].

Gibbons, William: Unknown; 1639; Hartford [HaBOP 305; CCCR 1:42; WetLR 1:77; HaVR 575; Manwaring 1:115, 355].

Gibbons, William: Unknown; 1640; New Haven [NHCR 1:42; FANH 641; NEHGR 11:160].

Gibbs, Francis: Unknown; 1640; Windsor (land grant only) [WiLR 1:86].

Gibbs, Giles: St. Sidwell, Exeter, Devon; 1632; Dorchester, Windsor [GMB 756-58].

Gibbs, Henry: Unknown; 1633; Charlestown, Hingham [GMB 758-59; HiBOP 45].

Gibbs, John: Unknown; 1637; Wethersfield, New Haven [CCCR 1:13; WetLR 1:163; NHCR 1:44; FANH 641; Wethersfield Hist 1:271]. (The "John Gibbs" who was granted land at Cambridge was actually John Gibson [CaBOP 332; GMN 22:13].)

Gibbs, Philip: Unknown; 1640; Massachusetts Bay (court appearance only) [Lechford 328].

Gibson, Ann: Unknown; 1635 on *Susan & Ellen*; passenger list only [GM 2:3:49].

Gibson, Christopher: Chesham, Buckinghamshire; 1630; Dorchester, Boston [GMB 759-63].

Gibson, Elizabeth: Unknown; 1630; Boston [GMB 764; NEHGR 95:362]. (She married John Endicott.)

Gibson, John: Unknown; 1634; Cambridge [GM 2:3:49-52].

Gibson, Mary: Unknown; 1634, Boston (servant; church admission only) [GM 2:3:52].

Gibson, Richard: Unknown; 1636; Richmond Island, Saco, Piscataqua; returned permanently to England in 1642 [Trelawny 86, 158; WJ 2:79; MPCR 1:6, 44; NHPP 1:113; Nicholas Davis Anc 121-23; WP 4:96-97; Abandoning 116-17].

Giddings, George: St. Albans, Hertfordshire; 1635 on *Planter*; Ipswich [GM 2:3:52-56].

Gifford, Abigail: Willesden, Middlesex; 1634 on *Griffin*; Boston; returned permanently to England later the same year [GM 2:3:56].

Gilberd, Nicholas: Unknown; 1640; Watertown (servant; court appearance only) [MBCR 1:314].

Gilbert, John: Bridgewater, Somerset; 1635 on *Hopewell*; Dorchester, Taunton [GM 2:3:56-60; NGSQ 71:176].

Gilbert, Matthew: Unknown; 1639; New Haven [NHCR 1:20; WP 4:161; Gilberts of NE 377-410; FANH 642-43; Waters 573-74].

Gilbert, Thomas: Yardley, Worcestershire; 1639; Braintree, Wethersfield [BTR 1:50; WP 4:268; Gilbert Gen; TAG 67:161-66].

Gilbert, William: Unknown; 1639; Windsor (admission to freemanship only) [CCCR 1:46].

Gildersleeve, Richard: Unknown; 1636; Wethersfield, Stamford, Hempstead [CCCR 1:3, 445; WetLR 1:81, 160; SmTR 4; Parke-Gildersleeve 32-35].

Giles, Edward: Unknown; 1633; Salem [GMB 764-66; TAG 72:285-300].

Gilham, Robert: Unknown; 1637; Boston [BTR 1:19; WP 4:128; RICR 1:91; GMN 22:22].

Gill, Arthur: Plymouth, Devon; 1638; Richmond Island, Dorchester, Boston; returned permanently to England by 1654 [Trelawny 133; MBCR 1:379; NEHGR 2:188; SPR Case #152; GDMNH 261; TAG 73:223-25; Abandoning 117-18].

Gill, Isabel: Unknown; 1638; Dorchester (church admission only) [DChR 3]. (She probably married Jeffrey Turner.)

Gill, John: Eastwell, Kent; 1637; Weymouth [NEHGR 75:221; Lechford 373; WP 4:232].

Gill, John: Unknown; 1640; Dorchester [DChR 5, 12, 22, 153, 160; Woolson-Fenno 99; SPR Case #1956; SPR 6:424, 9:137].

Gill, Thomas: Unknown; 1635; Hingham [HiBOP 64; NEHGR 33:340; Hingham Hist 2:268-69].

Gillam, Benjamin: Wapping, Middlesex; 1634; Boston [GM 2:3:60-65].

Gillett, Jonathan: Chaffcombe, Somerset; 1633; Dorchester, Windsor [GMB 766-70; TAG 42:160-63; NEHGR 162:113-14].

Gillett, Matthew: Unknown; 1634 on *Mary & John*; Salem, Marblehead [GM 2:3:65-66].

Gillett, Nathan: Chaffcombe, Somerset; 1633; Dorchester, Windsor [GMB 770-72; TAG 42:160-63; NEHGR 162:113-14].

Gillow, John: Unknown; 1636; Lynn [EQC 1:2, 5, 156, 348, 392; WJ 1:330; ELR 2:29r; EPR 2:353-55 (will of son)].

Gilman, Edward: Hingham, Norfolk; 1638 on *Diligent*; Hingham, Ipswich, Exeter [NEHGR 15:26; HiTR 3; HiBOP 98; Lechford 304; MBCR 1:375; ReTR 1:2; MD 25:65; TAG 11:137-38; Abel Lunt Anc 153-60].

Gilpin, Anthony: Unknown; 1640; Yarmouth, Barnstable [PCR 3:83, 7:21; MD 14:21-23 (clue); Otis 406].

Gilson, William: Unknown; 1632; Scituate [GMB 773-75; PM 223-26]. (He was accompanied to New England by his nephew and niece, John and Hannah Damon.)

Gilven, Thomas: Unknown; 1637; Ipswich [ITR 25, 48; Ipswich Hist 1:483]. (This entry assumes that the first record cited here should read "Gilven" rather than "Silver." If correct, then this immigrant has no connection with the Thomas Silver who appeared at Newbury a few years later [Phoebe Tilton Anc 243].)

Ginkin, Reynold: Unknown; 1636; Richmond Island; not seen after 1639 [Trelawny 183, 194, 290]. (Possibly the same as the Reynold Jenkins who appeared at Kittery by 1647 [GDMNH 377].)

Girling, Richard: Ipswich, Suffolk; 1635; Cambridge [GM 2:3:66-69].

Gladwell, Amos: Unknown; 1635 on *Increase*; passenger list only [GM 2:3:70].

Glass, Amy: Taunton, Somerset; 1639; Plymouth [PCR 1:134; NEHGR 111:172-73, 177]. (She married Richard Willis and Edward Holman.)

Glass, James: Taunton, Somerset; 1639; Barnstable [PCR 1:139, 3:16; MD 11:94-95; NEHGR 111:172-73, 178].

Glass, Roger: Taunton, Somerset; 1639; Scituate [PCR 1:141; NEHGR 111:172-73, 178].

Glover, Charles: Unknown; 1638; Salem, Gloucester, Southold [STR 1:86; SChR 9, 11; MBCR 1:378; Perley 2:75; NEHGR 53:414].

Glover, Henry: Unknown; 1634 on *Elizabeth*; passenger list only [GM 2:3:70-71].

Glover, John: Prescot, Lancashire; 1635; Boston, Dorchester [GM 2:3:72-76].

Glover, Jose: Sutton, Surrey; 1638 on *John*; Cambridge [WJ 1:348; BTR 1:29; SuTR 8; CaBOP 49; Lechford 90; SLR 1:66, 254; PCR 12:44; NEHGR 23:135-37, 30:26-28; Waters 33, 772-78; Morison 379-80; George Parker Winship, *The Cambridge Press, 1638-1692* (Philadelphia 1945); Glover Gen 560-72; Abandoning 118-19].

Glover, Ralph: Unknown; 1630; Charlestown [GMB 775-76; WF 332-34].

Glower, Charles: Unknown; 1632 on *Lyon*; passenger list only [GMB 776].

Goad, Abigail: Unknown; 1640; Salem [WP 4:306; SChR 10; GM 2:3:77]. (She married Robert Moulton.)

Goad, Thomas: London; 1635 on *Abigail*; Ipswich; departed for Spain in 1635 [GM 2:3:76-78].

Goadby, John: Unknown; 1635 on *Hopewell*; passenger list only [GM 2:3:78].

Goard, Richard: Unknown; 1635 on *Elizabeth & Ann*; Roxbury [GM 2:3:78-81; LENE 47].

Goble, Thomas: Unknown; 1634; Charlestown, Concord [GM 2:3:81-83].

Godbertson, Godbert: Leiden, Holland; 1623 on *Anne*; Plymouth [GMB 776-78; PM 226-28].

Goddard, John: Unknown; 1634 on *Pied Cow*; Piscataqua, Dover [GM 2:3:84-88].

Goddard, Thomas: Marlborough, Wiltshire; 1635 on *James*; passenger list only [GM 2:3:88].

Godden, William: Unknown; 1640; Duxbury (servant; court appearance only) [PCR 1:159].

Godfrey, Edward: London; 1630; Piscataqua, York; returned permanently to England about 1655 [GMB 778-83; Abandoning 120].

Godfrey, Francis: Unknown; 1638; Duxbury, Marshfield, Bridgewater [PCR 1:95, 109; PCPR 2:2:57; MD 17:155-56].

Godfrey, John: Unknown; 1634 on *Mary & John*; Newbury, Andover, Rowley, Haverhill, Dover, Ipswich, Salem [GM 2:3:88-91].

Godfrey, William: Unknown; 1638; Watertown, Hampton [WaVR 1:7; WaBOP 30; MBCR 1:377; Aspinwall 132; NEHGR 63:32-33, 142:267 (clue); TAG 46:150-54 (clue); Hampton Hist 727-28; GDMNH 269]. (William Godfrey was accompanied to New England by his stepson Thomas Webster.)

Godson, Francis: Unknown; 1634; Lynn [GM 2:3:91; Lechford 91].

Goffe, Edward: Ipswich, Suffolk; 1635; Watertown, Cambridge [GM 2:3:92-98; NEHGR 158:101-4].

Goffe, Elizabeth: Unknown; 1635 on *James*; passenger list only (with caveat) [GM 2:3:98-99].

Goffe, John: Unknown; 1638; Newbury [NeTR 26; MBCR 1:375; EPR 1:13-15; TAG 77:282-89, 78:291-92].

Goffe, Samuel: London; 1639; Massachusetts Bay (land transaction only) [Lechford 77].

Goit *see* **Coit**

Gold, Francis: Unknown; 1639; Massachusetts Bay (court appearance only) [MBCR 1:270].

Goldsmith, Thomas: Unknown; 1640; Salem, Southampton [EQC 1:20; STR 1:122, 123, 127, 167; MHSC 3:10:88; Wickham-Billard 49].

Goldstone, Henry: Wickham Skeith, Suffolk; 1634 on *Elizabeth*; Watertown [GM 2:3:99-101].

Goldthwait, Thomas: Unknown; 1630; Roxbury, Salem [GMB 783-86; WF 334-37].

Gooch, John: Unknown; 1639; York, Wells [MPCR 1:54, 58; Maine Wills 32-33 (clue); GDMNH 270; Stevens-Miller 2:97-105].

Good, Thomas: Unknown; 1638 on *Bevis*; passenger list only [Drake's Founders 60].

Goodale, Richard: Great Yarmouth, Norfolk; 1638; Newbury, Salisbury [NeTR 23; SyTR 9; TAG 22:17-21, 85:134-40; Abel Lunt Anc 101-7]. (His stepmother Elizabeth and half-sister Elizabeth came with him or soon after.)

Goodale, Robert: Unknown; 1634 on *Elizabeth*; Salem [GM 2:3:101-8].

Goodenow, Edmund: Donhead St. Andrew, Wiltshire; 1638 on *Confidence*; Sudbury [Drake's Founders 58; MBCR 1:296, 377; SuTR 3; TAG 52:208-9, 59:5-10, 61:65-69; Kempton Anc 3:160-76].

Goodenow, John: Semley, Wiltshire; 1638 on *Confidence*; Sudbury [Drake's Founders 58; MBCR 1:378; SuTR 3; TAG 52:208-9, 59:5-10, 61:65-69; Kempton Anc 3:160-68].

Goodenow, Thomas: Shaftesbury, Dorset; 1638 on *Confidence*; Sudbury, Marlborough [Drake's Founders 58; SuTR 1; TAG 52:208-9, 59:5-10, 61:65-69; Kempton Anc 3:160-68].

Goodenow, Ursula: Shaftesbury, Dorset; 1638 on *Confidence*; Sudbury [Drake's Founders 58; TAG 52:208-9, 59:5-10, 61:65-69; Kempton Anc 3:160-68].

Goodhue, Nicholas: Unknown; 1635 on *James*; passenger list only [GM 2:3:108].

Goodhue, William: Unknown; 1635; Ipswich [GM 2:3:108-14].

Goodin, Adam: Ormesby, Norfolk; 1637 on *John & Dorothy* or *Rose*; Providence [Hotten 291; PrTR 1:86-87, 2:7-10, 55-56, 104, 15:5, 21].

Goodin, Anne: Great Yarmouth, Norfolk; 1637 on *Mary Anne*; passenger list only [Hotten 293].

Goodman, John: Unknown; 1620 on *Mayflower*; Plymouth [GMB 786; PM 228-29].

Goodman, Richard: Unknown; 1633; Cambridge, Hartford, Hadley [GMB 786-90].

Goodman, Thomas: Unknown; 1639; Duxbury; not seen after 1641 [Lechford 194, 199; PCR 2:12].

Goodrich, Richard: Unknown; 1639; Guilford [Guilford Hist 25; TAG 18:105-10].

Goodrich, William: Woolverstone, Suffolk; 1636; Watertown [WaBOP 5, 52; MBCR 1:270; WaVR 1:5; SPR Case #50; TAG 13:78-82, 43:43-49; Hale, House 550-51; Edwin Alonzo Goodridge, *The Goodridge Genealogy: A History of the Descendants of William Goodridge* (New York 1918)]. (The two early Watertown land grants to "John Gutterige" were almost certainly clerical errors and were actually grants to this William Goodrich [WaBOP 5, 8].)

Goodwin, Edward: Unknown; 1639; Boston [BTR 1:53; BChR 35; MBCR 2:291; SPR Case #2192].

Goodwin, Ozias: Bocking, Essex; 1639; Hartford [HaBOP 158; HaTR 6; Manwaring 1:308; Moore Anc 281-84; Goodwin Gen 95-102; Frank Farnsworth Starr, *English Goodwin Family Papers*, 3 volumes (Hartford 1921) 492].

Goodwin, Susanna: Unknown; 1636; Salem (church admission only) [SChR 6].

Goodwin, William: Braintree, Essex; 1632 on *Lyon*; Cambridge, Hartford, Hadley, Farmington [GMB 790-94; TAG 75:225-28].

Goodyear, Stephen: London; 1640; New Haven; returned permanently to England in 1657 [Lechford 315; NHCR 1:51; Waters 888-89; TAG 16:193-200, 57:1-11, 100-2; NEHGR 61:189, 168:271; CA 48:149-57; Grace Goodyear Kirkman, *Genealogy of the Goodyear Family* (San Francisco 1899); Abandoning 120-21].

Goordley, John: Unknown; 1638; Boston (servant; death record only) [NEHGR 2:189].

Goose, William: Great Yarmouth, Norfolk; 1636; Salem [STR 1:23, 102; MBCR 1:247; SChR 7; EQC 1:26; EPR 1:435-36; Perley 1:390; Essex Ant 10:24; NEHGR 154:215-16].

Goouch, Mr.: Unknown; 1638; Newbury (court appearance only) [MBCR 1:266].

Gordon, Edmond: Unknown; 1635 on *Susan & Ellen*; passenger list only [GM 2:3:114].

Gore, John: Ippollitts, Hertfordshire; 1635; Roxbury [GM 2:3:114-20].

Gorges, Robert: London; 1623; Wessagusset; returned permanently to England in 1624 [GMB 794-95; PM 229-30; Abandoning 339-40].

Gorges, Thomas: London; 1640; York; returned permanently to England in 1643 [Trelawny 252; Gorges 1; WJ 2:11; WP 4:219; GDMNH 276; Abandoning 123].

Gorges, William: Wraxall, Somerset; 1635; York; returned permanently to England in 1636 [GM 2:3:120-21; Abandoning 340].

Gorham, Ralph: Unknown; 1637; Plymouth; not seen after 1642 [PCR 1:66, 118, 128, 2:37-38, 7:8, 17, 19]. (No evidence connects Ralph Gorham with the John Gorham who married Desire Howland [MD 5:174-75]. The first New England record for John Gorham is in 1643 [PCR 8:188.)

Gorton, Samuel: London; 1637; Plymouth, Portsmouth, Providence, Warwick [PCR 1:61, 100, 105; PoTR 1; RICR 1:91, 131; RWCorr 215; NEHGR 70:115-18, 82:185-93, 333-42; TAG 20:186-87; Adelos Gorton, *The Life and Times of Samuel Gorton* (Philadelphia 1907)].

Gorton, Thomas: Manchester, Lancashire; 1637; Plymouth, Portsmouth [PCR 1:61; PoTR 15; RICR 1:110; NEHGR 82:185-93, 333-42; TAG 20:186-87].

Gosmer, John: Fordwich, Kent; 1639; Southampton [SoTR 1:7, 2:236-37; SLR 2:189; Francis E. Woodruff, *The Woodruffs of New Jersey* (New York 1919) 5-8].

Gosnall, Henry: Sudbury, Suffolk; 1630; Boston [GMB 795; WF 337-38].

Gosse, John: Little Waldingfield, Suffolk; 1630; Watertown [GMB 795-98; WF 338-41].

Gostlin, Margaret: Unknown; 1638; Massachusetts Bay (mention in letter only) [WP 4:64].

Gott, Charles: Cambridge, Cambridgeshire; 1628 on *Abigail*; Salem, Wenham [GMB 798-800].

Gouge, William: Unknown; 1638; Lynn [EQC 2:270; EPR 1:50].

Gould, Edward: Unknown; 1635 on *Elizabeth*; Hingham, Boston [GM 2:3:121-23].

Gould, Jarvis: Unknown; 1635 on *Elizabeth*; Hingham, Boston [GM 2:3:123-24].

Gould, Jeremy: Chesham, Buckinghamshire; 1639; Weymouth; returned permanently to England in 1651 [SPR 1:25; RICR 1:92; WP 4:279; Cotton 346; NEHGR 11:103-4, 17:266-67, 119:174-76; Dudley Wildes Anc 102; Abandoning 123].

Gould, John: Towcester, Northamptonshire; 1635 on *Defence*; passenger list only (with caveat) [GM 2:3:125].

Gould, John: Unknown; 1636; Charlestown [ChChR 9, 46; Lechford 238; ChBOP 65; NEHGR 4:184; MBCR 1:374; ChTR 22; MLR 15:167-68; Wyman 425].

Gould, Thomas: Unknown; 1639; Charlestown [ChChR 10, 50; MBCR 1:378; NEHGR 32:409, 133:127-28; Wyman 428].

Gould, Zaccheus: Great Missenden, Buckinghamshire; 1639; Weymouth, Lynn, Ipswich, Topsfield [SPR 1:25; Lechford 322; EPR 1:33; EQC 1:24; Dudley Wildes Anc 101-8; NEHGR 119:174-76; Benjamin Apthorp Gould, *The Family of Zaccheus Gould of Topsfield* (Lynn, Massachusetts, 1895)].

Goulder, Francis: Unknown; 1638; Plymouth [PCR 1:93, 8:11, 25, 181, 188, 197, 12:36].

Goulworth, John: Unknown; 1630; Massachusetts Bay [GMB 801].

Gowen, Robert: Unknown; 1639; Dedham, Wenham, Lynn [DeChR 21; DeTR 1:75; DeVR 126; TEG 8:39-42].

Goyte, John: Unknown; 1632; Dorchester; returned permanently to England by 1634 [GMB 801].

Grafton, Joseph: Great Yarmouth, Norfolk; 1636; Salem [MBCR 1:373; SChR 16; STR 1:21, 51; WJ 1:400; WP 3:452, 4:107; EIHC 64:49-60; NEHGR 154:216].

Grange, Bryan: Unknown; 1637; Salem (land grant only) [STR 1:53].

Granger, Thomas: Canterbury, Kent; 1637 on *Hercules*; Scituate [NEHGR 75:222, 159:220-34; PCR 2: 45, 50; MD 2:5, 9:85. 14:23, 42:55; Bradford 320-21]. (Thomas Granger, Grace Granger, John Granger, Steven Granger and another Thomas Granger were listed separately as servants in the households of four families on this vessel [NEHGR 75:222]. They constitute the family seen a few years later at Scituate.)

Grant, Christopher: Unknown; 1634; Watertown [GM 2:3:126-32].

Grant, Ferdinando: Unknown; 1640; Saco [MPCR 1:56, 58, 66-67, 69].

Grant, Matthew: Unknown; 1630; Dorchester, Windsor [GMB 801-4].

Grant, Seth: Unknown; 1632 on *Lyon*; Cambridge, Hartford [GMB 804-5].

Grant, Thomas: Cottingham, Yorkshire; 1638; Rowley [RowBOP 3; Rowley Fam 124-25; GMN 18:27; Pillsbury 1001].

Grave, Joan: Unknown; 1635 on *Hopewell*; passenger list only [GM 2:3:132].

Grave, Mary: Unknown; 1635 on *Hopewell*; passenger list only [GM 2:3:132].

Grave, Samuel: Unknown; 1636; Plymouth (sale of land only) [PCR 1:43].

Grave, William: Unknown; 1635 on *Marygould*; passenger list only [GM 2:3:132-33].

Graves, George: London; 1639; Hartford [HaBOP 249; Dawes-Gates 2:380-83; TAG 31:172-74; NEHGR 161:245-49; Kenneth Vance Graves, *Deacon George Graves* (Wrentham, Massachusetts, 1995)].

Graves, Goodman: Unknown; 1638; Ipswich (land record only) [ITR 30].

Graves, John: Nazeing, Essex; 1635; Roxbury [GM 2:3:133-36].

Graves, Richard: Unknown; 1635 on *Abigail*; Salem, Boston [GM 2:3:136-40; MBCR 1:248 (as "Richard Geaves")].

Graves, Richard: Unknown; 1636; Connecticut (mention in letter only) [WP 3:320].

Graves, Thomas: Gravesend, Kent; 1629; Charlestown; apparently left New England in 1633 [GMB 805-7; WF 341-44].

Graves, Thomas: Unknown; 1638; Charlestown; returned permanently to England by 1653 [ChBOP 52; NEHGR 4:184, 34:253-59, 138:39-41; Lechford 26; ChChR 9, 48; MBCR 1:376; WoTR 2; TAG 32:14; EIHC 31:166-80; Abandoning 124].

Gray, Henry: Harrow-on-the-Hill, Middlesex; 1637; Boston, Fairfield [BTR 1:31; Lechford 10, 74-75, 232, 317; FOOF 1:232; TAG 64:161-67, 208-13].

Gray, John: Harrow-on-the-Hill, Middlesex; 1638; Boston, Fairfield, Newtown [NY] [Lechford 139-40, 194; FOOF 1:233; TAG 64:161-67, 208-13].

Gray, Katherine: Unknown; 1634; Massachusetts Bay (court appearance only) [GM 2:3:140].

Gray, Thomas: Unknown; 1630; Marblehead [GMB 807-9; Lechford 252].

Gray, Thomas: Unknown; 1638; Plymouth; not seen after 1643 (servant) [PCR 1:121, 8:187].

Graygoose, Nathaniel: Unknown; 1640; Boston [BChR 30; WP 4:354].

Greeley, Andrew: Unknown; 1640; Salisbury [SyTR 28; Pillsbury Anc 493-504; George Hiram Greeley, *Genealogy of the Greely-Greeley Family* (Boston 1905)].

Green, Bartholomew: Unknown; 1633; Cambridge [GMB 809-10].

Greene, Dorcas: Unknown; 1634 on *Francis*; passenger list only (with caveat) [GM 2:3:140-41].

Greene, Henry: Cambridge, Cambridgeshire; 1639; Watertown, Reading [MBCR 1:377; WaBOP 14, 18; WJ 2:183, 310; MLR 3:336; Bond 776; GM 2:6:556; Morison 380].

Greene, James: Unknown; 1636; Charlestown, Malden [ChTR 22; ChBOP 36; Wyman 437].

Green, John: Unknown; 1632 on *James*; Charlestown [GMB 811-13].

Greene, John: Unknown; 1634 on *Francis*; passenger list only (with caveat) [GM 2:3:140-41].

Greene, John: Salisbury, Wiltshire; 1635 on *James*; Boston, Salem, Providence, Warwick [GM 2:3:141-48; WP 3:458; NEHGR 103:185-88, 164:296-97].

Greene, John: Unknown; 1636; Saybrook (mention in Lyon Gardiner narrative only) [MHSC 3:3:147].

Greene, John: Unknown; 1638; Roxbury [MBCR 1:248; RChR 83; Granberry 232; Parker-Ruggles 474-77].

Green, Joseph: Unknown; 1640; Plymouth [PCR 1:164, 7:27, 8:189]. (Perhaps the Joseph Green who appears later at Weymouth [Weymouth Hist 3:248-49].)

Greene, Mary: Hadleigh, Suffolk; 1639; Boston (apprenticeship record only) [Lechford 153-54].

Greene, Percival: Unknown; 1635 on *Susan & Ellen*; Cambridge [GM 2:3:148-50].

Greene, Richard: Unknown; 1622; Wessagusset [GMB 814; PM 230].

Greene, Solomon: Hadleigh, Suffolk; 1639; Boston (apprenticeship record only) [Lechford 153-54].

Greene, Susan: Unknown; 1637; Salem; not seen after 1641 [STR 1:62, 64, 103; SChR 8; EQC 1:26].

Greene, Thomas: Unknown; 1635 on *Planter* or *Hopewell*; passenger list only (with caveat) [GM 2:3:150-51].

Greene, Widow: Unknown; 1640; New Haven; not seen after 1640 [NHCR 1:50, 92, 194; GMN 13:19].

Greene, William: Unknown; 1640; Charlestown, Woburn [WoTr 2; ChChR 10; NEHGR 16:74, 61:65 (clue); Stevens-Miller 1:101-3; Dawes-Gates 1:330-35].

Greenfield, Samuel: Norwich, Norfolk; 1637 on *Mary Anne*; Salem, Ipswich, Hampton, Exeter, Boston [Hotten 294; STR 1:54; MBCR 1:236, 317; GDMNH 55, 288; ITR 41; EPR 1:11; EIHC 53:241-42; WP 4:4; HmTR 44; TAG 68:216-24; GM 2:7:548-52].

Greenhill, Samuel: Staplehurst, Kent; 1634; Cambridge, Hartford [GM 2:3:151-53; TAG 83:267-77].

Greenland, John: Unknown; 1638; Charlestown [Lechford 320; ChTR 55; MBCR 1:309; SPR 1:1; MPR Case #9871; Wyman 443-44].

Greenleaf, Edmund: Ipswich, Suffolk; 1637; Newbury, Boston [NeTR 21; MBCR 1:258, 266, 375; NHPP 40:13; NEHGR 38:299-301, 69:358-59, 122:28-36; TAG 43:14-18, 56:107; Pillsbury Anc 589-91].

Greensmith, Stephen: Unknown; 1636; Boston [BTR 1:12; MBCR 1:189, 190; HAHAC 1:62; WJ 1:256, 280, 2:426; WP 3:461, 4:276].

Greenway, Clement: Unknown; 1635; Saco [GM 2:3:153-54].

Greenway, John: Mildenhall, Wiltshire; 1630; Dorchester [GMB 814-18; TAG 74:193-95].

Greenway, Richard: Unknown; 1637; Marblehead (land grant and tax assessment only) [STR 1:59, 63].

Gregory, Henry: Nottinghamshire; 1639; Springfield, Stratford [Pynchon Court 204, 211; SpTR 167; Waters 717-18; Ackley-Bosworth 228-30; NEHGR 23:304-7; TAG 38:171-74; Grant Gregory, *Ancestors and Descendants of Henry Gregory* (Provincetown, Massachusetts, 1938)].

Gregory, John: Unknown; 1638; Plymouth (land grant and sale of land only) [PCR 1:109, 12:64].

Gregson, Thomas: London, 1637; New Haven; died at sea 1646 while returning to England [NHCR 1:25; NHChR 1; Waters 563-65; NEHGR 81:124, 127:167-77, 260-27, 128:65-73, 105-12; Abandoning 124-25].

Grennill, Thomas: Unknown; 1635; Lynn (legatee in will only) [Waters 6-7; GM 2:3:43].

Gridley, Richard: Groton, Suffolk; 1631; Boston [GMB 818-23].

Gridley, Thomas: Unknown; 1637; Windsor, Hartford [CCCR 1:33, 2:161; HaBOP 341; HaVR 605; Manwaring 1:122].

Griffin, Hugh: Unknown; 1639; Sudbury [SuTr 4; Rodgers 1:255-57; Dawes-Gates 1:639-41; Brewer 383-85].

Griffin, Humfrey: Unknown; 1639; Ipswich [ITR 42; EPR 1:27, 353; Annis Spear Anc 145-48].

Griffin, Richard: Unknown; 1637; Concord [MBCR 1:264, 374; WP 4:124; Rodgers 2:32-33].

Griffin, Thomas: Unknown; 1638; Boston (business transaction only) [Lechford 69].

Griffith, Henry: Unknown; 1639; Cambridge (death record only) [NEHGR 4:56].

Griffith, Joshua: Stepney, Middlesex; 1635 on *Abigail*; Southampton (not seen after 1640) [GM 2:3:154; SoTr 14].

Griggs, George: Lavendon, Buckinghamshire; 1635 on *Hopewell*; Boston [GM 2:3:154-59; NYGBR 136:243-47].

Griggs, Thomas: Unknown; 1638; Roxbury [RChR 83; RBOP 1; NEHGR 6:183, 123:171-72; SPR Case #57; Parker-Ruggles 474-80].

Grigs, John: Unknown; 1636; Watertown (three land grants only) [WaBOP 3, 6, 10 (as "John Brigs"); GM 2:1:400].

Grimes, Samuel: Unknown; 1638; Boston [BTR 1:35, 40, 46; MBCR 1:314, 2:291; NEHGR 2:189; Lechford 298; BChR 35, 290].

Grinder, Alice: Unknown; 1633 on *James*; Plymouth [GMB 823].

Grinnell, Matthew: Lexden, Essex; 1640; Portsmouth, Newport [PoTR 17; RICR 1:92; GMN 23:4; TG 7-8:144-46; NEHGR 147:71-72; Austin 308-11].

Grissell, Francis: Unknown; 1636; Cambridge, Charlestown [CaTR 24; ChTR 42; Shepard 187; NEHGR 4:56; Rodgers 1:167-73; Wyman 447;

Glenn E. Griswold, *The Griswold Family, England-America* (Middleboro, Massachusetts, 1935) 13-15].

Griswold, Edward: Kenilworth, Warwickshire; 1639; Windsor [Manwaring 1:60; Dawes-Gates 2:398-404; NEHGR 155:245-50; TAG 39:176-80, 40:43-46, 41:100-1, 214, 249, 43:238, 44:115; CN 25:190-91; Waterman Gen 1:665-67; Glenn E. Griswold, *The Griswold Family, England-America* (Middleboro, Massachusetts, 1935)].

Groomes, John: Unknown; 1638; Plymouth; not seen after 1648 [PCR 1:85, 107, 2:26, 29, 48, 67, 75, 76, 120, 122, 7:29, 34, 39, 8:181, 188; PTR 1:7; PCPR 1:48; Lechford 169-70, 194, 199]. (Records for this man have been frequently combined with or confused for those of John Gorham.)

Gross, Isaac: Kings Lynn, Norfolk; 1635; Boston, Exeter [GM 2:3:159-63; NEHGR 146:296].

Gross, Joseph: Unknown; 1638; Plymouth; not seen after 1640 (servant) [PCR 1:158, 12:34].

Grove, Edward: Unknown; 1636; Massachusetts Bay (court appearance only) [WJ 2:423].

Grove, Mary: Unknown; 1630; Massachusetts Bay [GMB 823]. (She married Thomas Purchase.)

Grover, Edmund: Unknown; 1633; Salem, Beverly [GMB 824-26].

Grover, John: Unknown; 1640; Charlestown [NEHGR 4:267; ChTR 60; Wyman 448; MPR Case #9977].

Grover, Samuel: Unknown; 1635 on *Truelove*; passenger list only [GM 2:3:163-64].

Grubb, Thomas: Kings Lynn, Norfolk; 1633; Boston [GMB 826-29].

Gryme, Elizabeth: Unknown; 1639; Boston (church admission only) [BChR 26].

Guild, Ann: Unknown; 1638; Dedham [DeVR 126]. (She married James Allin.)

Guild, John: Unknown; 1640; Dedham [DeChR 23; TAG 83:217-22; SPR Case #1251; Margaret C. Guild Lambert, *Descendants of John Guild and Elizabeth Crooke of Dedham, Ma., Circa 1636-2006* (Scarborough, Ontario, 2006) (clue)].

Gullett, Peter: Unknown; 1636; Richmond Island [Trelawny 109, 113, 125].

Gunn, Jasper: Unknown; 1635 on *Defence*; Roxbury, Milford, Hartford [GM 2:3:164-69].

Gunn, Thomas: Unknown; 1634; Dorchester, Windsor, Westfield [GM 2:3:170-73].

Gunnison, Hugh: Unknown; 1635; Boston, Kittery [GM 2:3:173-80; NEHGR 163:16-18].

Gunter, Lester: Unknown; 1635 on *Truelove*; Boston [GM 2:3:180-81].

Guppy, Reuben: Unknown; 1640; Salem, York [WP 4:323; EQC 1:25, 143; STR 1:151, 152; Coltman Anc 81-85].

Gurdon, Edmund: Assington, Suffolk; 1637; Boston (mention in letter only) [WP 3:387].

Gurnell, John: Unknown; 1638; Dorchester [DChR 3; HAHAC 1:130; TAG 10:71; NEHGR 4:166, 40:258-59; SPR 5:278; Pillsbury Anc 433-39].

Gurney, John: Unknown; 1636; Boston, Braintree [WJ 2:422; MBCR 1:331; NEHGR 62:94; SPR Case #338; Weymouth Hist 3:251; TAG 10:70-73].

Gutch, Robert: Glastonbury, Somerset; 1637; Salem, Kennebec [STR 1:63, 94; SChR 11; EQC 1:24; RChR 124; GDMNH 293-94; NEHGR 34:313-14, 62:95-96; TAG 83:46-49; M&JCH 25:36-38].

Gutsall, Walter: Unknown; 1635 on *Abigail*; passenger list only [GM 2:3:182].

Guy, John: Unknown; 1639; Lynn (court appearance only) [Lechford 418].

Guy, Nicholas: Upton Grey, Hampshire; 1638 on *Confidence*; Watertown [Drake's Founders 58; WaBOP 21; MBCR 1:375; SPR 1:24, 2:59; TAG 65:17-23].

Gyver, Bridget: Unknown; 1632; Boston (church admission only) [GMB 829].

H

Haborne, George: Unknown; 1638; Exeter, Wells, Hampton [NHPP 1:133, 31:25-26; EQC 1:270; GDMNH 294; GM 2:3:310].

Hackford, William: Unknown; 1636; Salem (two land grants only) [STR 1:33, 103].

Hackwell, John: Unknown; 1635 on *Increase*; passenger list only [GM 2:3:183].

Haddon, Garrett: Unknown; 1630; Boston, Cambridge, Salisbury, Amesbury [GMB 831-33; WF 345-48].

Haddon, Katherine: Unknown; 1639; Cambridge (two land records and witness to will only) [CaBOP 66, 88; SPR 1:25].

Hadley, George: Unknown; 1639; Ipswich, Rowley [ITR 60; Rowley Fam 127; Samuel Page Hadley, *Genealogical Record of the Descendants of Moses Hadley and Rebecca Page ... Together with Some Account of George Hadley of Ipswich, Mass.* (Lowell, Massachusetts, 1887)].

Hadlock, Nathaniel: Unknown; 1640; Charlestown [NEHGR 4:267; ChChR 10, 11; MLR 3:362; Granberry 235-38; TAG 81:1-17].

Hadson, John: Unknown; 1639; Newport (court appearance only) [RICR 1:94].

Haffield, Richard: Sudbury, Suffolk; 1635 on *Planter*; Ipswich [GM 2:3:183-87].

Hagborne, Abraham: Unknown; 1639; Boston [NEHGR 2:189, 11:199; BTR 1:59, 78; BChR 35, 84, 291, 303, 324; SPR 1:23].

Hagborne, Samuel: Gloucester, Gloucestershire; 1637; Roxbury [RChR 82; MBCR 1:374; RBOP 2; Lechford 60, 208; SPR 1:22; Sibley 1:574; NEHGR 2:261-62, 6:183; Waters 552; TAG 9:221-22].

Haines *see also* **Haynes**

Haines, Richard: Unknown; 1639; Massachusetts Bay (court appearance only) [MBCR 1:298]. (Possibly the Richard Haines who appeared at Salem in the 1640s [Perley 2:192].)

Haines, Richard: Unknown; 1640; Portsmouth (servant; apprenticeship record only) [Lechford 314].

Haines, Samuel: Westbury Leigh, Wiltshire; 1635 on *Angel Gabriel*; Ipswich, Dover, Portsmouth [NH] [GM 2:3:187-92; NHPP 10:701].

Hale, Robert: Unknown; 1630; Boston, Charlestown [GMB 834-38; WF 348-54].

Hale, Samuel: Unknown; 1637; Hartford, Wethersfield, Norwalk [CCCR 2:151; HaBOP 369; Hale, House 3-8; TAG 38:237-39 (clue)].

Hale, Sarah: Unknown; 1635 on *Truelove*; passenger list only [GM 2:3:193].

Hale, Thomas: Unknown; 1633; Roxbury, Hartford, Norwalk, Charlestown [GMB 838-40].

Hale, Thomas: Watton-at-Stone, Hertfordshire; 1637; Newbury, Haverhill, Salem [WP 4:310; NeTR 10, 13; ITR 73; EPR 1:21; MBCR 1:295, 374; NEHGR 35:367-76, 64:186, 76:75-76, 141:128-34; TAG 22:180-83, 69:212-18; Phoebe Tilton Anc 193-96; GMC50 169-96; Robert Safford Hale, *Genealogy of the Descendants of Thomas Hale of Watton, England, and of Newbury, Mass.* (Albany, New York, 1889)].

Hales, John: Unknown; 1637; Massachusetts Bay (passenger list only) [WP 3:409].

Hales, Mr.: Unknown; 1640; Portsmouth (land grant and mention by Winthrop only) [PoTR 16; WJ 2:10].

Hales, William: Unknown; 1640; Charlestown; not seen after 1641 (business transaction and court appearance only) [Lechford 268; WJ 2:61-62; MBCR 1:335].

Haley, Thomas: Unknown; 1640; Saco [MPCR 1:70; GDMNH 298; Charity Haley Anc 3-4].

Halford, Thomas: Unknown; 1635 on *Christian*; passenger list only [GM 2:3:193].

Hall, Beatrice: Unknown; 1639; Boston [BChR 30, 42]. (She married George Bullard.)

Hall, Edward: Heddon, Northumberland; 1637; Cambridge [MBCR 1:374; Shepard 31-34; CaBOP 63; CaChR 21; SPR 1:6; MPR Case #10111].

Hall, Edward: Henborough, Gloucestershire; 1637; Duxbury; left Plymouth Colony by 1652 [PCR 1:66, 75, 112, 168, 3:20, 21, 34, 8:182, 190, 12:25, 41, 88; Lechford 263-64, 396; PCPR 1:30].

Hall, Edward: Unknown; 1637; Salem (servant; two court appearances only) [EQC 1:7, 43; MBCR 1:234].

Hall, Edward: Unknown; 1638; Ipswich (servant; deposition only) [Lechford 229-31].

Hall, Edward: Unknown; 1640; Taunton (servant; court appearance only) [PCR 2:9, 12].

Hall, Francis: Bulkington, Warwickshire; 1640; New Haven, Fairfield, Stratford [NHCR 1:92; Aspinwall 101-2; FOOF 1:249-56; NGSQ 85:195-218; CA 51:23-35]. (Francis Hall was accompanied to New England by his two wards, John and Thomas Whitehead [NHCR 1:60, 365; NEHGR 55:180-84].)

Hall, George: Unknown; 1637; Plymouth, Taunton [PCR 1:66, 143; Kempton Anc 4:318-27; NEHGR 161:37].

Hall, John: Unknown; 1630; Boston, Charlestown, Barnstable, Yarmouth [GMB 840-44; WF 354-58]. ✓

Hall, John: Unknown; 1634; admission as freeman only (with caveat) [GM 2:3:193-94].

Hall, John: Unknown; 1637; Lynn; not seen after 1647 [EQC 1:6, 10 (as "John Hale"), 135; MBCR 1:261; ELR 3:7].

Hall, John: Unknown; 1637; Hartford, New Haven, Wallingford [HaBOP 116, 352, 501; NHCR 1:50; CCCR 4:276; FANH 238, 693-95; GMB 1991; James Shepard, *John Hall of Wallingford, Conn.* (New Britain, Connecticut, 1902)].

Hall, John: Unknown; 1637; Salem, Roxbury, Salisbury [STR 1:56; RChR 84; MBCR 1:241, 271, 377, 2:245; Essex Ant 4:12; SyTR 14 (wife Rebecca); MBCR 2:245, 254; Hoyt 194].

Hall, John: Unknown; 1639; Dover [MPCR 1:42; NHPP 1:128, 10:701, 40:11; GDMNH 299].

Hall, John: Unknown; 1639; Portsmouth, Newport [RICR 1:83, 92; PoTR 32, 40; NEHGR 87:352-53].

Hall, John: Unknown; 1640; Hartford, Middletown [HaBOP 42, 286, 293, 373; Manwaring 1:205; Moore Anc 285-91].

Hall, Nathaniel: Unknown; 1634; Dorchester (land grant only) [GM 2:3:194-95].

Hall, Ralph: Unknown; 1638; Exeter [NHPP 1:133; GDMNH 301].

Hall, Samuel: Unknown; 1633; Ipswich, Salisbury; returned permanently to England after 1662 [GMB 844-48; Abandoning 362-63].

Hall, Samuel: Unknown; 1635 on *Elizabeth & Ann*; passenger list only (with caveat) [GM 2:3:195].

Hall, Samuel: Unknown; 1637; Charlestown [NEHGR 75:222; HAHAC 1:62; ChTR 30; ChBOP 39; ChChR 9, 49; SPR NS 1:11, 2:11; SPR Case #7; Wyman 455].

Hall, William: Unknown; 1638; Portsmouth [PoTR 1; RICR 1:91; Austin 91].

Hall, William: Unknown; 1639; Guilford [Guilford Hist 25; TAG 13:99; Hall-Baldwin 93-94].

Hallett, Andrew Jr.: Symondsbury, Dorset; 1635 on *Marygould*; Dorchester, Sandwich, Yarmouth [GM 2:3:195-200].

Hallett, Andrew Sr.: Stoke Abbot, Dorset; 1638; Plymouth, Yarmouth [PTR 1:4; PCR 1:117; GM 2:3:198-200; Crosby 2:357-63].

Hallett, John: Unknown; 1639; Scituate [PCR 2:16, 102, 8:183; ScitTR 1:237; MD 34:113-14].

Halliack, John: Unknown; 1635 on *Abigail*; passenger list only [GM 2:3:200-1].

Halloway *see* **Holloway**

Halsey, John: Unknown; 1635 on *Elizabeth & Ann*; passenger list only [GM 2:3:201].

Halsey, Thomas: Kempston, Bedfordshire; 1638; Lynn, Southampton [EQC 2:270; SoTR 1:2; Suffolk Sessions 87-89; TAG 26:216, 32:111-12; Goodwin-Morgan 2:319-32; SCHSR 4:22-23; TG 7-8:103].

Halstead, Nathan: Unknown; 1640; Concord [MBCR 1:379; CoVR 2; SPR 2:19; SPR Case #37; Pillsbury Anc 863-64].

Halstead, Susanna: Halifax, Yorkshire; 1635; Charlestown, Watertown [GM 2:3:201-2].

Ham, William: Plymouth, Devon; 1638; Richmond Island, Cape Neddick, Portsmouth [NH] [Trelawny 93, 95, 181; GDMNH 303; NHGR 10:131-32].

Hames, ____: Unknown; 1640; New Haven (land grant only) [NHCR 1:50].

Hammett, Thomas: Unknown; 1638; Richmond Island, Scarborough [Trelawny 193 (as "Thomas Hammecke"); GDMNH 303].

Hammon, Benjamin: Unknown; 1640; Salem (servant; two court appearances only) [EQC 1:23, 35].

Hammon, Widow: Unknown; 1638; Lynn (land grant only) [EQC 2:270].

Hammond, Frances: Unknown; 1633; Boston (church admission only) [GMB 849].

Hammond, George: Sudbury, Suffolk; 1630; Boston [GMB 850; WF 358-59].

Hammond, Margery: Unknown; 1632; Roxbury [GMB 849-50]. (She married John Ruggles.)

Hammond, Thomas: Unknown; 1636; Hingham, Cambridge [MBCR 1:372; Lechford 175; HiBOP 90; NEHGR 121:13; Bond 272, 779; Hingham Hist 2:286; Frederick Stam Hammond, *History and Genealogy of the Hammond Families in America*, volume 2 (Oneida, New York, 1904) 1-5 (proposed English origin not proved)].

Hammond, William: Lavenham, Suffolk; 1631; Watertown [GMB 850-54; NEHGR 163:113-16].

Hamon, Richard: Unknown; 1639; Newbury (court appearance only) [WP 4:128].

Hamonds, William: Unknown; 1634; Plymouth (servant; court appearance only) [GM 2:3:202-3].

Hampden, John: Unknown; 1622; Plymouth; returned permanently to England soon after 1622 [GMB 848-49; PM 231-32].

Hampton, Thomas: Unknown; 1637; Lynn, Sandwich [PCPR 1:32; PCR 1:97, 118, 133].

Hanbury, Daniel: Unknown; 1635 on *Planter*; passenger list only [GM 2:3:203].

Hanbury, Luke: Ealing, Middlesex; 1637; Massachusetts Bay; apparently returned to England by 1646 (two court appearances only) [MBCR 1:218, 241; Waters 461-62; NEHGR 67:342].

Hanbury, William: Wolverhampton, Staffordshire; 1640; Plymouth, Boston [PCR 7:31, 12:60; PCPR 1:40; WP 4:291; SPR Case #89; NEHGR 40:106; TAG 42:219-20].

Hancock, Elizabeth: Unknown; 1640; Charlestown (church admission only) [ChChR 10].

Hancock, Henry: Unknown; 1638; Richmond Island; returned permanently to England in 1641 [Trelawny 165, 188, 194, 288].

Hancock, Nathaniel: Unknown; 1634; Cambridge [GM 2:3:203-5].

Handford, Nathaniel: London; 1638; Lynn [ELR 1:3v; EQC 1:50, 2:270, 3:256; EIHC 18:30].

Hanford, Eglin: Alverdiscott, Devon; 1635 on *Planter*; Scituate [GM 2:3:205-7].

Hangert, Henry: Unknown; 1638 on *Confidence*; passenger list only (servant) [Drake's Founders 59]. (Possibly the same as Henry Haggett who appeared at Salem in 1642 [GMC50 165-67].)

Hanmer, John: Unknown; 1635; Scituate, Duxbury [GM 2:3:207-10].

Hannum, William: Unknown; 1635; Dorchester, Windsor, Northampton [GM 2:3:210-13].

Hanscombe, Thomas: Unknown; 1629; probably never sailed for New England [GMB 854; WF 359-60].

Hansett, John: Unknown; 1634; Boston, Ipswich, Braintree, Roxbury [GM 2:3:213-16].

Harbert, John: Unknown; 1639; Braintree [BTR 1:49; MBCR 1:309, 378; SLR 3:279-80; SPR Case #894; Parker-Ruggles 533-34; Scott Gen 323-24].

Harbottle, Dorothy: Unknown; 1638; Roxbury [RChR 74, 84; RVR MS 128]. (She married Thomas Lamb and Thomas Hawley [GMB 1154].)

Harding, Abraham: Boreham, Essex; 1640; Boston, Medfield [Lechford 296; TAG 34:208-10; Medfield Hist 405].

Harding, Elizabeth: Boreham, Essex; 1635 on *Abigail*; Boston [GM 2:3:217-18]. (She married Henry Bridgham.)

Harding, John: Unknown; 1639; Weymouth [MBCR 1:377; SPR Case #1250; Weymouth Hist 2:254].

Harding, Martha: Unknown; 1632; Plymouth [GMB 854-55; PM 232-33].

Harding, Phebe: Unknown; 1632; Plymouth [PCR 1:26]. (She married John Brown.)

Harding, Robert: Boreham, Essex; 1630; Boston, Portsmouth, Newport; returned permanently to England by 1654 [GMB 855-58; WF 360-64; TAG 58:131; Abandoning 126-28].

Harding, Winifred: Unknown; 1639; Plymouth [PCR 1:134]. (She married Thomas Whitton.)

Hardwick, Daniel: Unknown; 1635; Massachusetts Bay (servant; mention in letter only) [GM 2:3:217].

Hardy, Christopher: Unknown; 1640; Massachusetts Bay (legal transaction only) [Lechford 270].

Hardy, John: Unknown; 1634 on *Recovery*; Salem [GM 2:3:218-21].

Hardy, Thomas: Unknown; 1633; Ipswich, Rowley, Bradford [GMB 858-61].

Harker, Anthony: Unknown; 1633; Boston [GMB 861-63].

Harker, William: Unknown; 1638; Lynn, Southampton [EQC 1:33, 53, 64, 99, 193, 2:270; EPR 1:368; SoTR 1:2; NYColHist 2:149 (clue), 14:30-31].

Harlakenden, Roger: Earls Colne, Essex; 1635 on *Defence*; Cambridge [GM 2:3:221-25; NEHGR 154:78-108].

Harlow, William: Unknown; 1637; Sandwich [PCPR 1:32; PCR 1:97, 107, 117, 150; MD 12:193-94].

Harman, Francis: Unknown; 1635; passenger list only [GM 2:3:225].

Harmon, John: London; 1636; Plymouth, Duxbury [PCR 1:46-47, 2:90, 8:181, 187, 12:113-14].

Harmon, Nathaniel: Unknown; 1640; Braintree [NEHGR 3:127; MBCR 2:293; Artemas C. Harmon, *The Harmon Genealogy Comprising All Branches in New England* (Washington, D.C. 1920) 251].

Harnett, Edward: Kent; 1638; Salem [NEHGR 75:222; SChR 8; STR 1:79; NYGBR 61:14-39; Freeman 627-47]. (Edward Harnett, son of Edward Harnett, had come to New England in 1637 as servant to Joseph Bachiler [NEHGR 75:222].)

Harrington, Joseph: Unknown; 1640; Boston (servant; court appearance only) [EQC 1:26].

Harris, Arthur: Unknown; 1639; Duxbury, Bridgewater, Boston [PCR 1:153 (as "Arthur Harrison"); NEHGR 159:261-73, 349-59].

Harris, George: Unknown; 1636; Salem [STR 1:20, 23, 50, 65, 103, 123, 124; EQC 1:3, 12, 16, 28, 33, 45, 49, 197; Perley 1:407].

Harris, Jane: London; 1635; Scituate (church admission only) [GM 2:3:225-26].

Harris, John: Unknown; 1635 on *Christian*; passenger list only [GM 2:3:226].

Harris, Joshua: Unknown; 1633; Massachusetts Bay (apprenticeship record only) [GMB 863-64].

Harris, Nathaniel: Unknown; 1632; passenger list only [WP 3:68].

Harris, Parnell: London; 1635 on *Hercules*; Providence [GM 2:3:226-27]. (She married Thomas Roberts.)

Harris, Thomas: Hatherup, Gloucestershire; 1630; Winnissimmett [GMB 864-66; WF 364-66].

Harris, Thomas: London; 1637; Providence [PrTR 1:1, 15:5; NEHGR 167:96-104].

Harris, Thomas: Unknown; 1640; Roxbury (servant; death record only) [NEHGR 6:183].

Harris, Walter: Unknown; 1632; Plymouth (servant) [GMB 866; PM 233-34].

Harris, Walter: Unknown; 1637 on *Speedwell*; Weymouth, New London [NGSQ 71:176; MBCR 1:378; SPR 2:18; NEHGR 156:145-58, 262-79, 357-72].

Harris, William: London; 1636; Providence [PrTR 15:2; TG 20:168-71; NEHGR 167:96-99].

Harrison, John: Unknown; 1637; Boston; returned permanently to England in 1639 [WP 3:517, 4:87, 193; Lechford 127; HAHAC 1:62; GMN 17:22; Abandoning 340-41].

Harrison, John: Unknown; 1639; Salisbury, Boston [SyTR 5; MBCR 1:378; BChR 40; ChBOP 127-28; GMB 818-21; GMN 17:20; Hoyt 195].

Harrison, William: Unknown; 1635 on *Pied Cow*; passenger list only [GM 2:3:227].

Hart, Edmund: Unknown; 1632; Dorchester, Weymouth. Westfield [GMB 866-69; TAG 72:42-48].

Hart, Isaac: Scratby, Norfolk; 1637 on *John & Dorothy* or *Rose*; Watertown, Reading, Lynn [Hotten 291; MBCR 1:298; WaBOP 37; James M. Hart, *Genealogical History of Samuell Hartt* (n.p. 1903) 237-39; TEG 18:40-46].

Hart, John: Unknown; 1632 on *William & Francis*; passenger list only [GMB 869].

Hart, John: Unknown; 1635 on *James*; Marblehead [GM 2:3:227-30].

Hart, Stephen: Unknown; 1633; Cambridge, Hartford, Farmington [GMB 869-73; Waters 818-20 (clue)].

Hart, Thomas: Unknown; 1635 on *Defence*; passenger list only [GM 2:3:230-31].

Hart, Thomas: Unknown; 1639; Ipswich [ITR 55; James M. Hart, *Genealogical History of Samuell Hartt* (n.p. 1903) 314-15; Hammatt Papers 131-32].

Hart, William: Unknown; 1636; Maine (mention in letter only) [WP 3:277].

Hartwell, William: Unknown; 1640; Concord [CoVR 2; MPR Case #10598; Joy F. Peach, *The Descendants of William Hartwell, Concord Settler, 1636, Through Five Generations* (Foxborough, Massachusetts, 2007) (clue)].

Harvard, John: Southwark, Surrey; 1637; Charlestown [ChChR 9; ChTR 31; MBCR 1:206, 373; Waters 117-34, 180, 187-98, 782-83; NEHGR 62:200-1; Morison 380; Wyman 479].

Harvey, Edmond: Unknown; 1639; Milford, Fairfield [MiTR 2; MiChR 1; FOOF 1:261; McCormick-Hamilton 520-23].

Harvey, Joseph: Colne Engaine, Essex; 1638; died at sea [SPR 1:11, 2:7; NEHGR 2:181].

Harvey, Richard: Ilkeston, Derbyshire; 1635 on *Planter*; Concord, Stratford [GM 2:3:231-33].

Harvey, Thomas: Unknown; 1638; Taunton [PCR 12:38; MD 8:195; Oscar Jewell Harvey, *The Harvey Book* (Wilkes-Barre, Pennsylvania, 1899)].

Harvey, William: Unknown; 1637; Taunton, Boston [NGSQ 71:176; PCR 1:120; MD 13:85; BChR 294; NEHGR 2:189; Waters 645-46 (clue); Snow-Estes 2:299-308; Gen Adv 4:60; Oscar Jewell Harvey, *The Harvey Book* (Wilkes-Barre, Pennsylvania, 1899)].

Harwood, George: Unknown; 1636; Boston, New London [BTR 1:15, 34; BChR 291; NEHGR 2:189; MBCR 1:238; TG 13:178-88].

Harwood, Henry: Unknown; 1630; Charlestown [GMB 873-74; WF 366-68].

Harwood, Henry: Unknown; 1638; Salem [STR 1:75, 92; SChR 10; EQC 1:9; EPR 1:446-49; Essex Ant 10:30; Perley 2:48].

Haseltine, John: Unknown; 1639; Rowley [MBCR 1:376; HvBOP54; RowBOP 4; EQC 2:157-58; EIHC 70:152; NGSQ 68:10-11 (clue); Rowley Fam 144].

Haseltine, Robert: Unknown; 1639; Rowley [MBCR 1:376; RowBOP 4; NGSQ 68:10-11 (clue); Rowley Fam 142; Pillsbury Anc 381-85; Hoyt 975].

Haskell, Roger: Charlton Musgrove, Somerset; 1636; Salem [STR 1:23; EPR 2:87-89; NEHGR 86:257, 138:223-27; TAG 57:77-81; TEG 6:25-33; Sarah Stone Anc 3-4].

Haslewood, John: Unknown; 1638; Massachusetts Bay (court appearance only) [MBCR 1:246].

Hassell, John: Unknown; 1635; Ipswich [GM 2:3:234-35].

Hastings, Thomas: Unknown; 1634 on *Elizabeth*; Watertown [GM 2:3:235-40].

Hatch, Charles: Newton Ferrers, Devon; 1633; Richmond Island [GDMNH 317; Annis Spear Anc 59-60].

Hatch, Phillip: Newton Ferrers, Devon; 1638; Richmond Island, York [Trelawny 140, 182; Annis Spear Anc 59-63].

Hatch, Thomas: Unknown; 1633; Dorchester, Yarmouth, Barnstable [GMB 875-76].

Hatch, Thomas: Tenterden, Kent; 1638; Scituate [PCR 1:108, 116; Joseph Neal Anc 111-16; NEHGR 70:245-60].

Hatch, William: Sandwich, Kent; 1635 on *Hercules*; Scituate [GM 2:3:241-44].

Hathaway, John: Unknown; 1635 on *Blessing*; Massachusetts Bay [GM 2:3:245-46].

Hathaway, Nicholas: Unknown; 1639; Braintree [BTR 1:50; Elizabeth Starr Versailles, *Hathaways of America* (Northampton, Massachusetts, 1970)].

Hathaway, Susan: Unknown; 1635 on *Abigail*; passenger list only [GM 2:3:246].

Hatherly, Timothy: Southwark, Surrey; 1623; Plymouth, Scituate [GMB 876-81; PM 234-40].

Hathorne, William: Bray, Berkshire; 1633; Dorchester, Salem [GMB 881-87].

Hatley, Philip: Unknown; 1639; Milford; returned permanently to England by 1648 [MiTR 2; MiChR 2; Abandoning 132].

Haughton, Henry: Unknown; 1629; Salem [GMB 887; WF 368-69].

Haukes, Samuel: Unknown; 1640; Massachusetts Bay (court appearance only) [MBCR 1:313].

Haukins, John: Unknown; 1630; Boston (church admission only) [GMB 887; WF 369].

Haulton, William: Unknown; 1634 on *Francis*; passenger list only (with caveat) [GM 2:3:246-47]. (Later research has shown that this passenger very likely was William Holton of Hartford [TG 25:3-28].)

Havens, William: Unknown; 1638; Portsmouth [PoTR 2; RICR 1:91; Austin 93-94; TAG 20:185; Wickham-Billard 146].

Haward, Richard: Unknown; 1629; hired by Massachusetts Bay Company but no New England record [GMB 900; WF 369-70].

Hawes, Edmund: London; 1635 on *James*; Duxbury, Yarmouth [GM 2:3:247-50; NEHGR 164:250-53; Raymond Gordon Hawes, *Edmond Hawes and His American Descendants* (Baltimore 2000)].

Hawes, Richard: Great Missenden, Buckinghamshire; 1635 on *Truelove*; Dorchester [GM 2:3:250-53; Raymond Gordon Hawes, *The Richard Hawes Genealogy* (Baltimore 2003)].

Hawkes, Adam: Hingham, Norfolk; 1634; Charlestown, Lynn [GM 2:3:253-57].

Hawkes, John: Unknown; 1634; Dorchester, Windsor, Hadley [GM 2:3:257-61].

Hawkes, Matthew: Cambridge, Cambridgeshire; 1638 on *Diligent*; Hingham [NEHGR 15:27, 121:11; HiBOP 78; SPR Case #1390; Hingham Hist 2:294-95].

Hawkins, Abraham: Unknown; 1639; Charlestown [Lechford 119; ChChR 10; SPR Case #68; Wyman 482].

Hawkins, James: Unknown; 1635; Boston [GM 2:3:261-66].

Hawkins, Job: Unknown; 1635 on *Planter*; Boston, Portsmouth, Newport [GM 2:3:266-70].

Hawkins, Narias: Unknown; 1635; Richmond Island; returned permanently to England in 1640 [GM 2:3:270-72].

Hawkins, Richard: Unknown; 1635 on *Susan & Ellen*; passenger list only [GM 2:3:272-73].

Hawkins, Richard: Unknown; 1637; Massachusetts Bay, Portsmouth [MBCR 1:224, 329, 3:228; PoTR 6; Portsmouth Misc; NEHGR 14:207-11; Austin 94; GM 2:3:264-65; Blake-Glidden 137-40].

Hawkins, Robert: Unknown; 1635; Charlestown, Fairfield [GM 2:3:273-75].

Hawkins, Thomas: Whitechapel, Middlesex; 1636; Charlestown, Dorchester, Boston; died at sea in 1648 [ChTR 22; WP 4:132, 153; DTR 26; Lechford 116, 210; DChR 4; MBCR 1:276, 375; BChR 40; BBOP 8; SPR Case #168; NEHGR 8:140, 33:421-23, 151:192-216; NYGBR 47:112; Abandoning 363].

Hawkins, Thomas: Unknown; 1636; Boston [BTR 1:31, 52; MBCR 1:225; WP 3:439; BChR 40, 288; BBOP 15; Lechford 314; NEHGR 2:190; Blake-Glidden 138; Austin 94].

Hawkins, Timothy: Unknown; 1633; Watertown [GMB 887-90].

Hawkins, William: Unknown; 1640; New Haven; not seen after 1644 [NHCR 1:91, 142, 502; GMN 13:13].

Hawksworth, Thomas: Unknown; 1635 on *Christian*; Salisbury [GM 2:3:275-77; SyTR 4, 7].

Haybell, Elizabeth: Unknown; 1637; Plymouth (servant; court appearance only) [PCR 1:65].

Hayden, James: Unknown; 1635; Charlestown; died at Barbados in 1665 [GM 2:3:277-80; Abandoning 363-64].

Hayden, John: Unknown; 1632; Dorchester, Braintree [GMB 890-93].

Hayden, William: Unknown; 1637; Hartford, Windsor, Killingworth [HaBOP 405-6; MHSC 2:8:139; Grant 45; FOOF 1:267-68].

Hayes, Robert: Unknown; 1635 on *Elizabeth & Ann*; Ipswich [GM 2:3:281].

Haynes *see also* **Haines**

Haynes, John: Essex; 1633; Cambridge, Hartford [GMB 893-97].

Haynes, Thomas: Unknown; 1639; Sudbury (land grant and death record only) [SuTR 3; Sudbury VR].

Haynes, Walter: Sutton Mandeville, Wiltshire; 1638 on *Confidence*; Sudbury [Drake's Founders 57; SuTR 1; SPR NS 1:21; MBCR 1:271, 377; HAHAC 1:90; NEHGR 39:263-64, 65:295-97; TAG 61:65-69; Kempton Anc 1:453-54; Frances Haynes, *Walter Haynes of Sutton Mandeville, Wiltshire, England, and Sudbury, Massachusetts* (Haverhill, Massachusetts, 1929)].

Hayward *see also* **Howard**

Hayward, George: Unknown; 1637; Charlestown, Concord [ChTR 22; MBCR 1:374; CoVR 2; Rodgers 3:22-26; Blake-Glidden 141-42].

Hayward, Henry: Unknown; 1634 on *Francis*; Cambridge, Hartford, Wethersfield [GM 2:3:282-86].

Hayward, James: Stepney, Middlesex; 1635 on *Planter*; Charlestown, Woburn [GM 2:3:286-87].

Hayward, John: Unknown; 1633; Watertown, Dedham, Charlestown [GMB 898-900].

Hayward, John: Unknown; 1637; Plymouth [PCR 1:61, 2:48]. (More than one man of this name resided in early Plymouth Colony; further study required.)

Hayward, Samuel: Unknown; 1635 on *Elizabeth*; passenger list only (with caveat) [GM 2:3:288].

Hayward, Thomas: Unknown; 1632 on *William & Francis*; passenger list only [GMB 900].

Hayward, Thomas: Aylesford, Kent; 1635 on *Hercules*; Cambridge, Duxbury, Bridgewater [GM 2:3:288-94].

Hayward, William: Unknown; 1637; Charlestown (admission as inhabitant only) [ChTR 29]. (See Stevens-Miller 247 and Kempton Anc 3:238.)

Hazard, Thomas: Unknown; 1635; Boston, Newport, Portsmouth [GM 2:3:294-98].

Heald, John: Unknown; 1640; Concord [MBCR 1:379; Rodgers 2:105-6; TAG 10:15 (clue); Hale, House 262-73; GMC26 133; GMC50 199-202].

Heald, Sarah: Unknown; 1640; Springfield [SpVR 19; Hale-House 678]. (She married John Leonard.)

Heard, Arthur: Unknown; 1633; Richmond Island (business transaction only) [Trelawny Papers 40]. (See also Gorges 100.)

Heard, John: Unknown; 1639; Piscataqua [MPCR 1:42; NHPP 10:701, 40:9; GDMNH 322].

Heard, Luke: Unknown; 1639; Newbury, Salisbury, Ipswich [MBCR 1:376; NeTR 37; SyTR 5; EPR 1:81-82; NEHGR 38:81, 143:220; Hoyt 198].

Heard, Thomas: Unknown; 1639; Saco (court appearance only) [MPCR 1:52].

Heard, William: Unknown; 1623 on *Anne*; Plymouth (land grant only) [GMB 900; PM 240].

Hearker, John: Unknown; 1636; Scituate [PCR 1:61, 156, 2:66, 7:36, 12:92, 107].

Hearle, William: Unknown; 1638; Richmond Island [Trelawny 189, 194 (as "William Harell"), 282, 293, 300; GDMNH 323].

Hearne, Matthew: Unknown; 1635 on *Hopewell*; Hingham; returned permanently to England by 1641 [GM 2:3:298-99].

Heath, Isaac: Ware, Hertfordshire; 1635 on *Hopewell*; Roxbury [GM 2:3:299-302; NEHGR 149:173-86].

Heath, William: Nazeing, Essex; 1632 on *Lyon*; Roxbury [GMB 901-4; TAG 82:81-90, 187-95, 273-89].

Heaton, Nathaniel: Alford, Lincolnshire; 1634 on *Griffin*; Boston [GM 2:3:303-5].

Hecknell, John: Unknown; 1638; Braintree (birth of child only) [NEHGR 3:127].

Hedger, Thomas: Unknown; 1638; Boston (appearance in notarial record only) [Lechford 73]. (A Thomas Hedger appeared at Warwick in the mid-1650s.)

Hedges, William: Adstone, Northamptonshire; 1633; Lynn, Sandwich, Yarmouth [GMB 904-8; NEHGR 167:165-79].

Hedsall, Thomas: Unknown; 1635 on *Elizabeth & Ann*; passenger list only (with caveat) [GM 2:3:306].

Heffer, Andrew: Unknown; 1636; Richmond Island, Piscataqua, Spurwink [Trelawny 113, 183, 194; MPCR 1:42; GDMNH 324].

Hefford, Samuel: Unknown; 1640; Ipswich; returned permanently to England soon after 1651 [MBCR 1:311; EQC 1:147, 2:232-33; Ipswich Hist 1:469].

Heford, Nathan: St. Albans, Hertfordshire; 1635 on *Planter*; passenger list only [GM 2:3:306].

Heliere, John: Unknown; 1635; Scituate (land record only) [GM 2:3:306-7].

Helme, Christopher: Long Sutton, Lincolnshire; 1638; Exeter, Warwick [NHPP 1:133; WP 4:179, 185; NEHGR 98:11-25, 127:214-15; Donald Henry Strahle et al., *Some Descendants of Christopher Helme of Rhode Island*, second ed. (Markham, Ontario, 2002)].

Hemingway, Ralph: Unknown; 1633; Roxbury [GMB 908-10; NEHGR 162:15-17].

Hempenstall, Robert: Southwold, Suffolk; 1640; Boston (business transaction only) [Lechford 374].

Hempson, John: Unknown; 1637; Richmond Island [Trelawny 182, 184, 194 (as "John Imson"), 219-21, 289; GDMNH 324].

Hendrick, Daniel: Unknown; 1637; Sable Island, Hampton, Newbury, Haverhill [WP 4:28; GDMNH 55; HmTR 45; HvBOP23; Essex Ant 1:117, 3:140; GMC50 203-4; Charles T. Hendrick, *The Hendrick Genealogy: Daniel Hendrick of Haverhill, Mass., and His Descendants* (Rutland, Vermont, 1923)].

Henfield, Robert: Unknown; 1640; Salem (court appearance only) [EQC 1:26].

Hepburne, George: Stepney, Middlesex; 1635 on *Abigail*; Charlestown [GM 2:3:307-11].

Herbert, John: Northampton, Northamptonshire; 1635 on *Abigail*; Salem, Southold [GM 2:3:311-13].

Herman, Nathaniel: Unknown; 1640; Braintree [NEHGR 3:127; MD 8:85; Lydia Harmon Anc 4].

Herne, ____: Unknown; 1638; Portsmouth [WJ 1:338].

Herrick, Henry: Unknown; 1630; Salem, Beverly [GMB 910-14].

Herrick, William: Unknown; 1638; Boston; not seen after 1640 [BTR 1:37 (as "William Hyricke"); Lechford 227, 273, 286].

Herring, James: Unknown; 1639; Dedham (purchase and grant of land only) [DeTR 1:56, 94, 96, 168].

Hersey, William: Unknown; 1636; Hingham [HiBOP 50; MBCR 1:295, 374; NEHGR 121:10; HiTR 3; SPR Case #208; Hingham Hist 2:298; Stephen E. Hersey, *The Hersey Family: Tracing the Descendants of William Hersey of Hingham, Massachusetts, 1635-1994* (n.p. 1994) (clue)].

Hesseldon, Francis: Unknown; 1630; Boston (church admission only) [GMB 915; WF 370].

Hethersay, Robert: Unknown; 1640; Concord, Charlestown, Exeter, Dover, Hampton, York, Wells, Falmouth [SLR 1:26, 42, 47; EQC 1:58, 88, 149-50; GDMNH 326].

Hett, Thomas: Folkingham, Lincolnshire; 1635; Cambridge, Hingham, Rehoboth, Hull, Malden, Charlestown [GMB 915-18; NEHGR 155:357-58].

Heward, John: Unknown; 1634; Massachusetts Bay [GM 2:3:314].

Hewes, John: Unknown; 1632; Scituate [GMB 918-21; PM 240-43].

Hewes, Joshua: London; 1633; Roxbury, Boston, Wickford [GMB 921-24].

Hewett, Ephraim: Wroxhall, Warwickshire; 1639; Hingham, Windsor [NEHGR 121:11; CCCR 1:46; SLR 1:90; Cotton 266; Grant 79; Manwaring 1:19-20, 60; WP 4:151; SPR 7:120; Windsor Hist 2:415; Morison 383].

Hewett, Humphrey: Unknown; 1636; Plymouth (oath of fidelity only) [PCR 1:48, 8:181].

Hewett, Nicholas: Unknown; 1639; Dorchester, Boston [Lechford 116; NEHGR 8:38].

Hewlett, Lewis: Unknown; 1636; Charlestown, Salisbury [ChTR 23; MBCR 1:284; SyTR 10; Lechford 364].

Hewlett, Matthew: Unknown; 1634 on *Hercules*; passenger list only (but probably did not sail) [GM 2:3:314].

Hewlett, Mr.: Unknown; 1636; Lynn (business transaction only) [STR 1:28]. (Possibly the same as Lewis Hewlett above.)

Heylei, Richard: Unknown; 1635 on *Christian*; passenger list only [GM 2:3:315].

Heyman, Penticost: Unknown; 1638; Richmond Island [Trelawny 188, 194, 283, 294, 301].

Hibbard, Robert: Unknown; 1640; Salem, Beverly [EQC 6:247, 9:296-98; NEHGR 51:316-17; Farr Anc 165-67; Augustine George Hibbard, *Genealogy of the Hibbard Family Who Are Descendants Of Robert Hibbard of Salem, Massachusetts* (Woodstock, Connecticut, 1901)].

Hibbens, William: Unknown; 1634 on *Mary & John*; passenger list only (with caveat) [GM 2:3:315-17].

Hibbins, William: Unknown; 1638; Boston [BTR 1:41; BChR 26; Lechford 93; WJ 1:385; WP 4:113, 128; NEHGR 6:287-88, 48:74; GM 2:3:315-17; Legal Executions 28-29; Abandoning 364].

Hickbourne, Davy: Unknown; 1640; Massachusetts Bay (court appearance only) [MBCR 1:318]. (Possibly the David Hitchborne who appeared at Boston by 1650 [BTR 1:100; NEHGR 9:254].)

Hickford, John: London; 1636; Saco; returned permanently to England after 1640 [MPCR 1:5, 43, 47-48, 57; WP 4:123; Trelawny 194; Gorges 102; Two Voyages 21-22; GDMNH 326].

Hickoks, Mr.: Unknown; 1640; New Haven [NHCR 1:57, 91, 502; GMN 13:12-13]. (He probably never came to New England.)

Hicks, John: Unknown; 1639; Weymouth, Newport, Newtown [NY], Hempstead [RICR 1:92, 108, 110; TAG 21:191-200, 39:2; Weymouth Hist 1:196, 3:266-67; NYGBR 70:116; *Rhode Island History* 11:84-92].

Hicks, Robert: London; 1621 on *Fortune*; Plymouth [GMB 924-28; PM 243-48].

Hide, John: Marlborough, Wiltshire; 1635 on *James*; passenger list only [GM 2:3:317].

Higdon, Peter: Unknown; 1635 on *James*; Newbury [GM 2:3:317].

Higgins, Alexander: Unknown; 1636; Plymouth, Salem (not seen after 1637) [PCR 1:48, 8:181, 12:24; STR 1:59, 102].

Higgins, Richard: Unknown; 1632; Plymouth, Eastham, Piscataway [NJ] [GMB 929-32; PM 249-53].

Higgins, Thomas: Unknown; 1633; Plymouth (court appearance only) [GMB 932; PM 253-54].

Higginson, Francis: Claybrook, Leicestershire; 1629 on *Talbot*; Salem [GMB 933-37; WF 370-75].

Hill, Abraham: Unknown; 1636; Charlestown, Malden [ChTR 21; ChChR 9, 49; ChBOP 57; MBCR 1:376; NEHGR 4:267; Rodgers 2:603-5; Wyman 499-502].

Hill, Bartholomew: Unknown; 1630; Dorchester (court appearance only) [GMB 937].

Hill, Elizabeth: Unknown; 1638; Boston (church admission only) [BChR 24].

Hill, John: Unknown; 1631; Plymouth (single mention in letter, with caveat) [GMB 937; PM 254].

Hill, John: Unknown; 1639; Boston [Lechford 159; MBCR 1:301].

Hill, John: Unknown; 1633; Dorchester [DTR 5 (as "John Iles"); NEHGR 5:243, 58:157-59; DChR 4, 150; J. Gardner Bartlett, *John Hill of Dorchester, Mass., 1633* (Boston 1904)].

Hill, John: Unknown; 1640; Charlestown; probably returned to England in late 1640 [WP 4:255, 293; see also Lechford 327].

Hill, Peter: Unknown; 1633; Richmond Island, Saco [GMB 2080-81].

Hill, Prudence: Unknown; 1638; Plymouth [PCR 1:110]. (She married William Sherman.)

Hill, Ralph: Unknown; 1638; Plymouth [PCR 1:93, 107; NGSQ 72:3-32, 77:141].

Hill, Robert: Unknown; 1635 on *Defence*; passenger list only (with caveat) [GM 2:3:318].

Hill, Robert: Unknown; 1638; New Haven [NHCR 1:13, 50, 93; FANH 741; NEHGR 56:133].

Hill, Thomas: Unknown; 1637; Plymouth (not seen after 1640) [PCR 1:53, 57, 60, 61, 76, 90, 155, 7:12, 8:174, 12:68; PTR 1:4].

Hill, Tobias: Unknown; 1639; Massachusetts Bay (court appearance only) [EQC 1:17-18].

Hill, Valentine: London; 1635; Boston, Dover [GM 2:3:318-28; Jean A. Sargent, *Valentine Hill: Sparkplug of Early New England* (Laurel, Maryland, 1981)].

Hill, William: Exeter, Devon; 1633; Dorchester, Windsor, Fairfield [GMB 937-41; NEHGR 39:78-79, 52:83].

Hill, William: Unknown; 1635 on *James*; passenger list only [GM 2:3:329].

Hilliard, Anthony: Unknown; 1639; Hingham (land grant only) [HiBOP 75v; Hingham Hist 331-32].

Hilliard, William: Unknown; 1635 on *Elizabeth & Ann*; Plymouth, Duxbury [GM 2:3:329-31; MD 49:95-98; GMN 12:29-30].

Hillier *see also* **Tilley**

Hillier, John: Unknown; 1636; Windsor [Grant 61; WiLR 1:54; Manwaring 1:127; TAG 17:27-30].

Hillman, Eleanor: Unknown; 1635 on *Abigail*; passenger list only [GM 2:3:331].

Hills, Joseph: Maldon, Essex; 1638; Charlestown, Malden [ChBOP 4; ChChR 10, 48; NEHGR 4:267, 120:74; Lechford 137; Kempton Anc 4:394-419].

Hills, Thomas: Unknown; 1633; Roxbury [GMB 941].

Hills, William: Unknown; 1632 on *William & Francis*; Roxbury, Hartford [GMB 941-46].

Hilton, Edward: London; 1628; Dover, Exeter [GMB 947-51].

Hilton, William: London; 1621 on *Fortune*; Plymouth, Dover, Kittery, York [GMB 951-57; PM 254-61].

Hinckley, Samuel: Tenterden, Kent; 1635 on *Hercules*; Scituate, Barnstable [GM 2:3:331-35].

Hindersam, Margaret: Unknown; 1639; Massachusetts Bay (court appearance only) [MBCR 1:284].

Hindes, James: Unknown; 1637; Salem, Southold [SChR 7, 17; STR 1:51, 60, 102; EPR 1:24; EQC 1:9; MBCR 1:374; NEHGR 37:161-62; Albert Henry Hinds, *History and Genealogy of the Hinds Family* (Portland, Maine, 1899)].

Hindes, Margery: Unknown; 1633; Boston (church admission only) [GMB 957].

Hinds, Elizabeth: Unknown; 1633; Roxbury [GMB 958]. (She married Alexander Beck.)

Hines, Ann: Unknown; 1638; Plymouth [PCR 1:107]. (She married William Hoskins.)

Hingston, Philip: Holbeton, Devon; 1638; Richmond Island [Trelawny 193, 296; Aspinwall 23; YLR 1:123; GDMNH 338].

Hingston, William: Unknown; 1638; Richmond Island [Trelawny 147; GDMNH 339].

Hinsdale, Robert: Pulham St. Mary the Virgin, Norfolk; 1637; Dedham, Medfield, Hadley, Deerfield [DeTR 1:32; DeVR 1; DeChR 6; MBCR 1:331, 375; TAG 68:159; Herbert Cornelius Andrews, *Hinsdale Genealogy: Descendants of Robert Hinsdale of Dedham, Medfield, Hadley and Deerfield* (Lombard, Illinois, 1906)].

Hitchcock, Matthew: Unknown; 1635 on *Susan & Ellen*; Watertown, Cambridge, New Haven [GM 2:3:336-38].

Hitchcock, Richard: Unknown; 1634; Massachusetts Bay, Saco [GM 2:3:339-42].

Hitchen, Edward: Unknown; 1634; Boston (church admission and freemanship admission only) [GM 2:3:342].

Hoadley, John: Unknown; 1639; Guilford; returned permanently to England in 1653 [Guilford Hist 25; NEHGR 53:208; Abandoning 135-36; Francis Bacon Trowbridge, *The Hoadley Genealogy: A History of the Descendants of William Hoadley of Branford, Connecticut* (New Haven 1894) 205-6].

Hoames, Margaret: Unknown; 1630; Boston (church admission only) [GMB 958; WF 376].

Hoar, Hezekiah: Sidmouth, Devon; 1634 on *Recovery*; Taunton [GM 2:3:342-46].

Hobart, Edmund: Hingham, Norfolk; 1633; Charlestown, Hingham [GMB 958-60].

Hobby, John: Unknown; 1637; Dorchester [WJ 1:288 (as "John Hoddy"), 2:425; MBCR 1:202].

Hobell, John: Unknown; 1640; Springfield (court appearance and death record only) [Pynchon 209; SpVR 60].

Hoble, John: Unknown; 1635 on *Marygould*; passenger list only [GM 2:3:346].

Hoble, Widow: Unknown; 1640; Plymouth (court appearance only) [PCR 2:12].

Hobson, Henry: Unknown; 1640; Braintree (two apprenticeship records only) [WP 4:299; RCA 2:122].

Hocke, William: Unknown; 1637 on *Elizabeth*; passenger list only [NGSQ 71:177]. (Possibly William Hooke of Taunton.)

Hocking, John: Unknown; 1632; Kennebec [GMB 960-62; PM 261-62].

Hodges, Andrew: Unknown; 1639; Ipswich [ITR 56; MBCR 1:379; EPR 1:24-26; TAG 20:236-37; Almon D. Hodges Jr., *Genealogical Record of the Hodges Family of New England* (Boston 1896) 19-20].

Hodges, John: Wapping, Middlesex; 1633; Charlestown [GMB 962-64; Lechford 349].

Hodges, John: Unknown; 1639; Salisbury; returned permanently to England by 1647 [SyTR 6; Hoyt 203].

Hodgkins *see* **Hoskins**

Hodsdon *see also* **Hutchen**

Hodsdon, Nicholas: Unknown; 1637; Hingham, Kittery [HiBOP 89; NEHGR 121:12; MBCR 1:372 (as "Nicolas Hudson"); GDMNH 343; GM 2:7:476; Andrew Jackson Hodgdon, *Genealogy of the Descendants of Nicholas Hodsdon-Hodgdon* (Haverhill, Massachusetts, 1904)].

Hogg, Peter: Unknown; 1635; Saco (servant; court appearance only) [GM 2:3:347].

Hogg, Richard: Unknown; 1636; Boston [NEHGR 2:190; BChR 24, 55, 56, 57, 284, 288, 294, 304; WP 4:286; MBCR 1:377; BTR 1:45; BBOP 36, 81-82; Almon D. Hodges Jr., *Genealogical Record of the Hodges Family of New England* (Boston 1896) 18].

Holbeck, Grace: Unknown; 1635; Boston (church admission only) [GM 2:3:347-48].

Holbeck, William: Unknown; 1620 on *Mayflower*; Plymouth [GMB 964; PM 262-63].

Holbidge, Arthur: Unknown; 1635; Boston, New Haven [GM 2:3:348-50].

Holbrook, Thomas: Broadway, Somerset; 1635 on *Marygould*; Weymouth [GM 2:3:350-55; M&JCH 25:38, 26:41-42, 27:33-34].

Holcombe, Thomas: Unknown; 1633; Dorchester, Windsor [GMB 964-67].

Holden, Justinian: Lindsey, Suffolk; 1634 on *Francis*; Watertown, Cambridge [GM 2:3:355-62].

Holden, Randall: Unknown; 1638; Portsmouth, Warwick [RICR 1:47, 52, 100, 131; PoTR 16; MHSC 3:1:5-15; NEHGR 129:78-79; Austin 100-1; Eben Putnam, *The Holden Genealogy*, 2 volumes [Boston 1923, 1926] 1:379-89 (clue)].

Holden, Richard: Lindsey, Suffolk; 1634 on *Francis*; Watertown, Woburn, Groton [GM 2:3:363-68].

Holder, Thomas: Unknown; 1640; Rhode Island (mention in letter only) [Cotton Corr 346].

Holdred, William: London; 1635 on *Elizabeth*; Ipswich, Salisbury, Haverhill, Exeter [GM 2:3:368-72].

Hole, John: Unknown; 1638; Richmond Island [Trelawny 182; GDMNH 344].

Holgrave, John: Unknown; 1633; Salem, Maine [GMB 967-70].

Holland, John: Plymouth, Devon; 1634; Dorchester [GM 2:3:373-77, 380].

Holland, Thomas: Unknown; 1640; Barnstable (birth record of son only) [NEHGR 9:282].

Hollard, Angel: Beaminster, Dorset; 1635 on *Marygould*; Weymouth, Boston [GM 2:3:377-80; Abandoning 137].

Hollidge, Richard: Unknown; 1638; Boston [BChR 23, 24; BTR 1:38, 88, 95; MBCR 1:376; BBOP 39, 80; SLR 12:1; Gleaner 26-28; SPR Case #1240].

Holliman, Ezekiel: Tring, Hertfordshire; 1636; Dedham [DeTR 1:21; WJ 1:353, 2:423; Perley 1:271; MBCR 1:221; PoTR 14; STR 1:104;

PrTR 1:4; Waters 798-99; NEHGR 12:305-6; TAG 30:125, 53:28-30; Austin 102; Perley 1:269-72].

Hollingsworth, Richard: Southwold, Suffolk; 1635 on *Blessing*; Salem [GM 2:3:380-84; TAG 78:241-44].

Holloway *see also* **Halloway**

Holloway, John: Unknown; 1635 on *Elizabeth & Ann*; Hartford [GM 2:3:384-87].

Holloway, Joseph: Unknown; 1639; Sandwich [PCR 1:147, 2:15, 8:6, 184, 192; Lechford 321, 372-73; SLR 1:16; PCPR 1:71; MD 8:207-9; Everett Hall Pendleton, *William Holloway of Taunton, Mass., in 1637* (n.p. 1949) 8].

Holloway, Thomas: Unknown; 1637; Plymouth; not seen after 1638 [PCR 1:61, 93; WP 4:1; MBCR 1:234, 245; Everett Hall Pendleton, *William Holloway of Taunton, Mass., in 1637* (n.p. 1949) 8].

Holloway, William: Unknown; 1637; Duxbury, Marshfield [PCR 1:75, 80, 8:196; PCPR 1:120; Granberry 300-1; Everett Hall Pendleton, *William Holloway of Taunton, Mass., in 1637* (n.p. 1949) 8].

Holloway, William: Unknown; 1639; Taunton, Dorchester, Boston [PCR 1:132; Lechford 306, 318; NEHGR 9:251; SLR 1:133, 139; DChR 37, 160; Gen Mag 4:43; SPR Case #375; SPR 6:333, 9:4; Everett Hall Pendleton, *William Holloway of Taunton, Mass., in 1637* (n.p. 1949)].

Holly, Elizabeth: Unknown; 1635 on *Blessing*; passenger list only (with caveat) [GM 2:3:387].

Holly, Joseph: Unknown; 1634; Dorchester [GM 2:3:388].

Holly, Samuel: Unknown; 1636; Cambridge [MBCR 1:179; CaBOP 69; SPR 1:30, 2:19; SPR Case #26; CaBOP 119; Gillespie Anc 224-26].

Holman, Arthur: Unknown; 1635 on *Unity*; passenger list only [GM 2:3:388].

Holman, Edward: Unknown; 1623 on *Anne*; Plymouth [GMB 970-72; PM 263-65].

Holman, John: Swyre, Dorset; 1630 on *Mary & John*; Dorchester [GMB 973-76].

Holman, William: Northampton, Northamptonshire; 1635 on *Defence*; Cambridge [GM 2:3:389-91].

Holmar, Edward: Unknown; 1632 on *Lyon*; passenger list only [Hotten 150].

Holmes, Deborah: Unknown; 1636; Salem; not seen after 1637 [SChR 7; Fiske Notebook 243 (as "Deborah Holden"); STR 1:32].

Holmes, George: Nazeing, Essex; 1638; Roxbury [RChR 83; MBCR 1:376; NEHGR 6:183, 7:30-31, 58:21-22; TG 23:132-33; George Arthur Gray, *The Descendants of George Holmes of Roxbury, 1594-1908* (Boston 1908)].

Holmes, John: Unknown; 1632; Plymouth [GMB 977-78; PM 265-67; NGSQ 77:143-44].

Holmes, Obadiah: Stockport, Lancashire; 1638; Salem, Rehoboth, Newport [STR 1:80; SChR 8; EQC 1:25; ReTR 1:2; NEHGR 64:237-39, 67:21-23; Austin 103-4; Stillwell 3:301-7; Brady Anc 227-36; J. T. Holmes, *The American Family of Rev. Obadiah Holmes* (Columbus, Ohio, 1915)].

Holmes, Robert: Newcastle-upon-Tyne, Northumberland; 1638; Cambridge [NEHGR 4:181; BChR 28; CaBOP 62; Shepard 76, 142-43; MBCR 1:378; Rodgers 2:151-54].

Holmes, William: Unknown; 1632; Plymouth, Duxbury, Boston [GMB 979-81; PM 267-70].

Holmes, William: Sandwich, Kent; 1635 on *Hercules*; Scituate Marshfield [GM 2:3:392-97; NEHGR 145:374].

Holt, Mary: Unknown; 1638; Connecticut (servant; court appearance only) [CCCR 1:28, 29].

Holt, Nicholas: Romsey, Hampshire; 1635 on *James*; Newbury, Andover [GM 2:3:397-401].

Holton, William: Nayland, Suffolk; 1634 on *Francis*; Cambridge, Hartford, Northampton [Hotten 279; HaTR 23; NEHGR 159:25-34; TG 25:3-28].

Holyoke, Edward: Tanworth, Warwickshire; 1638; Lynn [MBCR 1:254, 375; EQC 2:270; NHPP 40:4; WP 4:104; Waters 149-50; SPR Case #242; NEHGR 40:41, 147:11-34, 164-73; Hale, House 641-46; Pillsbury Anc 287-91; NGSQ 69:11-12; NEQ 71:290-97].

Homes, Thomas: Norwich, Norfolk; 1637 on *John & Dorothy* or *Rose*; passenger list only (servant) [Hotten 290].

Hompste, Edmund: Unknown; 1639; Cambridge (land grant only) [CaTR 40]. (This is probably a garbled version of some other surname.)

Honywell, William: Unknown; 1633; Plymouth [GMB 981-82; PM 270-71].

Hood, John: Halstead, Essex; 1638; Cambridge [Lechford 10; EIHC 45:49-50; Essex Ant 2:14; Chase-Wigglesworth 249-54; Snow-Estes 2:63-66].

Hood, Mary: Halstead, Essex; 1634; Boston [GM 2:3:401-2; Gilberts of NE 433 (citing SJC Case #2335)].

Hooke, John: Leiden, Holland; 1620 on *Mayflower*; Plymouth [GMB 98; PM 271; TAG 80:100-1].

Hooke, John: Sandwich, Kent; 1637; Salem [NEHGR 75:223; WJ 1:384; MBCR 1:269, 283, 286].

Hooke, William: Bristol; 1634; York, Salisbury; returned permanently to England in 1650 [GM 2:3:403-10; Abandoning 140-41].

Hooke, William: Axmouth, Devon; 1639; Taunton, New Haven; returned permanently to England in 1656 [PCR 1:143; NEHGR 50:67-68; FANH 791; WP 6:408-9; Morison 381-82; Abandoning 137-40]. (He was possibly the "William Hocke" who came from England on the *Elizabeth* in 1637 [NGSQ 71:177].)

Hooker, Thomas: Rotterdam; 1633 on *Griffin*; Cambridge, Hartford [GMB 982-85; TAG 65:13-16, 75:225-28, 76:216; NEQ 66:67-109; Abandoning 141-42].

Hooper, Abraham: Unknown; 1637; Plymouth (two court appearance only) [PCR 1:68, 75].

Hooper, William: Unknown; 1635 on *James*; passenger list only (with caveat) [GM 2:3:410].

Hopcott, Sarah: Unknown; 1640; Salem (church admission only) [SChR 10]. (She is said to have married Thomas Macy [TAG 26:108, 30:157-58].)

Hopkins, Edward: London; 1637; New Haven, Hartford; returned permanently to England in 1652 [WJ 1:272; NHCR 1:24; HaBOP 5; Waters 61-65; Rodney Horace Yale, *Yale Genealogy* (Beatrice, Nebraska, 1908), 99-100; Abandoning 142-44].

Hopkins, John: Unknown; 1634; Cambridge, Hartford [GM 2:3:411-13].

Hopkins, Mr.: Unknown; 1633; Cambridge (land grant only) [GMB 985].

Hopkins, Richard: Unknown; 1632; Massachusetts Bay (court appearance only) [GMB 986].

Hopkins, Stephen: London; 1620 on *Mayflower*; Plymouth [GMB 986-89; PM 271-75; TAG 79:241-49; MD 61:38-59, 134-54].

Hopkins, Thomas: Ilchester, Somerset; 1640; Providence, Oyster Bay [PrTR 15:5; M&JCH 27:34; Austin 324-27; RIHSC 17:47].

Hopkins, William: Unknown; 1640; Stratford [CCCR 1:53, 71; Emerson-Benson 300].

Hopkinson, Michael: Unknown; 1638; Boston, Rowley [BChR 23; MBCR 1:376; RowBOP 2; EPR 1:253-54, 390; Parker-Ruggles 310-18; Rowley Fam 161-64; Laura Huffman et al., *Hopkinson and Allied Families* (n.p. 1965)].

Hore, Richard: Unknown; 1640; Yarmouth [PCR 2:16, 23, 8:176, 185, 194, 200; MD 15:64].

Horne, George: Unknown; 1638; Boston (court appearance only) [MBCR 1:234; see also MBCR 1:296].

Horne, John: Unknown; 1630; Salem [GMB 990-94].

Horrockes, Lydia: Unknown; 1638; Dorchester (church admission only) [DChR 3].

Horton, Barnabas: Unknown; 1638; Hampton, Ipswich, Southold [HmTR 45; EPR 1:25; ITR 74; Suffolk Sessions 100-3; NEHGR 55:302; NYGBR 102:69-77].

Horton, Thomas: Unknown; 1638; Springfield [SpTR 161, 162, 167; Pynchon 204-6, 208, 210-11; NEHGR 33:310-11; Hale, House 537-38].

Horton, Walter: Unknown; 1637; Plymouth (court appearance only) [PCR 1:88].

Horwood, James: Unknown; 1635 on *Christian*; passenger list only [GM 2:3:414].

Hosford, William: Beaminster, Dorset; 1633; Dorchester, Windsor, Springfield; returned permanently to England in 1654 [GMB 994-97; TAG 37:197-203; Abandoning 144-45].

Hosier, Samuel: Unknown; 1630; Watertown [GMB 997-99; WF 376-79].

Hoskin, John: Unknown; 1634; Richmond Island (business transaction only) [Trelawny Papers 41].

Hoskins, John: Unknown; 1630; Dorchester, Windsor [GMB 999-1002; NEHGR 146:297-98].

Hoskins, William: Ireland; 1634; Plymouth, Taunton [GM 2:3:414-20].

Hosmer, James: Hawkhurst, Kent; 1635 on *Elizabeth*; Cambridge, Concord [GM 2:3:421-23].

Hosmer, Thomas: Hawkhurst, Kent; 1633; Cambridge, Hartford, Farmington [GMB 1002-5].

Houchin, Jeremiah: Pulham St. Mary the Virgin, Norfolk; 1639; Dorchester, Boston [DChR 5; NEHGR 2:190; BChR 40, 292; MBCR 1:377; SPR Case #326, #541; SPR 13:32; HAHAC 1:115; TAG 67:54; Coltman Anc 110-11].

Hough, Atherton: Boston, Lincolnshire; 1633; Charlestown, Boston, Cambridge [GMB 1005-10].

Houghton, John: Eaton Bray, Bedfordshire; 1635 on *Abigail*; passenger list only (with caveat) [GM 2:3:423-24].

Houghton, William: Unknown; 1635 on *Increase*; passenger list only (with caveat) [GM 2:3:424].

Houlder, Nathaniel: Unknown; 1638; Dorchester (church admission only) [DChR 3].

Houlton, Robert: Unknown; 1633; Boston [GMB 1010-11].

House, Samuel: London; 1634; Scituate, Cambridge, Barnstable [GM 2:3:424-28].

Housegoe, John: Unknown; 1639; Guilford (signed founding covenant only) [Guilford Hist 25, 47].

Hovey, Daniel: Waltham Abbey, Essex; 1636; Ipswich [ITR 19, 25; EPR 1:28; EQC 9:101-3, 120-22; NEHGR 36:195, 67:342-43; Glover Gen 57-58; Daniel Hovey Association, *The Hovey Book* (Haverhill, Massachusetts, 1913)].

Howard *see also* **Hayward**

Howard, Elizabeth: Unknown; 1634; Roxbury (servant; church admission only) [GM 2:3:428].

Howard, Robert: Unknown; 1639; Dorchester, Boston [DChR 5, 7, 10, 17, 152, 162; BChR 61; NEHGR 33:236-37; SPR Case #1326; SPR 6:421].

Howard, Samuel: Unknown; 1637; Boston (land grant only) [BTR 1:32].

Howard, William: Unknown; 1639; Hampton, Topsfield, Boston [GDMNH 55, 351; HmTR 43; MBCR 1:291, 377].

Howard, William: Unknown; 1639; Salem [SChR 9, 19; EPR 1:20].

Howe, Abraham: Unknown; 1637; Roxbury [RChR 82; MBCR 1:374; NEHGR 6:183; SPR Case #844; Daniel Wait Howe, *Howe Genealogies*, volume two (Boston 1929) 1-7].

Howe, Anthony: Unknown; 1637; Saco (court appearance only) [MPCR 1:8].

Howe, Daniel: Unknown; 1633; Lynn, Southampton, New Haven, Easthampton; returned permanently to England by 1653 [GMB 1011-13].

Howe, Edward: Boxted, Essex; 1633; Watertown [GMB 1013-16; Kempton Anc 1:336-42].

Howe, Edward: Unknown; 1635 on *Truelove*; Lynn [GM 2:3:428-31].

Howe, James: Bishops Stortford, Hertfordshire; 1635; Roxbury, Ipswich [GM 2:3:431-35].

Howe, John: Unknown; 1639; Sudbury, Marlborough [MBCR 1:377; SuTR 4; Kempton Anc 3:256-69].

Howell, Edward: Marsh Gibbon, Buckinghamshire; 1638; Lynn, Southampton [EQC 1:14, 2:270; Lechford 322, 323; MBCR 1:375; WP 4:104; SoTR 11; TAG 55:178-81; NYGBR 106:217-20, 118:210-11; Goodwin-Morgan 2:333-43; TG 5:3-63, 157; SCHSR 4:21-27; David Faris, *Descendants of Edward Howell (1584-1655)* (Baltimore 1985)].

Howell, Morgan: Unknown; 1636; Saco, Cape Porpus [MPCR 1:5; GDMNH 352].

Howen, Robert: Unknown; 1639; Boston [WP 4:197; BChR 34, 36, 287, 290; NEHGR 2:190; BTR 1:54, 69, 83, 84, 108; BBOP 4, 112-13; SPR Case #133].

Howes, Thomas: Unknown; 1638; Yarmouth [EQC 1:9; PCR 1:107, 132, 7:20; Lechford 50; MD 6:157-65; NEHGR 67:261; Bassett-Preston 150-53; CCL #31].

Howland, Arthur: Fenstanton, Huntingdonshire; 1640; Duxbury, Marshfield [Lechford 297-99; NEHGR 104:221-25; Annis Spear Anc 103-7; NGSQ 71:84-93].

Howland, Henry: Fenstanton, Huntingdonshire; 1632; Plymouth [GMB 1016-19; PM 275-79].

Howland, John: Fenstanton, Huntingdonshire; 1620 on *Mayflower*; Plymouth [GMB 1020-24; PM 279-84; MF 23].

Howlett, Thomas: Unknown; 1630; Boston, Ipswich [GMB 1024-28; WF 379-85].

Howson, Peter: London; 1635; passenger list only [GM 2:3:435-36].

Hoyt, John: Unknown; 1639; Salisbury, Amesbury [SyTR 7; Lydia Harmon Anc 57-65; Pillsbury Anc 579-83].

Hoyt, Simon: West Hatch, Somerset; 1629; Charlestown, Dorchester, Scituate, Windsor, Fairfield, Stamford [GMB 1028-32; M&JCH 25:38-43, 27:34-35].

Hubbard, Ann: Unknown; 1638; Dedham [DeVR 126]. (She married William Barstow.)

Hubbard, Benjamin: Unknown; 1633; Charlestown; returned permanently to England in 1644 [GMB 1032-35; Abandoning 147].

Hubbard, George: Unknown; 1635; Wethersfield, Milford, Guilford [CCCR 1:2, 452; WetLR 1:161; MiTR 2; Ackley-Bosworth 58-60; TAG 10:17-18, 11:47-49, 29:127-28].

Hubbard, George: Unknown; 1639; Hartford, Middletown [HaBOP 264; Manwaring 1:160-61, 247-48, 325-26; TAG 22:161; Stevens-Miller 1:331-34].

Hubbard, James: Langham, Rutland; 1637; Charlestown, Lynn, Gravesend [ChTR 31; ChBOP 25; MBCR 1:311; EQC 1:28, 45, 48, 52-54; SLR 1:46; Kings County Settlers 148; Edward Warren Day, *One Thousand Years of Hubbard History, 866 to 1895* (New York 1895) 63-64].

Hubbard, James: Unknown; 1638; Watertown [WaVR 1:6; MBCR 1:346; CaChR 17; Bond 795; Pillsbury Anc 481].

Hubbard, Joseph: Unknown; 1637; Newbury (land grant only) [NeTR 8].

Hubbard, Mary: Unknown; 1635 on *Hopewell*; passenger list only [GM 2:3:436].

Hubbard, Samuel: Mendlesham, Suffolk; 1633; Salem, Watertown, Windsor, Wethersfield, Springfield, Newport [MBCR 1:370; Pynchon Court 204; SpTR 166; SpVR 9; NEHGR 70:183; Austin 106-7; *Magazine of New England History* 1:172-79, 193-201, 2:59-65, 170-76, 243-46].

Hubbard, William: Unknown; 1635 on *Elizabeth* or *Elizabeth & Ann*; passenger list only [GM 2:3:436-37].

Hubbard, William: Essex; 1635 on *Defence*; Ipswich, Boston [GM 2:3:437-43; Douglas Richardson, *Magna Carta Ancestry: A Study in Colonial and Medieval Families*, second edition, four volumes (Salt Lake City, Utah, 2011) 2:507-8].

Hubbard, William: Unknown; 1640; Windsor (business transaction only) [Lechford 342].

Hucker, Joan: Unknown; 1638; Taunton (marriage record only) [PCR 1:120]. (She married William Harvey.)

Huckins, Robert: Unknown; 1640; Dover [NHPP 1:128, 10:701, 40:11; GDMNH 354-55; NEHGR 33:96, 67:81-82].

Hudson, John: Hull, Yorkshire; 1635 on *Susan & Ellen*; Boston [GM 2:3:443-44].

Hudson, John: Unknown; 1640; Lynn [EQC 1:24; WJ 2:54-58].

Hudson, Ralph: Hull, Yorkshire; 1635 on *Susan & Ellen*; Cambridge, Boston [GM 2:3:445-48].

Hudson, Thomas: Unknown; 1638; Lynn [EQC 1:74, 77, 2:270; SLR 1:67]. (See also Parker-Ruggles 459; NEHGR 55:135.)

Hudson, William: Unknown; 1630; Charlestown, Boston; returned permanently to England by 1656 [GMB 1035-37; WF 385-88; Abandoning 148].

Huestis, Robert: Bridport, Dorset; 1635 on *Marygould*; Boston, Stamford, Greenwich [GM 2:3:448-50; TAG 73:201-6].

Huet, William: Unknown; 1637; Massachusetts Bay (court appearance only) [MBCR 1:218].

Huggins, John: Unknown; 1636; Dedham, Hampton [DeTR 1:20; HampVR 1:4; HmTR 44; EQC 2:230; GDMNH 55, 355-56; NHPP 31:118-19, 234-35; Essex Ant 6:84; EIHC 49:29].

Huitt, Robert: Unknown; 1632; Massachusetts Bay (court appearance only) [GMB 1037].

Hulbird, William: Unknown; 1630; Dorchester, Windsor, Hartford, Northampton [GMB 1038-40].

Hull, Andrew: Unknown; 1635 on *Hopewell*; New Haven [GM 2:3:451-52].

Hull, Edmund: Unknown; 1640; Boston (business transaction only) [Lechford 268].

Hull, George: Crewkerne, Somerset; 1632; Dorchester, Windsor, Fairfield [GMB 1040-43; Evans Festschrift 44-51; Robert E. Hull, *The Ancestors and Descendants of George Hull (ca 1590-1659)* (Baltimore 1994)].

Hull, John: Unknown; 1632, Dorchester [GMB 1043-44].

Hull, Joseph: Broadway, Somerset; 1635 on *Marygould*; Weymouth, Hingham, Barnstable, Yarmouth, York, Oyster River, Isles of Shoals

[GM 2:3:452-60; TAG 68:149; Evans Festschrift 44-51; Abandoning 148-49].

Hull, Richard: Unknown; 1633; Massachusetts Bay (admission to freemanship only) [GMB 1044].

Hull, Richard: Unknown; 1637; Boston (land transaction only) [BTR 1:19].

Hull, Richard: Unknown; 1639; New Haven [NHCR 1:20, 91; Pynchon Court 211; NEHGR 81:126; FANH 872-74; Charles H. Weygant, *The Hull Family in America* (Pittsfield, Massachusetts, 1913) 463-65].

Hull, Robert: Market Harborough, Leicestershire; 1635 on *George*; Boston [GM 2:3:460-62].

Hulling, ____: Unknown; 1638; Massachusetts Bay (admission to freemanship only) [MBCR 1:375].

Humfrey, John: Dorchester, Dorset; 1634; Lynn; returned permanently to England by 1641 [GM 2:3:462-68; Abandoning 150-54].

Humfrey, Jonas: Wendover, Buckinghamshire; 1637; Dedham, Dorchester [DeTR 1:42; DTR 24, 30; DChR 4; NEHGR 5:243, 18:328-30; MBCR 1:377; TAG 68:14-22].

Hunn, George: Unknown; 1635; Boston [GM 2:3:468-69].

Hunt, Bartholomew: Unknown; 1640; Dover [NHPP 1:128, 10:701]. (No obvious connection with the Bartholomew Hunt who appeared some years later at Newport.)

Hunt, Edmond: Unknown; 1634; Cambridge, Duxbury [GM 2:3:469-72].

Hunt, Enoch: Lee, Buckinghamshire; 1639; Newport, Weymouth [RICR 1:92; MBCR 1:317; Lechford 430 (as "Enoch Lunt"); Aspinwall 50 (son Ephraim Hunt); NEHGR 8:357; Weymouth Hist 3:312; GMN 23:4; Chase-Wigglesworth 255-56].

Hunt, Mary: Unknown; 1640; Salem (church admission only) [SChR 10].

Hunt, Robert: Unknown; 1637; Charlestown, Sudbury [ChTR 35; SuTR 3; SPR NS 1:18, 2:18; SPR Case #20, #23; Wyman 528; NEHGR 56:182].

Hunt, William: Unknown; 1640; Concord, Marlborough [CoVR 2; MBCR 1:379; SPR 1:31; TAG 30:100-3, 175; Hoyt 211; Smith-Hale 135-38].

Hunter, Christian: Southwold, Suffolk; 1635 on *Blessing*; Salem [GM 2:3:472-73; TAG 78:241-44]. (She married Richard More.)

Hunter, Elizabeth: Southwold, Suffolk; 1635 on *Blessing*; Salem [GM 2:3:473-74; TAG 78:241-44]. (She married Humphrey Woodbury.)

Hunter, Robert: Unknown; 1640; Rowley [MBCR 1:378; RowBOP 5; EQC 1:40, 93, 104; EPR 1:80-81; Essex Ant 3:8-9; Rowley Fam 165].

Hunter, Thomas: Southwold, Suffolk; 1635 on *Blessing*; Salem [GM 2:3:474; TAG 78:241-44].

Hunter, William: Southwold, Suffolk; 1635 on *Blessing*; Salem, Boston [GM 2:3:475-77; TAG 78:241-44, 85:217-21].

Hunting, Anna: Hoxne, Suffolk; 1640; Dedham [DeVR 126; NGSQ 78:90]. (She married Henry Phillips.)

Hunting, John: Oakley, Suffolk; 1638; Dedham [DeChR 7, 27; DeTR 1:48; DeVR 1; MBCR 1:375; NGSQ 74:3-6, 78:85-97].

Hunting, Susanna: Hoxne, Suffolk; 1638; Dedham [DeVR 126; NGSQ 78:90]. (She married Edward Richards.)

Huntington, Simon: Norwich, Norfolk; 1633; Roxbury [GMB 1044-46].

Huntridge, Alexander: Unknown; 1638; Massachusetts Bay (business transaction only) [Lechford 76].

Hurd, John: Unknown; 1638; Boston [BTR 1:39, 42; BChR 24; MBCR 1:377; Lechford 236; HAHAC 1:105; NEHGR 132:83-85].

Hurd, John: Unknown; 1640; Windsor, Stratford [Windsor Hist 1:160, 2:417; FOOF 1:312-13; TAG 30:7-10, 50:1-10].

Hurlbut, Thomas: Unknown; 1636; Wethersfield [MHSC 3:3:139; WetLR 1:16; CCCR 2:161; Manwaring 1:473; FOOF 1:315-16; Wethersfield Hist 2:442-43].

Hurne, George: Unknown; 1639; Massachusetts Bay (court appearance only) [MBCR 1:296; Pope 227; see also MBCR 1:234].

Hurst, _____: Unknown; 1640; Cambridge (business transaction only) [Lechford 298].

Hurst, James: Amsterdam, Holland; 1631; Plymouth [GMB 1046-48; PM 284-86].

Hurst, Margaret: Unknown; 1642; Charlestown (church admission only) [ChChR 10; see Wyman 535].

Hurst, William: Unknown; 1637; Sandwich [PCR 1:143, 149, 2:18; PCPR 1:32].

Huse, Abel: Unknown; 1639; Newbury [NeTR 37; EIHC 5:42; EPR Case #14322; Hoyt 202; GDMNH 333; Harry Pinckney Huse, *The Descendants of Abel Huse of Newbury (1602-1690)* (Washington D.C. 1935)].

Huson, William: Unknown; 1637; Salem (land grant only) [STR 1:53, 54].

Hussey, Christopher: Dorking, Surrey; 1633; Lynn, Newbury, Hampton [GMB 1048-52; TAG 79:177-78].

Hussey, Widow: Unknown; 1639; Hampton [HmTR 44; GDMNH 364-65; TAG 79:177-78].

Hutchen, George: Newcastle-upon-Tyne, Northumberland; 1639; Cambridge [NEHGR 4:181; CaTR 43; CaBOP 63; Aspinwall 90; MLR 2:49; Abandoning 154].

Hutchins, Daniel: Unknown; 1639; Massachusetts Bay (court appearance only) [MBCR 1:298].

Hutchins, John: Unknown; 1638 on *Bevis*; Newbury, Haverhill [Drake's Founders 61 (as "John Huchinson"); NeVR; HvBOP 38; Moore Anc 326-33; TEG 21:46-49, 27:71-78; GDMNH 366; Edwin Colby Byam, *Descendants of John Hutchins of Newbury and Haverhill, Massachusetts* (Rockville, Maryland, 1975)].

Hutchins, Richard: Unknown; 1630; Massachusetts Bay (admission to freemanship only) [GMB 1052; WF 388].

Hutchinson, Edward: Alford, Lincolnshire; 1633; Boston, Portsmouth; returned permanently to England by 1644 [GMB 1052-54; Abandoning 155].

Hutchinson, George: Unknown; 1630; Charlestown [GMB 1054-55; WF 389-91].

Hutchinson, Richard: Unknown; 1636; Salem [SChR 6, 16; Cotton Corr 306; EQC 1:4, 8:433-35; STR 1:21; Sarah Johnson Anc 63-65 (clue)]. (The Richard Hutchinson who was admitted to freemanship on 4 March 1634/5 was son of William Hutchinson.)

Hutchinson, Samuel: Alford, Lincolnshire; 1637; Boston, Portsmouth [WJ 1:278; Cotton Corr 306, 313, 317; RICR 1:70, 90; NHPP 1:134; SPR Case #453].

Hutchinson, Samuel: Unknown; 1638; Lynn [EQC 1:95, 2:271; ELR 1:25v]. (Possibly stepson of Adam Hawkes.)

Hutchinson, Susan: Alford, Lincolnshire; 1636; Boston, Exeter, Wells [BChR 22; GDMNH 367].

Hutchinson, Thomas: Unknown; 1630; Charlestown [GMB 1056; WF 391].

Hutchinson, William: Alford, Lincolnshire; 1634 on *Griffin*; Boston, Portsmouth [GM 2:3:477-84; TG 13:189-98; Abandoning 155-56; NEHGR 123:180-81, 138:317-20, 153:164-72].

Hutley, Richard: Unknown; 1635 on *Hopewell*; Ipswich [GM 2:3:484-85].

Hutson, Barbara: Unknown; 1640; Cambridge (death record only) [NEHGR 4:181].

Hyatt, Thomas: Unknown; 1633; Dorchester (mention in will only) [MBCR 1:153]. (No evidence that he is the man of the same name who appeared at Stamford in 1641 [FOOF 1:318].)

Hyde, Samuel: Unknown; 1639 on *Jonathan*; Cambridge [NEHGR 32:409, 71:144-46; Ackley-Bosworth 276; Bond 304-5].

Hyde, William: Unknown; 1639; Hartford, Saybrook, Norwich [HaTR 22; HaBOP 243; Stonington Hist 445; Reuben H. Walworth, *Hyde Genealogy*, two volumes (Albany, New York, 1864)].

Hyland, Thomas: Tenterden, Kent; 1637; Scituate [NEHGR 10:43, 66:61-67; PCR 1:110].

I

Ibrook, Richard: Southwold, Suffolk; 1635; Hingham [GM 4:1-2; TAG 78:242].

Iggleden, Elizabeth: Biddenden, Kent; 1638 on *Castle*; Roxbury [SPR 1:16; NEHGR 2:183, 65:174-87; GM 2:5:382-83]. (She married Joseph Patchen.)

Iles, Richard: Bristol; 1638; Charlestown [Lechford 58; SPR 1:1; SLR 1:1; ChTR 38; NEHGR 2:102-3, 218-21 (use with caution); Bethia Harris Anc 2-6].

Ilsley, John: Unknown; 1638 on *Confidence*; Salisbury [Drake's Founders 59; SyTR 9; MBCR 1:376; TAG 34:164-68; Hoyt 214-15].

Ilsley, William: Caversham, Oxfordshire; 1638 on *Confidence*; Newbury [Drake's Founders 59; TAG 34:164-68, 50:61-62; Hoyt 215-16].

Ince, Jonathan: Unknown; 1637; Hartford [HaTR 23; HaBOP 358; Savage 2:518; Sibley 1:256-58].

Ines, Matthew: Unknown; 1633; Boston [GMB 1057-59].

Ingalls, Edward: Sutterton, Lincolnshire; 1638; Lynn [EQC 2:270; WP 4:135; NEHGR 50:71-72; TAG 52:241-43, 55:109-10; Pillsbury Anc 2:1055-64; TEG 19:43-46, 23:51-52, 59].

Ingalls, Francis: Boston, Lincolnshire; 1638; Lynn, Boston [EQC 2:270; EPR 1:27; WP 4:135; NEHGR 50:71-72; TAG 52:241-43, 55:109-10; Pillsbury Anc 2:1955-57; TEG 19:43-44].

Ingersoll, Richard: Sutton, Bedfordshire; 1629; Salem [GMB 1060-63; WF 393-96].

Ingles, Maudit: Marlborough, Wiltshire; 1635; Boston [GM 4:2-4].

Ingram, Edward: Unknown; 1635; Salem [GM 4:4-5].

Ireland, Samuel: Unknown; 1635 on *Increase*; Wethersfield [GM 4:5-6].

Ireson, Edward: Unknown; 1629; Lynn [GMB 1063-65; WF 397-99].

Irish, John: "Clisdon, Somerset"; 1630; Plymouth, Duxbury [GMB 1065-68; PM 287-89].

Isaac, Joseph: Unknown; 1636; Cambridge [MBCR 1:220, 342, 372; CaTR 34, 37, 38, 42, 45; CaBOP 40, 52-53, 68, 109-10; NEHGR 4:182; SPR 1:11].

Isaac, Rebecca: Unknown; 1634 on *Elizabeth*; passenger list only [GM 4:6-7].

Isbell, Robert: Unknown; 1636; Salem [STR 1:23, 103; EQC 1:21; Edna Warren Mason, *The Descendants of Robert Isbell in America* (New Haven 1944)].

Islin, Thomas: Unknown; 1639; Sudbury [SuTR 3; MBCR 1:377]. (He died at Sudbury on 21 February 1663[/4?].)

Iver, Micha: Unknown; 1639; Salem [EQC 1:14; MBCR 1:286].

Ives, Miles: Unknown; 1639; Watertown [WaVR 1:6; WaBOP 68; CaBOP 68; Waters 76; Bond 306; TAG 41:206-8].

Ives, William: Unknown; 1639; New Haven [NHCR 1:28, 92; FANH 910-11].

Ivory, William: Unknown; 1638; Lynn [EQC 1:14, 2:270; EPR 1:152-53; NEHGR 67:341; Arthur Coon Ives, *Genealogy of the Ives Family* (Watertown, New York, 1928); TEG 10:33-37].

J

Jacklin, Edmund: Unknown; 1634; Boston [GM 2:4:9-13].

Jackson, Edmund: Unknown; 1635; Boston [GM 2:4:13-18].

Jackson, Henry: Unknown; 1635 on *Elizabeth & Ann*; Watertown, Fairfield [GM 2:4:19-22].

Jackson, John: Unknown; 1635 on *Elizabeth & Ann*; passenger list only [GM 2:4:22].

Jackson, John: Unknown; 1635 on *Defence*; passenger list only [GM 2:4:22].

Jackson, John: Unknown; 1635 on *Blessing*; Salem [GM 2:4:23-25].

Jackson, John: Unknown; 1635; Ipswich [GM 2:4:25-28; Kempton Anc 2:192-99].

Jackson, John: Unknown; 1637; Boston [BTR 1:31, 95, 153; BBOP 8, 91; BChR 31, 286, 287, 293, 300, 307, 317; NEHGR 2:191; SPR Case #630].

Jackson, John: London (but not fully documented); 1639; Cambridge [CaBOP 68; GMN 12:24; NEHGR 66:84; Parker-Ruggles 269-79, 401-3].

Jackson, Manus: Unknown; 1639; Charlestown [ChTR 49; ChVR 1:9].

Jackson, Richard: Unknown; 1636; Cambridge [CaTR 23; CaBOP 64; MBCR 1:210, 220; Lechford 318; Shepard 114, 119; WMQ 48:446-50; Rodgers 3:152-57; MPR Case #12417; Cameos 145-48, 183-88].

Jackson, Samuel: Unknown; 1636; Scituate, Barnstable [PCR 1:49, 134, 7:23; NEHGR 9:280, 10:41; MBCR 1:232; PCPR 4:2:17; MD 13:94-96; Otis 2:113-14].

Jackson, Thomas: Unknown; 1638; Plymouth [PCR 1:96, 97; Bradford 299; Legal Executions 7].

Jackson, William: Rowley, Yorkshire; 1639; Rowley [RowVR; RowBOP 2; Rowley Fam 166; GMN 18:21].

Jacob, Nicholas: Hingham, Norfolk; 1633; Watertown, Hingham [GMB 1069-71].

Jacob, Richard: Unknown; 1634 on *Mary & John*; Ipswich [GM 2:4:28-32].

Jagger, Jeremiah: Unknown; 1637; Wethersfield, Stamford [CCCR 2:150; WetLR 1:162; SmTR 4; Gillespie Anc 312-15].

James, Edmund: Unknown; 1630; Watertown [GMB 1071-72; WF 401-3].

James, Erasmus: Unknown; 1637; Marblehead [STR 1:58, 63, 74; EQC 1:11; EPR 1:314-16, 2:160; Marblehead 81-82].

James, Francis: Hingham, Norfolk; 1638 on *Diligent*; Hingham [NEHGR 15:26, 151:61-86; HiBOP 79].

James, Gawdy: Unknown (but of Winfarthing, Norfolk, in 1660); 1639; Charlestown, Boston [ChBOP 65, 67, 142; ChChR 10; ChTR 47; SPR 6:528, 9:280; Wyman 547].

James, Philip: Hingham, Norfolk; 1638 on *Diligent*; Hingham [NEHGR 15:26, 121:12, 151:61-86; HiBOP 80].

James, Thomas: Boston, Lincolnshire; 1632; Charlestown, Providence, New Haven, Virginia; returned permanently to England by 1649 [GMB 1072-76; Abandoning 157-59].

James, Thomas: Unknown; 1638; Salem; removed to Carolina by 1666 [STR 1:83; EQC 1:21; NEHGR 63:164; Aspinwall 7; EQC 3:338; ELR 1:13, 2:72; 4:133, 181; EPR 2:46-47, 449-50].

James, William: Unknown; 1630; Massachusetts Bay [GMB 1077; WF 403].

James, William: Unknown; 1632 on *Lyon*; passenger list only [GMB 1077; WF 403].

James, William: Unknown; 1636; Salem [STR 1:23, 32; EQC 1:3, 19, 123-24, 133; MBCR 1:193; Perley 1:272]. (Possibly the same as the William James seen in the 1640s at Kittery [GDMNH 373-74].)

James, William: London; 1640; Boston (business transaction only) [Lechford 323].

Janes, William: Unknown; 1640; New Haven, Wethersfield, Northampton [Lechford 315; NHCR 1:91; Wethersfield Hist 2:459-60; Ackley-Bosworth 161-63].

Jarman, Priscilla: Unknown; 1635 on *Susan & Ellen*; passenger list only [GM 2:4:32].

Jarrat, John: Unknown; 1639; Rowley [MBCR 1:376; RowBOP 4; EPR 1:98-99; Rowley Fam 168].

Jarvis, John: Unknown; 1630; Massachusetts Bay [GMB 1077; WF 404].

Jeffrey, Thomas: Unknown; 1633; Dorchester, New Haven [GMB 1077-82].

Jeffreys, Edward: Unknown; 1635 on *Truelove*; passenger list only [GM 2:4:32-33].

Jeffreys, Robert: Unknown; 1635 on *Elizabeth & Ann*; Weymouth, Charlestown, Boston, Portsmouth, Newport; returned permanently to England about 1646 [GM 2:4:33-36; Abandoning 159-60].

Jeffreys, William: Chiddingly, Sussex; 1623; Weymouth, Newport [GMB 1082-85].

Jefts, Henry: Unknown; 1640; Woburn, Billerica [WoTR 2; TEG 30:76-78].

Jeggles, William: Unknown; 1636; Salem [STR 1:21, 80, 102; WP 3:434, 4:4, 66; SChR 6; EQC 1:4; EPR 1:287-88; Waters 1408-9; Perley 1:390-91].

Jenkin, Richard: Eastwell, Kent; 1637; passenger list only [NEHGR 75:221].

Jenkins, ____: Unknown; 1632; Dorchester, Cape Porpus [GMB 1085].

Jenkins, Edward: Bethersden, Kent; 1635 on *Hercules*; Scituate [GM 2:4:36-41; NEHGR 161:165-66].

Jenkins, Elizabeth: Unknown; 1635 on *Truelove*; passenger list only [GM 2:4:41].

Jenkins, Joel: Unknown; 1640; Braintree, Boston, Malden [MBCR 1:298; NEHGR 3:127; WP 4:268; BChR 317, 319; Kempton Anc 4:420-27; TAG 30:98-100; Gilbert Gen 24, 53].

Jenkins, John: Unknown; 1635 on *Defence*; Plymouth, Eastham, Barnstable [GM 2:4:41-46].

Jenner, John: Unknown; 1639; New Haven, Stratford, Brookhaven [NHCR 1:29; Manwaring 1:62; FOOF 1:31; NEHGR 55:302; Suffolk Sessions 93-96].

Jenner, Thomas: Fordham, Essex; 1635; Roxbury, Charlestown, Weymouth, Saco; returned permanently to England in 1650 [GM 2:4:46-50; Abandoning 160-62].

Jennings, John: Unknown; 1639; Hartford [HaTR 7; HaBOP 170; GM 2:4:54-56]. (His son Nicholas Jennings had preceded him to New England, sailing on the *Francis* in 1634 [GM 2:4:50-58].)

Jennings, Richard: Ipswich, Suffolk; 1636; Ipswich; returned permanently to England in 1638 [Abandoning 342-43].

Jennings, Robert: Sandwich, Kent; 1635 on *Hercules*; passenger list only [GM 2:4:58-59].

Jennison, Robert: Unknown; 1636; Watertown [WaBOP 3, 54; WaVR 1:5; Dawes-Gates 1:369-71].

Jennison, William: Unknown; 1630; Charlestown, Watertown; returned permanently to England soon after 1645 [GMB 1086-89; WF 404-11; Abandoning 162-63].

Jenny, John: Leiden, Holland; 1623 on *Little James*; Plymouth [GMB 1089-94; PM 291-96; TG 22:1-28].

Jepson, John: Guildford, Surrey; 1639; Boston [BTR 1:41; TAG 20:85-97, 173-80, 78:253-55].

Jess, William: Unknown; 1640; Windsor, Springfield [WiLR 1:40; Grant 45, 92; Manwaring 1:125; FOOF 1:295; Savage 4:547].

Jesop, Walter: Unknown; 1635 on *Marygould*; passenger list only [GM 2:4:59].

Jessop, John: Unknown; 1637; Watertown, Wethersfield [MBCR 1:218; CCCR 1:12; SmTR 4; FOOF 1:336-37; TAG 63:28].

Jewell, George: Unknown; 1632; Saco [GMB 1094-95].

Jewell, Thomas: Unknown; 1635 on *Planter*; Boston, Braintree [GM 2:4:59-62].

Jewett, Joseph: Bradford, Yorkshire; 1638; Massachusetts Bay [MBCR 1:376; DChR 4; RowBOP 2; NEHGR 94:99-107; Rowley Fam 186-202;

Pillsbury Anc 1:375-78; Frederic Clarke Jewett, *History and Genealogy of the Jewetts of America*, two volumes (New York 1908)].

Jewett, Maximilian: Bradford, Yorkshire; 1639; Rowley [MBCR 1:318, 376; RowBOP 2; NEHGR 94:99-107; Rowley Fam 168-186; Snow-Estes 1:84-96; Frederic Clarke Jewett, *History and Genealogy of the Jewetts of America*, two volumes (New York 1908)].

Joes, William: Unknown; 1635 on *Truelove*; passenger list only [GM 2:4:62].

Johnson, Davy: Unknown; 1630; Dorchester [GMB 1095-96].

Johnson, Edmund: Unknown; 1635 on *James*; Newbury, Hampton [GM 2:4:62-65].

Johnson, Edward: Unknown; 1622; Wessagusset, York [GMB 1096-99].

Johnson, Edward: Canterbury, Kent; 1637; Charlestown, Woburn [NEHGR 59:79-86, 67:169-80, 68:142, 75:221, 139:60-61, 321-24; ChBOP 21; HAHAC 1:45; MBCR 1:316, 374; TG 2:136-37; GMC26 149-53].

Johnson, Francis: Unknown; 1630; Salem, Marblehead, Boston [GMB 1100-3].

Johnson, Isaac: Sempringham, Lincolnshire; 1630 in *Arbella*; Charlestown, Boston [GMB 1104-5; WF 411-15].

Johnson, James: Little Bowden, Northamptonshire; 1635; Boston [GM 2:4:66-78].

Johnson, James: Unknown; 1636; Kittery, Dover [Pope MNH 112; GDMNH 382].

Johnson, John: Ware, Hertfordshire; 1630; Roxbury [GMB 1105-10; WF 415-21].

Johnson, John: Unknown; 1635 on *Elizabeth*; passenger list only [GM 2:4:78].

Johnson, John: Strood, Kent; 1635 on *James*; Ipswich, Andover [GM 2:4:78-81].

Johnson, John: Unknown; 1637; Braintree, Portsmouth [MBCR 1:223; RICR 1:91].

Johnson, John: Unknown; 1638; Massachusetts Bay (apprenticeship record only) [Lechford 93].

Johnson, John: Unknown; 1640; New Haven, Rowley [NHCR 1:13, 31, 50, 93; Lechford 208; FANH 1029; Rowley Fams 208; TAG 20:237-38].

Johnson, Peter: Unknown; 1632 on *Plough*; removed to Virginia in 1632 [GMB 1110].

Johnson, Peter (called "Dutchman"): Unknown; 1638; Boston, Fairfield [BTR 1:35, 53; EQC 1:9; Manwaring 1:132; FOOF 1:339; FANH 952-53].

Johnson, Richard: Unknown; 1630; Charlestown [GMB 1110-11; WF 421-22].

Johnson, Richard: Unknown; 1636; Salem, Lynn [STR 1:50, 103; EQC 1:8, 2:270; MBCR 1:373; EPR 2:76-78; Chase-Wigglesworth 287-93; TEG 11:82-85].

Johnson, Samuel: Unknown; 1634; Massachusetts Bay (court appearance only) [GM 2:4:81-82; see also NEHGR 156:213-21].

Johnson, Solomon: Unknown; 1639; Sudbury [SuTR 4; NEHGR 66:233-43; Parker-Ruggles 254-56].

Johnson, Susan: London; 1635; passenger list only (ship's name not provided) [GM 2:4:82].

Johnson, Thomas: Unknown; 1635 on *Speedwell*; Hingham [GM 2:4:82-84].

Johnson, Thomas: Unknown; 1639; Hartford (probate proceedings only) [CCCR 1:49, 55, 453].

Johnson, Thomas: Unknown; 1639; New Haven [NHCR 1:31, 39; NEHGR 66:15; FANH 1029-30; Parke-Gildersleeve 73-76].

Johnson, Thomas: Unknown; 1639; Piscataqua [MPCR 1:48; NHPP 40:4].

Johnson, William: Dunstable, Bedfordshire; 1634; Charlestown [GM 2:4:84-90].

Johnson, William: Unknown; 1640; Boston (business transaction only) [Lechford 268].

Joiner, Isabel: Unknown; 1640; Milford [MiChR 2; TAG 16:29]. (She married Miles Moore [Milford Fams 456].)

Jolliffe, John: East Stower, Dorset; 1636; Boston [WP 3:308, 378, 502; Lechford 1; Waters 261-63].

Jones, ____: Unknown; 1639; Salem (court appearance only) [EQC 1:15].

Jones, Alice: Unknown; 1635 on *James*; passenger list only [GM 2:4:90].

Jones, Bethia: Unknown; 1630; Boston [GMB 1111; WF 422-23]. (She probably married Daniel Ray.)

Jones, Charles: London; 1635 on *Abigail*; passenger list only [GM 2:4:91].

Jones, Edward: Unknown; 1630; Charlestown, Southampton [GMB 1111-12; WF 423-26].

Jones, Edward: Titchmarsh, Northamptonshire; 1639; Boston (apprenticeship record only) [Lechford 427].

Jones, John: Unknown; 1635 on *Hopewell*; passenger list only [GM 2:4:91].

Jones, John: Unknown; 1635 on *Susan & Ellen*; passenger list only [GM 2:4:91-92].

Jones, John: Unknown; 1635 on *Abigail*; passenger list only [GM 2:4:92].

Jones, John: London; 1635 on *Defence*; Concord, Fairfield [GM 2:4:92-97; NEA 8:1:37-39].

Jones, John: Unknown; 1639; Piscataqua [NHPP 1:113; GDMNH 387; NHGR 11:57-63].

Jones, John: Unknown; 1639; Plymouth (servant; court appearance only) [PCR 1:156].

Jones, Lewis: Unknown; 1640; Roxbury, Watertown [RChR 84; GMN 21:12-13; Kempston Anc 1:345-51].

Jones, Margaret: Sandwich, Kent; 1634 on *Hercules*; passenger list only [GM 2:4:97-98].

Jones, Mary: Unknown; 1635 on *Abigail*; passenger list only [GM 2:4:98-99].

Jones, Mary: Unknown; 1637; Boston (poor relief only) [MBCR 1:230, 312, 318].

Jones, Richard: Dinder, Somerset; 1635 on *Marygould*; Dorchester [GM 2:4:99-102].

Jones, Robert: Caversham, Oxfordshire; 1638; Hingham [HiBOP 90; NEHGR 121:10, 143:121-24; Lechford 175; ReTR 1:2; Aspinwall 49; TAG 31:96-98; Hingham Hist 2:386-87; GMC50: 205-8].

Jones, Sarah: Unknown; 1632 on *James*; passenger list only [GMB 1112].

Jones, Thomas: Unknown; 1635 on *Abigail*; Dorchester [GM 2:4:102-6].

Jones, Thomas: Unknown; 1635; York [GM 2:4:106-7].

Jones, Thomas: Elsing, Norfolk; 1637 on *Mary Anne*; Newbury, Hampton, Exeter, Charlestown [Hotten 295; ILR 1:146; EQC 7:194; HampVR 1:3; GDMNH 55, 388; HmTR 40; MBCR 1:375; TAG 68:220].

Jones, Thomas: Caversham, Oxfordshire; 1638 on *Confidence*; Hingham, Hull, Manchester [Drake's Founders 59; HiBOP 89; NEHGR 113:42-44].

Jones, Thomas: Unknown; 1639; Guilford; returned permanently to England by 1652 [Guilford Hist 25, 46-47; NEHGR 59:386-87; Abandoning 163].

Jones, Thomas: Unknown; 1640; Massachusetts Bay [Lechford 339; see also GM 2:4:107].

Jones, Thomas: Unknown; 1640; Gloucester [Gloucester VR (1640 birth); EQC 3:327; TEG 18:83-85].

Jones, Widow: Unknown; 1640; Dorchester (church admission only) [DChR 5].

Jones, William: Unknown; 1635; Cambridge; probably returned permanently to England in 1636 or later [GM 2:4:107-9].

Jones, William: Wherwell, Hampshire; 1638 on *Confidence*; passenger list only [Drake's Founders 59; TAG 83:154-55].

Jones, William: Unknown; 1639; Strawberry Bank [NHPP 1:113]. (This and the following two entries do not necessarily represent three distinct men [GDMNH 389].)

Jones, William: Unknown; 1640; Dover [NHPP 1:128, 10:701, 40:4, 5, 7, 12, 15, 16].

Jones, William: Unknown; 1640; Saco [MPCR 1:81].

Jope, Samson: Unknown; 1636; Richmond Island [Trelawny 113, 165, 335, 355].

Jope, William: Unknown; 1635 on *Bachelor*; passenger list only [GM 2:4:110].

Jordan, Francis: Unknown; 1634; Ipswich [GM 2:4:110-14].

Jordan, James: Unknown; 1640; Dedham [DeTR 1:60, 74; DeChR 24; SPR 1:106, 3:75].

Jordan, Joan: Stepney, Middlesex; 1635 on *Abigail*; passenger list only [GM 2:4:114].

Jordan, John: Unknown; 1639; Guilford [Guilford Hist 25, 45; FOOF 1:346-47; NEHGR 62:333; Ackley-Bosworth 97].

Jordan, John: Unknown; 1640; Plymouth [PCR 2:5, 8:11, 183, 188, 203; PVR 85, 135, 136, 658; PPR 1:317-18].

Jordan, Robert: Worcester, Worcestershire; 1640; Pejepscot, Richmond Island, Spurwink, Portsmouth [NH] [MPCR 1:78; WP 4:276; Trelawny 269; GDMNH 390-91; NEHGR 96:303-4; Adelbert Jean "Andy" Annonson, *The Family Jordan*, three volumes (Camden, Maine, 2001)].

Jordan, Stephen: Unknown; 1634 on *Mary & John*; Ipswich, Newbury [GM 2:4:114-16].

Jordan, Thomas: Unknown; 1639; Guilford; returned permanently to England in 1654 [Guilford Hist 25, 31, 45; FOOF 1:346; NEHGR 62:333; Abandoning 164].

Joslin, Thomas: Barham, Suffolk; 1635 on *Increase*; Hingham, Lancaster [GM 2:4:117-21; TAG 64:148-49].

Josselyn, Thomas: Willingale-Doe, Essex; 1638; Black Point; returned permanently to England in 1639 [Trelawny 139-40; MPCR 1:30-36; NEHGR 71:248-50; TAG 52:77]. (He was father of Henry Josselyn who came to New England in 1630 [GMB 1113-16] and of John Josselyn who came to New England with his father in 1638, went home with him in 1639, and then came back to New England from 1663 to 1672 [NEHGR 71:249-50; ODNB].)

Joy, Richard: Unknown; 1640; Richmond Island [Trelawny 283].

Joy, Thomas: Unknown; 1636; Boston, Hingham [BTR 1:16; Lechford 188, 283, 364; BChR 287; SPR Case #993; NEHGR 2:191; Hingham Hist 2:396; Hoyt 219-20; Helen Bourne Joy Lee, *The Joy Genealogy* (Essex, Connecticut, 1968)].

Joyce, John: Unknown; 1639; Sandwich, Yarmouth [PCR 1:150; NEHGR 9:283; MD 16:160-61; TAG 43:1-13].

Judd, Thomas: Unknown; 1634; Cambridge, Hartford, Farmington, Northampton [GM 2:4:121-26].

Judkins, Job: Southam, Warwickshire; 1639; Boston [Lechford 235, 330; BChR 288; BTR 1:63; BBOP 36; GDMNH 393-94; Kempton Anc 1:352-62].

Judson, William: Unknown; 1638; Massachusetts Bay, Stratford, New Haven [MBCR 1:249; NEHGR 81:127; FOOF 1:349; McCormick-Hamilton 575-78].

Jupe, Alice: Unknown; 1640; Boston (church admission only) [BChR 33].

Jupe, Mrs.: Unknown; 1638; Ipswich (court appearance only) [MBCR 1:258].

Jusall, Sarah: Unknown; 1638; Massachusetts Bay (court appearance only) [MBCR 1:249].

K

Keayne, Robert: London; 1635 on *Defence*; Boston [GM 2:4:127-33; Abandoning 166-67].

Kedby, Lewis: Groton, Suffolk; 1630; Boston [GMB 1117; WF 427].

Keele, Edward: Unknown; 1635 on *Hopewell*; passenger list only [GM 2:4:134].

Keeler, Ralph: Unknown; 1639; Hartford, Norwalk [HaTR 24; HaBOP 42; FOOF 1:355-56; TAG 35:154, 58:32-34, 80:177-87; CN 38:380-88].

Keene, Martha: Checkenden, Oxfordshire; 1638 on *Confidence*; Boston [Drake's Founders 59; Aspinwall 249-50; Hale, House 11; TAG 41:95-97].

Keene, William: Unknown; 1638; Marblehead, Gloucester, Boston, New London [STR 1:74; EQC 1:31, 36, 47, 48, 50, 76, 77, 93, 157; BChR 46, 54, 302; New London Hist 291, 306; Miner Anc 117-18].

Kellogg, Nathaniel: Great Leighs, Essex; 1639; Hartford, Farmington [HaTR 24; HaBOP 312; Manwaring 1:132; Timothy Hopkins, *The Kelloggs in the Old World and the New*, three volumes (San Francisco 1903) 23-24].

Kelly, Abel: Unknown; 1640; Salem [SChR 10; EQC 1:27; EPR 1:13; MBCR 1:378].

Kelly, John: Unknown; 1640; Newbury [Newbury VR; NeBOP 44v; Hoyt 220; Sarah Hildreth Anc 71-72; Pillsbury Anc 1:165-66].

Kelsey, William: Unknown; 1633; Cambridge, Hartford, Killingworth [GMB 1117-19].

Kemp, Edward: Unknown; 1638; Dedham, Wenham, Chelmsford [DeTR 1:47; DeChR 14 (as "Robert Kemp"), 22, 29; MBCR 1:375; Fiske 91, 93-95; MPR Case #13008; Arthur James Weise, *The New-England Kemps* (Troy, New York, 1904) 27-44].

Kemp, John: Unknown; 1639; Massachusetts Bay (court appearance only) [MBCR 1:269].

Kemp, William: Unknown; 1635 on *James*; passenger list only (with caveat) [GM 2:4:134-35].

Kemp, William: Unknown; 1638; Plymouth [PCR 1:109, 137, 2:27, 37, 7:15, 8:175-182, 12:56; PCPR 1:40; MD 4:75-82, 14:228-30; TAG 86:119 (clue)].

Kempton, Manasseh: London; 1623 on *Anne*; Plymouth [GMB 1119-23; PM 297-301].

Kendall, Francis: Westmill, Hertfordshire; 1640; Woburn [WoTR 2; Stevens-Miller 1:116-24; Dawes-Gates 1:375-95; Sarah Hildreth Anc 25-27].

Kendall, Priscilla: Unknown; 1636; Salem (church admission only) [SChR 6].

Kendrick, John: Unknown; 1639; Boston, Cambridge [BChR 24, 30; MBCR 1:377; NEHGR 2:191; DChR 23, 44 (as "John Kimwright"); SPR Case #1490; Parker-Ruggles 274-76].

Kendrick, George: Unknown; 1635 on *James* of Bristol; Plymouth, Scituate, Boston, Providence, Newport [GM 2:4:135-39].

Keniston, Allen: Unknown; 1636; Salem [SChR 8; STR 1:29, 81, 103; EPR 1:101; Perley 2:142]. (His wife Dorothy had arrived by 1636, but he is not seen in the records until 1638.)

Kenning, Henry: Unknown; 1639; Massachusetts Bay (apprenticeship record only) [Lechford 101].

Kent, Richard Sr.: Over Wallop, Hampshire; 1634 on *Mary & John*; Ipswich, Newbury [GM 2:4:140-42; NEHGR 162:245-54, 163:51-65].

Kent, Richard Jr.: Unknown; 1634 on *Mary & John*; Ipswich, Newbury [GM 2:4:142-45].

Kent, Stephen: Salisbury, Wiltshire; 1638 on *Confidence*; Newbury, Haverhill, Woodbridge [NJ] [Drake's Founders 58; HvBOP 16; MBCR 1:375; NeTR 27; NEHGR 68:107, 162:245-54, 163:51-65].

Kerley, Edmund: Ashmore, Dorset; 1638 on *Confidence*; passenger list only [Drake's Founders 58].

Kerley, William: Ashmore, Dorset; 1638 on *Confidence*; Sudbury, Lancaster [Drake's Founders 58; SuTR 7; NEHGR 16:355; Rodgers 2:626-27; Stevens-Miller 1:74, 85; Warner-Harrington 369-71].

Ketcham, Edward: Cambridge, Cambridgeshire; 1636; Ipswich, Southold, Stratford [MBCR 1:372; ITR 38; TAG 30:2-6; FOOF 1:359-60; Seversmith 4:1729-36; Stevens-Miller 1:511].

Ketcham, Hester: Unknown; 1639; Charlestown (servant, court appearance only) [MBCR 1:286].

Ketcherell, Joseph: Sandwich, Kent; 1635 on *Hercules*; Charlestown [GM 2:4:145-47].

Ketcherell, Simon: Sandwich, Kent; 1635 on *Hercules*; passenger list only [GM 2:4:147].

Kettell, Peter: Unknown; 1635 on *Abigail*; passenger list only [GM 2:4:148].

Kettle, Richard: Unknown; 1633; Charlestown [GMB 1124-28].

Keyes, Robert: Unknown; 1633; Watertown, Newbury [GMB 1128-31].

Keyser, George: Leighton Buzzard, Bedfordshire; 1639; Lynn, Salem [WJ 1:387; EQC 1:14; MBCR 1:375; Aspinwall 15; Pillsbury Anc 1:275-83].

Keyser, Thomas: Unknown; 1639; Lynn, Boston [Lechford 418-21; EQC 1:26, 28, 31, 32, 42, 43; BChR 44].

Kibby, Henry: Taunton, Somerset; 1636; Dorchester [MBCR 1:193; DTR 1:39; DChR 4; SPR Case #278; Waters 406, 442; TAG 81:36-47; NEHGR 22:43-46; Stevens-Miller 1:98-100].

Kidby, John; Unknown; 1638; Plymouth (grant of land only) [PCR 1:120, 161].

Kidder, Stephen: Unknown; 1633; Piscataqua [GMB 1131]. (See also Stephen Tedder.)

Kilborne, George: Unknown; 1638; Roxbury, Rowley [RChR 84; MBCR 1:376; RowBOP 3; EQC 9:561-62; NEHGR 161:22-26; Sarah Stone Anc 95-100]. (He was not the son of Thomas Kilbourn.)

Kilbourn, Thomas: Wood Ditton, Cambridgeshire; 1635 on *Increase*; Wethersfield [GM 2:4:148-51; TAG 64:1-11; John Dwight Kilbourne, *The Ancestry of Thomas Kilbourn (1578-c.1637) of Wood Ditton, Cambridgeshire, England, and Wethersfield, Connecticut* (Washington D. C. 1991) {some date for members of the immigrant family differ from the dates in earlier printed sources}].

Kilcup, William: Unknown; 1639; Lynn; Charlestown, Boston [MBCR 1:298; ChBOP 102, 146-47; Wyman 588].

Kilham, Austin: Wrentham, Suffolk; 1637 on *Mary Anne*; Salem, Dedham, Wenham [Hotten 294; STR 1:53; EPR 1:12; EQC 1:18; DeTR 1:76; DeChR 24; MBCR 1:379; Fiske Notebook 89-90; TAG 67:53-54; Waters 1403-5; EIHC 49:210-38].

Kilin, John: Brampton, Suffolk; 1637 on *Mary Anne*; passenger list only (servant) [Hotten 293].

Killinghall, Margaret: Unknown; 1635 on *Truelove*; passenger list only [GM 2:4:151].

Kimball, Henry: Mistley, Essex; 1634 on *Elizabeth*; Watertown [GM 2:4:152-54].

Kimball, Richard: Rattlesden, Suffolk; 1634 on *Elizabeth*; Watertown, Ipswich [GM 2:4:154-60].

Kimberly, Thomas: Wotton-under-Edge, Gloucestershire; 1635; Dorchester, New Haven, Stratford [GM 2:4:160-66].

King, Daniel: High Wycombe, Buckinghamshire; 1639; Lynn [Lechford 385; EQC 3:92-94; NEHGR 65:84; NYGBR 31:136-39; TEG 9:82-87].

King, George: Unknown; 1634 on *Hercules*; Massachusetts Bay [GM 2:4:166-67].

King, Henry: Unknown; 1635 on *James*; passenger list only [GM 2:4:167].

King, Joanna: Unknown; 1638; Boston (servant; church admission only) [BChR 24].

King, John: Unknown; 1638; Massachusetts Bay [MBCR 1:245]. (Possibly one of the two following men.)

King, John: Unknown; 1639; Lynn [Lechford 307-8]. (Not necessarily the same as the next.)

King, John: Unknown; 1639; Weymouth [Lechford 392; Gen Adv 1:94-95; SPR 1:68, 2:84; Weymouth Hist 3:349-50].

King, Joseph: Unknown; 1640; Massachusetts Bay (court appearance only) [MBCR 1:315].

King, Persis: Unknown; 1635 on *Elizabeth & Ann*; passenger list only [GM 2:4:167].

King, Richard: Unknown; 1634; Salem [GM 2:4:167-68].

King, Robert: Unknown; 1638 on *Confidence*; passenger list only (servant) [Drake's Founders 58]. (See Robert Ring.)

King, Samuel: Taunton, Somerset; 1637; Plymouth [PCR 1:139, 12:47; TAG 30:11-14; NEHGR 148:326-27; M&JCH 27:35-36].

King, Sarah: Unknown; 1639; Boston (court appearance only) [MBCR 1:273].

King, Thomas: Unknown; 1634 on *Francis*; Watertown [GM 2:4:168-70].

King, Thomas: Unknown; 1634 on *Elizabeth*; passenger list only (with caveat) [GM 2:4:170].

King, Thomas: Cold Norton, Essex; 1635 on *Blessing*; Scituate [GM 2:4:171-73].

King, Thomas: Unknown; 1639; Hampton, Exeter [GDMNH 55, 401; HmTR 45; EQC 1:41, 44; NHPP 31:93-95; NEHGR 141:327; Pillsbury Anc 1:326].

King, William: Unknown; 1635 on *Marygould*; Salem [GM 2:4:174-77].

King, William: Unknown; 1635 on *Abigail*; passenger list only [GM 2:4:178].

Kingman, Henry: Unknown; 1635 on *Marygould*; Weymouth [GM 2:4:178-82].

Kingsbury, Henry: Assington, Suffolk; 1630; Boston [GMB 1131-33; WF 427-29].

Kingsbury, Henry: Unknown; 1638; Ipswich [ITR 34; NEHGR 54:260; Moore Anc 334-47; Granberry 265-66; Kingsbury Gen 85-89].

Kingsbury, John: Unknown; 1635; Watertown, Dedham [GM 2:4:183-88].

Kingsbury, Joseph: Unknown; 1637; Dedham [DeTR 1:32; DeVR 1; DeChR 6; MBCR 1:379; Moore Anc 334-36; Kingsbury Gen 83-85].

Kingsbury, William: Unknown; 1638; Dedham (court appearance only) [MBCR 1:241]. (No other record found for this name; possibly an error for John or Joseph above.)

Kingsley, John: Unknown; 1636; Dorchester, Rehoboth [DChR 2, 3; DTR 26; NEHGR 5:244; PCPR 4:1:4-5; Early Rehoboth 3:20-23; Parker-Ruggles 427; NYGBR 42:78].

Kingsley, Stephen: Unknown; 1636; Boston, Braintree, Dorchester [BTR 1:17, 41; WP 4:299; BrTR 1; NEHGR 3:127, 62:94; MBCR 1:377; SPR Case #655; TAG 10:15 (clue)].

Kingsnorth, Henry: Unknown; 1639; Guilford [Guilford Hist 25, 46; TAG 13:93; NEHGR 56:356-57; Stevens-Miller 1:214-15].

Kinham, Alice: Unknown; 1635 on *Marygould*; passenger list only [GM 2:4:188].

Kinsman, Robert: Highworth, Wiltshire; 1634 on *Mary & John*; Ipswich [GM 2:4:188-91; TAG 84:18-25].

Kirby, John: Unknown; 1635 on *Hopewell*; passenger list only (with caveat) [GM 2:4:191].

Kirby, Richard: Unknown; 1637; Sandwich, Dartmouth [PCPR 1:32; PCR 1:107, 149, 2:75, 172-73, 8:9, 184, 192; BrPR 4:119-20; NEHGR 128:250; Melatiah Everett Dwight, *The Kirbys of New England* (New York 1898) 229-336].

Kirby (or Kirkby), William: Unknown; 1639; Boston [BTR 1:49; NEHGR 2:191]. (Other early Boston records may be for this man or another of the same name [BBOP 13, 113-14; BTR 1:95; BChR 52; SLR 3:322].)

Kirby, ____: Unknown; 1640 on *William & George*; passenger list only [WP 4:203, 224, 242]. (This is apparently Francis Kirby's biological son Joshua, and not his stepson Joseph Carter who had come to New England the year before [NEHGR 35:373-75].)

Kirk, Judith: Unknown; 1635 on *Susan & Ellen*; Boston [GM 2:4:191-92].

Kirkby *see* **Kirby**

Kirman, John: Unknown; 1631 on *Plough*; Cambridge, Lynn, Sandwich; possibly returned to England shortly after 1640 [GMB 1133-35].

Kirtland, Nathaniel: Sherington, Buckinghamshire; 1635 on *Hopewell*; Lynn, Southampton [GM 2:4:192-98].

Kirtland, Philip: Sherington, Buckinghamshire; 1635 on *Hopewell*; Lynn, Southampton [GM 2:4:198-201].

Kitchell, Robert: Rolvenden, Kent; 1639; Guilford [Guilford Hist 25; SPR 2:17; NEHGR 55:208-20; TAG 15:69-80, 22:85-94, 83:267-77].

Kitcherell, Joseph: Unknown; 1638; Salem [SChR 8; STR 1:86, 88; GM 2:4:147].

Kitchin, John: Unknown; 1635 on *Marygould*; Weymouth, Salem [GM 2:4:201-7; MBCR 1:269].

Kitson, Alice: Unknown; 1638; Duxbury [PCR 1:94]. (She married William Reynolds.)

Kittwell, Samuel: Unknown; 1639; Connecticut (court appearance only) [CCCR 1:29].

Knapp, Nicholas: Unknown; 1630; Watertown, Stamford [GMB 1135-37; WF 430-33].

Knevitt, Ruth: Unknown; 1640; Boston (servant; church admission only) [BChR 34].

Knight, Alexander: Chelmsford, Essex; 1636; Ipswich [ITR 18; MHSC 3:6:41; WP 3:433; Waters 842-43; TAG 76:1-16; NEHGR 162:116-17; Dawes-Gates 1:397-99].

Knight, Apria: Unknown; 1637; Charlestown (admission as inhabitant only) [ChTR 31]. (Wyman thought this man was the same as a Philip Knight who appeared at Charlestown about 1650 [Wyman 590].)

Knight, Daniel: Unknown; 1640; York (court appearance only) [MPCR 1:58, 71-72].

Knight, Dorothy: Unknown; 1635 on *Defence*; passenger list only [GM 2:4:207].

Knight, Ezekiel: Unknown; 1637; Salem, Braintree, Wells, Dover [STR 1:53; NEHGR 3:127; GDMNH 403].

Knight, Francis: Bristol; 1640; Pemaquid [MPCR 1:57, 78; GDMNH 403].

Knight, George: Barrow, Suffolk; 1638; Hingham [NEHGR 15:26; HiBOP 99].

Knight, John: Unknown; 1632; Dorchester (probate of estate only) [GMB 1137-38].

Knight, John: Unknown; 1634; Dorchester [GM 2:4:207-8].

Knight, John: Romsey, Hampshire; 1635 on *James*; Newbury [GM 2:4:208-12].

Knight, John: Unknown; 1637; Cambridge (land transactions only) [CaBOP 44, 49; CaTR 29].

Knight, John: Unknown; 1638 on *Bevis*; Watertown, Sudbury, Charlestown, Woburn [Drakes's Founders 60; Lechford 390; WP 4:128; MBCR 1:300; WaBOP 9, 10, 13, 43; WaTR 1:14, 15; SLR 1:44, 47; SuTR 4; MLR 1:155; Rodgers 3:244-46; Stevens-Miller 1:229-32].

Knight, Mary: Unknown; 1639; Dorchester (church admission only) [DChR 4].

Knight, Matling: Unknown; 1639; Boston [Lechford 228; RCA 2:116; BChR 38; BTR 1:83, 114, 115, 116, 128, 137].

Knight, Mrs.: Unknown; 1637; Dorchester [DTR 30; DChR 3; WJ 2:426].

Knight, Richard: Romsey, Hampshire; 1635 on *James*; Newbury [GM 2:4:212-14].

Knight, Richard: Unknown; 1637; Weymouth (court appearance only) [WJ 2:426].

Knight, Richard: Unknown; 1640; Hampton, Newport [HmTR 47, 48; TAG 20:225-26; NEHGR 87:264-66].

Knight, Robert: Unknown; 1638 on *Bevis*; Marblehead [Drake's Founders 60; Ordway Anc 357-63].

Knight, Robert: Bristol; 1639; Pemaquid [WP 4:123; MPCR 1:78; GDMNH 404].

Knight, Roger: Unknown; 1630; Piscataqua [GMB 1138-39].

Knight, Sarah: Unknown; 1635 on *Defence*; passenger list only [GM 2:4:215].

Knight, Sarah: Unknown; 1638; Boston (church admission only) [BChR 24].

Knight, Thomas: Unknown; 1640; Piscataqua (witness to deed only) [GDMNH 405].

Knight, Toby: Unknown; 1639; Newport [RICR 1:92, 100, 111, 127; RICR (MS) 14, 30, 32].

Knight, Walter: Unknown; 1626; Cape Ann, Salem [GMB 1139-42].

Knight, Walter: Unknown; 1637; Duxbury (not seen after 1640) [PCR 1:95, 2:4, 12:38].

Knight, William: Unknown; 1636; Salem (land grant only) [STR 1:28].

Knight, William: Unknown; 1637; Charlestown (land transaction only) [ChTR 29].

Knight, William: Unknown; 1637; Lynn [MBCR 1:374; EQC 1:17, 2:270; Lechford 153; EPR 1:213-14; EIHC 2:102-3; TEG 18:71-74].

Knight, William: Southwark, Surrey; 1638; Ipswich; returned permanently to England in 1643 [ITR 40; Plain Dealing 93; TAG 33:108-12; Morison 385-86; Douglas Richardson, *Magna Carta Ancestry: A Study in Colonial and Medieval Families*, second edition, four volumes (Salt Lake City, Utah, 2011) 2:507-8; Abandoning 167-68].

Knill, Charles: Unknown; 1633; Piscataqua [GMB 1142].

Knollys, Hanserd: London; 1638; Boston, Dover; returned permanently to England in 1641 [WJ 1:351; WP 4:140, 176; Cotton 306; NHPP 10:701, 40:3; MBCR 1:278; NEHGR 19:131-33, 70:184; Abandoning 168-70; ODNB].

Knopp, William: Bures St. Mary, Suffolk; 1630; Watertown [GMB 1143-46; WF 433-38].

Knott, George: Unknown; 1636; Sandwich [PCR 1:57, 149, 8:6, 11; PCPR 1:1:82, 3:1:100; MD 9:157-59, 25:89-90; Rufus Babcock Tobey and Charles Henry Pope, *Tobey (Tobie, Toby) Genealogy* (Boston 1905) 15-23].

Knower, George: Unknown; 1631; Charlestown, Malden [GMB 1146-48].

Knower, Thomas: Unknown; 1630; Charlestown [GMB 1148-50].

Knowles, Alexander: Unknown; 1636; Concord, Fairfield [MBCR 1:372; FOOF 1:368-69; CN 38:542-63].

Knowles, Henry: Unknown; 1635 on *Susan & Ellen*; passenger list only (with caveat) [GM 2:4:215-16].

Knowles, John: Colchester, Essex; 1638; Boston, Watertown; returned permanently to England in 1651 [MBCR 1:235; WaBOP 70; BChR 25; WJ 2:21; Lechford 106; WaVR 1:9; SPR NS 1:18; WoTR 4; NEHGR 30:463; TAG 41:117; Abandoning 170-73; ODNB; WF 408].

Knowles, Richard: Unknown; 1637; Plymouth, Cambridge, Eastham [PCR 1:75, 109, 129; MD 5:23; NEHGR 21:213, 79:288-93].

Knowlton, John: Unknown; 1639; Ipswich [ITR 58; MBCR 1:379; EPR 1:163-65; TAG 35:17-18; NEHGR 163:14-15].

L

Ladd, Daniel: Unknown; 1634 on *Mary & John*; Ipswich, Salisbury, Haverhill [GM 2:4:217-21].

Laham, Richard: Unknown; 1640; Dover [NHPP 10:701]. (Probably a misreading of some other early Dover name [GDMNH 49, List 351b].)

Lahorne, Rowland: Unknown; 1635; Duxbury, Charlestown; returned permanently to England between 1654 and 1663 [GM 2:4:221-22; Abandoning 174].

Lake, Margaret: North Benfleet, Essex; 1638; Salem, New London, Ipswich [WP 4:63, 165; Bethia Harris Anc 53-56].

Lake, Thomas: Unknown; 1640; Dorchester [DChR 5; MBCR 1:378; NEHGR 4:167; TAG 12:18; SPR Case #1001].

Lamb, Edward: Unknown; 1633; Watertown, Boston [GMB 1151-52].

Lamb, Thomas: (possibly) Barnardiston, Suffolk; 1630; Roxbury [GMB 1153-55; WF 439-42].

Lambart, William: Unknown; 1635 on *Susan & Ellen*; passenger list only [GM 2:4:222].

Lambert, Francis: Holme-upon-Spalding-Moor, Yorkshire; 1639; Rowley [Lechford 208; MBCR 1:376; RowBOP 5; EPR 1:94, 300-1; NGSQ 68:13-14; Pillsbury Anc 1:417; Rowley Fam 220-21; GMN 18:27].

Lambert, Michael: Unknown; 1637; Salem [STR 1:66; EQC 1:6; BVR 71; EPR 3:106; EIHC 49-50].

Lambert, Richard: Unknown; 1634; Boston, Salem [GM 2:4:223-25].

Lamberton, George: Stepney, Middlesex; 1639; New Haven; died at sea in 1646 while returning to England [WP 4:115, 326; NHCR 1:27; NHChR 1; Cotton 346; Manwaring 1:49-50; NEHGR 61:189, 68:283-85; TAG 12:77-79, 185, 80:194; Ackley-Bosworth 139-40; Abandoning 174].

Lambson, Barnabas: Ridgewell, Essex; 1635; Cambridge [GM 2:4:226-28].

Lampson, William: Unknown; 1636; Ipswich [MBCR 1:373; ITR 25, 48; EPR 1:282-84; William J. Lamson, *Descendants of William Lamson of Ipswich, Mass., 1634-1917* (New York 1917)].

Lanckford, Richard: Unknown; 1632; Plymouth [GMB 1156; PM 303].

Lancton, Roger: Unknown; 1634; Ipswich, Haverhill [GM 2:4:228-30].

Lander, John: Unknown; 1635; Richmond Island [Trelawny 91; NHPP 1:113, 40:3; MPCR 1:42; GDMNH 410].

Lane, John: Unknown; 1639; Milford [MiTR 2; James Hill Fitts, *Lane Genealogies*, Volume II (Exeter, New Hampshire, 1897)].

Lane, Mary: Unknown; 1640; Weymouth (servant) [Lechford 391]. (She may have married Edward Poole.)

Lane, Matthew: Unknown; 1640; Hingham (land grant only) [HiBOP 96r].

Lane, Thomas: Unknown; 1633; Weymouth, Dorchester (servant; court appearance only) [MBCR 1:121; Weymouth Hist 3:363].

Lane, William: Beaminster, Dorset; 1635 on *Hopewell*; Dorchester [GM 2:4:230-33; M&JCH 27:36].

Lang, Richard: Unknown; 1634; Weymouth [GM 2:4:233-34].

Langer, Richard: Unknown; 1636; Hingham [HiBOP 46; SPR Case #258; Hingham Hist 3:422].

Langmore, John: Unknown; 1620 on *Mayflower*; Plymouth (died soon after arrival) [GMB 1156; PM 303].

Langstaff, Henry: Unknown; 1631; Piscataqua [GMB 1156-60; NHPP 10:701].

Lapham, Thomas: Tenterden, Kent; 1635 on *Hercules*; Scituate [GM 2:4:234-36].

Lapthorne, Mr.: Unknown; 1638; Salem (mention in letter only) [WP 4:71].

Lapthorne, Stephen: Unknown; 1637; Richmond Island; returned permanently to England in 1640 [Trelawny 112, 182, 184, 194, 220, 292, 300; MPCR 1:73; GDMNH 415].

Large, Jarvis: Unknown; 1636; Scituate (servant; death record only) [NEHGR 9:285].

Large, William: Norfolk; 1635; Hingham [GM 2:4:237-38].

Larkham, Thomas: Northam, Devon; 1639; Dover; returned permanently to England in 1642 [NHPP 1:128, 10:701, 40:3; WJ 2:32, 79; WP 4:289; Abandoning 175-81].

Larkin, Edward: Unknown; 1638; Charlestown [ChTR 39; ChBOP 43; ChChR 9; MBCR 1:376; NEHGR 4:268; Stevens-Miller 1:144-48; TAG 62:118-20; Kempton Anc 3:290-97].

Larmore, Henry: Unknown; 1637; Massachusetts Bay (court appearance only) [WJ 2:426].

Larremore, George: Unknown; 1640; New Haven; not seen after 1653 [NHCR 1:50, 94, 124, 135, 138, 164, 388, 424, 2:29, 306; NHTR 1:32, 110, 131, 188, 215, 246].

Lary, Sarah: Unknown; 1639; Charlestown (church admission only) [ChChR 9].

Laskin, Hugh: Unknown; 1635; Salem [GM 2:4:238-40].

Latcome, William: Unknown; 1634 on *Hercules*; passenger list only [GM 2:4:240].

Latham, Cary: Aldenham, Hertfordshire; 1639; Cambridge, New London [NEHGR 4:181, 61:385, 157:392; SPR 1:11; Waters 759; New London Hist 312].

Latham, William: Unknown; 1620 on *Mayflower*; Plymouth [GMB 1160; PM 304; MQ 75:49-53; LENE 10-11; Abandoning 182].

Lattimore, John: Unknown; 1639; Hartford, Wethersfield [CCCR 1:29; HaTR 46, 47, 50; TAG 10:107; Manwaring 1:134-35; Miner Anc 119; Wethersfield Hist 2:478].

Laughton *see also* **Lawton, Layton, and Leighton**

Laughton, Thomas: Great Missenden, Buckinghamshire; 1638; Lynn [MBCR 1:375; EQC 1:19, 270; TG 19:222-30; TEG 17:45-47].

Launder, Thomas: Unknown; 1635 on *Abigail*; Lynn, Sandwich [GM 2:4:240-44].

Lauson, Henry: Unknown; 1631; Massachusetts Bay [GMB 1160-61].

Laverick, John: Unknown; 1634 on *Elizabeth*; passenger list only [Hotten 282].

Lavis, John: Unknown; 1640; York [GDMNH 184, 419].

Law, Richard: Unknown; 1637; Wethersfield, Stamford [CCCR 1:20, 445; SmTR 4; WetLR 1:149; FOOF 1:375; Hale, House 655].

Lawes, Francis: Norwich, Norfolk; 1637 on *John & Dorothy* or *Rose*; Salem [Hotten 290; STR 1:59; SChR 10; MBCR 1:378; EQC 1:22; Sarah Stone Anc 77-82].

Lawrence, Henry: Unknown; 1635; Charlestown [GM 2:4:244-46].

Lawrence, John: Unknown; 1635; Watertown, Groton [GM 2:4:246-54].

Lawrence, John: St. Albans, Hertfordshire; 1635 on *Planter*; Ipswich, Flushing, New Amsterdam [GM 2:4:254-58].

Lawrence, Mary: St. Albans, Hertfordshire; 1635 on *Planter*; Ipswich [GM 2:4:258-59]. (She married Thomas Burnham.)

Lawrence, Thomas: St. Albans, Hertfordshire; 1635 on *Planter*; Ipswich, Flushing, Newtown [NY] [GM 2:4:259-63].

Lawrence, Thomas: Unknown; 1638; Hingham [HiBOP 76; Hingham Hist 2:426-27; GM 2:4:245-46].

Lawrence, Thomas: Unknown; 1639; Milford [MiTR 2; Milford Fam 407-8].

Lawrence, William: St. Albans, Hertfordshire; 1635 on *Planter*; Ipswich, Flushing [GM 2:4:263-68].

Lawson, Christopher: Lincolnshire; 1638; Exeter, Boston, Haverhill, Kennebec [NHPP 1:133; Aspinwall 23-24, 31-32, 172; NEHGR 2:274, 8:39, 98:11; SPR Case #1254; MHSP 46:479-84; GDMNH 419-20; Wentworth 1:76; Walter Eliot Thwing, *Thwing: A Genealogical, Biographical and Historical Account of the Family* (Boston 1883) 18].

Lawton *see also* **Laughton, Layton, and Leighton**

Lawton, George: Unknown; 1638; Portsmouth, Westerly [RICR 1:91; PoTR 2; Austin 121-22].

Lawton, Thomas: Unknown; 1638; Portsmouth [RICR 1:91; PoTR 2; Austin 122-23].

Lay, Edward: Unknown; 1639; Hartford, Saybrook [HaBOP 206, 357; HaTR 42; CCCR 1:302-3; see also Austin 123].

Layton *see also* **Laughton, Lawton, and Leighton**

Layton, John: Unknown; 1639; Newport [RICR 1:92; RICR (MS) 32, 37, 44].

Lazell, Henry: Unknown; 1637; Scituate (church admission only) [NEHGR 10:42].

Leach, John: Unknown; 1636; Salem [STR 1:33; EQC 1:8, 137; EPR 1:288-89; NEHGR 162:98].

Leach, Lawrence: Sonning, Berkshire; 1629; Salem [GMB 1161-64; WF 443-47].

Leach, Margaret: Unknown; 1635 on *Defence*; passenger list only [GM 2:268].

Leach, Margaret: Unknown; 1635 on *Susan & Ellen*; passenger list only [GM 2:4:268-69].

Leach, Robert: Unknown; 1637; Charlestown [ChTR 31; ChBOP 64, 70; ChChR 9; Wyman 610].

Leader, Thomas: Unknown; 1638; Dedham, Boston [DeTR 1:48; DeChR 25; Essex Ant 2:48; SPR Case #353; GDMNH 294, 421; NEHGR 54:350].

Leager, Jacob: Kersey, Suffolk; 1637; Boston [BChR 24, 33; Lechford 158; BTR 1:34; MBCR 1:379; NEHGR 69:353-57; TAG 19:193-97]. (Probably the "Jacob Segar" who held land briefly at Watertown [WaBOP 20, 75, 116].)

Leake, Anne: Unknown; 1635 on *Defence*; passenger list only [GM 2:4:269].

Learned, William: Bermondsey, Surrey; 1631; Charlestown, Woburn [GMB 1164-66; Kempton Anc 4:429-50].

Leaver, Thomas: Howden, Yorkshire; 1640; New Haven, Rowley [NHCR 1:50; RowBOP 4; EPR Case #16735; Rowley Fam 228; Parker-Ruggles 320-22; GMN 18:27].

Leaves, Ellen: Unknown; 1635 on *Hopewell*; passenger list only [GM 2:4:269].

Leavitt, John: Unknown; 1634; Dorchester, Hingham [GM 2:4:270-76].

Leavitt, Thomas: Unknown; 1638; Exeter, Hampton [NHPP 1:133; Exeter Hist 436; NEHGR 21:316, 67:66-81; GDMNH 425].

Lechford, Thomas: London; 1638; Boston; returned permanently to England in 1641 [Lechford 1; ODNB; Abandoning 182-83].

Lee, John: Unknown; 1633; Massachusetts Bay [GMB 2081-82].

Lee, John: Unknown; 1634 on *Francis*; passenger list only (with caveat) [GM 2:4:276-77].

Lee, John: Unknown; 1640; Ipswich [ITR 68; EQC 1:38; EPR 2:236-38; Hammatt Papers 203-4; William Lee, *John Leigh of Agawam (Ipswich) Massachusetts 1634-1671* (Albany, New York, 1888) {material prior to 1640 in this volume should be used with caution}].

Lee, John: Unknown; 1640; Saco, Boston [MPCR 1:69; GDMNH 425].

Lee, Robert: Unknown; 1636; Plymouth [PCR 1:48, 12:29; MD 5:153-59, 11:32, 200-6; Emerson-Benson 338-39].

Lee, William: Unknown; 1635 on *Planter*; passenger list only [GM 2:4:277].

Leeds, ____: Unknown; 1637; Salem (land grant only) [STR 1:103; Dawes-Gates 1:403].

Leeds, Richard: Great Yarmouth, Norfolk; 1637 on *John & Dorothy* or *Rose*; Dorchester [Hotten 292; DTR 40; DChR 149; NEHGR 4:169; Dawes-Gates 1:402-8].

Leete, William: Hail Weston, Huntingdonshire; 1639; Guilford, Hartford [Lechford 427; Guilford Hist 25; Manwaring 1:330; NEHGR 81:127; TAG 31:114-17; Eugene A. Stratton, *Applied Genealogy* (Salt Lake City, Utah, 1988) 70-72, 165].

Legatt, John: Theydon Garnon, Essex; 1640; Hampton [HmTR 48; NHPP 31:14; SPR 1:28; GDMNH 426; Phyllis O. Whitten, *Samuel Fogg, 1628-1672: His Ancestors and Descendants* (Annandale, Virginia, 1976)].

Legge, John: Unknown; 1630; Lynn, Marblehead [GMB 1166-68; WF 447-49].

Leighorne, James: Unknown; 1638; Plymouth (servant; court appearance only) [PCR 1:115].

Leighton *see also* **Laughton, Lawton, and Layton**

Leighton, Thomas: Unknown; 1640; Dover [NHPP 1:128, 10:701, 40:6; Perley M. Leighton, *A Leighton Genealogy: Descendants of Thomas Leighton of Dover, New Hampshire*, 2 volumes (Boston 1989)].

Leister, Edward: Unknown; 1620 on Mayflower; Plymouth; soon removed to Virginia [GMB 1168-69; PM 304-5].

Lemon, Robert: Unknown; 1636; Salem [STR 1:23; SChR 8, 10; EPR 2:90-92; Perley 1:391].

Lenthall, Robert: Great Missenden, Buckinghamshire; 1638; Weymouth, Newport; returned permanently to England by 1643 [WJ 1:346; RICR 1:92, 104; WP 4:86; MBCR 1:254; Weymouth Hist 3:367-68; GMN 22:30; TG 19:222-30; Frank Farnsworth Starr, *The Eells*

Family of Dorchester ...: With Notes on the Lenthall Family (Hartford 1903) 173-90; Abandoning 183-84].

Leonard, John: Unknown; 1638; Springfield [SpTR 161; SpVR 19; Pynchon Court 205 ; Hale-House 678-82].

Leonard, Solomon: Unknown; 1637; Duxbury, Bridgewater [PCR 1:83, 8:189; TAG 27:1-6, 37:212-15; MF 15:8-9; MD 57:68-75].

Leppinwell, Michael: Unknown; 1638; Cambridge, Woburn [NEHGR 4:181; WoVR; Flagg Anc 196 (clue)].

Letherland, William: Unknown; 1630; Boston, Newport [GMB 1169-73; WF 450-55].

Lettice, Thomas: Unknown; 1638; Plymouth [PTR 1:4; PCR 1:136, 7:5; PCPR 4:2:11; PPR 1:42; Scott Gen 289].

Lettin, Richard: Salford, Bedfordshire; 1640; Concord, Fairfield, Hempstead, Oyster Bay, Huntington [CoVR 2; FOOF 1:373-74; NYGBR 117:219-24].

Lettyne, Thomas: Unknown; 1635 on *Elizabeth*; passenger list only [GM 2:4:278].

Levens, John: Unknown; 1632 on *William & Francis*; Roxbury [GMB 1173-75].

Lever, Margery: Unknown; 1639; Dorchester [DChR 5, 17; SPR 1:432, 3:101, 4:206].

Leverett, Thomas: Boston, Lincolnshire; 1633; Boston [GMB 1175-78].

Leverich, Henry: Salisbury, Wiltshire; 1635 on *James*; passenger list only [GM 2:4:278].

Leverich, William: Great Livermere, Suffolk; 1633 on *James*; Dover, Boston, Duxbury, Sandwich, Oyster Bay, Newtown, Huntington [GMB 1178-80; Michael E. Leveridge, *A Godly Minister* (Cambridge, England, 2008)].

Levett, Christopher: Yorkshire; 1623; New England [GMB 1180-81; NEHGR 67:75-77].

Lewis, Edmond: Unknown; 1634 on *Elizabeth*; Watertown, Lynn [GM 2:4:278-81].

Lewis, George: Staplehurst, Kent; 1634; Scituate, Barnstable [GM 2:4:281-84].

Lewis, George: Unknown; 1639; Saco [MPCR 1:48; Trelawny 213; GDMNH 428-29].

Lewis, John: Unknown; 1634; Charlestown, Malden [GM 2:4:287-92].

Lewis, John: Tenterden, Kent; 1635 on *Hercules*; Scituate, Boston [GM 2:4:284-87].

Lewis, Morgan: Unknown; 1640; Plymouth (court appearance only) [Lechford 270; NHPP 40:4].

Lewis, Robert: Unknown; 1635 on *Blessing*; Salem [GM 2:4:292-93].

Lewis, Thomas: Shrewsbury, Shropshire; 1628; Saco [GMB 1181-84].

Lewis, Thomas: Unknown; 1637; Dorchester (church admission and grant of land only) [DTR 24; DChR 3].

Lewis, William: Unknown; 1632 on *Lyon*; Cambridge, Hartford, Hadley, Farmington [GMB 1184-86].

Lewis, William: Unknown; 1640; Roxbury, Lancaster [RVR MS 1, 3; RChR 85; MBCR 2:291; MLR 12:156; Rodgers 3:84-86].

Ley, James: Unknown; 1637; Boston; returned permanently to England the same year [WJ 1:274; WP 3:437; Abandoning 343; ODNB]. (In 1637 he was styled Lord Ley, but in 1638 succeeded his father as Earl of Marlborough [CP 8:490].)

Libby, John: Unknown; 1636; Richmond Island, Scarborough [Trelawny 190, 290; GDMNH 432; NEHGR 34:200-1; TAG 36:182-84, 73:258-71; Joseph Waterhouse Anc 115-20; Charles T. Libby, *The Libby Family in America: 1602-1881* (Portland, Maine, 1882)].

Lightfoot, Francis: Unknown; 1636; Lynn [MBCR 1:372; EQC 1:7, 11, 2:270; EPR 1:55-56].

Lincoln, Samuel: Norwich, Norfolk; 1637 on *John & Dorothy* or *Rose*; Salem, Hingham [Hotten 290; NEHGR 15:26, 121:10, 143:131-33; Hingham Hist 2:459-60; NYGBR 60:115, 117; GMB 1215; PM 311].

Lincoln, Stephen: Wymondham, Norfolk; 1638; Hingham [NEHGR 15:27; Hingham Hist 2:476; SPR Case #199].

Lincoln, Thomas, weaver: Hingham, Norfolk; 1633; Watertown, Charlestown, Hingham [GMB 1187-88; HiBOP 57v-58r].

Lincoln, Thomas, cooper: Beaminster, Dorset; 1635, Hingham [HiBOP 47r; TAG 64:214-15, 65:106; Hingham Hist 3:3].

Lincoln, Thomas, husbandman: Unknown; 1636; Hingham [HiBOP 48v; Hingham Hist 3:15-16].

Lincoln, Thomas, miller: Unknown; 1636; Hingham, Taunton [HiBOP 61r; Hingham Hist 3:20-21]. (Two early records for the name Thomas

Lincoln in Hingham cannot be confidently allocated to any one of these four men [WP 4:297; MBCR 1:374].)

Lindell, James: Unknown; 1639; Duxbury [PCR 1:145, 3:22; Farr Anc 194-95; Waters 743 (clue); PCPR 1:111-13; MD 11:87-92].

Ling, Benjamin: London; 1636; Charlestown, New Haven [ChTR 22; NHCR 1:28, 41; TAG 66:45-48, 76:1-16; NEHGR 81:127; Abandoning 187].

Linkes, Philip: Unknown; 1637; Scituate (death and probate only) [NEHGR 9:285; PCR 1:105].

Linnell, Robert: Unknown; 1638; Scituate, Barnstable [NEHGR 9:280, 67:260-61, 69:284; PCR 1:110; MD 15:58-59; Rachel Linnell Wynn, *The Descendants of Robert Linnell* (Baltimore 1994)].

Linsey, Christopher: Unknown; 1632, Lynn [EQC 1:26, 2:43; MBCR 3:387, 4:1:233; TEG 7:17-18].

Linsey, Daniel: Norwich, Norfolk; 1637 on *John & Dorothy* or *Rose*; passenger list only (servant) [Hotten 290].

Linsford, Francis: Unknown; 1638; Marblehead, Yarmouth [EQC 1:10, 114, 135, 152, 362, 414, 2:419, 441, 3:109, 5:257; ELR 2:97; PCR 2:27, 28, 36-37].

Linton, Richard: Unknown; 1630; Massachusetts Bay [GMB 1188-89; WF 455-56].

Lippet, John: Unknown; 1640; Providence, Warwick [PrTR 2:2, 15:5; NEHGR 27:70; Austin 336-39].

Lippincott, Richard: Unknown; 1639; Dorchester, Boston [DTR 1:42; DChR 5; MBCR 1:377; Judith M. Olsen, *Lippincott: Five Generations of the Descendants of Richard and Abigail Lippincott* (Woodbury, New Jersey, 1982)].

Lishe, Sarah: Unknown; 1639; Dorchester (probate proceedings only) [MBCR 1:285].

Lisle, Francis: Unknown; 1638; Boston; returned permanently to England by 1645 [BTR 1:35, 43; BChR 26; MBCR 1:377 (as "Francis Seyle"); SPR 4:275, 5:125; SPR Case #414; NEHGR 2:191; HAHAC 1:107; Abandoning 188].

Lissen, Thomas: Plymouth, Devonshire; 1638; Richmond Island (soon ran away) [Trelawny 181].

Listen, Nicholas: Unknown; 1637; Salem, Marblehead, Gloucester, Exeter [STR 1:53, 58, 63, 74; Essex Ant 3:43-44, 10:110, 12:84; GDMNH 436; Marblehead 90].

Little, Thomas: Unknown; 1632; Plymouth, Marshfield [GMB 1189-92; PM 305-9].

Littlefield, Edmond: Titchfield, Hampshire; 1638 on *Bevis*; Exeter [Drake's Founders 60; NHPP 1:133; Annis Spear Anc 77-84; TAG 75:16-25; NEHGR 67:343-48, 86:71-77].

Littlehale, Richard: Unknown; 1634 on *Mary & John*; Newbury, Haverhill [GM 2:4:294-96].

Livermore, John: Wethersfield, Essex; 1634 on *Francis*; Watertown, Wethersfield, New Haven [GM 2:4:297-302].

Lloyd, Walter: Unknown; 1635 on *Hopewell*; passenger list only [GM 2:4:302].

Lobden, Nicholas: Northam, Devon; 1636; Hingham [HiBOP 38; NEHGR 121:13, 142:394; TAG 54:35-37].

Locke, William: Stepney, Middlesex; 1635 on *Planter*; Charlestown, Woburn [GM 2:4:302-8].

Lockwood, Edmund: Combs, Suffolk; 1630; (probably) Watertown, Cambridge [GMB 1192-94; WF 456-58; CA 48:53-58].

Lockwood, Robert: Combs, Suffolk; 1633; Watertown, Stamford, Fairfield [GM 2:4:308-15; CA 48:53-58].

Lodge, Grace: Unknown; 1633; Boston [GMB 1194].

Loker, Henry: Bures St. Mary, Suffolk; 1639; Sudbury [SuTR 3; HAHAC 1:107; Stevens-Miller 1:142-43; NEHGR 63:280, 64:136, 143:325-31].

Loker, John: Bures St. Mary, Suffolk; 1639; Sudbury [SuTR 3; Stevens-Miller 1:142-43; NEHGR 49:341-42, 55:226, 63:280, 64:136, 143:325-31].

Lombard, Thomas: Thorncombe, Dorset; 1630 on *Mary & John*; Dorchester, Barnstable [GMB 1194-98; M&JCH 26:43-47].

Long, ____: Bristol; 1640; York; not seen after 1642 [WP 4:263; Gorges 100].

Long, Ellen: London; 1635 on *Increase*; passenger list only [GM 2:4:315].

Long, John: Unknown; 1638; Plymouth (servant; court appearance only) [PCR 1:100].

Long, John: Unknown; 1639; Massachusetts Bay [Lechford 176; SPR 2:1; MBCR 1:316, 318]. (These records are all dated 1639. If they do all pertain to the same John Long, he may have been a transient merchant or mariner.)

Long, John: Unknown; 1640; Weymouth (deposition only) [Lechford 391].

Long, Nicholas: Unknown; 1635 on *Blessing*; passenger list only [GM 2:4:315].

Long, Robert: Unknown; 1623 on *Anne*; Plymouth [GMB 1198; PM 309].

Long, Robert: Dunstable, Bedfordshire; 1635 on *Defence*; Charlestown [GM 2:4:316-20].

Long, Thomas: Unknown; 1634 on *Recovery*; passenger list only [GM 2:4:320-21].

Long, William: Unknown; 1637 on *Speedwell*; passenger list only [NGSQ 71:176].

Longley, William: Firsby, Lincolnshire; 1638; Lynn, Groton [EQC 1:17, 2:270; MBCR 1:375; Lechford 294; Bond 751; Wyman 413, 628; TAG 62:26]. (This immigrant appeared in Lynn records in 1638 as "Richard Langley" [EQC 2:268-71].)

Lonnin, James: Stepney, Middlesex; 1635 on *Planter*; passenger list only [GM 2:4:321].

Looke, Robert: Unknown; 1635 on *Unity*; Dorchester; perhaps returned to England permanently about 1640 [GM 2:4:321-22].

Looman, Ann: Unknown; 1634; Roxbury, Weymouth [GM 2:4:322-24].

Loomis, Joseph: Braintree, Essex; 1638; Windsor [Lechford 137; WiLR 1:49; Grant 10; CCCR 1:446; NEHGR 55:23-24; Dawes-Gates 2:567-72; Brainerd Anc 207-9; Elisha S. Loomis, *Descendants of Joseph Loomis in America* (n.p. 1909)].

Lopes, John: Unknown; 1638; Richmond Island (servant) [Trelawny 191].

Lord, Jane: Unknown; 1635; Roxbury, Hartford [GM 2:4:324-25]. (She married Thomas Hale.)

Lord, Nathan: Wittersham, Kent; 1638; Kittery [TAG 84:81-94; MG 33:3-6].

Lord, Robert: Finchingfield, Essex; 1635; Ipswich [GM 2:4:325-30].

Lord, Thomas: Towcester, Northamptonshire; 1635 on *Elizabeth & Ann*; Cambridge, Hartford [GM 2:4:331-35]. (Thomas Lord was preceded to New England in 1633 by his son Richard Lord [GMB 1198-1201].)

Lord, William: Unknown; 1635; Salem [GM 2:4:335-40].

Loring, Thomas: Axminster, Devon; 1635; Hingham, Hull [GM 2:4:340-45; M&JCH 27:37-38].

Lothrop, John: London; 1634 on *Griffin*; Scituate, Barnstable [GM 2:4:345-51; NEHGR 161:123-26].

Lothrop, Thomas: Unknown; 1633; Salem, Beverly [GMB 1201-6].

Louge, Richard: Unknown; 1630 on *Mary & John*; Dorchester [GMB 1206].

Love, Agnes: Ashford, Kent; 1635 on *Hercules*; passenger list only [GM 2:4:351].

Love, Goodman: Unknown; 1639; New Haven (court appearance only) [NHCR 1: 29].

Love, James: Unknown; 1640; Saco [Lechford 278; MHGR 5:124].

Love, John: Unknown; 1635; Massachusetts Bay [GM 2:4:351].

Love, John: Unknown; 1637; Boston (land grant only) [BTR 1:31].

Love, John: Unknown; 1640; Saco (court appearance only) [MPCR 1:57, 91, 98].

Lovejoy, Grace: Caversham, Oxfordshire; 1638 on *Confidence*; Newbury [Drake's Founders 59; NEHGR 163:27-32]. (She almost certainly married William Ballard of Andover.)

Lovejoy, John: Caversham, Oxfordshire; 1638 on *Confidence*; Newbury, Andover [Drake's Founders 59; NEHGR 163:27-32].

Lovell, Robert: Unknown; 1635 on *Marygould*; Weymouth [GM 2:4:352-54].

Lovell, William: Unknown; 1633; Dorchester, Marblehead; returned to England permanently by 1637 [GMB 1206-8].

Lovering, John: Ardleigh, Essex; 1635; Watertown [GM 2:4:354-57].

Lovett, Daniel: Unknown; 1639; Braintree [BTR 1:51 (as "Danyell Lovell"); Lyon-Rice 457-58 (no evidence provided for claimed relation with John Lovett)].

Lovett, John: Unknown; 1639; Salem, Beverly [STR 1:90; EQC 1:27; Perley 2:270; Granberry 270-72; Lyon-Rice 453-54 (no evidence provided for claimed relation with Daniel Lovett)].

Lovett, Mary: Unknown; 1638; Dorchester (church admission only) [DChR 3].

Low, Andrew: Unknown; 1638; New Haven [NHCR 1:13, 35; NEHGR 81:128; FANH 1110].

Low, Dorothy: Unknown; 1635 on *Truelove*; passenger list only [GM 2:4:357].

Low, John: Unknown; 1636; Boston [BTR 1:15, 20; Lechford 284, 316; BBOP 10, 92; SLR 1:96, 165, 252, 2:16-20; NEHGR 10:217; Aspinwall 111, 265; SPR Case #147; Austin 338-39].

Low, Thomas: Unknown; 1640; Ipswich [ITR 85; Phoebe Tilton Anc 173-76].

Lowden, Richard: Unknown; 1638; Charlestown [ChTR 40; ChChR 10; NEHGR 4:268, 5:175; WoTR 2; Wyman 632-33].

Lowell, Percival: Portbury, Somerset; 1639; Newbury [NeTR 43; Phoebe Tilton Anc 207-24; NEHGR 157:309-19; M&JCH 25:46-47; Scott C. Steward, *The Descendants of Judge John Lowell of Newburyport, Massachusetts* (Boston 2011) 2-7].

Lucas, Mr.: London; 1640; New Haven [NHCR 1:49, 93, 94, 95, 196; TAG 18:60]. (Probably never came to New England.)

Lucas, William: Unknown; 1638; Richmond Island; not seen after 1640 [Trelawny 182, 189, 194, 283, 292, 300]. (See also GDMNH 448.)

Ludden, James: Unknown; 1632; Weymouth [WJ 1:110; MBCR 1:164, 249, 331; SPR 1:5; RCA 2:61; Weymouth Hist 3:411-12; Savage 3:127-28].

Luddington, Christian: Unknown; 1635 on *Hopewell*; passenger list only [GM 2:4:357-58].

Luddington, William: Wrawby, Lincolnshire; 1639; Charlestown, Malden, New Haven [MBCR 1:291; NEHGR 4:268; TAG 74:81-96, 209-24].

Ludkin, George: Unknown; 1635; Hingham, Braintree [GM 2:4:358-59].

Ludkin, William: Norwich, Norfolk; 1637 on *John & Dorothy* or *Rose*; Hingham [Hotten 290; NEHGR 8:39, 10:71, 15:27, 121:10, 14; HiBOP 68; MBCR 1:374; BTR 1:95, 107, 108; BChR 57; Aspinwall 26, 285, 310, 311; SPR Case #122, Case #841; Hingham Hist 3:47].

Ludlow, George: Wiltshire; 1630 on *Mary & John*; Dorchester; soon moved permanently to Virginia [GMB 1208-11].

Ludlow, Roger: Warminster, Wiltshire; 1630 on *Mary & John*; Dorchester, Windsor, Fairfield; to Ireland permanently in 1654 [GMB 1211-13; Abandoning 190-91; M&JCH 26:49-51].

Ludwell, John: Unknown; 1638 on *Confidence*; passenger list only [Drake's Founders 59].

Luff, John: Unknown; 1634 on *Mary & John*; Salem, Beverly [GM 2:4:359-61].

Lugg, John: Gloucester, Gloucestershire; 1637; Boston [NEHGR 2:274; BChR 23, 291; BTR 1:47; Waters 551-52, 54; TAG 9:212-22; TG 6:195-97; Kempton 4:478-94].

Lukas, Mary: Unknown; 1633; Boston (church admission only) [GMB 1214].

Luker, Robert: Unknown; 1639; Massachusetts Bay (three business transactions only) [Lechford 247, 381; SLR 1:43].

Lummus, Edward: Unknown; 1635 on *Susan & Ellen*; Ipswich [GM 2:4:361-65; NHGR 27:1-10, 140].

Lumpkin, Richard: Boxted, Essex; 1637; Ipswich [ITR 30; MBCR 1:236, 375; EPR 1:11, 43-44, 138; Ipswich Hist 1:337, 340, 495-96; MPR 2:128-30; GM 2:6:555-56, 2:7:244-45, 298].

Lumpkin, William: Unknown; 1638; Yarmouth [PCR 1:108, 141, 7:9; PCPR 3:1:30; MD 12:139-41, 17:99-100; Bassett-Preston 181-82].

Lund, Thomas: London; 1640; Hingham, Boston [Lechford 306, 326; Aspinwall 302, 305-6, 319, 320, 329, 416; SLR 2:74].

Lunt, Henry: Unknown; 1634 on *Mary & John*; Ipswich, Newbury [GM 2:4:365-68].

Lush, Henry: Symondsbury, Dorset; 1635 on *Marygould*; Windsor [GM 2:4:368-69; Grant 78].

Lusher, Eleazer: Starston, Norfolk; 1637; Dedham [DeTR 1:32; DeChR 6; DeVR 127; HAHAC 1:70; MBCR 1:375; NEHGR 8:328, 96:372-74; DeHR 2:130-35; TAG 67:54].

Luson, John: Unknown; 1637; Dedham [DeTR 1:32; DeChR 6; MBCR 1:263, 374; SPR Case #268; TAG 66:134; NEHGR 151:180]. (See also ChTR 29.)

Lutner, John: Unknown; 1638; Portsmouth; left Portsmouth in 1638 (two court appearances only) [RICR 1:60, 62].

Luxford, James: Unknown; 1637; Cambridge, Plymouth [WP 3:516, 4:123-27; MHSC 4:6:167, 5:1:127-47; NEHGR 4:181; CaChR 9;

Shepard 38-41; Lechford 58, 229, 370; MBCR 1:283, 295; PCR 2:22-24, 39, 7:21-27; MHSP 2:7:127-43; Cambridge Hist 600-1].

Lyford, John: Loughall, Armagh, Ireland; 1624; Plymouth, Nantasket, Salem; to Virginia permanently in 1627 [GMB 1214-17; PM 309-13; NEHGR 121:11; TAG 83:174-78, 84:176].

Lyman, Richard: High Ongar, Essex; 1631; Roxbury, Hartford [GMB 1217-20].

Lynde, Thomas: Dunstable, Bedfordshire; 1634; Charlestown [GM 2:4:369-78].

Lyne, Mary: Unknown; 1635 on *Abigail*; passenger list only [GM 2:4:378].

Lynn, Henry: Unknown; 1630; Boston, York; to Virginia permanently in 1643 [GMB 1220-22; York Hist 1:97; GM 2:7:55-56].

Lyon, John: Unknown; 1637; Marblehead [STR 1:63, 74; EQC 1:77, 106, 114, 380, 2:160, 167; ELR 1:28v; Perley 1:235, 2:179; Marblehead 91-92].

Lyon, Susanna: Unknown; 1639; Dorchester (church admission only) [DChR 4].

Lyon, William: Unknown; 1635 on *Hopewell*; Roxbury, Rowley [GM 2:4:379-82].

Lyvars, Judith: Unknown; 1635; Boston [GM 2:4:382].

M

Mackworth, Arthur: Unknown; 1634; Saco, Falmouth [MPCR 1:6, 43; Trelawny 106, 266; GDMNH 451 (clue); TG 3:45-95; TAG 26:157, 30:175].

Macomber, John: Bridport, Dorset; 1639; Newport, Taunton [RICR 1:92; GMN 23:3; TG 2:170-71; Everett S. Stackpole, *Macomber Genealogy* (Lewiston, Maine, 1908)].

Macomber, William: Bridport, Dorset; 1637; Dorchester [PCR 1:82, 159; PCPR 3:1:9; TG 2:170-71; Everett S. Stackpole, *Macomber Genealogy* (Lewiston, Maine, 1908)].

Macy, Thomas: Unknown; 1639; Newbury, Salisbury, Amesbury, Nantucket [NeTR 37; MBCR 1:376; SyTR 3; EPR 1:23; Hoyt 236-37; TAG 30:158; Silvanus J. Macy, *Genealogy of the Macy Family from 1635-1868* (Albany, New York, 1868)].

Maddox, John: Stepney, Middlesex; 1635 on *Planter*; Salem [GM 2:5:1-2].

Mahoney, Dorman: Ireland; 1639; Hingham, Lynn, Boston [Lechford 251-52; EQC 1:26, 47, 53, 57, 64; BTR 1:141; BVR 79, 80, 82; MBCR 2:20; SPR Case #266; NEHGR 9:165, 10:221, 95:134; Aspinwall 374; GDMNH 468].

Makepeace, Thomas: Burton Dassett, Warwickshire; 1635; Dorchester, Boston [GM 2:5:2-8].

Malbon, Richard: London; 1639; New Haven; returned permanently to England about 1650 [NHCR 1:27; WP 4:254; WJ 2:114; Abandoning 192-94].

Malton, William: Unknown; 1635 on *Hopewell*; passenger list only [GM 2:5:8]. (Possibly a clerical error for William Walton [NEHGR 167:82].)

Manchester, Thomas: Unknown; 1639; New Haven (servant; two court appearances only) [NHCR 1:26, 31]. (A Thomas Manchester appeared at Portsmouth by 1655 [Austin 127].)

Manifold, John: Unknown; 1635 on *Blessing*; passenger list only [GM 2:5:8].

Mann, Susanna: Unknown; 1640; New Haven (servant; court appearance only) [NHCR 1:51].

Mann, William: Unknown; 1634; Cambridge [GM 2:5:9-11].

Mann, William: Unknown; 1640; Providence [PrTR 2:1, 15:5; TAG 20:53, 24:5; Austin 129-30; RIHSC 14:47].

Mannering, Joseph: Unknown; 1632 on *William & Francis*; Dorchester [GMB 1223].

Manning, Anne: Ormesby St. Michael, Norfolk; 1637 on *John & Dorothy* or *Rose*; passenger list only (servant) [Hotten 292].

Manning, Clement: Unknown; 1638; Massachusetts Bay (servant; court appearance only) [MBCR 1:234].

Manning, John: Unknown; 1634; Ipswich [GM 2:5:11-13].

Manning, Susan: Unknown; 1638; Ipswich [ITR 41; GM 2:5:12-13].

Manning, Thomas: Unknown; 1638; Ipswich [ITR 63; EPR 2:144-46; Hammatt 225-26; GM 2:5:12-13].

Manning, William: Unknown; 1639; Roxbury, Cambridge, Boston [Shepard 93; MBCR 1:377; CaChR 9; SPR Case #403; William H. Manning, *The Genealogical and Biographical History of the Manning Families of New England and Descendants* (Salem, Massachusetts, 1902)].

Mansfelt, Daniel: Unknown; 1638; Massachusetts Bay (court appearance only) [MBCR 1:290].

Mansfield, John: London; 1635 on *Susan & Ellen*; Boston, Charlestown [GM 2:5:14-17; NHGR 11:174-79].

Mansfield, Mr.: Unknown; 1640; New Haven [NHCR 1:91, 276, 317; GMN 13:9-13]. (Probably never came to New England.)

Mansfield, Richard: Exeter, Devon; 1640; New Haven [Lechford 250; NHCR 1:41, 91; NEHGR 66:308-10, 81:128; TAG 74:225; GMN 13:12; FANH 1137-38].

Mantell, Robert: Unknown; 1640; Dorchester (business transaction only); returned permanently to England in 1640 [Lechford 326].

Mapes, John: Unknown; 1634 on *Francis*; passenger list only [GM 2:5:17-18].

March, Hugh: Unknown; 1638 on *Confidence*; Newbury [Drake's Founders 58; Abel Lunt 125-32 (clue); GDMNH 456-57].

March, John: Unknown; 1638; Charlestown [NEHGR 4:268; ChBOP 64; ChChR 10; ChTR 44; Wyman 654-55; Rodgers 2:305-8].

Margesson, Edmund: Unknown; 1620 on *Mayflower*; Plymouth [GMB 1223; PM 315].

Marport, Mabel: Unknown; 1633; Boston [GMB 1223].

Marrett, Thomas: Ipswich, Suffolk; 1635; Cambridge [GM 2:5:18-22].

Marriner, Thomas: Unknown; 1639; Massachusetts Bay (servant; court appearance only) [MBCR 1:282].

Marriott, Thomas: Wapping, Middlesex; 1636; Massachusetts Bay (letter to John Winthrop only); returned permanently to England by 1637 [WP 3:422].

Marryner, ____: Unknown; 1634; Massachusetts Bay [GM 2:5:22-23].

Marsh, George: Unknown; 1635; Hingham [GM 2:5:23-25].

Marsh, John: Unknown; 1634 on *Mary & John*; Salem [GM 2:5:26-30].

Marsh, John: Braintree, Essex; 1639; Hartford, Hadley [HaBOP 347; TAG 58:223-28; Moore Anc 357-72; Dwight Whitney Marsh, *Marsh Genealogy* (Amherst, Massachusetts, 1895)].

Marshall, Ann: Unknown; 1638; Connecticut (court appearance only) [CCCR 1:28].

Marshall, Christopher: Alford, Lincolnshire; 1634; Boston, Exeter; returned permanently to England after 1639 [GM 2:5:30-35; Abandoning 194-95].

Marshall, Edmund: Unknown; 1635 on *Hopewell*; Salem, Manchester, New London, Ipswich [GM 2:5:35-40; NEHGR 160:312, 161:300-1].

Marshall, Francis: Unknown; 1635 on *Christian*; passenger list only (with caveat) [GM 2:5:40-41].

Marshall, James: Exeter, Devon; 1638; Dorchester, Windsor, New Haven [DTR 1:34, 53, 297; Lechford 250; NHCR 1:50, 80, 93, 196;

GMN 13:11-12, 20; M&JCH 18:100-2]. (Granted land at Dorchester, Windsor and New Haven, but probably never came to New England.)

Marshall, John: Unknown; 1635 on *Hopewell*; passenger list only [GM 2:5:41].

Marshall, John: Lincolnshire; 1639; Portsmouth, Boston [RICR 1:66, 91; BTR 1:48; GM 2:5:33, 41; GMN 22:27].

Marshall, Mr.: Unknown; 1638; Richmond Island (mention in letter only) [WP 4:118].

Marshall, Thomas: Unknown; 1634; Boston [GM 2:5:41; MA Arch 38B:213; Lechford 236].

Marshall, Thomas: Unknown; 1635 on *James*; passenger list only (with caveat) [GM 2:5:46-47].

Marshall, Thomas: Unknown; 1638; Lynn, Reading [EQC 2:270; MBCR 1:379; HAHAC 1:108; GM 2:5:46-47; TEG 16:161-68].

Marshall, William: Unknown; 1635 on *Abigail*; passenger list only [GM 2:5:47-48].

Marshfield, Thomas: Exeter, Devon; 1634 on *Regard*; Dorchester, Windsor [GM 2:5:48-54; TAG 67:11-14].

Marson, Elizabeth: Unknown; 1632; Boston [GMB 1224]. (She probably married John Pemberton.)

Marston, John: Ormesby St. Margaret, Norfolk; 1637 on *John & Dorothy* or *Rose*; Salem [Hotten 291; MBCR 1:378; SChR 10; EQC 1:12, 28, 8:362-63; Sarah Stone Anc 129-30; NEHGR 27:291-92; Perley 2:78-79; Sibley 3:423].

Marston, Robert: Unknown; 1639; Newbury, Hampton [NeTR 35; HmTR 45; GDMNH 55, 461; NEHGR 142:265, 163:166; Sarah Stone Anc 129-30; Pillsbury Anc 351-54].

Marston, William: Hemsby, Norfolk; 1636; Salem, Hampton [STR 1:23; GDMNH 55, 462; HmTR 44; NEHGR 69:342-45; Sarah Stone Anc 129-34; Pillsbury Anc 351-57].

Martin, Abraham: Unknown; 1635; Hingham, Rehoboth [GM 2:5:54-56].

Martin, Alice: Unknown; 1638; Plymouth [PCR 1:108]. (She married George Clark.)

Martin, Ambrose: Unknown; 1637; Dorchester, Concord; not seen after 1642 [DTR 24, 28, 30; DChR 4; CoVR 2; MBCR 1:252].

Martin, Christopher: Billericay, Great Burstead, Essex; 1620 on *Mayflower*; Plymouth [GMB 1124-25; PM 315-16; TAG 80:264; MQ 76:242-46].

Martin, Edward: Unknown; 1635 on *Abigail*; passenger list only [GM 2:5:56].

Martin, Francis: Plymouth, Devon; 1640; Richmond Island; returned permanently to England after 1642 [Trelawny 219, 312-13; WJ 2:368; GDMNH 462; Legal Executions 12-13; Abandoning 195-96].

Martin, George: Unknown; 1639; Salisbury, Amesbury [SJC Case #3231; TAG 56:155-59, 58:193-204, 59:11-22].

Martin, Isaac: Unknown; 1639; Hingham; not seen after 1643 [Lechford 175; ReTR 1:2; Early Rehoboth 4:4; GM 2:5:60 (clue)].

Martin, John: Unknown; 1637; Boston, Charlestown, Portsmouth [NH] [BTR 1:22; ChTR 43; ChBOP 56; ChChR 9, 48; NEHGR 4:268; MBCR 1:312, 376; NHPP 31:72-73; GDMNH 463; Wyman 658].

Martin, Mary: Unknown; 1635 on *Elizabeth*; Boston [GM 2:5:56-57].

Martin, Richard: Unknown; 1635 on *Elizabeth & Ann*; passenger list only [GM 2:5:57].

Martin, Richard: Unknown; 1638; Richmond Island, Black Point [Trelawny 183, 292; GDMNH 463].

Martin, Robert: Batcombe, Somerset; 1635 on *Marygould*; Weymouth, Rehoboth [GM 2:5:57-60; NEHGR 67:382].

Martin, Robin: Unknown; 1639; Richmond Island (business transaction only) [Trelawny 298].

Martin, Solomon: Unknown; 1635 on *James*; Gloucester, Andover [GM 2:5:60-62].

Martin, Thomas: Unknown; 1638; Charlestown; not seen after 1639 [ChTR 43; ChChR 9; Lechford 214; MBCR 1:375]. (A Thomas Martin appeared at Woburn and Cambridge in the early 1650s.)

Marvin, Matthew: Great Bentley, Essex; 1635 on *Increase*; Hartford, Norwalk [GM 2:5:63-71].

Marvin, Reynold: Great Bentley, Essex; 1640; Hartford, Farmington, Saybrook, Lyme [HaTR 36; Manwaring 1:219-20; TAG 18:12-13;

Brainerd Anc 213-14; McCormick-Hamilton 732-36; George Franklin Marvin and William T. R. Marvin, *Descendants of Reinold and Matthew Marvin* (Boston 1904)].

Mascall, Robert: Unknown; 1639; Boston; returned permanently to England by 1646 [BChR 30, 46; Abandoning 196-97].

Mason, Edmond: Unknown; 1636; Watertown; not seen after 1636 [WaBOP 4 (as "Thomas Mason"), 74].

Mason, Edward: Unknown; 1639; Wethersfield [CCCR 1:43, 57; WetLR 1:154; Manwaring 1:23-24; Wethersfield Hist 2:499; NEHGR 61:93].

Mason, Emma: Eastwell, Kent; 1635 on *Hercules*; Salem [GM 2:5:71-74].

Mason, Hugh: Maldon, Essex; 1634 on *Francis*; Watertown [GM 2:5:74-81; NEHGR 113:73-74].

Mason, John: Unknown; 1632; Dorchester, Windsor, Saybrook, Norwich [GMB 1225-30].

Mason, John: Unknown; 1640; New Haven; not seen after 1643 (three court appearances only) [NHCR 1:46, 80, 124].

Mason, Ralph: St. Olave Southwark, Surrey; 1635 on *Abigail*; Boston [GM 2:5:81-84].

Mason, Robert: Sudbury, Suffolk; 1637; Roxbury, Dedham [NEHGR 6:184; RBOP 1; DeTR 1:61; SPR Case #472; Medfield Hist 429; TAG 55:149-50].

Massey, Jeffrey: Unknown; 1630; Salem [GMB 1230-34].

Masters, John: Unknown; 1630; Watertown, Cambridge [GMB 1234-36; WF 459-61].

Masterson, Richard: Leiden, Holland; 1629; Plymouth [GMB 1236-38; PM 316-18].

Mather, Richard: Much Woolton, Lancashire; 1635 on *James*; Boston, Dorchester [GM 2:5:84-90; TG 21:108-28, 191-217].

Matson, Thomas: London; 1630; Boston, Braintree [GMB 1238-41; WF 461-65].

Matthews *see also* **Mahoney**

Matthews, Edmond: Unknown; 1640; Massachusetts Bay (court appearance only) [MBCR 1:300].

Matthews, Francis: Ottery St. Mary, Devon; 1637; Dover [GDMNH 468; NHPP 1:133, 40:8; NEHGR 9:220].

Matthews, James: London; 1634; Charlestown, Yarmouth [GM 2:5:90-95].

Matthews, John: Unknown; 1639; Roxbury [Lechford 344-48; RChR 84, 85, 115, 149; RBOP 20, 43; MBCR 2:291 (as "John Mathis"); SLR 1:67]. (Pope thought this man removed to Charlestown [Pope 306; Rodgers 1:421].)

Matthews, Marmaduke: Penmaen, Glamorganshire; 1638; Boston, Yarmouth, Hull, Malden; returned permanently to England by 1655 [BChR 23, 39, 307; PCR 1:107, 140; WJ 1:329; NEHGR 9:282; Abandoning 205-10].

Matthews, Mary: Unknown; 1640; Boston (servant; church admission only) [BChR 29].

Matthews, Nicholas: Unknown; 1638; Richmond Island; not seen after 1640 [Trelawny 184, 194, 297].

Matthews, Roger: Unknown; 1634; Dorchester [GM 2:5:95].

Mattocks, James: Unknown; 1637; Boston [BTR 1:34, 123; BChR 23; MBCR 1:375; SPR Case #462].

Maude, Daniel: Halifax, Yorkshire; 1635 on *James*; Boston, Dover [GM 2:5:96-100].

Maudsley, Henry: Unknown; 1635 on *Hopewell*; Dorchester, Braintree, Boston [GM 2:5:100-2].

Maudsley, John: Unknown; 1638; Dorchester [DChR 3; DTR 1:38; MBCR 1:375; SPR Case #277, Case #297; NEHGR 5:244; TAG 68:239-41; Windsor Hist 2:508].

Maulder, Phebe: Unknown; 1635 on *Defence*; passenger list only [GM 2:5:102].

Maverick, John: Beaworthy, Devon; 1630 on *Mary & John*; Dorchester [GMB 1241-43; NEHGR 122:282-83].

Mawer, William: Unknown; 1636; Boston; not seen after 1640 [BTR 1:12, 31, 51; BBOP 78].

Maxell, Mary: Unknown; 1637; Massachusetts Bay (court appearance only) [EQC 1:8].

Maxson, Richard: Unknown; 1634; Boston, Portsmouth [GM 2:5:102-4].

Maycock, Peter: Unknown; 1638; Plymouth; not seen after 1640 [PCR 1:156, 12:34, 36-37]. (No obvious connection with the Peter Meacock who appeared at Fairfield in the early 1650s [FOOF 1:398-99; TAG 33:40-41, 34:72-74; NYGBR 63:362].)

Mayer, Thomas: Norfolk; 1638 on *Diligent*; passenger list only [NEHGR 15:27].

Mayers, Mr.: Unknown; 1640; New Haven (two land records only) [NHCR 1:50, 93; GMN 13:19]. (Probably never came to New England.)

Mayhew, Thomas: Tisbury, Wiltshire; 1632; Medford, Watertown, Martha's Vineyard [GMB 1243-46; TAG 76:94-98].

Maynard, John: Unknown; 1634; Cambridge, Hartford [GM 2:5:104-6].

Maynard, John: Unknown; 1637; Duxbury, Boston [PCR 1:75, 115, 153, 7:36, 8:182, 12:66, 138, 143; PCPR 1:30; SPR Case #214; GM 2:6:492; NEHGR 95:253-57; Wyman 685].

Maynard, John: Unknown; 1639; Sudbury [SuTR 4; NEHGR 53:359; Hale, House 554; Wyman 662; Rodgers 3:190-93].

Mayo, John: Kent; 1632; Roxbury [Lechford 295-96; RChR 77; SPR Case #1862; NEHGR 14:53; Chester Garst Mayo, *John Mayo of Roxbury, Massachusetts, 1630-1688* (Huntington, Vermont, 1965)].

Mayo, John: Oxford, Oxfordshire; 1640; Barnstable, Eastham, Boston [WP 4:262; NEHGR 10:38, 95:39-49, 100-8, 103:32-42; Morison 390].

Mayo, Mary: Kent; 1640; Dorchester (mention in notarial record only) [Lechford 295-96].

Mays, John: Unknown; 1640; Roxbury [RChR 84; RBOP 35; MBCR 1:378; SPR Case #533; Dawes-Gates 1:412-24].

Mead, William: Unknown; 1639; Gloucester, Charlestown, New London, Roxbury [EQC 1:1, 16, 17, 22, 32, 69, 158, 159, 184; ChBOP 116-17, 130; SPR 6:428, 429, 9:169; GM 2:6:475; Winthrop-Babcock 347; Gen Mag 2:283].

Meade, Gabriel: Unknown; 1637; Dorchester [DChR 3; DTR 27; MBCR 1:374; TAG 73:1-3; SPR Case #455].

Meadows, Philip: Unknown; 1640; Roxbury [RVR MS 128; NEHGR 65:187; Powers-Banks 45 (use with caution)].

Meakins, Thomas: Thorpe Achurch, Northamptonshire; 1633; Boston, Braintree [GMB 1246-47; NEHGR 157:31-33].

Meane, John: Unknown; 1638; Cambridge [NEHGR 4:181; CaBOP 60; Rodgers 2:308-10].

Mears, Robert: Ringstead, Northamptonshire; 1635 on *Abigail*; Boston [GM 2:5:106-9].

Meech, John: Unknown; 1629; Charlestown [GMB 1248].

Mellen, Richard: Unknown; 1639; Weymouth, Charlestown [MBCR 1:376; NEHGR 4:269; Flagg 257, 288; Wyman 664].

Mellin, William: Unknown; 1638; Richmond Island; not seen after 1643 [Trelawny 193, 296, 312, 327, 331, 356, 357; GDMNH 475].

Mellowes, Abraham: Boston, Lincolnshire; 1633; Charlestown [GMB 1248-50]. (Oliver Mellowes, son of Abraham Mellowes, was accompanied to New England by his stepson, John Coney [Mary Lovering Holman, *Ancestors and Descendants of John Coney of Boston, England, and Boston, Massachusetts* (Concord, New Hampshire, 1928)].)

Mendlove, Mark: Unknown; 1637; Plymouth, Stamford; removed to Virginia by 1653 [PCR 1:74; PoTR 16; TAG 61:71-76].

Mendlove, William: Unknown; 1633; Plymouth [GMB 1250-51; PM 318-19].

Mendum, Robert: Unknown; 1630; Plymouth, Duxbury, Kittery [GMB 1251-55; PM 319-24; NEA 8:3:55-57].

Mepham, John: Unknown; 1639; Guilford [Guilford Hist 25; Botsford-Marble 29; Hale, House 781].

Mercer, Lucy: Unknown; 1635 on *Defence*; passenger list only [GM 2:5:109-10].

Mercer, Thomas: Unknown; 1639; Lynn (court appearance only) [EQC 1:13, 16]. (See GDMNH 476.)

Merchant, John: Unknown; 1638; Braintree; not seen after 1639 [NEHGR 3:247; RICR 1:92; BTR 1:49; GMN 23:4]. (No obvious connection with the John Merchant who appeared at Yarmouth in 1648 [PCR 2:124].)

Merriam, George: Kent; 1640; Concord [MBCR 1:379; CoVR 2; MPR Case #15059; Waters 1214-18; Blake-Glidden 176-77; Charles Henry Pope, *Merriam Genealogy in England and America* (Boston 1906)].

Merriam, Joseph: Kent; 1638 on *Castle*; Concord [Lechford 140, 163-68, 174; CoVR 2; PCR 7:13; MBCR 1:375; SPR 1:19, 2:10; Waters 1214-18; Blake-Glidden 176-77; Charles Henry Pope, *Merriam Genealogy in England and America* (Boston 1906); Mower Anc 438-41].

Merriam, Robert: Kent; 1638; Concord [Lechford 140, 162-63, 166-68, 174; ChBOP 70; MBCR 1:375; SPR 1:20, 2:12; MPR Case #15101; Waters 1214-18; Blake-Glidden 176-77; TAG 15:71; Charles Henry Pope, *Merriam Genealogy in England and America* (Boston 1906)].

Merrick, John: Unknown; 1637; Hingham [HiBOP 52; SLR 1:109-10; Hingham Hist 3:70; SPR Case #59, Case #90 ("Elizabeth Moricke")].

Merrick, Thomas: Unknown; 1637; Hartford, Springfield [CCCR 1:17; SpTR 161; SpVR 19; Pynchon Court 204].

Merrick, William: Unknown; 1636; Plymouth, Eastham [PCR 1:44, 66, 7:24, 8:182, 190, 202, 208; Dawes-Gates 2:580-86; Ackley-Bosworth 35-36; MF 6:22-25].

Merrill, John: Wherstead, Suffolk; 1636; Ipswich, Newbury [ITR 18; NeTR 27; MBCR 1:377; Pillsbury Anc 1031-36].

Merrill, Nathaniel: Wherstead, Suffolk; 1638; Newbury [NeTR 27 (as "John Merrill's brother"); EPR 1:204-6; Sarah Hildreth Anc 65-66; TAG 68:174-75; Pillsbury Anc 1031-44].

Merriman, Nathaniel: London; 1632; Massachusetts Bay, New Haven, Wallingford [WP 4:68; NGSQ 72:205-9; Waters 1445; Donald Lines Jacobus, *Reunion of Descendants of Nathaniel Merriman* (New Haven 1914); TAG 9:91-93].

Merritt, Henry: Unknown; 1638; Scituate [PCR 1:110, 3:51, 8:19, 182, 191; NEHGR 9:280; ScitTR 1:247; MD 11:198-200; Bartlett-Jenkins 70-71].

Merritt, Hezekiah: Unknown; 1639; Newport (admission as town inhabitant only) [RICR 1:92; GMN 23:3].

Merritt, Nicholas: Unknown; 1635; Marblehead [GM 2:5:110-14; MBCR 1:268].

Merry, Walter: Unknown; 1633; Boston [GMB 1255-57].

Messant, Ann: Unknown; 1639; Dover [YLR 3:116, 4:20; NHPP 40:11; Gorges 41; GDMNH 477-78]. (She married Edward Godfrey.)

Messenger, Andrew: Unknown; 1639; New Haven, Greenwich, Hempstead, Jamaica [NY] [NHCR 1:18; NEHGR 152:353-72].

Messenger, Henry: Unknown; 1639; Boston [BTR 1:46; BChR 32, 286; MBCR 1:300; NEHGR 16:309, 87:282, 135:301, 152:353-58; Richard Taft Messinger, Harley Bryce Messinger and Glenn A. Messinger, *The Descendants of Henry Messinger of Boston, 1637* (Yarmouthport, Massachusetts, 1994)].

Metcalf, Joseph: Strood near Rochester, Kent; 1634; Ipswich [GM 2:5:114-17].

Metcalfe, James: Unknown; 1638; Piscataqua [MBCR 1:249, 265, 283; GDMNH 478].

Metcalfe, Michael: Norwich, Norfolk; 1637 on *John & Dorothy* or *Rose*; Dedham [Hotten 289-90; DeTR 1:32; DeChR 21; SPR 1:440, 4:214; MBCR 1:295, 377; NEHGR 6:171-73, 16:279-84, 78:63-65, 80:312-13, 138:80, 166:28-39; TAG 41:207].

Metcalfe, Steven: Unknown; 1640; New Haven; returned permanently to England by 1646 [NHCR 1:50, 59, 105, 126, 138, 151, 157, 164, 176-77, 235, 300].

Mether, Henry: Unknown; 1638; Boston (servant; apprenticeship record only) [Lechford 78].

Micklethwait, Nathaniel: Unknown; 1639; Boston (business transactions only) [Lechford 144, 184, 186, 241, 234; see TAG 76:1-16].

Mighill, Thomas: Unknown; 1638; Roxbury, Rowley [RChR 83; MBCR 1:376; RowBOP 4; EPR 1:206-10; Rowley Fam 234-41; GMN 18:21 (clue); NEHGR 158:255-79, 364-79].

Miles, John: Unknown; 1638; Concord [MBCR 1:375; CoVR 2; MPR Case #15169].

Miles, Joseph: Unknown; 1639; Kittery [MPCR 1:113-15; GDMNH 479].

Miles, Richard: Great Munden, Hertfordshire; 1639; New Haven [NHCR 1:31; MiTR 2; MiChR 1; TAG 31:24-29, 33:129-37, 34:216, 35:247-54, 75:72-73; NEHGR 81:128; Stevens-Miller 1:492-95].

Millard, Thomas: Unknown; 1639; Boston [BTR 1:42; Lechford 394; MBCR 1:270; SPR Case #517; NEHGR forthcoming].

Millard, Thomas: Unknown; 1640; Gloucester, Newbury [Lechford 290; WP 4:69, 123; GlTR 1:1; EPR 1:160-61; Hoyt 176; NYGBR 47:246; NEHGR 29:273, 275; Phoebe Tilton Anc 218-19].

Miller, Alexander: Unknown; 1632; Dorchester [GMB 1258].

/**Miller, John:** Unknown; 1635; Dorchester [GM 2:5:117-19].

Miller, John: Cambridge, Cambridgeshire; 1638; Roxbury, Rowley, Yarmouth, Groton [RChR 83; RowBOP 4; MPR Case #15194; GM 2:5:118-19; Abel Lunt 84-85; Rowley Fam 242; Morison 390].

Miller, John: Unknown; 1639; Yarmouth, Sandwich (land grant and oath of fidelity only) [PCR 1:150, 8:185; GM 2:5:119].

Miller, John: Unknown; 1640; Wethersfield, Stamford [WetLR 1:169; SmTR 6; FOOF 1:410; NYGBR 76:19].

Miller, Joseph: Bishops Stortford, Hertfordshire; 1635 on *Hopewell*; passenger list only [GM 2:5:119; NYGBR 71:167-71 (connection of 1635 passenger to Newton resident not proved)].

Miller, Richard: Unknown; 1638; Charlestown [ChBOP 62; NYGBR 71:168-69; Wyman 668].

Miller, Sydrach: London; 1630; Piscataqua; returned permanently to England by 1632 [GMB 1258-59; WF 465-66].

Miller, Thomas: Unknown; 1640; Dorchester (church admission only) [DChR 5]. (Possibly the same as the next.)

Miller, Thomas: Unknown; 1640; Rowley, Middletown [Lechford 289; RowBOP 5; Rowley Fam 242; NYGBR 70:143-44; Stevens-Miller 1:301-15; Moore Anc 373-82; NEHGR 161:280-81].

Millett, Richard: Unknown; 1630; Massachusetts Bay [GMB 1259; WF 466].

Millett, Thomas: St. Saviour Southwark, Surrey; 1635 on *Elizabeth*; Dorchester, Gloucester, Brookfield [GM 2:5:120-24].

Mills, Edward: Unknown; 1637; Richmond Island; not seen after 1640 [Trelawny 182, 300].

Mills, John: Unknown; 1630; Boston, Braintree [GMB 1259-62; WF 467-69; NEHGR 168:48 (clue)].

Mills, John: Unknown; 1633; Richmond Island, Scarborough [GMB 2082-83].

Mills, Richard: Unknown; 1640; Wethersfield, Stratford, Southampton, Stamford, Newtown, Westchester [WetLR 1:128; NEHGR 154:189-210].

Mills, Robert: Unknown; 1636; Saco [MPCR 1:6, 7, 117; GDMNH 483].

Mills, Samuel: Unknown; 1640; Weymouth, Dedham [Lechford 373; DeChR 29; DeVR 126; SPR Case #2215].

Mills, Simon: Unknown; 1639; Windsor [WiLR 1:75; WMJ 447, 798; TAG 36:127-28, 54:73-75; Goodwin-Morgan 1:111-22; Eunice M. Lamb, *The John-Simon Mills Line of Windsor and Simsbury, Connecticut* (Burlington, Vermont, 1968)].

Milner, Michael: Unknown; 1635 on *James*; Lynn, Flushing [GM 2:5:124-25].

Mingay, Jeffrey: Denton, Norfolk; 1637; Dedham, Hampton [DeTR 1:34; Essex Ant 2:84; GDMNH 483; NHGR 8:145-56].

Minor, Thomas: Chew Magna, Somerset; 1632; Charlestown, Hingham, New London, Stonington [GMB 1262-67].

Minot, George: Saffron Walden, Essex; 1633; Dorchester [GMB 1267-69; Kempton Anc 3:298-326].

Minter, Desire: (possibly) Leiden, Holland; 1620 on *Mayflower*; Plymouth [GMB 1269-70; PM 324].

Mitchell, Edward: Hingham, Norfolk; 1638 on *Diligent*; passenger list only (servant) [NEHGR 15:25]. (An Edward Mitchell appeared at Plymouth court on 1 March 1641/2 [PCR 2:35].)

Mitchell, Experience: Leiden, Holland; 1623 on *Anne*; Plymouth, Duxbury, Bridgewater [GMB 1270-73; PM 324-29].

Mitchell, Matthew: Halifax, Yorkshire; 1635 on *James*; Charlestown, Concord, Springfield, Saybrook, Wethersfield, Stamford [GM 2:5:125-31].

Mitchell, Paul: Sheviock, Cornwall; 1638; Richmond Island, Saco [Trelawny 182, 186, 282-83, 300, 342-43; MPCR 2:27; GDMNH 484].

Mitchell, Thomas: Unknown; 1636; Charlestown (with wife Anne, admission to church only) [ChChR 9; Wyman 678].

Mitchell, Thomas: Unknown; 1640; New Haven [NHCR 1:50; NEHGR 81:128; FANH 1194; Parke-Gildersleeve 84-88; Dawes-Gates 2:588-92].

Mitchelson, Edward: Unknown; 1637; Cambridge [MBCR 1:217; CaBOP 66; CaChR 8, 17; Lechford 208; NEHGR 4:181; WP 4:183; HAHAC 1:71; Sibley 2:189-90; GM 2:1:507].

Mitton, Michael: Unknown; 1639; Casco [MPCR 1:42; Trelawny 211-12, 299; Two Voyages 20-21; Legal Executions 12-13; GDMNH 485; Blake-Glidden 180-81].

Mixer, Isaac: Capel St. Mary, Suffolk; 1634 on *Elizabeth*; Watertown [GM 2:5:132-35].

Montague, Griffin: Unknown; 1634; Muddy River, Exeter, Cape Porpus [MBCR 1:144, 164, 244; PCR 1:51; Exeter Hist 436; Maine Wills 22-23; Waters 759-60; GDMNH 486].

Moody, Deborah: Garsdon, Wiltshire; 1639; Salem, Lynn, Gravesend [SChR 9; Lechford 67; EQC 1:33, 48, 241-43; WJ 2:148-49, 164, 339-40; NEHGR 55:377-78; EIHC 31:96-102].

Moody, John: Moulton, Suffolk; 1633; Roxbury, Hartford [GMB 1273-76].

Moody, William: Unknown; 1634 on *Mary & John*; Ipswich, Newbury [GM 2:5:135-37].

Moore, Enoch: Unknown; 1637; Cambridge (land grant only) [CaTR 28; see NEHGR 122:28-36].

Moore, Francis: Maldon, Essex; 1638; Cambridge, Boston [MBCR 1:375; Shepard 35-37; CaChR 11; NEHGR 55:378, 122:28-36; Lyon-Rice 467-68; Rodgers 3:52-53].

Moore, Golden: Unknown; 1640; Cambridge, Billerica [MBCR 1:378; Shepard 122; CaChR 13].

Moore, Jeremiah: Wymondham, Norfolk; 1638 on *Diligent*; Hingham, Boston [NEHGR 15:27, 55:378; HiBOP 49; BChR 38; SLR 6:7; SPR Case #104].

Moore, John: Unknown; 1630; Dorchester, Windsor [GMB 1276-78].

Moore, John: Unknown; 1632; Salem [GMB 1278-80].

Moore, John: Unknown; 1636; Cambridge [CaTR 28-29, 34, 36, 41; CaBOP 61, 64, 69, 70, 102, 331, 333, 336; MBCR 1:295, 372].

Moore, John: Unknown; 1638; Portsmouth; not seen after 1640 [PoTR 2; RICR 1:91; GMN 22:22].

Moore, John: Unknown; 1639; Boston, Braintree; not seen after 1643 [BTR 1:49; Lechford 16; NEHGR 3:247].

Moore, John: Unknown; 1639; Duxbury (business transaction only) [Lechford 194].

Moore, John: Unknown; 1640; Southampton, Hempstead, Newtown [NY] [SoTR 1:223; TG 5:5-6; NYGBR 137:245-63; SCHSR 4:23-25].

Moore, Samuel: Unknown; 1631; Salem [GMB 1280-81].

Moore, Thomas: Unknown; 1630; Dorchester, Windsor [GMB 1281-82].

Moore, Thomas: Unknown; 1636; Salem [STR 1:17, 21, 25, 37, 67, 92, 102, 132; SChR 6; ELR 2:100v, 3:48-49, 4:209; NYGBR 15:57-68; SCHSR 1:4-5; EIHC 64:49-51; Winthrop-Babcock 357-58].

Moore, William: Unknown; 1639; Salem (land grant only) [STR 1:92].

Moore, William: Unknown; 1639; Exeter, Ipswich [Exeter Hist 436; GDMNH 490; EPR 2:235-36].

Mooteham, Thomas: Unknown; 1633; Massachusetts Bay [GMB 2083].

More, Ellen: Shipton, Shropshire; 1620 on *Mayflower*; Plymouth [GMB 1282-83; PM 329-30].

More, Isaac: Unknown; 1635 on *Increase*; Hartford, Farmington, Norwalk [GM 2:5:137-45].

More, Jasper: Shipton, Shropshire; 1620 on *Mayflower*; Plymouth [GMB 1282-83; PM 329-30].

More, John: Stepney, Middlesex; 1635 on *Planter*; passenger list only [GM 2:5:145-46].

More, John: Unknown; 1635 on *Susan & Ellen*; passenger list only [GM 2:5:146].

More, Mary: Shipton, Shropshire; 1620 on *Mayflower*; Plymouth [GMB 1282-83; PM 329-30].

More, Richard: Shipton, Shropshire; 1620 on *Mayflower*; Plymouth, Salem [GMB 1283-87; PM 330-35; MQ 64:44-48].

Morecock, Bennett: Benenden, Kent; 1635 on *Elizabeth & Ann*; Plymouth [GM 2:5:146-47].

Morecock, Mary: Benenden, Kent; 1635 on *Elizabeth & Ann*; Plymouth [GM 2:5:147-48]. (She married William Brown.)

Morecock, Nicholas: Benenden, Kent; 1635 on *Elizabeth & Ann*; passenger list only [GM 2:5:148].

Morecroft, John: Unknown; 1639; Boston (two court appearances only); not seen after 1641 [WP 4:128, 324, 456; Lechford 373; MBCR 1:314].

Morehouse, Thomas: Unknown; 1640; Wethersfield, Stamford, Fairfield [Wethersfield Hist 1:287; SmTR 4; FOOF 1:418-19].

Morfield, John: Hingham, Norfolk; 1638 on *Diligent*; passenger list only (servant) [NEHGR 15:26].

Morgan, Bennett: Unknown; 1621 on *Fortune*; returned permanently to England by 1624 [GMB 1287; PM 335].

Morgan, James: Unknown; 1640; Roxbury, New London [RBOP 3; TG 14:118-28].

Morgan, Robert: Unknown; 1636; Salem [STR 1:23; EQC 1:7; MBCR 1:234; EPR 2:355-57; Sarah Stone Anc 46; NEHGR 160:99-100].

Morgan, Robert: Unknown; 1636; Saco, Pemaquid [MPCR 1:lxii; Lechford 402; GDMNH 194, 492].

Morley, Ralph: Unknown; 1630; Charlestown [GMB 1287-88; WF 469-71].

Morley, Robert: Unknown; 1628; hired by Massachusetts Bay Company but probably did not sail for New England [MBCR 1:30].

Morley, Sarah: Unknown; 1631; Lynn [GMB 1288].

Morrell, Edward: Unknown; 1637; Yarmouth; left Plymouth Colony in 1641 [PCPR 1:32; PCR 1:135, 2:9, 18, 7:23].

Morrell, George: Unknown; 1638; Massachusetts Bay (court appearance only) [MBCR 1:241].

Morrell, George: Unknown; 1639; Plymouth (court appearance only) [PCR 1:130].

Morrell, William: Unknown; 1623; Wessagusset; returned permanently to England by 1625 [GMB 1289; PM 335-36].

Morres, Edmund: Kington Magna, Dorset; 1638 on *Confidence*; passenger list only [Drake's Founders 58].

Morrey, George: Unknown; 1635 on *Truelove*; Duxbury, Scituate [GM 2:5:149-51].

Morrice, Sarah: Unknown; 1633; Boston (church admission only) [BChR 16; GMB 450].

Morrill, Abraham: Unknown; 1635; Cambridge, Salisbury [GM 2:5:151-56].

Morrill, Isaac: Unknown; 1632 on *Lyon*; Roxbury [GMB 1289-92].

Morrill, Vashti: Unknown; 1639; Cambridge [GM 2:1:383-84]. (She married Robert Bradish.)

Morris, John: Unknown; 1639; Hartford [HaTR 24; HaBOP 168; Manwaring 1:222].

Morris, Rice: Unknown; 1633; Charlestown [GMB 1292-93].

Morris, Richard: The Hague, Holland; 1630; Boston, Roxbury, Exeter, Portsmouth [GMB 1293-96; WF 471-74].

Morris, Thomas: Alcester, Warwickshire; 1640; Rehoboth, New Haven [PCR 12:76; NHCR 1:50; FANH 1210-12; TAG 24:57-58; NEHGR 71:5, 81:129, 147:11-20].

Morris, William: Royston, Hertfordshire; 1637; Duxbury (apprenticeship record only) [PCR 1:64].

Morrison, Elizabeth: Ware, Hertfordshire; 1635 on *Planter*; Roxbury [GM 2:5:156-59].

Morse, Anthony: Marlborough, Wiltshire; 1635 on *James*; Newbury [GM 2:5:159-67].

Morse, Joseph: Unknown; 1634 on *Elizabeth*; Watertown [GM 2:5:167-70].

Morse, Joseph: Unknown; 1637; Ipswich [ITR 27 (as "Goodman Moss"), 52; EPR 1:53-55; NEHGR 83:292-93].

Morse, Samuel: Burgate, Suffolk; 1635 on *Increase*; Watertown, Dedham, Medfield [GM 2:5:170-77].

Morse, William: Marlborough, Wiltshire; 1635 on *James*; Newbury [GM 2:5:177-80].

Morton, George: Leiden, Holland; 1623 on *Anne*; Plymouth [GMB 1296-97; PM 336-37].

Morton, Mary: Unknown; 1630; Boston [GMB 1298; WF 474].

Morton, Thomas: Unknown; 1621 on *Fortune*; Plymouth [GMB 1298-99; PM 338-39].

Morton, Thomas: London; 1622; Merrymount and elsewhere; returned permanently to England in early 1640s [GMB 1299-1300; NEQ 82:490-513; NEHGR 134:282-90].

Mory, John: Unknown; 1635 on *Blessing*; passenger list only [GM 2:5:180-81].

Moses, John: Unknown; 1631; Casco, Piscataqua [GMB 1300-2].

Moses, John: Unknown; 1639; Duxbury (business transaction only) [Lechford 418].

Mosher, Hugh: Unknown; 1632 on *James*; Casco [GMB 1302-4].

Mosse, John: Unknown; 1636; Charlestown (servant; admission as town inhabitant only) [ChTR 25]. (Possibly the same as the next.)

Mosse, John: Unknown; 1639; New Haven, Wallingford [NHCR 1:29, 32; NHChR 1; FANH 1219-21; Boardman Anc 228-31].

Motley, Robert: Unknown; 1636; Ipswich (estate appraiser only) [EPR 1:4].

Mott, Adam: Horseheath, Cambridgeshire; 1635 on *Defence*; Roxbury, Hingham, Portsmouth [GM 2:5:181-85]. (Adam Mott's father, John Mott, had arrived in New England by 1639 [GM 2:5:184-85].)

Mott, Adam: Essex; 1638 on *Bevis*; New Netherland, Hempstead [Hotten 300; Stillwell 4:71-73; NYGBR 25:49-50, 45:117-18; NYChR 1:14; TAG 35:108 (clue); GM 2:5:185].

Moulenor, Thomas: Unknown; 1639; New Haven, Branford [NHCR 1:28, 29, 32, 42, 47, 122, 123, 153, 259, 281, 369; FANH 1285].

Moulthrop, Mathew: Wrawby, Lincolnshire; 1640; New Haven [NHCR 1:92; NEHGR 81:129; TAG 74:81-96, 209-24; FANH 1234].

Moulton, James: Ormesby St. Margaret, Norfolk; 1637; Salem [SChR 7; Fiske 243; MBCR 1:374; STR 1:53; NEHGR 141:313-16, 323-27, 144:245-63, 147:129-45; 163:165-69, 273-75].

Moulton, John: Ormesby St. Margaret, Norfolk; 1637 on *John & Dorothy* or *Rose*; Newbury, Hampton [Hotten 291; GDMNH 55, 498; NeTR 4; MBCR 1:236, 375; HmTR 39; HampVR 1:3; NEHGR 141:313-16, 323-28, 142:260-63, 144:245-63, 147:129-45, 163:165-69, 273-75].

Moulton, Mary: Unknown; 1637 on *John & Dorothy* or *Rose*; passenger list only [Hotten 291; NEHGR 141:313-16; GDMNH 499].

Moulton, Miriam: Ormesby St. Margaret, Norfolk; 1637 on *John & Dorothy* or *Rose*; Salem [Hotten 291; NEHGR 141:313-16, 323-27, 144:245-63, 147:129-45, 163:165-69, 273-75; GDMNH 499]. (She married Thomas King.)

Moulton, Robert: Unknown; 1629; Salem, Charlestown [GMB 1304-6; WF 474-77; NEHGR 141:313-16, 154:217; TAG 74:305].

Moulton, Ruth: Ormesby St. Margaret, Norfolk; 1637 on *John & Dorothy* or *Rose*; passenger list only [Hotten 291; NEHGR 141:313-16, 323-27, 144:245-63, 147:129-45, 163:165-69, 273-75].

Moulton, Thomas: Unknown; 1630; Charlestown, Malden [GMB 1306-9; WF 477-80; NEHGR 141:313-16].

Moulton, Thomas: Ormesby St. Margaret, Norfolk; 1637; Newbury [NeTR 4; GDMNH 55, 500; HmTR 40; HampVR 1:3; MBCR 1:236, 375; TAG 82:150-52; NEHGR 141:313-16, 323-29, 144:245-63, 147:129-45, 163:165-69, 273-75].

Moulton, William: Ormesby St. Margaret, Norfolk; 1637 on *John & Dorothy* or *Rose*; Hampton [Hotten 291; GDMNH 500; NEHGR 141:313-23, 142:259, 144:245-58, 163:165-73, 273-77].

Mountford, Ann: Unknown; 1632; Roxbury [RVR MS 128]. (She married John Eliot.)

Mousall, John: Unknown; 1634; Charlestown, Woburn [GM 2:5:186-90].

Mousall, Ralph: Unknown; 1630; Charlestown [GMB 1309-12; WF 480-85].

Mousar, John: Unknown; 1639; Salem [STR 1:91, 94; GM 2:5:189-90].

Mowry, Roger: Unknown; 1630; Salem, Lynn, Providence [GMB 1312-15; Angell Anc 414-34].

Moxon, George: Prescot, Lancashire; 1637; Dorchester, Springfield; returned permanently to England in 1652 [DChR 3; SpTR 161; MBCR 1:202, 373; Glover Gen 454-55; Morison 390-91; Abandoning 213-15; ODNB].

Moyse, Joseph: Unknown; 1638; Dedham, Salisbury [DeTR 1:48; SyTR 1; Hoyt 262, 992 (clue); Waters 1120-21 (clue); Pillsbury Anc 507-8].

Mudge, Jarvis: Unknown; 1638; Massachusetts Bay, Wethersfield, New London [MBCR 1:248, 269; HaTR 47; Manwaring 1:7-8, 139; TAG 36:187, 81:18-30; Alfred Mudge, *Memorials: Being a Genealogical, Biographical and Historical Account of the Name of Mudge in America, from 1638 to 1868* (Boston 1868)].

Mullinder, ____: Unknown; 1637; Massachusetts Bay (court appearance only) [MBCR 1:219].

Mullins, William: Dorking, Surrey; 1620 on *Mayflower*; Plymouth [GMB 1315-16; PM 339-40; MD 44:39-44, 61:17-27].

Mullyn, ____: Unknown; 1635; Boston [GM 2:5:190].

Munday, Henry: Unknown; 1638; Salisbury [MBCR 1:277, 376; SyTR 4; Essex Ant 2:11; Hoyt 263].

Munn, Benjamin: Unknown; 1637; Hartford, Springfield [HaBOP 56; NEHGR 86:219; McCormick-Hamilton 768-71].

Munnings, Edmund: Tillingham, Essex; 1635 on *Abigail*; Dorchester; returned permanently to England after 1643 [GM 2:5:190-95; Abandoning 215-16].

Munnings, George: Rattlesden, Suffolk; 1634 on *Elizabeth*; Watertown, Sudbury, Boston [GM 2:5:195-299].

Munsall, Ruth: Unknown; 1640; Salem (church admission only) [SChR 10; GM 2:5:189-90].

Munson, Susan: Unknown; 1634 on *Elizabeth*; passenger list only [GM 2:5:200; TAG 17:134].

Munson, Thomas: Unknown; 1637; Hartford, New Haven [NHCR 1:32; CCCR 1:66; HaBOP 82, 194, 312, 348; TAG 17:129-34; FANH 1285-87; NEHGR 57:331-32 (clue), 81:129; Myron A. Munson, *The Munson Record*, volume one (New Haven 1895)].

Munson, Thomasine: Unknown; 1635 on *Blessing*; Scituate [GM 2:5:201; PCR 2:66]. (She married Henry Advord.)

Munt, Thomas: Unknown; 1630; Boston [GMB 1316-18; WF 485-88].

Mussell, John: Hawkhurst, Kent; 1635 on *Elizabeth*; passenger list only [GM 2:5:201].

Musselwhite, John: Landford, Wiltshire; 1635 on *James*; Newbury [GM 2:5:201-3].

Mussey, Abraham: Unknown; 1634 on *Mary & John*; passenger list only [GM 2:5:203-4].

Mussey, John: Unknown; 1634 on *Mary & John*; Ipswich [GM 2:5:204-6].

Mussey, Robert: Unknown; 1634; Ipswich [GM 2:5:206-9].

Muste, Edward: Unknown; 1633; Cambridge [GMB 1319-20].

Mygate, Joseph: Messing, Essex; 1634; Cambridge, Hartford [GM 2:5:209-12; TAG 83:195-98, 86:315-16].

Mylam, John: Unknown; 1635; Boston [GM 2:5:212-16].

Myles, Joseph: Unknown; 1634 on *Mary & John*; passenger list only [GM 2:5:216-17].

N

Nanney, Robert: London; 1635 on *Increase*; Saco, Dover, Hampton, Boston [GM 2:5:219-29].

Nash, Gregory: Unknown; 1630; Charlestown [GMB 1321; WF 489].

Nash, James: Great Missenden, Buckinghamshire; 1640; Weymouth [Lechford 430; NEHGR 151:166-70; Richard H. Benson, *The Nash Family of Weymouth, Massachusetts* (Boston 1998)].

Nash, Robert: Unknown; 1640; Charlestown, Boston [ChTR 51; Lechford 411; EQC 1:26; BChR 38; BVR 48; NEHGR 61:47-48; Scott Gen 180-81].

Nash, Samuel: Leiden; 1632; Plymouth, Duxbury [GMB 1321-24; PM 341-43; Plooij 83-84].

Nash, Thomas: Unknown; 1639; Guilford, New Haven [Guilford Hist 25; NHCR 1:40; FOOF 1:430; FANH 1312; Flagg 245 (clue)].

Nash, William: Maidstone, Kent; 1634; Charlestown [GM 2:5:229-31].

Nash, _____: Unknown; 1632; Boston [GMB 1321].

Neale, Charles: Unknown; 1633; Piscataqua [GMB 1324].

Neale, Henry: Unknown; 1638; Braintree, Providence [MBCR 1:249; BTR 1:50; NEHGR 3:247; WP 4:299; TAG 25:157-59; Bartlett-Jenkins 75-78].

Neale, John: Unknown; 1639; Hingham, Marblehead (servant) [WP 4:128; MBCR 1:268; EQC 1:35]. (Probably not identical with John Neale of Salem [Sarah Stone Anc 57].)

Neale, Walter: Unknown; 1630 on *Warwick*; Piscataqua; returned permanently to England in 1633 [GMB 1324-26; Abandoning 344].

Neave, Margaret: Great Yarmouth, Norfolk; 1637 on *Mary Ann*; Salem [Hotten 293; SChR 12; STR 1:206, 227; NEHGR 154:216-17].

Needham, Anne: Unknown; 1630; Boston [GMB 1326-27; WF 489-90]. (She married Thomas Hett.)

Needham, Edmond: London; 1639; Lynn, Southampton [SoTR 1:1; Waters 543, 1239-40; TAG 47:146-48, 49:170-71; TEG 9:25-30].

Needham, Nicholas: Mancetter, Warwickshire; 1636; Braintree, Exeter [BTR 1:15; NHPP 1:133, 134, 135, 40:5; GDMNH 507-8; NHGR 26:52].

Needham, William: Unknown; 1638; Braintree, Boston [RICR 1:91; BTR 1:41, 51; SPR 8:11, 204; Savage 3:266; Pope 325; GMN 22:21].

Negus, Benjamin: Unknown; 1639; Boston [BTR 1:47; NEHGR 2:274; TG 6:195, 198-200].

Negus, Grace: Unknown; 1634; Boston, Dorchester [GM 2:5:231-32]. (She married Barnabas Fawer.)

Negus, Jonathan: Unknown; 1634; Boston [GM 2:5:233-35].

Nelson, Thomas: Rowley, Yorkshire; 1638; Boston, Rowley; returned permanently to England in 1646 [Lechford 57; MBCR 1:289, 376; RowBOP 5; WP 4:208; NEHGR 128:82, 148:130-40; Waters 83-84; Aspinwall 254; Rowley Fam 242-55; Abandoning 217-18].

Nelson, William: Unknown; 1636; Plymouth, Middleborough [PTR 1:3; PCR 1:153, 159; TAG 42:39, 56:32-35].

Neuley, Thomas: Unknown; 1635 on *Hercules*; passenger list only [GM 2:5:235].

Neve, Richard: Unknown; 1640; Massachusetts Bay (court appearance only) [MBCR 1:311].

Newberry, Thomas: Whitchurch Canonicorum, Dorset; 1634 on *Recovery*; Dorchester [GM 2:5:235-42].

Newbey, William: Unknown; 1634 on *Mary & John*; passenger list only [GM 2:5:242].

Newcomb, Francis: Sudbury, Suffolk; 1635 on *Planter*; Boston, Braintree [GM 2:5:242-45].

Newcomen, John: Unknown; 1630; Plymouth [GMB 1327; PM 344].

Newell, Abraham: Unknown; 1634 on *Francis*; Roxbury [GM 2:5:245-50].

Newgate, John: Southwark, Surrey; 1633; Boston, [GMB 1327-1332; Abandoning 371].

Newhall, Anthony: Sherington, Buckinghamshire; 1638; Lynn [EQC 2:270; TAG 65:66, 73:119-21; EIHC 18:1-2, 4-6; TEG 17:215-19].

Newhall, Thomas: Sherington, Buckinghamshire; 1638; Lynn [EQC 2:270; SoTR 1:5; TAG 65:66, 66:9, 73:119-21, 74:50-52; EIHC 18:1-4; TEG 15:38-47].

Newland, William: Unknown; 1640; Weymouth, Sandwich [Lechford 392-93; PCR 7:19, 20; MD 23:66, 24:61-63; Weymouth Hist 4:443-44].

Newman, Elizabeth: Unknown; 1635 on *James*; passenger list only [GM 2:5:250].

Newman, Francis: Unknown; 1639; New Haven [NHCR 1:35; WP 4:161; WMJ 412; NEHGR 81:127, 129; FANH 1313; Isabel Calder, *Letters of John Davenport, Puritan Divine* (New Haven 1937) 122, 178-79, 182-83].

Newman, George: Bristol; 1634; York, Pemaquid [YLR 8:209; MPCR 1:8, 251; Trelawny 106; Aspinwall 230, 298, 321; NEHGR 4:285; York Hist 1:96].

Newman, John: Unknown; 1634 on *Mary & John*; Ipswich [GM 2:5:251-53].

Newman, John: Unknown; 1634 on *Mary & John*; passenger list only [GM 2:5:253].

Newman, Richard: Unknown; 1640; New Haven [NHCR 1:50, 122, 138, 145, 261; FANH 1313].

Newman, Robert: Unknown; 1634 on *Mary & John*; passenger list only [GM 2:5:253-54].

Newman, Robert: London; 1639; New Haven; returned permanently to England by 1650 [NHCR 1:20; WP 4:161; FANH 1313; Abandoning 218-19].

Newman, Samuel: Ecclesfield, Yorkshire; 1637; Dorchester, Weymouth, Rehoboth [DChR 3; WP 4:310; MBCR 1:313, 316, 375; ReTR 1:1; MD 15:234-36; Weymouth Hist 4:444; Magnalia 428-33; Morison 391; Sylvanus Chace Newman, *Rehoboth in the Past* (Pawtucket 1860), 11-33].

Newman, Thomas: Unknown; 1634 on *Mary & John*; Ipswich [GM 2:5:254-57].

Newton, Anthony: Colyton, Devon; 1637; Dorchester, Milton [DTR 1:28; BTR 1:50; Waters 1040-41; TAG 65:13-16; M&JCH 19:108-10, 27:38-39].

Newton, Ellen: Unknown; 1623 on *Anne*; Plymouth [GMB 1332; PM 344]. (She married John Adams and Kenelm Winslow.)

Newton, Joan: Colyton, Devon; 1640; Windsor [Grant 22; Waters 1040-41; TAG 65:13-16; M&JCH 19:108-10]. (She married Benedict Alvord.)

Newton, John: Unknown; 1632; Dorchester [GMB 1333].

Newton, Richard: Bures St. Mary, Suffolk; 1639; Sudbury, Marlborough [SuTR 3; Moore Anc 399-403; Stevens-Miller 138-41; TAG 55:86-87; NEHGR 143:330-31; Ermina Newton Leonard, *Newton Genealogy* (De Pere, Wisconsin, 1915)].

Newton, Thomas: Unknown; 1639; Fairfield [Fairfield Hist 9; FOOF 1:432-33; LENE 18-19, 397-98].

Nicholas, Austen: Unknown; 1621 on *Fortune*; Plymouth [GMB 1333; PM 344].

Nichols, Adam: Unknown; 1639; New Haven, Hartford [NHCR 1:35; FANH 1319; GMB 1901; TAG 74:94, 79:208].

Nichols, Elizabeth: Unknown; 1635 on *Susan & Ellen*; passenger list only [GM 2:5:257].

Nichols, Francis: Sedgeberrow, Worcestershire; 1639; Stratford [CCCR 1:36; FOOF 1:434; TAG 9:9-12, 68:113-14, 75:267-71, 76:38].

Nichols, Jane: Unknown; 1638; Boston (servant; church admission only) [BChR 24].

Nichols, Richard: Unknown; 1640; Massachusetts Bay (court appearance only) [MBCR 1:311].

Nichols, Walter: Great Coggeshall, Essex; 1635; Cambridge; returned permanently to England in 1638 [GM 2:5:257-60].

Nichols, William: Unknown; 1638; Salem, Topsfield [STR 1:74; TAG 32:180; NEHGR 9:377; NYGBR 69:37-38; Essex Ant 1:53-56; TEG 8:128-31].

Nickerson, John: Unknown; 1636; Watertown; not seen after 1638 [WaBOP 8, 9, 11, 113; MBCR 1:374 (as "Will[iam] Nickerson")].

Nickerson, William: Norwich, Norfolk; 1637 on *John & Dorothy* or *Rose*; Yarmouth [Hotten 290; PCR 2:3, 7:21; TAG 85:242-53].

Nidds, Anne: Unknown; 1633; Boston [GMB 1333].

Niles, John: Unknown; 1634; Dorchester, Braintree [GM 2:5:260-62].

Niles, Richard: Unknown; 1637; Richmond Island [Trelawny 121, 184, 194, 200, 294, 300, 323, 328, 335, 339].

Nixon, Matthew: Unknown; 1639; Salem [STR 1:91; EQC 1:18, 123-24; EPR 1:12; Perley 2:73].

Noddle, William: Unknown; 1630; Massachusetts Bay [GMB 1334; WF 491].

Nolton, William: Unknown; 1635; Hingham [GM 2:5:263-66].

Norcott, Ann: Canterbury, Kent; 1637; passenger list only (servant) [NEHGR 75:221].

Norcott, Daniel: Unknown; 1634 on *Recovery*; Boston [GM 2:5:266].

Norcross, Jeremiah: London; 1639; Watertown; returned permanently to England by 1656 [WaTR 1:5; WaBOP 20; MBCR 1:311; CaBOP 115-16, 121; Rodgers 1:288-90; Waters 1041; NYGBR 40:183-84; TAG 61:18-31; Granberry 283-84; Abandoning 219-21].

Norman, Hugh: Orchard Portman, Somerset; 1638; Massachusetts Bay, Yarmouth; returned permanently to England about 1649 [EQC 1:10; PCR 1:134, 2:137, 148, 163, 8:7, 194; MD 6:102-3; PCLR 2:105; NEHGR 68:62-63].

Norman, Matthew: Unknown; 1640; Pemaquid (appearance as bondsman only) [Lechford 377; GDMNH 512].

Norman, Richard: Charminster, Dorset; 1626; Salem, Marblehead [GMB 1334-36; TAG 77:102-3].

Norman, Samuel: 1639; Massachusetts Bay (court appearance only) [MBCR 1:265].

Norris, Edward: Horsley, Gloucestershire; 1639; Boston, Salem [BChR 24; WP 4:168; SChR 9; EPR 1:34; MBCR 1:377; WJ 1:197, 2:78; TAG 84:200-11]. (His daughter Mary preceded him to New England by 1635 [GM 2:5:266-67].)

North, Alice: Unknown; 1638; Dorchester (church admission only) [DChR 3].

North, John: Unknown; 1635 on *Susan & Ellen*; Ipswich [GM 2:5:267].

North, Richard: Olney, Buckinghamshire; 1640; Salisbury [SyTR 4; MBCR 1:378; EPR 2:125-27; EIHC 68:186-87; Essex Ant 2:81, 11:174; TAG 58:193-204, 59:11-22, 68:65-70].

Northam, James: Unknown; 1639; Hartford, Wethersfield [CCCR 1:45; Manwaring 1:139; Wethersfield Hist 2:520].

Northend, Jeremiah: Unknown; 1638; Rowley; returned permanently to England after 1650 [GMN 18:22; NEHGR 66:352; EIHC 12:71-73, 17:85-88].

Northend, John: Unknown; 1640; Wethersfield, Stamford [WetLR 1:140; SmTR 4, 6, 16].

Norton, Francis: London; 1637; Charlestown [ChTR 31; ChBOP 55; ChChR 9, 10; CCCR 1:41; HAHAC 1:132; NEHGR 165:273-79].

Norton, George: Unknown; 1629, Salem, Gloucester, Wenham [GMB 1336-39; WF 491-95].

Norton, Henry: Stepney, Middlesex; 1634; Boston, York; returned permanently to England in 1657 [GM 2:5:267-72; NEHGR 150:327-28].

Norton, James: Unknown; 1639; New Haven (three court appearances only) [CCCR 1:49, 109; NHCR 1:124].

Norton, John: Bishops Stortford, Hertfordshire; 1635; Plymouth, Ipswich, Boston [GM 2:5:272-80].

Norton, Nicholas: Broadway, Somerset; 1637; Weymouth [SJC Case #377; PCR 1:160, 7:16; Martha's Vineyard Hist 2:Edgartown:85-90, 3:341-45; TAG 65:15; M&JCH 26:51-52].

Norton, Thomas: Dean, Bedfordshire; 1639; Guilford [Guilford Hist 25; NEHGR 51:221, 54:269-76; TAG 54:179-80, 56:170-72].

Norton, Walter: Low Countries; 1630; Charlestown, York [GMB 1339-41; NEHGR 327-28].

Norton, William: Unknown; 1632 on *William & Francis*; passenger list only [GMB 1341-42; WF 496-99].

Norton, William: Unknown; 1635 on *Hopewell*; passenger list only [GM 2:5:280-82].

Norwick, John: Unknown; 1639; Massachusetts Bay (admission to freemanship only) [MBCR 1:377].

Nott, John: Unknown; 1637; Wethersfield [MBCR 1:218, 235; CCCR 1:55; WP 3:320; WetLR 1:165; SmTR 4; Manwaring 1:342-43; Wethersfield Hist 2:521-23; Hale, House 20-21].

Nowell, Increase: Stepney, Middlesex; 1630; Charlestown [GMB 1342-46; WF 499-504; TAG 82:172-77].

Noyes, James: Cholderton, Wiltshire; 1634 on *Mary & John*; Ipswich, Newbury [GM 2:5:282-86].

Noyes, Nicholas: Cholderton, Wiltshire; 1634 on *Mary & John*; Ipswich, Newbury [GM 2:5:286-93].

Noyes, Peter: Weyhill, Hampshire; 1638 on *Confidence*; Sudbury [Drake's Founders 57; MBCR 1:238, 271, 377; SuTR 1; WaBOP 46; NEHGR 152:259-85, 492].

Nudd, Thomas: Ormesby St. Margaret, Norfolk; 1637 on *John & Dorothy* or *Rose*; Watertown, Hampton [Hotten 292; NEHGR 142:257, 263-66].

Nunn, Richard: Unknown; 1635 on *Increase*; passenger list only [GM 2:5:293].

Nurse, Francis: Unknown; 1639; Salem [EQC 1:16; Sarah Johnson Anc 13-20; TAG 69:81-85].

Nutbrowne, Francis: Unknown; 1635 on *Defence*; passenger list only [GM 2:5:293].

Nute, James: Unknown; 1640; Dover [NHPP 10:701, 40:11; GDMNH 515].

Nutt, Miles: Barking, Suffolk; 1636; Watertown, Woburn, Charlestown, Malden [WaBOP 5, 44, 129; MBCR 1:316, 373; TAG 31:90-93, 52:21-22; NEHGR 141:56].

Nutter, Hatevil: Warwickshire; 1636; Dover [NHPP 1:204, 31:13, 40:3; TAG 72:263-84; Frederick R. Boyle, *Hatevil Nutter of Dover, New Hampshire, and His Descendants* (Portsmouth, New Hampshire, 1997)].

Nye, Benjamin: Unknown; 1635; Lynn, Sandwich [GM 2:3:43; PCR 1:149, 153; NEHGR 158:345-60, 159:69-80; TAG 41:176-78, 80:53-55].

O

Oakes, Richard: Unknown; 1635; Boston (land record only) [GM 2:5:295].

Oakley, Sarah: Virginia; 1634; Charlestown [WP 3:174]. (She was the widow of John Lyford and (possibly) of Robert Oakley and then married Edmond Hobart [GMB 958-60, 1214-17; PM 309-13; TAG 83:174-78].)

Oates, John: Unknown; 1640; Scituate (burial record only) [NEHGR 9:285].

Odding, Sarah: Essex (Braintree or vicinity); 1633; Roxbury [GMB 1347; TAG 73:176-80]. (She married Philip Sherman.)

Oddingsell, Thomas: Epperstone, Nottinghamshire; 1639; Salem [EQC 1:13, 14, 22, 30, 34, 36, 43, 54, 77, 119, 157; Lechford 300].

Odell, William: Newport Pagnell, Buckinghamshire; 1639; Concord, Southampton, Fairfield [CoVR 2; TAG 14:224-28, 15:55-57, 21:69-83, 26:8-9; FOOF 1:445; NYGBR 44:118; NEHGR 45:7-12, 60:91].

Odlin, John: Unknown; 1632; Boston [GMB 1347-50; RIR 15:85-90].

Offitt *see* **Ufford**

Offley, David: Unknown; 1637; Boston [BTR 1:34, 42; BBOP 34; Lechford 102, 161-62, 191, 238, 240, 363, 437; SLR 1:20, 41; SPR 1:9; WaBOP 56; PCR 2:57; Aspinwall 19; WP 5:57-58; CSM 25:19; HAHAC 1:73; GM 2:7:535-36].

Okam, Thomas: Unknown; 1634; Dorchester (court appearance only) [GM 2:5:295].

Okers, Rowland: Unknown; 1633; Richmond Island [GMB 1350].

Olbon, Elizabeth: Unknown; 1638; Cambridge [Shepard 38-41; CaChR 9; MBCR 1:283, 295]. (She had two children with James Luxford.)

Olcott, Thomas: London; 1639; Hartford; probably died in Virginia in 1654 or 1655 [HaTR 11; WetLR 1:133; NEHGR 16:342-43; TAG

14:229-37; TG 20:174-76, 21:41-42, 171-72; Frank Farnsworth Starr, *The Olcott Family of Hartford, Connecticut* (Hartford 1899)].

Oldage, Richard: Unknown; 1640; Windsor [WiLR 1:96; Grant 54, 82; Levi Elmore Coe, *Coe-Ward Memorial and Immigrant Ancestors* (Meriden, Connecticut, 1897) 86].

Oldham, John: Derby, Derbyshire; 1623; Plymouth, Nantasket, Watertown [GMB 1350-53; PM 345-48].

Oldham, John: Derby, Derbyshire; 1635 on *Elizabeth & Ann*; Unknown [GM 2:5:296-97].

Oldham, Thomas: Derby, Derbyshire; 1635 on *Elizabeth & Ann*; Duxbury, Scituate [GM 2:5:297-301].

Oliver, Christopher: Unknown; 1634; Dorchester (court appearance only) [GM 2:5:301].

Oliver, John: Bristol; 1639; Newbury [MBCR 1:376, 2:11-12, 164, 275-76, 282; EPR 1:15-18; Aspinwall 45-46; SLR 1:51; Phoebe Tilton Anc 217-18].

Oliver, Thomas: Thorpe Achurch, Northamptonshire; 1632 on *William & Francis*; Boston [GMB 1354-57; NEHGR 130:196-207, 157:34-36].

Oliver, Thomas: Norwich, Norfolk; 1637 on *Mary Anne*; Salem [Hotten 295; MBCR 1:247; STR 1:54; EQC 1:8; Legal Executions 64-69; TAG 57:129-38, 58:163, 64:207].

Olmstead, James: Fairstead, Essex; 1632 on *Lyon*; Cambridge, Hartford [GMB 1357-60].

Olmstead, John: Fairstead, Essex; 1639; Hartford [HaBOP 252; CCCR 1:45, 447; Manwaring 1:343; FOOF 1:451-53; TAG 82:32-38].

Olmstead, Rebecca: Fairstead, Essex; 1640; Hartford [CCCR 1:447; Goodwin-Morgan 1:181-90; TAG 82:32-38]. (She married Thomas Newell.)

Olmstead, Richard: Fairstead, Essex; 1637; Hartford, Norwalk [HaBOP 254; CCCR 1:447; FOOF 1:451-53; TAG 82:32-38; Miner Anc 137-38].

Olney, Thomas: St. Albans, Hertfordshire; 1635 on *Planter*; Salem, Providence [GM 2:5:302-8].

Onge, Frances: Lavenham, Suffolk; 1631 on *Lyon*; Watertown [GMB 1360].

Onge, Mary: Unknown; 1634 on *Francis*; Watertown [GM 2:5:308-9]. (Probably daughter of Frances Onge.)

Onion, John: Unknown; 1639; Braintree (land grant only) [BTR 1:51].

Onion, Robert: Unknown; 1635 on *Blessing*; Roxbury, Dedham [GM 2:5:309-12].

Ormsby, Anne: Unknown; 1634; Boston, New Haven [GM 2:5:313].

Ormsby, Edmund: Unknown; 1637; Boston (land grant only) [BTR 1:33; GM 2:5:313].

Ormsby, Richard: Unknown; 1640; York, Salisbury, Haverhill, Rehoboth [Trelawny 269; NHPP 40:11; HvBOP 11; MD 16:127; PCR 4:105, 164, 167; GDMNH 520; York Hist 1:163; Hoyt 267-68].

Orris, George: Unknown; 1635 on *Elizabeth & Ann*; Boston [GM 2:5:314-17].

Orton, Thomas: Unknown; 1640; Windsor, Farmington [Grant 53; Bassett-Preston 205; Edward Orton, *An Account of the Descendants of Thomas Orton of Windsor, Connecticut, 1641* (Columbus, Ohio, 1896)].

Osborn, Christopher: Unknown; 1638; Duxbury (court appearance only) [PCR 1:107].

Osborn, John: Unknown; 1639; Weymouth, Braintree [NEHGR 3:247; Weymouth Hist 4:452].

Osborn, Mary: Unknown; 1637; Massachusetts Bay [MBCR 1:202, 334]. (Probably wife of John Osborn.)

Osborn, Mathew: Unknown; 1637; Weymouth, Plymouth (apprenticeship record only) [PCR 1:65]. (See John Osborn.)

Osborn, Richard: Unknown; 1635; Hingham [GM 2:5:317-18].

Osborn, Richard: Unknown; 1637; New Haven, Fairfield, Westchester [CCCR 2:151; NHCR 1:39, 46, 92; FOOF 1:455-56; GM 2:5:317-18; NYGBR 54:281, 137:257 (footnote 72)].

Osborn, Thomas: Ashford, Kent; 1640; New Haven, Easthampton [NHCR 1:92; TAG 12:248-55, 13:63; FANH 1322].

Osborn, William: Unknown; 1638; Salem, Dorchester, Braintree, Boston, New Haven [STR 1:70; SChR 8; MBCR 1:376; NEHGR 5:334, 9:167, 249, 10:68, 81:129; DChR 156-57; NHVR 18, 20; SPR 4:106-8; FANH 1322; Sibley 2:88-89].

Osgood, Christopher: Marlborough, Wiltshire; 1634 on *Mary & John*; Ipswich [GM 2:5:318-22; TAG 83:51-58].

Osgood, John: Wherwell, Hampshire; 1638 on *Confidence*; Newbury, Andover [Drake's Founders 59; MBCR 1:236, 375; NeTR 30; NEHGR 20:22-28; Pillsbury Anc 2:1067-72; TAG 17:99-101, 83:141-55].

Osgood, William: Unknown; 1639; Salisbury [SyTR 7; Pillsbury Anc 2:703-7; TAG 83:141-55].

Otis, John: Glastonbury, Somerset; 1635; Hingham, Weymouth [GM 2:5:322-26].

Ovell, Nathaniel: Unknown; 1637; passenger list only [NEHGR 75:222].

Owdie, John: Unknown; 1635 on *Increase*; passenger list only [GM 2:7:326].

Owen, Thomas: Unknown; 1640; Boston; removed soon, probably to Virginia [Lechford 337, 341, 352-53, 355-56, 360, 362; MBCR 1:309, 335, 337, 2:21; WJ 2:61; Aspinwall 166-69; HAHAC 1:94].

P

Packard, Samuel: Wymondham, Norfolk; 1638 on *Diligent*; Hingham, Weymouth, Bridgewater [NEHGR 15:27, 59:107-8; MD 15:253-56; Weymouth Hist 4:454; Bartlett-Jenkins 79-81].

Packett, John: Unknown; 1639; Saco (court appearance only) [MPCR 1:51; GDMNH 522].

Pacy, Nicholas: Unknown (but resided at Lowestoft, Suffolk, upon return to England); 1638; Salem; returned permanently to England by 1646 [STR 1:78; EQC 1:23, 96; NEHGR 32:235; SChR 11, 19; Dudley Wildes Anc 122; Perley 2:42].

Paddock, Robert: Unknown; 1637; Duxbury [PCR 1:85, 7:32; PCPR 1:30; TAG 31:100-1, 32:39-45; M&JCH 25:49-50; Brainerd Anc 221].

Paddy, William: London; 1635 on *James*; Plymouth, Boston [GM 2:5:327-36].

Pafflin, John: Unknown; 1639; Braintree (land grant and court appearance only) [BTR 1:49; MBCR 1:265].

Page, Edward: Canterbury, Kent; 1637; Charlestown (passenger list and court appearance only) [NEHGR 75:222; MBCR 1:315]. (No obvious connection with the Edward Page who appeared at Boston in the early 1650s [GM 2:1:508].)

Page, John: Dedham, Essex; 1630; Watertown [GMB 1365-69; WF 505-10].

Page, John: Unknown; 1640; Hingham, Haverhill [MBCR 1:378; Hingham Hist 3:105; Hoyt 273].

Page, Robert: Ormesby St. Margaret, Norfolk; 1637 on *John & Dorothy* or *Rose*; Salem, Hampton [Hotten 291; SChR 8, 17; STR 1:72; GDMNH 55, 522; HmTR 43; NEHGR 66:180-83, 141:114-27; Hoyt 272-73].

Page, Thomas: London; 1635 on *Increase*; Saco [GM 2:5:336-39].

Paine, _____: Unknown; 1632; Massachusetts Bay [GMB 2083].

Paine, Anthony: Unknown; 1638; Portsmouth [PoTR 2; RICR 1:91; TG 7-8:146; Austin 142; Hall-Baldwin 143-44].

Paine, Edward: Unknown (but resided at Wapping, Middlesex, upon return to England); 1638; Charlestown; returned permanently to England in 1640s [ChTR 39; ChBOP 68; SLR 1:17, 55, 109; Wyman 720-21; NYGBR 47:252].

Paine, Edward: Unknown; 1640; Dover [Lechford 289; NHPP 40:5, 9, 13; EQC 1:48, 87, 94, 99, 100; GDMNH 523].

Paine, John: Unknown; 1635 on *Abigail*; passenger list only [GM 2:5:339].

Paine, John: Unknown; 1639; Saco [MPCR 1:51; GDMNH 523].

Paine, Moses: Tenterden, Kent; 1638; Cambridge, Braintree [CaTR 40; BTR 1:37; NEHGR 3:247, 65:290-91; SPR 1:26, 2:17; MBCR 1:378; TAG 21:181-89, 83:267-77].

Paine, Richard: Unknown; 1640; Wethersfield (appearance in notarial record only) [Lechford 313].

Paine, Robert: Suffolk; 1639; Ipswich [ITR 67; EPR 1:31; MBCR 1:379; NEHGR 4:180, 31:161; Hammatt Papers 241-42; Waters 1171-18, 1123].

Paine, Stephen: Great Ellingham, Norfolk; 1638 on *Diligent*; Hingham, Rehoboth [NEHGR 15:25, 143:291-302; HiBOP 84; MBCR 1:376; TAG 62:107].

Paine, Thomas: Sandwich, Kent; 1632 on *William & Francis*; passenger list only [GMB 2084].

Paine, Thomas: Wrentham, Suffolk; 1637 on *Mary Anne*; Salem [Hotten 293; STR 1:55; EPR 1:37; WP 4:293-94; NEHGR 5:331-32; Nathaniel Emmons Paine, *Thomas Payne of Salem and His Descendants* (Haverhill, Massachusetts, 1928)].

Paine, Thomas: Unknown; 1638; Yarmouth; not seen after 1650 [PCR 1:126, 2:20, 57, 70, 128, 7:21, 50, 8:176, 194]. (Possible relation to Thomas Paine who appeared at Eastham in the late 1650s [CCL 32:21-28; MF 6:13-14].)

Paine, William: Unknown; 1634; Massachusetts Bay [GM 2:5:339].

Paine, William: Unknown; 1635 on *Abigail*; passenger list only [GM 2:5:340].

Paine, William: Lavenham, Suffolk; 1635 on *Increase*; Watertown, Ipswich, Boston [GM 2:5:340-47].

Painter *see also* **Paynter**

Painter, Thomas: Unknown; 1636; Boston, Hingham, Rowley, Charlestown, New Haven, Newport, Westerly [BTR 1:13, 36, 47; BChR 31, 286; MBCR 1:260, 378; WJ 2:213-14; WP 4:272; Lechford 33; HiBOP 62; NEHGR 2:275, 68:273; Austin 143]. (This collection of records deserves further research; they do not necessarily all apply to one man.)

Palfrey, Jane: Newcastle-upon-Tyne, Northumberland; 1638; Cambridge [Shepard 150-52]. (She married George Willis.)

Palfrey, Peter: Unknown; 1626; Salem, Reading [GMB 1369-72].

Palgrave, Richard: Wymondham, Norfolk; 1630; Charlestown [GMB 1373-76; WF 510-15].

Palmer, Abraham: London; 1629; Charlestown; died at Barbados [GMB 1376-79; TAG 85:9].

Palmer, Edward: Unknown; 1638; Massachusetts Bay (court appearance only) [MBCR 1:260, 291; Lechford 242].

Palmer, George: Unknown; 1639; Massachusetts Bay (court appearance only) [MBCR 1:287].

Palmer, Henry: Unknown; 1640; Newbury, Haverhill [MBCR 1:314; HvBOP 19; Hoyt 994; Pillsbury Anc 1093-95].

Palmer, John: Unknown; 1634 on *Elizabeth*; passenger list only [GM 2:5:348].

Palmer, John: Unknown; 1635; Boston [GM 2:5:348-49].

Palmer, John: Unknown; 1635; Hingham, Scituate [GM 2:5:349-54].

Palmer, John: Unknown; 1640; Boston [Lechford 349-50; SLR 1:313; MBCR 3:192; BTR 1:51, 63, 85; BBOP 37, 79, 82; GM 2:5:349].

Palmer, Nicholas: Unknown; 1636; Windsor [Grant 59, 77; WiLR 1:16; HaVR 607; WMJ 267; TAG 34:69-70; Windsor Hist 2:548-49].

Palmer, Richard: Unknown; 1635 on *James*; passenger list only [GM 2:5:354].

Palmer, Walter: Unknown; 1629; Charlestown, Rehoboth, Stonington [GMB 1379-83; Doris Palmer Buys, *Walter Palmer of Charlestown and*

Rehoboth, Massachusetts, and Stonington, Connecticut (Orem, Utah, 1986)].

Palmer, William: Unknown; 1621 on *Fortune*; Plymouth, Duxbury [GMB 1383-86; PM 349-52].

Palmer, William: Unknown; 1636; Watertown, Yarmouth, Newtown [NY] [WaBOP 7; Lechford 231; PCR 1:108, 132; TAG 26:95, 101, 183-89; NYGBR 63:360, 64:30; Miner Anc 142-43].

Palmer, William: Ormesby St. Margaret, Norfolk; 1637; Newbury, Hampton [NeTR 4; MBCR 1:236, 375; GDMNH 55; HmTR 39; NEHGR 69:284-85, 75:79-80; EIHC 53:243-44; John Calvin Palmer, *A Genealogical Record of the Descendants of William Palmer of Hampton, New Hampshire, 1638*, 2 volumes (n.p. 1998)].

Palmer, William: Unknown; 1639; Strawberry Bank, Kittery [NHPP 1:113, 40:7; GDMNH 527].

Palmer, William: Unknown; 1640; Wethersfield, Branford, Westchester [WetLR 1:171; TAG 26:95-101; David A. Parker, *The Genealogy of One Line of Descendants of William Palmer of Wethersfield, Conn., and Westchester, N.Y.* (n.p. 1994)].

Palmerley, John: Unknown; 1635 on *Elizabeth & Ann*; passenger list only [GM 2:5:355].

Pane, Thomas: Unknown; 1636; Lynn (court appearance only) [EQC 1:5].

Pankhurst, Ann: Iford, Sussex; 1635 on *Abigail*; Lynn, Ipswich, Newport, Hempstead [GM 2:5:355-57]. (She married Michael Williamson and Henry Pearsall.)

Pantry, William: Willesborough, Kent; 1634; Cambridge, Hartford [Manwaring 1:119; TAG 30:7-10, 38:205; NEHGR 80:131, 95:255, 96:370-71; GM 2:7:423; Hale, House 774; Goodman Anc 351-56].

Parish, Thomas: Nayland, Suffolk; 1635 on *Increase*; Watertown, Cambridge; returned permanently to England by 1649 [GM 2:5:357-60; Abandoning 227-29].

Park, Richard: Unknown; 1635 on *Defence*; Cambridge [GM 2:5:360-63].

Parke, Joseph: Unknown; 1639; Hingham (appearance in notarial record only) [Lechford 176].

Parke, Margery: Wherwell, Hampshire; 1638 on *Confidence*; passenger list only (servant) [Drake's Founders 59].

Parke, Robert: Bildeston, Suffolk; 1639; Wethersfield [CCCR 1:46, 55; WetLR 1:80; Wethersfield Hist 1:289; TAG 13:1-8, 14:16, 145-46, 29:215-18, 33:11-13, 82:250-60; TG 4:173-86]. (His son William Parke preceded him to New England in 1631 [GMB 1386-91].)

Parker, Basil *see* **Thomas Brooks**

Parker, George: Unknown; 1635 on *Elizabeth & Ann*; passenger list only (with caveat) [GM 2:5:363-64].

Parker, George: Unknown; 1638; Portsmouth [RICR 1:60, 91; PoTR 18; TAG 20:54, 57:15-23; Austin 143-44].

Parker, James: Unknown; 1631; Piscataqua, Dorchester, Weymouth, Strawberry Bank; removed permanently to Barbados in 1646 [GMB 1391-93].

Parker, James: Great Burstead, Essex; 1640; Woburn, Chelmsford, Groton [WoTR 2; WoVR; NEHGR 30:236, 153:81-96, 159:360; TEG 16:225-28].

Parker, John: Marlborough, Wiltshire; 1635 on *James*; Boston [GM 2:5:364-67].

Parker, John: Unknown; 1636; Saco [MPCR 1:lxii; GDMNH 528].

Parker, John: Unknown, 1636, Hingham (land grant only) [HiBOP 95v].

Parker, John: Unknown; 1639; Dedham (land transaction only) [Lechford 244-47].

Parker, John: Unknown; 1640; Massachusetts Bay (court appearance only) [MBCR 1:309].

Parker, John: Unknown; 1640; Taunton [Lechford 326; PCR 2:17; PCPR 2:2:47A; MD 17:26-28, 18:169].

Parker, Joseph: Newbury, Berkshire; 1638 on *Confidence*; Salisbury, Newbury, Andover [Drake's Founders 59; SyTR 5; Hoyt 277-78; TEG 18:154-57].

Parker, Judith: Unknown; 1639; Hampton [HmTR 45; GDMNH 55, 529; Waters 625].

Parker, Nathaniel: London; 1638 on *Bevis*; passenger list only (servant) [Drake's Founders 61].

Parker, Nicholas: Unknown; 1633; Roxbury, Boston; returned permanently to England after 1651 [GMB 1394-96; Abandoning 229-30].

Parker, Richard: Unknown; 1638; Boston [NEHGR 2:275; BTR 1:42, 48; BChR 33; Lechford 68, 116, 244-47, 409; MBCR 1:378; SPR Case #638].

Parker, Robert: Unknown; 1633; Boston, Cambridge [GMB 1396-99; TEG 24:46-47].

Parker, Robert: Unknown; 1640; Wethersfield (appearance in notarial record only) [Lechford 313]. (Possibly a clerical error for Robert Parke.)

Parker, Samuel: Unknown; 1638; Hingham (land grant only) [HiBOP 49].

Parker, Sarah: Stepney, Middlesex; 1630; Charlestown [TAG 82:172-77]. (She married Hugh Williams.)

Parker, Thomas: Newbury, Berkshire; 1634 on *Mary & John*; Ipswich, Newbury [GM 2:5:367-70].

Parker, Thomas: Unknown; 1635 on *Susan & Ellen*; passenger list only (with caveat) [GM 2:5:370-71].

Parker, Thomas: Unknown; 1636; Lynn, Reading [MBCR 1:373; EQC 1:6, 10, 26, 2:270; NEHGR 33:61, 35:86; TEG 15:48-49; Mower Anc 461-65].

Parker, Walter: Unknown; 1635 on *Love*; passenger list only [GM 2:5:371].

Parker, William: Unknown; 1637; Scituate [NEHGR 5:335, 10:43; PCR 1:110, 143, 2:3; MD 1:236; TAG 41:102-8; Scott Gen 263].

Parker, William: Unknown; 1638; Boston (Boston town committee only) [BTR 1:38]. (Possibly a clerical error for some other name.)

Parker, William: Unknown; 1639; Hartford, Saybrook [HaTR 22; HaBOP 113; Granberry 288-90].

Parker, William: Unknown; 1639; Newport (admission as Newport inhabitant only) [RICR 1:92; GMN 23:3]. (Probably the same as the next.)

Parker, William: Unknown; 1639; Taunton [PCR 1:132, 7:28; MD 17:216; NEHGR 6:95].

Parker, William: Unknown; 1640; Watertown [WaVR 1:8; WaBOP 29; SuTR 3; MBCR 1:378; BChR 313; Bond 388, 868].

Parkman, Elias: Unknown; 1633; Dorchester, Windsor, Saybrook, Boston [GMB 1399-1403; M&JCH 26:52-53 (clue)].

Parmelee, John: Unknown; 1639; Guilford, New Haven [Guilford Hist 25; NEHGR 53:405-6, 81:130; Hall-Baldwin 145-49].

Parmenter, Benjamin: Unknown; 1636; Marblehead, Manchester [STR 1:29, 47; EQC 1:9; Marblehead 104-5].

Parmenter, John: Bures St. Mary, Suffolk; 1639; Sudbury, Roxbury [MBCR 1:271, 377; SPR 2:7; SuTR 1; NEHGR 68:262-73, 143:325-31, 147:377-82; TG 11:173-75].

Parratt, Francis: Unknown; 1639; New Haven, Rowley [NHCR 1:24; MBCR 1:301, 376; RowBOP 4; EPR 1:244-45; Pillsbury Anc 271-72; Rowley Fam 266].

Parrie, Edward: Unknown; 1635 on *Truelove*; passenger list only [GM 2:5:372].

Parsons, Joseph: Beaminster, Dorset; 1636; Springfield [NEHGR 15:140-41, 143:101-19, 148:215-21; Gerald James Parsons, *The Parsons Family*, Volume One (Baltimore 2002)].

Parsons, Richard: Unknown; 1639; Windsor (admission to freemanship only) [CCCR 1:46; see GM 2:5:442].

Parsons, Robert: Unknown; 1638; Lynn, Easthampton [EQC 1:11, 2:270; MBCR 1:375; TAG 20:148-59, 21:116-18].

Parsons, Thomas: Unknown; 1636; Wethersfield, New Haven [NHCR 1:38; Grant 59; TAG 21:118; NEHGR 143:105-7 (clue), 148:215, 226-38, 345-59].

Parsons, William: Salisbury, Wiltshire; 1635 on *James*; passenger list only [GM 2:5:372].

Partridge, George: Unknown; 1635; Duxbury [GM 2:5:372-81].

Partridge, Ralph: Sutton-by-Dover, Kent; 1636; Duxbury [WJ 1:244, 245; PCR 1:73, 12:18, 54; MD 14:228-30; NYGBR 35:101-7; TAG 86:81-95].

Partridge, William: Olney, Buckinghamshire; 1638; Lynn, Salisbury [EQC 2:270; MBCR 1:375; SyTR 1; NHPP 40:11; NEHGR 63:283-84, 164:15-22, 296; TAG 65:68; NHGR 9:180-81].

Pasmer, Bartholomew: Unknown; 1640; Boston; not seen after 1645 [NEHGR 2:275; BBOP 11, 127].

Patch, Edmund: South Petherton, Somerset; 1639; Salem, Ipswich [STR 1:90; EPR 3:395-98; NEHGR 4:289, 71:169].

Patch, Nicholas: South Petherton, Somerset; 1639; Salem [STR 1:90; EQC 5:255; NEHGR 71:166-70, 100:72].

Patchen, Joseph: Ashford, Kent; 1635 on *Hercules*; Scituate, Roxbury, Fairfield [GM 2:5:382-83].

Patience, Thomas: Unknown; 1640; Lynn; returned permanently to England by 1642 [MBCR 1:316; EQC 1:52; Abandoning 231-32; ODNB].

Patrick, Daniel: The Hague, Holland; 1630; Watertown, Cambridge, Greenwich [GMB 1403-8; WF 516-21].

Patricson, ____: Unknown; 1635; Medford; returned permanently to England in 1635 [GM 2:5:383-84].

Patten, Nathaniel: Crewkerne, Somerset; 1640; Dorchester [DTR 1:43; Lechford 318; NEHGR 35:166, 86:456-57, 87:270-79; M&JCH 27:43].

Patten, William: Earls Colne, Essex; 1635; Cambridge [GM 2:5:384-86].

Patteson, Edward: Unknown; 1635 on *Christian*; New Haven [GM 2:5:387-89].

Paul, Daniel: Ipswich, Suffolk; 1640; Boston, New Haven, Kittery [Lechford 293; NHCR 1:92, 105, 125, 138, 273, 282, 302; GDMNH 534-35; NYGBR 47:332-33].

Paul, Richard: Unknown; 1636; Boston, Taunton [WJ 2:423; PCR 1:103, 159; PCPR 1:31; NEHGR 75:142].

Paulmin, Sebastian: London; 1636; Boston (servant; apparently returned to England in 1637) [WJ 2:422; WP 3:352; Abandoning 344-45].

Pauly, Benjamin: Unknown; 1640; Salem [MBCR 1:309; STR 1:152, 197, 213; ELR 1:29v]. (Possibly also at New Haven [MHCR 1:18, 51].)

Paybody, John: Unknown; 1637; Duxbury [PCR 1:72, 74; MD 17:23; Selim Hobart Peabody, *Peabody (Paybody, Pabody, Pabodie) Genealogy* (Boston 1909); MF 16:1:23-27].

Paynter *see also* **Painter**

Paynter, Thomas: Unknown; 1630; Mystic [GMB 1408; WF 521].

Payson, Edward: Nazeing, Essex; 1634; Roxbury, Dorchester [GM 2:5:389-95].

Payson, Giles: Nazeing, Essex; 1635 on *Hopewell*; Roxbury [GM 2:5:396-400].

Peabody, Francis: Unknown; 1635 on *Planter*; Ipswich, Hampton, Topsfield [GM 2:5:400-10].

Peach, Arthur: Unknown; 1637; Plymouth [WJ 1:323; WP 4:49; PCR 1:96, 113; Legal Executions 7].

Peach, John: Unknown; 1630; Salem, Marblehead [GMB 1408-12].

Peach, John: Unknown; 1639; Marblehead [EQC 1:62, 78, 5:4-5; EPR Case #20912; GMN 1410-12; Weymouth Hist 4:637; Noyes-Gilman 328; Marblehead 106-7; NEHGR 54:276-79].

Peacock, John: Radwell, Bedfordshire; 1639; Milford [MiTR 2; FOOF 1:466-67; Ackley-Bosworth 166].

Peacock, Richard: Unknown; 1638; Roxbury [RChR 83; MBCR 1:376; NEHGR 6:184; MD 22:114].

Peacock, William: Stanstead Abbots, Hertford; 1635 on *Hopewell*; Roxbury [GM 2:5:411-13].

Peake, Christopher: Unknown; 1634; Roxbury [GMB 1413-14].

Peake, Mary: Unknown; 1635 on *Hopewell*; passenger list only [GM 2:5:413-14].

Peakes, John: Unknown; 1640; Massachusetts Bay (business transaction only) [Lechford 283].

Pease, Henry: Unknown; 1631; Boston [GMB 1415-17].

Pease, John: Great Baddow, Essex; 1634 on *Francis*; Salem, Edgartown [GM 2:5:414-18; Richard Bart, *The Pease Family from Great Baddow, England* (n.p. 1999)].

Pease, Robert: Great Baddow, Essex; 1634 on *Francis*; Salem [GM 2:5:418-20; Richard Bart, *The Pease Family from Great Baddow, England* (n.p. 1999)].

Peat, John: Duffield, Derbyshire; 1635 on *Hopewell*; passenger list only (with caveat) [GM 2:5:420].

Peck, Joseph: Hingham, Norfolk; 1638 on *Diligent*; Hingham, Rehoboth [NEHGR 15:26, 89:327-39; MBCR 1:375; HiBOP 65; MD 15:236-39; TAG 13:153; Ackley-Bosworth 120-24; GMC50 291-92; Ira

B. Peck, *A Genealogical History of the Descendants of Joseph Peck* (Boston 1868)].

Peck, Nathaniel: Unknown; 1635, Hingham (land grant only) [HiBOP 38].

Peck, Paul: Unknown; 1639; Hartford [HaBOP 283; TAG 9:82-89, 154, 38:237-39, 50:236; Hale, House 256-61].

Peck, Peter: Unknown; 1634; Dorchester (land record only) [GM 2:5:420].

Peck, Robert: Hingham, Norfolk; 1638 on *Diligent*; Hingham; returned permanently to England in 1641 [NEHGR 15:26, 37:193, 89:327-39; MBCR 1:375; HiBOP 65; WJ 1:331; Ackley-Bosworth 120-21; GMC50 289-90; Abandoning 232-35].

Peck, William: Unknown; 1640; New Haven, Lyme [NHCR 1:44, 50, 51, 92; NHChR 1; FANH 1383-85; TAG 13:122; NEHGR 121:81].

Peckham, John: Unknown; 1639; Newport [RICR 1:92; NEHGR 57:31-32, 63:198; TAG 24:72, 71:151-54; Austin 147-48].

Peeters, Anne: Unknown; 1630; Salem, Boston (church admission only) [GMB 1417; WF 521-22].

Pelham, Herbert: Boston, Lincolnshire; 1637; Cambridge; returned permanently to England in 1647 [CaTR 33; SuTR 21; WaBOP 49; WJ 2:23; HAHAC 1:94; MBCR 1:292; TAG 18:138-46; NEHGR 154:78-108; Abandoning 235; ODNB].

Pelham, John: Bures, Essex; 1635 on *Susan & Ellen*; passenger list only [GM 2:5:421].

Pelham, Penelope: Bures, Essex; 1635; Boston [GM 2:5:421]. (She married Richard Bellingham.)

Pelham, William: Boston, Lincolnshire; 1630; Watertown, Sudbury; returned permanently to England by 1652 [GMB 1417-19; WF 522-24; Abandoning 239].

Pell, Joseph: Unknown; 1638; Lynn, Boston [EQC 2:270; MBCR 1:375; SPR Case #90; Essex Ant 2:101; Snow-Estes 1:126-27].

Pell, Margaret: Unknown; 1640; Windsor [Grant 53]. (She married Thomas Orton.)

Pell, Thomas: Unknown; 1635 on *Planter*; passenger list only [GM 2:5:422].

Pell, Thomas: Unknown; 1635 on *Hopewell*; passenger list only (with caveat) [GM 2:5:422].

Pell, Thomas: Unknown; 1636; Saybrook, New Haven, Fairfield [MHSC 3:3:144; Aspinwall 161, 193, 248; FOOF 1:471-72].

Pell, William: Unknown; 1634; Boston [GM 2:5:423-25].

Pemberton, James: Unknown; 1630; Nantasket, Charlestown, Malden [GMB 1419-21; SLR 1:82; NEHGR 142:114].

Pemberton, John: Unknown; 1632; Boston, Newbury; returned permanently to England in 1648 or after [GMB 1421-22; Abandoning 239-40].

Pendleton, Brian: London; 1634; Watertown, Sudbury, Topsfield, Portsmouth [NH], Saco [GM 2:5:425-28].

Pengry, Moses: Unknown; 1640; Ipswich [ITR 85; Aspinwall 282 (clue); Rowley Fam 302; Pillsbury 981-84; William M. Pingry, *A Genealogical Record of the Descendants of Moses Pengry* (Ludlow, Vermont, 1881)].

Penn, Christian: Unknown; 1623 on *Anne*; Plymouth [GMB 1423; PM 352]. (She married Francis Eaton and Francis Billington.)

Penn, Hannah: Unknown; 1634; Boston [GM 2:5:429]. (She married William Townsend.)

Penn, James: Unknown; 1630; Boston [GMB 1423-26; WF 524-28].

Penn, Mary: Unknown; 1632; Boston (church membership only, with caveat) [GMB 1426].

Penn, Richard: Unknown; 1639; Boston (court appearance and business transaction only) [MBCR 1:282; Lechford 272].

Penn, Robert: Unknown; 1638; Salem (admission as town inhabitant and land grant only) [STR 1:73, 74].

Penn, William: Unknown; 1630; Charlestown [GMB 1426; WF 528].

Penn, William: Unknown; 1640; Braintree, Boston [WP 4:299; SLR 1:299; Aspinwall 123; NEHGR 40:63; SPR Case #2127].

Penniman, James: High Laver, Essex; 1631 on *Lyon*; Boston, Braintree [GMB 1426-30; NEHGR 162:136].

Pennington, Deborah: Unknown; 1636; Salem (land grant only) [STR 1:29].

Pennoyer, Robert: Bristol; 1635 on *Hopewell*; Medford, New Amsterdam, Gravesend, Stamford, Mamaroneck [GM 2:5:429-37].

Pennoyer, Thomas: Unknown; 1635 on *Hopewell*; passenger list only [GM 2:5:437].

Penny, Elinor: Unknown; 1639; Plymouth [PCR 1:129]. (She married Thomas Redding.)

Pentecost, John: Cranbrook, Kent; 1638; Charlestown [ChTR 39; ChChR 9; ChBOP 10; SPR 2:9; MBCR 1:376; Wyman 737; TAG 62:118-20].

Pepper, Phyllis: Unknown; 1636; Roxbury (church admission only) [RChR 82].

Pepper, Richard: Unknown; 1634 on *Francis*; Roxbury [GM 2:5:437-38].

Pepper, Robert: Unknown; 1639; Roxbury [RChR 84; SPR Case #523 (son John Pepper); Stevens-Miller 1:321; Winthrop-Babcock 387; Emily Clark Landon, *Pepper Genealogy: Ancestors and Descendants of Robert Pepper of Roxbury, Mass.* (Angola, New York, 1932); NEA 9:3:48-49].

Perien, Mary: Unknown; 1635 on *Hercules*; passenger list only [GM 2:5:438].

Perkins, Abraham: Unknown; 1638; Ipswich, Hampton [EPR 1:11; HmTR 40; HampVR 1:3; MBCR 1:377; GDMNH 55, 541; Pillsbury Anc 339-41; Dudley Wildes Anc 89; Carolyn C. Perkins, *Descendants of Abraham Perkins of Hampton, New Hampshire, to the Eighth Generation* (Portsmouth, New Hampshire, 1993)].

Perkins, Isaac: Unknown; 1637; Ipswich [ITR 28, 52-53; Essex Ant 8:2; Dudley Wildes Anc 89].

Perkins, Isaac: Unknown; 1639; Hampton [GDMNH 55, 541-42; HampVR 1:3; Dudley Wildes Anc 89].

Perkins, John: Hillmorton, Warwickshire; 1631 on *Lyon*; Boston, Ipswich [GMB 1431-33].

Perkins, William: London; 1632 on *William & Francis*; Roxbury, Weymouth, Gloucester, Topsfield [GMB 1433-38].

Perley, Allen: St. Albans, Hertford; 1635 on *Planter*; Ipswich [GM 2:5:438-41].

Perrin, John: Unknown; 1640; Braintree, Rehoboth [NEHGR 3:247, 96:256-60; ReTR 1:2; MD 34:35-36].

Perrin, Mr.: Unknown; 1639; Salem (appearance in notarial record only) [Lechford 230].

Perry, Abraham: Unknown; 1640; Boston (land sale only) [BTR 1:59]. (Probably a clerical error for Arthur or Isaac Perry.)

Perry, Arthur: Unknown; 1638; Boston [BTR 1:36; BChR 24; MBCR 1:377; NEHGR 2:276, 96:323, 125:231-36; HAHAC 1:76; Lechford 91; WP 4:286; FOOF 1:474-75].

Perry, Francis: Unknown; 1631; Salem, Lynn; removed to Barbados by 1655 [GMB 1438-41].

Perry, Isaac: Sawbridgeworth, Hertfordshire; 1631; Boston [GMB 1441; TAG 82:81-90, 187-95, 273-89].

Perry, John: Sawbridgeworth, Hertfordshire; 1632; Roxbury [GMB 1442-43; TAG 82:81-90, 187-95, 273-89].

Perry, Richard: London; 1636; Charlestown, New Haven; returned permanently to England in 1651 [ChTR 22; MBCR 1:270; NHCR 1:26, 39, 41, 91; FANH 1439; FOOF 1:472; TAG 10:61-62, 20:supp:27; Jacob M. Price, *Perry of London: A Family and a Firm on the Seaborne Frontier, 1615-1753* (Cambridge, Massachusetts, 1992)].

Perry, William : Unknown; 1638; Scituate [PCR 1:110; Gen Adv 3:91, 112; TAG 70:42-48, 84; NEHGR 146:230-34].

Persons, Richard: Unknown; 1635 on *Marygould*; passenger list only [GM 2:5:442].

Pester, William: Unknown; 1636; Salem; returned permanently to England about 1642 [STR 1:24; EQC 1:6, 30, 78; Lechford 233-34, 255, 300; SLR 1:17, 52; MBCR 1:225, 247, 3:277; Abandoning 240].

Peter, Hugh: Rotterdam; 1635 on *Abigail* or *Defence*; Salem; returned permanently to England in 1641 [GM 2:5:442-45; Abandoning 241-49].

Petfree, ____: Unknown; 1636; Piscataqua [WJ 1:270].

Pettee, William: Unknown; 1637; Weymouth [Weymouth VR; Weymouth Hist 4:460].

Pettingill, Richard: Unknown; 1640; Salem, Wenham, Newbury [SChR 10; MBCR 1:378; EPR 1:19; NEHGR 55:194; Abel Lunt Anc 51-60 (clue)].

Pettit, Thomas: Unknown; 1634; Boston, Exeter [BTR 1:22; MBCR 1:193; NHPP 1:133; Essex Ant 5:15; GDMNH 544].

Phelps, George: Unknown; 1634; Dorchester, Windsor, Westfield [GM 2:5:445-50].

Phelps, Henry: Unknown; 1634 on *Hercules*; passenger list only [GM 2:5:450].

Phelps, Richard: Unknown; 1632; Dorchester [GMB 1443-44].

Phelps, William: Crewkerne, Somerset; 1630 on *Mary & John*; Dorchester, Windsor [GMB 1444-46; TAG 75:26; M&JCH 25:50-51, 26:54-55].

Philbrick, Robert: Unknown; 1637; Ipswich [ITR 43; EQC 1:147, 160, 224, 278, 305, 368; EPR 1:192].

Philbrick, Thomas: Bures St. Mary, Suffolk; 1636; Watertown [WaBOP 5, 62; NEHGR 108:252-58, 147:327; GDMNH 546; GMC26 223-26].

Phillipp, Phillip: Unknown; 1635 on *Hopewell*; passenger list only [GM 2:5:450-51].

Phillips, George: Boxted, Essex; 1630; Watertown [GMB 1446-50; WF 528-33].

Phillips, George: Unknown; 1632; Dorchester, Windsor [GMB 1450-52].

Phillips, Hannah: Unknown; 1638; Dedham [DeVR 126]. (She married Joseph Morse.)

Phillips, Henry: Unknown; 1637; Dedham [DeTR 1:32; DeVR 126; DeChR 14; SPR 1:19; HAHAC 1:109; MBCR 1:375; NGSQ 78:90; DeHR 3:158-59].

Phillips, John: Unknown; 1630; Dorchester, Boston [GMB 1452-56].

Phillips, John: Unknown; 1631; Plymouth Colony (mention in letter only) [WP 3:65].

Phillips, John: Unknown; 1637; Duxbury, Marshfield [PCR 1:87, 145, 12:31; PPR 1:140-41; MD 34:35-37; Azel Ames, *The Family and Vicissitudes of John Phillips, Senior, of Duxbury and Marshfield* (Malden, Massachusetts, 1903)].

Phillips, John: Wrentham, Suffolk; 1638; Salem, Dedham; returned permanently to England in 1641 [STR 1:77; WJ 2:103; WP 4:109, 197, 293-94; MBCR 1:253; DeChR 7; DeTR 1:48; Abandoning 250-54].

Phillips, John: Unknown; 1640; Portsmouth (court appearance only) [PoTR 17-18].

Phillips, John: Unknown; 1640; Dover [NHPP 10:701, 31:13, 40:7; GDMNH 547].

Phillips, Martin: Unknown; 1637; Dedham; not seen after 1639 [DeTR 1:33, 91].

Phillips, Nicholas: Unknown; 1636; Dedham, Weymouth [DeTR 1:20; MBCR 1:295, 377; NEHGR 163:113-16; Weymouth Hist 4:464-65; Backus Anc 131-32].

Phillips, William: Great Berkhamsted, Hertfordshire; 1639; Charlestown, Boston, Saco [ChChR 9, 49; ChTR 49; Lechford 377; NEHGR 4:269; MBCR 1:376; TAG 14:157, 86:296-301; Wyman 740; GDMNH 548; NEQ 79:461-72].

Phillips, William: Unknown; 1640; Hartford [HaBOP 82, 161-63; HaTR 35; Manwaring 1:143-44, 225-26].

Phippen, David: Weymouth, Dorset; 1634 on *Recovery*; Hingham, Boston [GM 2:5:451-56].

Phippen, Judith: Wedmore, Somerset; 1635 on *Planter*; Woburn [GM 2:5:456-57]. (She married James Hayward and William Simons.)

Phips, William: Unknown; 1630; Penobscot [GMB 1456-57; PM 352-53].

Pickeram, John: Unknown; 1630; Watertown [GMB 1457-58; WF 533-35].

Pickering, John: Unknown; 1630; Piscataqua [GMB 1458-61].

Pickering, John: Coventry, Warwickshire; 1636; Salem [STR 1:35; SChR 8; Aspinwall 334; EPR 1:254-55; GMB 1461; NEA 13:3:29-31; Harrison Ellery and Charles Pickering Bowditch, *The Pickering Genealogy Being an Account of the First Three Generations of the Pickering Family of Salem, Mass.* (n.p. 1897)].

Pickering, John: Unknown; 1638; Cambridge (births of two children only) [NEHGR 4:182; GMB 1461].

Pickton, Thomas: Unknown; 1639; Salem [STR 1:89; EQC 1:26; EPR 3:185-86; EIHC 4:63].

Pickus, John: Unknown; 1639; Piscataqua (court appearance only) [MPCR 1:42].

Pickworth, John: Unknown; 1631; Massachusetts Bay, Plymouth, Salem, Manchester [GMB 1462-64; PM 353-56].

Pidcock, George: Unknown; 1639; Duxbury, Scituate [PCR 1:153, 2:67, 135; PCPR 1:48, 3:1:23; MD 19:31].

Pidge, Thomas: Saffron Walden, Essex; 1633; Roxbury [GMB 1464-66].

Pierce, Abraham: Unknown; 1623 on *Anne*; Plymouth, Duxbury [GMB 1466-69; PM 356-59].

Pierce, Daniel: Unknown; 1634 on *Elizabeth*; Watertown, Newbury [GM 2:5:457-62; Lechford 93].

Pierce, John: Unknown; 1630; Dorchester, Boston [GMB 1469-72].

Pierce, John: Norwich, Norfolk; 1636; Watertown [TAG 84:177-84; MBCR 1:374; WaBOP 63, 142; EQC 1:15]. (His son Anthony Pierce had preceded him to New England in 1633.)

Pierce, John: Unknown; 1637; Hartford; not seen after 1640 [HaBOP 84, 157, 302-3; HaTR 24; CCCR 1:45; Lechford 311].

Pierce, John: Unknown; 1639; Massachusetts Bay (business transaction only) [Lechford 215].

Pierce, John: Unknown; 1639; Noddle's Island, Kittery [MBCR 1:265, 284, 318; WP 4:167; GDMNH 553].

Pierce, Mark: Unknown; 1638; Cambridge, New Haven; returned permanently to England by 1653 [MBCR 1:261; CaBOP 114; NHCR 1:50, 93, 156; Waters 199, 1080-81; Abandoning 254-55].

Pierce, Marmaduke: Sandwich, Kent; 1637; Salem; not seen after 1640 [NEHGR 75:223, 225; STR 1:53, 103; MBCR 1:269, 283, 286; Lechford 229-31; WJ 1:384 (as "Marmaduke Percy")].

Pierce, Phebe: Unknown; 1635 on *Increase*; passenger list only [GM 2:5:462-63].

Pierce, Robert: Unknown; 1639; Dorchester [DChR 5; NEHGR 4:169, 5:244, 32:57; SPR 1:444, 4:224].

Pierce, Thomas: Unknown; 1633; Charlestown, Woburn [ChBOP 42; WoVR; Rodgers 2:340-43; Wyman 756; Frederic Beech Pierce, *Pierce Genealogy, Being the Record of the Posterity of Thomas Pierce, An Early Inhabitant of Charlestown* (Worcester, Massachusetts, 1882)].

Pierce, William: Ratcliffe, Middlesex; 1632; Boston [GMB 1472-78].

Pierson, Abraham: Yorkshire; 1640; Boston, Southampton, Branford, Newark [BChR 31; SoTR 1:14; WJ 2:7; TAG 9:37-40; Parke-Gildersleeve 80-82; Magnalia 1:397-98; Sibley 2:253-58].

Pierson, Bartholomew: Unknown; 1640; Watertown, Woburn [WaVR 1:8, 9, 11, 14, 15; WaBOP 63; SPR Case #1541; Bond 406, 910].

Pierson, Henry: Olney, Buckinghamshire; 1639; Lynn, Southampton [WP 4:240; NEHGR 65:298; TAG 64:193-202; NYGBR 121:72-73].

Pigge, Robert: Unknown; 1640; New Haven [NHCR 1:46, 50; NEHGR 81:130; Manwaring 1:62-63; NHVR 19; FANH 1449; Wickham-Billard 82-84].

Pike, John: Landford, Wiltshire; 1635 on *James*; Ipswich, Newbury, Salisbury [GM 2:5:463-66; TAG 73:256-57; NEHGR 121:161-62].

Pike, Tabitha: Unknown; Boston; 1640 (servant; church admission only) [BChR 32].

Pile, Henry: Unknown; 1637 on *Prosperous*; passenger list only [NGSQ 71:177].

Pillsbury, William: Unknown; 1640; Dorchester, Newbury [MBCR 1:318, 334; SPR Case #1486; Pillsbury Anc 1:1-9; David B. Pilsbury and Emily A. Getchell, *The Pillsbury Family* (Everett, Massachusetts, 1898)].

Pinder, Henry: Cambridge, Cambridgeshire; 1635 on *Susan & Ellen*; Ipswich [GM 2:5:466-68].

Pinkham, Richard: Unknown; 1640; Dover [NHPP 1:128, 10:701; GDMNH 557; NHGR 22:1-3].

Pinney, Humphrey: Broadway, Somerset; 1633; Dorchester, Windsor [GMB 1478-81; M&JCH 27:43; CN 26:542-46].

Pinney, John: Unknown; 1634 on *Recovery*; passenger list only [GM 2:5:468].

Pinny, Thomas: Unknown; 1640; Weymouth (business transaction only) [Lechford 281-82].

Pinson, Thomas: Unknown; 1636; Scituate [ScTR 1:248; PCR 1:110, 134; PN&Q 2:154; PPR Case #15932; TAG 32:194-95, 50:97-104].

Pitcher, Andrew: Unknown; 1634; Dorchester [GM 2:5:468-71].

Pitford, Peter: Unknown; 1639; Marblehead [WP 4:128, 165; EQC 1:27; Marblehead 109].

Pithouse, John: Marlborough, Wiltshire; 1635 on *James*; Ipswich [GM 2:5:471-72].

Pitman, Nathaniel: Unknown; 1639; Salem [STR 1:89; EPR 1:13; EQC 1:17; EPR Case #22065; Essex Ant 11:72; EIHC 4:172; George Francis Dow, *The Diary and Letters of Benjamin Pickman (1740-1819) of Salem, Massachusetts, with a Biographical Sketch and Genealogy of the Pickman Family* (Newport, Rhode Island, 1928)].

Pitney, James: Unknown; 1635 on *Planter*; Ipswich, Marshfield, Boston [GM 2:5:472-74].

Pitney, Margaret: Unknown; 1635 on *Planter*; passenger list only [GM 2:5:475].

Pitt, William: Unknown; 1623 on *Fortune*; Plymouth (land grant only) [GMB 1481; PM 359].

Pitts, Edith: Unknown; 1636; Scituate (servant; court appearance only) [PCR 1:48-49; MBCR 1:193].

Pitts, Edmond: Hingham, Norfolk; 1639; Hingham [NEHGR 15:27, 113:45; HiBOP 24; MBCR 1:377; SPR Case #1407; Hingham Hist 3:113-14].

Pitts, Elizabeth: Unknown; 1638; Dorchester [EQC 1:12; DChR 4; ChChR 10; SPR 3:26; Weymouth Hist 4:472].

Pitts, Henry: Unknown; 1640; Massachusetts Bay (court appearance only) [MBCR 1:315].

Pitts, Leonard: Hingham, Norfolk; 1639; Hingham [NEHGR 15:27; WJ 2:372; SLR 1:97; Aspinwall 48-49].

Pitts, William: Hingham, Norfolk; 1638 on *Diligent*; passenger list only [NEHGR 15:26]. (A William Pitts appeared at Marblehead in the 1650s [Hingham Hist 3:114].)

Place, Peter: Unknown; 1635 on *Truelove*; Boston [GM 2:5:475-77].

Place, Thomas: Unknown; 1639; Cambridge, Braintree; not seen after 1640 [CaBOP 65; BTR 1:49; MBCR 1:377].

Plaine, William: Unknown; 1639; Guilford [Guilford Hist 25; NEHGR 53:406; WJ 2:324; Legal Executions 12].

Plasse, William: London; 1637; Salem [STR 1:50; EQC 1:108; EPR 1:49; EIHC 28:88; Waters 1334-35, 1340-43].

Plastowe, Josias: Unknown; 1630; Massachusetts Bay; returned permanently to England in 1631 [GMB 1481-82; WF 535-36].

Platt, Richard: Ware, Hertfordshire; 1639; Milford [MiTR 2; MiChR 1; FOOF 1:483-84; TAG 30:232-42, 31:155-70, 38:223; Miner Anc 147-49].

Player, Giles: Unknown; 1638; Massachusetts Bay (two court appearances only) [MBCR 1:246, 310].

Plimpton, Elizabeth: Hampshire; 1639 on *Jonathan*; Sudbury [NEHGR 32:407-10; Levi B. Chase, *A Genealogy and Historical Notices of the Family of Plimpton or Plympton in America* (Hartford, Connecticut, 1884) 59]. (She married John Rutter.)

Plimpton, John: Unknown; 1640; Roxbury, Dedham, Medfield, Deerfield [SPR 1:7; DeChR 26; HAHAC 1:133; Medfield Hist 456-57; Levi B. Chase, *A Genealogy and Historical Notices of the Family of Plimpton or Plympton in America* (Hartford, Connecticut, 1884)].

Plimpton, Thomas: Unknown; 1640; Sudbury [SuTR 13; NEHGR 32:407, 47:73; MPR Case #17672; Levi B. Chase, *A Genealogy and Historical Notices of the Family of Plimpton or Plympton in America* (Hartford, Connecticut, 1884)].

Plum, John: Ridgewell, Essex; 1636; Wethersfield [MHSC 3:3:147; CCCR 1:3; WetLR 1:49; TAG 70:65-74, 149-55, 82:250-60].

Plumer, Mary: Unknown; 1633; Plymouth [GMB 1482; PM 359]. (She married John Barnes.)

Plumley, Alexander: Unknown; 1639; Braintree [BTR 1:42; SPR Case #1222].

Plummer, Anne: Unknown; 1635; Plymouth [PCR 1:36]. (She married Henry Samson.)

Plummer, Francis: Unknown; 1633; Newbury [GMB 1482-86; NGSQ 83:112 (clue)].

Pocock, Mr.: Unknown; 1640; New Haven (land grant only) [NHCR 1:49, 79, 196]. (Probably never came to New England.)

Podd, Samuel: Unknown; 1635 on *Susan & Ellen*; Ipswich [GM 2:5:477-79].

Pollard, John: "Belcham," Essex; 1640; Boston; not seen after 1641 [Lechford 314, 351-52, 362, 396, 413].

Pollard, Katherine: Unknown; 1639; Boston (church admission only) [BChR 26].

Pollard, George: Stoke by Clare, Suffolk; 1639; Duxbury; departed Duxbury by 1646 [PCR 1:145, 152, 158, 2:41, 12:49, 72-74, 139-40; Lechford 413]. (Possibly the same as the George Pollard who died testate at Marblehead in 1646 [EPR 1:59-60; Marblehead 111].)

Pomeroy, Eltweed: Crewkerne, Somerset; 1632; Dorchester, Windsor [GMB 1486-90; M&JCH 25:51; MHSC 2:8:148 (as "Edward Pomeroy")].

Pomfret, William: Unknown; 1640; Dover [NHPP 1:128, 10:701; Lechford 326, 328; GDMNH 562].

Pond, John: Edwardstone, Suffolk; 1630; Watertown; apparently returned permanently to England in 1631 [GMB 1490-91; WF 536-37].

Pond, Rebecca: Unknown; 1638 on *Bevis*; passenger list only (servant) [Drake's Founders 60].

Ponderson, John: Unknown; 1639; New Haven [NHCR 1:20; Lechford 208; NEHGR 81:130; FANH 1494-98].

Ponton, Richard: Unknown; 1640; Braintree, Boston, Hartford, Westchester [MBCR 1:314; BChR 43; TG forthcoming].

Pontus, William: Leiden, Holland; 1632; Plymouth [GMB 1491-93; PM 360-62].

Poole, Edward: Unknown; 1635 on *Marygould*; Weymouth, Newport [GM 2:5:479-83].

Poole, Elizabeth: Colyton, Devon; 1637; Taunton [NGSQ 71:175; Lechford 177; PCPR 1:31, 2:1:24; PCR 1:143; WJ 1:302; NEHGR 61:280; Waters 925-31; TAG 14:222-23].

Poole, John: Unknown; 1632; Cambridge, Lynn, Reading [GMB 1493-96; GM 2:2:45; TEG 21:209-11].

Poole, Samuel: Unknown; 1640; Scituate, Boston; not seen after 1642 [PCR 12:70; BChR 36, 290; NEHGR 14:124].

Poole, William: Unknown; 1638; Salem (two court appearances only) [EQC 1:9, 25]. (Probably not the same as the William Poole who was refused admittance as an inhabitant of Salem in 1656 [STR 1:190].)

Poole, William: Colyton, Devon; 1636; Taunton, Dorchester [PCR 1:53, 105, 7:36; PCPR 1:31; NEHGR 2:381, 61:280; Aspinwall 48; DChR 24,

170; SPR 8:46; Waters 925-31; TAG 14:222-23; M&JCH 26:55-56; Winthrop-Babcock 389-91].

Poor, Alice: Unknown; 1638 on *Bevis*; passenger list only [Drake's Founders 61].

Poor, Daniel: Unknown; 1638 on *Bevis*; Andover [Drake's Founders 61; NEHGR 3:65; EPR Case #22323; EIHC 4:237; NYGBR 49:307-8].

Poor, Nicholas: Unknown; 1636; Lynn (court appearance only) [EQC 1:5].

Poor, Samuel: Unknown; 1638 on *Bevis*; Newbury [Drake's Founders 61; EQC 9:420; EPR Case #22378].

Pope, Ephraim: Unknown; 1639; Massachusetts Bay [MBCR 1:270; GM 2:7:474-77].

Pope, John: Unknown; 1634 on *Recovery*; Dorchester [GM 2:5:483-87].

Pope, John: Eastwell, Kent; 1637; Dorchester [NEHGR 4:276, 75:221, 225-26; MBCR 1:287; DeTR 1:52; SPR Case #1512; Charles Henry Pope, *A History of the Dorchester Pope Family. 1634-1888* (Boston 1888)]. (This man is not the son of the earlier John Pope of Dorchester [GM 2:5:486-87].)

Pope, Joseph: Unknown; 1634 on *Mary & John*; Salem [GM 2:5:487-91].

Pope, Thomas: Unknown; 1632; Plymouth, Dartmouth [GMB 1496-99; PM 362-65].

Pope, Walter: Unknown; 1630; Charlestown [GMB 1499-1500].

Pormort, Philemon: Alford, Lincolnshire; 1634; Boston, Exeter, Wells [GM 2:5:491-94].

Porter, Abel: Unknown; 1633; Boston [BTR 1:31; BChR 33, 295; MBCR 1:379 (as "Abel Parr"); SPR Case #1453, Case #1464; GDMNH 563; NEHGR 53:128].

Porter, Edward: Chelmsford, Essex; 1636; Roxbury, Boston [RChR 82; MBCR 1:373; TAG 27:19-21; NEHGR 148:45-60].

Porter, Elizabeth: Ware, Hertfordshire, 1636; Roxbury [NEHGR 148:45-51]. (She married Isaac Johnson.)

Porter, John: Unknown; 1633; Roxbury, Boston, Portsmouth, Pettaquamscutt [GMB 1501-4; TAG 73:176-80].

Porter, John: Unknown; 1637; Hingham, Salem [HiBOP 98r; Hingham Hist 3:115; Dudley Wildes 135-38; TAG 30:157-58; Mower Anc 494-500].

Porter, John: Felsted, Essex; 1639; Windsor [Grant 57; WiLR 1:64; Manwaring 1:29-30; TAG 16:49-58, 122, 17:86-87, 18:56-60; NEHGR 55:22-31; FOOF 1:487].

Porter, Jonathan: Unknown; 1636; Salem [STR 1:24, 157, 179; SChR 8, 9; MBCR 1:378; Putnam's Mag 7:292; NYGBR 61:16-17; FOOF 1:490].

Porter, Nathaniel: Unknown; 1636; Salem [STR 1:21, 73-74, 93, 106, 107; MBCR 1:373; EPR 1:26].

Porter, Richard: Unknown; 1635 on *Marygould*; Weymouth [GM 2:5:494-97].

Porter, Roger: Long Sutton, Hampshire; 1638 on *Confidence*; Watertown [Drake's Founders 58; WaBOP 59; MBCR 1:376; Rodgers 1:151-54; TAG 61:79-82, 62:65-77, 64:44].

Porter, Thomas: Unknown; 1640; Hartford [HaTR 32; HaVR 606; Manwaring 1:579; Bassett-Preston 217-18; Flagg Anc 270-1].

Post, Stephen: Otham, Kent; 1634; Cambridge, Hartford, Saybrook [GM 2:5:497-500].

Potter, George: Unknown; 1638; Portsmouth [PoTR 2; RICR 1:91; Austin 155-56].

Potter, John: Unknown; 1636; Charlestown (land grant only) [ChTR 22, 57].

Potter, John: Lewes, Sussex; 1640; New Haven [NHCR 1:92; TAG 79:28-33, 81:133-40].

Potter, Luke: Newport Pagnell, Buckinghamshire; 1638; Concord [MBCR 1:375; CoVR 2; MPR Case #17812; GMC26 227-40].

Potter, Nathaniel: Unknown; 1638; Portsmouth [PoTR 2; RICR 1:91; Austin 354-57].

Potter, Nicholas: Newport Pagnell, Buckinghamshire; 1638; Lynn, Salem [EQC 2:270; TEG 19:142-45; Essex Ant 8:24; GMC26 232].

Potter, Robert: Unknown; 1634; Portsmouth, Warwick [GM 2:5:500-5].

Potter, Vincent: Unknown; 1635 on *Elizabeth & Ann*; Boston, Sandwich; returned permanently to England in 1639 [GM 2:5:505-6; Abandoning 345-46].

Potter, William: Unknown; 1635 on *Increase*; passenger list only (with caveat) [GM 2:5:506-7].

Potter, William: Lewes, Sussex; 1635 on *Abigail*; New Haven [GM 2:5:507-13; TAG 81:133-40].

Potter, William: Unknown; 1637; Watertown, Stamford [WaBOP 11, 55; SLR 1:66; SmTR 118; GMN 1:8; GM 2:5:506-7].

Potter, William: Unknown; 1638; Braintree [MBCR 1:249, 377; BTR 1:44; BrTR 1; SPR Case #143; GM 2:5:506-7].

Pount, Thomas: Unknown; 1635 on *Elizabeth & Ann*; passenger list only [GM 2:5:513].

Powell, Michael: Romford, Essex; 1639; Dedham [DeTR 1:62; DeChR 25; DeVR 1; MBCR 1:379; Romford parish register; NEHGR 131:173-74; Abandoning 373].

Powell, Thomas: Unknown; 1640; New Haven [NHCR 1:50, 93; NEHGR 81:130-31; FANH 1476-77; Moore Anc 429-38].

Powell, William: Unknown; 1636; Charlestown; residing in England by 1656 [ChTR 21; NEHGR 4:269; MBCR 1:194, 282. 296; Wyman 768].

Poyett, Lucy: Norwich, Norfolk; 1637 on *Mary Anne*; passenger list only [Hotten 293].

Pratt, Abraham: London; 1629; Charlestown, Roxbury, Cambridge; died at sea in 1645 returning to England [GMB 1504-7; WF 537-40; Abandoning 255-56].

Pratt, John: Unknown; 1633; Cambridge, Hartford [GMB 1507-10].

Pratt, Joshua: Unknown; 1623 on *Anne*; Plymouth [GMB 1510-13; PM 365-69].

Pratt, Macuth: Aston Clinton, Buckinghamshire; 1639; Weymouth [MBCR 1:377; ReTR 1:2; TAG 65:33-43, 89-96, 68:29-32].

Pratt, Phineas: Unknown; 1622 on *Sparrow*; Weymouth, Plymouth, Charlestown [GMB 1514-18; PM 369-74; TAG 74:122-27].

Pratt, William: Unknown; 1637; Hartford, Saybrook [HaBOP 177; Dawes-Gates 2:674-81; Moore Anc 434-44; Hale, House 719-21; NEHGR 149:374-78].

Preble, Abraham: Unknown; 1638; Scituate [ScitTR 1:242; NEHGR 22:311-17; GDMNH 565-66; George Henry Preble, *Genealogical Sketch of the First Three Generations of Prebles in America* (Boston 1868)].

Prence, Thomas: London; 1621 on *Fortune*; Plymouth, Duxbury, Eastham [GMB 1518-24; PM 374-81].

Prentice, Henry: Unknown; 1639; Sudbury, Cambridge [SuTR 3; CaChR 20, 27; GMC26 241-45; NEHGR 143:24; Dawes-Gates 1:501-8; C. J. F. Binney, *The History and Genealogy of the Prentice, or Prentiss Family, in New England, Etc., from 1631 to 1883* (Boston 1883)].

Prentice, Robert: Unknown; 1639; Roxbury [RBOP 1, 36; SPR Case #401; C. J. F. Binney, *The History and Genealogy of the Prentice, or Prentiss Family, in New England, Etc., from 1631 to 1883* (Boston 1883)].

Prentice, Thomas: Unknown; 1640; Cambridge (mention in will only) [SPR 1:14]. (Unless he returned soon to England, married and had a child, and came back to New England in the late 1640s, this 1640 record does not pertain to Captain Thomas Prentice of Cambridge [CaChR 21].)

Prentice, Valentine: Chelmsford, Essex; 1631; Roxbury [GMB 1525; TAG 77:173-75].

Presbury, John: Unknown; 1640; Sandwich [Gen Adv 3:76; MD 14:169, 15:28; TAG 30:69, 31:53; Martha's Vineyard Hist 3:410].

Presgrave, Peter: Unknown; 1638; Massachusetts Bay (servant; court appearance only) [MBCR 1:238].

Prestland, Nicholas: Unknown; 1634; Plymouth [GM 2:5:513-14].

Preston, Roger: London; 1635 on *Elizabeth*; Ipswich, Salem [GM 2:5:514-18].

Preston, William: Chesham, Buckinghamshire; 1635 on *Truelove*; Dorchester, New Haven [GM 2:5:519-25].

Price, David: Ilminster, Somerset; 1635 on *Hopewell*; Dorchester [GM 2:5:525-26].

Price, John: Unknown; 1638; Plymouth (servant; court appearance only) [PCR 1:92].

Price, Rebecca: Unknown; 1635 on *Abigail*; passenger list only [GM 2:5:527].

Price, Richard: Shrewsbury, Shropshire; 1639; Piscataqua (appearance in notarial record only) [Lechford 257].

Prichard, Hugh: Unknown; 1640; Plymouth, Gloucester, Roxbury; returned permanently to England in 1650 [PCR 2:8; HAHAC 1:133; Abandoning 256].

Prichard, Roger: Unknown; 1640; Wethersfield, Springfield, Milford, New Haven [CCCR 1:452; Wethersfield Hist 2:536; TAG 44:193-94; Moore Anc 445-48].

Pride, John: Unknown; 1636; Salem [STR 1:24, 41; EQC 1:4; EPR 1:91-92; Perley 1:427; GDMNH 569].

Priest, Degory: Leiden, Holland; 1620 on *Mayflower*; Plymouth [GMB 1526; PM 382-83; TAG 80:241-60].

Priest, James: Unknown; 1637; Dorchester [DTR 1:29; NEHGR 65:63, 66, 93:206-7; Weymouth Hist 4:57-58].

Prince, John: East Shefford, Berkshire; 1634; Cambridge, Hingham, Hull [GM 2:5:527-32].

Prince, Mary: Unknown; 1637; Salem [TAG 14:83-86].

Prince, Richard: Unknown; 1639; Salem [STR 1:91; EPR 3:32-35; EIHC 14:249-50].

Prior, Thomas: Watford, Hertfordshire; 1638; Scituate [PCR 1:110; PCPR 1:34; Lechford 296; NEHGR 9:285; GM 2:5:533-34]. (Thomas Prior was preceded to New England by his sons Daniel Prior and John Prior in 1635 [GM 2:5:532-36].)

Prior, _____: Unknown; 1638; Salem (land grant only) [STR 1:76].

Proctor, George: Pitminster, Somerset; 1634; Dorchester [GM 2:5:536-40; M&JCH 25:51-55, 26:56].

Proctor, John: Assington, Suffolk; 1635 on *Susan & Ellen*; Ipswich [GM 2:5:540-44].

Prout, John: Unknown; 1639; New Haven (court appearance only) [NHCR 1:29].

Prower, Solomon: Billericay, Great Burstead, Essex; 1620 on *Mayflower*; Plymouth [GMB 1527; PM 383; MQ 76:242-46].

Prudden, James: Kings Walden, Hertfordshire; 1639; Milford [MiChR 1; MiTR 2; NHCR 1:92; FOOF 1:495; Goodwin-Morgan 2:163-70; Ackley-Bosworth 203; TAG 16:28].

Prudden, Peter: Herefordshire; 1637; Massachusetts Bay, Milford [WJ 1:311; WP 4:4; MiChR 2; MiTR 2; DeTR 1:33; NHCR 1:92; TAG 16:1-27, 122-23, 177-79, 17:52-55, 18:60, 19:135-41, 232; NEHGR 84:62-68; FOOF 1:494-95; CSMP 17:244-48].

Puckett, Thomas: Unknown; 1630; Salem [GMB 1527].

Puddington, George: Tiverton, Devon; 1640; York [Gorges 9-11, 41; MPCR 1:44; GDMNH 571; CCL 30; Putnam's Mag 7:47-53, 140-44, 193-98; York Hist 1:100-4; M&JCH 18:121-26].

Puddington, Robert: Tiverton, Devon; 1639; Strawberry Bank [NHPP 1:113, 40:5; Putnam's Mag 7:47-53, 140-44, 193-98; GDMNH 571; CCL 30; M&JCH 18:121-26].

Puffer, George: Unknown; 1639; Braintree [NEHGR 3:247, 22:288, 37:285, 151:31-37; BTR 1:49; Charles Nutt, *Descendants of George Puffer of Braintree, Massachusetts, 1639-1915* (Worcester, Massachusetts, 1915)].

Purchase, Aquila: Dorchester, Dorset; 1633; Dorchester [GMB 1527-28; M&JCH 25:7].

Purchase, John: Unknown; 1639; Hartford [HaBOP 155; HaTR 24; HaVR 607; CCCR 1:466-68; TAG 34:69-70].

Purchase, John: Unknown; 1640; Massachusetts Bay (witness to deed only) [PCR 1:160].

Purchase, Thomas: Dorchester, Dorset; 1630; Pejepscot, Lynn [GMB 1529-34].

Purrier, William: Olney, Buckinghamshire; 1635 on *Hopewell*; Ipswich, Salisbury, Southold [GM 2:5:544-47].

Purton, Elizabeth: Unknown; 1633; Boston [GMB 1535-36].

Putnam, _____: Unknown; 1639; Massachusetts Bay (appearance in notarial record only) [Lechford 238].

Putnam, John: Aston Abbots, Buckinghamshire; 1640; Salem [STR 1:109; SChR 10; EPR 1:18; Dawes-Gates 1:520-26; NEHGR 108:110-13, 119:174-76; TAG 15:8-15, 23:93-95, 24:257].

Pyce, Alice: Unknown; 1636; Boston (servant; church admission only) [BChR 21].

Pyford, Peter: Unknown; 1635; Massachusetts Bay (servant; court appearance only) [GM 2:5:547-48].

Pynchon, William: Essex; 1630; Roxbury, Springfield; returned permanently to England in 1652 [GMB 1536-38; WF 541-45; Abandoning 257-59; NEQ 71:290-97].

Pyne, Thomas: Unknown; 1634; Massachusetts Bay (admission to freemanship only) [GM 2:5:548-49].

Q

Quick, Anne: Unknown; 1639; Charlestown [SLR 1:16].

Quick, William: Unknown; 1636; Charlestown, Newport [ChTR 23; ChBOP 62; RICR 1:91; CCCR 1:6; NHCR 1:46, 74; MBCR 1:284; WP 3:320, 430, 4:128; Lechford 271, 330, 342].

Quilter, Mark: Assington, Suffolk; 1637; Ipswich [ITR 27; EPR 1:167-68; NEHGR 68:189-90].

Quincy, Edmund: Thorpe Achurch, Northamptonshire; 1633; Boston [GMB 1539-42; NEHGR 157:31-33].

R

Rabey, Katherine: Great Yarmouth, Norfolk; 1637 on *John & Dorothy* or *Rose*; Salem [Hotten 292; SChR 11; NEHGR 154:216].

Raborne *see* **Haborne**

Rainend, Mathew: Unknown; 1638; Windsor (death record only) [Grant 78].

Rainsborough, William: Wapping, Middlesex; 1639; Charlestown, Boston; returned permanently to England by 1642 [ChTR 46; Lechford 271; HAHAC 1:95; SLR 1:16; WaBOP 56, 139; Waters 159-71; Bond 911; Abandoning 260-61; ODNB; Adrian Tinniswood, *The Rainborowes* (New York 2013)].

Rainsford, Edward: London; 1630; Boston [GMB 1543-48; WF 547-53].

Ram, George: Unknown; 1635 on *Abigail*; passenger list only [GM 2:6:1].

Ramsden, John: Unknown; 1632; Lynn [EQC 1:7, 26, 2:43; TEG 10:25-27].

Rand, Francis: Unknown; 1640; Strawberry Bank [NHPP 40:4; GDMNH 573-74].

Rand, James: Unknown; 1623 on *Anne*; Plymouth (land grant only) [GMB 1548; PM 385].

Rand, Robert: Ridgewell, Essex; 1635; Charlestown [GM 2:6:1-5; NEHGR 165:183-86].

Randall, ____: Unknown; 1637; Braintree (servant; court appearance only) [MBCR 1:223].

Randall, Philip: Unknown; 1633; Dorchester, Windsor [GMB 1548-50].

Randall, Robert: Wendover, Buckinghamshire; 1640; Weymouth [MBCR 1:310; MA Arch 129:16; NEHGR 8:357, 63:98; Weymouth Hist

4:559; William L. Chaffin, *A Biographical History of Robert Randall and His Descendants 1608-1909* (New York 1909)].

Randall, William: Unknown; 1640; Scituate [PCR 7:23; Gen Adv 3:110; NEHGR 57:82, 146:230-34; Frank Alfred Randall, *Randall and Allied Families: William Randall (1609-1693) of Scituate and His Descendants with Ancestral Families* (Chicago 1943)].

Rasdall, Humphrey: London; 1624; Massachusetts Bay; soon departed [GMB 1550].

Rashley, Thomas: Cambridge, Cambridgeshire; 1639; Boston, Gloucester, Exeter; returned permanently to England by 1648 [BChR 28, 298; Gorges 35; GDMNH 577; Plain Dealing 99-100; Abandoning 261-62].

Ratcliff, Philip: Unknown; 1629 or 1630; Mystic; returned permanently to England in 1631 [GMB 1550-51; WF 553-54; Abandoning 346].

Rattlife, Robert: Unknown; 1623 on *Anne*; Plymouth (land grant only) [GMB 1551; PM 385].

Ravensdale, John: Unknown; 1629; Nahant [GMB 1551; WF 554-55].

Rawlin, Jane: Unknown; 1635 on *Increase*; passenger list only [GM 2:6:5].

Rawlins, James: Unknown; 1633; Newbury, Dover [GMB 1552-55].

Rawlins, Jasper: Ingatestone, Essex; 1633; Roxbury, Wethersfield, Windsor, Boston [GMB 1555-57].

Rawlins, Richard: Unknown; 1638; Boston [BTR 1:35; BChR 36, 38; BBOP 10, 126; MBCR 2:293].

Rawlins, Thomas: Little Baddow, Essex; 1630; Roxbury, Scituate, Boston [GMB 1557-60; WF 555-60; NEHGR 148:342-44].

Rawlins, Thomas: Unknown; 1634; Dorchester, Weymouth, Boston [GM 2:6:6-10; DTR 7-9, 57; SLR 3:394-95].

Rawson, Edward: London; 1637; Newbury, Boston [NGSQ 71:176; NeTR 10; MBCR 1:230, 236, 374; Waters 57-59; TAG 83:207-16; NEHGR 3:201-8, 297-330; Abandoning 262-63; E. B. Crane, *The Rawson Family: A Revised Memoir of Edward Rawson* (Worcester, Massachusetts, 1875); Ellery Bicknell Crane, *The Ancestry of Edward Rawson* (Worcester, Massachusetts, 1887)].

Rawson, Henry: Unknown; 1637 on *Elizabeth*; passenger list only [NGSQ 71:177].

Ray, Daniel: Unknown; 1630; Plymouth, Salem [GMB 1560-62; PM 385-88; Joseph W. Ray, *Descendants of Daniel Ray Of Plymouth and Salem*, two volumes (Baltimore 2005)].

Rayment, Richard: Unknown; 1631; Salem, Norwalk, Saybrook [GMB 1563-65].

Raynor, Edward: Elmsett, Suffolk; 1634 on *Elizabeth*; Watertown, Wethersfield, Stamford, Hempstead [GM 2:6:10-14].

Raynor, Thurston: Elmsett, Suffolk; 1634 on *Elizabeth*; Watertown, Wethersfield, Stamford, Southampton [GM 2:6:14-19].

Read, Esdras: Southwark, Surrey; 1638; Boston, Salem, Wenham, Chelmsford, Woburn [BTR 1:36; STR 1:84; SChR 9, 10; WnTR 1:1; MBCR 1:378; TAG 28:149-53; NEHGR 60:137-39, 63:200-1, 140:180; GMC 50:307-10].

Read, John: Unknown; 1637; Weymouth, Braintree, Rehoboth [NGSQ 71:176; Lechford 96-102; PCR 1:65; BTR 1:49; MBCR 1:314, 377; NEHGR 3:247; SPR 2:17; ReTR 1:1; Aspinwall 11; Weymouth Hist 4:564-65].

Read, Matthew: Unknown; 1638; Salem (servant; court appearance only) [EQC 1:10].

Read, Robert: Unknown; 1635; Boston, Exeter, Hampton [GM 2:6:19-24].

Read, Thomas: Unknown; 1630; Mystic (court appearance only) [WF 560].

Read, Thomas: North Benfleet, Essex; 1633; Salem; returned permanently to England in the late 1640s [MBCR 1:114, 191, 368; STR 13, 19, 102; SChR 10; Bethia Harris Anc 69-75; GMB 1565-67 (as partially corrected by WF 560); Abandoning 263-64].

Read, Thomas: Unknown; 1636; Salem [STR 1:24, 44, 47, 70, 78, 103; GMB 1567; Richard H. Benson, *The Read Family of Salem, Massachusetts* (Boston 2005)].

Read, William: Batcombe, Somerset; 1635 on *Marygould*; Weymouth, Boston, Rhode Island [GM 2:6:24-30; CN 40:28-31].

Read, William: Unknown; 1635 on *Defence*; Dorchester, Scituate, Roxbury, Woburn; returned permanently to England between 1648 and 1656 [GM 2:6:30-35].

Redding, Joseph: Unknown; 1630; Boston, Cambridge, Ipswich [GMB 1567-69; WF 561-64].

Redding, Miles: Unknown; 1630; Boston [GMB 1569-71; WF 564-67].

Redding, Thomas: Unknown; 1637; Plymouth, Scituate, Saco, North Yarmouth [PCR 1:61, 129; TG 3:161-71; GDMNH 578-79; Weymouth Hist 4:567; NGSQ 60:248; Billie Redding Lewis, *The Redding Family and Its Relatives* (Lake Wales, Florida, 1982)].

Rediat, John: Sutton Mandeville, Wiltshire; 1638 on *Confidence*; Sudbury, Marlborough [Drake's Founders 57; SuTR 13; SPR Case #1549].

Redknap, Joseph: Hampton, Middlesex; 1634; Lynn [GM 2:6:35-40].

Redman, Richard: Unknown; 1639; Massachusetts Bay [WP 4:128; WJ 2:289-90; MBCR 1:270, 2:153, 166, 3:1:68, 83, 84].

Reeder, John: Unknown; 1635; Springfield, New Haven, Stratford, Newtown [SpTR 159; NHCR 1:28, 51; McArthur-Barnes 51-56].

Reeves, Jane: Unknown; 1640; Salem (church admission only) [SChR 10]. (She may have been the wife of John Reeves, who appeared at Salem by 1642 [Kempton Anc 1:390-97].)

Reeves, John: Unknown; 1635 on *Christian*; Windsor [GM 2:6:40-41].

Reeves, Margery: Unknown; 1639; Plymouth [PCR 1:139]. (She married Francis West [NEHGR 60:142].)

Reeves, Thomas: Salisbury, Wiltshire; 1638 on *Bevis*; Newbury [Drake's Founders 60; Noyes-Gilman 271-74]. (Savage and Pope claim that this passenger was identical with a Thomas Reeves who appeared at Roxbury in 1642 [Savage 3:523; Pope 382; GMN 21:13-14].)

Reeves, Widow: Unknown; 1639; Salem [Perley 1:271].

Reeves, William: Unknown; 1635 on *Elizabeth & Ann*; Boston [GM 2:6:41].

Reld, Gabriel: Unknown; 1635 on *Hopewell*; passenger list only [GM 2:6:42].

Remick, John: Unknown; 1639; Boston (land grant only) [BTR 1:44]. (Possibly a clerical error for John Kenrick.)

Remington, John: Unknown; 1637; Newbury, Rowley, Roxbury [NeTR 21; MBCR 1:291, 375; RowBOP 3; Stevens-Miller 1:149-50; Rowley Fam 319-21; NEHGR 147:371-76].

Rennolls, William: Unknown; 1639; Salem (church admission only) [SChR 9].

Revell, John: Unknown; 1630; Massachusetts Bay; returned permanently to England in 1630 [GMB 1571-72; WF 567-68; Abandoning 346].

Rew, Edward: Unknown; 1639; Newport, Taunton [RICR 1:92; MD 19:60; PCR 8:69; PCPR 3:2:124-25; Snow-Estes 1:404; TAG 54:97-98].

Reyner, John: Gildersome, Yorkshire; 1636; Plymouth, Dover [PCR 1:50, 79; Cotton Corr 291; WP 4:292; NEHGR 7:206, 11:102-12, 231-41, 26:331-32, 109:5-11, 156:322-26; GDMNH 583; Morison 397; Sibley 2:138-39].

Reynolds, John: Unknown; 1634; Watertown, Wethersfield, Stamford [GM 2:6:42-45].

Reynolds, John: Unknown; 1639; Dover, Portsmouth [NH] [GDMNH 582; NHPP 40:7].

Reynolds, Richard: Unknown; 1634 on *Mary & John*; passenger list only [GM 2:6:45].

Reynolds, Robert: Unknown; 1634; Boston [GM 2:6:43-49].

Reynolds, Sarah: Unknown; 1634 on *Elizabeth*; passenger list only [GM 2:6:49].

Reynolds, William: Unknown; 1633; Plymouth [GMB 1572]. (Probably the same as the next.)

Reynolds, William: Unknown; 1636; Duxbury [PCR 1:50, 75, 12:31; NEHGR 162:91-92; GDMNH 582-83; NHGR 25:145-62].

Reynolds, William: Unknown; 1637; Providence [PTR 1:1, 15:5; Austin 362-65].

Rhoads, Henry: Unknown; 1640; Lynn [Lynn VR; TEG 14:156-61].

Rice, Edmund: Great Berkhamsted, Hertfordshire; 1639; Sudbury, Marlborough [SuTR 1; MBCR 1:271, 377; WP 4:222; TAG 10:133-39, 11:14-21, 15:227, 26:10-11, 61:161-66, 63:129-37, 65:241-47; TG 6:131-41; Stevens-Miller 2:109-40; NEA 3:4:50-51, 6:4:48-50, 9:4:48-50; Ray Lowther Ellis, *A Genealogical Register of Edmund Rice Descendants* (Rutland, Vermont, 1970)].

Rice, Philip: Unknown; 1640; Boston [BTR 1:59; BChR 35; SPR 4:216].

Rice, Richard: Unknown; 1635; Cambridge, Concord [GM 2:6:49-57].

Richards, Anne: Maidstone, Kent; 1635 on *Hercules*; passenger list only [GM 2:6:57-58].

Richards, Edward: Unknown; 1633; Lynn [ELR 4:203; EQC 1:83, 4:411, 6:362-63; EIHC 4:237-38; TEG 12:142-56].

Richards, Edward: Unknown; 1638; Dedham [DeTR 1:50; DeVR 1, 126; DeChR 23; MBCR 1:379; NGSQ 78:90; TAG 24:87-95, 143-46].

Richards, George: Unknown; 1638; Massachusetts Bay (court appearance only) [MBCR 1:247].

Richards, John: Unknown; 1637; Plymouth; not seen after 1638 (court appearance and land grant only) [PCR 1:63, 102].

Richards, Nathaniel: Unknown; 1632 on *Lyon*; Cambridge, Hartford, Norwalk [GMB 1572-74].

Richards, Thomas: Unknown; 1631; Penobscot [GMB 1574-75].

✓ **Richards, Thomas:** Pitminster, Somerset; 1633; Dorchester, Weymouth [GMB 1575-79; NEHGR 163:85-97, 199-211, 278-95, 167:182; M&JCH 25:55-56, 26:57].

Richards, Thomas: Unknown; 1639; Hartford [HaBOP 365; Wethersfield Hist 2:542; Manwaring 1:146, 226-27; Brainerd Anc 292].

Richards, William: Unknown; 1632; Plymouth (tax list only) [GMB 1579; PM 388-89].

Richards, William: Unknown; 1640; Boston (servant; coroner's inquest only) [WP 4:285].

Richards, William: Unknown; 1640; Weymouth [MBCR 1:300; SPR Case #1234; Weymouth Hist 1:195, 4:589].

Richardson, Ezekiel: Westmill, Hertfordshire; 1630; Charlestown, Woburn [GMB 1580-83; WF 568-72; NEHGR 139:147-48].

Richardson, George: Wapping, Middlesex; 1635 on *Susan & Ellen*; Watertown, Salem; returned permanently to England after 1644 [GM 2:6:58-61].

Richardson, Henry: Canterbury, Kent; 1637; passenger list only [NEHGR 75:222].

Richardson, Mary: Unknown; 1635; Charlestown [GM 2:6:61-62].

Richardson, Samuel: Westmill, Hertfordshire; 1636; Charlestown, Woburn [ChTR 22; ChChR 9, 47; MBCR 1:374; ChBOP 5; WoTR 2; WoVR; NEHGR 57:298-300, 139:147-48; Sarah Hildreth Anc 25-27; GMC50 533-34].

Richardson, Thomas: Westmill, Hertfordshire; 1636; Charlestown, Woburn [ChTR 22; ChChR 9, 47; MBCR 1:374; ChBOP 7; WoTR 2; WoVR; NEHGR 57:298-300, 139:147-48; Sarah Hildreth Anc 25-27; Stone-Gregg 223-27].

Richardson, William: Unknown; 1638; Portsmouth [PoTR 2; RICR 1:91]. (Possibly the William Richardson who appeared at Newport in the 1650s [Austin 163; GMN 22:22].)

Richmond, John: Unknown; 1636; Saco (court appearance only) [MPCR 1:5-7].

Richmond, John: Unknown; 1639; Taunton, Newport [PCR 8:186; MD 18:248-49; TAG 54:96-99; Chase-Wigglesworth 357-58].

Rickard, Giles: Taunton, Somerset; 1637 on *Speedwell*; Plymouth [NGSQ 71:176; PCR 1:70, 75, 7:29; PCPR 1:52, 4:2:101-2; TAG 30:11; NEHGR 111:172, 112:154; M&JCH 18:127-28, 25:56-57, 27:44-45].

Rickard, Sarah: Unknown; 1639; Plymouth [PCR 1:153]. (She married George Pidcock. No proven relation to Giles Rickard.)

Rickard, Thomas: Unknown; 1638; Scituate [PCR 1:141, 2:81, 12:167-68; PCPR 1:34, 80; MD 9:155-56]. (His will does not indicate any relation to Giles Rickard.)

Rickards, George: Unknown; 1637; Providence [PrTR 1:1, 50, 14:19-24, 15:33, 173, 201].

Rickdall, Alice: Unknown; 1638; Dorchester (church admission only) [DChR 3].

Rickman, Isaac: Unknown; 1629; hired as a company servant but perhaps never sailed [WF 572].

Ricroft, Frances: Hingham, Norfolk; 1638 on *Diligent*; Hingham [NEHGR 15:26]. (She "died in a few weeks after she came" [NEHGR 15:27].)

Riddlesden, Mary: Unknown; 1635 on *Susan & Ellen*; passenger list only (with caveat) [GM 2:6:62].

Rider, Samuel: Northampton, Northamptonshire; 1638; Yarmouth [PCR 1:108, 7:21, 8:185, 194; NEHGR 79:316; MD 11:49-55, 170-72, 182-87; TAG 36:193-98, 43:117-23, 80:128-39].

Rider, Thomas: Unknown; 1634 on *Hercules*; passenger list only (with caveat) [GM 2:6:62-64].

Ridge, Mary: Unknown; 1632; Massachusetts Bay [GMB 1583].

Ridley, Richard: Unknown; 1635 on *Planter*; passenger list only [GM 2:6:64].

Rigby, John: Unknown; 1637; Dorchester [DTR 1:31; DChR 3; SPR Case #64; NEHGR 72:196].

Riggs, Edward: Nazeing, Essex; 1633; Roxbury [GMB 1583-85; TAG 82:120-29; TG 23:131-73; NEHGR 164:95-103].

Rigsdale, John: Unknown; 1620 on *Mayflower*; Plymouth [GMB 1585; PM 389].

Ring, Mary: Leiden, Holland; 1629 or 1630; Plymouth [GMB 1586-88; PM 389-91].

Ring, Robert: Unknown; 1639; Salisbury [SyTR 2; MBCR 1:378; Hoyt 297-98, 1002].

Ring, Thomas: Unknown; 1636; Salem (land grant only) [STR 1:24].

Ringe, John: Unknown; 1635; Cambridge (land grant only) [GM 2:6:64-65].

Ripley, William: Hingham, Norfolk; 1638; Hingham [NEHGR 2:252, 15:27; HiBOP 82; SPR 1:285, 3:64; Hingham Hist 3:131-32; Granberry 304-5].

Rishworth, Edward: Laceby, Lincolnshire; 1638; Exeter, Wells, Hampton, York [NHPP 1:133; Lechford 141; GDMNH 588; Essex Ant 2:82; NEHGR 31:218-19; *Genealogists' Magazine* 30 (2012):443-51].

Risley, Richard: Unknown; 1639; Hartford [HaBOP 266; HaTR 23; TAG 25:233-46, 70:162-70].

Rix, William: Kenninghall, Norfolk; 1640; Boston [Lechford 302; WaBOP 30; BChR 45; Guy S. Rix, *History and Genealogy of the Rix Family in America* (New York 1906)].

Robbins, John: Unknown; 1640; Wethersfield [WetLR 1:13, 72, 122; Manwaring 1:146-47; Hale, House 801-3; TAG 10:51].

Robbins, Nicholas: Dover, Kent; 1635 on *Blessing*; Cambridge, Duxbury [GM 2:6:65-67; TAG 61:129-32; NEHGR 167:245-50].

Robbins, Richard: Unknown; 1639; Charlestown, Cambridge [ChChR 10, 49; ChTR 46, 59; MBCR 1:378 (as "Robinson"); CaChR 11; Wyman 816; Granberry 306-7; Noyes-Gilman 282].

Roberts, Henry: Unknown; 1633; Richmond Island [Trelawny 36].

Roberts, John: Unknown; 1637; Richmond Island [Trelawny 121].

Roberts, John: Unknown; 1638; Roxbury [RChR 84, 172, 175; MBCR 1:376; SPR 2:135; Pillsbury 835; Carlton Lee Starkweather, *A Brief Genealogical History of Robert Starkweather of Roxbury and Ipswich, Massachusetts* (Occoquan, Virginia, 1904) 11-16].

Roberts, Joseph: Unknown; 1632 on *Lyon*; passenger list only [GMB 1588].

Roberts, Robert: Unknown; 1636; Ipswich [EQC 2:169-71; Small Gen 928-1099].

Roberts, Thomas: Unknown; 1637; Boston (servant; mention in letter only) [WP 3:445].

Roberts, Thomas: Unknown; 1637; Plymouth, Duxbury, Marshfield, Eastham, Dartmouth [PCR 1:64, 2:6, 12, 8:11, 188, 196, 12:53, 55; TAG 32:39-45].

Roberts, Thomas: London; 1640; Dover [NHPP 1:128, 10:701, 40:4; Lydia Harmon Anc 25; WJ 1:394; GDMNH 589; Wentworth 1:503].

Roberts, William: Unknown; 1640; Taunton (apprenticeship record only) [Lechford 255].

Robinson, _____: Little Waldingfield, Suffolk; 1636; passenger list only [WP 3:295-96].

Robinson, Abraham: Unknown; 1640; Gloucester [Lechford 406; EPR 1:102].

Robinson, Anne: Unknown; 1637; Salem (church admission and land grant only) [SChR 7 (annotated "dead"); STR 1:104].

Robinson, Anthony: Unknown; 1636; Massachusetts Bay, Portsmouth (two court appearances only) [MBCR 1:184; RICR 1:60].

Robinson, Edward: Unknown; 1639; Saco; not seen after 1640 (appearances as petit jury member only) [MPCR 1:44, 46, 47, 65, 67, 70].

Robinson, Ellen: Unknown; 1637 on *John & Dorothy* or *Rose*; passenger list only [Hotten 292].

Robinson, Francis: Unknown; 1631; Saco, Barbados, Nevis, Black Point, Boston [GMB 1588-90].

Robinson, Isaac: Leiden, Holland; 1631; Plymouth, Scituate, Barnstable, Falmouth, Tisbury [GMB 1590-94; PM 391-95; MD 43:183-86; MQ 74:317-31].

Robinson, Isaac: Unknown; 1635 on *Hopewell*; Lynn [GM 2:6:68].

Robinson, Jane: Unknown; 1639; Massachusetts Bay (court appearance only) [MBCR 1:284].

Robinson, John: Unknown; 1635; Ipswich [GM 2:6:68-69].

Robinson, John: Unknown; 1638; Salem [STR 1:78, 104, 142, 150, 160; EQC 1:28, 181, 230; SChR 8; MBCR 1:378; EPR 1:159-60].

Robinson, John: Unknown; 1639; Boston (land grant only) [BTR 1:43, 53].

Robinson, Joseph: Unknown; 1637; Plymouth (servant; military service only) [PCR 1:61].

Robinson, Lydia: Tenterden, Kent; 1635 on *Hercules*; passenger list only [GM 2:6:69]. (She was step-daughter of Jonas Austin.)

Robinson, Robert: Unknown; 1635 on *Christian*; passenger list only [GM 2:6:69].

Robinson, Thomas: Halifax, Yorkshire; 1638; Roxbury, Scituate, Boston [RChR 83; GMN 6:25; Lechford 308; MD 1:93-95; SLR 2:134, 136, 4:70; NEHGR 10:223, 111:16-17; SPR Case #402; SPR 6:9-10; Waters 751; TAG 19:138-39].

Robinson, Thomas: Unknown; 1636; Boston [MBCR 1:187, 269; WP 3:320, 434, 480; Lechford 271-72, 279, 283, 301]. (These records all appear to pertain to the same man, a mariner of Boston. Further research is recommended.)

Robinson, Thomas: Unknown; 1640; Connecticut (court appearance only) [CCCR 1:54].

Robinson, William: Unknown; 1637; Salem [SChR 7; STR 1:65; EQC 1:108; EPR 3:285-86; Perley 2:3-4].

Robinson, William: Unknown; 1638; Dorchester [DChR 3; Lechford 210; HAHAC 1:133; NEHGR 53:198-200; Dawes-Gates 1:527-32;

Edward Doubleday Harris, *William and Anne Robinson of Dorchester, Mass.* (Boston 1890)].

Roby, Henry: Castle Donington, Leicestershire; 1638; Exeter [NHPP 1:133; NEHGR 60:92-93, 65:293-94; GDMNH 590; William Grafton Robey, *Robey, Roby, Robie: The Family History from Early England to America*, two volumes (Bowie, Maryland, 1994)].

Rockett, John: Unknown; 1633; Dorchester [GMB 1594].

Rockett, Richard: Unknown; 1636; Dorchester, Braintree [MBCR 1:189; DTR 32; BTR 1:50; NEHGR 3:247; SPR Case #254, Case #364; Medfield Hist 471-72].

Rockwell, John: Fitzhead, Somerset; 1635 on *Hopewell*; Windsor [GM 2:6:70-72].

Rockwell, William: Dorchester, Dorset; 1630 on *Mary & John*; Dorchester, Windsor [GMB 1594-97].

Rogers, ____: Unknown; 1628; Plymouth; returned permanently to England in 1631 [GMB 1597; PM 395-96].

Rogers, Christopher: Cheddar, Somerset; 1640; York [Gorges 2; NEHGR 140:203-4; GDMNH 593].

Rogers, David: Unknown; 1639; Braintree [BTR 1:51; NEHGR 3:247].

Rogers, Ezekiel: Rowley, Yorkshire; 1638; Rowley [WJ 1:334, 354; MBCR 1:376; RowBOP 4; EPR 1:331-36; EQC 3:229-35, 263, 275, 313; Waters 209-36; NEHGR 5:105-52, 17:43-50, 50:65-68; TAG 36:34-35; Rowley Fam 323-24; Morison 397-98; ODNB].

Rogers, George: Unknown; 1639; Richmond Island, Kittery [Trelawny 172, 186; GDMNH 593].

Rogers, James: Unknown; 1635 on *Increase*; Saybrook, Stratford, Milford, New London [GM 2:6:72-84].

Rogers, James: Unknown; 1639; Newport [RICR 1:92, 108; Austin 368-71; TAG 20:229].

Rogers, John: Chelmsford, Essex; 1636; Watertown, Dedham, Chelmsford [MBCR 1:373; WaBOP 29, 120; DeTR 1:20, 58; BChR 33; Lechford 186; Aspinwall 14; Fiske Notebook 95, 99-101, 120; Waters 216-17; SPR Case #1568; Rodgers 3:40-43; NEHGR 33:443, 56:379; TEG 21:169-70].

Rogers, John: Unknown; 1638; Weymouth [MBCR 1:375; Kempton Anc 1:398-404].

Rogers, John: Unknown; 1639; Milford [MiTR 2; McCormick-Hamilton 853-54].

Rogers, John: Cheddar, Somerset; 1640; York [Lechford 339; Gorges 23; NEHGR 140:203-4; GDMNH 593].

Rogers, Nathaniel: Assington, Suffolk; 1636; Ipswich [WJ 1:244; WP 3:258, 380; MBCR 1:236, 374, 376; EPR 1:222-25; Waters 209-36; NEHGR 4:179-80, 5:105-52, 311-30, 12:337-42, 13:61-69, 17:43-50, 21:284, 63:356, 64:59-60, 68:63; Morison 398].

Rogers, Richard: Unknown; 1637; Dover (court appearance and land grant only) [NHPP 40:3, 4; GDMNH 593].

Rogers, Robert: Cheddar, Somerset; 1640; Boston, Newbury [Lechford 339; Gorges 96; TAG 64:147; NEHGR 140:203-10].

Rogers, Simon: Unknown; 1635 on *Defence*; Concord, Boston [GM 2:6:84-87].

Rogers, Thomas: Leiden, Holland; 1620 on *Mayflower*; Plymouth [GMB 1597-99; PM 396-97].

Rogers, Thomas: Dedham, Essex; 1634; Watertown [GM 2:6:88-90; TAG 64:44].

Rogers, William: Unknown; 1640; Wethersfield, Southampton [CA 50:64-68; NYGBR 60:102 (clue); Wethersfield Hist 1:293].

Roice, Robert: Unknown; 1632; Boston [GMB 1599-1600].

Rolfe, Barbara: London; 1635 on *Hopewell*; Maine; soon removed to "another plantation" [GM 2:6:72; GDMNH 595].

Rolfe, Henry: Whiteparish, Wiltshire; 1637; Newbury [NeTR 23; EPR 1:21-22, 137-38; NEHGR 3:151, 36:143-44, 66:247-51; Hoyt 301-2; Pillsbury 525-28].

Rolfe, John: Melchet Park, Wiltshire; 1638 on *Confidence*; Salisbury [Drake's Founders 58; SyTR 4; MBCR 1:376; EPR 1:438-39; TAG 75:185; NEHGR 36:143-44, 66:247-51; Hoyt 300-1; Pillsbury 525-28].

Roman, John: Unknown; 1638; Cambridge (death record only) [NEHGR 4:182].

Rookeman, John: Unknown; 1635 on *Abigail*; passenger list only [GM 2:6:90].

Roome, John: Bristol; 1639; Portsmouth [RICR 1:70, 91; PoTR 1; NEHGR 145:122-24, 147:162-63; Austin 167].

Roosa, Elizabeth: Unknown; 1634; Roxbury [GM 2:6:90-91]. (She married Edward Riggs.)

Root, John: Unknown; 1639; Wethersfield, Farmington [GM 2:4:150; Hale, House 655; Wethersfield Hist 2:588; James Pierce Root, *Root Genealogical Records. 1600-1870* (New York 1870) 314-15].

Root, Robert: Unknown; 1639; Newport; not seen after 1642 [RICR 1:92; Chapin 2:136].

Root, Thomas: Unknown; 1639; Hartford, Northampton [HaBOP 32; James Pierce Root, *Root Genealogical Records. 1600-1870* (New York 1870) 101-3, 309-13].

Roote, Mary: Unknown; 1635 on *Abigail*; passenger list only [GM 2:6:91].

Roote, Ralph: Unknown; 1635 on *Abigail*; Boston [GM 2:6:91-93].

Rooten, Richard: Unknown; 1635 on *Susan & Ellen*; Lynn [GM 2:6:94-95].

Rootes, Joseph: Great Chart, Kent; 1635 on *Hercules*; Salem [GM 2:6:95-96].

Roper, John: New Buckenham, Norfolk; 1637 on *John & Dorothy* or *Rose*; Dedham, Charlestown [Hotten 292; DeTR 1:33; DeVR 1; DeChR 21; MBCR 1:379; TAG 85:222-34].

Roper, Walter: Unknown; 1640; Hampton, Ipswich [GDMNH 55, 596; HampVR 1:4; Phoebe Tilton Anc 123-25].

Ropes, George: Unknown; 1635; Salem [GM 2:6:96-99].

Ropus, _____: Unknown; 1637; Richmond Island [Trelawny 121].

Rose, George: Unknown; 1639; Braintree [WP 4:199; MBCR 1:377; BTR 1:49]. (Possibly the George Rowes who appeared at Plymouth a year earlier.)

Rose, Henry: Plaitford, Wiltshire; 1635 on *James*; passenger list only [GM 2:6:100].

Rose, John: Unknown; 1636; Watertown, Cambridge (two land grants and death record only) [WaBOP 3, 7; NEHGR 4:182].

Rose, Robert: Unknown; 1634 on *Elizabeth*; Wethersfield, Branford [GM 2:6:100-4].

Rossiter, Edward: Combe St. Nicholas, Somerset; 1630; Dorchester [GMB 1600-1; M&JCH 25:7-8, 21-31].

Rouse, John: Unknown; 1634; Marshfield [GM 2:6:104-9].

Rouse, Nicholas: Unknown; 1630; Casco; returned permanently to England by 1640 [GMB 1601].

Row, Nicholas: Unknown; 1639; Piscataqua [NHPP 1:113, 40:37-39, 42-43; GDMNH 598; Joseph Waterhouse Anc 72].

Rowe, John: Unknown; 1637; Duxbury [PCPR 1:30; PCR 1:109, 118, 2:41]. (These records possibly, but not certainly, pertain to John Rouse above [GM 2:6:108].)

Rowell, Thomas: Mancetter, Warwickshire; 1639; Salisbury, Ipswich, Andover [SyTR 4; NEHGR 109:243-48, 138:128-29; Hoyt 304-6; Pillsbury Anc 213-17; Herbert W. Hildebrand, *Thomas Rowell: 400 Years & 8461 Descendants Later* (Kettering, Ohio, 1973)].

Rowes, George: Unknown; 1638; Plymouth (two land grants only) [PCR 1:95, 99]. (Possibly the George Rose who appeared at Braintree a year later.)

Rowland, ____: Unknown; 1632; Plymouth (tax list only) [GMB 1602; PM 397-98].

Rowlandson, Thomas: Unknown; 1637; Ipswich, Lancaster [ITR 21, 58; EPR 1:32; MBCR 1:374; Rodgers 1:309-12; Putnam's Mag 7:123; Hoyt 306-8; Hammatt Papers 288-89; Sibley 1:311-21].

Rowley, Henry: Unknown; 1632; Plymouth, Scituate, Barnstable [GMB 1602-4; PM 398-400].

Ruchman, George: Unknown; 1637; Sandwich (mention in will only) [PCPR 1:32].

Ruck, Thomas: Maldon, Essex; 1637; Charlestown, Salem, Boston [ChTR 38; EQC 1:19; Lechford 118, 138; MBCR 1:377; SChR 9; STR 1:91; WaBOP 22; SPR Case #495; SPR 1:75, 82, 83 (son Thomas); TAG 15:69-80, 85:92-104; NEHGR 66:358-59; Perley 2:97-98].

Rudd, Jonathan: Unknown; 1639; Hartford, New Haven, Saybrook [CCCR 1:45, 2:558-59; Granberry 310-12].

Ruddock, John: Unknown; 1639; Sudbury, Marlborough [SuTR 4; MBCR 1:377; TAG 59:5-10; Kempton Anc 3:160-68].

Ruggles, Jeffrey: Sudbury, Suffolk; 1630; Boston [GMB 1607-8; WF 572-74].

Ruggles, John: Sudbury, Suffolk; 1630; Boston [GMB 1608-9; WF 574-77]. (Son George Ruggles came to New England in 1633 [GMB 1604-7].)

Ruggles, John: Nazeing, Essex; 1635 on *Hopewell*; Roxbury [GM 2:6:109-12].

Ruggles, Thomas: Nazeing, Essex; 1637; Roxbury [RChR 82, 172; RBOP 1; MBCR 1:375; NEHGR 6:377; Parker-Ruggles 448-52]. (His son John sailed to New England in 1635 on the *Hopewell* [GM 2:6:112-14].)

Rugs, Margery: Unknown; 1639; Massachusetts Bay (court appearance only) [MBCR 1:287].

Rumball, Daniel: Unknown; 1639; Salem [PCPR 1:35; JIC 32; Essex Ant 8:160-61, 11:13, 167]. (Pope has inserted in his entry for this man the unconnected 1677 will of John Reeves of Salem.)

Rumball, Thomas: Unknown; 1635 on *Truelove*; Saybrook, Stratford [GM 2:6:114-17].

Ruscoe, William: Billericay, Great Burstead, Essex; 1635 on *Increase*; Cambridge, Hartford, Norwalk, Jamaica [NY] [GM 2:6:117-24].

Russe, John: Unknown; 1637; Newbury, Andover [NeTR 13; EQC 2:307-10; Noyes-Gilman 413-14; EPR Case #24365].

Russe, Widow: Unknown; 1637; Newbury (land grant only) [NeTR 13].

Russell, Elizabeth: Unknown; 1634; Charlestown (church admission only) [GM 2:6:124-25].

Russell, George: Hawkhurst, Kent; 1635 on *Elizabeth*; passenger list only [GM 2:6:125-33].

Russell, George: Unknown; 1636; Hingham, Plymouth, Scituate, Marshfield [HiBOP 60; NEHGR 121:12; PCR 1:76; GM 2:6:125-33].

Russell, Henry: Chalfont St. Giles, Buckinghamshire; 1639; Weymouth [SPR 1:25; Lechford 323; Weymouth Hist 4:606-7].

Russell, James: Unknown; 1640; New Haven [NHCR 1:93; NEHGR 54:96 (clue); TAG 10:208-12].

Russell, John: Unknown; 1633; Dorchester [GMB 1609].

Russell, John: Unknown; 1635; Cambridge, Wethersfield, Hadley [GM 2:6:134-39].

Russell, John: Unknown; 1637; Marblehead [STR 1:63; EQC 1:36, 57, 59; EIHC 69:226; Marblehead 114].

Russell, John: Unknown; 1640; Woburn [WoTR 2; Snow-Estes 2:286-87 (ignoring intrusive material pertaining to John Russell of Cambridge); NEHGR 133:125-33; John Russell Bartlett, *Genealogy of That Branch of the Russell Family Which Comprises the Descendants of John Russell of Woburn, Massachusetts, 1640-1878* (Providence, Rhode Island, 1879)].

Russell, Richard: Unknown; 1640; Charlestown [ChTR 50; ChChR 10, 50; NEHGR 4:270, 7:343, 22:338, 33:298, 68:181; MBCR 1:378; Wyman 829-30; GDMNH 601; Wethersfield Hist 2:209].

Russell, William: Unknown; 1640; New Haven [NHCR 1:50; FANH 1572; Wethersfield Hist 2:597-614; NEHGR 7:53-59, 81:123, 131-32].

Rust, Henry: Unknown; 1637; Hingham, Boston [HiBOP 60; MBCR 1:374; NEHGR 121:11; Hingham Hist 3:142; Albert D. Rust, *Record of the Rust Family* (Waco, Texas, 1891)].

Rutherford, Henry: Unknown; 1640; New Haven [NHCR 1:92; NEHGR 81:132; FANH 1582].

Rutter, John: Weyhill, Hampshire; 1638 on *Confidence*; Sudbury [Drake's Founders 58; SuTR 18; Dawes-Gates 1:533-39].

Ryall, William: Unknown; 1629; Salem, Casco [GMB 1610-13; WF 577-81].

S

Sabell, John: Unknown; 1639; Hartford [HaTR 23; HaBOP 117-18, 257, 501; CCCR 1:202, 315].

Sackett, Simon: St. John Margate, Isle of Thanet, Kent; 1632; Cambridge [GMB 1615-16].

Sadler, Anthony: Unknown; 1638 on *Confidence*; Newbury, Salisbury [Drake's Founders 58; MBCR 1:254, 375; WP 4:104; Essex Ant 1:22-23; EPR 1:121; Phoebe Tilton Anc 147-48; Hoyt 308, 1004].

Sadler, John: Unknown; 1640; Plymouth, Gloucester [PCR 2:8; GlTR 1:1; EQC 1:43; Gloucester Hist 146].

Sadler, Richard: Cambridge, Cambridgeshire; 1638; Lynn; returned permanently to England in 1646 [EQC 1:14, 2:270; MBCR 1:254, 375; WP 4:104; Lynn Hist 157-58, 174; Abandoning 266-67; NEQ 42:411-25].

Saffery, Solomon: Unknown; 1639; Charlestown [Lechford 214; Hutchinson 1:178, 2:152-53].

Sale, Edward: Chesham, Buckinghamshire; 1635 on *Elizabeth & Ann*; Marblehead, Hingham, Weymouth, Rehoboth [GM 2:6:141-45].

Sales, John: Little Waldingfield, Suffolk; 1630; Charlestown, Boston, New Amsterdam [GMB 1616-18; WF 583-87; NEHGR 168:43-57].

Sallowes, Michael: Unknown; 1635; Salem [GM 2:6:145-48].

Salmon, Daniel: Unknown; 1638; Lynn [EQC 1:11, 2:194, 211, 331, 394, 3:11, 273; PCR 12:62; Driver Gen 69].

Salsbery, ____: Unknown; 1622; Wessagusset [GMB 2084].

Salter, Sampson: Unknown; 1635 on *James*; Newport [GM 2:6:148-50].

Salter, William: Unknown; 1635; Boston [GM 2:6:150-56].

Saltonstall, Richard: London; 1630; Watertown; returned permanently to England in 1631 [GMB 1618-21; WF 587-91; Scott C. Steward, *The Descendants of Dr. Nathaniel Saltonstall of Haverhill, Massachusetts* (Boston 2013)].

Samond, William: Unknown; 1635 on *Elizabeth & Ann*; passenger list only [GM 2:6:156-57].

Sampson, John: Rotherhithe, Surrey; 1636; Lynn; not seen after 1641 (but see SPR 3:11) [MBCR 1:315; Lechford 403-5].

Sampson, Samuel: Kersey, Suffolk; 1630; Massachusetts Bay; returned permanently to England in 1630 [WF 591-92].

Sams, John: Unknown; 1640; Roxbury; returned permanently to England in 1642 [SLR 1:37, 81; Waters 516-17; Abandoning 271-72].

Sams, Thomas: Unknown; 1637; Roxbury [SPR NS 1:107]. (Possibly the same as the next.)

Sams, Thomas: Unknown; 1638; Marblehead; not seen after 1647 [STR 1:74; EQC 1:13, 24, 26, 90, 106; Perley 2:179; Marblehead 114].

Samson, Abraham: Unknown; 1638; Duxbury [PCR 1:107, 120, 8:182, 189; TAG 15:165-67, 28:1-4, 56:141-43 (clue), 63:207-10].

Samson, Henry: Henlow, Bedfordshire; 1620 on *Mayflower*; Plymouth, Duxbury [GMB 1621-24; PM 401-4; MD 6170-75].

Samson, Thomas: Unknown; 1636; Richmond Island; returned permanently to England in 1637 [Trelawny 113-14].

Samwise, Richard: Unknown; 1640; Windsor [WiLR 1:63; Grant 81, 93; CCCR 1:190, 202; Manwaring 1:148-49; Windsor Hist 2:674; NYGBR 66:205].

Sanborn, John: London; 1639; Hampton [HmTR 44; Waters 519-20; GDMNH 603-4; NEHGR 51:57-64; NHGR 13:145-51, 14:80-83; V. C. Sanborn, *Genealogy of the Family of Samborne or Sanborn in England and America. 1194-1898* (n.p. 1899)].

Sanborn, Stephen: London; 1639; Hampton; returned permanently to England in 1654 [HmTR 45; Waters 519-20; GDMNH 605; NEHGR 51:57-64; V. C. Sanborn, *Genealogy of the Family of Samborne or Sanborn in England and America. 1194-1898* (n.p. 1899); Abandoning 272].

Sanborn, William: London; 1639; Hampton [HmTR 39; Waters 519-20; GDMNH 605; NEHGR 51:57-64; V. C. Sanborn, *Genealogy of the*

Family of Samborne or Sanborn in England and America. 1194-1898 (n.p. 1899)].

Sandbrooke, John: Unknown; 1633; Boston [GMB 1624-25].

Sandbrooke, Sarah: Unknown; 1633; Boston [GMB 1624-25].

Sanden, Arthur: Unknown; 1639; Marblehead [MBCR 1:290, 332; EQC 1:16; STR 1:95; EPR 2:73-74; GM 2:5:110, 112; EIHC 47:154; Marblehead 114-15].

Sanders *see also* **Saunders**

Sanders, John: Unknown; 1622; Wessagusset [GMB 1625].

Sanders, John: Unknown; 1636; Salem [STR 1:20; SChR 6, 9; EPR 1:26; EQC 1:14; TEG 23:229-35].

Sanders, John: Unknown; 1638; Salisbury; returned permanently to England in 1655 [Drake's Founders 58; SyTR 1; MBCR 1:237, 277, 376; TEG 23:229-35].

Sanders, Robert: Unknown; 1639; Richmond Island [Trelawny 293, 300; MPCR 1:48; GDMNH 606].

Sanders, William: Unknown; 1636; Massachusetts Bay (servant; court appearance only) [WJ 2:424].

Sanderson, Edward: Unknown; 1638; Watertown [MBCR 1:249; GDMNH 605-6; NEHGR 52:23; Bond 416-21, 930-31].

Sanderson, Robert: Unknown; 1639; Hampton, Watertown, Boston [HampVR 1:3; HmTR 40; GDMNH 55, 607; MBCR 1:376; WaBOP 45; SLR 12:125-26; NEHGR 52:23-24, 70:185; Bond 416, 930].

Sandys, Henry: Unknown; 1638; Boston [BChR 22; MBCR 1:378; RowBOP 4; NEHGR 165:261-72].

Sanford, Frances: Dorchester, Dorset; 1630; Dorchester [Whiteway 110; RChR 77; NEHGR 143:109-10, 146:297]. (She married William Pynchon.)

Sanford, John: Unknown; 1631 on *Lyon*; Boston, Portsmouth [GMB 1626-29].

Sanford, Richard: Unknown; 1640; Boston [BTR 1:59; BChR 32; Lechford 363; MBCR 1:378; NEHGR 2:400; SPR Case #881 (son John); SPR 6:450, 9:167 (son Thomas); Carlton E. Sanford, *Thomas Sanford, the Emigrant to New England* (Rutland, Vermont, 1911) 1394-95].

Sanford, Thomas: Stansted Mountfitchet, Essex; 1634; Dorchester, Milford [GM 2:6:157-62].

Sanger, Richard: Donhead St. Andrew, Wiltshire; 1638 on *Confidence*; Sudbury, Watertown [Drake's Founders 58; SuBOP 124; Bond 421-23, 931-32].

Sankey, Robert: London; 1635 on *Increase*; Saco [GM 2:6:162-64].

Sanson, Richard: Unknown; 1635 on *Elizabeth & Ann*; passenger list only [GM 2:6:164].

Santly, John: Unknown; 1635; Cambridge (land record only) [GM 2:6:165].

Sape, Mary: Norwich, Norfolk; 1637 on *Mary Anne*; passenger list only (servant) [Hotten 295].

Sargent, Stephen: Unknown; 1638; Richmond Island [Trelawny 159, 188; SPR Case #91; GDMNH 608].

Sargent, William: Unknown; 1632; Ipswich, Newbury, Hampton, Salisbury [GMB 1630-33; HmTR 44; NeTR 8; SyTR 5].

Sargent, William: Northampton, Northamptonshire; 1638; Charlestown, Malden, Barnstable [ChTR 41; ChChR 9, 48; NEHGR 4:270, 74:231-37, 267-83, 75:57-63, 129-42, 163:192-98; Lechford 224; MBCR 1:375].

Sary, Ralph: Unknown; 1639; Roxbury (court appearance only) [MBCR 1:257]. (Probably a misreading of some other surname.)

Satterly, Roger: Unknown; 1638; Richmond Island [Trelawny 173,182, 187, 194, 220-21, 295, 301, 375; GDMNH 609].

Saule, Thomas: Unknown; 1639; New Haven; not seen after 1644 [NHCR 1:26, 28, 41, 145].

Saunders *see also* **Sanders**

Saunders, ____: Unknown; 1637; Boston (purchase of land only) [BTR 1:19]. (Probably not the same as Silvester Saunders.)

Saunders, Daniel: Unknown; 1639; Cambridge (death record only) [NEHGR 4:182].

Saunders, John: Unknown; 1634; Ipswich, Hampton, Wells, Cape Porpus [GM 2:6:165-71].

Saunders, John: Unknown; 1639; Piscataqua [SPR 1:22; NEHGR 2:261; Trelawny 327; GDMNH 606].

Saunders, Martin: Sudbury, Suffolk; 1635 on *Planter*; Boston, Braintree [GM 2:6:171-76].

Saunders, Robert: Unknown; 1638; Cambridge; not seen after 1645 [MBCR 1:283, 376; Shepard 70; CaTR 37, 43; CaBOP 69, 70, 100, 153, 332; Aspinwall 13, 49].

Saunders, Silvester: Unknown; 1637; Boston (two land grants only) [BTR 1:31, 43].

Savage, Thomas: Unknown; 1635 on *Planter*; Boston [GM 2:6:177-89].

Savil, William: Unknown; 1640; Cambridge, Braintree [Lechford 410; BrVR 633; NEHGR 3:247; SPR Case #501; Stevens-Miller 126].

Savory, Anthony: Unknown; 1632; Plymouth [GMB 1633-34; PM 405].

Savory, Thomas: Unknown; 1633; Plymouth [GMB 1634-38; PM 405-9].

Savory, Thomas: Unknown; 1634 on *Mary & John*; Essex County [GM 2:6:190].

Savory, William: Unknown; 1634 on *Mary & John*; passenger list only [GM 2:6:191].

Sawkynn, William: Unknown; 1635 on *Defence*; passenger list only [GM 2:6:191].

Sawtell, Richard: Aller, Somerset; 1636; Watertown [WaBOP 5, 53; WaVR 1:6; NEHGR 126:3-5, 128:153-54; GMC50 343-47; M&JCH 25:57-61].

Saxton, Peter: Edlington, Yorkshire; 1640; Scituate; returned permanently to England in 1641 [Magnalia 1:587; NEHGR 14:123-24; Plain Dealing 96; Abandoning 272-73].

Say, Thomas: Unknown; 1638; Massachusetts Bay (admission to freemanship only) [MBCR 1:376].

Sayer, Elizabeth: Hingham, Norfolk; 1638 on *Diligent*; passenger list only [NEHGR 15:26].

Sayer, Mary: Hingham, Norfolk; 1638 on *Diligent*; passenger list only [NEHGR 15:26].

Sayers, James: Northbourne, Kent; 1635 on *Hercules*; passenger list only [GM 2:6:191; NEHGR 167:96].

Sayres, Job: Leighton Buzzard, Bedfordshire; 1638; Lynn, Southampton [EQC 2:270; SoTR 1:1; Stevens-Miller 1:473-76; Theodore M. Banta, *Sayre Family* (New York 1901)].

Sayres, Thomas: Leighton Buzzard, Bedfordshire; 1638; Lynn, Southampton [EQC 1:12, 2:270; SoTR 1:1; Suffolk Sessions 21-23; TAG 38:225-28; Stevens-Miller Anc 1:473-78; Theodore M. Banta, *Sayre Family* (New York 1901)].

Sayward, Edmund: Unknown; 1635; Ipswich [GM 2:6:192-93].

Sayward, Henry: Unknown; 1640; Hampton, Strawberry Bank, York [HmTR 50, 51; Essex Ant 10:111; GDMNH 611-12; York Hist 1:226-29; Emerson-Benson 499-506; Charles A. Sayward, *The Sayward Family* (Ipswich, Massachusetts, 1890)].

Sayward, Robert: Unknown; 1639; Exeter, Hampton, Strawberry Bank [NHPP 1:133; HmTR 45; GDMNH 611].

Saywell, Robert: Rayleigh, Essex; 1635 on *Blessing*; passenger list only [GM 2:6:193-94].

Scadding, William: Unknown; 1637 on *Speedwell*; Taunton [NGSQ 71:176; PCPR 1:31; PCR 8:186]. (Possibly the William Scaddin who appeared some years later at Hempstead.)

Scadlock, William: Unknown; 1635; Saco, Cape Porpus [GM 2:6:194-98].

Scales, William: Rowley, Yorkshire; 1639; Rowley [MBCR 1:376; RowBOP 3; NEHGR 66:42-43; Rowley Fam 327-29; GMN 18:23].

Scant, Joanna: Unknown; 1639; Springfield [SpVR 19]. (She married William Warrener.)

Scarborough, John: Unknown; 1639; Roxbury [MBCR 1:377; NEHGR 40:63; HAHAC 1:133; SPR Case #48].

Scarlett, Anne: Unknown; 1636; Salem [SChR 6, 9; STR 1:21; EPR 1:24; Amos Towne Anc 19; NEA 7:3:27-28 (clue)].

Scarlett, Jane: Kersey, Suffolk; 1635; Boston [GM 2:6:199-200].

Scarlett, Robert: Great Yarmouth, Norfolk; 1635; Salem [GM 2:6:200-1].

Schoolee, Mary: Unknown; 1637; Newbury [MBCR 1:202; WJ 1:288-90; Legal Executions 6].

Schooler, William: London; 1636; Massachusetts Bay [MBCR 1:199, 202; WJ 1:288-90, 387; Legal Executions 6].

Scoates, Thomas: Salisbury, Wiltshire; 1635 on *James*; passenger list only [GM 2:6:201].

Scobell, John: Unknown; 1639; Boston (appearance in notarial records only) [Lechford 342-49].

Scofield, Richard: Unknown; 1635 on *Susan & Ellen*; passenger list only (with caveat) [GM 2:6:201-2].

Scott, Benjamin: Unknown; 1640; Braintree [NEHGR 3:247; SPR Case #150; Scott Gen 323-24].

Scott, John: Unknown; 1638; Massachusetts Bay (admission to freemanship only) [MBCR 1:376].

Scott, Ralph: Unknown; 1639; Massachusetts Bay (appearance in notarial records only) [Lechford 216].

Scott, Richard: Great Berkhamsted, Hertfordshire; 1634; Boston, Providence [GM 2:6:202-9; NEHGR 96:192-94; TAG 63:135-37].

Scott, Robert: Unknown; 1633; Boston [GMB 1638-41].

Scott, Roger: Unknown; 1639; Lynn; not seen after 1643 [EQC 1:13, 14, 51, 52, 59].

Scott, Thomas: Rattlesden, Suffolk; 1634 on *Elizabeth*; Ipswich [GM 2:6:209-13].

Scott, Thomas: Unknown; 1634; Cambridge, Hartford [GM 2:6:213-18].

Scottow, Thomasine: Great Yarmouth, Norfolk; 1634; Boston [GM 2:6:218-20].

Scruggs, Thomas: Great Yarmouth, Norfolk; 1635; Salem [GM 2:6:221-23].

Scudder, John: Strood, Kent; 1635 on *James*; Charlestown, Barnstable [GM 2:6:223-25; TAG 82:227-32].

Scudder, Thomas: Horton Kirby, Kent; 1637; Salem [STR 1:103, 115, 158, 159; NEHGR 100:222; TAG 72:285-97].

Scullard, Samuel: Abbots Ann, Hampshire; 1637; Newbury [NeTR 11, 36; MBCR 1:236; TAG 75:181-86].

Seaberry, John: Unknown; 1639; Boston; died in Barbados [BTR 1:43; BChR 289; NEHGR 2:401; Lechford 350, 432; Blake-Torrey 154].

Seaborn, John: Unknown; 1636; Boston [BTR 1:42; Lechford 253; NEHGR 2:401; BChR 43; Walter Lee Sheppard Jr., *The Ancestry and Descendants of Thomas Stickney Evans and Sarah Ann Fifield His Wife Both of Fryeburg, Maine* (n.p. 1940) 130].

Seager, Lawrence: Southampton, Hampshire; 1635 on *James*; passenger list only [GM 2:6:226].

Seager, Thomas: Unknown; 1637; Newbury (land grant only) [NeTR 2].

Seaman, John: Unknown; 1640; Stamford [SmTR 4, 6, 16]. (Probably the man of the same name who appeared at Hempstead by the mid-1640s [Winthrop-Babcock 432-33].)

Search, John: Unknown; 1640; Boston [BTR 1:61; SPR 1:9; BChR 35, 84; MBCR 2:291; SPR Case #1957].

Searle, Ephraim: Unknown; 1637; Hingham (baptismal record only) [NEHGR 121:10; Hingham Hist 3:143].

Searle, John: Unknown; 1637; Springfield [SpTR 161, 162; Pynchon Court 204, 205, 208, 213-14; SpVR 9, 19, 60; Warner-Harrington 562-64].

Searle, Richard: Unknown; 1637; Dorchester, Portsmouth; not seen after 1639 [WJ 2:425; RICR 1:49, (as "Richard Sawell), 91; PoTR 420; GMN 22:27].

Searle, Samuel: Unknown; 1640; New Haven (business transaction only) [Lechford 286].

Sears, John: Unknown; 1638; Charlestown, Woburn [ChTR 44; ChChR 10; WoTR 2; MBCR 1:378; NEHGR 6:321; GDMNH 618; Putnam's Mag 4:40].

Sears, Richard: Unknown; 1632; Plymouth, Marblehead, Yarmouth [GMB 1642-44; PM 409-12].

Seaver, Robert: Unknown; 1634 on *Mary & John*; Roxbury [Drake's Founders 70; GMB 1644-46].

Seavey, William: Unknown; 1632; Isles of Shoals, Portsmouth [NH] [GDMNH 619; MPCR 1:52; TAG 18:76-77 (clue); Kittery Hist 34].

Sedgwick, John: Unknown; 1635 on *Truelove*; passenger list only [GM 2:6:226].

Sedgwick, Robert: London; 1636; Charlestown; returned permanently to England in 1653 [ChTR 21; ChChR 9, 48; ChBOP 2; MBCR 1:190, 205, 373; Lechford 51; WP 3:441; SPR NS 1:19; NEHGR 70:366-67; Wyman 852-53; Waters 47-48, 257-61, 277-78; Abandoning 273-75].

Sedley, James: Unknown; 1632; Wessagusset [GMB 1646].

Seeley, Robert: London; 1630; Watertown, Wethersfield, New Haven, Saybrook, Stratford, Huntington [GMB 1647-50; WF 592-96; NEA 6:2:46-47, 51].

Selden, Thomas: Wadhurst, Sussex; 1639; Hartford [HaTR 23; HaBOP 269; CCCR 1:46; Manwaring 1:149-50; Brainerd Anc 259-63; Sophie Selden Rogers, Elizabeth Selden Lane and Edwin van Deusen Selden, *Selden Ancestry: A Family History* (Oil City, Pennsylvania, 1931)].

Sellanova, Peter de: Unknown; 1635; Weymouth [GM 2:6:226-27; WP 4:133-34, 189-90].

Selleck, David: Taunton, Somerset; 1638; Dorchester, Boston; died in Virginia [NEHGR 2:401, 163:85-97, 199-211, 278-88, 164:63-74; Lechford 101, 216; DTR 43; DChR 5; BChR 40, 293; SPR Case #178; NYGBR 47:115; TAG 81:36-47; TG 19:3-40; FOOF 1:534-35].

Sellen, Thomas: Unknown; 1633; Ipswich, Boston [GMB 1651].

Sellin, Joan: Unknown; 1635 on *Elizabeth*; passenger list only [GM 2:6:227].

Sension, Matthew: London; 1634; Dorchester, Windsor, Wethersfield, Norwalk [GM 2:6:228-34; NEHGR 167:85-95].

Sension, Nicholas: London; 1635 on *Elizabeth & Ann*; Dorchester, Windsor [GM 2:6:234-42; NEHGR 167:85-95].

Severance, John: Unknown; 1636; Ipswich, Salisbury [ITR 20, 22; MBCR 1:373; WP 3:433; SyTR 5; EIHC 57:157; HAHAC 1:117; NEHGR 27:364; Phoebe Tilton Anc 112-13; David C. Dewsnap, *The Severance Genealogy* (Bowie, Maryland, 1995)].

Sewall, Henry: Manchester, Lancashire; 1635; Ipswich, Newbury, Rowley [GM 2:6:243-49; NEHGR 159:35-39].

Sexton, Giles: Unknown; 1630; Mystic [GMB 1651; WF 597].

Sexton, Richard: Unknown; 1635 on *Blessing*; passenger list only (with caveat) [GM 2:6:250].

Seymour, Richard: Sawbridgeworth, Hertfordshire; 1639; Hartford, Norwalk [HaBOP 160; FOOF 1:536; Dawes-Gates 2:729-30; CN 22:24;

NEHGR 71:105-12, 72:209; Donald Lines Jacobus, *A History of the Seymour Family* (New Haven, Connecticut, 1939)].

Shaflin, Michael: Salisbury, Wiltshire; 1635 on *James*; Charlestown, Salem [GM 2:6:250-55].

Sharp, Robert: Unknown; 1635 on *Abigail*; Boston, Braintree, Rehoboth [GM 2:6:255-59].

Sharp, Samuel: London; 1629 on the *George Bonaventure*; Salem [GMB 1652-55; WF 597-602; GDMNH 624].

Sharp, Thomas: Chelmsford, Essex; 1630; Boston; returned permanently to England in 1631 [GMB 1655-56; WF 602-4; Abandoning 347-48].

Shatswell, John: Sibbertoft, Northamptonshire; 1633; Ipswich [GMB 1656-58].

Shatswell, Theophilus: Sibbertoft, Northamptonshire; 1639; Ipswich [ITR 67; NEHGR 150:180-89; Annis Spear Anc 160-62].

Shatswell, William: Unknown; 1637; Ipswich [EPR 1:7; Annis Spear Anc 157-58].

Shaw, Abraham: Halifax, Yorkshire; 1636; Watertown, Dedham [WaBOP 4; WJ 1:239; MBCR 1:206, 241, 372; SPR 1:10, 2:4; DeTR 1:20, 51; CaTR 43; Lechford 329; NEHGR 48:346, 49:64, 106:50-52; TAG 57:85-87, 68:23; TG 10:86-97, 104-8; GMC50 353-58; Weymouth Hist 4:611].

Shaw, Edward: Unknown; 1632; Plymouth [GMB 1658-59; PM 412-13].

Shaw, John: Unknown; 1627; Plymouth [GMB 1659-62; PM 413-16].

Shaw, Robert: Unknown; 1632; Massachusetts Bay [GMB 1662].

Shaw, Roger: Gawsworth, Cheshire; 1638; Cambridge, Hampton [MBCR 1:283, 375; CaTR 36; CaBOP 49; NEHGR 4:182, 158:309-18; Phoebe Tilton Anc 8-9].

Shaw, Thomas: Unknown; 1634 on *Recovery*; Hingham, Barnstable [GM 2:6:259-61].

Sheafe, Jacob: Cranbrook, Kent; 1639; Guilford, Roxbury, Boston [Guilford Hist 25; NEHGR 55:208-20; TAG 15:69-80].

Sheafe, Widow: Unknown; 1638; Roxbury [RChR 83; RBOP 4]. (Possibly mother of Jacob Sheafe above.)

Sheele, Margaret: Unknown; 1636; Boston (servant; church admission only) [BChR 22; GMB 1663].

Sheffield, Deliverance: Unknown; 1638; Boston [BChR 24, 26-27; WP 4:109]. (She married Hugh Peter [Abandoning 241-42].)

Shelley, Robert: Unknown; 1632 on *Lyon*; Boston or Roxbury [GMB 1662-63].

Shepard, George: Unknown; 1639; Braintree (land grant only) [BTR 1:50].

Shepard, Humphrey: Unknown; 1635 on *Marygould*; passenger list only [GM 2:6:262].

Shepard, Ralph: Stepney, Middlesex; 1635 on *Abigail*; Watertown, Dedham, Weymouth, Malden, Concord [GM 2:6:262-69].

Shepard, Samuel: Towcester, Northamptonshire, or Banbury, Oxfordshire; 1635 on *Defence*; Cambridge; returned permanently to England by 1650 [GM 2:6:269-73; Abandoning 277-78].

Shepard, Thomas: London; 1635 on *Defence*; Cambridge [GM 2:6:273-81; WMQ 48:432-66].

Shepard, Thomas: Unknown; 1638; Richmond Island, North Yarmouth [Trelawny 185; GDMNH 628].

Shepard, William: Unknown; 1635; Dorchester (court appearance only) [GM 2:6:281-82].

Shepardson, Daniel: Unknown; 1633; Charlestown [GMB 1663-66].

Shepheard, ____: Unknown; 1631; Massachusetts Bay [GMB 2084-85].

Shepley, John: Unknown; 1636; Salem, Wenham, Chelmsford [STR 1:24, 34, 47; EPR 1:35; Fiske Notebook 61, 83, 115; Kempton Anc 4:562-66].

Sheppe, Thomas: Unknown; 1639; Charlestown [MBCR 1:282; Wyman 863].

Sherbone, Elizabeth: Unknown; 1639; Cambridge (landholding only) [CaBOP 67, 98].

Sherborn, Henry: Odiham, Hampshire; 1632 on *James*; Piscataqua [GMB 1666-69].

Sherin, Robert: Unknown; 1634 on *Elizabeth*; passenger list only [GM 2:6:282].

Sherman, Edmund: Dedham, Essex; 1635; Watertown, Wethersfield, New Haven [GM 2:6:282-87; NEHGR 166:245-58, 167:213-24, 275-84, 168:16-33].

Sherman, John: Dedham, Essex; 1634 on *Elizabeth*; Watertown [GM 2:6:287-94; NEHGR 166:245-58, 167:35-54].

Sherman, Philip: Dedham, Essex; 1633; Roxbury, Portsmouth [GMB 1670-73; TAG 73:176-80; NEHGR 166:245-58, 167:35-54, 149-56].

Sherman, Richard: Dedham, Essex; 1635; Boston [GM 2:6:294-302; NEHGR 166:245-58, 167:213-24, 275-84, 168:16-33].

Sherman, Samuel: Dedham, Essex; 1636; Ipswich [ITR 19; WP 3:433; BChR 28; BTR 1:34; MBCR 1:377; NEHGR 2:401, 166:245-58, 167:35-54, 149-56].

Sherman, Thomas: Unknown; 1637; Ipswich; not seen after 1638 [WP 3:454; ITR 25].

Sherman, William: Unknown; 1632; Plymouth, Duxbury, Marshfield [GMB 1673-75; PM 416-19].

Sherrat, Hugh: Unknown; 1634; Ipswich, Haverhill [GM 2:6:302-4].

Sherwood, Thomas: Kettle Baston, Suffolk; 1634 on *Francis*; Wethersfield, Stamford, Fairfield [GM 2:6:304-12].

Short, Anthony: Unknown; 1634; Ipswich, Newbury [GM 2:6:312-13].

Short, Henry: Unknown; 1634 on *Mary & John*; Ipswich, Newbury [GM 2:6:313-19].

Short, Rebecca: Unknown; 1632; Roxbury [GMB 1675]. (She married Walter Palmer.)

Short, Tobias: Unknown; 1639; Richmond Island [Trelawny 172, 175, 327, 331, 355, 356; GDMNH 632].

Shorthose, Robert: Unknown; 1634; Charlestown [GM 2:6:319-20].

Shotton, Samson: Cropston, Leicestershire; 1636; Boston, Portsmouth, Warwick [BTR 1:15 (as "Sampson Shelton"); Lechford 16; PoTR 1; RICR 1:91, 131; Austin 180; GMN 22:22].

Shove, Margery: Elsham, Lincolnshire; 1638; Boston, Rowley, Taunton [BChR 23; RowBOP 4; Sibley 1:554-55; Rowley Fam 343; GMN 18:28; NEHGR 157:338-54; Benjamin Jay Shove, *The Family Shove* (n.p. 1941)].

Shrimpton, Henry: Unknown; 1638; Boston [BTR 1:40; BChR 26; Lechford 241; SPR Case #409; SPR 1:389-91 (brother Edward); Stevens-Miller Anc 2:53].

Shurt, Abraham: Bristol; 1626; Pemaquid [GMB 1675-77].

Shurtleff, William: Unknown; 1634; Plymouth, Marshfield [GM 2:6:320-24].

Shute, Robert: Unknown; 1640; Winnegance [MPCR 1:58, 80; Lechford 377, 402-3; SPR NS 2:276].

Shuter, ____: Unknown; 1630; Massachusetts Bay; returned permanently to England in 1631 [GMB 2085; WF 605].

Sibley, John: Bradpole, Dorset; 1629; Nahant, Salem, Manchester [WF 605-8].

Sibley, John: Unknown; 1634; Charlestown [GM 2:6:325-28].

Sill, John: Newcastle-upon-Tyne; Northumberland; 1637; Cambridge [MBCR 1:374; CaBOP 57; Shepard 44; SPR 2:17; CaTR 40; MLR 1:87; NEHGR 38:79].

Sillis, Richard: Unknown; 1637; Scituate [NEHGR 9:280, 65:319-22, 70:349; PCR 1:96, 134, 12:70].

Silsby, Henry: Unknown; 1639; Salem, Ipswich, Lynn [STR 1:89; Waters 700-8 (clue); EIHC 17:257-59; Granberry 312; TEG 18:99-102; Snow-Estes 2:216-17].

Silsby, Thomas: Unknown; 1640; Massachusetts Bay (court appearance only) [EQC 1:21].

Silvester, Richard: Unknown; 1630; Weymouth, Marshfield [GMB 1677-81; NEHGR 162:47-53].

Simes, Sarah: Earls Colne, Essex; 1635 on *Defence*; Cambridge [GM 2:6:328-29].

Simkins, Nicholas: London; 1635; Dorchester, Cambridge, Yarmouth, Barnstable, Scituate, Boston [GM 2:6:330-36].

Simkins, Vincent: Unknown; 1640; Stamford [SmTR 4, 72-73; Wethersfield Hist 1:297].

Simmons *see also* **Symonds**

Simmons, John: Unknown; 1635; Richmond Island, Piscataqua [Trelawny 93, 98; GDMNH 633-34]

Simmons, William: Unknown; 1635; Ipswich, Haverhill [GM 2:6:336-40].

Simmons, William: Unknown; 1639; Charlestown, Concord, Woburn [ChTR 46; CoVR 3; SPR 2:16; Rodgers 3:96-102, 168-69 (son William); GM 2:5:456-57; NEHGR 148:239; NEHGR forthcoming].

Simmons, William: Unknown; 1640; Boston [NEHGR 2:401, 165:10-14; SPR 1:27; BChR 292].

Simonds, Edward: Unknown; 1639; Newbury (court appearance only) [WP 4:128].

Simonson, Moses: Leiden, Holland; 1621 on *Fortune*; Plymouth, Duxbury [GMB 1681-83; PM 419-22].

Simpson, Henry: Unknown; 1638; York [Gorges 9; GDMNH 634; York Hist 1:110-13].

Simpson, John: Unknown; 1635 on *Truelove*; passenger list only [GM 2:6:340].

Simson, John: Unknown; 1634; Watertown [GM 2:6:341-45].

Singletary, Richard: Unknown; 1637; Salem, Newbury, Salisbury, Haverhill [STR 1:57; NeTR 4; MBCR 1:374; HvBOP 36; SyTR 6; GMC26 283-88; Hoyt 317-18].

Sinnott, Walter: Unknown; 1637; Boston [BTR 1:32, 49; NEHGR 2:401; SLR 5:378-79; BChR 47, 308].

Skelton, Samuel: Tattershall, Lincolnshire; 1629 on *George Bonaventure*; Salem [GMB 1684-87; WF 608-12].

Skerry, Francis: Unknown; 1636; Salem [STR 1:24; SChR 6; MBCR 1:373; EQC 1:13; EIHC 4:65; EPR Case #25358].

Skerry, Henry: Great Yarmouth, Norfolk; 1637 on *John & Dorothy* or *Rose*; Salem [Hotten 291; SChR 7; STR 1:51; EQC 1:9; MBCR 1:374; EPR Case #25363; NEHGR 147:146-47; Perley 1:433-34].

Skidmer, John: Unknown; 1640; Massachusetts Bay (court appearance only) [MBCR 1:317].

Skidmore, Thomas: Westerleigh, Gloucestershire; 1636; Saybrook, Cambridge, New London, Stratford, Fairfield, Huntington [WP 3:268; NEHGR 4:182; Lechford 256-58; FOOF 1:564-65; Warren Skidmore,

Thomas Skidmore (Scudamore), 1605-1684, of Westerleigh, Gloucestershire, and Fairfield, Connecticut (n.p. 1980)].

Skiffe, James: Unknown; 1636; Sandwich [PCR 1:43, 47, 82, 106, 12:26, 55; MD 14:167, 170; Martha's Vineyard Hist 2: West Tisbury:71-72, 3:432-33].

Skilling, Thomas: Unknown; 1639; Salem, Gloucester, Falmouth [EQC 1:16, 93, 2:37; GDMNH 636; MHGR 2:45-46].

Skinner, John: Unknown; 1638; Hartford [CCCR 1:29; HaTR 23; HaBOP 309; Manwaring 1:150-52; TAG 74:97-100; Windsor Hist 2:687].

Skinner, Nathaniel: Unknown; 1638; Lynn (court appearance only) [EQC 1:9].

Skipper, William: Boston, Lincolnshire; 1639; Boston or Lynn [Lechford 244; TAG 20:77-85, 69:129-39].

Skouling, Robert: Hingham, Norfolk; 1638 in *Diligent*; Hingham (passenger list only) [NEHGR 15:25].

Slaid, Thomas: Unknown; 1639; Portsmouth (land grant only) [PoTR 6; RICR 1:72].

Slate, Robert: Unknown; 1640; Sudbury (land grant only) [SuTR 15].

Slawson, George: Unknown; 1638; Sandwich, Stamford [PCR 1:101, 107; SmTR 186-88; FOOF 1:565-67; CA 50:158-60; McCormick-Hamilton 880-83; George C. Slawson, *The Slason-Slauson-Slawson-Slosson Family* (Waverly, New York, 1946)].

Sleeper, Thomas: Unknown; 1640; Hampton, Haverhill [HmTR 48; SLR 1:61; Essex Ant 2:47; GDMNH 638].

Sloffe, John: Unknown; 1638; Portsmouth (admission as town inhabitant only) [PoTR 1; RICR 1:91].

Small, Edward: Bideford, Devonshire; 1639; Piscataqua, Isles of Shoals [MPCR 1:42; GDMNH 639; Lois Altine Woodbury Underhill, *Descendants of Edward Small of New England and the Allied Families with Tracings of English Ancestry*, revised edition, three volumes (Boston and New York 1934)]

Small, John: Salisbury, Wiltshire; 1635 on *James*; Salem [GM 2:6:345-47].

Smalley, John: Unknown; 1632 on *William & Francis*; Plymouth, Eastham, Piscataway [NJ] [GMB 1687-89; PM 422-24].

Smart, John: Norfolk (near Hingham); 1635; Hingham, Exeter [GM 2:6:348-49].

Smead, Judith: Unknown; 1637; Dorchester [DTR 1:27; DChR 4; MBCR 1:259; SPR Case #15]. (She was accompanied to New England by her three children from two earlier marriages, John Denman, Mary Denman and William Smead [TAG 41:30-35].)

Smith, Anne: Norwich, Norfolk; 1637 on *John & Dorothy* or *Rose*; passenger list only (servant) [Hotten 290].

Smith, Arthur: Unknown; 1637; Hartford [MHSC 2:8:140; HaTR 22; CCCR 1:62; HaBOP 247; Manwaring 1:152, 463-64].

Smith, Bartholomew: Unknown; 1640; Dover [NHPP 1:128, 10:701; GDMNH 642].

Smith, Benjamin: Unknown; 1640; Dedham [DeChR 25; MBCR 1:379; NGSQ 74:3-6; NEHGR 152:19].

Smith, Christopher: Unknown; 1639; Dedham [DeTR 1:67; DeChR 26; SPR Case #854; Parker-Ruggles 332, 334; CN 23:68-77, 36:559-64].

Smith, Christopher: Unknown; 1640; Roxbury (mention in notarial records only) [Lechford 349].

Smith, Dorothy: Unknown; 1635 on *Elizabeth*; passenger list only (with caveat) [GM 2:6:350-51].

Smith, Ellen: Unknown; 1640; Boston (church admission only) [BChR 33].

Smith, Francis: Unknown; 1630; Roxbury [GMB 1690; WF 612-14].

/ **Smith, Francis:** Unknown; 1635 on *Planter*; Watertown, Winnissimmett; Reading [GM 2:6:351-54].

Smith, Francis: Unknown; 1635; Hingham, Taunton [GM 2:6:355-58].

Smith, George: Salisbury, Wiltshire; 1635 on *James*; Salem [GM 2:6:359-60; STR 1:24 ("widow Smith")].

Smith, George: Unknown; 1639; Exeter, Dover; not seen after 1653 [GDMNH 52, 642; NHPP 31:13].

Smith, George: Unknown; 1640; New Haven [NHCR 1:92; FANH 1619-45; Ackley-Bosworth 58-59; Parke-Gildersleeve 180-81].

Smith, Giles: Unknown; 1639; Hartford, New London, Fairfield [HaBOP 268; FOOF 568-69].

Smith, Hannah: Unknown; 1635 on *Planter*; passenger list only [GM 2:6:361].

Smith, Hannah: Unknown; 1635 on *Susan & Ellen*; passenger list only [GM 2:6:361].

Smith, Henry: Dorchester, Dorset; 1630 on *Mary & John*; Dorchester, Springfield; returned permanently to England in 1653 [GMB 1691-92; Abandoning 278-79].

Smith, Henry: Unknown; 1637; Charlestown, Wethersfield [NGSQ 71:176; ChChR 9; WetLR 1:16; Bassett-Preston 257-59; Hale, House 729-33; GM 2:6:350-51; Morison 401; TAG 10:7-14].

Smith, Henry: New Buckenham, Norfolk; 1637 on *John & Dorothy* or *Rose*; Dedham, Medfield [Hotten 292; DeTR 1:34; DeVR 1; DeChR 21; MBCR 1:377; SPR Case #1524; NEHGR 59:107-8; TAG 85:216; Medfield Hist 479-80; Marjorie Little Napoli, *The Smith Genealogy* (n.p. 1974)].

Smith, Henry: Norfolk; 1638 on *Diligent*; Hingham, Rehoboth [NEHGR 15:27, 97:256-57, 121:12; Lechford 176, 304; ReTR 1:2; MBCR 1:297, 375; HiBOP 76; MD 10:159-62; Waters 1120-22; Ackley-Bosworth 110-12].

Smith, Henry: Unknown; 1640; Stamford [SmTR 4; CA 45:3-6, 50:114-15].

Smith, Jacob: Unknown; 1637; Massachusetts Bay (court appearance only) [MBCR 1:203].

Smith, James: Unknown; 1635; Salem, Gloucester, Marblehead [GM 2:6:361-73; TEG 17:209-14].

Smith, James: Unknown; 1640; Casco Bay [Lechford 402; GDMNH 642-43].

Smith, James: Unknown; 1640; Weymouth [Lechford 268; SPR Case #102; Weymouth Hist 4:632-33; Granberry 323-35].

Smith, John: Unknown; 1631; Massachusetts Bay [GMB 1693-94].

Smith, John: Unknown; 1633; Plymouth [GMB 1693; PM 424-25].

Smith, John: Unknown; 1635; Dorchester [GM 2:6:373-87].

Smith, John: Unknown; 1635 on *Elizabeth*; passenger list only (with caveat) [GM 2:6:387].

Smith, John: Unknown; 1635; Dorchester, Providence [GM 2:6:387-90].

Smith *alias* Bland, John: Colchester, Essex; 1635; Watertown, Martha's Vineyard [GM 2:6:391-94].

Smith, John: Unknown; 1636; Watertown [WaBOP 4, 8, 10, 11; MBCR 1:311; TAG 61:18-31]. (Possibly the same as the John Smith later of Hampton and Martha's Vineyard [GDMNH 644].)

Smith, John: Unknown; 1636; Lynn [EQC 1:3, 10, 2:270]. (This John Smith was not the man who appeared at Reading in the 1640s [GM 2:6:353].)

Smith, John: Unknown; 1636; Massachusetts Bay [MBCR 1:373]. (This admission to freemanship cannot be confidently assigned to any of the John Smiths listed, but does not necessarily imply the existence of an additional John Smith.)

Smith, John: Unknown; 1636; Saco [MPCR 1:lxii, 43; Trelawny 214; GDMNH 643].

Smith, John: Unknown; 1637; Massachusetts Bay [MBCR 1:219, 233, 234; WP 4:70]. (These four records do not necessarily all apply to the same man, and may apply to one or more of the other John Smiths.)

Smith, John: Unknown; 1638; Weymouth [MBCR 1:252, 254, 258; WP 1:347]. (Probably the same as one of the two John Smiths who appeared at Newport in 1639.)

Smith, John: Unknown; 1638; Boston [BChR 23, 41; BTR 1:41; SPR Case #692].

Smith, John: Unknown; 1638; Plymouth [PCR 1:103, 107, 127, 12:51; MD 13:84; GMB 1693; GM 2:5:146-47].

Smith, John: Unknown; 1638; Massachusetts Bay [MBCR 1:376]. (This admission to freemanship cannot be confidently assigned to any of the John Smiths listed, but does not necessarily imply the existence of an additional John Smith.)

Smith, John: Dublin, Ireland; 1639; Dedham, Boston; not seen after 1640 [DeTR 1:68; BChR 33; Aspinwall 39].

Smith, John: Unknown; 1639; Taunton, Newtown [NY] [PCR 1:132; TAG 25:66-67].

Smith, John: Unknown; 1639; Newport [RICR 1:92; GMN 23:3]. (One of these two John Smiths of Newport may be the man who was earlier at Weymouth.)

Smith, John: Unknown; 1639; Newport [RICR 1:92; GMN 23:4].

Smith, John: Unknown; 1640; York [MPCR 1:81; GDMNH 643-44].

Smith, John "Rock": Unknown; 1640; Stamford, Hempstead [NYGBR 88:5-16 (citing Fairfield PR 3:349); TAG 25:144].

Smith, Judith: Alford, Lincolnshire; 1634; Boston, Portsmouth [GM 2:6:394-95]. (She married Edward Fisher.)

Smith, Lucy: Unknown; 1631; Dorchester [GMB 1694].

Smith, Mary: Unknown; 1635 on *Planter*; passenger list only [GM 2:6:395].

Smith, Mary: Unknown; 1635 on *Susan & Ellen*; passenger list only [GM 2:6:395].

Smith, Matthew: Sandwich, Kent; 1637; Charlestown [NEHGR 75:223; ChTR 29; ChChR 10; TAG 19:203-4; TG 10:120-21].

Smith, Matthew: Unknown; 1637; Salem (land grant only) [STR 1:54].

Smith, Matthew: Unknown; 1639; Dorchester (land purchase only) [DTR 1:39].

Smith, Matthew: Unknown; 1639; Braintree (land grant only) [BTR 1:50].

Smith, Nehemiah: Unknown; 1637; Marshfield, New Haven, New London, Norwich [PCR 1:79, 138; PCPR 1:48; MD 13:85; TAG 11:12-14; Granberry 322-23; FANH 1664; Waterman Gen 1:621-23; H. Allen Smith, *A Genealogical History of the Descendants of the Rev. Nehemiah Smith* (Albany, New York, 1889)].

Smith, Ralph: Unknown; 1629; Nantasket, Plymouth, Manchester, Ipswich, Boston [GMB 1694-97; PM 425-28].

Smith, Ralph: Hingham, Norfolk; 1633; Charlestown, Hingham, Eastham [GMB 1697-99].

Smith, Richard: Unknown; 1633; Maine [GMB 1699].

Smith, Richard: Unknown; 1635 on *Planter*; passenger list only [GM 2:6:396].

Smith, Richard: Thornbury, Gloucestershire; 1637; Taunton, Portsmouth, New Amsterdam, Wickford [NGSQ 71:176; PCR 1:103, 132, 8:186; MD 13:86; RICR 1:92; PoTR 16; GMN 23:3; Austin 185; TAG 27:222-23, 84:257-64].

Smith, Richard: Unknown; 1639; Southampton, Smithtown [WP 4:230-32; GMB 852; NYGBR 121:19-22; Frederick Kinsman Smith, *The*

Family of Richard Smith of Smithtown, Long Island (Smithtown, New York, 1967)].

Smith, Richard: Burghfield, Berkshire; 1640; Watertown, Sudbury, Boston, York [TAG 61:29-31].

Smith, Robert: London; 1637; unknown; returned permanently to England [NEHGR 40:63; Abandoning 280; Parker-Ruggles 275].

Smith, Robert: Unknown; 1638; Exeter, Hampton [NHPP 1:133, 40:12; GDMNH 647; DeHR 8:38-42].

Smith, Robert: Unknown; 1638; Ipswich [EQC 1:381, 2:141; Amos Towne Anc 25-27; GMC50 371-76].

Smith, Robert: Unknown; 1639; Massachusetts Bay (court appearance only) [MBCR 1:282]. (This record might pertain to one of the three men above.)

Smith, Samuel: Hadleigh, Suffolk; 1634 on *Elizabeth*; Watertown, Wethersfield, Hadley [GM 2:6:396-402; NEA 4:5/6:35-37].

Smith, Samuel: Unknown; 1636; Salem, Wenham [STR 1:24, 69; EQC 1:16; EPR 1:18-21; GMC50 377-83].

Smith, Samuel: Unknown; 1638; Massachusetts Bay (business transaction only) [Lechford 50-51].

Smith, Samuel: Unknown; 1638; Portsmouth (court appearance only) [RICR 1:60].

Smith, Thomas: Unknown; 1633; Lynn; not seen after 1635 [GMB 1699-1700].

Smith, Thomas: Romsey, Hampshire; 1635 on *James*; Newbury [GM 2:6:402-5].

Smith, Thomas: Unknown; 1636; Salem [SChR 16; STR 1:103; EQC 1:3, 21, 22]. (These records may or may not pertain to the son of Samuel Smith of Salem and Wenham [Sarah Johnson Anc 47-48; GMB 1700; GMC50 382-83].)

Smith, Thomas: Unknown; 1636; Watertown [WaBOP 4, 31; TAG 61:28-29; Kempton Anc 1:424-37].

Smith, Thomas: Unknown; 1638; Ipswich [ITR 44-45; GMC50 385-89; NEHGR 142:51-55].

Smith, Thomas: Unknown; 1639; Saco [MPCR 1:43; Trelawny 214; NHPP 40:8; GDMNH 647].

Smith, Thomas: Unknown; 1639; Hampton [HmTR 45; GDMNH 55, 647].

Smith, William: Unknown; 1635; Black Point (Scarborough) [GM 2:6:406-8].

Smith, William: Unknown; 1635; Weymouth, Rehoboth, Huntington, Jamaica [NY] [GM 2:6:408-12].

Smith, William: Unknown; 1638; Charlestown [ChBOP 12; ChChR 10, 49; NEHGR 4:270; Rodgers 1:102-3; Wyman 872].

Snell, Mary: Unknown; 1633; Charlestown (church admission only) [GMB 1700].

Snow, Anthony: Unknown; 1637; Plymouth, Marshfield [PCR 1:83, 134, 12:53; MD 13:85; Gen Adv 3:90; Moore Anc 470-76; MF 18:7-8].

Snow, Nicholas: Unknown; 1623 in *Anne*; Plymouth, Eastham [GMB 1701-4; PM 428-32; MD 62:39-41].

Snow, Thomas: Unknown; 1635; Boston [GM 2:6:413-17].

Snow, William: Unknown; 1635 on *Susan & Ellen*; passenger list only [GM 2:6:417-18].

Snow, William: Unknown; 1638; Plymouth, Bridgewater [PCR 1:94, 8:188; MD 5:33-35; MF 7:7-8; Edwin H. Snow, *The William Snow Family* (Providence, Rhode Island, 1908)].

Solling, ____: Unknown; 1636; Massachusetts Bay (mention in letter only) [WP 3:269].

Somerby, Anthony: Little Bytham, Lincolnshire; 1639 on *Jonathan*; Newbury [NEHGR 32:441; Sarah Hildreth Anc 71; EPR Case #25839].

Sougth, John: Unknown; 1635; Dorchester (death record only) [GM 2:6:418].

Soule, George: Unknown; 1620 on *Mayflower*; Plymouth, Duxbury [GMB 1704-8; PM 432-36; MQ 74:140-43, 75:245-61; MD 60:134-35].

South, Thomas: Unknown; 1638; Lynn; not seen after 1646 [EQC 1:24, 60, 61, 84, 95, 2:270].

South, William: Unknown; 1638; Massachusetts Bay (court appearance only) [MBCR 1:234].

Southcott, Richard: Unknown; 1630; Dorchester [GMB 1708].

Southcott, Thomas: Unknown; 1630; Dorchester [GMB 1708].

Southwick, Lawrence: Kingswinford, Staffordshire 1638; Salem, Shelter Island [STR 1:87; SChR 8; MBCR 1:376; EPR 1:318-19; TG 12:223-31, 16:40-41; NEHGR 54:60; Essex Ant 135-36; TAG 71:193-97; James M. Caller and Mrs. M. A. Ober, *Genealogy of the Descendants of Lawrence and Cassandra Southwick* (Salem, Massachusetts, 1881); Neal S. Southwick, *The English Ancestry and American Posterity of Joseph Southwick, 1703-1980* (Rexburg, Idaho, 1981)].

Southworth, Constant: Unknown; 1628; Plymouth, Duxbury [GMB 1709-12; PM 437-40].

Southworth, Thomas: Unknown; 1628; Plymouth [GMB 1712-13; PM 440-43].

Soutly, John: Unknown; 1637; Plymouth (mention in probate inventory only) [PCPR 1:29].

Sowther, Nathaniel: Derby, Derbyshire; 1636; Plymouth [PCR 1:44, 12:29; PTR 1:4; SPR 3:21, 23; TAG 42:210-21, 43:14-18].

Spalding, Edward: Unknown; 1639; Braintree, Wenham, Chelmsford [MBCR 1:377; NEHGR 3:247; Backus Anc 169-72; Charles Warren Spalding, *The Spalding Memorial* (Chicago, Illinois, 1897)]. (Proposed connection with Virginia highly unlikely.)

Sparhawk, Nathaniel: Great Coggeshall, Essex; 1636; Cambridge [CaBOP 40; MBCR 1:376; NEHGR 4:182, 19:125-27, 21:172-73; Shepard 62; SPR 2:15; SPR Case #53; WP 4:134; Aspinwall 5; Waters 1194-1204; EIHC 25:30-31; Cecil Hampden Cutts Howard, *Materials for a Genealogy of the Sparhawk Family in New England* (Salem, Massachusetts, 1892)].

Sparks, Edward: Unknown; 1635 on *Increase*; passenger list only [GM 2:6:418-19].

Sparrow, John: Unknown; 1639; Boston (coroner's jury duty only) [SPR 2:1].

Sparrow, Richard: Unknown; 1632; Plymouth, Eastham [GMB 1715-18; PM 443-47].

Spencer, George: Unknown; 1637; Massachusetts Bay, New Haven [MBCR 1:203; NHCR 1:29, 31, 32, 62-73; Legal Executions 9].

Spencer, Goodman: Unknown; 1639; died at sea on voyage to New England [NHCR 1:33].

Spencer, Jared: Stotfold, Bedfordshire; 1634; Cambridge, Lynn, Hartford, Haddam [GM 2:6:419-28; CN 29:592-615].

Spencer, John: Unknown; 1634 on *Mary & John*; Ipswich, Newbury; returned permanently to England between 1637 and 1648 [GM 2:6:428-36; Abandoning 348].

Spencer, John: Unknown; 1636; Connecticut (Pequot War service only) [MHSC 3:3:143].

Spencer, Michael: Stotfold, Bedfordshire; 1634; Cambridge, Lynn [GM 2:6:436-39].

Spencer, Thomas: Unknown; 1630; Piscataqua [MPCR 1:6, 42; GDMNH 651-52].

Spencer, Thomas: Stotfold, Bedfordshire; 1633; Cambridge, Hartford [GMB 1718-21; CN 29:14-27].

Spencer, William: Stotfold, Bedfordshire; 1631; Cambridge, Hartford [GMB 1721-25; CN 27:32-37].

Spencer, William: Unknown; 1634 on *Mary & John*; passenger list only [GM 2:6:439].

Spicer, Christian: Eastwell, Kent; 1637; Roxbury (servant; passenger list and church admission only) [NEHGR 75:221; RChR 82].

Spicer, Thomas: Sandwich, Kent; 1638; Portsmouth, New Amsterdam, Gravesend [PoTR 1; RICR 1:91; Susan Spicer Meech and Susan Billings Meech, *History of the Descendants of Peter Spicer* (Boston 1911) 8-16; Susan Billings Meech, *A Supplement to the Descendants of Peter Spicer* (Groton, Connecticut, 1923) 25-30; Stillwell 4:289-94].

Spinnage, Humphrey: Unknown; 1639; New Haven [NHCR 1:26, 28, 41, 140; NEHGR 59:267-69, 80:107-9, 81:132, 83:127-28; FANH 1697].

Spofford, William: Unknown; 1637; Massachusetts Bay (mention in two letters only) [WP 3:488, 493].

Spooner, Thomas: Unknown; 1637; Salem [STR 1:51; SChR 7; MBCR 1:374; EIHC 28:124; Perley 1:433; NEHGR 23:348 (clue)].

Spooner, William: Unknown; 1637; Plymouth [PCR 12:19; MD 15:27, 16:238; NEHGR 23:407-8; Thomas Spooner, *Records of William Spooner of Plymouth, Mass., and His Descendants* (Cincinnati, Ohio, 1883)].

Spour (or Spurr), John: Clapton, Somerset; 1637; Boston; not seen after 1651 [BTR 1:34, 45; BBOP 27, 76, 101; BChR 24, 52, 284, 289, 298, 309, 320; MBCR 1:254, 376; NEHGR 2:401; SLR 1:95, 152].

Sprague, Francis: Unknown; 1623 on *Anne*; Plymouth, Duxbury [GMB 1725-28; PM 447-50].

Sprague, Ralph: Fordington St., Dorset; 1629; Charlestown, Malden [GMB 1728-31].

Sprague, Richard: Upway, Dorset; 1629; Charlestown [GMB 1731-35].

Sprague, William: Upway, Dorset; 1629; Charlestown, Hingham [GMB 1735-39].

Spratt, Mary: Unknown; 1635 on *Blessing*; passenger list only [GM 2:6:439-40].

Spring, John: Unknown; 1634 on *Elizabeth*; Watertown [GM 2:6:440-46].

Squance, Philip: Unknown; 1636; Massachusetts Bay (court appearance only) [WJ 2:425].

Squire, John: Unknown; 1640; York (three business transactions only) [Lechford 265-66; Trelawny 326, 328; York Hist 1:119].

Squire, Nicholas: Unknown; 1640; York (business transaction only) [Lechford 265-66; York Hist 1:118-19].

Squire, Thomas: Unknown; 1630; Charlestown, Malden [GMB 1739-41; WF 614-17].

Stackhouse, Richard: Unknown; 1638; Salem, Beverly [STR 1:75; EQC 1:15, 28; EPR Case #26049; Perley 2:48].

Stacy, Hugh: Unknown; 1621 on *Fortune*; Plymouth [GMB 1741; PM 450].

Stacy, Hugh: Unknown; 1639; Salem, Dedham [STR 1:98; DeVR 1; DeChR 24; DeTR 1:73; Perley 2:149; Marblehead 118].

Stacy, John: Unknown; 1639; Massachusetts Bay [MBCR 1:268; EQC 1:332; EPR 2:271-72; Marblehead 119].

Stacy, Simon: Bocking, Essex; 1637; Ipswich [ITR 27, 36; NEHGR 58:91-92, 160:17-29; Dawes-Gates 1:557-61].

Stafford, Thomas: Unknown; 1639; Newport [RICR 1:92; EQC 3:292; Austin 384-89].

Stagg, _____: Unknown; 1634; Massachusetts Bay (court appearance only) [GM 2:6:446].

Stanborough, Josias: Canons Ashby, Northamptonshire; 1638; Lynn, Southampton [EQC 1:12, 2:270; Lechford 197; Aspinwall 103-4, 165; SoTR 1:1, 2:8-12; NEHGR 63:166; TAG 26:61-62, 31:1-15].

Stanbury, Thomas: Unknown; 1640; Boston [BTR 1:58; BChR 44, 84, 301, 315; NEHGR 10:72; SPR Case #2412; GMN 7:4].

Standish, James: Unknown; 1636; Salem [STR 1:20; SChR 7, 8; EQC 1:28; MBCR 1:376; EPR 3:293-94].

Standish, Miles: Holland; 1620 on *Mayflower*; Plymouth, Duxbury [GMB 1741-47; PM 451-57].

Standish, Thomas: Unknown; 1640; Wethersfield [WetLR 1:130; TAG 25:126; Wethersfield Hist 2:658-62; Lyon-Rice 550-52].

Standlake, Daniel: Unknown; 1635 on *Hopewell*; Scituate [GM 2:6:447-50].

Standy, Robert: Unknown; 1635 on *Elizabeth & Ann*; passenger list only [GM 2:6:450].

Stanley, Christopher: Unknown; 1635 on *Elizabeth & Ann*; Boston [GM 2:6:450-54].

Stanley, Joan: Unknown; 1639; Plymouth [PCR 1:134]. (She married Thomas Pinson.)

Stanley, John: Tenterden, Kent; 1634; died at sea, family settled at Hartford [GM 2:6:455-56].

Stanley, Thomas: Ashford, Kent; 1634; Lynn, Hartford, Hadley [GM 2:6:456-62].

Stanley, Timothy: Tenterden, Kent; 1634; Cambridge, Hartford [GM 2:6:462-66].

Stansby, John: Unknown; 1637; Cambridge; not seen after 1642 [WP 3:381; Shepard 85-88; CaBOP 54].

Stansley, Thomas: Unknown; 1635 on *Planter*; passenger list only [GM 2:6:467].

Stantley, John: Unknown; 1635 on *Abigail*; passenger list only [Hotten 98].

Stanton, Robert: Unknown; 1638; Portsmouth, Newport [PoTR 2; RICR 1:60, 66, 91; NHM 67; RIVR 7:75, 122; Austin 388-91; Stonington Hist 601-4].

Stanton, Thomas: Unknown; 1635; Cambridge, Hartford, New London, Stonington [GM 2:6:467-79; NYGBR 60:31].

Stanyan, Anthony: Unknown; 1635 on *Planter*; Boston, Exeter, Hampton [GM 2:6:479-86].

Staples, Jeffrey: Wendover, Buckinghamshire; 1639; Weymouth [Weymouth VR; SLR 3:356; SPR Case 58½; NEHGR 161:95-100; Weymouth Hist 4:637-38].

Starbuck, Edward: Unknown; 1639; Dover, Nantucket [MPCR 1:42; NHPP 1:128, 10:701, 31:13, 40:3, 454; WP 4:179; GDMNH 656-57; Nantucket Hist 802; Farr Anc 252-23].

Starcy, John: Unknown; 1637; Dorchester; not seen after 1638 [DTR 1:32, 34].

Stares, Thomas: London; 1635; Windsor; left New England soon after 1640 [GM 2:6:486-87].

Stark, Aaron: Unknown; 1638; Windsor, New London [CCCR 1:28, 55, 84; New London Hist 313-14; Charles R. Stark, *The Aaron Stark Family* (Boston 1927)].

Starr, Comfort: Ashford, Kent; 1635 on *Hercules*; Cambridge, Duxbury, Boston [GMB 2:6:487-94].

Starr, Thomas: Canterbury, Kent; 1637; Dorchester [NEHGR 75:221, 95:260; DChR 4; DTR 286; MBCR 1:314; Fiske Notebook 13; GM 2:6:492-93].

Starr, Truth-Shall-Prevail: Ashford, Kent; 1635 on *Hercules*; passenger list only [GM 2:6:494].

Stearns, Isaac: Nayland, Suffolk; 1630; Watertown [GMB 1747-50; WF 617-21].

Stebbins, Edward: (probably) Braintree, Essex; 1633; Cambridge, Hartford [GMB 1750-53].

Stebbins, John: Unknown; 1633; Watertown [Lechford 242-43, 318; MBCR 1:314; WaVR 2:8; WaBOP 66; Bond 582; Ralph Stebbins Greenlee and Robert Lemuel Greenlee, *The Stebbins Genealogy*, two volumes (Chicago, Illinois, 1904) 1021-22].

Stebbins, Martin: Unknown; 1639; Roxbury, Boston [Lechford 210; RChR 85; NEHGR 6:377, 20:143, 32:317-19; SPR Case #223; TAG 41:95-97; Parker-Ruggles 477; Ralph Stebbins Greenlee and Robert Lemuel Greenlee, *The Stebbins Genealogy*, two volumes (Chicago, Illinois, 1904) 1117-19].

Stebbins, Rowland: Bocking, Essex; 1634 on *Francis*; Roxbury, Springfield, Northampton [GM 2:6:494-98].

Stedman, Isaac: Biddenden, Kent; 1635 on *Abigail*; Scituate, Boston [GM 2:6:498-504].

Stedman, John: Unknown; 1639; Cambridge [CaBOP 59; CaTR 43; Shepard 73; MBCR 1:377; CaChR 6; MPR Case #21358; GM 2:2:181].

Stedman, Robert: Unknown; 1638; Cambridge [MBCR 1:314, 375; CaBOP 59; NEHGR 4:183; CaChR 9; Rodgers 2:371-74].

Steele, George: Fairstead, Essex; 1633; Cambridge, Hartford [GMB 1754-56; TAG 81:18-30].

Steele, John: Fairstead, Essex; 1633; Cambridge, Hartford, Farmington [GMB 1756-59; Edward Eugene Steele, *A Steele Family History* (St. Louis, Missouri, 2001)].

Steerer, Elizabeth: Unknown; 1635 on *Defence*; passenger list only [GM 2:6:504].

Stevens, Benjamin: Unknown; 1638; Richmond Island [Trelawny 182, 291; GDMNH 658].

Stevens, Henry: Unknown; 1635 on *Defence*; Lynn, Boston [GM 2:6:504-11].

Stevens, John: Caversham, Oxfordshire; 1638 on *Confidence*; Newbury, Andover [Drake's Founders 59; NEHGR 85:396-401, 163:27-28; Hoyt 322-23, 1009-10]

Stevens, John: Unknown; 1639; Boston (mention in notarial records only) [Lechford 199].

Stevens, John: Unknown; 1639; Salisbury [SyTR 7; MBCR 1:378; Essex Ant 1:24; Hoyt 325-26; Stone-Gregg 245-46].

Stevens, Robert: Unknown; 1635 on *Planter*; Boston, Braintree [GM 2:6:511-112].

Stevens, Thomas: Unknown; 1635 on *Abigail*; passenger list only (with caveat) [GM 2:6:512-13].

Stevens, William: Unknown; 1632; Boston, Salem, Marblehead, Gloucester [MHSC 3:8:324-25; STR 1:54; SChR 9; MBCR 1:377; WP 4:15, 189; GlTR 1:1; Dawes-Gates 1:562-68; GMB 2085 (incomplete)].

Stevens, William: Caversham, Oxfordshire; 1638 on *Confidence*; Newbury [Drake's Founders 59; EPR 1:153-54; NEHGR 85:396-401; Hoyt 324; TAG 67:236-42].

Stevenson, Edward: Unknown; 1640; Southampton [SoTR 1:14]. (Possibly the Edward Stevenson who appeared later at Newtown [TAG 33:36; John R. Stevenson, *Thomas Stevenson of London, England, and His Descendants* (Flemington, New Jersey, 1902) 131-33].)

Steward, James: Unknown; 1621 on *Fortune*; Plymouth (land grant only) [GMB 1759; PM 457].

Stewart, James: Unknown; 1639; New Haven; not seen after 1646 [NHCR 1:26, 88, 122, 123, 125, 260, 261].

Stibbins, William: Unknown; 1640; Boston (business transaction only) [Lechford 314].

Stickney, William: Cottingham, Yorkshire; 1638; Boston, Rowley [BChR 23, 25; MBCR 1:378; RowBOP 3; EPR 2:5-8; Rowley Fam 364; NEHGR 139:319-20; Parker-Ruggles 320-22; GMN 18:28; Matthew Adams Stickney, *The Stickney Family* (Salem, Massachusetts, 1869)].

Stileman, Elias: London; 1629; Salem [GMB 1759-62; WF 621-24].

Stiles, Francis: London; 1635 on *Christian*; Windsor, Saybrook, Stratford [GM 2:6:513-21].

Stiles, Henry: London; 1635 on *Christian*; Windsor [GM 2:6:521-24].

Stiles, Joan: Millbrook, Bedfordshire; 1635 on *Christian*; passenger list only [GM 2:6:524-25].

Stiles, John: Millbrook, Bedfordshire; 1635 on *Christian*; Windsor [GM 2:6:525-28].

Stiles, Thomas: London; 1635 on *Christian*; Windsor, Flushing [GM 2:6:528-33].

Stinnings, Richard: Unknown; 1635; Plymouth [GM 2:6:533].

Stitson, William: Unknown; 1632; Winnissimmet, Charlestown [GMB 1763-67].

Stockbridge, John: Rayleigh, Essex; 1635 on *Blessing*; Scituate, Boston [GM 2:6:534-40].

Stocker, Thomas: Unknown; 1639; Lynn [Lechford 241; Backus Anc 173-74; TEG 10:155-56].

Stocking, George: Unknown; 1634; Cambridge, Hartford [GM 2:6:540-45].

Stockton, Thomas: Unknown; 1635 on *Truelove*; passenger list only [GM 2:6:545-46].

Stoddard, Anthony: London; 1639; Boston [BTR 1:42; BChR 26; MBCR 1:318, 377; WJ 2:46; SPR Case #1559; NEHGR 61:92; HAHAC 1:96; Hale, House 734-46; TAG 65:17-23; NGSQ 71:179; Ralph Coffman, *Solomon Stoddard* (Boston 1978)].

Stodder, John: Unknown; 1638; Hingham [HiBOP 67; NEHGR 121:13; SPR Case #290; Hingham Hist 3:191-92; Francis Russell Stoddard Jr., *The Stoddard Family* (New York 1912)].

Stokes, Grace: Unknown; 1635 on *Hopewell*; passenger list only [GM 2:6:546].

Stone, Gregory: Nayland, Suffolk; 1635; Watertown, Cambridge [GM 2:6:546-52]. (He was accompanied to New England by his stepchildren John and Lydia Cooper.)

Stone, John: Unknown; 1633; Massachusetts Bay [GMB 1767-68].

Stone, John: Unknown; 1635 on *Elizabeth*; passenger list only (with caveat) [GM 2:6:552-53].

Stone, John: Unknown; 1636; Salem, Beverly [STR 1:24; EQC 1:17; Sarah Stone Anc 3-23].

Stone, John: Unknown; 1639; Hartford (land transaction only) [HaBOP 347].

Stone, John: Unknown; 1639; Guilford [Guilford Hist 25; Guilford Fam 131-32].

Stone, Samuel: Stisted, Essex; 1633 on *Griffin*; Cambridge, Hartford [GMB 1768-73].

Stone, Simon: Boxted, Essex; 1635 on *Increase*; Watertown [GM 2:6:553-58].

Stone, William: Unknown; 1639; Guilford [Guilford Hist 25; Guilford Fam 1131].

Stonehill, Henry: Unknown; 1639; Milford; returned permanently to England by 1648 [MiTR 2; MiChR 2; NHCR 1:92; Abandoning 285].

Storer, Richard: London; 1639; Braintree; returned permanently to England by 1643 [BTR 1:43; NEHGR 15:322-23; WP 4:374-75; GM 2:3:460-62; Abandoning 285].

Storer, William: Unknown; 1640; Dover [NHPP 1:128, 10:701, 40:11; NEHGR 23:474; GDMNH 665-66; Malcom Storer, *Annals of the Storer Family* (Boston 1927)]. (William Storer was not son of Augustine Storre.)

Storre, Augustine: Alford, Lincolnshire; 1638; Exeter [NHPP 1:132, 134; GDMNH 666; GMB 1005-10].

Story, Andrew: Unknown; 1635; Ipswich [GM 2:6:558-59].

Story, Elias: Unknown; 1620 on *Mayflower*; Plymouth [GMB 1773; PM 457].

Story, Elizabeth: Unknown; 1638; Boston [BChR 24]. (She married Wentworth Day.)

Story, George: Unknown; 1638; Boston; not seen after 1643 [Lechford 67, 127, 187; WJ 2:84; NHPP 40:7; EQC 1:28; GM 2:6:300-1].

Story, William: Norwich, Norfolk; 1637 on *John & Dorothy* or *Rose*; Ipswich [Hotten 290; TAG 43:238-39; NEHGR 90:308-9; Robert L. Pratt, *The Descendants of William Story* (Baltimore, Maryland, 2000)].

Stoughton, Israel: Rotherhithe, Surrey; 1632; Dorchester; returned permanently to England in 1644 [GMB 1773-77; Abandoning 286-87; NEHGR 165:245-60, 166:46-70; Foundations 1:46-50].

Stoughton, Thomas: Aller, Somerset; 1630; Dorchester, Windsor [GMB 1777-79].

Stow, John: Biddenden, Kent; 1634; Roxbury, Concord [GM 2:6:559-65].

Stow, John: Unknown; 1639; Plymouth (court appearance only) [PCR 7:16].

Stowers, John: Unknown; 1634; Watertown, Newport [GM 2:6:565-70].

Stowers, Nicholas: Unknown; 1629; Charlestown [GMB 1779-82; M&JCH 27:52-63 (clue)].

Strange, George: Unknown; 1634; Dorchester, Hingham; probably returned permanently to England in 1641 [GM 2:6:570-72].

Stratton, John: Shotley, Suffolk; 1628; Cape Porpus, Salem [GMB 1782-85; NeTR 29; WP 4:165; NEHGR 155:367-90, 156:39-61, 390, 157:394, 160:101-8; GDMNH 667].

Stratton, John: Unknown; 1638; Charlestown; not seen after 1638 [ChTR 41, 42; ChBOP 16; GMB 1784].

Stream, John: London; 1635 on *Truelove*; Weymouth, Milford [GM 2:6:573-77].

Stream, Thomas: London; 1635 on *Truelove*; Weymouth [GM 2:6:578-80].

Streaton, Elizabeth: Unknown; 1635 on *Increase*; passenger list only [GM 2:6:580].

Street, Alice: Unknown; 1635 on *Susan & Ellen*; passenger list only (with caveat) [GM 2:6:580].

Street, Nicholas: Norton Fitzwarren, Somerset; 1637 on *Elizabeth*; Taunton, New Haven [NGSQ 71:177; PCR 1:143; Lechford 319; M&JCH 25:61-64, 26:58-59; TAG 27:9-11; NEHGR 46:256-67, 47:348-49; Henry A. Street, *The Street Genealogy* (Exeter, New Hampshire, 1895)].

Streson, Robert: Unknown; 1639; Dorchester (mention in notarial records only) [Lechford 346].

Stret, William: Unknown; 1639 on *Jonathan*; passenger list only [NEHGR 32:410].

Strickland, Edward: Unknown; 1640; Wethersfield, Fairfield, Newtown [NY] [Wethersfield Hist 1:303; TAG 20:210-12, 21:85-88].

Strickland, John: Unknown; 1629; Charlestown, Watertown, Wethersfield, Fairfield, Hempstead, Huntington, Jamaica [NY] [GMB 1785-87].

Strickland, Thwaits: Unknown; 1640; Dedham, Westerly, Hartford [DeTR 1:72; WMJ 808, 810; Manwaring 1:243; NEHGR 39:192; TAG 21:89-92].

Stringer, John: Unknown; 1637; Dorchester (servant; court appearance only) [WJ 2:426].

Strong, John: Chard, Somerset; 1635 on *Hopewell*; Hingham, Taunton, Windsor, Northampton [GM 2:6:581-88; M&JCH 25:64-65, 26:59, 27:63].

Strowde, John: Unknown; 1635 on *Abigail*; passenger list only [GM 2:6:588].

Stuckely, John: Unknown; 1637; Sandwich; not seen after 1639 [PCR 1:107, 8:184].

Stuckey, George: Unknown; 1640; Windsor, Fairfield, Stamford [WiLR 1:74; SmTR 84-86; FOOF 1:592].

Sturges, Edward: Unknown; 1634; Charlestown, Yarmouth [GM 2:6:588-97].

Stuttin, Joan: Unknown; 1634; Charlestown (church admission only) [GM 2:6:598].

Styth, Margaret: Unknown; 1638; Dorchester (church admission only) [DChR 3].

Sucklin, Thomas: Hingham, Norfolk; 1638 on *Diligent*; Hingham, Providence [NEHGR 15:26; Austin 194].

Sumner, Elizabeth: Unknown; 1635 on *Abigail*; passenger list only [GM 2:6:598].

Sumner, Henry: Unknown; 1635 on *Abigail*; passenger list only [GM 2:6:598].

Sumner, William: Bicester, Oxfordshire; 1635; Dorchester [GM 2:6:598-604].

Sunderland, John: Unknown; 1638; Boston, Eastham [NEHGR 2:402; MD 12:139-40, 17:99-100; TAG 78:256-64; Wickham-Billard 97-98].

Sutherland, Matthew: Unknown; 1638; Plymouth, Portsmouth, Newport; died at Long Island [PCR 1:100; RICR 1:91; RICR (MS) 12; Lechford 283, 301; GMN 22:28].

Sutton, Ambrose: Westwell, Oxfordshire; 1638; Charlestown (servant; mention in notarial records only) [Lechford 58-59].

Sutton, Elizabeth: London; 1640; Charlestown (business transaction only) [Lechford 393-35, 429].

Sutton, George: Tenterden, Kent; 1635 on *Hercules*; Scituate; removed to North Carolina by 1668 [GM 2:6:604-7].

Sutton, John: Attleborough, Norfolk; 1638 on *Diligent*; Hingham [NEHGR 15:26, 91:61-65, 167:7-14; HiBOP 75; MBCR 1:315].

Sutton, Lambert: Unknown; 1640; Charlestown, Woburn [ChChR 10; MLR 1:14-15].

Sutton, Simon: Unknown; 1635 on *Hercules*; Scituate [GM 2:6:607-8].

Swaddon, Philip: Unknown; 1630; Watertown, Kittery, Dover, St. George [GMB 1787-89; WF 624-26; NHPP 10:701].

Swain, Elizabeth: Unknown; 1635 on *Planter*; passenger list only [GM 2:6:608].

Swain, Elizabeth: Unknown; 1635 on *Susan & Ellen*; passenger list only [GM 2:6:608].

Swain, Henry: Unknown; 1638; Charlestown (admission as town inhabitant only) [ChTR 39].

Swain, Richard: Easthamstead, Berkshire; (probably) 1635 on *Truelove*; Newbury, Hampton, Nantucket [GM 2:6:609-17].

Swain, William: Unknown; 1635 on *Elizabeth & Ann*; Watertown, Wethersfield, Branford [GM 2:6:618-21].

Swan, Henry: Unknown; 1638 (possibly on *Castle*); Salem [Lechford 165; STR 1:83, 84; SChR 8, 19, 21; MBCR 1:376; NEHGR 10:71, 18:325; TAG 62:33-40].

Swan, John: Unknown; 1640; Cambridge [SPR 1:25, 2:10; MD 59:21-31; MF 8:10-11].

Swan, Richard: Unknown; 1638; Boston, Rowley [BChR 23, 25, 283; WP 4:283; MBCR 1:376; RowBOP 5; Parker-Ruggles 310-29; Rowley Fam 371-72; NEHGR 31:115-16; Pillsbury Anc 2:897-901].

Swanson, Anna: Unknown; 1632; Boston (church admission only) [GMB 1789].

Sweet, John: Unknown; 1632; Salem [GMB 1789-90; PrTR 1:3; TAG 53:28-30].

Sweet, John: Unknown; 1638; Boston [BChR 23, 32; BTR 1:59; Lechford 253; MBCR 1:379; SPR 1:22; NEHGR 2:391; SPR Case #1403].

Sweet, Thomas: Unknown; 1634 on *Mary & John*; passenger list only [GM 2:6:621].

Sweetser, Seth: Tring, Hertfordshire; 1637; Charlestown [ChTR 31; ChChR 9, 47; NEHGR 4:270; MBCR 1:375; Aspinwall 43; Rodgers 2:90-95; Wyman 921-26; Philip Starr Sweetser, *Seth Sweetser and His Descendants* (Philadelphia, Pennsylvania, 1938)].

Swetman, Thomas: Unknown; 1637; Cambridge [MBCR 1:374; CaChR 13; MPR Case #22046].

Swift, Margaret: Unknown; 1636; Salem (court appearance only) [EQC 1:3].

Swift, Thomas: Dorchester, Dorset; 1634 on *Recovery*; Dorchester [GM 2:6:621-26].

Swift, William: Bermondsey, Surrey; 1634; Watertown, Sandwich [GM 2:6:626-32].

Swimmer, Anthony: Unknown; 1638; Lynn (two appearances in notarial records only) [Lechford 4, 25, 381].

Swinden, William: Unknown; 1635 on *Elizabeth & Ann*; Ipswich [GM 2:6:633].

Swinforth, John: Unknown; 1639; Massachusetts Bay (business transaction only) [Lechford 279].

Swinnerton, Job: Unknown; 1637; Salem [STR 1:53; SChR 8; MBCR 1:376; Perley 1:438-40].

Swinnerton, Joanna: Unknown; 1640; New Haven [NHCR 1:50; NEHGR 124:133; MD 63:213-24]. (She married Isaac Allerton.)

Sydlie, Thomas: Unknown; 1635 on *Susan & Ellen*; passenger list only [GM 2:6:634].

Sykes, Richard: Unknown; 1639; Dorchester, Springfield [DChR 4, 5, 153; MBCR 1:377; Pynchon Court 213; SpTR 167; Arthur M. Sikes Jr., *Richard Sikes and His Descendants, the First Seven Generations* (n.p. 2000)].

Symmes, Zachariah: Dunstable, Bedfordshire; 1634 on *Griffin*; Boston, Charlestown [GM 2:6:634-43].

Symonds *see also* **Simmons**

Symonds, Henry: Unknown; 1640; Lynn, Southampton, Boston [Plain Dealing 98; SoTR 1:23; BTR 1:71, 74; BChR 295; NEHGR 2:402; MBCR 2:104, 293].

Symonds, John: Great Yarmouth, Norfolk; 1636; Salem [STR 1:24; SChR 7; EQC 1:3; MBCR 1:374; NEHGR 96:205; Dudley Wildes 129-31].

Symonds, John: Unknown; 1639; Braintree (death of daughter only) [NEHGR 3:248].

Symonds, Mark: Unknown; 1637; Ipswich [ITR 28; MBCR 1:374; TAG 74:114-16 (clue); Hoyt 600; EPR 1:285-86, 2:33-34; EQC 1:149; Parker-Ruggles 438-44].

Symonds, Samuel: Toppesfield, Essex; 1637; Ipswich [WP 3:518, 4:11; MBCR 1:374; TAG 70:152-53; Hoyt 597-600; William S. Appleton, *Ancestry of Priscilla Baker* (Cambridge, Massachusetts, 1870)].

Symonds, Thomas: Unknown; 1638; Braintree [NEHGR 3:248; Lechford 351; BTR 1:49; MBCR 1:282].

Symons, Thomas: Unknown; 1633; Plymouth [GMB 1790; PM 457-58].

T

Tabor, Philip: Unknown; 1633; Watertown, Yarmouth, Martha's Vineyard, New London, Portsmouth, Providence [GMB 1791-94; TAG 72:329-32].

Tabor, Timothy: Batcombe, Somerset; 1635 on *Marygould*; passenger list only [GM 2:7:1].

Tacy, ____: Unknown; 1639; Massachusetts Bay (court appearance only) [MBCR 1: 283].

Tainter, Joseph: Upton Grey, Hampshire; 1638 on *Confidence*; Watertown, Sudbury [Drake's Founders 58; WaBOP 46; SPR 1:24; SuTR 4; MD 1:89-90; TAG 65:17-23; Dean W. Tainter, *A History and Genealogy of the Descendants of Joseph Taynter* (Boston 1859)].

Talbot, Peter: Unknown; 1636; Plymouth (servant; land transaction only) [PCR 1:43, 47].

Talby, John: Spalding, Lincolnshire; 1636; Salem [STR 1:17; SChR 16; EQC 1:6; Fiske 245; Perley 1:272; WJ 1:335; MBCR 1:246; TAG 78: 1-8, 256-64].

Talcott, John: Braintree, Essex; 1632 on *Lyon*; Cambridge, Hartford [GMB 1794-97; NEHGR 148:240-58].

Talmage, Thomas: Barton Stacey, Hampshire; 1633; Lynn, Southampton, Easthampton [GMB 1798-1800].

Talmage, William: Unknown; 1630; Boston [WF 626].

Tanner, Nicholas: Unknown; 1639; New Haven (servant; two court appearances only) [NHCR 1:26, 56].

Tapp, Edmond: Bennington, Hertfordshire; 1637; New Haven, Milford [NHCR 1:28; MiTR 2; MiChR 1; NEHGR 54:352; TAG 72:65-80, 73:65-73].

Tapp, Joan: Unknown; 1639; Salem (court appearance only) [EQC 1:12].

Tarbox, John: Unknown; 1638; Massachusetts Bay [EQC 1:11; NEHGR 42:27-29; TEG 20:132-33].

Tarling, Christopher: Unknown; 1633; Massachusetts Bay [GMB 1800].

Tarne, Miles: Unknown; 1638; Boston [NEHGR 2:402, 10:265; BTR 1:57; BChR 24, 287; SLR 9:352-54, 393-94; Stevens-Miller 2:157-63].

Tarr, James: Unknown; 1638; Portsmouth (land grant and admission as inhabitant only) [RICR 1:59, 91].

Tart, Edward: Unknown; 1640; Scituate [PCPR 1:37; PCR 7:45, 66, 8:191].

Tart, Elizabeth: Unknown; 1638; Scituate [PCR 1:103, 2:14-15]. (She married Thomas Williams [GM 2:7:437].)

Tart, Thomas: Unknown; 1639; Scituate; removed to Barbados after 1649 [PCR 1:156, 162, 2:14-15, 141, 7:20, 66, 8:183, 191, 12:70, 158, 174; PCPR 1:37; BChR 286; MD 9:165; ScitTR 1:106, 397, 2:107, 218, 236, 3:120; Aspinwall 172, 224, 411]. (Probably sibling, possibly parent of the two above.)

Taselie, Elizabeth: Unknown; 1635 on *Abigail*; Lynn [GM 2:7:1].

Tatman, John: Unknown; 1632 on *Lyon*; Roxbury [GMB 1800-2].

Taylor, Anthony: Unknown; 1639; Hampton [GDMNH 55; HmTR 45; Harold Murdock Taylor, *Family History: Anthony Taylor of Hampton, New Hampshire* (Rutland, Vermont, 1935)].

Taylor, Dyonis: Unknown; 1635 on *Susan & Ellen*; Boston [GM 2:7:2].

Taylor, Elizabeth: Unknown; 1635 on *Susan & Ellen*; passenger list only [GM 2:7:2].

Taylor, Elizabeth: Unknown; 1638; Charlestown (church admission only) [ChChR 9]. (Wyman thought she was wife of Thomas Taylor of Watertown and Reading, who did have a wife Elizabeth [Wyman 932].)

Taylor, George: Unknown; 1635 on *Truelove*; passenger list only (unless he was one of the following) [GM 2:7:2-4].

Taylor, George: Unknown; 1636; Saco [EQC 2:25; MPCR 1:48; GDMNH 674; GM 2:7:2-4].

Taylor, George: Unknown; 1638; Lynn [EQC 1:19, 2:270; WJ 2:25; GM 2:7:2-4].

Taylor, Gregory: Haverhill, Suffolk; 1630; Boston, Watertown, Stamford [GMB 1802-3; WF 627-29].

Taylor, Henry: Unknown; 1639; Strawberry Bank [NHPP 1:113, 31:18, 40:19, 40, 43-44, 49, 51, 56-57; MBCR 3:140; GDMNH 674].

Taylor, Humphrey: Unknown; 1636; Maine (mention in letter only) [WP 3:383].

Taylor, John: Unknown; 1630; Massachusetts Bay [GMB 1803-4; WF 629-30].

Taylor, John: Unknown; 1640; Windsor [WP 4:288; WiLR 1:10; TAG 37:197, 38:1-7, 53:241-43; Dawes-Gates 2:784-90; Stevens-Miller 1:509-10; FOOF 1:599-601].

Taylor, Katherine: London; 1635 on *Increase*; passenger list only [GM 2:7:4].

Taylor, Nathaniel: Unknown; 1640; Massachusetts Bay (court appearance only) [EQC 1:26].

Taylor, Nicholas: Unknown; 1635 on *Unity*; passenger list only [GM 2:7:5].

Taylor, Samuel: Dover, Kent; 1637; Ipswich [NEHGR 75:222, 163:5-15].

Taylor, Thomas: Unknown; 1636; Salem (grant of land only) [STR 1:35].

Taylor, Thomas: Unknown; 1640; Massachusetts Bay (business transaction only) [Lechford 289]. (Possibly the same as the next.)

Taylor, Thomas: Unknown; 1640; Watertown [Lechford 304; WaBOP 65, 142; WaVR 1:10; MLR 3:39-41; Wyman 932-33].

Taylor, William: Beddington, Cornwall; 1638; Plymouth (servant; apprenticeship only) [PCR 1:119].

Tedder, Stephen: Unknown; 1640; Dover [NHPP 10:701, 40:7,12]. (See also Stephen Kidder.)

Teed, John: Norwich, Norfolk; 1637 on *Mary Anne*; passenger list only (servant) [Hotten 294]. (He was not the son of John Tidd of Charlestown [Stevens-Miller 1:127]. He may have been the John Tedd who appeared at Exeter in 1649 [GDMNH 676].)

Teff, William: Unknown; 1638; Boston [BTR 1:36, 51; BChR 30; MBCR 1:378; NEHGR 11:310; Austin 392].

Temple, Abraham: Unknown; 1636; Salem [STR 1:24, 55, 78, 102; EQC 1:9, 11; Levi Daniel Temple, *Some Temple Pedigrees* (Boston 1900)].

Temple, Dorothy: Unknown; 1638; Plymouth (servant) [PCR 1:111, 112, 113, 127].

Tench, Edward: Unknown; 1639; New Haven [NHCR 1:26, 50, 93, 196, 278; GMN 13:19-20].

Tench, William: Unknown; 1623 on *Fortune*; Plymouth [GMB 1804; PM 459].

Tenney, Thomas: Great Limber, Lincolnshire; 1640; Rowley [RowVR; RowBOP 4; Rowley Fam 373-81; NEHGR 151:329-41; M. J. Tenney, *The Tenney Family* (Concord, New Hampshire, 1904)].

Terry, John: Unknown; 1635 on *Abigail*; passenger list only [GM 2:7:5].

Terry, Richard: Unknown; 1635 on *James*; Lynn, Southampton, Southold [GM 2:7:5-9].

Terry, Robert: Unknown; 1635 on *James*; Lynn, Southampton, Flushing [GM 2:7:9-11].

Terry, Stephen: Dorchester, Dorset; 1630 on *Mary & John*; Dorchester, Windsor, Hadley [GMB 1804-6].

Terry, Thomas: Unknown; 1635 on *James*; Lynn, Southampton, Southold [GM 2:7:11-14].

Thacher, Anthony: Salisbury, Wiltshire; 1635 on *James*; Newbury, Marblehead, Yarmouth [GM 2:7:14-22].

Thacher, Peter: Unknown; 1637 on *Prosperous*; passenger list only [NGSQ 71:177]. (Probably not the Peter Thacher seen in Massachusetts Bay records in 1642 [EQC 1:35; RCA 2:118; GM 2:7:20].)

Thacher, Thomas: Salisbury, Wiltshire; 1637; Newbury, Weymouth, Boston [GM 2:7:19-20; EQC 1:162; NEHGR 7:344, 8:177-78; NYGBR 35:101-7, 42:62-63; Weymouth Hist 4:641-42; Magnalia 488-97; Sibley 2:370-79].

Thaxter, Thomas: Unknown; 1638; Hingham [HiBOP 83r; SPR Case #148; Hingham Hist 3:229-30].

Thayeler, Faithful: Unknown; 1636; Springfield (witness only) [NEHGR 15:141].

Thayer, Thomas: Thornbury, Gloucestershire; 1637; Braintree [NGSQ 71:176; BTR 1:50; NEHGR 60:281-91, 64:185; TAG 59:175-79, 73:81-90, 209-19; Pillsbury Anc 443-49; Kempton Anc 3:368-93; SPR Case #383].

Theale, Nicholas: Unknown; 1637; Watertown, Stamford [MBCR 1:220; WaBOP 42; WaVR 1:8; SLR 1:62; GMN 1:8; SmTR 24, 62-63; FOOF 1:601-2].

Thickston, Katherine: Unknown; 1639; Sandwich [PCR 1:143]. (She married William Hurst.)

Thing, Jonathan: Unknown; 1640; Hampton, Wells [MBCR 1:317, 2:76; GDMNH 678; EQC 5:409-10; Noyes-Gilman 236-37].

Thomas, ____: Unknown; 1639; Windsor (death record only) [Grant 78].

Thomas, Evan: Unknown; 1640; Boston [MBCR 1:300, 379; BTR 1:56; BChR 33, 45, 287, 291; EPR 1:343-45; GM 2:4:201].

Thomas, John: Unknown; 1635 on *Hopewell*; passenger list only [GM 2:7:22].

Thomas, John: Unknown; 1640; New Haven [NHCR 1:51; NEHGR 78:154-59, 81:132; FANH 1727-29].

Thomas, Thomas: Unknown; 1632 on *William & Francis*; passenger list only [GMB 1806-7].

Thomas, William: Unknown; 1636; Plymouth, Marshfield [PCR 1:45, 105, 126, 7:4, 8:173, 177; MD 10:162-64; NEHGR 4:317].

Thomas, William: Great Comberton, Worcestershire; 1637 on *Mary Anne*; passenger list only [Hotten 293].

Thomlins, Benjamin: Unknown; 1635 on *Susan & Ellen*; passenger list only [GM 2:7:23].

Thomlins, Edward: Unknown; 1635 on *Susan & Ellen*; passenger list only [GM 2:7:23].

Thompson *see also* **Tompson**

Thompson, Alice: Preston Capes, Northamptonshire; 1640; Roxbury [Lechford 308, 381; Granberry 333; Stevens-Miller 1:419-26; TAG 13:1-8, 145-46, 29:215-18, 56:80; TG 4:173-86].

Thompson, Robert: Unknown; 1639; Boston; not seen in New England after 1640 [SLR 3:386-87; Lechford 374; MBCR 1:315, 5:408; Waters 65-67, 74-75; ODNB (under "George Thomson")].

Thompson, Simon: Unknown; 1636; Ipswich [ITR 18, 22; MBCR 1:379; WoVR; WP 4:14; EPR 3:59-62; Hammatt Papers 369].

Thompson, William: Winwick, Lancashire; 1639; Dorchester, York, Braintree [BTR 1:47, 80; MBCR 1:292, 377; NEHGR 3:248, 9:151, 15:112-16, 81:133, 140:3-16; DChR 3; WP 4:31, 268; WJ 1:376; TAG 14:123-26, 60:231-35; GDMNH 682; NYGBR 60:31].

Thomson, David: Plymouth, Devon; 1623; Piscataqua, Thompson's Island (Boston Harbor) [GMB 1807-9].

Thomson, Edmond: Unknown; 1637; Salem; returned permanently to England after 1647 [SChR 9; STR 1:92; EQC 1:12, 16; Aspinwall 186-87; NEHGR 62:303-4 (clue), 88:273; WP 4:464; Abandoning 291].

Thomson, Edward: Unknown; 1620 on *Mayflower*; Plymouth [GMB 1809; PM 459].

Thomson, James: Fishtoft, Lincolnshire; 1633; Charlestown, Woburn [GMB 1809-11; TAG 74:101-4].

Thomson, John: Unknown; 1635 on *Elizabeth & Ann*; passenger list only [GM 2:7:23].

Thomson, Thomas: Unknown; 1635 on *Abigail*; passenger list only [GM 2:7:24].

Thorley, Richard: Holme-upon-Spalding-Moor, Yorkshire; 1639; Rowley, Newbury [RowVR; RowBOP 5; GMN 18:28; Rowley Fam 382-83; Snow-Estes 1:131-32; GMC50 477-78].

Thorn, Peter: Unknown; 1635 on *Elizabeth*; passenger list only [Hotten 56].

Thorn, William: Unknown; 1637; Lynn, Gravesend, Flushing, Jamaica [EQC 1:28, 2:270; MBCR 1:374; NYGBR 53:18, 92:1-12, 91-95].

Thorndike, John: Lincolnshire; 1632; Ipswich, Salem; returned permanently to England shortly after 1668 [GMB 1811-14; NEHGR 154:459-76; Scott C. Steward and John Bradley Arthaud, *A Thorndike Family History: Descendants of John and Elizabeth (Stratton) Thorndike* (Boston 2000)].

Thornton, John: Unknown; 1637; Ipswich [ITR 28, 59; Essex Ant 8:3; GMB 294].

Thornton, Robert: Unknown; 1635 on *Elizabeth*; passenger list only [GM 2:7:24-25].

Thornton, Thomas: London; 1633; Dorchester, Windsor, Stratford, Yarmouth [GMB 1814-17].

Thornton, Walter: Unknown; 1635 on *Susan & Ellen*; passenger list only [GM 2:7:25].

Thorpe, John: Unknown; 1632; Duxbury [GMB 1817-18; PM 459-61].

Thorpe, Robert: Unknown; 1638; Massachusetts Bay (court appearance only) [MBCR 1:249].

Thorpe, William: Unknown; 1639; New Haven [NHCR 1:28, 93; NEHGR 59:392, 81:133; TAG 20:237-38; FANH 1776-77; FOOF 1:607-8].

Thrall, William: Unknown; 1640; Windsor [CCCR 2:150; WiLR 1:57; Dawes-Gates 2:792-97].

Throckmorton, John: Unknown; 1631 on *Lyon*; Salem, Providence [GMB 1818 (incorrect); WJ 1:49-51; MBCR 1:366 (as "Mr. George Throckmorton"); TAG 12:79-85, 20:116-18, 77:110-24, 229-34, 290-97; NEHGR 98:67-72, 279, 101:290-91; Frances Grimes Sitherwood, *Throckmorton Family History* (Bloomington, Illinois, 1929)].

Thurston, Daniel: Unknown; 1638; Newbury [NeTR 33; EPR 2:30-31; NEHGR 42:249-50; Snow-Estes 1:117-25].

Thurston, John: Wrentham, Suffolk; 1637 on *Mary Anne*; Salem, Dedham, Medfield [Hotten 293; STR 1:62, 64, 98, 103; EPR 1:37; DeVR 1; DeChR 24; TAG 54:176-77; Kempton Anc 3:394-407].

Thwaits, Alexander: Unknown; 1635 on *Hopewell*; Concord, Maquoit, Kennebec [GM 2:7:25-32].

Thwing, Benjamin: Hull, Yorkshire; 1635 on *Susan & Ellen*; Cambridge, Boston [GM 2:7:32-35].

Tibballs, Thomas: Ellesborough, Buckinghamshire; 1635 on *Truelove*; Dorchester (or Weymouth), New Haven, Milford [GM 2:7:35-38].

Tibbetts, Henry: Unknown; 1635 on *James*; Dover [GM 2:7:38-40].

Tibbetts, Remembrance: Unknown; 1635 on *James*; Dover [GM 2:7:41]. (She married John Ault.)

Tibbot, Walter: Unknown; 1640; Marshfield, Gloucester [PCR 2:8; GlTR 1:1; EPR 1:132-33; Dawes-Gates 1:606-9].

Ticknall, Henry: Unknown; 1635 on *Hopewell*; passenger list only [GM 2:7:42].

Tidd, John: Hertford, Hertfordshire; 1637; Charlestown, Woburn [ChTR 31; ChBOP 58; WoTR 2; Rodgers 1:250-52; Stevens-Miller 1:125-27; Dawes-Gates 1:595-98; TG 12:223-31]. (John Dane, a tailor, more likely "wrought" with John Tidd, a tailor, than with Joshua Tidd, a mariner [NEHGR 132:22].)

Tidd, Joshua: Unknown; 1637; Charlestown, Boston [ChTR 30; ChChR 9, 48; ChBOP 57; STR 1:56; MBCR 1:376; Gen Adv 1:90-95; SCC 1011, 1014, 1139; SPR Case #986; Wyman 945].

Tike, Robert: Unknown; 1640; Salem; not seen after 1643 [EQC 1:22, 59; STR 1:115].

Tilden, Nathaniel: Tenterden, Kent; 1635 on *Hercules*; Scituate [GM 2:7:42-46].

Tilden, Thomas: Unknown; 1623 on *Anne*; Plymouth [GMB 1819; PM 461].

Tiler, Job: Cranbrook, Kent; 1637; Braintree, Andover, Roxbury, Mendon [WJ 2:426; RICR 1:92; GMN 22:30; EQC 2:367; NEHGR 115:75-76; Willard I. Tyler Brigham, *The Tyler Genealogy: The Descendants of Job Tyler, of Andover, Massachusetts, 1619-1700* (Plainfield, New Jersey, and Tylerville, Connecticut)].

Tilestone, Thomas: Unknown; 1634; Dorchester [GM 2:7:46-50].

Till, James: Unknown; 1638; Scituate, New Haven; departed by 1651 [PCR 1:118, 131, 132, 143, 2:68, 69, 8:191, 12:101; Aspinwall 22; NHCR 1:163, 293, 413, 416, 418-19, 420, 437, 454-55; NHTR 1:28, 40, 46, 57, 104, 225].

Tilley, Eady: Unknown; 1640; Windsor [WiLR 1:31]. (She married Nicholas Camp [Parke-Gildersleeve 171; CN 28:387-89; GMB 1823-25].)

Tilley, Edward: Leiden, Holland; 1620 on *Mayflower*; Plymouth [GMB 1819-20; PM 461-62; MQ 76:125-26].

Tilley, Hugh: Unknown; 1629 on *Lyon's Whelp*; Nahant, Salem, Yarmouth [GMB 1820-22; WF 630-32].

Tilley, John: Leiden, Holland; 1620 on *Mayflower*; Plymouth [GMB 1822; PM 462-63; TAG 85:1-8; MQ 65:322-25, 76:125-26].

Tilley, John: Dorchester, Dorset; 1624; Cape Ann, Dorchester [GMB 1823-25].

Tilley, Nathaniel: Unknown; 1635 on *Abigail*; passenger list only [GM 2:7:51].

Tilley, William: Holy Trinity Minories, London; 1635 on *Abigail*; Barnstable, Boston, Cape Porpus [GM 2:7:51-56].

Tilson, Edmond: Unknown; 1638; Plymouth [PCR 1:95, 2:14, 7:31; TAG 69:37-44].

Tilton, Peter: Unknown; 1640; Windsor, Hadley [Grant 67; Phoebe Tilton Anc 12-16].

Tingley, Palmer: Kingston-upon-Thames, Surrey; 1635 on *Planter*; Ipswich [GM 2:7:56-57].

Tinker, John: New Windsor, Berkshire; 1636; Boston, Lancaster, Windsor, New London [Lechford 2; WP 4:92, 129; WetLR 1:146; SPR NS 1:10, 2:19; NEHGR 149:401-32].

Tinker, Sarah: New Windsor, Berkshire; 1636; Scituate [NEHGR 9:280, 149:401-32]. (She married Thomas King of Scituate.)

Tinker, Thomas: Unknown; 1620 on *Mayflower*; Plymouth [GMB 1825; PM 461].

Tinkham, Ephraim: Barnstaple, Devon; 1634; Plymouth [GM 2:7:57-63].

Tisdale, John: Unknown; 1636; Plymouth, Taunton [PCR 1:42, 66, 102; MD 21:29-35; Granberry 331-33; Rosa D. Tisdale, *Meet the Tisdales:Descendants of John Tisdale of Taunton, Mass., 1634-1980* (Baltimore, Maryland, 1981)].

Tise, John: Unknown; 1635 on *Unity*; passenger list only [GM 2:7:63].

Titcomb, William: Ogbourne St. George, Wiltshire; 1638; Newbury [NeTR 34; Kempton Anc 2:280-97]. (Savage thought this immigrant was the same as William Latcome, who probably did not sail on the *Mary & John* or the *Hercules* in 1634 [Savage 4:307; GM 2:4:240].)

Titus, Robert: Unknown; 1635 on *Hopewell*; Boston, Weymouth, Rehoboth, Huntington [GM 2:7:63-67].

Tobey, Francis: Unknown; 1634; Massachusetts Bay [GM 2:7:67].

Tod, John: Unknown; 1639; Massachusetts Bay (court appearance only) [MBCR 1:262].

Todd, Christopher: Unknown; 1640; New Haven [NHCR 1:50; NEHGR 62:48, 81:133].

Toll, John: Unknown; 1639; Sudbury [SuTR 7; NEHGR 6:378].

Toll, Roger: Unknown; 1639; Boston; not seen after 1644 (servant) [MBCR 1:312, 2:293; Lechford 412; BChR 41].

Toller, Mary: Unknown; 1635 on *Increase*; passenger list only [GM 2:7:67-68].

Tolman, Thomas: Unknown; 1639; Dorchester [MBCR 1:377; DChR 4; NEHGR 14:247; Mower 611-14]. (No evidence for claim of Salcombe Regis, Devon, as English origin.)

Tomkins, Micah: Unknown; 1639; Milford [MiTR 2; Wethersfield Hist 2:705; FANH 1847].

Tomlins, Edward: Todenham, Gloucestershire; 1630; Lynn; returned permanently to England by 1648 [GMB 1825-28; WF 632-36; Abandoning 293].

Tomlins, Timothy: Todenham, Gloucestershire; 1632; Cambridge, Lynn [GMB 1828-30].

Tompkins, John: Unknown; 1640; Concord, Fairfield [CoVR 3; FOOF 1:612].

Tompkins, Ralph: Wendover, Buckinghamshire; 1635 on *Truelove*; Dorchester, Salem [GM 2:7:68-72].

Tompson *see also* **Thompson**

Tompson, Anthony: Unknown; 1640; New Haven [NHCR 1:41; NEHGR 66:198-99, 81:132-33; FANH 1749-50].

Tompson, John: Unknown; 1640; New Haven [NHCR 1:47, 50]. (Insufficient evidence to connect these records with either of the men of this name who appeared in New Haven in the early 1650s [NEHGR 66:197-200].)

Tompson, Mary: Unknown; 1640; Massachusetts Bay (servant; mention in letter only) [WP 4:223].

Tomson, ____: Unknown; 1639; Richmond Island (death record only) [Trelawny 169].

Tomson, Archibald: Unknown; 1637; Marblehead [EQC 1:6; STR 1:63; WJ 2:52].

Tomson, John: Unknown; 1634; Watertown [GM 2:7:73-75].

Tomson, John: Unknown; 1640; Wethersfield [WetLR 1:131]. (Possibly the John Tomson who appeared at Stratford in 1641 [FOOF 1:605].)

Tomson, Widow: Unknown; 1638; Marblehead (land grant only) [STR 1:74].

Toothaker, Roger: Unknown; 1635 on *Hopewell*; Plymouth [GM 2:7:75-76].

Topliff, Clement: Unknown; 1636; Dorchester [NEHGR 4:166, 169, 5:333, 58:117-18; DChR 4, 5; DTR 31; MBCR 1:377; McCormick-Hamilton 994-98].

Toppan, Abraham: Great Yarmouth, Norfolk; 1637 on *Mary Anne*; Newbury [Hotten 293; NeTR 5; MBCR 1:374; WP 4:124; Abel Lunt Anc 103-5, 185; NEHGR 161:92-94].

Topping, Richard: Unknown; 1633; Boston; returned permanently to England soon after 1654 [GMB 1830-32; Abandoning 293].

Topping, Thomas: Unknown; 1639; Wethersfield, Milford, Southampton, Branford [CCCR 1:29; MiTR 2; MiChR 1; Miner Anc 172-74; Wethersfield 2:699].

Torrey, Philip: Combe St. Nicholas, Somerset; 1640; Roxbury [SLR 8:392; M&JCH 25:65-67; NEHGR 61:189, 163:85-97, 199-211, 278-95, 164:63-74; Waters 546-51].

Torrey, William: Combe St. Nicholas, Somerset; 1640; Weymouth [SLR 8:392; M&JCH 25:65-67; NEHGR 61:189, 163:85-97, 199-211, 278-95, 164:63-74; Weymouth Hist 4:677-78; Waters 546-51; HAHAC 1:117].

Tose, John: Unknown; 1638; Hingham (dispute over land only) [Lechford 83].

Tottingham, Henry: Unknown; 1640; Woburn [WoTR 2; MPR Case #22656].

Tower, John: Hingham, Norfolk; 1637; Hingham [NEHGR 15:26, 121:11; HiBOP 68; MBCR 1:297, 375; Hingham Hist 3:251-52; Annis Spear Anc 49-52].

Towne, Edmund: Great Yarmouth, Norfolk; 1637 on *John & Dorothy* or *Rose*; passenger list only (servant) [Hotten 291]. (Age on passenger list does not match age of Edmund, son of William Towne of Salem.)

Towne, William: Unknown; 1635; Cambridge [GM 2:7:76-78].

Towne, William: Great Yarmouth, Norfolk; 1639; Salem, Topsfield [EQC 1:19; STR 1:108; Amos Towne Anc 3-6; Dudley-Wildes Anc 111-14].

Townsend, Henry: Unknown; 1633; Richmond Island [GMB 1832].

Townsend, Henry: Unknown; 1639; Portsmouth, Warwick, Oyster Bay [PoTR 14; Winthrop-Babcock 495-502].

Townsend, Thomas: Unknown; 1638; Lynn [MBCR 1:375; EQC 1:26, 2:270; NEHGR 33:61; GMB 1332; TEG 13:152-55 (clue)].

Townsend, William: Unknown; 1634; Boston [GM 2:7:78-82].

Tracy, Stephen: Leiden, Holland; 1623 on *Anne*; Plymouth, Duxbury; returned permanently to England by 1654 [GMB 1832-34; PM 463-65; Abandoning 294].

Tracy, Thomas: Unknown; 1636; Watertown, Salem, Wethersfield, Saybrook, Norwich [STR 1:33, 101; TAG 41:250-52 (clue); Granberry 334-35; NEHGR 61:93; Moore Anc 506-13; Waterman 1:691-95].

Tracy, William: Unknown; 1634 on *Mary & John*; passenger list only [GM 2:7:83].

Train, John: Unknown; 1635 on *Susan & Ellen*; Watertown [GM 2:7:83-87].

Trask, Henry: Unknown; 1634 on *Mary & John*; passenger list only [GM 2:7:87].

Trask, William: East Coker, Somerset; 1628; Salem [GMB 1834-37].

Travell, Nathaniel: Unknown; 1639; Massachusetts Bay (court appearance only) [MBCR 1:287].

Travers, Henry: Unknown; 1634 on *Mary & John*; Newbury; returned permanently to England about 1648 [GM 2:7:88-93; Abandoning 294].

Treadway, Nathaniel: Essex; 1639; Sudbury, Watertown [SuTR 4; Kempton Anc 1:450-61]

Trebie, Edward: Unknown; 1638; Richmond Island; not seen after 1642 [Trelawny 185, 194, 295, 301, 324, 328].

Treble, John: Unknown; 1631; Winnissimmet [GMB 1838].

Tredwell, Edward: Epwell, Oxfordshire; 1637; Ipswich, Branford, Southold, Huntington [ITR 25; MBCR 1:206; NYGBR 42:177-84, 104:195-204; FOOF 1:613; Kempton Anc 2:303-7; NGSQ 68:117].

Tredwell, Thomas: London; 1635 on *Hopewell*; Dorchester, Ipswich [GM 2:7:94-97].

Trelawny, Edward: Plymouth, Devon; 1635; Richmond Island, Boston, Piscataqua; returned permanently to England in 1636 [Trelawny 81; WP 3:392; GDMNH 691].

Trentum, Thomas: Unknown; 1635 on *Blessing*; passenger list only [GM 2:7:98].

Trerice, Nicholas: Stepney, Middlesex; 1636; Charlestown, Woburn [ChTR 23; ChBOP 54, 71; NEHGR 4:270, 143:25-39, 159:235; WoTR 2; RCA 2:118; WJ 1:385; ChChR 9, 48; WoVR].

Trevor, William: Unknown; 1620 on *Mayflower*; Plymouth [GMB 1838; PM 466].

Treworthy, James: Kingsweare, Devon; 1639; Piscataqua [MPCR 1:42; NEHGR 50:219-20; TAG 84:46-49; GDMNH 691; Brian J. L. Berry, *The Shapleigh, Shapley and Shappley Families, A Comprehensive Genealogy: 1635-1993* (Baltimore 1993); M&JCH 26:59-60, 27:82-84].

Tripp, John: Lincolnshire; 1636; Boston, Portsmouth [PoTR 2; RICR 1:91; TG 4:59-128, 5:257-62, 10:195-99].

Tritton, Rose: Ashford, Kent; 1635 on *Hercules*; passenger list only [GM 2:7:98 (source for baptism not given in sketch); NYGBR 138:178-88].

Trott, Simon: Unknown; 1634; Plymouth, Cape Porpus [GM 2:7:99-104].

Trowbridge, Thomas: Exeter, Devon; 1637; Dorchester, New Haven; returned permanently to England in 1644 [DTR 1:27; DChR 4; NHCR 1:92; HAHAC 1:80; TG 9:3-39; NEHGR 59:291-97; TAG 18:129-37, 57:31; Abandoning 295; Francis Bacon Trowbridge, *The Trowbridge Genealogy* (New Haven, Connecticut, 1908)].

Truant, Morris: Unknown; 1630; Massachusetts Bay, Duxbury, Marshfield [GMB 1838-40; WF 636-39].

Truesdale, Richard: (probably) Boston, Lincolnshire; 1634; Boston [GM 2:7:104-8].

Trumble, John: Newcastle-upon-Tyne, Northumberland; 1637; Cambridge, Charlestown [CaBOP 62; MBCR 1:194, 198, 245, 377; SPR Case #1576; NEHGR 4:183, 38:79, 49:148-49; Shepard 106; Wyman 954; Pillsbury Anc 867-71].

Trumble, John: Unknown; 1639; Roxbury, Rowley [RChR 84; MBCR 1:377; RowBOP 4; EPR 1:259-60; Rowley Fam 398-99; Parker-Ruggles 310-18; NEHGR 49:148; DeTR 1:50].

Trusler, Thomas: Unknown; 1638; Salem [STR 1:73; SChR 9; EPR 1:183-84, 211-12; SPR Case #154; NGSQ 75:289-302].

Try, Michael: Unknown; 1639; Windsor, Fairfield [CCCR 1:46; WiLR 1:93; FOOF 1:617-18; Stevens-Miller 1:501].

Tubbs, William: Unknown; 1634; Plymouth, Duxbury [GM 2:7:108-17].

Tuchill, Francis: Unknown; 1634; Dorchester [GM 2:7:117-18].

Tuck, Robert: Unknown; 1636; Watertown, Hampton [WaBOP 4; GDMNH 55, 695; HmTR 40; MBCR 1:236, 376; NHPP 31:79-81; EIHC 53:246-47; Joseph Dow, *Tuck Genealogy: Robert Tuck, of Hampton, N.H. and His Descendants. 1638-1877* (Boston 1877)]. (Evidence not provided for Gorleston, Suffolk, as English origin.)

Tuck, Thomas: Unknown; 1636; Salem [STR 1:25; EQC 1:14, 197, 3:421; Perley 1:399-401].

Tucker, Adrian: Unknown; 1630; Piscataqua [GMB 1841].

Tucker, Henry: Unknown; 1639; York (witness only) [YLR 1:119].

Tucker, John: Unknown; 1635; Hingham, Watertown [GM 2:7:118-22].

Tucker, John: Unknown; 1640; Salem; not seen after 1647 [Lechford 404; STR 1:134, 163; EQC 1:51, 81, 105, 118; Perley 2:99, 203].

Tucker, Margaret: Unknown; 1635 on *Abigail*; passenger list only [GM 2:7:122].

Tucker, Richard: Unknown; 1630; Spurwink, Casco, Piscataqua [GMB 1841-43].

Tucker, Robert: Unknown; 1639; Weymouth, Gloucester, Milton [MBCR 1:296; Granberry 335; Weymouth Hist 4:700-1; Parker-Ruggles 361-66; NEHGR 76:232-40].

Tufts, John: Hingham, Norfolk; 1638 on *Diligent*; passenger list only (servant) [NEHGR 15:26].

Tupper, Thomas: Unknown; 1635; Lynn, Sandwich [PCC 79 Campbell; PCR 1:57, 98, 149, 153; PCPR 1:32; MD 14:170, 21:39-40; NEHGR 159:73 (clue); Scott Gen 278; Noyes-Gilman 384-86].

Turkey, John: Unknown; 1635 on *Hercules*; passenger list only [GM 2:7:122-23]. (Possibly "Turvey" or "Turbey" [NEHGR 79:108].)

Turland, Ann: Unknown; 1635; Salem [GM 2:7:123].

Turner, _____: Unknown; 1637; Charlestown [ChTR 38; WJ 2:73].

Turner, Charles: Unknown; 1639; Salem [EQC 1:14, 15, 26; STR 1:119; EPR 1:26; Perley 2:78].

Turner, Elizabeth: Unknown; 1635 on *Hopewell*; passenger list only [GM 2:7:123-24].

Turner, Elizabeth: Unknown; 1635; Salem [GM 2:7:124].

Turner, Humphrey: Little Baddow, Essex; 1632; Plymouth, Scituate [GMB 1843-46; PM 466-70].

Turner, Jeffrey: Unknown; 1637; Dorchester [DChR 3, 11, 12, 152, 155; DTR 40; NEHGR 5:333, 466; SPR 1:102, 3:9; SPR Case #257 (widow Isabel)].

Turner, John: Leiden, Holland; 1620 on *Mayflower*; Plymouth [GMB 1846-47; PM 470-71].

Turner, John: Unknown; 1640; Weymouth (court appearance only) [MBCR 1:300].

Turner, Margery: Unknown; 1638; Taunton [PCR 1:103]. (She married Richard Paul.)

Turner, Michael: Unknown; 1637; Sandwich [PCR 1:149, 2:34, 40, 75, 102, 155, 3:101, 4:77, 84, 99, 101, 5:27, 94, 99, 110-11, 7:7, 8:184, 192; MQ 53:248-54, 54:44-46].

Turner, Nathaniel: Unknown; 1630; Lynn, New Haven; sailed for England in 1646 and died at sea [GMB 1847-50; WF 639-43; Abandoning 295-96].

Turner, Richard: Unknown; 1633; Boston [GMB 1850-51].

Turner, Robert: Unknown; 1633; Boston [GMB 1851-55].

Turner, Robert: Unknown; 1635 on *Blessing*; passenger list only [Hotten 93]. (This passenger is probably not the Robert Turner, shoemaker, who appeared at Boston by 1643 [GMB 1854; NEHGR 74:143; TAG 30:160-61].)

Turner, Thomas: Unknown; 1635 on *Hopewell*; passenger list only (with caveat) [GM 2:7:124-25].

Turner, Thomas: Unknown; 1637; Hingham [HiBOP 9; Lechford 306; MBCR 1:268, 315; Hingham Hist 3:270; GM 2:7:125].

Turney, Benjamin: Soulbury, Buckinghamshire; 1639; Concord, Fairfield [CoVR 3; MBCR 1:379; TAG 13:125-44, 14:224-28; Gillespie Anc 472-76; FOOF 1:618-19].

Tuttill, Henry: Unknown; 1637; Hingham [NEHGR 15:26, 121:13; HiBOP 67; MBCR 1:299, 374; NYGBR 29:124-25 (clue); Hingham Hist 3:271].

Tuttle, John: St. Albans, Hertfordshire; 1635 on *Planter*; Ipswich, Boston; removed permanently to Ireland in 1650, followed by his wife Joanna in 1654 [GM 2:7:125-35; Abandoning 296-98].

Tuttle, John: Unknown; 1640; Dover [NHPP 1:128, 40:12; GDMNH 700; NEHGR 21:132-35].

Tuttle, Richard: Ringstead, Northamptonshire; 1635 on *Planter*; Boston [GM 2:7:136-38].

Tuttle, William: Ringstead, Northamptonshire; 1635 on *Planter*; Charlestown, Boston, New Haven [GM 2:7:138-45].

Twining, William: Unknown; 1640; Yarmouth, Eastham [PCR 2:19, 7:21; MD 6:202, 17:201; Emerson-Benson 568-69].

Twisden, John: Frittenden, Kent; 1636; Scituate [NEHGR 9:285, 10:42; PCR 7:32; Gorges 130; Joseph Neal Anc 81-84; York Hist 1:151-52; TAG 86:46-53].

Twitchell, Joseph: Chesham, Buckinghamshire; 1633; Dorchester [GMB 1855-56; Kempton Anc 3:424-37; TG 23:136-39].

Twogood, John: Unknown; 1640; Massachusetts Bay (court appearance only) [MBCR 1:311].

Tylls, Peter: Unknown; 1639; Watertown (servant; court appearance only) [MBCR 1:282]. (Probably not the Peter Till who first appeared at Boston in 1651 [NEHGR 10:222; SLR 4:112; Pope 454].)

Tyndall, Arthur: Great Maplestead, Essex; 1630; Boston; returned permanently to England in 1630 [WF 643-44].

Tyng, Edward: London; 1639; Boston [WP 4:148; BTR 1:43; MBCR 1:378; SPR Case #1212; EIHC 28:149; NEHGR 3:39, 8:19; TAG 50:92-93 (clue); GDMNH 701; HAHAC 1:123].

Tyng, William: Wapping, Middlesex; 1638; Boston [BChR 23, 32; Lechford 62; HAHAC 1:30; ITR 73; MBCR 1:374; BTR 1:12, 47; SPR

Case #128; NEHGR 3:38, 63:28, 138:39-41; TAG 32:16-19, 50:92-93 (clue); NGSQ 69:115; WP 4:173].

Tynkler, Sarah: Unknown; 1635 on *Blessing*; passenger list only [GM 2:7:145]. (Probably the Sarah Tinker who married Thomas King of Scituate.)

U

Ufford, Thomas: Nazeing, Essex; 1632 on *Lyon*; Roxbury, Springfield, Wethersfield, Milford [GMB 1857-58].

Ugrove, John: Unknown; 1638; Kittery, Dover [NHPP 40:3; MPCR 1:42; GDMNH 701-2; YLR 5:102].

Underhill, John: Holland; 1630; Boston, Exeter, Stamford, New Amsterdam, Southold, Setauket, Oyster Bay [GMB 1859-65; WF 645-52].

Underwood, James: Unknown; 1637; Salem [STR 1:55; EQC 1:13, 14, 274, 360, 2:316, 3:217; MA Arch 9:22; Perley 1:444].

Underwood, Joseph: Unknown; 1637; Hingham, Watertown [HiBOP 86; Lucien Marcus Underwood, *The Underwood Families of America*, 2 volumes (Lancaster, Pennsylvania, 1913) 1:4-6].

Underwood, Marable: Unknown; 1637; passenger list only [Hotten 291].

Underwood, Martin: Great Bentley, Essex; 1634 on *Elizabeth*; Watertown [GM 2:7:147-49].

Underwood, Peter: Unknown; 1635 on *Rebecca*; passenger list only [GM 2:7:149].

Underwood, Thomas: Unknown; 1636; Hingham, Watertown [MBCR 1:205, 372; HiTR 3; HiBOP 88; Lechford 176; Lucien Marcus Underwood, *The Underwood Families of America*, 2 volumes (Lancaster, Pennsylvania, 1913), 1:2-4, 317-20].

Underwood, William: Unknown; 1639; Concord, Chelmsford [CoVR 3; Sarah Hildreth Anc 41-43; Snow-Estes 1:294-95].

Unthank, Christopher: Unknown; 1640; Providence [PrTR 15:5; Austin 211].

Upham, John: Bicton, Devon; 1635 on *Marygould*; Weymouth, Malden [GM 2:7:149-58].

Upham, Sarah: Bicton, Devon; 1635 on *Marygould*; Weymouth [GM 2:7:158; GDMNH 520]. (She married Richard Ormsby.)

Upsall, Nicholas: Dorchester, Dorset; 1630 on *Mary & John*; Dorchester, Boston [GMB 1865-69].

Upson, Stephen: Unknown; 1635 on *Increase*; unknown [GM 2:7:159-60].

Upson, Thomas: Unknown; 1639; Connecticut [CCCR 1:29; HaBOP 41; HaTR 24].

Upton, John: Unknown; 1640; Massachusetts Bay (servant; court appearance only) [Lechford 365].

Usher, Hezekiah: London; 1638; Cambridge, Boston [MBCR 1:375; NEHGR 4:183; HAHAC 1:80; Shepard 182; TAG 84:265-78].

Utting, Anne: Stradbroke, Suffolk; 1640; Dedham [DeChR 24; MBCR 1:313; SPR 1:19; NEHGR 144:131-32].

Uzell, Richard: Unknown; 1639; Massachusetts Bay, Southampton, Gravesend, Portsmouth [EQC 1:17; SoTR 1:5; RICR 1:263, 300, 349, 359, 360, 365; RITR 1:18, 22, 28, 31, 37; Austin 163].

V

Vale, Jeremiah: Unknown; 1639; Salem, Southold [EQC 1:12; SChR 12, 20, 21, 22; ELR 1:8, 11; William Penn Vail, *Moses Vail of Huntington, L.I.* (n.p. 1947) 3-4].

Vane *see also* **Fane**

Vane, Henry: London; 1635; Boston; returned permanently to England in 1637 [GM 2:7:161-71; Abandoning 350-1].

Varnum, George: Unknown; 1635; Ipswich [GM 2:7:171-72].

Vassall, William: London; 1630; Boston, Scituate; returned to England in 1646 and then moved on to Barbados where he died in 1655 or soon after [GMB 1871-75; WF 653-57; Abandoning 299-300].

Vaughan, George: Unknown; 1631; Piscataqua; returned permanently to England in 1633 [GMB 1875].

Vaughan, John: Unknown; 1633; Watertown (court appearance and land grant only) [GMB 1876-77].

Vaughan, John: Unknown; 1638; Portsmouth [RICR 1:60, 92; PoTR 5; Austin 400-1; TAG 35:72; H. Vaughan Griffin Sr., *John Vaughan Settled Newport, Rhode Island, 1638* (Rutland, Vermont, 1976)].

Vaughan, John: Unknown; 1639; Massachusetts Bay (two court appearances only) [MBCR 1:284, 285].

Veazy, Robert: Unknown; 1636; Watertown [WaBOP 3, 6, 10, 30, 57, 106, 139; WaVR 1:15; Bond 616; MLR 17:509].

Venner *see also* **Fenner**

Venner, Thomas: London; 1637; Salem, Boston; returned permanently to England in 1651 [SChR 7; STR 1:51; MBCR 1:374; EQC 1:7; NEHGR 47:437-44; M&JCH 18:145; GDMNH 705; Abandoning 300-1; ODNB].

Vere, Edward: Unknown; 1639; Wethersfield [CCCR 1:50, 81, 129, 143, 463].

Veren, Philip: Salisbury, Wiltshire; 1635 on *James*; Salem [GM 2:7:173-76].

Vermayes, Alice: Great Yarmouth, Norfolk; 1638; Salem, Boston [SChR 8; STR 1:72, 73; EQC 1:23; MBCR 1:377; Sarah Johnson Anc 37-43; Dudley Wildes Anc 119-25].

Vernam, Margaret: Unknown; 1635; Boston (church admission only) [GM 2:7:176].

Very, Bridget: Strood, Kent; 1635; Salem [TAG 60:174-76, 72:298-300].

Viall, Jillian: Unknown; 1639; Boston (church admission only) [BChR 30].

Viall, John: Unknown; 1639; Boston, Swansea [NEHGR 3:39; BTR 1:47; BChR 34; MBCR 1:379; TAG 37:153-54, 42:158-59; *Narragansett Historical Register* 3:97-107].

Vicars, William: Unknown; 1640; Wethersfield (two notarial records only) [Lechford 271, 328].

Vicary, George: Unknown; 1637; Salem, Hull [STR 1:63; TAG 17:7; NEHGR 143:338-46].

Vinall, Stephen: Unknown; 1638; Plymouth [PCR 1:116, 4:81, 7:158; ScitTR 1:302; PCLR 3:1:26, 53; PCPR 2:2:26; Lyon-Rice 586-88].

Vincent, Adrian: Unknown; 1634 on *Mary & John*; passsenger list only [GM 2:7:176].

Vincent, Humphrey: Unknown; 1634; Cambridge, Ipswich [GM 2:7:177-79].

Vincent, John: Unknown; 1636; Duxbury, Sandwich, Yarmouth [PCR 1:53, 67, 80, 150, 7:28; Harl Preslar Aldrich Jr., *George Lathrop Cooley and Clara Elizabeth Hull* (Rockport, Maine, 2001) 213-15].

Vincent, John: Unknown; 1640; New Haven [NHCR 1:50; NEHGR 81:134; FANH 1930].

Vincent, Philip: London; 1637; Connecticut (but unclear whether he ever came to New England) [MHSC 3:6:29-43, 4:1:86-90; ODNB].

Vincent, William: Unknown; 1636; Salem, Gloucester [EQC 1:4, 8; STR 1:24, 51; Charity Haley Anc 83-84; Nicholas Davis Anc 223-28].

Vincent, William: Unknown; 1638; Plymouth (court appearance only) [PCR 1:100].

Vines, Edward: Unknown; 1640; Sudbury (servant; death record only) [NEHGR 6:378].

Vines, Richard: London; 1630; Richmond Island; removed permanently to Barbados in 1646 [GMB 1877-81].

Vivion, John: Unknown; 1635; Richmond Island; returned permanently to England in 1641 [Trelawny 91, 119, 123, 192-93, 282, 283, 297, 298].

Vobes, John: Unknown; 1636; Plymouth [PCR 1:44, 66; Granberry 216-18].

Vore, Richard: Crewkerne, Somerset; 1635; Dorchester, Windsor [Grant 10; Windsor Hist 2:774; TAG 26:65-70].

W

Wad, William: Unknown; 1638; Plymouth (proposed for freemanship only) [PCR 1:117].

Wade, Jonathan: Unknown; 1632 on *Lyon*; Charlestown, Ipswich [GMB 1883-88; NEHGR 160:198; Abandoning 375].

Wade, Nicholas: Unknown; 1638; Scituate [PCR 1:110; PCPR 4:2:136-37; Stevens-Miller 1:487; Lyon-Rice 595-98].

Wade, Richard: Symondsbury, Dorset; 1635 on *Marygould*; Dorchester, Sandwich [GM 2:7:181-82].

Wade, Robert: Unknown; 1639; Hartford, Saybrook [HaTR 24; HaBOP 157; CCCR 1:46, 301, 2:523; TAG 35:22].

Wade, Samuel: London; 1639; Lynn; returned permanently to England by 1643 [MBCR 1:268; WP 4:129; EQC1:53].

Wade, Thomas: Unknown; 1635; perhaps never came to New England [GM 2:7:182-83].

Wadleigh, John: Unknown; 1636; Saco, Wells [MPCR 1:lxii; Trelawny 234; GDMNH 707; Pillsbury Anc 227-29 (clue)].

Wadsworth, Christopher: Unknown; 1632; Plymouth, Duxbury [GMB 1888-91; PM 473-76].

Wadsworth, William: Unknown; 1632 on *Lyon*; Cambridge, Hartford [GMB 1892-96].

Wainwright, Francis: Chelmsford, Essex; 1637; Ipswich [ITR 43; MHSC 3:6:41; ChTR 29; HmTR 49; Aspinwall 112-13; GDMNH 708; Hammatt 384-87; SPR Case #1954].

Wait, Gamaliel: Rigsby, Lincolnshire; 1633; Boston [GMB 1896-99].

Wait, Richard: Rigsby, Lincolnshire; 1634; Boston [GM 2:7:183-88].

Wait, Richard: Unknown; 1638; Watertown [WaVR 1:6; WaBOP 38; Bond 617-18, 960; MPR Case #23477, Case #23497].

Wait, Thomas: Rigsby, Lincolnshire; 1639; Portsmouth [PoTR 6; RICR 1:111; WP 4:135; NEHGR 69:188, 73:291-92; TAG 20:230-32, 67:193-200; Austin 404-7].

Wake, William: Unknown; 1637; Salem [STR 1:52; MBCR 1:311; EQC 1:22, 25, 26, 49, 51, 59, 137, 159, 231, 274, 283; EPR 1:181-82; Perley 1:437-38].

Wakefield, Anne: Unknown; 1638 on *Bevis*; passenger list only (servant) [Drake's Founders 61].

Wakefield, John: Unknown; 1637; Marblehead, Wells, Scarborough, Saco [STR 1:63, 74; GDMNH 708].

Wakefield, John: Unknown; 1638; Plymouth; not seen after 1640 [PCR 1:106, 122, 128, 162].

Wakefield, William: Unknown; 1638 on *Bevis*; Hampton; apparently returned permanently to England about 1649 [Drake's Founders 61; GDMNH 55, 709; HmTR 39; MBCR 1:375; EQC 1:162, 177, 202].

Wakely, James: Unknown; 1639; Hartford, Wethersfield, Providence [HaBOP 323; HaTR 32; FOOF 1:627; Ackley-Bosworth 88-90].

Wakely, Thomas: Unknown; 1634 on *Recovery*; Hingham, Gloucester, Casco [GM 2:7:188-93].

Wakeman, John: Bewdley, Worcestershire; 1640; New Haven [NHCR 1:41; NEHGR 81:134; TAG 48:208-14; FOOF 1:630-31; Brainerd Anc 290-92; Robert P. Wakeman, *Wakeman Genealogy. 1630-1899* (Meriden, Connecticut, 1900)].

Wakeman, Samuel: Bewdley, Worcestershire; 1631 on *Lyon*; Roxbury, Cambridge, Hartford; died at Providence Island 1641 [GMB 1899-91].

Walcott, William: Unknown; 1636; Salem [STR 1:19; Perley 1:272; EPR 1:25; Abel Lunt Anc 65-66].

Walden, Anne: Unknown; 1633; Boston (church admission only) [GMB 1901]. (Perhaps the same as the next.)

Walden, Anne: Unknown; 1638; Plymouth [PCR 1:103]. (She married John Smalley.)

Waldron, Richard: Alcester, Warwickshire; 1640; Dover [NHPP 1:128, 10:701, 40:3, 454; Lechford 289; GDMNH 711; NEHGR 8:78, 9:55-56, 33:99-100, 43:60-64, 258-59].

Waldron, William: Alcester, Warwickshire; 1640; Dover [NHPP 1:128, 10:701; Lechford 290; GDMNH 712; NEHGR 8:78, 9:56-57, 33:100, 43:60-64, 258-59].

Wales, Nathaniel: Calverley, Yorkshire; 1635 on *James*; Dorchester, Boston [GM 2:7:193-97].

Walford, Thomas: Unknown; 1628 (or earlier); Charlestown, Piscataqua [GMB 1902-6; Emerson W. Baker, *The Devil of Great Island* (New York 2007)].

Walgrave, Mr.: Unknown; 1639; Sudbury (land grant only) [MBCR 1:292].

Walker, Augustine: Unknown; 1638; Charlestown [ChBOP 43; ChChR 10, 49; ChTR 46; MBCR 1:378; SPR 2:8; NEHGR 4:270; Rodgers 1:178-83; Wyman 990].

Walker, Dorcas: Unknown; 1640; Roxbury (death record only) [NEHGR 6:377; GMB 1907-8].

Walker, James: London; 1635 on *Elizabeth*; Plymouth, Taunton [GM 2:7:197-205].

Walker, John: Unknown; 1633; Roxbury, Boston, Portsmouth [GMB 1906-8; Austin 214].

Walker, John: Unknown; 1640; New Haven [NHCR 1:51, 94, 326, 2:357; NHChR 1; FANH 1931].

Walker, Margery: Dover, Kent; 1637; passenger list only (servant) [NEHGR 75:222].

Walker, Persis: Unknown; 1639; Salem (admission to church [annotated "removed"] and baptism of two children only) [SChR 9, 17; GM 2:7:206]. (Possibly wife of Richard Walker [Perley 1:390].)

Walker, Richard: Unknown; 1633; Lynn, Reading, Boston [GMB 1908-12].

Walker, Richard: Unknown; 1635 on *Elizabeth*; passenger list only [GM 2:7:206].

Walker, Richard: Marlborough, Wiltshire; 1635 on *James*; passenger list only (but possibly one of the following two men) [GM 2:7:205-6].

Walker, Richard: Unknown; 1635; Boston [BTR 1:5, 9; BChR 22; WJ 2:427; GMB 2:1010-11; GM 2:7:205-6].

Walker, Richard: Unknown; 1636; Salem; not seen after 1639 [STR 1:24, 50, 103; EQC 7:125; MBCR 1:253; MA Arch 113:182; GM 2:7:206]. (Possibly the "brother Walker" of Salem in 1637 [Fiske Notebook 239-42]; William Walker of Salem is a less likely candidate for this record.)

Walker, Robert: Manchester, Lancashire; 1632; Boston [GMB 1912-15].

Walker, Samuel: Unknown; 1638; Exeter; not seen after 1644 [NHPP 1:133, 40:12; NEHGR 8:77; Exeter Hist 436; GDMNH 714].

Walker, Sarah: London; 1635 on *Elizabeth*; Plymouth [GM 2:7:207]. (She married John Tisdale.)

Walker, William: Unknown; 1635 on *Elizabeth*; passenger list only [GM 2:7:207].

Walker, William: Unknown; 1636; Hingham (land grant only) [HiBOP 52].

Walker, William: Norwich, Norfolk; 1636; Salem; not seen after 1639 [STR 1:39; Lechford 230].

Walker, William: Unknown; 1637 on *Mary Anne*; passenger list only (servant) [Hotten 294].

Wall, James: Witham, Essex; 1630; Massachusetts Bay; returned permanently to England in 1630 [WF 659-60].

Wall, James: Stratford, Suffolk; 1634 on *Pied Cow*; Kittery, Exeter, Dover, Hampton [MA Arch 3:437, 444; GM 2:2:34; TAG 80:1-10, 102-16, 201-7].

Wall, Joan: Unknown; 1635 on *Abigail*; passenger list only [GM 2:7:207-8].

Wall, John: Unknown; 1639; Strawberry Bank (signed land agreement only) [NHPP 1:113].

Wallen, Ralph: Unknown; 1623 on *Anne*; Plymouth [GMB 1915-16; PM 476-77; TAG 73:91-100].

Waller, Matthew: London; 1636; Salem, Providence, New London [STR 1:33, 101; EQC 1:26; PrTR 15:5; TAG 33:95-98, 68:171-72; Angell Anc 514-17].

Wallington (or Wallingford) Nicholas: Unknown; 1638 on *Confidence*; Newbury, Bradford [Drake's Founders 59; EQC 1:406, 8:184, 358; Waters 146-47 (clue); Rowley Fam 400-1; GDMNH 715].

Wallis, Ann: Unknown; 1638; Roxbury (servant; church admission only) [RChR 84].

Wallis, Henry: Unknown; 1640; Plymouth (disposal of estate only) [PCR 2:12, 12:73].

Wallis, Ralph: Unknown; 1635 on *Abigail*; passenger list only (with caveat) [GM 2:7:208].

Wallis, Robert: Unknown; 1638; Ipswich [ITR 40, 46, 58; EQC 1:125, 368; EPR 2:387; Hammatt Papers 389-91].

Wallis, Thomas: Unknown; 1639; Plymouth, Massachusetts Bay; not seen after 1643 [PCR 12:50-51, 59, 63, 76-77; PCPR 1:45; Lechford 377-78; MBCR 2:292].

Walston, Jane: Unknown; 1635 on *Truelove*; passenger list only [GM 2:7:208-9].

Walter, James: Unknown; 1636; Plymouth (court appearance only) [PCR 7:5].

Waltham, Henry: Unknown; 1635; Weymouth [GM 2:7:209-16].

Walton, George: Unknown; 1638; Massachusetts Bay [MBCR 1:245; NHPP 1:133, 40:6; Lydia Harmon Anc 81-108; NHGR 27:141-48; Emerson W. Baker, *The Devil of Great Island* (New York 2007)].

Walton, Henry: Unknown; 1638; Lynn, Portsmouth, Boston [EQC 2:270; SoTR 1:1; SLR 1:55; WP 4:190, 284; Aspinwall 21; NEHGR 9:166].

Walton, William: Seaton, Devon; 1635; Hingham, Marblehead [GM 2:7:216-23]. (See William Malton.)

Wange, Goodman: Unknown; 1639; Massachusetts Bay (mention in probate inventory only) [SPR 2:1].

Wannerton, Thomas: Unknown; 1633; Piscataqua [GMB 1916-18].

Ward, Alice: Unknown; 1640; Salem (church admission only) [SChR 10].

Ward, Andrew: Unknown; 1633; Watertown, Wethersfield, Stamford, Fairfield [GMB 1918-21].

Ward, Anne: Ormesby, St. Margaret, Norfolk; 1637 on *John & Dorothy* or *Rose*; Salem [Hotten 291 (as "Anne Wadd")]. (She married Edward Colcord [NEHGR 141:120-21].)

Ward, Benjamin: Stepney, Middlesex; 1635; Boston [GM 2:7:223-28].

Ward, Elizabeth: Unknown; 1635 on *Increase*; passenger list only [GM 2:7:228-29].

Ward, Elizabeth: Unknown; 1638; Scituate [PCR 1:100]. (She married Gowen White.)

Ward, Esther: Unknown; 1633; Boston, Charlestown [GMB 1921]. (She married Richard Kettle.)

Ward, George: Unknown; 1640; New Haven, Branford [NHCR 1:93, 184-85, 329-33; TAG 12:100; Clara Pierce Olson Overbo, *Ancestors & Descendants of Clark Proctor Nichols and Sarah (Sally) Stoughton* (Decorah, Iowa, 2002) 221-28 (dubious English origin)].

Ward, John: Unknown; 1640; Salem [EQC 1:27; STR 1:112; WJ 2:72]. (Possibly husband of Alice Ward of Salem.)

Ward, Joyce: Stretton, Rutland; 1640; Wethersfield [CCCR 1:451-53; Manwaring 1:38-39; NHCR 2:427; NYGBR 44:120, 49:262-64; Keeler-Wood 242-44].

Ward, Lawrence: Unknown; 1640; New Haven, Branford, Newark [NHCR 1:93, 329-33; *Collections of the New Jersey Historical Society*, Volume VI, Supplement (Newark, New Jersey, 1866) 136].

Ward, Marmaduke: Unknown; 1639; Newport [RICR 1:92, 108, 110, 301; EQC 1:314; RICR (MS) 37, 39, 40; RITR 2:58, 83, 3:1, 114].

Ward, Miles: Unknown; 1639; Salem [SChR 9, 10; STR 1:106; EQC 1:28, 123; MBCR 1:378; EPR 1:118-19; Perley 1:101].

Ward, Nathaniel: Stondon Massey, Essex: 1634; Ipswich; returned permanently to England in the winter of 1646-7 [GM 2:7:229-35; Abandoning 304-7].

Ward, Nathaniel: Little Wratting, Suffolk; 1639; Hartford, Hadley [HaBOP 296; HaTR 10; TAG 83:13-18; TG 28:137-54].

Ward, Samuel: Unknown; 1637; Hingham, Hull, Charlestown [MBCR 1:220, 372; HiBOP 87; MPR Case #23742; NEHGR 7:57, 121:11, 143:346-49; Wyman 993-94].

Ward, Thomas: Unknown; 1630; Mystic [GMB 1921; WF 661].

Ward, Thomas: Unknown; 1638; Dedham, Hampton [DeTR 1:50; GDMNH 55; HmTR 44, 719; NHPP 31:217-19; NEHGR 141:114-21 (clue)].

Ward, William: Unknown; 1639; Sudbury, Marlborough [SuTR 7; MPR Case # 23758; Charles Martyn, *The William Ward Genealogy* (New York 1925)].

Warden, Jane: Unknown; 1635; Plymouth [GM 2:7:236].

Wardwell, Thomas: Alford, Lincolnshire; 1634; Boston, Exeter [GM 2:7:236-39; TEG 21:85-88; TMG 18:147-49].

Wardwell, William: Alford, Lincolnshire; 1633; Boston, Exeter, Wells [GMB 1922-24; RIR 16:69-71].

Ware, Mary: Unknown; 1640; Newbury [WP 4:168]. (She married William White of Newbury [GM 2:7:346-48].)

Ware, Rebecca: Unknown; 1640; Dedham [WP 4:293]. (She married Thomas Paine.)

Ware, William: Unknown; 1639; Dorchester, Boston [Lechford 343; HAHAC 1:134; SPR Case #180; EIHC 28:145 (clue)].

Warham, John: Exeter, Devon; 1630 on *Mary & John*; Dorchester, Windsor [GMB 1925-28; M&JCH 25:68-69. 26:60, 27:84-85, 116-26].

Warner, Andrew: Hatfield Broadoak, Essex; 1633; Cambridge, Hartford, Farmington, Hadley [GMB 1928-32].

Warner, John: Unknown; 1635 on *Increase*; Hartford, Farmington [GM 2:7:239-43].

Warner, John: Unknown; 1636; Watertown (land grant only) [WaBOP 8].

Warner, John: Unknown; 1637; Providence, Warwick; returned permanently to England in 1652 [PrTR 1:1, 15:2; MBCR 3:274; Austin 408].

Warner, John: Unknown; 1639; Dorchester (mention in letter only) [WP 4:132].

Warner, Thomas: Unknown; 1639; Massachusetts Bay (two court appearances and one deposition only) [MBCR 1:270; WP 4:128, 165].

Warner, William: Boxted, Essex; 1635; Ipswich [GM 2:7:243-47].

Warren, Abraham: Unknown; 1635; Salem [GM 2:7:247-50].

Warren, Abraham: Unknown; 1640; Boston (land grant only) [BTR 1:58].

Warren, Arthur: Unknown; 1637; Weymouth [MBCR 1:219; RCA 2:116; SPR Case #2625; Weymouth Hist 4:724; Warren Woden Foster, *Some Descendants of Arthur Warren of Weymouth, Massachusetts Bay Colony* (Washington DC 1911)].

Warren, John: Nayland, Suffolk; 1630; Watertown [GMB 1932-34; WF 661-65].

Warren, Ralph: Unknown; 1638; Marblehead (land grant and court appearance only) [STR 1:74; MBCR 1:268].

Warren, Richard: London; 1620 on *Mayflower*; Plymouth [GMB 1935-37; PM 477-80].

Warren, Thomas: Unknown; 1639; Salem (witness to will only) [EPR 1:12; EQC 1:18].

Warrener, William: Unknown; 1639; Springfield [SpVR 9, 19; Pynchon 206; Brady Anc 372-77; Edwin Warriner, *The Warriner Family of New England Origin* (Albany, New York, 1899)].

Warwick, Henry: Unknown; 1636; Saco [MPCR 1:lxii, 7, 61; Trelawny 234; GDMNH 706-7].

Washburn, John: Bengeworth, Worcestershire; 1632; Plymouth, Duxbury [GMB 1937-39; PM 480-83].

Wason, Phebe: Unknown; 1638; Boston (church admission only) [BChR 24].

Waterbury, William: Sudbury, Suffolk; 1630; Boston [GMB 1939-40; WF 665-67].

Waterhouse, Jacob: Unknown; 1639; Wethersfield, New London [CCCR 1:40; WetLR 1:127; NEHGR 104:186-89, 108:36-38, 162:85-90].

Waterhouse, Thomas: Coddenham, Suffolk; 1639; Dorchester; returned permanently to England by 1643 [DTR 1:40; DChR 4, 5; MBCR 1:377; NEHGR 88:204; Abandoning 308-9].

Waterman, John: Unknown; 1639 on *Jonathon*; Sudbury (passenger list and land grant only) [NEHGR 32:410; SuTR 10].

Waterman, Richard: Unknown; 1629; Salem, Providence, Warwick [GMB 1941-43; WF 667-71].

Waterman, Robert: Unknown; 1638; Marshfield [PCR 1:107, 7:14, 12:42; WP 4:262; MaVR; MaTR 1:3; PCPR 1:118; MD 11:100-4; Moore Anc 572-78; Waterman Gen].

Waterman, Thomas: Unknown, 1640, Roxbury [SPR Case #774; SPR 6:415, 9:124 (wife Margaret); Waterman Gen 11-14; NEHGR 146:267].

Waters, John: Nayland, Suffolk; 1630; Boston [GMB 1943-44; WF 671-72].

Waters, Lawrence: Unknown; 1635; Watertown, Lancaster, Charlestown [GM 2:7:250-57].

Waters, Matthew: Unknown; 1635; Boston [GM 2:7:257-58].

Waters, Richard: Stepney, Middlesex; 1636; Salem [STR 1:24; SChR 11; MBCR 1:375; Waters 1340-43; TAG 81:172-91; NHGR 13:145-51; Jeanne Waters Strong, *One Waters Family* (Los Altos Hills, California, 1980)].

Wathen, George: Bristol; 1638; Lynn, Salem [EQC 1:19, 2:270; EPR 1:34; STR 1:110; SChR 11; NEHGR 148:67-78, 154:325-52].

Watkins, John: Unknown; 1640; Salem [EPR 1:13; EQC 1:27].

Watson, Elizabeth: Unknown; 1638; Plymouth [PCR 1:102, 12:32]. (She may have married John Gray of Fairfield.)

Watson, George: Unknown; 1631; Penobscot, Plymouth [GMB 1944-47; PM 483-87].

Watson, John: Unknown; 1632 on *Lyon*; Roxbury [GMB 1947-49].

Watson, Thomas: Unknown; 1636; Salem [STR 1:24, 79; SChR 6, 9; MBCR 1:377; Hoyt 1017].

Watson, Thomas: Unknown; 1638; Duxbury; returned permanently to England in 1639 [PCR 1:102, 12:32; Lechford 166-67, 169-70, 194, 199].

Watson Challis, Philip: Chelmsford, Essex; 1636; Ipswich, Salisbury [ITR 19; WP 4:108; SyTR 6; TAG 79:57-61, 82:261-66].

Wattels, Richard: Unknown; 1637; Ipswich [ITR 25; Ipswich Hist 1:361].

Wattlin, Richard: Unknown; 1634 on *Francis*; passenger list only [GM 2:7:258].

Watts, Henry: London; 1631; Saco, Scarborough [GMB 1949-51].

Watts, Richard: Unknown; 1639; Hartford [HaBOP 345; TAG 22:159-61; Manwaring 1:160-61, 247-48; Stevens-Miller Anc 335-37; Moore Anc 579-83].

Watts, William: Unknown; 1640; Hartford; returned permanently to England by 1668 [HaTR 47; HaBOP 399; Manwaring 1:248].

Way, George: Dorchester, Dorset; 1637; Dorchester (land grant only) [DTR 27; GDMNH 725; TAG 37:197-99, 61:253]. (Almost certainly never came to New England.)

Way, Henry: Bridport, Dorset; 1630; Dorchester [GMB 1951-53; M&JCH 27:85].

Way, Robert: Unknown; 1634; Massachusetts Bay (servant; not seen after 1636) [MBCR 1:122, 123, 163-64].

Weare, Nathaniel: Unknown; 1637; Newbury, Nantucket [NeTR 21; Farr Anc 311-13; Putnam's Mag 6:245-51; GDMNH 726].

Weare, Peter: Unknown; 1640; Dover, York [MPCR 1:42 (as "Peter Wyer"), 67; NHPP 40:3; GDMNH 727; NEHGR 39:184, 42:312 (clue), 55:56; Stevens-Miller Anc 2:77-94].

Weaver, Clement: Glastonbury, Somerset; 1639; Weymouth, Newport [MBCR 1:297; Joseph Neal Anc 128; Weymouth Hist 4:725; M&JCH 25:69-70; Lucius E. Weaver, *History and Genealogy of a Branch of the Weaver Family* (Rochester, New York, 1928)].

Weaver, Mr.: Unknown; 1630; Massachusetts Bay (court appearance only) [GMB 1953, 2085; WF 672].

Webb, Elizabeth: Unknown; 1631; Boston (church admission only) [GMB 1953].

Webb, George: Unknown; 1640; Dover [NHPP 10:701, 40:11; GDMNH 727-28].

Webb, Henry: Salisbury, Wiltshire; 1637; Boston [NGSQ 71:176; BTR 1:20, 31; BChR 23; MBCR 1:247, 375; Lechford 412; WP 4:128; SPR Case #246; NEHGR 10:177-80; GDMNH 728; Giles Memorial 497-98; W. P. W. Phillimore, *Wiltshire Parish Registers* 13:63, 67].

Webb, Henry: Unknown; 1640; Saco [MPCR 1:58; GDMNH 728].

Webb, John: Unknown; 1633; Roxbury, Boston [GMB 1954; MBCR 1:105, 372; SPR 2:1].

Webb, Mr.: Unknown; 1636; Salem (two land grants only) [STR 1:25, 103].

Webb, Richard: Unknown; 1632; Cambridge, Hartford, Norwalk [GMB 1954-56].

Webb, Richard: Unknown; 1640; Weymouth [Weymouth Hist 4:725; NEHGR 9:138-39; TAG 19:208-9].

Webb, William: Unknown; 1635; Roxbury, Boston [GM 2:7:258-60].

Webster, John: Unknown; 1634; Ipswich [GM 2:7:261-68].

Webster, John: Cossington, Leicestershire; 1636; Hartford [CCCR 1:9; HaBOP 16; Moore Anc 584-606; NYGBR 62:232-34; TAG 24:197-214, 29:80-86; William Holcomb Webster and Melville Reuben Webster, *History and Genealogy of the Gov. John Webster Family of Connecticut* (Rochester, New York, 1915)].

Webster, John: Unknown; 1637; Salem, Strawberry Bank [STR 1:65; EQC 1:13, 19; GDMNH 730-31; GM 2:7:264-65; Gen Mag 5:196-97].

Wedgewood, John: Unknown; 1637; Ipswich, Hampton [ITR 25; WP 3:454; HmTR 45; MBCR 1:269; Lechford 181; GDMNH 55, 731-32; NHPP 31:26-27; Essex Ant 1:179, 2:82].

Weed, Jonas: Unknown; 1630; Watertown, Wethersfield, Stamford [GMB 1956-59; WF 672-76].

Weeden, ____: Unknown; 1638; Dedham (land grant only) [DeTR 1:48].

Weeden, Edward: Unknown; 1635 on *Susan & Ellen*; Boston [GM 2:7:268-73].

Weedon, James: Chesham, Buckinghamshire; 1638 on *Martin*; Newport [Savage 1:105; TG 11:111; Austin 414-17; NEHGR 76:115-29, 78:147-53, 108:87-88].

Weekes, Francis: Unknown; 1635; Dorchester, Providence, Gravesend, Hempstead, Oyster Bay [GM 2:7:273-80].

Weeks, George: Seaton, Devon; 1637; Dorchester [DTR 1:28; DChR 5; MBCR 1:377; SPR Case #105; TAG 9:78-79, 23:82; Stevens-Miller Anc 1:271-75; NEHGR 156:150-52].

Weeks, Oliver: Unknown; 1633; Richmond Island; not seen after 1643 [GMB 1959-60].

Weeks, Thomas: Unknown; 1636; Charlestown, Salem [ChTR 23; ChChR 9; EQC 1:29; STR 1:86; SChR 8; EPR 1:241-43; Perley 2:65].

Weillust, Jost: Unknown; 1630; Massachusetts Bay; returned permanently to "his own country" in 1632 [GMB 1960-61].

Welch, Thomas: Bishops Stortford, Hertfordshire; 1639; Milford [MiChR 1; MiTR 2; NHCR 1:31; NEHGR 54:352; Milford Fam 793].

Weld, Daniel: Sudbury, Suffolk; 1639; Braintree, Roxbury [BTR 1:49; MBCR 1:378; NEHGR 3:248; TAG 55:145-48; Parker-Ruggles 502-4].

Weld, Joseph: Sudbury, Suffolk; 1635; Roxbury [GM 2:7:280-88].

Weld, Thomas: Terling, Essex; 1632 on *William & Francis*; Roxbury; returned permanently to England in 1641 [GMB 1961-63; Abandoning 310-13].

Welden, Robert: Unknown; 1630; Charlestown [GMB 1964-65; WF 676-77].

Weller, Richard: Unknown; 1640; Windsor [Grant 70; CTVR 39; WiLR 1:67; Moore Anc 606-17; TAG 26:248-56, 27:26-31, 192, 34:140-54, 36:125, 56:76-77].

Welles, Thomas: Tidmington, Worcestershire; 1635; Cambridge, Hartford, Wethersfield [GM 2:7:288-92; TAG 56:228-29; Barbara Jean Mathews, *The Descendants of Gov.Thomas Welles of Connecticut and His Wife, Alice Tomes*, Volume 1, second edition (Wethersfield, Connecticut, 2013)].

Wellington, Roger: Unknown; 1636; Watertown [WaBOP 5, 51, 136; WaVR 1:6; WJ 2:424; NEHGR 102:97; Bond 627-37, 963; McCormick-Hamilton 1067-70].

Wellman, William: Unknown; 1639; Salem (court appearance only) [EQC 1:17].

Wells, Ann: Unknown; 1635 on *Planter*; passenger list only [GM 2:7:292].

Wells, Ann: Unknown; 1635 on *Susan & Ellen*; passenger list only [GM 2:7:293].

Wells, Isaac: Unknown; 1638; Scituate [PCR 1:110; PCPR 3:1:99; MD 25:89].

Wells, Lydia: Sandwich, Kent; 1635 on *Hercules*; passenger list only (with caveat) [GM 2:7:293].

Wells, Richard: Unknown; 1638; Lynn, Salisbury [EQC 2:270; MBCR 1:375; SyTR 3, 7; EPR 2:296-97; Hoyt 348].

Wells, Thomas: Unknown; 1635 on *Susan & Ellen*; Ipswich [GM 2:7:294-300].

Welsh, Jacob: Unknown; 1635 on *Rebecca*; passenger list only [GM 2:7:300].

Wentworth, William: Alford, Lincolnshire; 1638; Exeter, Wells, Dover [NHPP 1:132; GDMNH 738-39; TG 7-8:127-31; NEHGR 22:120-39; John Wentworth, *The Wentworth Genealogy: English and American*, three volumes (Boston 1878)].

West, Francis: Unknown; 1640; Duxbury [PCR 1:164; DuTR 1; NEHGR 60:142; Martha's Vineyard Hist 2:Tisbury:25-27, 3:500-8].

West, John: Unknown; 1635 on *Abigail*; passenger list only (with caveat) [GM 2:7:301].

West, John: Unknown; 1636; Saco, Wells [MPCR 1:6, 43; NHPP 40:4; Trelawny 210; Charity Haley Anc 17-19; GDMNH 740].

West, Lancelot: Unknown; 1639; Lynn (two court appearances only) [EQC 1:12, 24].

West, Matthew: Unknown; 1636; Lynn, Newport [MBCR 1:372; EQC 2:270; Austin 218-19; Mary Elizabeth Sinnott, *Annals of the Sinnott, Rogers, Coffin, Corlies, Reeves, Bodine and Allied Families* (Philadelphia, Pennsylvania, 1905) 225-35].

West, Thomas: Unknown; 1634 on *Mary & John*; passenger list only (with caveat) [GM 2:7:301-2].

West, Thomas: Unknown; 1638; Salem; not seen after 1644 [STR 1:98; GM 2:7:301-2].

West, Twiford: Unknown; 1635 on *Hopewell*; Plymouth, Marshfield, Rowley, Ipswich [GM 2:7:303-9].

Westall, John: Unknown; 1640; Dover; not seen after 1642 [NHPP 10:701; GDMNH 49, 741]. (See Wethersfield Hist 2:752.)

Westcott, Richard: Unknown; 1637; Wethersfield, Fairfield [CCCR 1:40, 41; WetLR 1:168; FOOF 1:660].

Westcott, Stukeley: Yeovil, Somerset; 1636; Salem, Providence, Warwick [EQC 1:4; STR 1:20; MBCR 1:223; Perley 1:271; PrTR 15:5; Austin 416-21; TAG 45:157; M&JCH 25:70, 103, 26:60-61; Roscoe L. Whitman, *History and Genealogy of the Ancestors and Some Descendants of Stukely Westcott*, two volumes (n.p. 1932, 1939)].

Westgate, John: Unknown; 1640; Boston; returned permanently to England by 1645 [BChR 31, 49; HAHAC 1:118; Abandoning 313-14].

Westly, William: Unknown; 1639; Hartford [HaTR 24; HaBOP 343; CCCR 1:139; Savage 4:489].

Weston, Edmond: Unknown; 1635 on *Elizabeth & Ann*; Duxbury [GM 2:7:309-12].

Weston, Francis: Unknown; 1632; Plymouth, Salem, Providence, Warwick [GMB 1965-67; PM 487-90].

Weston, Matthew: Unknown; 1636; Massachusetts Bay (court appearance only) [EQC 1:4]. (Perhaps intended for Matthew West.)

Weston, Thomas: London; 1623; Weymouth; removed in 1624 to Virginia [GMB 1967-70; PM 490-93; MHSP 54:165-78; ODNB].

Westwood, William: Essex; 1634 on *Francis*; Cambridge, Hartford, Hadley [GM 2:7:312-17].

Wetherell, John: Unknown; 1639; Sudbury, Watertown [SuTR 4; WaBOP 45; MBCR 1:316 (as "John Witheredge"); Rodgers 3:117-18; Bond 637].

Wetherell, William: Maidstone, Kent; 1635 on *Hercules*; Cambridge, Charlestown, Duxbury, Scituate [GM 2:7:318-23].

Weymouth, Jonathan: Unknown; 1639; Massachusetts Bay [SPR 1:22; Lechford 216, 223-24].

Wheat, Jane: Unknown; 1636; Salem (servant; court appearance only) [EQC 1:5].

Wheat, Joshua: Unknown; 1635 on *Elizabeth*; Concord; returned permanently to England in 1640 or 1641 [GM 2:7:323-24].

Wheat, Moses: Unknown; 1640; Concord [CoVR 3; MPR Case #24203; GM 2:7:323-24; Silas C. Wheat, *Wheat Genealogy: A History of the Wheat Family in America* (Brooklyn, New York, 1903)].

Wheatley, Gabriel: Unknown; 1637; Watertown [SPR 1:34; Bond 638].

Wheaton, Robert: Unknown; 1636; Salem [STR 1:33, 74, 128; ReTR 1:2; William B. Saxbe Jr., *Richard Bowen (1594?-1675), of Rehoboth, Massachusetts, and His Descendants* (Williamstown, Massachusetts, 2011) 17-20; TAG 76:263-78, 80:68-78].

Wheeler, Ephraim: Cranfield, Bedfordshire; 1638; Concord, Fairfield [NYGBR 2:8; MBCR 1:375; Lechford 305; CoVR 3; TAG 12:5, 14:1-4, 28:259; FOOF 1:665-66; Ackley-Bosworth 52-56; Albert Gallatin Wheeler Jr., *History of the Wheeler Family in America* (Boston 1914) 491].

Wheeler, George: Cranfield, Bedfordshire; 1639; Concord [CoVR 3; MBCR 1:379; TAG 14:131-32; Kempton Anc 3:438-47; GMC50 495-97; Albert Gallatin Wheeler Jr., *History of the Wheeler Family in America* (Boston 1914) 17-20].

Wheeler, Isaac: Unknown; 1639; Charlestown [ChTR 47; ChChR 10; NEHGR 4:270; Wyman 1012; Parker-Ruggles 376-77; TAG 12:6 (clue); Albert Gallatin Wheeler Jr., *History of the Wheeler Family in America* (Boston 1914) 513-16].

Wheeler, John: Unknown; 1634 on *Mary & John*; passenger list only [GM 2:7:324].

Wheeler, John: Salisbury, Wiltshire; 1639; Salisbury, Newbury [SyTr 10; EPR 2:200-1; Annis Spear Anc 133-35; Drake's Founders 59 (son David); EIHC 44:290-92; Rowley Fam 403; Pillsbury Anc 1107-9].

Wheeler, Joseph: Cranfield, Bedfordshire; 1639; Concord [CoVR 3; MBCR 1:377; SPR 1:30; TAG 12:5, 14:1-4, 28:259; Ackley-Bosworth 52-53].

Wheeler, Moses: Unknown; 1640; New Haven, Stratford [NHCR 1:93; FOOF 1:676-77; Goodwin-Morgan 2:91-97; Albert Gallatin Wheeler Jr., *History of the Wheeler Family in America* (Boston 1914) 412; McCormick-Hamilton 1073-83].

Wheeler, Obadiah: Cranfield, Bedfordshire; 1640; Concord [CoVR 3; MBCR 1:379; Rodgers 3:61-65; TAG 12:4-6; Albert Gallatin Wheeler Jr., *History of the Wheeler Family in America* (Boston 1914) 350-53].

Wheeler, Thomas: Reading, Berkshire; 1635 on *James*; passenger list only (with caveat) [GM 2:7:324-26].

Wheeler, Thomas: Unknown; 1636; Boston [BTR 1:14, 43; BChR 21; SPR 1:101, 2:1, 155; WP 4:69, 124; MBCR 1:212, 373; NEHGR 3:39; Parker-Ruggles 465; GM 2:7:325-26; Albert Gallatin Wheeler Jr., *History of the Wheeler Family in America* (Boston 1914) 485-90].

Wheeler, Thomas: Unknown; 1639; Milford [MiTR 2; MiChR 1; FOOF 1:679-80; GM 2:7:324-26].

Wheeler, Thomas Sr.: Cranfield, Bedfordshire; 1640; Concord, Fairfield [NYGBR 2:8; FOOF 1:662-63; TAG 12:5-6, 14:1-4, 27:35-40, 119-25, 28:139-48, 257-59; GMC50 501-3].

Wheeler, Thomas Jr.: Cranfield, Bedfordshire; 1640; Concord, Fairfield, Stratford, Derby [NYGBR 2:8; FOOF 1:663-65; TAG 12:4-17, 14:1-4].

Wheeler, Timothy: Cranfield, Bedfordshire; 1639; Concord, Charlestown [NYGBR 2:8; MBCR 1:377; CoVR 3; WaBOP 145; SPR Case #1592; TAG 12:5, 14:1-4, 28:259; Wyman 1012-13; Ackley-Bosworth 52; Albert Gallatin Wheeler Jr., *History of the Wheeler Family in America* (Boston 1914) 134-42].

Wheelock, Ralph: Eccles, Norfolk; 1637; Dedham, Medfield [DeTR 1:32; DeChR 5; DeVR 1; MBCR 1:374; SPR Case #1339; Parker-Ruggles 459; NGSQ 74:3-6; Medfield Hist 506-7; NEHGR 152:3-23, 311-12].

Wheelwright, John: Bilsby, Lincolnshire; 1636; Boston [BChR 21; WJ 1:239-40; WP 3:392; NEHGR 22:83, 24:77, 68:73-77, 74:51-53; GDMNH 743-44; NEQ 64:22-45; ODNB].

Whelden, Gabriel: Basford, Nottinghamshire; 1638; Dedham, Yarmouth, Malden [PCR 1:95, 134; Lechford 102; ELR 1:24v; Rodgers 1:146-48; TAG 15:114-15, 48:4-11; NEHGR 163:253-61].

Whipple, John: Unknown; 1632; Dorchester, Providence [GMB 1970-74].

Whipple, John: Bocking, Essex; 1638; Ipswich [ITR 36; EQC 1:28; MBCR 1:295, 376; NEHGR 160:17-29; TG 20:191; Blaine Whipple, *History and Genealogy of "Elder" John Whipple of Ipswich, Massachusetts* (Victoria, British Columbia, 2003)].

Whipple, Matthew: Bocking, Essex; 1638; Ipswich [ITR 36; TG 20:191-217; Pillsbury Anc 43-48; Blaine Whipple, *15 Generations of Whipples: Descendants of Matthew Whipple of Ipswich, Massachusetts, Abt 1590-1647*, four volumes (Baltimore, Maryland, 2007)].

Whiston, John: Unknown; 1632 on *William & Francis*; Scituate [GMB 1974-76; PM 493-95].

Whitcomb, John: Taunton, Somerset; 1635 on *Hopewell*; Dorchester, Scituate, Lancaster [GM 2:7:326-31].

White, Anthony: Unknown; 1634 on *Francis*; Sudbury, Watertown [GM 2:7:332-34].

White, Charity: Unknown; 1640; Boston [BChR 34; NEHGR 10:265; SPR Case #256].

White, Daniel: Unknown; 1635; Massachusetts Bay (court appearance only) [GM 2:7:334].

White, Edie: Unknown; 1639; Weymouth (servant; court appearance only) [WP 4:232-33].

White, Edmond: London; 1637; Watertown [MBCR 1:232, 311; Lechford 425-27, 432; WaBOP 10, 47, 132-33]. (Perhaps never came to New England.)

White, Edward: Cranbrook, Kent; 1635 on *Abigail*; Dorchester [GM 2:7:335-36].

White, Emanuel: Unknown; 1636; Watertown, Yarmouth [WaBOP 4, 78; WJ 4:424; PCR 2:9, 7:20, 8:176, 185, 194, 200; TAG 17:205].

White, Francis: Unknown; 1635 on *Elizabeth*; passenger list only [GM 2:7:337].

White, Gowen: West Quantoxhead, Somerset; 1638; Scituate [PCR 1:100, 2:16; NEHGR 9:286; MD 16:126; Joseph Neal Anc 35-40; TAG 17:198-99].

White, James: Unknown; 1633; Marblehead (court appearance only) [GMB 1976].

White, John: Messing, Essex; 1632 on *Lyon*; Cambridge, Hartford, Hadley [GMB 1976-79].

White, John: Unknown; 1636; Massachusetts Bay [WJ 2:423; MBCR 1:177, 268, 298, 307, 317]. (These records do not necessarily pertain to the same man, but they cannot be confidently assigned to any of the other John Whites who had arrived by 1640.)

White, John: Unknown; 1638; Lynn, Southampton [EQC 2:270; SoTR 2:22-24; Miner Anc 187-88].

White, John: Unknown; 1639; Piscataqua [MPCR 1:42; GDMNH 746].

White, John: South Petherton, Somerset; 1639; Salem, Wenham, Lancaster [STR 1:90; EQC 1:16, 21; Rodgers 3:202-5; NEHGR 162:93-97; Essex Ant 1:182; Almira Larkin White, *Genealogy of the Descendants of John White of Wenham and Lancaster, Massachusetts*, four volumes (Haverhill, Massachusetts, 1900-1909) 4:15-26, 45-59; M&JCH 18:153-56 (for South Petherton baptisms)].

White, Nicholas: Unknown; 1639; Richmond Island [Trelawny 164, 182; GDMNH 748].

White, Philip: Unknown; 1637; Piscataqua, not seen after 1640 [WJ 2:426; Lechford 232, 330; GDMNH 748].

White, Richard: Unknown; 1635 on *Elizabeth & Ann*; Charlestown, Sudbury [GM 2:7:337-38].

White, Robert: Unknown; 1635; Winnissimmet (probate record only) [GM 2:7:338].

White, Sarah: Unknown; 1639; Yarmouth [PCR 1:134]. (She married Hugh Norman.)

✓ **White, Thomas:** Unknown; 1635; Weymouth [GM 2:7:339-42].

White, Thomas: Unknown; 1639; Cambridge (purchase and sale of land only) [CaBOP 60, 65]. (Possibly the same as the next.)

White, Thomas: Unknown; 1639; Sudbury, Charlestown [SuTR 4; SLR 1:44, 47; MBCR 1:377; Rodgers 2:224-29; Wyman 1015].

✓ **White, William:** Leiden, Holland; 1620 on *Mayflower*; Plymouth [GMB 980-81; PM 495-96; TAG 61:207-12].

White, William: Unknown; 1634 on *Mary & John*; Ipswich [GM 2:7:342-50].

White, William: Unknown; 1635 on *Increase*; passenger list only [GM 2:7:351].

✓ **White, William:** Unknown; 1639; Newbury, Haverhill [WP 4:168; HvBOP 12; NLR 2:209; GM 2:7:345-50].

Whitefield, Henry: Ockley, Surrey; 1639; Guilford; returned permanently to England in 1650 [Guilford Hist 25; WP 4:261; Davenport 76; Waters 1334, 1344-54, 1384, 1436-37; TAG 56:236-37; John Brooks Threlfall, *The Ancestry of Reverend Henry Whitfield (1590-1657) and His Wife Dorothy Sheafe (159?-1669) of Guilford, Connecticut* (Madison, Wisconsin, 1989); GMC50 509-18; Abandoning 316-20; NEHGR 137:291-305].

Whitefield, John: Unknown; 1638; Richmond Island; not seen after 1646 [Trelawny 193; MPCR 1:255].

Whitehand, George: Unknown; 1633; Charlestown [GMB 1981-82].

Whitehead, Richard: Unknown; 1640; Windsor [CCCR 1:55; Manwaring 1:215; Waters 463-65 (clue); NYGBR 46:388].

Whitehead, Samuel: Unknown; 1634; Cambridge, Hartford, New Haven [GM 2:7:351-56].

Whitehone, Thomas: Unknown; 1640; Southampton (witness to deed only) [SoTR 1:14].

Whitele, John: Unknown; 1640; Massachusetts Bay (court appearance only) [MBCR 1:176].

Whiteman, John: Maidstone, Kent; 1640; Charlestown [ChTR 51; ChChR 10; GMC26 85-88].

Whiting, Nathaniel: Unknown; 1638; Lynn, Dedham [EQC 2:270; DeChR 19, 25; SPR 6:408, 9:117; Theodore S. Lazell, *Whiting Genealogy: Nathaniel Whiting of Dedham, Mass., 1641* (Boston 1902)].

Whiting, Samuel: Skirbeck, Lincolnshire; 1636; Lynn [WJ 1:240, 243; MBCR 1:372; EQC 2:270; WP 4:94; NEHGR 8:19, 123:161-69; EPR 3:352-54; TAG 34:15-17, 46:256; Bulkeley Gen 29-33; TEG 23:218-28; Sibley 1:363-66; Abandoning 320].

Whiting, William: Unknown; 1636; Hartford [CCCR 1:9, 56; HaBOP 19; HaTR 14; Manwaring 1:40-42, 60; WP 4:116; NHPP 40:4; MBCR 1:324; GDMNH 749; Sibley 1:343-47; FANH 1971; Goodwin-Morgan 2:351-81].

Whitman, John: Unknown; 1638; Weymouth [MBCR 1:375; SPR Case #2012; Weymouth Hist 4:753; Charles H. Farnam, *History of the Descendants of John Whitman of Weymouth, Mass.* (New Haven, Connecticut, 1889)].

Whitman, Robert: Unknown; 1635 on *Abigail*; Ipswich [GM 2:7:356-58; NEHGR 162:116-17].

Whitman, Zachariah: Chesham, Buckinghamshire; 1635 on *Truelove*; Dorchester, New Haven, Milford [GM 2:7:359-63].

Whitmarsh, John: Shepton Mallett, Somerset: 1635 on *Marygould*; Weymouth [GM 2:7:363-66].

Whitmore, John: Unknown; 1639; Wethersfield, Stamford [CCCR 1:44, 197; WetLR 1:74, 137; SmTR 4; FOOF 1:336; Moore Anc 619].

Whitmore, Robert: Unknown; 1636; Dedham (land record only) [DeTR 1:27].

Whitnell, Jeremiah: Unknown; 1640; New Haven [NHCR 1:91; NEHGR 81:134; FANH 1975; Parke-Gildersleeve 84-88].

Whitney, John: London; 1635 on *Elizabeth & Ann*; Watertown [GM 2:7:366-72; TAG 81:249-62, 86:209-12].

Whittemore, Lawrence: Stanstead Abbots, Hertfordshire; 1635 on *Hopewell*; Roxbury [GM 2:7:372-73].

Whittemore, Thomas: Hitchin, Hertfordshire; 1640; Charlestown [Lechford 364-65; Rodgers 2:28-31; NEHGR 21:169-72, 106:31-36].

Whittered, William: Colkirk, Norfolk; 1635 on *Elizabeth*; Ipswich [GM 2:7:374-80].

Whittier, Abraham: Unknown; 1636; Marblehead, Manchester [EQC 1:5; STR 1:63; EPR 2:418-19; Perley 1:427; EIHC 49:37-39; Marblehead 130].

Whittier, Thomas: Melchet Park, Wiltshire; 1638 on *Confidence*; Salisbury, Haverhill [Drake's Founders 58 (as "Thomas Whittle"); HvBOP 9; Essex Ant 13:108; NEHGR 66:251-57; Hoyt 358, 1023-24; Pillsbury Anc 1:517-22; Charles Collyer Whittier, *The Descendants of Thomas Whittier and Ruth Green* (Rutland, Vermont, 1937)].

Whittingham, John: Boston, Lincolnshire; 1637; Ipswich [ITR 26; EQC 1:381-82; WP 4:106; HAHAC 1:82; EPR 1:103-6; Waters 111-14, 423-25; NEHGR 33:19-20, 70:185; Bulkeley Gen 33-35].

Whitton, Thomas: Benenden, Kent; 1635 on *Elizabeth & Ann*; Plymouth [GM 2:7:380-86].

Whityear, John: Unknown; 1635; Ipswich (land grant and sale of land only) [GM 2:7:386].

Wickenden, William: Unknown; 1637; Providence [PrTr 1:1, 15:5; Austin 224-25; TAG 37:139-40 (clue)].

Wickes, John: Staines, Middlesex; 1635 on *Hopewell*; Plymouth, Portsmouth, Warwick [GM 2:7:387-92].

Wickes, Thomas: Unknown; 1640; Wethersfield, Stamford, Huntington [WetLR 1:146; SmTR 4; Suffolk Sessions 18-19; Wickham-Billard 107-8; TAG 9:77-78 (clue)].

Wicksen (or Vixon), Robert: Unknown; 1638, Plymouth, Eastham [PCR 1:102, 2:166, 202, 208, 8:187; MD 2:177-78; CCL 33:20-21; J. H. Wixom and Ruth S. Widdison, *Wixom Family History* (Salt Lake City, Utah, 1963)].

Wiggin, Thomas: Unknown; 1630; Piscataqua, Squamscott [GMB 1982-85].

Wigglesworth, Edward: Wrawby, Lincolnshire; 1640; Charlestown, New Haven [NHChR 1; NHCR 1:49, 93; NEHGR 17:129-42, 81:134, 156:309-21; Wyman 1029; Chase-Wigglesworth 37-47].

Wight, Thomas: Unknown; 1637; Dedham, Medfield [DeTR 1:32; DeVR 1; DeChR 24; MBCR 1:378; William Ward Wight, *The Wights: A Record of Thomas Wight of Dedham and Medfield and of His Descendants 1635-1890* (Milwaukee, Wisconsin, 1890)].

Wight, Thomas: Unknown; 1639; Exeter [NHPP 1:132; GDMNH 753; NEHGR 68:77 (clue)].

Wignall, Alexander: Unknown; 1630; Charlestown [GMB 1985-86; WF 677-78].

Wilbore, Samuel: Sible Hedingham, Essex; 1633; Boston, Providence, Taunton [GMB 1986-88].

Wilby, George: Northamptonshire; 1635 on *Susan & Ellen*; Lynn [GM 2:7:393].

Wilcocks, Edward: Croft, Lincolnshire; 1639; Newport [RICR 1:91; NEHGR 87:73-74, 147:188-91; TAG 19:23-31, 20:233-34].

Wilcocks, John: Unknown; 1639; Hartford [HaBOP 220; HaTR 22; Manwaring 1:164-65, 255; Hale, House 803-8].

Wilcocks, John: Unknown; 1639; Saco [MPCR 1:48; GDMNH 753].

Wilcocks, William: Unknown; 1635; Watertown, Cambridge [GM 2:7:394-96].

Wilcockson, William: Derbyshire; 1635 on *Planter*; Concord, Stratford [GM 2:7:396-401].

Wild, Alice: Unknown; 1635 on *Elizabeth*; passenger list only (with caveat) [GM 2:7:401-2].

Wild, George: Unknown; 1635 on *Elizabeth & Ann*; passenger list only [GM 2:7:402].

Wild, John: Unknown; 1635 on *Elizabeth*; Topsfield [GM 2:7:402-7].

Wild, William: Unknown; 1635 on *Elizabeth*; Ipswich, Rowley [GM 2:7:407-12].

Wilder, Elizabeth: Unknown; 1638; Scituate [PCR 1:108]. (She married Thomas Ensign.)

Wilder, Martha: Shiplake, Oxfordshire; 1638 on *Confidence*; Hingham [Drake's Founders 59; HiBOP 85; Hingham Hist 3:311-29; Blake-Glidden 265-66; NEA 11:2:46-48].

Wilder, Roger: Unknown; 1620 on *Mayflower*; Plymouth [GMB 1989; PM 497].

Wilder, Thomas: Unknown; 1638; Charlestown, Lancaster [ChBOP 55; ChTR 51; ChChR 10; MBCR 1:378; Rodgers 2:450-52; NEHGR 4:270; Wyman 1030; Stevens-Miller Anc 1:43-46; NEA 11:2:46-48].

Wiley, John: Unknown; 1640; Watertown, Reading [MBCR 1:298; SPR 1:9; WaVR 1:11, 12, 13; TAG 24:115; GM 2:7:547-48; Goodman Anc 585-86].

Wilkes, William: Unknown; 1633; Boston, New Haven; returned permanently to England about 1644 [GMB 1989-91; Abandoning 320-21].

Wilkins, Bray: Unknown; 1633; Dorchester, Lynn, Salem [GMB 1991-94].

Wilkinson, Henry: Unknown; 1635 on *Elizabeth & Ann*; Ipswich [GM 2:7:412-13].

Wilkinson, Isabel: Unknown; 1638; Cambridge [CaBOP 56, 62, 94, 332, 336, 340; CaTR 64, 66, 68, 97; Rodgers 1:242-44, 353; GM 2:7:486]

Wilkinson, John: Unknown; 1636; Maine [GMB 1995].

Wilkinson, Prudence: Unknown; 1630; Charlestown, Malden [GMB 1995-97].

Willard, George: Horsmonden, Kent; 1638; Scituate; removed to Maryland by 1652 [PCR 1:110; Bassett-Preston 327-30; Joseph Willard and Charles Wilkes Walker, *Willard Genealogy* (Boston 1915) 10-14].

Willard, Simon: Marden, Kent; 1634; Cambridge, Concord, Lancaster, Groton, Charlestown [GM 2:7:413-27].

Willett, Thomas: Leiden, Holland; 1630; Penobscot, Plymouth, Rehoboth, New York, Swansea [GMB 1997-2002; PM 497-503].

Willett, Tobie: Unknown; 1632 on *Lyon*; passenger list only [Hotten 150].

Willey, Allen: Saleby, Lincolnshire; 1634; Boston [GM 2:7:427-29].

Willey, Isaac: Unknown; 1640; Boston, Charlestown, New London [BChR 285; New London Hist 310; McCormick-Hamilton 1099-1101; Henry Willey, *Isaac Willey, of New London, Conn., and His Descendants* (New Bedford, Massachusetts, 1888)].

Williams, Ann: Unknown; 1635 on *Abigail*; passenger list only [GM 2:7:429].

Williams, Ann: Norwich, Norfolk; 1637 on *John & Dorothy* or *Rose*; passenger list only [Hotten 290]. (Possibly the same as the next.)

Williams, Ann: Unknown; 1639; Salem (church admission only) [SChR 9].

Williams, Arthur: Unknown; 1639; Windsor, Northampton [CCCR 1:46; WiLR 1:80; TAG 24:114; Windsor Hist 2:791].

Williams, Eleazer: Unknown; 1637; Salem (church admission only) [SChR 7].

Williams, Elizabeth: Great Yarmouth, Norfolk; 1637 on *John & Dorothy* or *Rose*; passenger list only [Hotten 292].

Williams, Francis: Unknown; 1638; Dover; removed soon after 1645 to Barbados [MBCR 1:254 (as "Mr. Williams"); WP 4:144, 289; WJ 2:32; Gorges 80; NHPP 1:113, 40:5; GDMNH 755].

Williams, George: Unknown; 1633; Salem [GMB 2002-5].

Williams, John: Unknown; 1636; Scituate [NEHGR 10:43; PCPR 1:34, 2:2:50; MD 17:109; PM 32; MacDonough-Hackstaff 461-65].

Williams, John: Unknown; 1637; Massachusetts Bay [MBCR 1:202; WJ 1:288].

Williams, John: Unknown; 1638; Windsor [CCCR 1:28; Windsor Hist 2:791-92].

Williams, Matthew: Unknown; 1640; Marblehead [EQC 1:26, 42; ELR 2:62r].

Williams, Nathaniel: Unknown; 1639; Boston [BTR 1:42; BChR 25; MBCR 1:377; NEHGR 3:40; TAG 28:215-27, 82:161-71].

Williams, Owen: Cardiff, Glamorganshire; 1640; Portsmouth, Newport, Norwich [Lechford 315-16; RICR 1:301; Norwich Hist 252].

Williams, Philip: Unknown; 1639; Pemaquid (witness to deed only) [GDMNH 757 (citing YLR 35:55)].

Williams, Richard: Unknown; 1633; Watertown (court appearance only) [GMB 2005-6].

Williams, Richard: Unknown; 1634; Saco [GM 2:7:429-32].

Williams, Richard: Witcome Magna, Gloucestershire; 1639; Dorchester, Taunton [DChR 4; WJ 2:119; PCR 2:52, 8:176, 195, 199, 205; Waters 3-4, 8-9, 551-52; TAG 9:136-44, 212-22, 10:20-29, 118].

Williams, Richard: Unknown; 1640; Springfield (court appearance only) [Pynchon Court 210].

Williams, Robert: Norwich, Norfolk; 1637 on *John & Dorothy* or *Rose*; Roxbury [Hotten 290 (as interpreted in NEHGR 44:211-12); RChR 82; NEHGR 6:377, 47:363, 54:226; MBCR 1:374; DeTR 37, 40, 41; SPR Case #2073; Granberry Anc 347-48; TAG 36:117, 74:292-98; Harrison Williams, *The Life, Ancestors and Descendants of Robert Williams of Roxbury* (Washington DC 1934)].

Williams, Roger: Unknown; 1630 on *Mary & John*; Dorchester, Windsor, Boston [GMB 2006-7].

Williams, Roger: High Laver, Essex; 1631 on *Lyon*; Salem, Plymouth, Providence [GMB 2007-10; PM 503-6; NEQ 57:323-46, 63:624-48, 66:199-225; Roger Williams Family Association, *Descendants of Roger Williams*, three volumes (Baltimore, Maryland, and East Greenwich, Rhode Island, 1991, 1998, 2002)].

Williams, Thomas: Unknown; 1620 on *Mayflower*; Plymouth [GMB 2010; PM 506].

Williams, Thomas: Unknown; 1634; Saco [GM 2:7:432-35].

Williams, Thomas: Unknown; 1635; Plymouth, Eastham [GM 2:7:435-39].

Williams, Widow: Unknown; 1640; New Haven (two land records only) [NHCR 1:50, 93, 194; GMN 13:20].

Williams, William: Great Yarmouth, Norfolk; 1637 on *John & Dorothy* or *Rose*; Salem, Watertown; not seen after 1643 [Hotten 292; STR 1:52, 103; EQC 1:21, 24; MBCR 1:316; WaBOP 45].

Williamson, Ann: Unknown; 1635 on *Hopewell*; passenger list only [GM 2:7:439].

Williamson, Michael: Sharnbrook, Bedfordshire; 1635 on *Planter*; Ipswich, Newport, Hempstead [GM 2:7:439-41].

Williamson, Paul: Sharnbrook, Bedfordshire; 1635; Ipswich, New Haven [GM 2:7:441-42].

Williamson, William: Unknown; 1635 on *Defence*; passenger list only [GM 2:7:443].

Willing, Roger: Unknown; 1638; Richmond Island, Cape Porpus [Trelawny 187; GDMNH 759].

Willis *see also* **Wyllys**

Willis, Elizabeth: Unknown; 1635; Charlestown (death record only) [GM 2:7:443].

Willis, Henry: Unknown; 1637; Plymouth (military service only) [PCR 1:61].

Willis, Jeremy: Unknown; 1636; Lynn, Plymouth; not seen after 1639 (unless he is the man of that name at Newport in 1655 [RICR 1:301]) [EQC 1:5; Lechford 232; PCPR 1:30; PCR 1:107, 109].

Willis, John: Unknown; 1632; Boston, Lynn [GMB 2010-12].

Willis, John: Unknown; 1637; Duxbury, Bridgewater [PCPR 1:28, 44, 7:7, 8:182, 190, 202, 12:39; Lechford 299; PPR 1:169; Gen Adv 3:93; Bartlett-Jenkins 130-31].

Willis, Michael: Unknown; 1637; Dorchester, Boston [MBCR 1:312, 374; DChR 3; SPR Case #505, Case #1220; Pauline Willis, *Willis Records: or Records of the Willis Family of Haverhill, Portland, and Boston* (London 1908)].

Willis, Nathaniel: Unknown; 1639; Boston (mention in town records only) [BTR 1:53]. (Possibly a clerical error for Nicholas Willis.)

Willis, Nathaniel: Unknown; 1639; Sandwich, Bridgewater [PCR 2:9, 15, 8:184, 192; PPR 1:2; Gen Adv 1:17; MD 14:109; NEHGR 16:332 (Samuel Hutchinson will)].

Willis, Nicholas: Bury St. Edmunds, Suffolk; 1634; Boston [GM 2:7:443-46].

Willis, Richard: Unknown; 1634; Plymouth [GM 2:7:446-49].

Willis, Sergeant: Unknown; 1636; Saybrook (mention in two letters only) [WP 3:269, 276].

Willis, Thomas: Isleworth, Middlesex; 1638; Lynn; returned permanently to England by 1642 [EQC 1:11, 2:270; Lechford 329; WP 4:104; MBCR 1:375; NEHGR 30:463; TAG 41:109-18; Morison 407-8; Abandoning 321-22; ODNB].

Willix, Balthazar: Alford, Lincolnshire; 1639; Exeter, Salisbury [Exeter Hist 436; NHPP 40:6; EPR 1:130, 442-43; GDMNH 759; NEHGR 50:46-48; Snow-Estes 1:82; Dorothy Brewer Erikson, *Descendants of Thomas Brewer* (Boston 1996) 517-19].

Willmore, George: Unknown; 1638; Portsmouth (court appearance only) [RICR 1:60].

Willoughby, Francis: Stepney, Middlesex; 1638; Charlestown [ChTR 39; ChChR 10, 50; ChBOP 46; MBCR 1:376; NEHGR 4:270, 8:328, 30:67-78, 35:59-65, 40:50-56; Lechford 267; HAHAC 1:98; Rodgers

2:130-34, 3:11-21; Wyman 1036-37; Noyes-Gilman 142-46; TAG 56:12-13; Abandoning 322-24].

Willowes, George: Unknown; 1637; Cambridge [MBCR 1:374; CaBOP 65; CaTR 40; Shepard 43, 150; CaChR 12; NEHGR 4:183; MPR Case #25059].

Wills, William: Unknown; 1635; Dorchester [GM 2:7:449].

Wills, William: Unknown; 1638; Scituate [NEHGR 9:286; PN&Q 5:14-15].

Wilmot, Ralph: Unknown; 1640; Charlestown (court appearance and mention in town records only) [MBCR 1:306; ChTR 50].

Wilson, Edward: Unknown; 1638; Massachusetts Bay (probate record only) [MBCR 1:235; SPR Case #8; GMB 2018].

Wilson, Henry: Unknown; 1639; Dedham [DeTR 1:68; DeChR 23; MBCR 1:379; Ken Stevens, *Descendants of Henry Wilson of Dedham, Massachusetts* (Walpole, New Hampshire, 1996)].

Wilson, Jacob: Unknown; 1637; Boston [BTR 1:33, 37, 49; MBCR 1:378; NEHGR 3:248; SPR Case #336; Ken Stevens, *Descendants of Jacob Wilson of Braintree, Massachusetts* (Walpole, New Hampshire, 1988)].

Wilson, John: Sudbury, Suffolk; 1630; Boston [GMB 2012-15; WF 678-83].

Wilson, Joseph: Unknown; 1637; Dorchester; not seen after 1638 [DChR 3; DTR 32; MBCR 1:374].

Wilson, Lambert: Unknown; 1629; hired by Massachusetts Bay Company but no record in New England [GMB 2016; WF 683-84].

Wilson, Richard: Unknown; 1639; Lynn, Cambridge, Charlestown, Boston [WP 4:129; MBCR 1:268, 315; CaBOP 127; SLR 1:139, 274; ChBOP 96, 100, 103; SPR 1:101, 2:155, 157].

Wilson, Samuel: Unknown; 1640; Portsmouth [PoTR 17, 28; Austin 230; Blake-Torrey 100-1; NEHGR 69:380; TAG 24:74-75].

Wilson, Theophilus: Canterbury, Kent; 1636; Ipswich [ITR 21, 61; MBCR 1:375; Snow-Estes 1:355-58; NEHGR 163:5-15; TAG 35:17-18; Parker-Ruggles 322-24].

Wilson, Thomas: Unknown; 1633; Roxbury, Exeter [GMB 2016-19].

Wilson, William: Donington, Lincolnshire; 1635; Boston [GM 2:7:450-53].

Wilton, David: Beaminster, Dorset; 1632; Dorchester, Windsor, Northampton [GMB 2019-21; NEHGR 146:298].

Winborn, William: Unknown; 1638; Boston, Exeter [NEHGR 2:191, 9:166; NHPP 1:132, 133; GDMNH 762; Sibley 1:576].

Winch, Mary: Bocking, Essex; 1634 on *Francis*; Roxbury, Springfield [GM 2:7:453-54].

Winchell, Robert: Unknown; 1634; Dorchester, Windsor [GM 2:7:454-57].

Winchester, Alexander: Unknown; 1635 on *Defence*; Boston, Braintree, Rehoboth [GM 2:7:457-62].

Winchester, John: Cranbrook, Kent; 1635 on *Planter*; Hingham, Boston [GM 2:7:462-69].

Wincoll, Thomas: Unknown; 1632; Cambridge, Watertown [GMB 2021-23; WF 684-86].

Windsor, Joshua: Unknown; 1637; Providence [PrTR 1:1, 15:5; WP 3:267-68; Austin 434].

Wines, Barnabas: Ipswich, Suffolk; 1634; Watertown, Southold [GM 2:7:469-73].

Wines, Faintnot: Ashford, Kent; 1635 on *Hercules*; Charlestown [GM 2:7:474-77].

Wing, Elizabeth: Unknown; 1632; Boston (church admission only) [GMB 2023].

Wing, John: London; 1637; Sandwich [PCPR 1:32; PCR 1:150; EPR 1:11; Waters 519-20; Raymond T. Wing, *Wing Genealogy, Volume I* (Camden, Maine, 2006)]. (No contemporary evidence has been found to support the claim that John Wing's mother and brothers had also arrived in New England by 1640.)

Wing, Robert: Unknown; 1634 on *Francis*; Boston [GM 2:7:477-80].

Wing, Sarah: Unknown; 1638; Ipswich (servant; mention in letter only) [WP 4:68].

Winn, Edward: Unknown; 1639; Woburn [Lechford 379; WoTR 2; WoVR; TMG 26:116; Edmund James Cleveland and Horace Gillette

Cleveland, *The Genealogy of the Cleveland and Cleaveland Families* (Hartford, Connecticut, 1899) 2420-50].

Winship, Edward: Newcastle upon Tyne, Northumberland; 1634; Cambridge [GM 2:7:481-88].

Winsley, Samuel: Saxmundham, Suffolk; 1638; Salisbury [MBCR 1:237, 277, 375; SyTR 1; Essex Ant 2:49, 11:31; EPR 2:82-84; Hoyt 363-64; NEHGR forthcoming].

Winslow, Edward: Leiden, Holland; 1620 on *Mayflower*; Plymouth, Marshfield; returned permanently to England in 1646 [GMB 2023-26; PM 507-10; NEHGR 154:78-118, 242; MQ 75:137-38; TAG 54:31-34; MD 53:67-69, 60:27-29; NEA 4:5/6:56-59, 5:4:15-20; Abandoning 324-26].

Winslow, Gilbert: Droitwich, Worcestershire; 1620 on *Mayflower*; Plymouth; returned permanently to England by 1627 [GMB 2026-27; PM 510-11; TAG 81:246].

Winslow, John: Droitwich, Worcestershire; 1621 on *Fortune*; Plymouth, Boston [GMB 2027-30; PM 511-15].

Winslow, Josiah: Droitwich, Worcestershire; 1631; Plymouth, Marshfield [GMB 2031-33; PM 515-17].

Winslow, Kenelm: Droitwich, Worcestershire; 1631; Plymouth, Marshfield [GMB 2033-36; PM 518-21].

Winsor, Joseph: Unknown; 1638; Sandwich [PCR 1:118, 132, 7:19; PCPR 1:45; MQ 53:248-54, 54:44-46].

Winter, Christopher: Goathurst, Somerset; 1637; Scituate, Marshfield [NEHGR 9:280, 10:40, 42, 61:199; PCR 1:97, 12:57; PCPR 4:2:61-62; MD 2:252; M&JCH 25:71-76].

Winter, Elizabeth: Unknown; 1637 on *Speedwell*; passenger list only [NGSQ 71:176].

Winter, John: Holbeton, Devon; 1633; Richmond Island, Casco [GMB 2037-38; NEQ 57:184-204].

Winter, John: Goathurst, Somerset; 1636; Scituate [NEHGR 9:280; PCR 1:102, 12:53; PCPR 1:34; M&JCH 25:71-76].

Winter, John: Unknown; 1636; Watertown [WaBOP 5, 57; Rodgers 2:83-85; Bond 656].

Winter, Timothy: Unknown; 1640; Hingham (baptismal record only) [NEHGR 121:13; Hingham Hist 3:331].

Winthrop, John: Groton, Suffolk; 1630 on *Arbella*; Boston [GMB 2038-42; WF 686-91; TAG 79:283-91].

Wise, Elizabeth: Sudbury, Suffolk; 1635; Roxbury [GM 2:7:488].

Wise, Joseph: Unknown; 1640; Roxbury [SPR 1:7; TAG 56:80-82; TG 4:178-81; Sibley 2:428-41].

Wise, Thomas: Unknown; 1635; Saco, Casco [GM 2:7:489].

Wiseman, James: Unknown; 1639; Braintree, Boston [BTR 1:50; NEHGR 3:248; SPR Case #1174].

Wiswall, John: Winwick, Lancashire; 1636; Dorchester, Boston [DChR 3; DTR 37; MBCR 1:318, 375; Letters from NE 2; TAG 58:110-15; Parker-Ruggles 396-99; NEHGR 8:20, 18:71, 40:58-59].

Wiswall, Thomas: Winwick, Lancashire; 1636; Dorchester, Cambridge [DChR 3; DTR 28; TAG 58:110-15; Parker-Ruggles 262-69, 396-99; NEHGR 40:58-59].

Witchfield, John: Unknown; 1632 on *Lyon*; Dorchester, Windsor [GMB 2042-44].

Witherly, Thomas: Southwark, Surrey; 1639; Massachusetts Bay; not seen after 1640 [MBCR 1:261; Lechford 214, 235, 271-72, 342].

Withers, Thomas: Unknown; 1631; Piscataqua [GMB 2044-49].

With, Mary[ie]: Unknown; 1635 on *Hopewell*; passenger list only [GM 2:7:490].

Withington, Henry: Leigh, Lancashire; 1636; Dorchester [DChR 2; DTR 19, 33; Lechford 343; SPR Case #432; NEHGR 16:52-54, 75:142-44].

Withington, William: Unknown; 1639; Newport [RICR 1:91; Lechford 188, 314; Austin 306].

Witter, William: Unknown; 1640; Lynn [EQC 1:29; NEHGR 81:357-88; Harold John Witter, *The Descendants of William Witter and Hannah Churchman of Lynn, Massachusetts* (Baltimore, Maryland, 1991)].

Wolcott, Henry: Lidyard St. Lawrence, Somerset; 1630 on *Mary & John*; Dorchester, Windsor [GMB 2049-52; M&JCH 26:73-83, 27:86].

Wolhouston, Mary: Unknown; 1635 on *Planter*; passenger list only [GM 2:7:490].

Wollaston, Edward: Unknown; 1639; Sandwich; not seen after 1642 [PCR 1:150, 7:29; 12:84].

Wollaston, Richard: Unknown; 1624; Mount Wollaston; removed soon [GMB 2085-86].

Wolterton, Gregory: Norfolk; 1639; Hartford [HaTR 4; HaBOP 288; CCCR 1:55; TAG 68:160-75; Angell Anc 568-77].

Wood, Anne: Earls Colne, Essex; 1635 on *Defence*; Cambridge [GM 2:7:490-91].

Wood, Constant: Unknown; 1635 on *Abigail*; passenger list only [GM 2:7:491].

Wood, Edmund: Halifax, Yorkshire; 1635; Springfield, Wethersfield, Stamford, Hempstead, Huntington [GM 2:7:491-96].

Wood, Edward: Nuneaton, Warwickshire; 1639; Charlestown [ChChR 10, 50; ChTR 58; Lechford 174, 217; NEHGR 4:270, 123:230-31; MBCR 1:376; TG 9:90-159; TAG 21:123-33, 30:100-3; Kempton Anc 3:470-77].

Wood, Elizabeth: Unknown; 1635 on *Increase*; passenger list only [GM 2:7:496].

Wood, Henry: Unknown; 1637; Charlestown (court appearance only) [WJ 2:425].

Wood, Joan: Unknown; 1639; Charlestown; not seen after 1641 [ChTR 52; ChChR 10, 50].

Wood, John: Unknown; 1635 on *Marygould*; passenger list only (with caveat) [GM 2:7:497-98].

Wood, John: Unknown; 1635; Saybrook [GM 2:7:498].

Wood, John: Unknown; 1636; Salem (land grant only) [STR 1:25; GM 2:7:497].

Wood, John: Unknown; 1636; Plymouth [PCR 1:46, 70, 88, 2:4, 8:181, 188, 12:27; PTR 1:6; NEHGR 144:23-28; MQ 48:127-30; MD 44:137-42; TAG 41:200-5].

Wood, John: Unknown; 1638; Lynn [EQC 1:53, 57, 58, 62, 92, 2:270; MBCR 2:293; GM 2:7:497-98].

Wood, John: Bures St. Mary, Suffolk; 1639; Sudbury, Marlborough [SuTR 3; MBCR 1:377; MPR Case #25456; NEHGR 147:377-82; Emerson-Benson 601-2].

Wood, Jonas: Halifax, Yorkshire; 1640; Stamford [WetLR 1:138; SmTR 4; NYGBR 123:79-82, 135-44, 223-27, 124:22-28, 92-94, 144-46; TAG 11:148-53, 199-203].

Wood, Nathaniel: Unknown; 1635 on *Increase*; passenger list only [GM 2:7:499].

Wood, Nicholas: Unknown; 1638; Braintree, Dorchester, Medfield, Natick [DTR 1:38; MBCR 1:378; SPR Case #521; NEHGR 40:324; TAG 36:117; GMB 1465].

Wood, William: Unknown; 1629; Lynn, Sandwich [GMB 2052-54].

Wood, William: Unknown; 1635 on *Hopewell*; passenger list only (with caveat) [GM 2:7:499-500].

Wood, William: Unknown; 1638; Salem (land grant only) [STR 1:70].

Wood, William: Unknown; 1639; Concord [MBCR 1:295, 377; CoVR 3; Rodgers 3:30-31; TAG 21:123-24; Clay W. Holmes, *A Genealogy of the Lineal Descendants of William Wood* (Elmira, New York, 1901)].

Woodall, Phillips: Unknown; 1639; Plymouth (court appearance only) [PCR 1:156].

Woodbridge, John: Stanton Fitzwarren, Wiltshire; 1634 on *Mary & John*; Ipswich, Newbury, Boston, Andover [GM 2:7:500-10].

Woodbury, John: West Coker, Somerset; 1624; Cape Ann, Salem [GMB 2054-57; M&JCH 25:78-79; 26:83].

Woodbury, William: Misterton, Somerset; 1636; Salem [STR 1:26; SChR 9, 10; MBCR 1:378; NEHGR 71:168, 170; Dawes-Gates 2:829-38; M&JCH 25:78-79, 26:83].

Woodcliff, Edward: Unknown; 1639; New Haven (servant; court appearance only) [NHCR 1:35].

Woodcock, John: Unknown; 1635 on *Marygould*; passenger list only (with caveat) [GM 2:7:510-11].

Woodcock, John: Unknown; 1638; Springfield [SpTR 161; Pynchon 204; GM 2:7:511].

Woodford, Thomas: Unknown; 1632 on *William & Francis*; Roxbury, Hartford, Northampton [GMB 2057-60].

Woodhouse, Richard: Unknown; 1637; Boston [BTR 1:21, 44; BChR 292; NEHGR 3:40; SPR 12:11, 107; GDMNH 769; John A. Brayton,

The Ancestry of Tennessee Williams (Winston-Salem, North Carolina, 1993)].

Woodley, Edmund: Unknown; 1640; Massachusetts Bay (court appearance only) [EQC 1:26].

Woodley, Edward: Unknown; 1636; Massachusetts Bay (servant; court appearance only) [MBCR 1:177, 193].

Woodman, Archelaus: Christian Malford, Wiltshire; 1635 on *James*; Newbury [GM 2:7:511-16].

Woodman, Edward: Christian Malford, Wiltshire; 1635; Newbury [GM 2:7:516-22].

Woodman, Richard: Unknown; 1635 on *Abigail*; Lynn [GM 2:7:522-23].

Woodmansey, Robert: Unknown; 1635; Ipswich, Boston [GM 2:7:523-26].

Woodroffe, Elizabeth: Thorpe Achurch, Northamptonshire; 1633; Boston [GMB 2060; NEHGR 157:31-33].

Woodward, George: London; 1635 on *Rebecca*; Boston [GM 2:7:527-28].

Woodward, Henry: Unknown; 1639; Dorchester, Northampton [DChR 4, 11, 38; Stevens-Miller Anc 1:400-2; Dawes-Gates 2:841-49].

Woodward, James: Unknown; 1630; Watertown; not seen after 1632 [GMB 2060; WF 691-92].

Woodward, Lawrence: Unknown; 1640; Hartford (appearance in town meeting record only) [HaTR 35].

Woodward, Nathaniel: Puddington, Bedfordshire; 1637; Boston [BTR 1:24; TMG 20:147-68]. (He was preceded to New England by his son Nathaniel Woodward in 1633 [GMB 2061-64; NEHGR 158:213-27; ChTR 28].)

Woodward, Peter: Unknown; 1640; Dedham [DeTR 1:71; DeChR 26; NEHGR 6:72; DeHR 3:156-57; Waterman Gen 1:734-35].

Woodward, Ralph: Unknown; 1636; Hingham [HiBOP 56; MBCR 1:374; NEHGR 121:11; SPR Case #333; Hingham Hist 3:332-33].

Woodward, Richard: Unknown; 1634 on *Elizabeth*; Watertown [GM 2:7:528-31; Lindsay S. Reeks, *Woodward, Woodard Ancestors of New England* (Baltimore, Maryland, 1995)].

Woodward, Robert: Unknown; 1638; Dedham (death record only) [DeVR 127].

Woodward, William: Unknown; 1640; Portsmouth (land grant only) [PoTR 16].

Woodworth, Walter: Unknown; 1633; Plymouth, Scituate [GMB 2064-67; PM 521-24; Jeannette Woodworth Behan, *The Woodworth Family of America: Descendants of Walter Woodworth of 1630 Through Six Generations* (n.p. 1988)].

Woolcott, John: Axbridge, Somerset; 1634 on *Recovery*; Salem, Cambridge, Watertown [GM 2:7:531-42].

Woolfe, Peter: Unknown; 1633; Salem, Beverly [GMB 2067-69; TEG 14:109-10].

Woolridge, John: Unknown; 1630; Charlestown [GMB 2069-71; WF 692-95].

Woolsey, Joel: Unknown; 1631; York (land patent only) [GMB 2071-72].

Woolstone, Elizabeth: Unknown; 1634; Boston [GM 2:7:542].

Woory, Ralph: Unknown; 1640; Charlestown; not seen after 1651 [ChTR 53; Lechford 408; HAHAC 1:109; NEHGR 4:270; SPR 2:9; ChChR 10; ChBOP 111, 124].

Worcester, William: Olney, Buckinghamshire; 1639; Salisbury [MBCR 1:277, 376; SyTR 2; WP 4:239; Essex Ant 12:81; TAG 65:65-66, 71:50-51, 73:122; Hoyt 368-69; GDMNH 771; Morison 410; Sarah Alice Worcester, *The Descendants of Rev. William Worcester* (Boston 1914)].

Worden, Isaac: Unknown; 1635 on *Increase*; passenger list only [GM 2:7:542].

Worden, Jane: Unknown; 1635 on *Christian*; passenger list only (with caveat) [GM 2:7:542-43].

Worden, Peter: Lancashire; 1638; Yarmouth [PCPR 1:33; PCR 1:109, 117, 7:18; MD 3:75-76; Gilbert S. Bahn, *The Worden Surname from Peter Worden of Yarmouth to 1850* (n.p. 2002)].

Wormewood, ____: Unknown; 1630; Massachusetts Bay; apparently returned permanently to England in 1631 [GMB 2086; WF 695-96].

Wormwood, William: Unknown; 1639; Piscataqua, Isles of Shoals [MPCR 1:42; SPR 1:9; GDMNH 771-72; Annis Spear Anc 111-15].

Wotten, John: Unknown; 1635; Piscataqua [MPCR 1:1; NHPP 1:113; GDMNH 772].

Wotts, John: Unknown; 1634 on *Recovery*; passenger list only [GM 2:7:543].

Wrast, Mary: Unknown; 1635 on *Planter*; passenger list only [GM 2:7:543].

Wright, ____: Unknown; 1638; Plymouth (court appearance only) [PCR 1:109].

Wright, Anthony: Unknown; 1639; Sandwich, Oyster Bay [PCR 1:150, 2:84, 8:184, 192; NYGBR 3:35-37; Howland Delano Perrine, *The Wright Family of Oysterbay, L. I.* (New York 1923)].

Wright, Dorothy: Unknown; 1639; Sudbury [SuTR 3, 5, 11 (apparently mistranscribed as "widow Rice"); Dawes-Gates 1:678-86; Richard Morgan Wright, *Edward Wright of Sudbury, Massachusetts*, three volumes (Baltimore, Maryland, 2012)].

Wright, Elizabeth: Unknown; 1640; Salem (church admission only) [SChR 10 (annotated "removed")].

Wright, George: Unknown; 1636; Salem; not seen after 1643 [EQC 1:5, 10, 19, 49; STR 1:58, 104, 117, 118].

Wright, George: Unknown; 1639; Braintree (grant of land and admission to freemanship only) [BTR 1:45; MBCR 2:292].

Wright, Henry: Unknown; 1634; Dorchester [GM 2:7:543-45].

Wright, John: Unknown; 1640; Woburn [WoTR 2; NEHGR 37:76].

Wright, Nicholas: Unknown; 1639; Sandwich, Oyster Bay [PCR 1:150; NEHGR 55:380-81; NYGBR 3:35-45; Howland Delano Perrine, *The Wright Family of Oysterbay, L. I.* (New York 1923)].

Wright, Peter: Unknown; 1639; Sandwich, Oyster Bay [PCR 1:150; NEHGR 55:380-81; Howland Delano Perrine, *The Wright Family of Oysterbay, L. I.* (New York 1923)].

Wright, Rachel: Unknown; 1637; Roxbury [RChR 83]. (She married John Levens.)

Wright, Richard: Unknown; 1630; Lynn, Boston, Braintree, Rehoboth, Podunk [GMB 2072-74; WF 696-98].

Wright, Richard: Unknown; 1636; Plymouth [PCR 1:45, 67, 78, 12:24, 34; MD 4:165-67, 24:83-86; TAG 59:165-70; Small Gen 476-82].

Wright, Robert: Southwark, Surrey; 1630; Massachusetts Bay; returned permanently to England in 1631 [GMB 2074-75; WF 698].

Wright, Robert: Unknown; 1639; Cambridge (servant; mention in deposition only) [WP 4:131].

Wright, Samuel: Unknown; 1639; Springfield [Pynchon Court 204; SpTR 167; TAG 63:163; NEHGR 40:280-84; McCormick-Hamilton 1135-36].

Wright, Thomas: Unknown; 1640; Wethersfield [WetLR 1:170; Manwaring 1:9, 260-63; Wethersfield Hist 2:851].

Wright, William: Unknown; 1621 on *Fortune*; Plymouth [GMB 2075-76; PM 524-26].

Wyatt, Edward: Unknown; 1637 on *Speedwell*; Massachusetts Bay [NGSQ 71:176; WJ 2:426]. (Possibly the same as the Edward Wyatt who appeared at Dorchester in the mid-1640s [NEHGR 7:89; SPR Case #1173].)

Wyatt, John: Assington, Suffolk; 1635; Ipswich [GM 2:7:545-47]. (Accompanied to New England by his stepchildren Mary, Sarah and Dorcas Riddlesdale [NEHGR 143:213-20].)

Wyatt, William: Unknown; 1639; Massachusetts Bay (mention in notarial records only) [Lechford 158].

Wybert, Elizabeth: Unknown; 1633; Boston (church admission only) [GMB 2076].

Wybourne, Thomas: Tenterden, Kent; 1638; Duxbury, Scituate, Boston [SPR 1:16, 280, 3:55; PCR 1:109, 144, 160-61; S. Fletcher Weyburn, *Weyburn-Wyborn Genealogy* (New York 1911)].

Wylie, John: Unknown; 1635; *Elizabeth & Ann*; passenger list only (with caveat) [GM 2:7:547-48].

Wyllys, George: Fenny Compton, Warwickshire; 1639; Hartford [HaBOP 10; HaTR 22; MBCR 1:324; WetLR 1:78; Manwaring 1:42-43; Waters 595-99; NEHGR 33:356, 37:33, 53:217-24, 128:138; TAG 39:86-89, 44:1-8].

Wyman, Francis: Westmill, Hertfordshire; 1640; Woburn [WoTR 2; Waters 315; NEHGR 50:45-46, 139:147-48; Sarah Hildreth Anc 26].

Wyman, John: Westmill, Hertfordshire; 1640; Woburn [WoTR 2; Waters 315; NEHGR 50:45-46, 139:147-48; Sarah Hildreth Anc 26].

Wyndell, John: Unknown; 1635 on *Increase*; passenger list only [GM 2:7:548].

Wythe, Humphrey: Woolverstone, Suffolk; 1635; Ipswich [GM 2:7:548-55].

Y

Yale, David: London; 1638; New Haven; returned permanently to England in 1651 [WP 4:88; NHCR 1:50; Lechford 414; TAG 20:30-33, 32:71-79, 56:1-11, 101-5; NEHGR 53:82-83, 71:91-93; Waters 65; Rodney Horace Yale, *Yale Genealogy* (Beatrice, Nebraska, 1908) 91-99; Abandoning 332].

Yale, Thomas: London; 1638; New Haven [NHCR 1:92; TAG 20:30-33, 29:200, 32:71, 52:142-44, 56:1-11, 101-5; NEHGR 53:82-83, 81:135; Rodney Horace Yale, *Yale Genealogy* (Beatrice, Nebraska, 1908) 91-95, 100-1; Abandoning 333].

Yates, William: Unknown; 1635 on *Abigail*; passenger list only [GM 2:7:557].

Yelke, James: Unknown; 1637; Sable Island (servant) [WP 4:28].

Yeowe, Thomas: Unknown; 1638; Charlestown (witnessed a deed) [Lechford 59]. (Possibly the same as the man seen ten years later in Boston and then Fairfield [BBOP 45; Aspinwall 174, 320-21; SLR 1:150, 2:305; BChR 323-24, 328; FOOF 1:701; TAG 17:1-19.)

Yew, Allen: Unknown; 1640; Boston [Lechford 272, 273, 287; EQC 1:20].

Yonge, Paul: Unknown; 1640; Boston (court appearance only) [MBCR 1:318].

York, Richard: Unknown; 1635; Dover [NHPP 40:11; GDMNH 775].

Young, Rowland: Unknown; 1636; York [MA Arch 10:161, 128:243; GDMNH 776; York Hist 1:98].

Young, Widow: Unknown; 1638; Cambridge (land grant only) [CaBOP 331; GMN 22:11-14].

Younglove, Samuel: Epping, Essex; 1635 on *Hopewell*; Ipswich [GM 2:7:557-63].

Youngs, Christopher: Southwold, Suffolk; 1636; Salem, Wenham [STR 1:37; SChR 17; WnTR 1:1; Waters 1409-12; Selah Youngs Jr., *Youngs Family* (New York 1907) 17, 38-39, 45-46].

Youngs, John: Covehithe, Suffolk; 1637 on *Mary Ann*; Salem, Southold [Hotten 294; STR 1:54; EQC 1:18; Waters 1409-12; NYGBR 39:193-99, 45:114-16; Selah Youngs Jr., *Youngs Family* (New York 1907) 17, 38-43].

Youngs, Joseph: Southwold, Suffolk; 1638; Salem [Lechford 159; STR 1:79; MBCR 2:36; Waters 1409-12; Selah Youngs Jr., *Youngs Family* (New York 1907) 17, 38-39, 43-45].

Youngs, Richard: Unknown; 1638; Dedham (town meeting appearance only) [DeTR 1:48].

Africans

African immigrants had arrived in New England at least by early 1638. On 26 February 1637/8, Governor John Winthrop reported that "Mr. Peirce, in the Salem ship, the *Desire*, returned from the West Indies after seven months. He had been at Providence [in the western Caribbean], and brought some cotton, and tobacco, and negroes, etc., from thence, and salt from Tertugos" [WJ 1:305].

The three individuals listed here are the only such immigrants identified by name during our period (and we do not know whether or not any of them came on the *Desire*). George Pye, if he was in fact from Africa, was probably from North Africa, while the other two are likely sub-Saharan Africans. Their origins are listed here as "unknown," as they almost certainly did not come to New England directly from Africa.

Dorcas the blackamore: Unknown; 1640; Dorchester, Boston [DChR 5, 12; BChR 74, 90, 323].

George Pye a Moor: Unknown; 1638; Massachusetts Bay [MBCR 1:234].

Mingo a negro: Unknown; 1640; Boston [NEHGR 2:274].

INDEX SECTION

This final section contains four indices: supplemental names, European place names, American place names, and ship names. Because the entire directory is an alphabetical listing, we have not provided a full index of main entry names. The "supplemental" names are those that appear within other entries, e.g., John Adams and Kenelm Winslow in the listing for Ellen Newton:

Newton, Ellen: Unknown; 1623 on Anne; Plymouth [GMB 1332; PM 344]. (She married John Adams and Kenelm Winslow.)

The European places consist primarily of English ones, but locations in Holland and Ireland appear in this index as well. The American places also include Barbados.

INDEX OF SUPPLEMENTAL NAMES

Adams
John, 240
Allerton
Isaac, 326
Alvord
Benedict, 240
Ault
John, 335
Austin
Jonas, 286
Barber
Edward, 18
Barniston
Marmaduke, 21
Beats
John, 24
Beeford
Richard, 26
Billington
Francis, 259
Bloomfield
Thomas, 34
Brigs
John, 141
Briskow
Widow, 42
Buckminster
Thomas, 42
Burpee
Thomas, 50
Carpenter
Thomas, 57
Carpenter
William, 56
Caule
Thomas, 55
Claff
Thomas, 65

Clare
John, 68
Clipton
Thomas, 69
Cobham
Josiah, 70
Codmore
Goodman, 70
Colcord
Edward, 357
Coney
James, 80
Cook
Richard, 76
Cooper
John, 321
Lydia, 321
Copie
James, 80
Couve
James, 80
Couvey
James, 80
Dane
John, 336
Dawse
Priscilla, 88
Deare
Philip, 33
Denman
John, 308
Mary, 308
Dinny
Edward, 92
Eaton
Francis, 259
Edwards
Edmond, 103

Ensign
  Thomas, 373
Estick
  Elizabeth, 108
Evington
  Thomas, 107
Fawer
  Barnabas, 238
Fisher
  Edward, 311
Fownell
  John, 124
Gainer
  Thomas, 125
Geaves
  Richard, 138
Gibson
  John, 129
Gray
  John, 361
Gutterige
  John, 135
Haggett
  Henry, 150
Hale
  John, 147
Hammecke
  Thomas, 149
Harell
  William, 158
Harrison
  Arthur, 151
Hayward
  James, 263
Hett
  Thomas, 238
Hitchborne
  David, 160
Hobart
  Edmund, 245
Hocke
  William, 168
Hoddy
  John, 164
Holden
  Deborah, 167
Holton
  William, 155
Huchinson
  John, 176
Hudson
  Nicolas, 164
Hurst
  William, 333
Hyricke
  William, 159
Iles
  John, 161
Imson
  John, 149
Jenkins
  Reynold, 131
Johnson
  Isaac, 269
Kemp
  Robert, 191
Kettle
  Richard, 358
Kimwright
  John, 192
King
  Thomas, 337
Kirby
  Joshua, 196
Knight
  Philip, 197
Langley
  Richard, 211
Latcome
  William, 337
Levens
  John, 386
Lovell
  Danyell, 212
Lunt
  Enoch, 174
Luxford
  James, 245

Index of Supplemental Names

Lyford
  John, 245
Mason
  Thomas, 222
Mathis
  John, 223
Moss
  Goodman, 233
Newell
  Thomas, 246
Norris
  Mary, 241
Oakley
  Robert, 245
Ormsby
  Richard, 10, 348
Orton
  Thomas, 258
Osborn
  John, 247
Paine
  Thomas, 359
Palmer
  Walter, 304
Parke
  William, 253
Pearsall
  Henry, 252
Peter
  Hugh, 303
Pierce
  Anthony, 264
Pomeroy
  Edward, 268
Prior
  Daniel, 273
  John, 273
Pynchon
  William, 295
Redding
  Thomas, 260
Reeves
  John, 291
Riddlesdale
  Dorcas, 387
  Mary, 387
  Sarah, 387
Riggs
  Edward, 289
Ruggles
  George, 291
  John, 291
Samson
  Henry, 267
Sawell
  Richard, 300
Segar
  Jacob, 205
Seyle
  Francis, 209
Sherman
  Philip, 245
Silver
  Thomas, 131
Simons
  William, 263
Smead
  William, 308
Tedd/Tidd
  John, 331
  Joshua, 336
Till
  Peter, 344
Townsend
  William, 259
Walton
  William, 217
Waterman
  Margaret, 361
White
  Gowen, 358
  William, 359
Williams
  Hugh, 254
Williamson
  Michael, 252
Willis
  George, 251
Winslow
  Kenelm, 240

INDEX OF EUROPEAN PLACES

Bedfordshire
  Cranfield, 366, 367, 368
  Dean, 242
  Dunstable, 186, 211, 215, 326
  Eaton Bray, 170
  Henlow, 294
  Kempston, 6, 148
  Leighton Buzzard, 193, 298
  Millbrook, 320
  Odell, 48, 49
  Puddington, 34, 384
  Pulloxhill, 40
  Radwell, 257
  Salford, 207
  Sharnbrook, 376
  Stotfold, 315
  Sutton, 69, 179
  Woburn, 96
Berkshire
  Barkham, 49
  Bray, 154
  Easthamstead, 325
  East Shefford, 273
  Newbury, 70, 253, 254
  New Windsor, 75, 337
  Reading, 69, 367
  Sonning, 205
  Burghfield, 312
  Bristol, 40, 45, 102, 168, 179, 197, 198, 210, 239, 246, 260, 288, 305, 361
Buckinghamshire, 113
  Aston Abbots, 274
  Aston Clinton, 17, 22, 271
  Aylesbury, 46
  Chalfont St. Giles, 291

  Chesham, 129, 136, 272, 293, 344, 363, 371
  Cholesbury, 17
  Ellesborough, 335
  Great Missenden, 137, 155, 203, 206, 237
  High Wycombe, 44, 194
  Lavendon, 141
  Lee, 174
  Little Missenden, 94
  Marsh Gibbon, 171
  Newport Pagnell, 245, 270
  Olney, 77, 112, 123, 125, 242, 255, 265, 274, 385
  Sherington, 196, 239
  Soulbury, 344
  Wendover, 119, 174, 277, 318, 338
Cambridgeshire
  Cambridge, 8, 32, 34, 58, 91, 113, 136, 139, 155, 193, 228, 265, 293
  Cottenham, 77
  Eltisley, 93
  Horseheath, 234
  Wood Ditton, 193
Cheshire
  Gawsworth, 302
  Waverton, 59
Cornwall
  Beddington, 331
  Lezant, 8
  Milbrook, 5, 28, 103
  St. Breage, 35
  St. John, 128
  Saltash, 35
  Sheviock, 84, 229

Denbighshire
  Holt, 33
Derbyshire, 373
  Derby, 246, 314
  Duffield, 32, 257
  Ilkeston, 24, 153
  Matlock, 117
Devon
  Alverdiscott, 150
  Axminster, 212
  Axmouth, 168
  Barnstaple, 72, 74, 337
  Beaworthy, 223
  Berry Pomeroy, 61
  Bideford, 126, 307
  Braunton, 5, 6
  Chudleigh, 7
  Colyton, 240, 268
  Dartington, 60
  Exeter, 65, 71, 99, 129, 162, 218, 219, 220, 341, 359
  Harberton, 51
  Hartland, 52
  Holbeton, 163, 380
  Kingsweare, 341
  Newton Ferrers, 154
  Northam, 55, 74, 210
  Ottery St. Mary, 223
  Plymouth, 115, 130, 148, 165, 209, 221, 334, 341
  Bicton, 347
  Salcombe Regis, 65, 338
  Seaton, 357, 363
  Sidbury, 65
  Sidmouth, 164
  Tiverton, 274
Dorset, 104
  Affpuddle, 64
  Ashmore, 192
  Beaminster, 165, 169, 202, 208, 255, 379
  Bradpole, 305
  Bridport, 28, 100, 125, 173, 217, 362
  Burton Bradstock, 92
  Charminster, 241
  Dorchester, 39, 52, 56, 76, 119, 174, 274, 287, 295, 309, 326, 332, 337, 347, 362
  East Stower, 186
  Fordington, 101, 316
  Kington Magna, 232
  Netherbury, 76
  Shaftesbury, 134
  Stoke Abbot, 96, 148
  Swyre, 166
  Symondsbury, 148, 214, 353
  Thorncombe, 210
  Upway, 316
  Weymouth, 263
  Whitchurch Canonicorum, 238

Essex, 156, 172, 234, 274, 340, 366
  Ardleigh, 212
  Baddow, 92
  "Belcham," 267
  Billericay, Great Burstead, 221, 273, 291
  Bocking, 127, 135, 316, 319, 368, 379
  Boreham, 150
  Boxted, 103, 171, 214, 262, 321, 359
  Braintree, 135, 211, 219, 245, 318, 329
  Brentwood, South Weald, 72
  Bures, 258
  Castle Hedingham, 71
  Chelmsford, 123, 124, 197, 269, 272, 287, 302, 353, 361
  Childerditch, 43
  Colchester, 35, 73, 98, 199, 210
  Cold Norton, 195
  Colne Engaine, 153
  Dedham, 8, 13, 23, 65, 249, 288, 304
  Earls Colne, 46, 76, 77, 122, 151, 256, 305, 382
  Epping, 9, 24, 389
  Fairstead, 79, 246, 319

Index of European Places

Felsted, 270
Finchingfield, 211
Fordham, 184
[Great?] Baddow, 44
Great Baddow, 257
Great Bentley, 221, 347
Great Bromley, 86
Great Burstead, 253
Great Coggeshall, 81, 240, 314
Great Leighs, 191
Great Maplestead, 344
Halstead, 168
Hatfield Broadoak, 87, 359
High Laver, 259, 376
High Ongar, 215
Horsmonden, 374
Ingatestone, 278
Lawford, 63
Lexden, 141
Little Baddow, 53, 278, 343
Maldon, 121, 162, 222, 230, 290
Messing, 236, 369
Mistley, 84, 194
Navestock, 73
Nazeing, 55, 85, 105, 138, 158, 167, 257, 284, 291, 347
North Benfleet, 201, 279
North Weald, 25
Rayleigh, 41, 298, 320
Ridgewell, 202, 267, 277
Romford, 271
Roxwell, 44, 45
Saffron Walden, 21, 79, 93, 117, 229, 264
St. Lawrence, 49
Shalford, 118 Sible Hedingham, 373
South Weald, 76
Stansted Mountfitchet, 296
Stondon Massey, 358
Stisted, 60, 321
Terling, 30, 364
Theydon Garnon, 118, 119, 206
Tillingham, 236
Toppesfield, 327

Waltham Abbey, 170
Weeley, 116
Wethersfield, 210
Willingale-Doe, 188
Witham, 356
Glamorganshire
  Bridgend, 108
  Cardiff, 375
  Penmaen, 223
Gloucestershire
  Gloucester, 14, 89, 90, 145, 214
  Hatherup, 152
  Henborough, 147
  Horsley, 241
  Rangeworthy, 97
  Rodborough, 33
  Todenham, 338
  Tetbury, 88
  Thornbury, 96, 311, 333
  Westerleigh, 306
  Witcome Magna, 375
  Wotton-under-Edge, 194

Hampshire, 44, 267
  Abbots Ann, 299
  Barton Stacey, 329
  Basing, 123
  Bishopstoke, 12, 99
  Clatford, 19, 33
  Eling, 114
  Odiham, 303
  Over Wallop, 192
  Romsey, 12, 29, 102, 107, 167, 197, 198, 312
  Southampton, 3, 300
  South Stoneham, 13
  Titchfield, 210
  Upton Grey, 15, 143, 329
  Weyhill, 27, 89, 90, 243, 292
  Wherwell, 57, 188, 248, 252
Herefordshire, 273
Hertfordshire
  Aldenham, 203
  Bennington, 329
  Berkhamsted, 281, 299

Hertfordshire *cont.*
  Bishops Stortford, 60, 92, 93, 101, 106, 228, 242, 364
  Flamstead, 119
  Great Berkhamsted, 263
  Great Munden, 66, 227
  Hertford, 120, 336
  Hitchin, 52, 371
  Ippollitts, 120, 135
  Kings Walden, 273
  Little Hadham, 10, 127
  Minsden, 47
  Royston, 233
  St. Albans, 8, 12, 15, 64, 116, 130, 158, 204, 246, 260, 344
  Sawbridgeworth, 44, 261, 301
  Stanstead Abbots, 91, 257, 371
  Tring, 165, 325
  Ware, 97, 158, 185, 233, 267, 269
  Watford, 273
  Watton-at-Stone, 146
  Westmill, 192, 282, 283, 387
Holland, 242, 317, 347
  Amsterdam, 175
  Leiden, 5, 34, 38, 40, 56, 58, 60, 64, 76, 77, 81, 85, 92, 99, 117, 123, 124, 132, 168, 184, 222, 229, 233, 237, 268, 273, 284, 286, 288, 306, 336, 340, 343, 370, 374, 380
  Rotterdam, 126, 168, 261
  The Hague, 233, 256
Huntingdonshire
  Fenstanton, 171
  Hail Weston, 206

Ireland, 114, 217
  Dublin, 76, 310
  Loughall, 215

Kent, 151, 224, 225, 226
  Ashford, 11, 27, 60, 91, 212, 247, 256, 317, 318, 341, 379
  Ash-juxta-Sandwich, 60
  Aylesford, 157
  Benenden, 16, 231, 372
  Bethersden, 183
  Biddenden, 21, 119, 179, 319, 322
  Canterbury, 13, 28, 112, 137, 185, 241, 249, 282, 318, 378
  Cranbrook, 29, 103, 107, 260, 302, 336, 379
  Dover, 13, 87, 102, 285, 331, 355
  East Farleigh, 88
  Eastwell, 8, 53, 131, 183, 222, 269, 315
  Faversham, 41, 55
  Fordwich, 136
  Frittenden, 344
  Gravesend, 138
  Great Chart, 289
  Hawkhurst, 64, 84, 169, 170, 236, 291
  Hernehill, 4, 98
  High Halden, 39
  Horton Kirby, 299
  Hothfield, 16
  Isle of Thanet, 293
  Lenham, 11, 35
  Lydd, 21
  Maidstone, 17, 43, 125, 237, 282, 366, 371
  Marden, 374
  Northbourne, 297
  Otham, 270
  Rochester, 112, 227
  Rolvenden, 196
  Sandwich, 35, 72, 74, 109, 154, 167, 168, 184, 187, 193, 250, 264, 311, 315, 364
  Staple, 102
  Staplehurst, 140, 207
  Strood, 109, 185, 227, 299, 350
  Sutton-by-Dover, 255
  Tenterden, 12, 26, 55, 80, 103, 119, 154, 163, 177, 202, 208, 250, 286, 317, 324, 336, 387
  Thanington, 37

Index of European Places

Willesborough, 252
Wittersham, 75, 211
Lancashire, 385
  Bury, 99
  Leigh, 381
  Manchester, 10, 69, 136, 301, 356
  Much Woolton, 222
  Prescot, 40, 132, 235
  Stockport, 167
  Winwick, 334, 381
Leicestershire
  Blaby, 63
  Castle Donington, 287
  Claybrook, 161
  Cossington, 363
  Cottesbach, 94
  Cropston, 304
  Great Bowden, 73, 93, 115
  Husbands Bosworth, 53
  Leicester, 3, 63
  Market Harborough, 174
  South Kilworth, 6
  Wistow, 75
Lincolnshire, 36, 204, 220, 334, 341
  Alford, 121, 158, 176, 177, 219, 269, 311, 322, 359, 365, 377
  Billingborough, 94
  Bilsby, 368
  Boston, 26, 51, 62, 70, 80, 81, 89, 94, 112, 170, 179, 182, 207, 225, 258, 307, 341, 372
  Croft, 373
  Donington, 379
  Elsham, 304
  Farlsthorpe, 81
  Firsby, 211
  Fishtoft, 334
  Folkingham, 160
  Great Limber, 332
  Hannah, 92
  Horbling, 39, 72
  Horncastle, 121
  Laceby, 284
  Little Bytham, 313
  Long Sutton, 158, 270
  Rigsby, 353, 354
  Saleby, 374
  Sempringham, 99, 114, 185
  Skirbeck, 371
  Spalding, 29, 329
  Sutterton, 179
  Tattershall, 306
  Wrawby, 213, 234, 372
London, 1, 4, 6, 7, 9, 11, 15, 18, 20, 24, 28, 31, 32, 35, 37, 38, 42, 45, 46, 48, 52, 55, 57, 62, 63, 66, 67, 73, 75, 77, 82, 88, 97, 100, 101, 102, 104, 105, 108, 112, 113, 118, 121, 129, 132, 133, 135, 136, 138, 141, 150, 151, 152, 155, 160, 161, 162, 163, 165, 168, 170, 171, 181, 182, 186, 187, 191, 192, 199, 205, 209, 210, 212, 213, 214, 217, 218, 222, 223, 226, 228, 233, 237, 238, 239, 241, 242, 245, 249, 251, 253, 256, 259, 260, 261, 266, 271, 272, 277, 278, 285, 288, 294, 299, 301, 302, 303, 305, 312, 318, 320, 321, 322, 323, 324, 331, 335, 337, 341, 344, 347, 349, 350, 351, 353, 355, 356, 360, 361, 366, 369, 371, 379, 389

Middlesex
  Ealing, 149
  Hampton, 280
  Harrow-on-the-Hill, 138
  Isleworth, 377
  Ratcliffe, 264
  Staines, 372
  Stepney, 5, 28, 50, 74, 89, 118, 125, 141, 157, 159, 189, 201, 210, 211, 217, 231, 242, 243, 254, 303, 341, 361, 377
  Wapping, 12, 36, 64, 131, 164, 219, 250, 277, 282, 344
  Westminster, 19, 42
  Whitechapel, 156
  Willesden, 130

Norfolk, 118, 203, 224, 309, 382
  Attleborough, 324
  Banham, 67
  Colkirk, 372
  Denton, 115, 229
  Eccles, 368
  Elsing, 188
  Great Ellingham, 250
  Great Yarmouth, 7, 48, 50, 51, 95, 113, 128, 134, 135, 137, 206, 237, 277, 298, 299, 306, 326, 339, 340, 350, 375, 376
  Hemsby, 220
  Hingham, 23, 47, 59, 64, 77, 78, 85, 112, 118, 128, 131, 155, 164, 182, 208, 229, 232, 257, 258, 266, 283, 284, 297, 307, 308, 311, 324, 339, 342
  Kenninghall, 284
  Kings Lynn, 4, 142
  New Buckenham, 289, 309
  Norwich, 2, 5, 15, 30, 36, 52, 95, 96, 104, 121, 128, 140, 167, 175, 204, 208, 209, 213, 227, 240, 246, 264, 271, 296, 308, 322, 331, 356, 374, 376
  Ormesby, 103, 134
  Ormesby St. Margaret, 108, 220, 234, 235, 243, 249, 252, 357
  Ormesby St. Michael, 97, 218
  Pulham St. Mary the Virgin, 163, 170
  Redenhall, 115
  Saxlingham-juxta-Mare, 6, 116
  Scratby, 58, 117, 152
  Starston, 214
  Topcroft, 123
  Winfarthing, 182
  Wymondham, 208, 230, 249, 251
  Yarmouth, 10
Northamptonshire, 373
  Adstone, 158
  Canons Ashby, 317
  Guilsborough, 25
  Little Bowden, 78, 185
  Marston St. Lawrence, 62
  Northampton, 86, 159, 166, 284, 296
  Preston Capes, 333
  Ringstead, 29, 225, 344
  Sibbertoft, 85, 302
  Thorpe Achurch, 225, 246, 275, 384
  Titchmarsh, 187
  Towcester, 136, 211, 303
Northumberland
  Heddon, 146
  Newcastle-upon-Tyne, 17, 31, 63, 86, 107, 167, 176, 251, 305, 341, 380
Nottinghamshire, 140
  Basford, 368
  Epperstone, 245
  Lenton, 115
  Nottingham, 75, 103, 122
  Sutton-in-Ashfield, 116
  Worksop, 35

Oxfordshire
  Banbury, 303
  Bicester, 324
  Burford, 38
  Caversham, 27, 179, 188, 212, 319, 320
  Checkenden, 191
  Chipping Norton, 12
  Claydon, 28, 35
  Epwell, 340
  Oxford, 224
  Shiplake, 373
  Westwell, 324

Rutland
  Langham, 172
  Stretton, 358

Shropshire
  Bridgenorth, 23
  Shipton, 231
  Shrewsbury, 46, 69, 208, 272

Index of European Places 405

Somerset, 104
　Aller, 84, 297, 322
　Axbridge, 385
　Batcombe, 2, 27, 114, 221, 279, 329
　Bridgewater, 130
　Broadway, 6, 122, 165, 173, 242, 265
　Chaffcombe, 131
　Chard, 323
　Charlton Musgrove, 154
　Cheddar, 287, 288
　Chew Magna, 73, 229
　Clapton, 316
　"Clisdon,"* 180
　Combe St. Nicholas, 123, 289, 339
　Crewkerne, 21, 64, 128, 173, 256, 262, 268, 351
　Dinder, 187
　East Coker, 95, 340
　Fitzhead, 287
　Glastonbury, 143, 248, 362
　Goathurst, 380
　Ilchester, 10, 169
　Ilminster, 272
　Kingweston, 2
　Lidyard St. Lawrence, 381
　Middle Chinnock, 95
　Misterton, 383
　Norton Fitzwarren, 323
　Orchard Portman, 241
　Pitminster, 32, 273, 282
　Portbury, 213
　Shepton Mallett, 371
　South Chard, 91
　South Petherton, 256, 369
　Stradbroke, 42, 347
　Taunton, 71, 132, 193, 195, 283, 301, 368
　Wedmore, 263
　West Coker, 383
　West Hatch, 172
　West Quantoxhead, 369
　Wookey, 13, 54
　Wraxall, 136
　Wrington, 31
　Yeovil, 365

Staffordshire
　Kingswinford, 314
　Tamworth, 59
　Wolverhampton, 149
Suffolk, 250
　Assington, 59, 122, 143, 195, 273, 276, 288, 387
　Barham, 189
　Barking, 243
　Barnardiston, 201
　Barnham, 48, 67
　Barrow, 197
　Bildeston, 253
　Boxford, 72
　Bradwell, 49
　Brampton, 77, 94, 113, 194
　Brundish, 46
　Burgate, 233
　Burstall, 100
　Bury St. Edmunds, 5, 26, 38, 41, 109, 377
　Bures St. Mary, 199, 210, 240, 255, 262, 382
　Capel St. Mary, 230
　Coddenham, 360
　Combs, 210
　Covehithe, 390
　Dennington, 87
　Edwardstone, 39, 268
　Elmsett, 279
　Framlingham, 74, 87
　Fressingfield, 3
　Freston, 108
　Great Livermere, 207
　Great Wenham, 119
　Groton, 141, 191, 381
　Hadleigh, 26, 139, 312
　Haverhill, 331
　Hoxne, 175
　Ipswich, 2, 8, 68, 86, 119, 131, 133, 140, 184, 219, 256, 379
　Kersey, 7, 26, 205, 294, 298
　Kettle Baston, 304
　Lavenham, 149, 246, 251
　Lindsey, 165

Suffolk *cont.*
  Little Waldingfield, 9, 125, 136, 285, 293
  Little Wratting, 358
  Lowestoft, 249
  Mendlesham, 172
  Moulton, 230
  Nayland, 115, 167, 252, 318, 321, 360, 361
  Oakley, 175
  Rattlesden, 194, 236, 299
  Rickinghall Superior, 51
  Ringsfield, 63
  Rushbrooke, 61
  Saxmundham, 380
  Shotley, 323
  South Elmham, 116
  Southwold, 70, 159, 166, 175, 179, 390
  Stoke by Clare, 268
  Stowmarket, 33
  Stradishall, 18 Stratford, 356
  Sudbury, 22, 34, 38, 77, 115, 123, 136, 145, 149, 222, 238, 290, 291, 297, 360, 364, 378, 381
  Syleham, 115
  Thelnetham, 41
  Westhorpe, 67, 68
  Wherstead, 226
  Wickham Skeith, 133
  Wingfield, 116
  Winston, 13
  Woolverstone, 72, 87, 100, 108, 135, 388
  Wrentham, 63, 194, 250, 262, 335
Surrey
  Bermondsey, 205, 326
  Dorking, 21, 44, 45, 51, 176, 235
  Ewell, 119
  Guildford, 184
  Kingston-upon-Thamcs, 337
  Merstham, 106
  Ockley, 99, 370
  Rotherhithe, 294, 322

  Southwark, 41, 48, 61, 74, 153, 154, 199, 222, 228, 239, 279, 381, 387
  Sutton, 132
Sussex
  Billingshurst, 121
  Chiddingly, 183
  Horsham, 52
  Iford, 252
  Lewes, 25, 270, 271
  North Mundham, 62
  Ovingdean, 128
  Rye, 32, 107
  Wadhurst, 301

Warwickshire, 24, 243
  Alcester, 233, 354, 355
  Bulkington, 147
  Burton Dassett, 217
  Coventry, 14, 126, 263
  Fenny Compton, 387
  Fillongley, 103
  Hampton in Arden, 98
  Hatton, 78, 102
  Hillmorton, 260
  Kenilworth, 142
  Mancetter, 3, 25, 238, 290
  Nuneaton, 382
  Southam, 190
  Tanworth, 167
  Wroxhall, 160
Wiltshire, 213
  Amesbury, 56, 57
  Bromham, 14
  Cholderton, 243
  Christian Malford, 45, 384
  Donhead St. Andrew, 134, 296
  Downton, 85
  Garsdon, 230
  Highworth, 196
  Landford, 8, 80, 236, 265
  Marlborough, 53, 74, 80, 90, 108, 120, 133, 161, 179, 233, 248, 253, 266, 355
  Melchet Park, 288, 372
  Mildenhall, 140

Index of European Places

Ogbourne St. George, 337
Plaitford, 289
Salisbury, 9, 22, 32, 44, 54, 64, 84, 139, 192, 207, 255, 280, 299, 302, 307, 308, 332, 350, 362, 367
Semley, 134
Stanton Fitzwarren, 383
Sutton Mandeville, 29, 33, 156, 280
The Devizes, 22
Tisbury, 224
Warminster, 214
Westbury Leigh, 71, 146
Whiteparish, 288
Worcestershire
  Bengeworth, 360
  Bewdley, 354
  Droitwich, 380
  Great Comberton, 333
  Inkberrow, 45
  Sedgeberrow, 240
  Tidmington, 364
  Worcester, 189
  Yardley, 130
Yorkshire, 207, 265
  Bradford, 184, 185
  Buttercrambe, 52, 123
  Calverley, 355
  Cottingham, 137, 320
  Ecclesfield, 239
  Edlington, 297
  Everingham, 76
  Gildersome, 281
  Halifax, 20, 53, 92, 111, 148, 223, 229, 286, 302, 382, 383
  Heptonstall, 25
  Holme-upon-Spalding-Moor, 41, 83, 201, 334
  Howden, 205
  Hull, 173, 335
  Leeds, 38
  Ripplingham, 83
  Rowley, 182, 238, 287, 298
  York, 56

*Please note that Clisdon appears in quotation marks under Somerset because the original record lists it as such, but Clisdon does not exist.

INDEX OF AMERICAN PLACES

Amesbury, 19, 145, 171, 217, 221
Andover, 39, 123, 133, 167, 185, 212, 221, 248, 253, 269, 289, 291, 319, 336, 383

Barbados, 156, 251, 253, 261, 286, 300, 330
Barnstable, 5, 8, 18, 24, 28, 34, 36, 51, 57, 68, 70, 71, 77, 82, 84, 88, 93, 94, 109, 116, 121, 122, 131, 132, 147, 154, 163, 165, 170, 173, 181, 184, 207, 209, 210, 212, 224, 286, 290, 296, 299, 302, 305, 337
Beverly, 16, 31, 38, 64, 75, 79, 95, 105, 125, 142, 159, 160, 212, 214, 316, 321, 385
Billerica, 16, 30, 112, 119, 122, 183, 221, 230
Black Point, 34, 55, 92, 189, 221, 286, 313
Boston, 1, 2, 3, 4, 5, 7, 9, 10, 11, 12, 14, 15, 16, 19, 20, 22, 23, 24, 25, 26, 27, 28, 29, 30, 31, 32, 33, 34, 35, 36, 37, 38, 39, 40, 41, 42, 43, 44, 46, 47, 48, 49, 50, 51, 52, 53, 55, 56, 57, 58, 59, 60, 61, 62, 65, 66, 67, 68, 69, 70, 71, 72, 73, 74, 75, 77, 78, 79, 80, 81, 82, 83, 84, 88, 89, 90, 91, 92, 93, 94, 95, 96, 97, 98, 99, 100, 101, 102, 103, 105, 106, 107, 108, 109, 111, 112, 113, 114, 115, 116, 117, 118, 119, 120, 121, 122, 123, 125, 126, 127, 128, 129, 130, 131, 132, 135, 136, 138, 139, 140, 141, 142, 143, 145, 146, 147, 149, 150, 151, 152, 153, 155, 156, 157, 158, 159, 160, 161, 162, 163, 164, 165, 166, 167, 168, 169, 170, 171, 172, 173, 174, 175, 176, 177, 179, 181, 182, 183, 184, 185, 186, 187, 189, 190, 191, 192, 193, 194, 195, 196, 197, 198, 199, 201, 204, 205, 206, 207, 208, 209, 210, 212, 213, 214, 215, 217, 218, 219, 220, 221, 222, 223, 224, 225, 226, 227, 228, 230, 231, 232, 233, 235, 237, 238, 240, 241, 242, 245, 246, 247, 248, 249, 251, 253, 254, 255, 256, 257, 258, 259, 260, 261, 262, 263, 264, 265, 266, 267, 268, 269, 270, 274, 275, 277, 278, 279, 280, 281, 282, 284, 285, 286, 288, 289, 290, 291, 292, 293, 293, 295, 296, 297, 298, 299, 300, 301, 302, 303, 304, 305, 306, 307, 308, 310, 311, 312, 313, 314, 316, 317, 318, 319, 320, 321, 322, 324, 325, 326, 329, 330, 331, 332, 333, 334, 335, 336, 337, 338, 339, 340, 341, 343, 344, 347, 348, 349, 350, 353, 354, 355, 356, 357, 358, 359, 360, 361, 362, 363, 365, 367, 368, 373, 374, 375, 376, 377, 378, 379, 380, 381, 383, 384, 385, 386, 387, 389, 391
Bradford, 11, 125, 151, 356

Braintree, 2, 3, 5, 6, 7, 17, 21, 23, 25, 30, 31, 32, 33, 38, 44, 46, 56, 62, 66, 72, 74, 75, 80, 84, 88, 90, 91, 96, 97, 117, 119, 122, 130, 135, 143, 150, 151, 154, 156, 158, 159, 164, 183, 184, 185, 196, 197, 212, 213, 222, 223, 225, 228, 230, 237, 238, 241, 247, 249, 250, 259, 260, 266, 267, 268, 271, 274, 277, 279, 287, 289, 297, 299, 302, 303, 311, 314, 319, 322, 326, 327, 333, 334, 336, 364, 379, 381, 383, 386
Branford, 1, 33, 38, 61, 81, 234, 252, 265, 289, 325, 339, 340, 358
Bridgewater, 21, 40, 54, 56, 103, 133, 151, 157, 207, 229, 249, 313, 377
Brookfield, 81, 228
Brookhaven, 184

Cambridge, 1, 2, 6, 7, 8, 9, 10, 12, 14, 17, 19, 20, 21, 23, 24, 25, 26, 27, 28, 31, 33, 34, 37, 38, 39, 40, 41, 45, 46, 47, 48, 50, 52, 53, 55, 56, 60, 61, 62, 63, 66, 67, 69, 70, 72, 74, 76, 77, 81, 83, 85, 86, 87, 88, 91, 99, 101, 102, 106, 107, 114, 116, 120, 121, 122, 123, 124, 127, 128, 129, 130, 131, 132, 133, 134, 135, 137, 139, 140, 141, 145, 146, 149, 150, 151, 153, 156, 157, 160, 163, 165, 166, 167, 168, 169, 170, 173, 174, 175, 176, 177, 180, 181, 188, 190, 191, 192, 196, 197, 199, 202, 203, 207, 208, 210, 211, 214, 218, 219, 221, 222, 224, 225, 229, 230, 232, 234, 236, 240, 245, 246, 250, 251, 252, 254, 256, 258, 263, 264, 268, 270, 271, 272, 273, 280, 281, 282, 284, 285, 288, 289, 291, 293, 296, 297, 299, 301, 302, 303, 305, 306, 314, 315, 317, 318, 319, 321, 325, 326, 329, 335, 338, 339, 341, 348, 350, 353, 354, 359, 362, 364, 366, 369, 370, 373, 374, 378, 379, 380, 381, 385, 387, 389
Cape Ann, 5, 16, 75, 94, 126, 198, 337, 383
Cape Neddick, 148
Cape Porpus, 21, 66, 171, 183, 230, 298, 323, 337, 341, 376
Carolina, 187
Casco, 4, 15, 43, 73, 74, 80, 96, 113, 127, 129, 229, 233, 234, 290, 292, 342, 380, 381
Casco Bay, 309
Charlestown, 4, 5, 6, 7, 8, 10, 11, 12, 13, 15, 16, 20, 22, 25, 27, 29, 33, 34, 35, 36, 37, 38, 41, 42, 44, 45, 47, 49, 51, 53, 55, 57, 58, 59, 61, 62, 64, 69, 71, 72, 73, 74, 76, 82, 83, 84, 85, 87, 88, 89, 90, 98, 99, 101, 103, 104, 106, 107, 109, 111, 113, 114, 119, 120, 121, 122, 123, 127, 129, 132, 137, 138, 139, 140, 141, 142, 145, 146, 147, 148, 153, 155, 156, 157, 159, 160, 161, 162, 164, 170, 172, 173, 174, 175, 176, 177, 179, 181, 182, 183, 184, 185, 186, 187, 188, 193, 197, 198, 199, 201, 203, 204, 205, 208, 209, 210, 211, 213, 215, 218, 219, 221, 223, 224, 225, 228, 229, 232, 233, 234, 235, 237, 242, 243, 245, 249, 250, 251, 254, 259, 260, 261, 263, 264, 269, 270, 271, 275, 277, 282, 283, 285, 290, 291, 292, 293, 296, 299, 300, 301, 302, 303, 304, 305, 306, 309, 311, 313, 316, 320, 322, 323, 324, 325, 330, 331, 334, 336, 341, 343, 344, 353, 355, 358, 361, 363, 364, 366, 367, 368, 369, 370, 371, 372, 373, 374, 376, 377, 378, 379, 382, 385, 389
Chelmsford, 53, 54, 108, 112, 116, 191, 253, 279, 287, 303, 314, 347

Index of American Places

Concord, 11, 14, 18, 22, 24, 26, 29, 34, 35, 37, 42, 43, 46, 48, 52, 53, 60, 88, 96, 98, 104, 108, 112, 117, 120, 124, 126, 127, 132, 141, 148, 153, 156, 157, 159, 169, 174, 187, 199, 207, 221, 225, 226, 227, 229, 245, 270, 281, 306, 322, 335, 338, 344, 347, 366, 367, 368, 373, 374, 383

Connecticut, 10, 24, 27, 71, 79, 88, 90, 103, 108, 125, 138, 167, 197, 219, 286, 315, 348, 350

Damariscove, 122

Dartmouth, 196, 269, 285

Dedham, 2, 3, 5, 6, 8, 12, 13, 14, 15, 18, 20, 23, 42, 48, 49, 58, 63, 65, 67, 72, 73, 76, 84, 87, 97, 100, 101, 102, 104, 106, 108, 111, 115, 116, 118, 121, 123, 128, 137, 142, 157, 159, 163, 165, 172, 173, 174, 175, 189, 191, 194, 195, 205, 214, 222, 227, 229, 233, 235, 247, 253, 262, 263, 267, 271, 282, 287, 289, 302, 303, 308, 309, 310, 316, 323, 335, 348, 358, 359, 363, 368, 371, 372, 378, 384, 385, 390

Deerfield, 163, 267

Derby, 367

Dorchester, 3, 4, 5, 8, 10, 11, 14, 16, 18, 21, 23, 26, 28, 29, 30, 32, 39, 40, 41, 42, 49, 51, 53, 56, 57, 64, 65, 67, 68, 69, 71, 74, 76, 78, 81, 84, 88, 92, 93, 94, 97, 98, 99, 100, 101, 104, 105, 106, 108, 112, 113, 114, 118, 119, 120, 121, 122, 123, 125, 128, 129, 130, 131, 132, 137, 140, 143, 147, 148, 150, 152, 154, 155, 156, 160, 161, 162, 164, 165, 166, 169, 170, 172, 173, 174, 177, 183, 185, 187, 188, 193, 194, 195, 196, 197, 198, 201, 202, 205, 206, 207, 208, 209, 210, 211, 212, 213, 214, 215, 217, 218, 219, 220, 221, 222, 223, 224, 227, 228, 229, 230, 231, 235, 236, 238, 239, 240, 241, 245, 246, 247, 255, 256, 257, 258, 262, 264, 265, 266, 268, 269, 272, 273, 274, 277, 278, 279, 282, 283, 284, 286, 287, 289, 291, 295, 296, 300, 301, 303, 308, 309, 311, 313, 318, 322, 323, 324, 326, 332, 334, 335, 336, 337, 338, 339, 341, 342, 343, 344, 348, 351, 353, 355, 359, 360, 362, 363, 368, 369, 371, 374, 375, 376, 377, 378, 379, 381, 383, 384, 386, 387, 391

Dover, 11, 13, 15, 24, 34, 36, 48, 50, 55, 56, 72, 83, 87, 97, 100, 107, 109, 118, 124, 127, 129, 132, 133, 146, 147, 159, 162, 163, 173, 174, 185, 188, 197, 199, 201, 203, 206, 207, 223, 226, 237, 243, 250, 263, 265, 268, 278, 281, 285, 288, 308, 318, 322, 325, 331, 335, 344, 347, 354, 355, 356, 362, 365, 375, 389

Dracut, 72

Duxbury, 3, 18, 21, 25, 27, 28, 32, 34, 35, 40, 43, 44, 49, 50, 53, 56, 58, 60, 61, 65, 68, 72, 73, 74, 79, 88, 90, 92, 118, 126, 133, 134, 147, 150, 151, 155, 157, 162, 166, 167, 171, 174, 180, 197, 198, 201, 207, 209, 224, 225, 229, 230, 232, 233, 234, 237, 247, 249, 252, 255, 256, 262, 264, 268, 272, 281, 285, 290, 294, 304, 313, 314, 316, 317, 318, 335, 340, 341, 342, 350, 353, 361, 365, 366, 377, 387

Eastham, 17, 64, 72, 73, 77, 82, 95, 161, 184, 199, 224, 226, 285, 307, 311, 313, 314, 324, 344, 372, 376

Easthampton, 16, 75, 127, 171, 247, 255, 329

Edgartown, 19, 23, 30, 53, 70, 80, 118, 257

Essex County, 297

Exeter, 19, 32, 48, 73, 75, 78, 79, 81, 82, 92, 105, 115, 118, 131, 140, 142, 145, 148, 158, 159, 162, 165, 177, 188, 195, 204, 205, 209, 210, 219, 230, 231, 233, 238, 261, 269, 278, 279, 284, 287, 298, 308, 312, 318, 322, 331, 347, 356, 359, 365, 373, 377, 378, 379

Fairfield, 1, 7, 21, 22, 26, 50, 55, 61, 83, 114, 119, 122, 138, 147, 153, 156, 162, 172, 173, 181, 186, 187, 199, 207, 210, 214, 224, 231, 240, 245, 247, 304, 306, 308, 323, 324, 338, 342, 344, 365, 366, 367, 389
Falmouth, 69, 71, 74, 159, 217, 286, 307
Farmington, 19, 46, 135, 153, 170, 190, 191, 208, 221, 231, 247, 289, 319, 359
Flushing, 114, 204, 229, 320, 332, 334

Gloucester, 10, 13, 25, 33, 36, 46, 59, 71, 85, 89, 100, 106, 122, 132, 188, 191, 209, 221, 224, 227, 228, 242, 260, 272, 273, 278, 285, 293, 307, 309, 320, 335, 342, 350, 354
Gravesend, 9, 37, 69, 172, 230, 260, 315, 334, 348, 363
Greenwich, 81, 113, 114, 173, 226, 256
Groton, 82, 165, 204, 211, 228, 253, 374
Guilford, 31, 52, 55, 62, 64, 77, 84, 93, 96, 99, 108, 122, 134, 148, 163, 170, 172, 188, 189, 196, 206, 225, 237, 242, 255, 266, 302, 321, 370

Haddam, 68, 315
Hadley, 6, 19, 29, 64, 66, 68, 74, 83, 94, 126, 134, 135, 155, 163, 208, 219, 291, 312, 317, 332, 337, 358, 359, 366, 369
Hampton, 7, 12, 13, 38, 40, 42, 45, 58, 62, 65, 69, 72, 73, 74, 81, 82, 83, 87, 89, 97, 98, 104, 105, 107, 108, 114, 118, 123, 124, 128, 133, 140, 145, 159, 169, 170, 173, 176, 185, 188, 195, 198, 205, 206, 220, 229, 234, 235, 237, 243, 249, 252, 253, 257, 260, 279, 284, 289, 294, 295, 296, 298, 302, 307, 310, 312, 313, 318, 325, 330, 333, 342, 354, 356, 358, 363
Hartford, 2, 6, 7, 8, 9, 13, 18, 19, 21, 23, 28, 29, 30, 32, 33, 34, 45, 46, 48, 49, 50, 52, 53, 61, 63, 64, 66, 67, 68, 70, 73, 75, 79, 83, 84, 91, 93, 102, 104, 106, 107, 114, 122, 126, 127, 129, 134, 135, 137, 138, 140, 141, 143, 146, 147, 153, 155, 156, 157, 162, 166, 167, 168, 170, 172, 173, 177, 179, 184, 186, 190, 191, 203, 204, 206, 208, 211, 215, 219, 221, 224, 226, 230, 231, 233, 236, 240, 242, 245, 246, 252, 254, 258, 263, 264, 268, 270, 271, 274, 282, 282, 284, 289, 290, 291, 293, 299, 301, 307, 308, 315, 317, 318, 319, 321, 323, 353, 354, 358, 359, 361, 362, 363, 364, 366, 369, 370, 371, 373, 382, 383, 384, 387
Hatfield, 6
Haverhill, 12, 53, 89, 90, 102, 112, 133, 146, 159, 165, 176, 192, 201, 202, 204, 210, 247, 249, 251, 304, 306, 307, 370, 372
Hempstead, 9, 56, 68, 71, 92, 119, 130, 161, 207, 226, 230, 234, 252, 279, 300, 311, 323, 363, 376, 382
Hingham, 4, 8, 10, 12, 13, 16, 19, 20, 21, 23, 27, 28, 47, 51, 55, 57, 59, 61, 64, 65, 70, 74, 77, 78, 85, 98, 100, 101, 112, 113, 118, 120, 128, 129, 131, 136, 149, 155, 158, 159,

Index of American Places 413

160, 162, 164, 173, 179, 182, 186, 188, 189, 197, 202, 203, 204, 205, 208, 209, 210, 212, 213, 214, 217, 219, 220, 221, 226, 229, 230, 234, 237, 241, 247, 248, 249, 250, 251, 252, 253, 254, 257, 258, 263, 266, 270, 273, 283, 284, 291, 292, 293, 300, 302, 307, 308, 309, 311, 316, 321, 322, 323, 324, 332, 339, 342, 344, 347, 354, 356, 357, 358, 373, 379, 380, 384
Hull, 16, 28, 74, 160, 188, 212, 223, 273, 350, 358
Huntington, 75, 108, 207, 301, 313, 323, 337, 340, 372, 382

Ipswich, 2, 7, 9, 12, 13, 15, 20, 25, 29, 30, 31, 35, 36, 38, 39, 40, 44, 45, 47, 50, 53, 57, 58, 62, 63, 65, 68, 70, 71, 72, 74, 77, 80, 81, 83, 84, 85, 87, 89, 91, 94, 95, 96, 97, 99, 101, 102, 106, 107, 112, 113, 115, 119, 120, 121, 122, 123, 124, 125, 127, 130, 131, 132, 133, 134, 137, 138, 140, 141, 145, 146, 147, 148, 150, 151, 153, 154, 156, 157, 158, 164, 165, 169, 170, 171, 172, 177, 181, 182, 184, 185, 189, 190, 192, 193, 194, 195, 196, 197, 199, 201, 202, 204, 211, 213, 214, 218, 219, 226, 227, 230, 231, 233, 234, 236, 239, 241, 242, 243, 248, 250, 251, 252, 254, 256, 257, 259, 260, 262, 265, 266, 267, 272, 273, 274, 275, 280, 285, 286, 288, 289, 290, 296, 298, 299, 301, 302, 304, 305, 306, 311, 312, 315, 316, 322, 326, 327, 331, 334, 337, 340, 341, 344, 349, 350, 353, 357, 358, 359, 361, 363, 364, 365, 368, 370, 371, 372, 373, 374, 376, 378, 379, 383, 384, 388, 389Isles of Shoals, 82, 173, 300, 307, 385

Jamaica [NY], 71, 109, 226, 291, 313, 323, 334

Kennebec, 143, 164, 204, 335
Killingworth, 156, 191
Kittery, 7, 59, 60, 75, 82, 100, 107, 122, 129, 131, 143, 163, 164, 182, 185, 211, 225, 227, 252, 256, 264, 287, 325, 347, 356

Lancaster, 23, 40, 127, 128, 189, 192, 208, 290, 337, 361, 369, 373, 374
Long Island, 324
Lyme, 221, 258
Lynn, 5, 6, 8, 9, 11, 12, 13, 15, 17, 21, 22, 25, 27, 28, 36, 39, 40, 41, 43, 45, 49, 51, 59, 65, 70, 72, 74, 77, 78, 79, 80, 81, 89, 91, 92, 93, 94, 95, 98, 103, 104, 107, 112, 116, 118, 119, 121, 123, 125, 127, 128, 131, 133, 136, 137, 141, 143, 147, 148, 149, 150, 151, 152, 155, 158, 160, 167, 171, 172, 173, 174, 176, 179, 180, 186, 193, 194, 196, 199, 203, 206, 207, 208, 209, 211, 217, 220, 225, 229, 230, 232, 235, 238, 239, 243, 252, 254, 255, 258, 261, 265, 268, 269, 270, 274, 277, 280, 281, 282, 286, 289, 293, 293, 294, 298, 299, 305, 307, 310, 312, 313, 315, 317, 319, 321, 326, 329, 331, 332, 334, 338, 340, 342, 343, 353, 355, 357, 361, 364, 365, 369, 371, 373, 374, 377, 378, 381, 382, 383, 384, 386

Maine, 10, 153, 165, 288, 311, 331, 374
Malden, 2, 11, 28, 38, 57, 113, 139, 160, 161, 162, 183, 199, 208, 212, 223, 235, 243, 259, 296, 303, 316, 348, 368, 374
Mamaroneck, 260

Manchester, 4, 5, 27, 64, 188, 219, 255, 264, 305, 311, 372
Maquoit, 335
Marblehead, 4, 5, 18, 21, 23, 26, 32, 64, 66, 71, 76, 93, 95, 104, 106, 127, 128, 131, 138, 140, 152, 182, 185, 191, 198, 206, 209, 212, 215, 226, 237, 241, 255, 257, 265, 268, 292, 293, 294, 295, 300, 309, 320, 332, 338, 339, 354, 357, 360, 369, 372, 375
Marlborough, 26, 134, 171, 174, 240, 280, 281, 290, 359, 382
Marshfield, 18, 25, 27, 28, 33, 36, 43, 46, 49, 58, 60, 61, 63, 91, 95, 96, 101, 133, 166, 167, 171, 210, 262, 266, 285, 290, 291, 304, 305, 311, 313, 333, 335, 360, 365, 380
Martha's Vineyard, 310, 329
Maryland, 97, 374
Massachusetts Bay, 1, 3, 4, 7, 8, 14, 16, 19, 20, 21, 22, 24, 26, 28, 29, 30, 34, 35, 37, 38, 39, 40, 42, 46, 47, 49, 50, 52, 59, 63, 66, 67, 68, 69, 70, 71, 73, 75, 77, 79, 82, 83, 87, 88, 89, 91, 93, 95, 96, 97, 98, 100, 103, 104, 105, 106, 108, 116, 120, 125, 126, 129, 133, 136, 137, 138, 142, 146, 149, 151, 152, 154, 155, 157, 160, 162, 163, 168, 173, 174, 175, 176, 182, 183, 184, 185, 186, 188, 190, 192, 194, 203, 205, 209, 210, 212, 214, 218, 219, 222, 223, 226, 228, 231, 232, 235, 238, 240, 241, 242, 247, 250, 251, 253, 257, 264, 266, 267, 269, 272, 273, 274, 278, 280, 281, 282, 284, 285, 286, 291, 294, 295, 297, 299, 302, 303, 305, 306, 309, 310, 312, 313, 314, 315, 316, 317, 321, 326, 329, 330, 331, 332, 335, 337, 338, 340, 341, 344, 348, 349, 356, 357, 359, 362, 363, 366, 368, 370, 375, 378, 381, 384, 385, 387, 391

Medfield, 3, 18, 37, 48, 49, 100, 106, 124, 150, 163, 233, 267, 309, 335, 368, 372, 383
Medford, 21, 26, 88, 101, 256, 260
Mendon, 3, 336
Merrymount, 233
Middleborough, 18, 238
Middletown, 45, 79, 147, 172, 228
Middletown [NJ], 37
Milford, 1, 10, 11, 16, 17, 24, 30, 35, 36, 42, 46, 47, 52, 55, 66, 74, 101, 113, 117, 120, 143, 153, 154, 172, 186, 202, 204, 257, 267, 273, 287, 288, 296, 321, 323, 329, 335, 338, 339, 347, 364, 367, 371
Milton, 240, 342
Monhegan, 56
Mount Wollaston, 382
Muddy River, 230
Mystic, 39, 83, 106, 120, 256, 278, 279, 301, 358

Nahant, 278, 305, 336
Nantasket, 75, 215, 246, 259, 311, 362
Nantucket, 31, 74, 217, 318, 325
Natick, 383
Nevis, 286
New Amsterdam, 5, 21, 69, 97, 115, 204, 260, 293, 311, 315, 347
Newark, 46, 81, 265, 311, 358
Newbury, 2, 5, 12, 13, 14, 15, 20, 22, 31, 34, 44, 45, 52, 54, 57, 59, 62, 63, 64, 67, 70, 72, 74, 80, 81, 82, 83, 89, 90, 96, 99, 102, 107, 108, 114, 115, 116, 123, 131, 133, 134, 135, 140, 146, 149, 157, 159, 161, 167, 172, 176, 179, 185, 188, 189, 191, 192, 193, 197, 198, 210, 212, 213, 214, 217, 219, 220, 226, 227, 230, 233, 234, 235, 236, 243, 246, 248, 251, 252, 253, 254, 259, 261, 264, 265, 267, 269, 278, 280, 288, 291, 293, 296, 298, 299, 300, 301,

Index of American Places

304, 306, 312, 313, 315, 319, 320, 325, 332, 334, 335, 337, 339, 340, 356, 359, 362, 367, 370, 383, 384
New England, 207, 234
New Hampshire, 82
New Haven, 1, 5, 6, 7, 8, 10, 11, 12, 14, 15, 18, 24, 25, 26, 32, 33, 37, 38, 39, 40, 42, 44, 45, 46, 47, 55, 56, 60, 61, 62, 64, 66, 67, 70, 71, 75, 76, 78, 81, 88, 89, 90, 91, 93, 95, 102, 105, 106, 108, 114, 119, 121, 123, 125, 129, 130, 135, 140, 141, 147, 148, 156, 161, 162, 163, 165, 168, 171, 173, 174, 180, 182, 183, 184, 186, 190, 194, 201, 203, 205, 209, 210, 212, 213, 217, 218, 219, 220, 222, 224, 226, 227, 229, 233, 234, 236, 237, 239, 240, 242, 247, 251, 255, 256, 258, 259, 261, 264, 265, 267, 268, 270, 271, 272, 273, 280, 290, 291, 292, 296, 300, 301, 304, 308, 311, 314, 315, 320, 323, 326, 329, 332, 333, 335, 336, 338, 341, 343, 344, 350, 354, 355, 358, 367, 370, 371, 372, 374, 376, 383, 389
New London, 4, 33, 34, 46, 59, 61, 62, 71, 75, 80, 84, 97, 104, 152, 153, 191, 201, 203, 219, 224, 229, 232, 235, 287, 306, 308, 311, 318, 329, 337, 356, 360
New Netherland, 75, 234
Newport, 2, 5, 8, 9, 20, 25, 30, 33, 38, 40, 43, 48, 51, 52, 57, 66, 67, 68, 69, 70, 71, 79, 80, 90, 100, 101, 102, 114, 120, 121, 126, 141, 145, 147, 150, 155, 157, 161, 167, 172, 174, 183, 192, 198, 204, 206, 207, 217, 226, 251, 252, 254, 258, 268, 275, 281, 283, 287, 289, 293, 310, 316, 318, 322, 324, 358, 362, 363, 365, 373, 375, 376, 377, 381
Newtown [NY], 34, 71, 97, 112, 115, 138, 161, 204, 207, 228, 230, 252, 280, 310, 320, 323

New York, 374
Noddle's Island, 64, 264
Northampton, 15, 21, 68, 76, 84, 106, 114, 119, 150, 167, 173, 183, 190, 289, 319, 323, 375, 379, 383, 384
North Carolina, 324
North Yarmouth, 280, 303
Norwalk, 1, 106, 146, 191, 221, 231, 246, 279, 282, 291, 301, 362
Norwich, 30, 59, 104, 177, 222, 375

Oyster Bay, 9, 81, 169, 207, 340, 347, 363, 386

Pejepscot, 39, 126, 189, 274
Pemaquid, 22, 45, 50, 60, 90, 197, 198, 232, 239, 241, 305, 375
Penobscot, 55, 91, 263, 282, 361, 374
Pettaquamscutt, 269
Piscataqua, 10, 21, 27, 29, 32, 38, 43, 55, 56, 71, 78, 82, 96, 97, 114, 120, 122, 128, 129, 130, 132, 133, 157, 158, 176, 187, 193, 198, 199, 202, 227, 228, 233, 237, 253, 261, 263, 272, 290, 296, 303, 305, 307, 315, 334, 341, 342, 349, 355, 357, 369, 372, 381, 385, 386
Piscataway [NJ], 116, 161, 307
Plymouth, 2, 3, 4, 5, 8, 9, 11, 16, 17, 18, 19, 21, 23, 24, 27, 28, 29, 31, 34, 35, 36, 37, 38, 40, 41, 42, 43, 45, 47, 49, 56, 57, 58, 59, 60, 62, 64, 66, 67, 68, 69, 70, 72, 73, 74, 75, 76, 77, 78, 80, 81, 82, 83, 85, 89, 90, 91, 92, 93, 94, 95, 96, 99, 102, 103, 105, 106, 107, 108, 111, 112, 115, 117, 118, 119, 123, 124, 126, 132, 134, 136, 137, 138, 139, 140, 141, 142, 147, 148, 149, 150, 151, 152, 154, 156, 157, 158, 160, 161, 162, 163, 164, 165, 166, 167, 168, 169, 171, 175, 180, 181, 184, 187, 189, 192, 193, 195, 199, 202, 203, 206, 207, 208, 210, 211, 214, 215,

219, 220, 221, 222, 224, 225, 226, 229, 231, 232, 233, 235, 237, 238, 240, 242, 246, 247, 249, 252, 257, 259, 260, 264, 266, 267, 268, 269, 271, 272, 273, 277, 278, 279, 280, 281, 282, 284, 285, 286, 287, 288, 290, 291, 293, 294, 297, 300, 302, 304, 305, 306, 307, 309, 310, 311, 313, 314, 315, 316, 317, 320, 322, 324, 327, 329, 331, 332, 333, 334, 336, 337, 339, 341, 342, 343, 350, 351, 353, 354, 355, 356, 357, 359, 360, 361, 365, 366, 370, 372, 373, 374, 376, 377, 380, 382, 383, 385, 386, 387

Plymouth Colony, 3, 99, 147, 157, 232, 262

Podunk, 386

Portsmouth, 3, 6, 9, 10, 12, 16, 21, 22, 25, 35, 36, 40, 41, 45, 46, 48, 52, 57, 60, 66, 67, 69, 70, 71, 75, 76, 79, 80, 89, 90, 100, 101, 102, 107, 114, 115, 121, 126, 136, 141, 146, 147, 148, 150, 155, 157, 159, 165, 176, 177, 183, 185, 204, 214, 218, 220, 224, 230, 233, 234, 250, 253, 263, 269, 270, 283, 288, 295, 300, 304, 307, 311, 312, 315, 318, 324, 329, 330, 340, 341, 348, 349, 354, 355, 357, 372, 375, 377, 378, 385

Portsmouth [NH], 24, 146, 148, 189, 221, 259, 281, 300

Providence, 1, 8, 9, 10, 25, 28, 44, 51, 57, 74, 78, 114, 134, 136, 139, 152, 169, 182, 192, 209, 218, 235, 237, 246, 281, 299, 309, 329, 335, 347, 354, 356, 359, 360, 363, 365, 366, 368, 372, 373, 376, 379

Providence Island, 354

Reading, 13, 45, 51, 85, 88, 102, 104, 116, 139, 152, 220, 251, 254, 268, 308, 330, 355, 374

Rehoboth, 1, 7, 26, 33, 37, 43, 45, 47, 53, 57, 59, 62, 66, 69, 78, 90, 96, 116, 123, 160, 167, 195, 220, 221, 233, 247, 250, 251, 257, 260, 279, 293, 302, 309, 313, 337, 374, 379, 386

Rhode Island, 165

Richmond Island, 4, 5, 7, 10, 11, 14, 15, 28, 29, 35, 39, 47, 49, 51, 56, 61, 65, 67, 70, 79, 81, 84, 92, 100, 103, 104, 114, 115, 117, 121, 122, 126, 128, 129, 130, 131, 142, 148, 149, 150, 154, 155, 157, 158, 159, 160, 162, 163, 165, 169, 189, 202, 208, 209, 211, 213, 220, 221, 223, 225, 228, 229, 245, 285, 287, 289, 294, 295, 296, 303, 304, 305, 319, 338, 340, 341, 351, 363, 369, 370, 376, 380

Rowley, 9, 15, 18, 19, 26, 37, 38, 40, 41, 49, 50, 56, 83, 85, 94, 133, 137, 145, 151, 153, 154, 169, 175, 182, 183, 185, 186, 193, 201, 205, 215, 227, 228, 238, 242, 251, 255, 280, 287, 298, 301, 304, 320, 325, 332, 334, 342, 365, 373

Roxbury, 3, 7, 9, 10, 16, 17, 21, 23, 26, 30, 31, 32, 33, 34, 37, 38, 40, 48, 49, 50, 51, 55, 56, 58, 60, 61, 62, 63, 66, 71, 74, 75, 79, 81, 84, 85, 92, 93, 97, 99, 105, 112, 114, 121, 126, 127, 132, 133, 135, 138, 139, 141, 143, 145, 146, 147, 149, 150, 152, 158, 159, 160, 162, 163, 167, 170, 171, 175, 179, 184, 185, 187, 193, 201, 207, 208, 211, 215, 218, 222, 223, 224, 227, 228, 230, 232, 233, 234, 235, 238, 245, 247, 254, 255, 256, 257, 260, 261, 264, 267, 269, 271, 272, 274, 278, 279, 280, 284, 285, 286, 289, 291, 294, 296, 298, 300, 302, 303, 304, 308, 315, 319, 322, 330, 333, 336, 339, 342, 347, 354, 355, 357, 361, 362, 363, 364, 371, 376, 378, 379, 381, 383, 386

Index of American Places

Sable Island, 159, 389
Saco, 7, 14, 19, 22, 27, 34, 35, 39, 73, 74, 75, 77, 86, 90, 105, 122, 124, 127, 129, 130, 137, 140, 146, 157, 161, 162, 163, 164, 171, 184, 188, 206, 207, 208, 212, 217, 228, 229, 232, 237, 249, 250, 253, 263, 280, 283, 285, 286, 296, 298, 310, 312, 330, 353, 360, 361, 362, 365, 373, 375, 376, 381
Salem, 1, 2, 3, 4, 5, 7, 8, 9, 12, 13, 14, 16, 17, 18, 19, 20, 21, 22, 23, 24, 25, 27, 28, 30, 31, 32, 34, 36, 37, 38, 39, 40, 41, 42, 44, 45, 46, 47, 48, 49, 50, 51, 52, 54, 56, 57, 58, 59, 61, 63, 64, 65, 68, 70, 72, 74, 75, 76, 79, 85, 88, 89, 90, 91, 92, 93, 94, 95, 96, 97, 98, 99, 101, 102, 103, 104, 105, 107, 108, 111, 113, 114, 116, 117, 118, 122, 123, 124, 125, 126, 127, 128, 130, 131, 132, 133, 134, 135, 136, 137, 138, 139, 140, 142, 143, 145, 146, 147, 149, 150, 151, 153, 154, 159, 160, 161, 163, 165, 166, 167, 168, 169, 170, 172, 174, 175, 176, 179, 180, 181, 182, 183, 185, 186, 187, 191, 192, 193, 194, 195, 197, 198, 201, 202, 203, 204, 205, 206, 208, 209, 212, 214, 215, 217, 219, 220, 222, 230, 231, 232, 234, 235, 236, 237, 240, 241, 242, 243, 245, 246, 247, 249, 250, 251, 256, 257, 258, 259, 261, 262, 263, 264, 266, 268, 269, 270, 272, 273, 274, 277, 279, 280, 281, 282, 284, 285, 286, 289, 290, 291, 292, 293, 295, 298, 299, 302, 303, 305, 306, 307, 308, 309, 311, 312, 314, 315, 316, 317, 320, 321, 323, 325, 326, 329, 330, 331, 332, 334, 335, 336, 338, 339, 340, 342, 343, 347, 349, 350, 354, 355, 356, 357, 358, 359, 360, 361, 363, 364, 365, 366, 369, 374, 375, 376, 382, 383, 385, 386, 390

Salisbury, 5, 7, 12, 14, 19, 22, 32, 38, 44, 51, 53, 54, 57, 69, 70, 72, 73, 81, 84, 94, 97, 99, 101, 102, 113, 116, 118, 122, 123, 128, 134, 139, 145, 147, 148, 152, 156, 157, 160, 164, 165, 168, 171, 179, 201, 217, 221, 232, 235, 236, 242, 247, 248, 253, 255, 265, 274, 284, 288, 290, 293, 295, 296, 301, 306, 319, 361, 364, 367, 372, 377, 380, 385
Sandwich, 4, 6, 9, 19, 24, 28, 32, 33, 35, 36, 40, 41, 48, 50, 53, 59, 63, 65, 72, 93, 94, 95, 103, 108, 112, 115, 118, 121, 128, 148, 149, 151, 158, 166, 176, 190, 196, 199, 203, 207, 228, 238, 243, 270, 272, 290, 307, 324, 326, 333, 342, 343, 350, 353, 377, 379, 380, 381, 383, 386
Saybrook, 14, 23, 30, 39, 52, 53, 61, 70, 75, 113, 122, 126, 139, 177, 204, 221, 222, 229, 254, 255, 259, 270, 271, 279, 287, 290, 291, 301, 306, 320, 353, 377, 382
Scarborough, 4, 15, 19, 51, 74, 103, 120, 149, 208, 228, 313, 354, 361
Scituate, 4, 8, 13, 16, 20, 27, 28, 30, 32, 36, 37, 43, 47, 54, 55, 60, 62, 64, 65, 68, 70, 71, 74, 77, 82, 84, 85, 88, 92, 99, 103, 106, 107, 109, 116, 118, 119, 121, 126, 127, 131, 132, 137, 148, 150, 151, 154, 158, 160, 163, 167, 170, 172, 177, 181, 182, 192, 195, 202, 205, 207, 208, 209, 212, 226, 232, 236, 243, 251, 254, 256, 261, 264, 265, 266, 268, 271, 273, 278, 279, 280, 286, 290, 291, 297, 305, 317, 319, 320, 324, 325, 330, 336, 337, 343, 344, 345, 349, 353, 358, 364, 366, 368, 369, 374, 375, 378, 380, 385, 387
Setauket, 347
Shelter Island, 314
Smithtown, 311

Southampton, 19, 68, 77, 119, 133, 136, 141, 148, 151, 171, 187, 196, 228, 230, 238, 245, 265, 279, 288, 298, 311, 317, 320, 326, 329, 332, 339, 348, 369, 370

Southold, 26, 47, 58, 75, 85, 94, 108, 132, 159, 163, 169, 193, 274, 332, 340, 347, 349, 379, 390

Springfield, 4, 10, 17, 32, 45, 50, 51, 53, 55, 61, 78, 93, 99, 106, 109, 140, 157, 164, 169, 172, 184, 207, 226, 229, 235, 236, 255, 274, 280, 298, 300, 309, 319, 326, 333, 347, 360, 375, 379, 382, 383, 387Spurwink, 39, 69, 158, 189, 342

Squamscott, 372

Stamford, 1, 6, 9, 22, 25, 31, 45, 61, 68, 71, 81, 92, 105, 114, 116, 130, 172, 173, 177, 182, 197, 204, 210, 225, 228, 229, 231, 242, 260, 271, 279, 281, 304, 305, 307, 309, 311, 324, 331, 333, 347, 357, 371, 372, 382, 383

Stonington, 62, 229, 251, 318

Stratford, 6, 21, 24, 30, 32, 42, 111, 140, 147, 153, 169, 175, 184, 190, 193, 194, 228, 240, 280, 287, 291, 301, 306, 320, 335, 367, 373

Strawberry Bank, 13, 62, 80, 83, 188, 252, 253, 274, 277, 298, 331, 356, 363

Study Hill, 32

Sudbury, 19, 21, 25, 27, 28, 33, 44, 46, 47, 55, 85, 88, 89, 90, 98, 101, 119, 121, 134, 141, 156, 171, 174, 180, 186, 192, 198, 210, 224, 236, 240, 243, 255, 258, 259, 267, 272, 280, 281, 290, 292, 296, 307, 312, 329, 338, 340, 351, 355, 359, 360, 366, 368, 369, 370, 382, 386

Swansea, 3, 36, 59, 103, 350, 374

Taunton, 7, 12, 30, 31, 40, 45, 47, 49, 51, 58, 76, 91, 97, 112, 130, 132, 147, 153, 164, 166, 168, 169, 173, 208, 217, 253, 254, 256, 268, 281, 283, 285, 298, 304, 308, 310, 311, 323, 337, 343, 355, 373, 375

Ten Hills, 42

Thompson's Island, 334

Tisbury, 286

Topsfield, 46, 84, 96, 137, 170, 240, 257, 259, 340, 373

Virginia, 18, 29, 52, 97, 102, 182, 186, 206, 213, 215, 225, 245, 248, 301

Wallingford, 42, 147, 226, 234

Warwick, 21, 52, 56, 74, 107, 136, 139, 158, 165, 209, 270, 304, 340, 359, 360, 365, 366, 372

Watertown, 1, 5, 6, 9, 13, 16, 19, 20, 21, 25, 26, 28, 30, 34, 35, 37, 38, 41, 43, 44, 45, 46, 48, 49, 52, 55, 58, 59, 61, 63, 64, 68, 69, 71, 73, 77, 78, 82, 83, 84, 85, 86, 87, 88, 92, 94, 95, 96, 97, 100, 102, 103, 105, 109, 113, 114, 115, 116, 117, 118, 121, 125, 126, 128, 130, 133, 135, 136, 137, 139, 141, 143, 148, 149, 152, 154, 156, 157, 163, 165, 169, 171, 172, 180, 181, 182, 184, 187, 193, 194, 195, 198, 199, 201, 204, 205, 207, 208, 210, 212, 222, 224, 230, 233, 236, 240, 241, 243, 246, 247, 249, 251, 252, 255, 256, 258, 259, 262, 263, 264, 265, 268, 270, 271, 279, 281, 282, 287, 288, 289, 294, 295, 296, 297, 301, 302, 303, 304, 306, 308, 310, 312, 316, 318, 321, 322, 325, 326, 329, 330, 331, 333, 338, 340, 342, 344, 347, 349, 354, 357, 359, 360, 361, 363, 364, 366, 368, 369, 371, 373, 374, 375, 379, 380, 384, 385

Wells, 20, 34, 73, 83, 133, 145, 159, 177, 197, 269, 284, 296, 333, 353, 354, 359, 365
Wenham, 1, 54, 81, 116, 128, 136, 137, 191, 194, 242, 261, 279, 303, 312, 314, 369, 390
Wessagusset, 32, 129, 135, 139, 185, 232, 293, 295, 301
Westchester, 28, 247, 252, 268
Westerly, 60, 79, 204, 251, 323
Westfield, 76, 143, 152, 262
West Indies, 55, 97
Wethersfield, 1, 22, 24, 25, 32, 35, 38, 46, 61, 63, 64, 67, 68, 71, 74, 75, 81, 83, 85, 92, 94, 103, 104, 114, 117, 118, 126, 129, 130, 146, 157, 172, 175, 180, 182, 183, 184, 193, 203, 204, 210, 222, 228, 229, 231, 235, 242, 243, 250, 252, 253, 254, 255, 267, 272, 273, 278, 279, 281, 284, 288, 289, 291, 301, 304, 309, 312, 317, 323, 325, 339, 340, 347, 350, 354, 357, 358, 360, 363, 364, 365, 371, 372, 382, 387
Weymouth, 1, 2, 4, 7, 9, 15, 22, 26, 27, 28, 37, 41, 42, 51, 53, 54, 57, 64, 65, 69, 73, 75, 79, 82, 87, 96, 106, 119, 123, 124, 126, 131, 136, 136, 139, 150, 152, 161, 165, 173, 174, 183, 184, 194, 195, 197, 198, 202, 206, 211, 212, 213, 221, 225, 229, 237, 239, 242, 247, 248, 249, 253, 260, 261, 263, 265, 268, 270, 271, 277, 278, 279, 282, 287, 291, 293, 301, 303, 305, 309, 310, 313, 318, 323, 332, 335, 337, 339, 342, 343, 348, 357, 360, 362, 363, 366, 368, 370, 371, 377
Wickford, 160, 311
Windsor, 1, 5, 6, 18, 20, 21, 30, 31, 39, 47, 48, 57, 66, 67, 75, 76, 78, 83, 92, 93, 98, 99, 101, 104, 114, 119, 120, 122, 128, 129, 130, 131, 137, 131, 142, 143, 150, 155, 156, 160, 162, 165, 169, 172, 173, 175, 184, 211, 214, 219, 220, 222, 223, 229, 230, 231, 240, 246, 247, 251, 255, 258, 262, 265, 268, 270, 277, 278, 280, 287, 294, 301, 318, 320, 322, 323, 324, 331, 332, 333, 335, 336, 337, 342, 351, 359, 364, 370, 375, 376, 379, 381
Winnegance, 60, 305
Winnissimmett, 10, 32, 152, 308, 320, 340, 370
Woburn, 30, 35, 42, 53, 58, 62, 68, 72, 76, 89, 112, 124, 140, 157, 165, 183, 185, 192, 198, 205, 207, 210, 221, 235, 243, 253, 263, 264, 265, 279, 282, 283, 292, 300, 324, 334, 336, 339, 341, 379, 386, 387
Woodbridge [NJ], 31, 192
Worcester, 11

Yarmouth, 9, 13, 15, 19, 35, 55, 62, 73, 83, 92, 93, 105, 106, 111, 117, 131, 147, 148, 154, 155, 158, 169, 171, 173, 190, 209, 214, 223, 225, 228, 232, 240, 250, 252, 284, 300, 305, 324, 329, 332, 335, 336, 344, 350, 368, 369, 370, 385
York, 3, 8, 15, 19, 20, 32, 38, 39, 48, 50, 60, 78, 79, 82, 89, 90, 95, 96, 118, 122, 126, 133, 135, 136, 143, 154, 159, 163, 168, 173, 185, 188, 197, 203, 210, 215, 239, 242, 247, 274, 284, 287, 288, 298, 306, 311, 312, 316, 334, 342, 362, 385

INDEX OF SHIP NAMES

Abigail, 1, 2, 3, 4, 5, 6, 9, 21, 38, 39, 45, 49, 50, 51, 52, 53, 57, 71, 74, 77, 80, 88, 91, 93, 95, 96, 98, 106, 107, 118, 119, 120, 121, 123, 124, 128, 132, 136, 138, 141, 143, 148, 150, 154, 159, 162, 170, 187, 188, 189, 193, 195, 203, 215, 220, 221, 222, 225, 236, 250, 252, 261, 271, 272, 277, 288, 289, 302, 303, 317, 319, 324, 330, 332, 334, 337, 342, 356, 357, 365, 369, 371, 374, 382, 384, 389

Angel Gabriel, 71, 124, 146

Anne, 8, 17, 21, 41, 47, 49, 68, 94, 117, 132, 158, 166, 192, 211, 229, 233, 240, 259, 264, 271, 277, 278, 316, 336, 340, 356

Arbella, 381

Bachelor, 72, 126, 189

Bevis, 3, 12, 15, 18, 22, 32, 54, 57, 99, 100, 123, 134, 176, 198, 210, 234, 253, 268, 269, 280, 354

Blessing, 24, 29, 41, 43, 47, 50, 54, 78, 88, 90, 154, 166, 175, 181, 195, 208, 211, 218, 233, 236, 247, 285, 298, 301, 316, 320, 341, 343, 345

Castle, 10, 39, 179, 226, 325

Charles, 74

Christian, 18, 21, 52, 61, 78, 82, 100, 120, 146, 152, 156, 160, 169, 219, 256, 280, 286, 320, 385

Confidence, 15, 22, 24, 27, 29, 32, 33, 64, 73, 80, 89, 90, 96, 101, 134, 143, 150, 156, 179, 188, 191, 192, 194, 212, 214, 219, 232, 243, 248, 252, 253, 270, 280, 288, 292, 293, 296, 319, 320, 329, 356, 372, 373

Defence, 1, 10, 17, 27, 37, 44, 50, 60, 72, 76, 77, 92, 93, 96, 112, 113, 116, 122, 136, 143, 151, 153, 162, 166, 172, 181, 184, 187, 191, 197, 198, 205, 211, 223, 225, 234, 243, 252, 261, 279, 288, 297, 303, 305, 319, 376, 379, 382

Diligent, 4, 23, 47, 59, 78, 85, 113, 128, 131, 155, 182, 224, 229, 230, 232, 249, 250, 257, 258, 266, 283, 297, 309, 324, 342

Elizabeth, 19, 21, 23, 29, 34, 39, 42, 45, 48, 49, 61, 69, 83, 86, 88, 89, 91, 96, 97, 99, 119, 126, 132, 133, 134, 136, 154, 157, 164, 165, 168, 169, 172, 180, 185, 194, 195, 203, 207, 221, 228, 230, 233, 236, 246, 251, 264, 270, 272, 278, 279, 291, 299, 301, 303, 304, 308, 309, 312, 316, 321, 323, 334, 335, 347, 355, 356, 366, 369, 372, 373, 384

Elizabeth & Ann, 2, 6, 15, 16, 23, 35, 42, 43, 45, 57, 61, 70, 80, 85, 87, 91, 102, 111, 132, 148, 156, 158, 162, 166, 172, 181, 183, 194, 211, 221, 231, 247, 252, 253, 271, 280, 281, 289, 293, 294, 296, 301, 317, 325, 326, 334, 356, 366, 369, 371, 372, 373, 374

Elizabeth Dorcas, 36

Fortune, 2, 21, 23, 28, 41, 49, 56, 76, 85, 91, 92, 117, 118, 128, 161, 163, 232, 233, 240, 252, 266, 272, 306, 316, 320, 332, 380, 387
Francis, 3, 19, 24, 28, 37, 48, 68, 71, 98, 121, 127, 139, 155, 157, 165, 167, 184, 195, 205, 210, 219, 222, 238, 247, 257, 260, 304, 319, 361, 366, 368, 379
George, 174
George Bonaventure, 302, 306
Griffin, 20, 130, 158, 168, 177, 212, 321, 326
Handmaid, 103
Hercules, 12, 26, 27, 28, 35, 41, 43, 60, 61, 72, 80, 89, 99, 101, 104, 106, 109, 112, 114, 119, 120, 125, 137, 152, 154, 157, 160, 163, 167, 183, 184, 187, 193, 194, 202, 203, 208, 212, 222, 238, 256, 260, 262, 282, 284, 286, 289, 297, 318, 324, 325, 336, 337, 341, 343, 364, 366, 379
Hopewell, 1, 3, 10, 23, 26, 29, 32, 48, 50, 52, 60, 64, 65, 67, 69, 71, 77, 91, 93, 94, 98, 103, 104, 105, 112, 119, 121, 127, 128, 130, 132, 138, 140, 141, 158, 172, 173, 177, 187, 191, 196, 202, 205, 210, 213, 215, 217, 219, 220, 223, 228, 242, 257, 259, 259, 260, 262, 272, 274, 280, 286, 287, 288, 291, 317, 321, 323, 333, 335, 336, 337, 339, 341, 343, 365, 368, 371, 372, 376, 381, 383, 389
Increase, 7, 13, 20, 24, 31, 33, 47, 64, 83, 87, 89, 109, 117, 118, 129, 131, 145, 170, 180, 189, 193, 210, 221, 231, 233, 237, 243, 248, 249, 251, 252, 264, 271, 278, 287, 291, 296, 314, 321, 323, 331, 338, 348, 358, 359, 370, 382, 383, 385, 388
James, 8, 9, 12, 18, 22, 23, 24, 27, 28, 40, 44, 45, 46, 48, 53, 56, 57, 69, 74, 80, 85, 90, 107, 108, 109, 112, 126, 133, 134, 139, 141, 152, 155, 161, 162, 167, 168, 185, 187, 188, 192, 194, 197, 198, 207, 220, 221, 222, 223, 229, 233, 234, 236, 239, 249, 251, 253, 255, 265, 266, 289, 293, 299, 300, 302, 303, 307, 308, 312, 332, 335, 350, 355, 367, 384
John, 10, 34, 91, 132
John & Dorothy, 2, 6, 15, 36, 52, 58, 95, 97, 103, 128, 134, 152, 167, 204, 206, 208, 209, 213, 218, 220, 227, 234, 235, 240, 243, 249, 277, 286, 289, 306, 308, 309, 322, 339, 357, 374, 375, 376
Jonathan, 19, 177, 267, 313, 323
Little James, 184
Love, 46, 63, 254, 303, 335
Lyon, 6, 14, 21, 26, 44, 57, 65, 67, 71, 105, 106, 132, 135, 137, 158, 166, 182, 208, 232, 246, 259, 260, 282, 285, 295, 329, 330, 347, 353, 354, 361, 369, 374, 376, 381
Lyon's Whelp, 41, 95, 104, 336
Martin, 17, 35, 44, 363
Mary & John, 8, 12, 17, 44, 45, 65, 68, 72, 73, 76, 89, 102, 119, 120, 121, 128, 131, 133, 160, 166, 182, 189, 192, 196, 201, 210, 212, 213, 214, 219, 223, 230, 236, 238, 239, 243, 248, 254, 262, 269, 281, 287, 297, 300, 304, 309, 315, 325, 332, 337, 340, 348, 350, 359, 365, 367, 370, 376, 381, 383
Mary Anne, 2, 7, 51, 77, 88, 94, 95, 96, 128, 134, 140, 188, 194, 237, 246, 250, 271, 296, 331, 333, 335, 339, 356, 390

Index of Ship Names

Marygould, 2, 87, 114, 119, 122, 138, 148, 164, 165, 173, 184, 187, 195, 196, 197, 212, 214, 221, 261, 268, 270, 279, 303, 329, 348, 353, 371, 382, 383

Mayflower, 3, 5, 29, 38, 40, 42, 45, 53, 57, 48, 64, 67, 76, 77, 81, 96, 102, 106, 107, 117, 123, 123, 126, 134, 165, 168, 171, 202, 203, 206, 219, 221, 229, 231, 235, 273, 284, 288, 294, 313, 317, 322, 334, 336, 337, 341, 343, 360, 370, 373, 376, 380

Pied Cow, 16, 29, 59, 88, 132, 152, 356

Planter, 15, 24, 29, 52, 57, 64, 65, 89, 91, 93, 106, 111, 113, 123, 130, 140, 145, 149, 150, 153, 155, 157, 158, 184, 204, 206, 210, 211, 217, 231, 233, 238, 246, 257, 258, 260, 263, 266, 284, 297, 308, 309, 311, 317, 318, 319, 325, 337, 344, 364, 373, 376, 379, 381, 386

Plough, 186, 196

Prosperous, 6, 31, 71, 265, 332

Rebecca, 81, 347, 384

Recovery, 3, 21, 37, 94, 101, 106, 151, 164, 211, 238, 241, 263, 265, 269, 302, 326, 354, 365, 385, 386

Regard, 220

Rose, 2, 6, 15, 36, 52, 58, 95, 97, 103, 128, 134, 152, 167, 204, 206, 208, 209, 213, 218, 220, 227, 234, 235, 243, 322, 375, 376

Sparrow, 271

Speedwell, 29, 76, 82, 152, 186, 211, 283, 298, 380, 387

Susan & Ellen, 11, 25, 30, 33, 41, 43, 48, 51, 56, 69, 71, 72, 78, 79, 95, 118, 120, 129, 135, 139, 155, 163, 173, 183, 187, 196, 199, 201, 205, 214, 218, 231, 240, 241, 254, 258, 265, 267, 273, 282, 283, 289, 299, 309, 311, 313, 323, 325, 326, 330, 333, 335, 335, 340, 363, 364, 373

Talbot, 31, 161

Truelove, 20, 27, 30, 32, 34, 41, 43, 45, 96, 105, 113, 142, 143, 146, 155, 171, 183, 185, 194, 213, 232, 255, 266, 272, 291, 300, 306, 321, 323, 325, 330, 335, 338, 357, 371

Unity, 59, 79, 90, 106, 166, 211, 331, 337

Warwick, 237

Whale, 99

William & Francis, 13, 126, 152, 157, 162, 207, 218, 242, 246, 250, 260, 307, 333, 364, 368, 383

William & George, 196

Other NEHGS Titles by Robert Charles Anderson, FASG

The Great Migration Begins
Immigrants to New England,
1620–1633 (first series)

6 x 9, 2,386 pp. in 3 vols.
hdcvr, $125; pbk, $79.95

The Great Migration
Immigrants to New England,
1634–1635 (second series)

6 x 9, hdcvr
Vols. I–VII, $59.95–$64.95 per volume

The Pilgrim Migration
Immigrants to Plymouth Colony, 1620–1633

6 x 9 pbk, 708 pp., $29.95

The Winthrop Fleet
Massachusetts Bay Company Immigrants to New England,
1629–1630

6 x 9 hdcvr, 912 pp., $64.95

Available from shop.AmericanAncestors.org/collections/great-migration